Rights and Reproductions

AMERICAN ALLIANCE OF MUSEUMS

The American Alliance of Museums has been bringing museums together since 1906, helping to develop standards and best practices, gathering and sharing knowledge, and providing advocacy on issues of concern to the entire museum community. Representing more than 35,000 individual museum professionals and volunteers, institutions, and corporate partners serving the museum field, the Alliance stands for the broad scope of the museum community.

The American Alliance of Museums' mission is to champion museums and nurture excellence in partnership with its members and allies.

Books published by AAM further the Alliance's mission to make standards and best practices for the broad museum community widely available.

American
Alliance of
Museums

Rights and Reproductions

The Handbook for Cultural Institutions

Second Edition

EDITED BY
ANNE M. YOUNG

ROWMAN & LITTLEFIELD
Lanham • Boulder • New York • London

Published by Rowman & Littlefield
An imprint of The Rowman & Littlefield Publishing Group, Inc.
4501 Forbes Boulevard, Suite 200, Lanham, Maryland 20706
www.rowman.com

6 Tinworth Street, London SE11 5AL

The first edition of *Rights & Reproductions: The Handbook for Cultural Institutions* was made possible by a grant from the U.S. Institute of Museum and Library Services. That project utilized the OSCI Toolkit, which was supported by the Getty Foundation as a part of its Online Scholarly Catalogue Initiative.

NEWFIELDS | INSTITUTE of Museum and Library SERVICES | American Alliance of Museums | The Getty Foundation

British Library Cataloguing in Publication Information Available

Library of Congress Cataloging-in-Publication Data

Library of Congress Control Number: 2018959554
ISBN: 978-1-5381-1265-6 (cloth : alk. paper)
ISBN: 978-1-5381-1266-3 (pbk. : alk. paper)
ISBN: 978-1-5381-1267-0 (electronic)

™ The paper used in this publication meets the minimum requirements of American National Standard for Information Sciences—Permanence of Paper for Printed Library Materials, ANSI/NISO Z39.48-1992.

Printed in the United States of America

In memory of Marie C. Malaro (1933–2018),
whose enduring publication—*A Legal Primer on Managing Museum Collections*—
is still utilized by so many working in the rights and reproductions field today.

Contents

List of Videos (ebook only)

Figure 3.7:
Abraham Zapruder Film, November 1963. © 1967 (Renewed 1995). The Sixth Floor Museum at Dealey Plaza.

Figure 4.2:
Judith Braun, *Without Pleasure All We'd Have Is a Bunch of Stuff Vibrating,* 2012, powdered graphite on vinyl, dimensions variable. Courtesy of the artist. Commissioned by the Indianapolis Museum of Art. © 2013 Judith Braun. *Graphite* installation in progress. Time lapse video courtesy of the Indianapolis Museum of Art at Newfields.

List of Figures

Preface

WALTER G. LEHMANN AND ANNE M. YOUNG

Rights and Reproductions: The Handbook for Cultural Institutions, Second Edition, is a must-have, comprehensive resource for anyone in a cultural institution, including museums, libraries, archives, historical property associations, and universities, who has the responsibility of handling rights clearances, permissions, and intellectual property (IP) matters. Today, the management and dissemination of creative and historical content has become an essential task for cultural institutions. While they have long been in the content-creation business, many of these institutions are now recognizing the importance of the sound management of their IP assets.

Rights and reproductions specialists[1] need not become IP lawyers to accomplish their jobs, but they do need accurate and up-to-date resources to help them identify legal issues. They need to know how to respond to those issues and, in particular, when to seek the advice of experienced legal counsel. That is the primary goal of this book—to provide current, relevant, and accurate information as well as practical tips for those responsible for clearing rights, obtaining permissions, and otherwise managing IP on behalf of cultural institutions. The goal is not so much to turn rights and reproductions specialists into IP attorneys, but to give them the tools they need to perform their jobs and the knowledge to spot potential legal issues that may require expert analysis and advice.

Cultural institutions create and use a wide variety of IP on a daily basis. While the user communities may differ among museums and universities, archives and libraries, the overarching missions of these cultural institutions are based on providing access to information and artifacts that are in the institutions' collections. Scholarship, conservation, exhibition design, educational programming, fundraising and development, publishing, archiving, marketing and communications, human resources management—every aspect of these practices involves the creation and use of IP. In the past, many cultural institutions operated under the erroneous belief that their nonprofit tax-exempt status insulated them from the application of laws regulating the use of IP. Today, cultural institutions appropriately consider managing IP rights an important and even necessary part of their organizational mission. While these institutions create content and may own the IP rights to those creations, the rights for much of what is in their collections and much of the content they use on a daily basis are owned by others who may or may not be willing to grant the broad rights needed to accomplish the wide dissemination of knowledge at the core of each cultural institution's mission.

Rights and reproductions specialists are charged with the dual responsibility of ensuring the content created by their institutions is adequately protected and, perhaps more importantly, that any content used by their institutions does not infringe on the legitimate IP rights of others.[2] To accomplish this, they are routinely expected to apply legal concepts to minimize the institution's legal liability. They must determine if a work is protected by IP laws and if so, which particular laws apply; identify the current rights holder(s) and know what to do when they cannot identify or locate the presumed owner(s); analyze whether the proposed use requires permission or whether an exception such as fair use applies; or negotiate a license for the necessary rights for a proposed use such as a publication, website, or merchandise. These are all demanding tasks that require familiarity with the legal landscape of IP laws. Moreover, as global communications increase, so does the need to understand and apply both national and international laws. The nitty-gritty details of calculating a copyright term or weighing fair use factors are not glamorous and, depending on the available information about the creator of the work in question, can be exasperating.

The explosion of content generation and the ease of distribution in the digital realm pose new challenges. The ways in which IP can be created and exploited through ever-changing reproduction and distribution technologies are significantly impacting how people produce, protect, and use content. Applying legal concepts—copyright, trademark, privacy, publicity, trade secrets, and even patents—to rapidly changing technological situations and within an ever more international context can be difficult in any setting, and is particularly complex for cultural institutions because of their unique relationship with the content they create and manage.

While rights and reproductions specialists are usually not trained in the law, they typically bring to the rights clearance process something that even seasoned IP lawyers often lack: firsthand knowledge of their institution's collections and culture and an appreciation for the ethical policies and professional principles that govern the operations of cultural institutions. While lawyers may approach questions about IP from a strictly legal perspective ("What does the law require?"), rights and reproductions specialists must also consider their particular institutional mission and polices, as well as applicable professional guidelines and codes of ethics ("What does the museum or library profession expect?"). Sometimes the combination of legal and institutional thinking results in an approach that may seem conservative, such as asking for permission when fair use might apply, or refraining from posting certain images online despite a broad license granting the institution permission to do so. On the other hand, because cultural institution missions strongly favor the dissemination of knowledge, using the most current and viable tools for that purpose may make some creators and rights holders uncomfortable.

Institutional and professional practices may impose requirements that are distinct from applicable legal standards.[3] In some cases, ethical codes may impose a "higher" standard, but often they simply impose a different one. By adhering to institutional policies, generally accepted professional best practices, and ethical codes, the integrity of the institution and its reputation in the eyes of the public are preserved. Rights and reproductions specialists in cultural institutions are uniquely qualified to consider these nuances.

Ultimately, the goal of rights and reproductions specialists is to manage the intellectual assets of the institution to meet its legal, ethical, and mission goals as well as minimize the legal risks of infringement claims for both legal and reputational reasons. What may be considered the "right" approach from a legal standpoint may not necessarily reflect the values a given cultural institution wants to uphold.[4] While detailed and sometimes frustrating work (not all rights questions have clear and straightforward answers), rights management is dynamic and professionally satisfying, especially when a particular approach helps the institution do what it wants to do without rights problems. Within the realm of rights and reproductions, this difference manifests mainly as a conflict between private rights and public access.

Rights holders may vary in their approaches to this conflict between private rights and public access. Some are solely concerned about protecting their economic rights, while others are focused on their reputational or "moral" rights. Other rights holders are happy to provide public access to their work without restriction. Ironically, a number of contemporary artists maintain a distinctly hypocritical (or dysfunctional) approach to IP rights—aggressively enforcing rights in their own work but heavily relying on the rights of others.[5] When negotiating permissions from IP rights holders, rights and reproductions specialists should keep in mind these varying perspectives and seek to accommodate the rights holder's viewpoint when feasible. Rights and reproductions specialists must balance these considerations with their institution's mission.

The nature of each cultural institution will determine its approach to managing IP. Some institutions believe that their mission is to reflect the general norms of the society in which they operate and consider their primary mission as providing public access. Others feel a strong responsibility to prioritize creators' individual rights. Regardless of the approach, rights and reproductions specialists must clearly understand their institution's values and keep these in mind when dealing with IP rights.

Applying legal principles and ethical codes is a process of assessing and managing risk. The rights and reproductions specialist is responsible for applying legal and ethical concepts in an effort to minimize the risk that the use of the IP will infringe on another's rights, or otherwise create legal or reputational liability for the institution. While rights and reproductions specialists are not expected to become experts on IP law, they must be able to identify potential legal issues and know when to seek professional advice.

Following established professional best practices, such as the practices and procedures set forth in *Rights and Reproductions: The Handbook for Cultural Institutions, Second Edition*, will reduce an institution's exposure to risk. This publication was created specifically through the collaboration of archivists, lawyers, librarians, registrars, and rights and reproductions specialists who handle the myriad IP questions facing their institutions. Its goal is to provide an easily navigable and practical explanation of IP laws, rights research options, record-keeping and metadata systems, legal analysis that applies the law to the facts, and guidance on how rights professionals evaluate and resolve real-life IP matters.

While the second edition can be referenced at any time for advice on specific question(s), the content is structured to build upon each successive chapter to provide rights and reproductions specialists with an overall framework for managing IP at a cultural institution. Chapter 1 presents a general IP overview and outlines the legal principles that underscore rights and reproductions work. Chapter 2 builds upon this by reviewing the importance of institutional IP policies and audits to ensure proper ownership, use, and maintenance of the IP assets a cultural institution uses and maintains. Chapter 3 begins to synthesize the principles outlined in the first two chapters and provides practical steps for determining the rights status of works, finding rights holders, and considering the myriad IP rights that might be present in the collection works at a cultural institution. Chapters 4, 5, and 6 work together to delve into the activities that rights and reproductions specialists encounter on a daily basis, including institutional and external uses, as well as leveraging content with distribution partners. The second edition further investigates trends in rights and reproductions practices with the addition of chapter 7, which is devoted to expanding the discussion of fair use and open access. This *Handbook* concludes with three updated appendices with new references, resources, and court decisions, including more than fifty document and contract templates, as well as an updated and expanded glossary of terms commonly encountered, but defined with most of the legalese removed.

NOTES

1. For the purposes of this publication, the phrase "rights and reproductions specialist" refers to anyone working at a cultural institution who handles this type of work, including but not limited to registrars, rights and reproductions managers, archivists, librarians, and lawyers.

2. While the day-to-day responsibility for identifying and addressing institutional legal concerns falls squarely on the museum director (see Stephen E. Weil, "Vincible Ignorance: Museums and the Law," in *Beauty and the Beasts* [Washington, DC: Smithsonian Institution Press, 1983], 133–42), the responsibility for the day-to-day management of a museum's intellectual property

rights often falls on the museum registrar or rights and reproductions specialist.

3. For a discussion of the relationship between legal standards and ethical codes, see Marie C. Malaro, "Why Ethics?" in *Museum Governance: Mission, Ethics, Policy* (Washington, DC: Smithsonian Institution Press, 1994).

4. The outcome in *Massachusetts Museum of Contemporary Art Foundation, Inc. v. Büchel, 565 F. Supp. 2d 245* (D. Mass. 2008) is a good example of the difference between legal thinking and institutional thinking. In that case, which involved the scope of the Visual Artists Rights Act, the District Court determined that Mass MoCA had the right to display an unfinished work of art. Immediately after the verdict in Mass MoCA's favor was announced, the museum's director decided not to display the work in deference to the concerns of the artist. See Walter G. Lehmann, "The Mess at Mass MOCA," Lehmann PLC, accessed April 23, 2018, http://lehmannplc.com/article/exhibiting-unfinished-commissioned-work.

5. The aggressive assertion of copyrights in certain works of appropriation art by artists such as Shepard Fairey or Richard Prince reflects this conflict.

Acknowledgments

ANNE M. YOUNG

When *Rights & Reproductions: The Handbook for Cultural Institutions* was first published in 2015, I had no idea how quickly the field and practices would evolve. Barely six months passed before a list started to form of content that was already out-of-date and/or in need of an update. I also vastly underestimated how much people would want a physical, printed copy of this resource. Without a doubt the question I was asked the most was when it would be available in print and not just as the print-on-demand PDF version. Thankfully, readers have not had to wait too long for the print edition and many now have Rowman & Littlefield to thank for making that a reality.

Moving on a truncated timeline to update the content for the second edition required an all hands on deck effort to bring this to fruition. Over a few short months we furiously edited, updated, deleted, and expanded content to get it into a state that all the contributors felt comfortable committing to the printed page. My undying thanks are once again due to the contributing authors—Megan P. Bryant, Cherie C. Chen, Kenneth D. Crews, John ffrench, Walter G. Lehmann, Naomi Leibowitz, Melissa Levine, Sofía Galarza Liu, Michelle Gallagher Roberts, Nancy Sims, and Deborah Wythe—and the legal review panelists—Jeffrey P. Cunard, Kenan Farrell, Janet Benson Forville, Fred Goldstein, Cara Hirsch, Troy B. Klyber, Lynda Knowles, Pamela Kohanchi, Robert S. Meitus, Megan M. Mulford, Virginia Rutledge, Bridget Smith, and Maureen Whalen—all of whom eagerly agreed to their original contributions being part of the second edition. I owe a particular debt of gratitude to Megan, Cherie, John, Walt, Melissa, Michelle, and Deb for jumping in, reviewing chapters, catching edits, and serving as a general sounding board to the numerous revisions and Basecamp posts.

I am equally thankful to the staff at Rowman & Littlefield, particularly Charles Harmon and Michael Tan, for shepherding the manuscript through the final editing process and for gently nudging me along when deadlines neared. Additional thanks are due to Laura Lott of the American Alliance of Museums and Charles Venable of the Indianapolis Museum of Art at Newfields for agreeing to the new edition being produced. I owe an extra thanks to my Newfields colleagues for your patience as I ran around like a crazed woman for several months and to my ever-supportive boss, Kathryn Haigh, for helping me to retain sanity while I added this item to my already full plate. Naturally, there are many more individuals without whom this new edition would not be a reality and please know I am eminently grateful to all you have done to bring this about.

And finally to my family—Chris, Theo, and Jamie—thank you a thousand times over for your continued, unwavering love and support. I'm fairly certain I owe all of you an extended vacation or twelve.

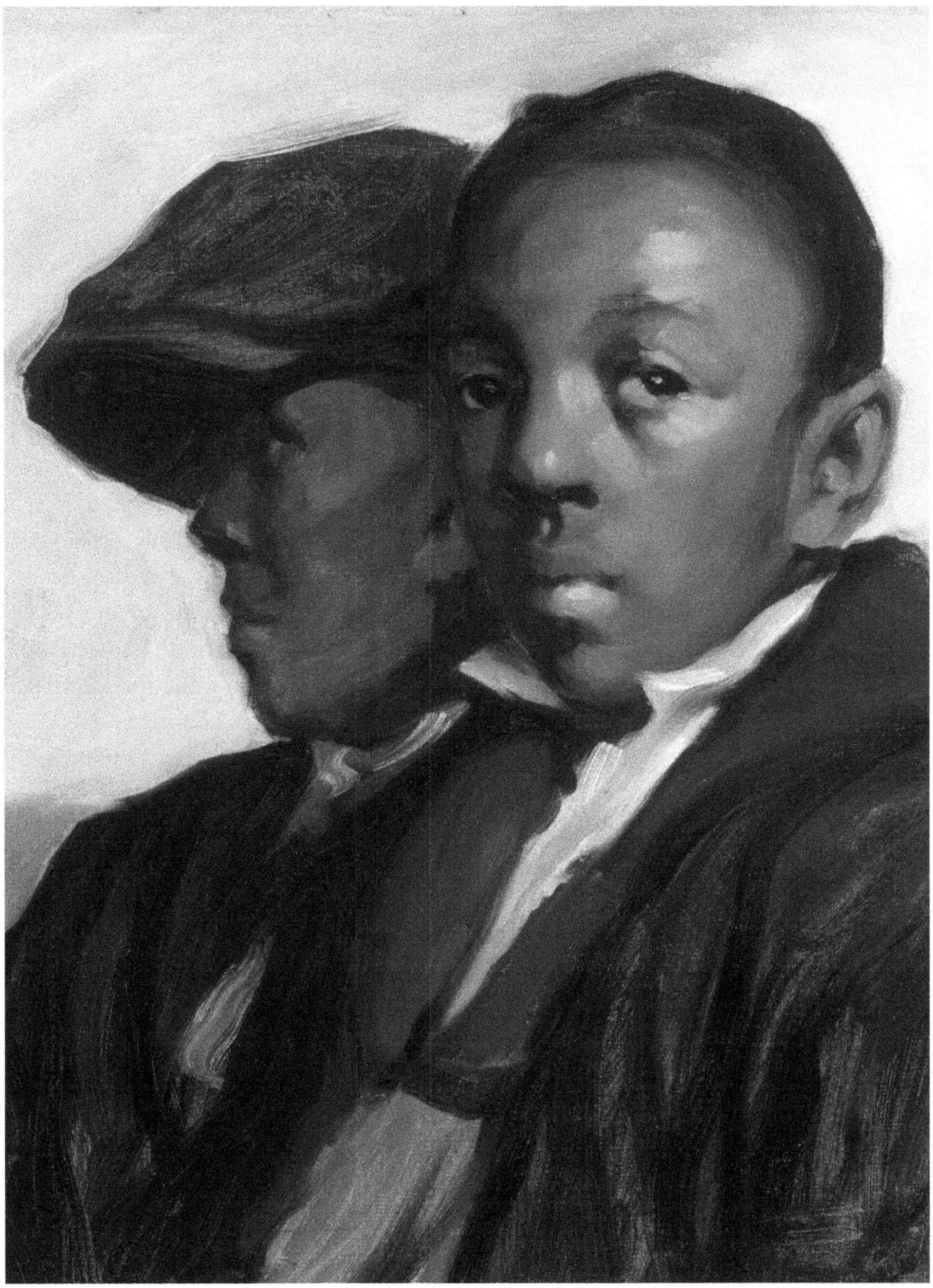

1

Intellectual Property

Kenneth D. Crews, Walter G. Lehmann, Melissa Levine, and Nancy Sims

WHAT IS INTELLECTUAL PROPERTY?

Intellectual property (IP) law is a broad expression that encompasses several bodies of law including *copyright*, *trademark*, *patent*, and *trade secret*. It refers generally to work products of the mind or products of human creativity, broadly referring to protection for inventions, ideas, and creative and artistic works. The term is often also associated with the law governing certain personal rights, including the right of privacy and the right of publicity. This chapter will explore some of the many legal considerations that arise from the creation and use of IP. While IP concepts in an international context will be addressed generally, the focus of this publication will be on US IP laws.

Why is IP different from other kinds of property such as physical or personal property? IP rights are intangible and bound with other considerations like freedom of speech, inquiry, expression, and privacy. Land can be conveyed from one owner to another, theoretically forever. Copyrights, trademarks, and patents have a different place in the context of human inquiry—they are legally designed to benefit the rights holder, typically for a defined period of time, and then become available for the public good for further inquiry and innovation. Similarly, personal rights are intended to protect a person's reputation and economic interests—their "personhood." Comparisons to land and personal property do not align with IP concepts because of this public policy element. Part of the legal notion of property is the right to exclude others from using it.

IP is unique because it is not "consumed" by use. A copy of a book can be lost or destroyed, but the copyright embodied in the text of that book still exists. This difference is fundamentally important in thinking about whether permissions are necessary or appropriate in the cultural institution context, and for thinking about the rights these institutions can or should assert over reproductions of works in their collections. It is also important in contemplating what permissions may or may not be needed from others for different kinds of projects—from educational materials, to information about collections online and in print, to product development and licensing. These uses range from noncommercial and mission driven to commercial activities that may have different legal and ethical frameworks.

The concept of IP rights has different meanings to different people and is often a highly contentious notion as the law struggles with adjusting a very tangible concept of property to the more ethereal world of creativity and innovation. IP concepts and the laws governing them vary from country to country as well. In the United States some IP laws such as copyrights are governed by federal statute while others, including privacy and publicity rights, vary by state.

To most lawyers, "IP rights" represent a broad range of many forms of legal protection. It is an umbrella term referring broadly to more specific forms of IP rights, such as copyrights, patents, and trademarks. IP can also encompass trade secrets, geographical indicators, rights of privacy and publicity, unfair competition, and even indigenous knowledge. A single situation can raise multiple IP rights issues. For example, a museum shop will often want to sell postcards and other commercial products based on objects in the collection. If the image on the postcard is a photograph of a well-known person, the museum may have to consider the copyright held by the photographer and the publicity and trademark rights held by the person in the image. Of all forms of IP, copyright is the most prevalent in the world of cultural institutions because copyright law protects the artworks, sculptures, designs, photographs, motion pictures, architectural works, books, manuscripts, and other objects that form the core of their collections.

COPYRIGHT

Copyright protects original creative expression fixed in a tangible medium of expression.[1] Copyright law provides the creator (referred to as the "author" in the US Copyright Act) the exclusive right to reproduce, distribute copies, prepare derivative works, and (for certain works) the right to publicly display or perform the work.[2] This is essentially the right to exclude others from using a work as mentioned above. This exclusive right is, however, limited under US law. Put another way, copyright is a monopoly in an original work that is granted by the federal government to the copyright owner for a limited period of time.

Copyright protects original works of authorship.[3] Ideas are not protected by copyright.[4] The expression of ideas is protected.[5] Each new expression of an underlying idea is a new, protectable expression. A work needs to be original but not necessarily highly original or radically new. At its simplest, independent creation is required—the work cannot be derived from another work. Further merit is not considered. All art is subject to copyright as long as it is nominally original.

Copyright is federal law provided for in the US Constitution and Title 17 of the US Code (the "Copyright Act").[6] The law establishes a set of rights that belong to the owner of the copyright which lasts for many decades. The law then proceeds to create exceptions or limitations on those rights, the best known of which is fair use. According to Article 1, Section 8 of the US Constitution, Congress is given the power to make laws in order "[t]o promote the Progress of Science and useful Arts, by securing for limited Times to Authors and Inventors the exclusive Right to their respective Writings and Discoveries."[7] Exercising that power, Congress enacted the first US copyright statute in 1790. Congress has revised and amended the Copyright Act many times since, and the most recent full revision was enacted in 1976. With a variety of amendments through the intervening years, the Copyright Act of 1976 is the fundamental American copyright law in force today.

Scope of Protection

Copyright law applies to a wide range of works, including text, images, motion pictures, artworks, computer programs, and much more. The scope of copyrightable works is defined conceptually: it applies to works that are "original works of authorship" and "fixed in any tangible medium of expression."[8] The concept of originality implies the work originates from an author and embodies some minimum amount of creativity.[9] A work can be "fixed" by many different means, including written on paper, spray painted on a wall, stored in a computer, or chiseled in stone.

Today, once a work meets these requirements, it receives automatic legal protection.[10] However, before 1989, there was a requirement in the law that published works have a formal copyright notice and sometimes be registered with the US Copyright Office. Those "formalities" of copyright are no longer required today. For new works created under the current law, copyright protection for the full duration allowed under the law vests instantly and automatically

WHY DOES THE THEORY MATTER?

The legal concept of IP is based on several philosophical approaches.[1] Theory provides the context for the pragmatics of applying IP. It is easier to apply IP concepts to real life with an understanding of the assumptions that underlie IP law. These theories evolved in Europe and the United States reflecting distinct notions of culture and ownership that may differ from other cultural notions of personal or private property. Thus, these philosophical differences arise in debates about IP in traditional knowledge.[2]

Labor theory is based on the work of John Locke and argues that an individual has a natural right to the results of their individual efforts. This natural right is inherent in the work product of each creator.

Moral theory argues that the results of individual creativity are the progeny of the person who created them. This approach was articulated by Immanuel Kant and Friedrich Hegel.

Utilitarian theory argues that the grant of exclusive rights to useful and creative works encourages their creation, which in turn benefits society as a whole. It looks at economic incentives for creation and investment in creation. From the perspective of *social planning,* a system that grants exclusive rights to creators fosters achievement and leads to a just and attractive culture (Fisher/Marx, Jefferson, and proponents of Legal Realist theory).

NOTES

1. See generally, "Intellectual Property," *Stanford Encyclopedia of Philosophy,* accessed April 20, 2018, https://plato.stanford.edu/entries/intellectual-property/.
2. "The term 'traditional knowledge' is used here as shorthand for the entire field of traditional knowledge (TK), genetic resources (GRs) and traditional cultural expressions (TCEs)." "Traditional Knowledge," World Intellectual Property Organization, accessed March 13, 2018, http://www.wipo.int/tk/en/.

upon creation of an eligible work. Copyright applies to published and unpublished works, works created in the United States, and those that originate in almost all countries of the world.

A few important categories of works are not eligible for protection. Perhaps the most common form of uncopyrightable works under US copyright law are those created by employees of the federal government acting within the scope of their employment.[11] Copyright may exist for works commissioned by or produced under a contract with the US federal government. The exclusion does not bar copyright protection for works produced by state and local governments, foreign governments, or organizations like the United Nations. Copyright also does not protect facts, ideas, data, names, slogans, formulas, and other short or factual works.[12] Nevertheless, a collection of nonprotected works can be copyrighted if the collection itself has originality in its selection, arrangement, or coordination.[13] The facts of personal names and telephone numbers are not protected under copyright.[14] The US Supreme Court ruled that conventional alphabetical listings of these facts are also outside the reach of copyright.[15] As a result, the digitization of public records and directories, and the creation of searchable databases based on these records, generally should not pose copyright concerns. However, a more creative collection of common information, arranged according to at least a somewhat original plan, could be within copyright's purview—for example, a catalogue raisonné.

Rights of Copyright Owners

Once a work has legal protection, the copyright owner enjoys a set of rights defined by the statutes and common law. These rights are often described as "economic rights" and "moral rights." As soon as a work gains its automatic copyright protection, the legal rights of the copyright owner apply.[16]

Economic Rights

The economic rights generally encompass the right to:

- reproduce the work in copies
- distribute the work in copies to the public
- prepare derivative works
- perform the work publicly
- display the work publicly[17]

Copyright is often referred to as a "bundle of rights" because copyright can embody several different kinds of rights—each one can be licensed, assigned, or transferred together or independently of the other. Thus, copyright includes all of these legal rights and the authority to license or permit others to exercise them in whole or in part. This is why you might see a contract that designates not only how a work can be presented but where—for example, "North American" publication rights in a book publishing contract.

The Copyright Holder

The law clearly establishes the initial ownership of a copyright, but under US law copyrights may be subsequently transferred. Copyrights may be transferred voluntarily, but the transfer must be documented in writing and signed by the transferor.[18] The law imposes no requirement to record the transfer document or to disclose it publicly.[19] As a result, often the only way to know if someone still holds the copyright in a particular work is to contact them directly. As a practical matter, potential rights holders often do not know if they are the copyright holder. In such cases, it is prudent to document the communication and, if warranted, ask if the person is willing to sign a "quitclaim" indicating they have no objection to your intended use.

Copyrights may also be transferred involuntarily.[20] Because copyrights last far beyond the life of the author, they are often devised by will and distributed through probate. Rights holders, probate judges, and lawyers often overlook copyrights in their estate planning, meaning that copyrights often go neglected and by default pass to unsuspecting heirs. Copyrights can also be redistributed in bankruptcy proceedings. They can be claimed in divorce actions and used to settle child support. They can be confiscated in criminal cases. They can be foreclosed on as a mortgaged asset. These are the unusual situations. Nevertheless, tracking the current ownership of a copyright from the distant past can be part law and part detective investigation.

The following scenarios address most situations for an initial copyright owner:

- *Single Author*
  The general rule of copyright ownership is that the author—the person who creates the copyrighted work—is the copyright owner.[21]
- *Joint Authorship*
  If two or more authors work together, contributing copyrighted content with the intent to commingle the content into a cohesive whole, the copyright in

the work is jointly owned.[22] Unless otherwise agreed, each joint owner holds an equal interest in the copyright. Each owner has authority acting alone to grant nonexclusive licenses to use the work but must share any proceeds with the other owners. Only by acting in unison may the authors grant an exclusive license or transfer all or part of the copyright.

- *Works Made for Hire and Employees*
  If a work is created by an employee within the scope of her employment, the work is deemed to be "for hire," and the copyright belongs to the employer.[23] Further, the law establishes the employer as not only the owner, but also the legal author of the work.[24] These works arise most commonly in the case of employees creating works as part of their employment. An artist may hire assistants to help complete works of art in their studio. If the assistants are truly employees, and their job involves helping create the artwork, then the copyrights in their contributions belong to the hiring artist. This demands careful planning—establishing that the person making the creative contribution is a proper and formal employee. If a work is created by an employee outside of their scope of employment (a novel written by a museum tour guide, for example), the employee retains their copyright in the work.
- *Works Made for Hire and Contractors*
  Sometimes an artist's assistants may not be formal employees. They may instead be hired as independent contractors. In that event, their works can still be "for hire" under the law, but only under rigorous

HIRING OR BEING HIRED?

In the 1989 case of *Community for Creative Non-Violence v. Reid*, the Supreme Court found that when Community for Creative Non-Violence (CCNV), a nonprofit organization, asked sculptor James Earl Reid to make a work of art expressing the plight of the homeless, the copyright in the resulting artwork was held by the artist and not CCNV. The court found Reid was neither a contractor with a written agreement nor an employee. Although CCNV gave Reid considerable direction in the creation of the work and was very engaged in the creative process, the court found that the sculpture was not a work for hire under the law at the time. In the end, Reid was recognized as the copyright holder in the sculpture while CCNV was found to be the owner of the sculpture itself.

This case underscores the importance of having strong provenance information about the creation of works in a collection and of having clear agreements with contractors for creative works that a cultural institution may commission. Additionally, it underscores the importance for employees who make creative works as part of their employment to understand the limits of their rights to control or use their creative output.[1]

NOTE

1. See generally *Community for Creative Non-Violence v. Reid*, 490 U.S. 730 (1989).

conditions.[25] The works they create must fit within a prescribed set of works listed in the statute, and the parties must have entered into a written and signed agreement stating that the works are "for hire."

Duration of Copyright

The Constitution empowers Congress to grant copyright protection for "limited times." Recent decisions from the US Supreme Court have reaffirmed Congress's wide discretion to determine the length of copyright protection.[26] But once the applicable term of copyright has run its course, the protection expires. This is the core of the law, which grants a set of rights that last for a specified term, but when the term ends the work enters the public domain, where the public has the right to use the work without restriction.

The rules affecting copyright terms have changed many times. Publication was once required for copyright ownership, as was registration and correct copyright notice.[27] Under previous versions of the US copyright law, copyright registrations had to be renewed after a set term of years. Today, copyright for all works comes into being when a work is created.[28] Neither registration, publication, nor copyright notice is currently required for a copyright to exist; however, registration is still available and provides benefits to copyright owners both in terms of enforcement of rights in courts and practically in terms of enabling contact from users requesting permissions.[29]

General rules for the copyright term are:[30]

- *Single Author*
  The basic rule is that copyright lasts for the life of the author, plus seventy years.[31] All copyrights terminate at the end of day on December 31 of the year in which they are scheduled to expire.
- *Joint Authorship*
  A jointly owned work may have two copyright owners or an unlimited number. The copyright lasts for the life of all initial copyright owners, plus seventy years.[32]
- *Work Made for Hire*
  The hiring party can be an individual, but more often it is a corporation or other legal entity. Because the "life" of a corporation can be indeterminate, works made for hire have a more defined term of protection. These works expire upon 95 years from publication or 120 years from creation, whichever comes first. Again, whatever the term, the copyrights expire on December 31 of the year in which they are scheduled to expire.[33]
- *Government Works*
  Works created by employees of the US federal government produced in the scope of their employment are not subject to copyright.[34] However, works produced under contract with or commissioned by the US federal government may be subject to copyright. The Federal Works exemption does not apply to state and local governments within the United States, [35] and other national and local governments outside of the United States may claim ownership of the works they create.[36] The interplay between state "public record" laws, which govern access to certain government-created works, and copyright ownership in those works, has long been a source of confusion. It is important to note that just because a work is considered "public record" (and those may be accessed by members of the public) does not necessarily mean that the work is "public domain" (i.e., not protected by copyright). On the contrary, you may need permission to use certain "public record" works created by state and local governments.

The rules of copyright duration are an arcane patchwork of legislation. Too often the bargain (rights in exchange for eventual public domain access) does not work well. They also expect individuals to have access to complete and accurate facts about the origin and publication of the work. Consider the museum that has a collection of European prints from the early twentieth century. Determining whether the copyright is still in effect can depend on some or all of the following:[37]

FORMALITIES, DURATION, AND WORKS CREATED BEFORE THE US COPYRIGHT ACT OF 1976

Due to changes in US copyright law over the years, the rules to determine whether copyright has expired are extremely technical—especially for works created prior to January 1, 1978, when the 1976 act took effect. Key issues include when and where the work was created, whom it was created by or for, whether and when the work was "published," and whether applicable statutory formalities, if any, were followed.

Many people have the impression that all "old" works are in the public domain. While this impression is not categorically correct, there is one large category of "older" works for which public domain status is relatively clear: those published in the United States prior to 1923. However, what constituted "publication" can be unclear, especially with some artworks. For the purposes of copyright term determination, public display (an exhibition), public performance, or the leasing or offering of a work (or copies of a work) for sale may have constituted, under limited circumstances, as "publication" of a work.[1] It is also important to remember that works *created* prior to 1923, but not *published* prior to 1923, may have much more complicated term rules and not be in the public domain.

For works that were not published prior to 1923, or that were created after or in 1923, it is quite possible that the copyright term may have ended. However, for a specific work, that determination may depend on whether the work was ever published (and if so, when), whether it was registered, whether the registration was renewed, when the author died, whether the work was created outside the United States, and even whether the author served in the military of some non-US countries.

Cultural institutions may want to invest in researching some of these factors; the payoff for determining that a work is in the public domain can be great. Peter Hirtle's "Copyright Term and the Public Domain in the United States" chart maintained by Cornell University can be a valuable tool for such investigations.[2]

NOTES

1. 17 U.S.C. § 101 (defining "publication").
2. Peter B. Hirtle, "Copyright Term and the Public Domain in the United States," Cornell University: Copyright Information Center, last modified January 1, 2015, http://copyright.cornell.edu/resources/publicdomain.cfm.

- where and when the works were created
- whether the United States had a copyright treaty with that country
- whether they were published
- in which country they were published
- if the publication included a copyright notice
- whether the copyright was renewed, if necessary
- if the US copyright was restored under the 1994 Uruguay Round on the General Agreement on Tariffs and Trade agreement[38]

Subject Matter of Copyright

The US Copyright Act lists many kinds of protected works; in addition to books, copyright applies to choreography, music, visual art, film, and architectural works.[39] However, the statutory list is not exhaustive—other kinds of creative works can be subject to copyright.

The US Copyright Act also lists things that are explicitly *not* protected by US copyright law.[40] Some of these exclusions are to preserve the separation of other types of legal protections: "methods of operation," for example, can sometimes be patentable, but would not otherwise be copyrightable. Other exclusions are related to public policy and the "bar-

WHAT MAKES A WORK "ORIGINAL"?

What makes a work sufficiently original to meet the criteria for copyright protection? The 1999 decision in *Bridgeman Art Library v. Corel Corp.* was made by the US District Court for the Southern District of New York. The Corel Corporation had made copies of images of works of art in museum collections; the underlying works of art were in the public domain. Bridgeman sold and licensed the reproductions of those works of art and claimed the images were subject to copyright. The court found that images (photographs) of two-dimensional works in the public domain were not sufficiently original to be protected by copyright under US law.[1] Although high-quality art photography takes considerable skill and experience, under US law, the skill or effort it takes to make the reproduction, the "sweat of the brow," is not relevant as it does not contribute to any new, original creation.[2]

Yet, museums still often assert copyright in the photographs they take to sell or license for art or objects in their collections. Under US law, this is a legally dubious practice—especially when the photographs are utilitarian reproductions of collection items. There is a "culture of permissioning" that reflects deference to museums but in many cases is without legal foundation. As such, many museums and cultural institutions are reexamining their policies and practices to see if they need to be reconsidered and updated.[3] While policy shifts in museums overall can take years, if not decades, to be realized field-wide, numerous museums are moving toward no longer claiming a copyright to photographs of *any* collection objects, whether those individual objects are in the public domain or under copyright, and thus consider all collection photography to be part of "slavish reproductions" to create truthful, accurate representations of the original objects themselves.

NOTES

1. This does not apply to photographs of three-dimensional works in the public domain, such as sculptures, which may be eligible for copyright protection.
2. *Bridgeman Art Library, Ltd. v. Corel Corp.*, 36 F. Supp. 2d 191, 197 (S.D.N.Y. 1999).
3. See Kenneth Crews, "Museum Policies and Art Images: Conflicting Objectives and Copyright Overreaching," *Fordham Intellectual Property, Media & Entertainment Law Journal* 22 (2012): 795.

gain" copyright strikes between private ownership and public access. The exclusion of ideas, concepts, and principles is often couched in terms related to First Amendment values—they are too important and fundamental to communication and inquiry to be subject to private ownership. Courts have also extended the "ideas" exclusion to facts, titles, and data.[41]

Publication

To "publish" a work is to distribute copies of it to the public by sale or other transfer of ownership, or by rental, lease, or lending. "Publication" also includes offering to distribute copies to a group of persons for purposes of further distribution, public performance, or public display. Under current law, a public performance or display of a work does not of itself constitute publication.[42]

Whether something is published or not for the purposes of calculating copyright can be opaque. In one famous example, Martin Luther King's 1963 "I Have a Dream" speech is considered to be unpublished despite the fact he gave the speech before more than one-quarter of a million people on the National Mall in Washington, DC. Printed copies of the speech did not include a copyright notice, which was required at the time. If the reading was considered publication, the speech would have entered the public domain. If it was considered "limited publication," then there was still a copyright. In *Estate of Martin Luther King, Jr., Inc. v. CBS, Inc.*, the King estate argued that the reading of the speech was a "performance," not a "publication," and thus was still subject to copyright held by the King estate.[43] This result is not intuitive for many people given the public importance of the speech and the size of the audience.

This case is an important indicator of the importance of publication under earlier law, the significance of understanding earlier copyright law given its influence on the collections of many cultural institutions, and the challenge of evaluating nuanced factual scenarios. For example, there are important implications for works of visual art. Unpublished works of art are rarely registered for copyright with the US Copyright Office. Ideally, the date of publication will appear on the work itself as part of a copyright notice, but a date is not required for works of art, so many do not have a date. The term "publication" for works of art generally refers to the date an image of the work was reproduced and distributed publicly, such as in a catalogue or magazine, or the year the work was sold or offered for sale by a gallery, dealer, or public auction.

Once the new copyright act went into effect in 1978, it became very difficult to "waive" or lose a copyright, accidentally or intentionally. However, prior to 1978, there were numerous ways rights holders could (usually accidentally) lose their copyright; the work would, as a result, become part of the public domain. One way an owner could lose or waive his copyright was to fail to register the work or, in certain time periods, fail to renew the registration within a specified time period. Another way an owner could lose his copyright prior to 1978 was to publish the work without the then-required copyright notice. Between 1978 and 1989, the notice requirement still applied unless the copyright owner corrected the error during a grace period. The notice requirement was abolished as of March 1, 1989, when the United States joined the Berne Convention, which prohibits such formalities. US rights holders received improved global copyright protection in exchange for complying with the "no formalities" requirement of the Berne Convention. As a practical matter, removing these formalities theoretically addressed the risk of owners accidentally losing rights via technicalities. Ironically, the absence of these formalities (i.e., notice and registration) has exacerbated the problem of "orphan works" in which a copyright is presumed to exist, but for whom no owner is readily identifiable.

Music, Sound Recordings, and Oral Histories

Sound recordings have unique requirements. Although musical compositions have been covered by US copyright law for a long time, sound recordings were not subject to federal copyright until February

15, 1972. Today, recordings do carry a copyright, and if they are based on an underlying musical composition (or book, play, etc.), the underlying work may carry a separate copyright.[44] Thus, although performers and performance venues might be able to perform a public domain musical work freely, a new recording of that performance may carry a new copyright protection.

Commercial recordings were big business well before 1976. As a result, many states passed laws protecting sound recordings prior to 1976. The continued applicability of state law protections for sound recordings is a matter of some debate, and this uncertainty has cast a pall on some music archiving projects.[45] Recent class action lawsuits brought by Flo and Eddie of The Turtles, best known for their 1967 hit "Happy Together," have done little to clarify the copyright status of pre-1972 sound recordings.[46]

Recordings that are not based on separately copyrightable works—such as recordings of impromptu speeches or improvisational performances—may only carry one copyright, but the question of whether the copyright belongs to the performer or the person who recorded it can be complex.[47] It is also worth noting that recordings may implicate personal rights such as rights of publicity, privacy, etc. Even with the permission of the person who *made* a recording, an institution should evaluate if others also hold rights.

With respect to recorded music: although fair use is not genre specific, an early case about music "sampling" declared that sampling of even one note required a license.[48] Subsequently, the commercial music recording industry has developed a fairly intricate internal system of licensing samples, and also the recording of "soundalike" clips to reduce licensing fees. Meanwhile, the concept of transformative use has been developing and is often invoked by musical remix artists. "Correct" practices in this area are not easy to determine, but cultural institutions may find some of the appropriation art copyright cases an interesting comparison when considering sound or video materials that incorporate samples.

Limitations and Exceptions to US Copyright Law

Copyrights are also subject to a series of statutory exceptions or limitations. These, too, are part of the larger bargain in the law. If copyright protection were complete and sweeping—without equitable limits—many common and socially beneficial activities that are fundamental to freedom of speech and expression in a democracy would be prohibited or penalized. Fair use may be the best known of the copyright exceptions. However, it is only one of many exceptions in the US Copyright Act that support socially significant interests, several of which are important to cultural institutions.

Fair Use

Fair use is a flexible limitation on the otherwise exclusive rights of the copyright holder. It allows for certain uses of copyrighted works without permission from the copyright owner, recognizing that the use of existing protected works is sometimes essential to creating new works and new technologies as well as fostering cultural and intellectual exchange.[49] Fair use is often acknowledged as providing "breathing room" for the constitutional right of freedom of speech under the First Amendment within the exclusive rights of copyright owners.

One reason the notion of "fair use" and related ideas of "fair dealing" in other countries have become increasing important is that the length of copyright term has continually expanded, dramatically since the Copyright Act of 1976, such that very few new works enter the public domain automatically.[50] With older works, it can be difficult to determine who the owner of the work is, or to locate the owner, if known, often leading to more so-called orphan works. If licenses or permissions were required for all new uses of such older works, this could impose significant restrictions on art, innovation, and cultural discourse.

The US Copyright Act states that use of an otherwise copyright-protected work "for purposes such as criticism, comment, news reporting, teaching (including multiple copies for classroom use), scholarship or research *is not an infringement of copyright.*" The statute includes four factors to be considered "[i]n determining whether the use made of a work in any particular case is a fair use":

1. purpose and character of use, including whether the use is commercial or noncommercial, and whether it is used for the purpose of comment and criticism, parody and satire, scholarship and research, news reporting or teaching
2. nature of copyrighted work, including the degree of creativity and originality, and whether the work is published or unpublished
3. amount and substantiality of use, including whether the degree of use is reasonable
4. impact of the use on the market for the copyrighted work, including the extent to which the use may harm or may have harmed the market or potential market for the copyrighted work[51]

One developing approach to discussing fair use reframes the issue more tightly around two points. This framework is closely tied to the evolving doctrine of transformative use and has been applied in some appropriation art cases:

1. whether the use "transformed" the material taken from the copyrighted work—use for a different purpose (e.g., comment, criticism or parody)[52]
2. whether the amount and kind of material taken from the copyrighted work was reasonable considering the nature of the copyrighted work and the way it is used in the new work[53]

Applying Fair Use[54]

Fair use is a judicially applied "rule of reason"—it is an "equitable" doctrine that examines what is sensible in a given fact situation in light of the factors provided by 17 U.S.C. § 107.[55] When applying fair use, cultural institutions need to consider the following:

- Determining whether a work is "fair use" requires an analysis of the facts on a case-by-case basis; the context in which the work is used is paramount.
- Judicial decisions applying fair use are often contextual and fact dependent.
- It can be very difficult to reconcile case law; the best way to understand fair use is to look at many examples of how it has been applied.[56]

A copyright holder cannot "preempt" fair use by claiming a licensing market (and thus market harm) for all fair uses. Similarly, a copyright holder cannot leverage copyright law to enforce censorship; withholding permission because one does not like the message may strengthen a fair use case. Nevertheless, fair use does not cover all possible uses, and ethical users *must* consider that permissions may be necessary.

Reproduction by Libraries and Archives

Section 108 of the US Copyright Act gives libraries and archives the flexibility to reproduce and distribute specific types of copyrighted works without first obtaining permission from the rights holder(s) on a limited basis for the purposes of preservation of the work, replacement of the work, and research about the work.[57] While libraries and archives have been able to rely upon this exception since the 1976 revision, other cultural institutions, namely museums, have not enjoyed a similar safe harbor for undertaking similar mission-related activities toward maintaining collections and providing visitor and researcher access to materials. In September 2017, the US Copyright Office published a Section 108 Discussion Document that proposes a variety of changes to Section 108 specifically including museums in Section 108.[58] The proposed changes expand the exceptions applicable to libraries and archives in many ways, including covering museums, adding exceptions for public performance and display, allowing multiple preservation copies, allowing preservation copies of published works, expanding access to digital preservation copies, amending the subsection 108(i) exclusions for copies made at the request of users, allowing more flexibility in making preservation copies of works covered by licensing or purchase agreements, and allowing the use of third-party vendors in some situations.

AN INSTRUCTIVE IMAGE FAIR USE CASE: *BILL GRAHAM ARCHIVES V. DORLING KINDERSLEY, LTD.*

In 2006, the Second Circuit Court of Appeals held that including reduced-size copies of concert posters in a time line in a commercially published book on the history of the Grateful Dead was fair use. Notably, permission had been sought, but the parties had been unable to agree upon licensing terms.

The court's ruling provides an overview of evolving points of fair use analysis:

- affirms that copying in service of biographical works, even in "less erudite" publications focused on pop cultural figures, is often fair use
- applies "transformative purpose" analysis to biographical use and concludes that both images specifically commented on in the text and images that are only tangentially related to the text can be fair use (although there is an implication here that the fair use argument is stronger for the former)
- observes that the small size of the images on the page and their use in concert with many other pieces of historical interest bolster the transformative nature of the use; illustrations on a timeline do not serve the same expressive purpose as the original art
- holds that the amount of the derivative work that is made up of the original is also relevant to the transformative nature of the use; the negligible contribution of the images to the overall biography also demonstrates they are not being used for their original artistic purpose
- agrees that as "creative works," the posters were of the "nature" that is normally not as available for fair use, but affirms that "the second factor may be of limited usefulness where the creative work of art is being used for a transformative purpose"
- concludes that the small size and low quality of the reproductions were tailored to the transformative purpose of the biography, and so the "amount and substantiality" factor did not weigh against fair use even though the posters were copied in their entirety
- finds that although the copyright holder would have *liked* to obtain a license fee for the use of the images, that was not relevant to the market harm analysis since the use was for a transformative purpose unlike that of traditional image licensing[1]

This case provides support for the idea that many uses of images in scholarship and cultural commentary are fair use and do not require permission or payment. This case and others like it helped to establish principles that have allowed cultural institutions to articulate fair use justifications for some important and commonplace image uses.

NOTE

1. *Bill Graham Archives v. Dorling Kindersley, Ltd.*, 448 F.3d 605 (2d Cir. 2006).

Instructional Displays and Performances

Section 110(1) of the US Copyright Act authorizes the display or performance of most copyrightable works without permission or payment "by instructors or pupils in the course of face-to-face teaching activities of a nonprofit educational institution, in a classroom or similar place devoted to instruction."[59] This certainty and straightforwardness can be helpful both in cultural institutions' own educational programs and in collaborations with other institutions.

Section 110(2) of the US Copyright Act addresses distance education.[60] In 1998, Congress revised this code section in an effort to clarify the ability to use copyrighted works in "transmissions" that are part of educational programs. This statute, The Technology, Education and Copyright Harmonization Act of 2002, colloquially known as the "TEACH Act," has had most attention for its potential application by nonprofit schools and universities. The exception may also be used by governmental agencies. Some museums qualify to use it. While the statute offers some assurance about the ability to use works in distance education, including internet-based courses, many educational institutions are finding the law to be too constrained and cumbersome to employ. Section 110(2) is worth noting here if only to indicate its failure in its current form to address the expectations most cultural institutions have regarding possible contributions to online teaching and learning.

Images of Utilitarian Works

Section 113 of the US Copyright Act outlines provisions for the exclusive right to reproduce a copyrighted pictorial, graphic, or sculptural work in or on any kind of article, whether useful or otherwise.[61] In 2000, the US Court of Appeals for the Ninth Circuit issued an opinion in the case of *Ets-Hokin v. Skyy Spirits, Inc.* A photographer was hired to make stylized photographs of a vodka bottle for Skyy Spirits. There was a written contract between the photographer and the company that governed the disposition of the resulting photographs. The photographer claimed copyright in the images and registered them for copyright protection in his name. He did not designate them as derivative works. The bottle itself was a unique shade of blue that was subject to a trademark, but was of a shape typical for vodka bottles. When the photographer sued Skyy Spirits for copyright infringement after a dispute about the scope of the contract, the court found the images were subject to the photographer's copyright and sufficiently original to warrant protection. The photographs were found to be original and not derivative of the vodka bottle. The bottle design was found to be utilitarian and not subject to copyright. Thus, it was not possible for the resulting photographs of the bottle to be derivations of the bottle design; they were found to be necessarily original.[62]

Architectural Works

Congress brought architectural works under copyright protection in 1990.[63] At the same time, Congress crafted an exception that permitted making photographs and other visual images of architectural works that have been constructed in a place that is easily and readily visible to the public.[64] Without this exception, infringements could occur with each photograph of a city skyline, with each postcard, and souvenir that depicts a protected building design.[65]

Accessible Formats

Section 121 of the US Copyright Act creates explicit permissions for adaptations of "previously published, nondramatic literary work[s]" to formats accessible to people with visual disabilities.[66] Courts noted that legislative history pointed to accessibility for blind persons "with no suggestion that anything more than a purpose to entertain or inform" as fair use.[67] More recently, courts have upheld the idea that noncommercial reformatting of works in general, to provide access for people with a wide range of disabilities, is fair use.[68] International support for accessible formats is also evident in efforts to ratify agreements such as the Marrakesh Treaty, which addresses access to works by the visually impaired.[69] Cultural institutions can increasingly feel confident that copyright presents few barriers when thoughtfully altering or reformatting materials to provide access to patrons with a variety of disabilities.

First-Sale Doctrine

Under the US Copyright Act, "The owner of a particular copy or phonorecord lawfully made under this title, or any person authorized by such owner, is entitled, without the authority of the copyright owner, to sell or otherwise dispose of the possession of that copy or phonorecord."[70] This means cultural institutions generally do have the right to sell, lend, or otherwise dispose of copyrightable items in their collections. But it also means that rights and reproductions specialists cannot assume an institution owns the copyright in a work just because it owns the work. When something is acquired, the seller or donor frequently only owns the object and not the accompanying IP rights. Increasingly, museums, libraries, and archives take care in their acquisition process to obtain rights, if possible, whether by a transfer, assignment, or nonexclusive license to reproduce the work in certain ways with or without additional compensation to the rights holder(s). Careful acquisition practices can help alleviate the orphan works problem over time and minimize the need for permissions, especially for routine, expected uses that might exceed fair use.

Public Displays

"The owner of a particular copy lawfully made under this title, or any person authorized by such owner, is entitled, without the authority of the copyright owner, to display that copy publicly, either directly or by the projection of no more than one image at a time, to viewers present at the place where the copy is located."[71] It is important to note that the public display right language "projection of not more than one image at a time" does not apply to movies and videos. Therefore, cultural institutions typically can display works in their collections—as well as works on loan to their institution—without permission from the copyright owner.

Appropriation Art

From the comic-panels-turned-paintings by Roy Lichtenstein to Sherrie Levine's "re-photography" of famous photographs, many artists make use of existing materials in creating new works. Reproduction of large portions of works by other artists, often without credit to or permission from the first artist, is a thread that connects a large body of work referred to as "appropriation art." Appropriation art largely includes the concept of recontextualization in which the work of one creator is placed into a new context by the appropriation artist.

When the pre-existing material is not under copyright, there is no legal IP problem. However, when an appropriation artist uses materials that are protected by copyright, the potential for copyright infringement arises. Unsurprisingly, the use of copyrighted works by other artists often attracts lawsuits, and the law around appropriation art is rapidly evolving. Often, the framing of the legal system conflicts with the norms and ethics of the art world, but the frequent reversals and multijudge panel reviews of judicial opinions in this area demonstrates that the legal world does not always know what to do with these situations either.

TRADEMARK

Trademark protects corporate identities and products and may include a word, name, symbol, or device (or combination thereof) used to identify goods and services and distinguish them from goods or services offered by others.[72] It protects the exclusive right to use the mark in connection with particular goods or services.[73] It is also often thought of as a consumer-protection provision, helping consumers ensure they are getting goods or services of the quality they expect and from the source they expect. Because trademark law is oriented to public perceptions, it most strongly protects marks that create strong impressions: fanciful and arbitrary marks are considered legally strongest. However, marks that are plainer or more descriptive can obtain "secondary meaning" (and stronger protection) through continued use.[74]

JEFF KOONS

Sued when he turned a photograph of people holding puppies into a sculpture that was subsequently sold, Koons claimed his work, which did include some differences from the photograph, was a parody. In 1992, the Second Circuit Court of Appeals found that the parodic point (critique of greeting-card-style photography) could have been made without use of that particular image and found that it was not fair use.[1]

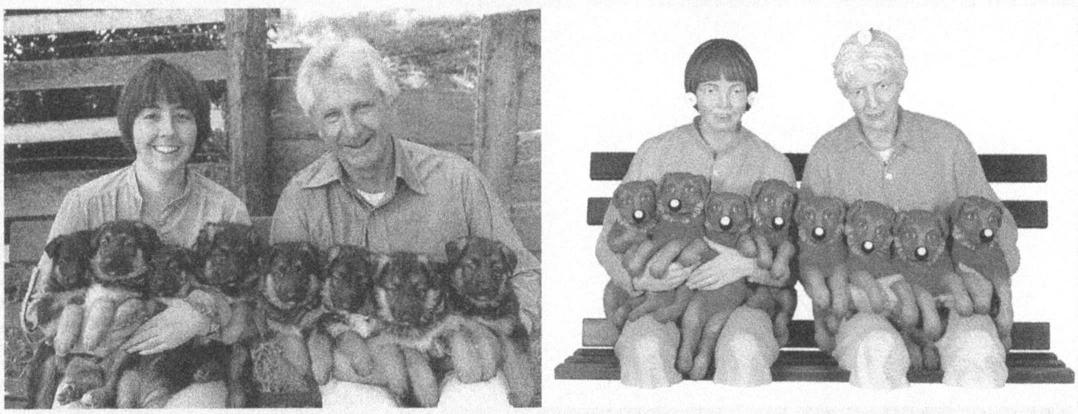

FIGURE 1.1
Photograph (left) and sculpture (right) that were the subject of *Rogers v. Koons.*

However, in 2006 Koons was involved with another case where the Second Circuit Court found in Koons's favor in a similar case where he included another artist's commercial photograph of someone's feet in a collage image. In contrast to the 1992 case, the court concluded that under the facts of this case, Koons's use was a transformative fair use; parody was not a key aspect of this analysis.[2] The key here is that fair use is a situational concept. Two cases involving the same artist, but not the same art, can lead to different results.

SHEPARD FAIREY

The famous "Hope" poster of then-presidential candidate Barack Obama is another instance of a lawsuit around use of one artist's uncredited work by another artist. Fairey was sued by the Associated Press for the use of photographer Mannie Garcia's image, but he maintained the poster was a fair use of the image—and many advocates agreed. Garcia also argued he had retained the rights to the image, and expressed both admiration for Fairey's use and objection to the uncredited appropriation.[3] A variety of procedural and other legal issues arose as the copyright case proceeded,[4] and the parties eventually settled out of court.

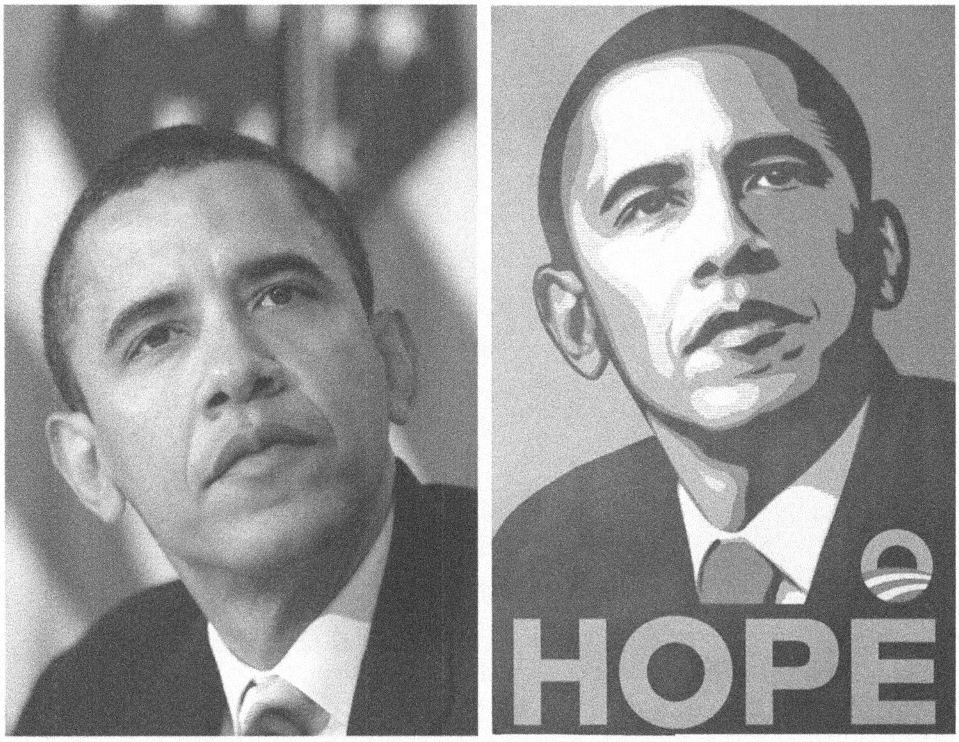

FIGURE 1.2
Mannie Garcia's photograph (left) and Shepard Fairey's poster (right) of President Barack Obama.

RICHARD PRINCE

Prince was sued by Patrick Cariou for his use of Cariou's photographs in a series of thirty works entitled *Canal Zone*. In many of the individual works, Cariou's photographs were reproduced largely intact, with some additional painted or drawn-on elements by Prince. Others involved greater recontextualization. Although the District Court initially held that all the works were infringing,[5] the Second Circuit Court reversed this on appeal, finding twenty-five of the works were transformative fair use and remanding the remaining five works (including "Graduation" on the right in Figure 1.3) for reconsideration. The Appellate Court specifically held that the lower court had been incorrect in ruling that for a work to be transformative it must comment on the work from which it copies.[6] Instead, the Second Circuit Court said a use can be transformative when it changes the aesthetic of the original.[7]

Cariou v. Prince raises an issue of great importance for cultural institutions and museums in particular: the liability of those who display or distribute copies of appropriation art. Cariou sued both the gallery hosting Prince's works and the publisher of the exhibition catalogue. The District Court ordered that the paintings and the exhibition catalogues be impounded and destroyed and held that the gallery was liable as a vicarious and contributory infringer (meaning the gallery was as responsible as the artist for the purported infringement and even "contributed" to the artist's action).[8] The Second Circuit Court, in

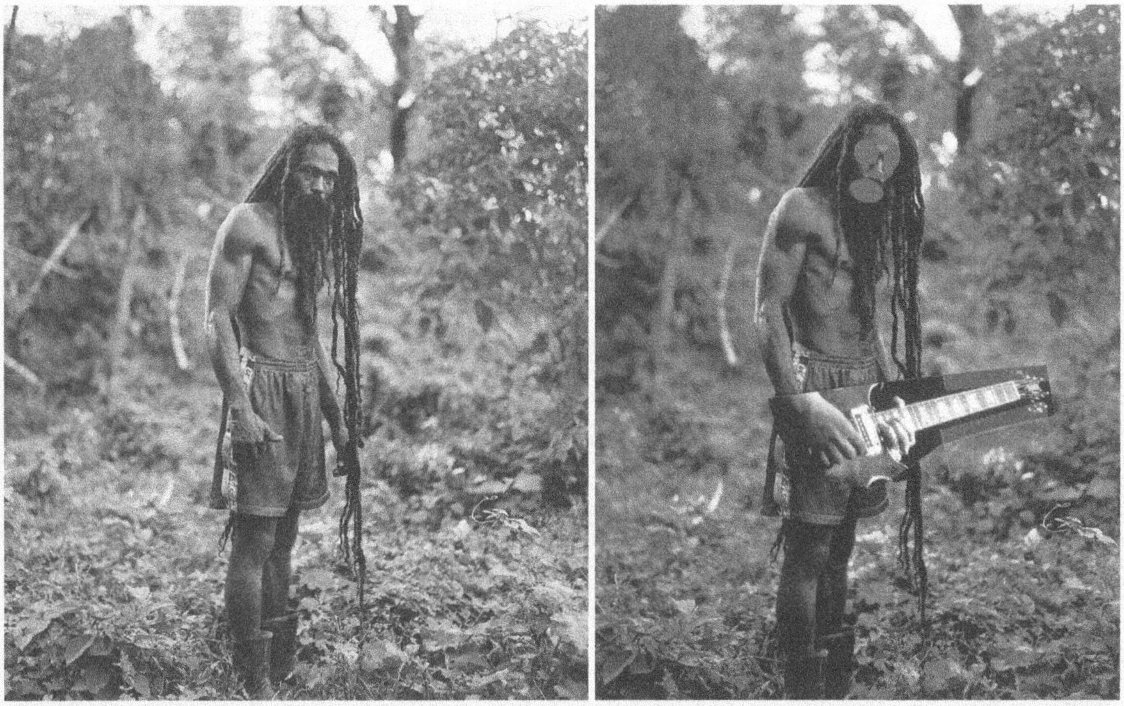

FIGURE 1.3
Patrick Cariou's photograph (left) and Richard Prince's photograph (right) that were part of the disputed works in *Cariou v. Prince.*

reversing the lower court's decision on appeal, determined that neither the gallery nor the publisher could be liable for most of the works. However, the Second Circuit Court remanded five images for further consideration by the District Court, and if the District Court had concluded those images were infringing, it may or may not also have concluded that the gallery or publisher bore some liability. Since the parties settled out of court, this question was ultimately never resolved.[9]

Because the gallery that displayed Prince's works was sued for liability as well, museums may have some hesitations about displaying appropriation art, especially given the District Court's initial opinion in *Cariou v. Prince.* The overall development of fair use law related to appropriation art has tended to find these are fair uses, but there may be instances where the copying is so egregious that a court will not allow it. Museums must balance the possible legal risks with their goals and missions of collecting, preserving art, and sharing art with the public.

NOTES

1. *Rogers v. Koons,* 960 F.2d 301 (2d Cir. 1992).
2. *Blanch v. Koons,* 467 F.3d 244 (2d Cir. 2006). It is worth noting that *Campbell v. Acuff-Rose,* the earliest Supreme Court case employing a transformative use analysis, was decided after Rogers, but well before

Blanch. The analysis in Blanch reflects several years of courts' evolving understanding of the transformative use analysis.

3. Randy Kennedy, "Artist Sues The A.P. Over Obama Image," *New York Times*, February 9, 2009, http://www.nytimes.com/2009/02/10/arts/design/10fair.html.
4. Fairey did not disclose necessary information to his own lawyers and destroyed evidence in such a way that he ultimately received a criminal sentence (of community service) for those actions.
5. *Cariou v. Prince*, 784 F.Supp.2d at 337 (S.D.N.Y. 2011).
6. *Cariou v. Prince*, 714 F.3d at 694 (2nd Cir. 2013).
7. "Where Cariou's serene and deliberately composed portraits and landscape photographs depict the natural beauty of Rastafarians and their surrounding environs, Prince's crude and jarring works, on the other hand, are hectic and provocative." Ibid. at 706 (2nd Cir. 2013). (Also citing, with approval, Prince's changes in the physical size of the images.)
8. *Cariou v. Prince*, 784 F. Supp. 2d at 354 (S.D.N.Y. 2011).
9. Randy Kennedy, "Richard Prince Settles Copyright Suit With Patrick Cariou Over Photographs," ArtsBeat Blog, March 18, 2014, 6:23 p.m., http://artsbeat.blogs.nytimes.com/2014/03/18/richard-prince-settles-copyright-suit-with-patrick-cariou-over-photographs/.

Trademarks may be identified by the symbols TMSM, or ®, (for formally registered marks), although use of such symbols is not all legally required to maintain a trademark. Registration with the US Patent and Trademark Office protects a trademark under federal law and creates legal presumptions that may benefit the rights holders.[75] But trademarks can also have protection without federal registration: trademark rights can be created just by using a mark in commerce. Such trademarks are referred to as "common law" trademarks.

Unlike copyrights, trademarks must be used *and* enforced to maintain rights. Trademarks can be lost if they are not enforced or, ironically, if the trademark is so successful that it becomes commonly used as a generic term for a whole category of products.[76] So-called generic trademarks include well-known items such as Kleenex, Band-Aid, and Velcro. Trademark owners sometimes fight against "dilution" of their marks (uses that make their marks less distinctive) and "tarnishment" (uses that might create negative associations in consumers' minds).

Cultural institutions may create (or may already have) trademarks in relation to their own services, products, and programming. Trademarks can be valuable branding tools. Therefore, cultural institutions should consider registering and enforcing their trademark rights, in institutional names and logos among other things, where appropriate.[77]

Trademark issues may also arise when using others' trademarks, particularly with sponsorships or other business partnerships. Importantly, uses of trademarks strictly to identify a product or service (especially in noncommercial contexts), or to critique, satirize, or parody a trademark owner are often legally permitted as trademark "fair use" (which is different in some critical ways from copyright fair use!). As long as a trademark is used in a way that does not create confusion about the source of the goods or services it identifies, the use is permissible. Thus, works that include or make reference to trademarks without implying sponsorship or endorsement, or that mislead consumers as to the origin of the work, often do not present legal issues to their creators or cultural institutions that acquire or display them. However, trademark owners may not always recognize that point. For example, Mattel, Inc. has sued often over artistic uses of its "Barbie" character, but has repeatedly lost those cases.[78]

PATENT

Patents protect novel, useful inventions (method, process, composition, design, etc.) and function as a limited monopoly for a limited period of time; the owner of the patent controls who gets to "practice" or use the invention.[79] There are formal patent registration processes administered by the US Patent and Trademark Office.

Patents last for a relatively short time (usually around twenty years in the United States).[80] Because of this short term, and because patent protection does not extend to *discussions* of an invention but only its actual *use*, patents are rarely a significantly large factor in the art museum context, but may be more applicable to nature or science museums[81] and where innovative techniques, procedures, or devices may be employed, such as certain conservation practices. Patent may be more relevant to innovations *produced by* cultural institutions, such as the development of new approaches to conservation science, innovations in programming and computer hardware, or even design innovations.

TRADE SECRET

Trade secret is an area of law that creates an exclusive right to ideas or information not generally known that gives their holder a competitive advantage.[82] Some items protectable as trade secrets may also be protectable under patent law (such as product recipes or formulas)—but patent protection requires public disclosure and lasts for a limited time, so sometimes trade secret is more appealing to a rights holder. Other items protectable as trade secrets, such as closely protected private donor lists, may not be patentable.

Trade secrets must be treated as confidential to maintain protection; if best efforts are used to maintain confidentiality, then courts will prevent others who circumvent the confidentiality from making use of the information in ways that create commercial harm. There is fairly limited applicability of trade secret law in the cultural institution context. Liability for violating trade secrets is almost never an issue without breaching someone else's confidentiality, although the potential could arise in situations such as illicitly obtaining another institution's confidential donor lists or disclosing secret "ingredients" in an artist's production methods.

PERSONAL RIGHTS

In addition to the IP rights arising from or embedded in a creative work, there may also be certain rights belonging to a person whose image, name, or likeness is used in or in conjunction with a creative work. These rights are generally referred to as "personal rights" because they are rights that arise from an individual's inherent "personhood." Personal rights are fundamentally human rights that include the right to control the use and exploitation of one's name, image, and likeness and the results and proceeds of one's personal efforts. Personal rights include the right to privacy, the right to publicity, and moral rights.[83] These rights may be recognized by statute or by common law and vary by jurisdiction. Privacy and publicity laws in particular are creatures of state law, and their scope varies. The individual controls personal rights; generally speaking these rights cannot be transferred or waived. In some situations, personal rights may be assigned to the person's agent and licensee, and in some jurisdictions personal rights may survive the person's death and be inherited.

The degree to which personal rights are recognized varies by country and jurisdiction. The nature and scope of these rights is a product of the culture and traditions of the society in which they are asserted. In the United States, the rights of privacy and publicity, and to a limited extent moral rights, are recognized through a variety of state and federal statutes and in common law through court decisions.

Privacy

The right of privacy protects private individuals against unwanted public exposure. Central to a claim for invasion of privacy is damage to one's reputation, personal dignity, or freedom. Claims for invasion of privacy take various forms and may include claims based on emotional distress or defamation, and may also involve the unwanted collection or disclosure of personal information. Generally, the right of privacy does not apply to so-called public figures—those who can be said to have "waived" their privacy rights as a result of their involvement in public events, even when that involvement was unintentional. In some cases, a person can be considered a "limited public figure" in the sense that they can be considered a public figure with respect to a single, public newsworthy event.[84]

The constitutional basis for the right of privacy in the United States arises from the Fourteenth Amendment. In his dissent to a 1928 Supreme Court case involving telephone wiretapping, *Olmstead v. United States*, Justice Brandeis articulated the right of privacy as the "right to be left alone."[85] The right of privacy also has a statutory basis in both federal and state law and is a highly litigated area of the law.

There are four basic forms of privacy rights recognized by US common law:[86]

1. *Unreasonable intrusion on personal solitude*
   These claims involve intrusions into a person's private life in a manner that would be considered highly offensive to a reasonable person.[87] Such claims are similar to claims of trespass: they are highly fact dependent and emphasize the sanctity of the home and personal space. There is no "public figure" exception for unreasonable intrusion claims. Examples of lawsuits involving claims of unreasonable intrusion include celebrity stalking cases and television "ride-along" cop shows.[88]
2. *Public disclosure of true but embarrassing private facts*
   These claims involve situations in which the disclosure of true private facts results in embarrassment or humiliation. These privacy rights can be waived in situations in which a person becomes involved in a public event, however involuntary, and are not actionable in situations where the public has a legitimate interest in the disclosure of otherwise private facts.[89] Examples of situations involving the public disclosure of private facts include the publication of truthful information contained in public records or posting photographs online.[90]
3. *False light*
   These claims involve publicly made statements that contain untrue facts. The statements must be highly offensive to a reasonable person and made with the intent to harm the person's reputation.[91] The focus is on the emotional or psychological harm suffered by the victim. Examples of situations involving false light include blog posts, YouTube videos, or statements made on social media platforms.[92]
4. *Appropriation of name and likeness*
   Privacy rights based on the appropriation of a person's name and likeness are similar to publicity rights. The appropriation of an individual's name and likeness focuses on the right to be able to control and benefit from the exploitation of one's own "personhood." The focus is on the economic harm that a victim may suffer as a result of the appropriation of their name and likeness. Examples of lawsuits involving appropriation include the use of a photograph of a person for commercial purposes, such as advertising or marketing, without permission.[93]

Defamation Claims

Defamation involves an intentionally false communication that injures another's reputation or good name. To be actionable, the communication must be made publicly, be false, be unprivileged, and cause harm to the claimant.[94] Defamation claims may be brought as civil or criminal actions. Defamation based on a written statement is called "libel," while defamation based on a spoken statement is called "slander." A higher standard of actual malice applies in the case of public figures. Truth is a defense to defamation; opinion may also be a defense.

The specific requirements to prevail in a lawsuit for defamation of character vary by jurisdiction. According to the Restatement (Second) of Torts, to succeed in a claim for defamation, including both libel and slander, a plaintiff must prove four elements:

1. The defendant made a false and defamatory statement concerning the plaintiff.
2. The defendant made an unprivileged publication to a third party.
3. The publisher acted at least negligently in publishing the communication.
4. In some cases, the plaintiff must also prove special damages.[95]

An essential element in any defamation claim is that the defendant published something defamatory about the plaintiff. The Restatement defines a communication as defamatory "if it tends so to harm the reputation of another as to lower him in the estimation of the community or to deter third persons from associating with him."[96]

Examples of defamatory statements include communications that:

- impute a serious crime involving moral turpitude or a felony
- expose the plaintiff to hatred
- reflect negatively on the plaintiff's character, morality, or integrity
- impair the plaintiff's financial well-being
- suggest that the plaintiff suffers from a physical or mental defect that would cause others to refrain from associating with the plaintiff

Since the statement must be false, generally speaking, truth is a defense to a defamation claim.[97] Objective statements based on facts that can be substantiated are unlikely to result in a successful defamation claim. Some courts have held that opinions—subjective statements of emotion or reaction based on facts—do not

PRIVACY RIGHTS AND CULTURAL INSTITUTIONS

Privacy rights may arise in cultural institutions in a variety of ways. Certain collections, such as photographs and videos, as well as other content-based materials, may contain readily identifiable names, images, voices, or depictions of real people. It is quite possible that in many cases personal releases were not obtained from those depicted in the works. Depending on the context in which the person is depicted, it is possible that certain privacy rights may be implicated. Works in which clearly identifiable people are depicted in embarrassing or humiliating situations are of particular concern. In displaying these images, there is a risk that the institution may be held contributorily or vicariously liable for violating the privacy rights of the person(s) depicted. If permission from the individuals cannot be obtained, efforts to conceal the identity of those depicted should be considered. Personal information may also be included in metadata and other archival materials associated with collections.

Institutions may also record and use photographs, videos, or other depictions of visitors, staff, volunteers, board members, donors, etc. and some uses may be for commercial purposes, including marketing and promotion. In such cases, written releases should be obtained from all clearly identifiable people. Member and donor lists may also pose privacy concerns. Social media presents many new concerns regarding privacy rights. An institutional policy regarding the management of personal information is advisable and having such a policy will help to minimize risks associated with privacy rights.

give rise to a defamation claim. However, if a statement implies defamatory facts as the basis of the opinion, then the statement may be actionable.[98] To minimize the potential for a defamation claim, it is considered best practice to state the facts first and express opinion separately. While very few defamation claims result in court proceedings, it is important to be sensitive to the reputational and emotional harm that may result from making potentially defamatory statements.

Publicity

Publicity rights are a form of personal property rights with increasing significance in social media uses. Publicity rights involve the right of an individual to control the commercial use of one's name, image, likeness, or other personal identifying characteristics. The concept that a person's identity represents a property interest was first recognized in US law in a 1953 case involving the rights of baseball players to control the licensing of their images for use on baseball cards.[99] Publicity rights are generally a function of state law. The scope and duration of publicity rights vary widely.[100] Roughly half of the states have specific statutes governing publicity rights. In some of these states, the publicity right is protected as a form of privacy rights involving the misappropriation of a person's name and likeness. Other states rely on common law court rulings to define publicity rights. In some states, publicity rights are protected under theories involving unfair competition or state trademark law. In these states, publicity rights claims are couched in terms of misappropriation of one's name or likeness, or as improperly implying endorsement or creating consumer confusion as to the source of particular goods or services.[101]

Publicity rights may also be protected under federal trademark law where a person's identity can be considered a personal "mark," the misappropriation of which creates a likelihood of consumer confusion as to the source or origin of the goods or services with which the mark is associated.[102] Federal trademark law has been asserted to protect publicity rights in cases involving false endorsement claims by celebrities.[103]

Traditionally, publicity rights terminate on death, but under US law the duration of publicity rights is also determined under state law and varies widely. In some states, such as New York, the publicity right terminates at death.[104] In others, the publicity right may survive after death for a period of years. In Florida, the right of publicity lasts for forty years after death,[105] while in Ohio the right lasts for sixty years after death,[106] and in Indiana the right lasts for one hundred years after death.[107] Publicity rights may also be inheritable under some state laws. The California Celebrity Rights Act recognizes a property interest in publicity rights and grants rights to the estate of a "deceased personality" for a period of seventy years. The statute established a successor-in-interest registry for deceased personalities.[108]

Although some state laws may apply more broadly, as an economic right, the publicity right generally applies only to commercial uses of a person's image and likeness. The publicity right is typically implicated in situations involving the use of a celebrity's name, image, or likeness in connection with advertising, marketing, or in situations that imply endorsement or sponsorship, and on merchandising. Publicity rights are not absolute. Courts are often asked to balance the competing private rights of publicity with public rights to freedom of speech and expression.[109] Numerous recent cases involving sports celebrities have dealt with these issues.[110] The death of a well-known celebrity often results in efforts to make legislative changes to state publicity rights laws.[111]

The publicity right is limited by the First Amendment's right to freedom of speech. For the most part, use of images of celebrities and other public figures in conjunction with news reporting, commentary, parody, or other expressive uses does not implicate publicity rights and is permitted without approval from the person being depicted.[112] Even so, privacy rights may be implicated in certain contexts.

MORAL RIGHTS

In addition to protecting the economic interests of artists, most Western European countries (as well as

MARILYN MONROE

In a well-known case involving the right of publicity, the US Court of Appeals for the Ninth Circuit was asked to determine whether the film actress Marilyn Monroe was a resident of New York or California at the time of her death.[1] It was important to determine which state she was domiciled in at the time of her death to resolve which state's publicity rights laws would apply to her estate, which held lucrative publicity rights. This would also determine which state's estate taxes would apply to Monroe's estate. The court held that because the Monroe estate had claimed for decades that Monroe died domiciled in New York in order to avoid paying California estate taxes, the estate was judicially estopped (prevented) from now claiming years later that the actress was domiciled in California at the time of her death to take advantage of the California right of publicity statutes.[2]

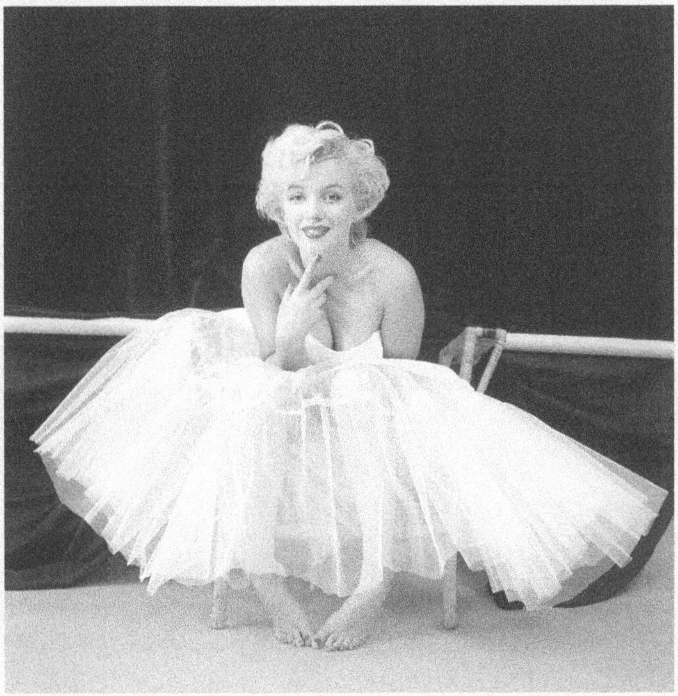

FIGURE 1.4
Marilyn Monroe in New York City in 1954.

NOTES

1. *Milton H. Greene Archives, Inc. v. Marilyn Monroe LLC*, 692 F.3d 983 (9th Cir. 2012).
2. Tamlin H. Bason, "9th Circuit: Marilyn Monroe Not Protected by California's Post-Mortem Publicity Statute," Bloomberg BNA, Sept. 7, 2012, www.bna.com/9th-circuit-marilyn-n17179869601/.

THE THREE STOOGES

In a case involving the use of artistic portraits of The Three Stooges on merchandise including lithographs and T-shirts, the California Supreme Court focused on the economic value of using images of these iconic film stars and the commercial exploitation of their fame.[1] The court determined that the works in question lacked sufficient creativity to warrant First Amendment protection. The court cited works by Andy Warhol incorporating celebrity images and indicated that those uses would be protected expression. "Through distortion and the careful manipulation of context, Warhol was able to convey a message that went beyond the commercial exploitation of celebrity images and became a form of ironic social comment on the dehumanization of celebrity itself."[2]

Recently, cases have been brought against social media entities by noncelebrities (private persons) using publicity rights theories. These include a class action suit involving Facebook's use of user testimonials for commercial purposes as part of its "Sponsored Stories" advertising campaign,[3] testing Andy Warhol's concept of "15 minutes of fame."

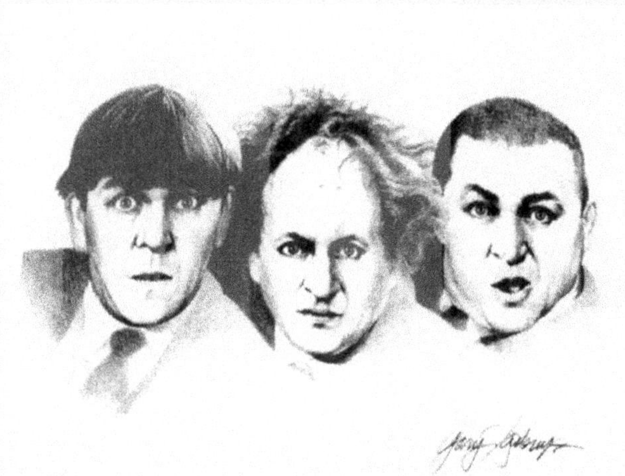

FIGURE 1.5
Gary Saderup's drawing of The Three Stooges.

NOTES

1. *Comedy III Productions, Inc. v. Gary Saderup, Inc.*, 21 P.3d at 797 (Cal. 2001).
2. Ibid. at 811.
3. *Fraley v. Facebook, Inc.*, 830 F. Supp. 2d 785 (N.D. Cal. 2011).

Canada and Australia) have long incorporated the concept of "moral rights" to varying degrees in their IP laws.[113] Viewing the work of an artist as an extension of the artist's self, moral rights seek to preserve the reputation of the artist by protecting the integrity of the work.[114] Moral rights primarily consist of the right of attribution and the right of integrity.[115] Select moral rights concepts in some countries also protect an artist's right to determine when and how a work may be distributed to the public.[116] French law, for example, recognizes the right of "divulgence" (*droit de divulgation*) under which an artist has the exclusive right to "divulge" the work—to determine when it is finished. As early as 1845, French courts held that only the artist knows when his work is finished and that "unauthorized exposure of unfinished paintings is an infringement of the right of divulgence."[117] The scope of moral rights varies by jurisdiction and are generally broader under European laws than in the United States.

Although European copyright traditions provide an interesting contrast to the American approach, it is important to keep in mind Stephen Weil's admonition that "copyright law is essentially territorial."[118] Regardless of an artist's birthplace, citizenship, domicile, or habitual residence, and regardless of where the artist's work was created, ordinarily the only copyright provisions that US courts will apply to the artist's work are those to be found in the US Copyright Act.[119]

Moral Rights in the United States

Unlike some other countries, US IP law has traditionally focused exclusively on protecting economic rights in creative works.[120] Subject to exceptions such as fair use,[121] US copyright laws provide artists with exclusive rights to control the exploitation of their work(s), including the rights of reproduction, adaptation, distribution and, for certain works, the rights of performance and display.[122] These rights can be alienated or transferred by the artist under certain circumstances.[123] Importantly, these copyrights are separate and distinct from ownership of the physical object created by the artist[124] and do not preclude the owner of the work from displaying it publicly.[125]

Economic rights function somewhat like a property interest. The rights last beyond the life of the author and can be bought and sold. By contrast, under US law, moral rights are not transferrable. Only the author may exercise them, and for the most part, moral rights in the United States are effective only during the lifetime of the author.[126] Congress was not very partial to the concept of moral rights, arguing that US law already protects comparable rights through legal theories of publicity, privacy, trademark, and even defamation. On the other hand, to the extent that the rights exist, they can apply to many works in cultural institutions.

In the United States, moral rights of an author are limited in many respects, but do include the right to:[127]

- have the author's name on the work
- remove the author's name from a work that has been altered in a manner that is harmful to the author's reputation
- prevent the willful destruction or alteration of a work of "recognized stature"[128]

In many countries, moral rights are broader and apply to many different types of works. Under US law, moral rights apply only to "works of visual art."[129] Even then, the rights apply only if the work has been produced in a single copy or in a series of not more than two hundred originals, each signed and numbered.[130]

Congress added moral rights provisions in a limited way in 1990 in order to comply with international treaty obligations when the United States joined the Berne Convention for the Protection of Literary and Artistic Works, originally signed in Berne, Switzerland, on September 9, 1886. The United States joined the Berne Convention effective March 1, 1989, to improve global protection for copyrights originating in the United States. At that time, Congress amended the US Copyright Act, adding section 106A, which applied moral rights to "works of visual art" only if the works were created or sold by the author (the artist) after the effective date of the law.[131]

Visual Artists Rights Act

Several notable examples of the limitations of the traditional American approach to copyright protection include the mutilation of important sculptures by Alexander Calder, Isamu Noguchi, and Richard Serra, and the misattribution of a mural by William Smith.[132] None of these artists had recourse under then-existing copyright laws. In response, beginning with California in 1979, ten states enacted laws to protect the attribution and integrity rights of artists.[133] When the United States became a member of the Berne Convention for the Protection of Literary and Artistic Works in 1989, US copyright law nominally included moral rights by virtue of that treaty. The following year, Congress enacted the Visual Artists Rights Act of 1990 (VARA) to further codify moral rights in a greater capacity.

VARA provides specific attribution and integrity rights for creators of works of visual art, including the right to prevent the destruction of works of "recognized stature."[134] VARA applies only to certain types of visual art, including paintings, drawings, prints, sculptures, and still photographs produced in limited editions of two hundred or fewer copies.[135] Other common forms of "visual art," including posters, books, and videos, are specifically excluded from this definition, as are advertisements[136] and works made for hire.[137] Whether a work falls within the definition is based not on the media or materials used, but on the "generally accepted standards of the artistic community." A work does not need to be "final" to be covered by VARA.[138]

Under VARA, artists have the right to claim authorship in a work and to prevent the use of the artist's name in connection with any work the artists did not create or which has been altered in a way that "would be prejudicial to his or her honor or reputation."[139] Artists also have the right to prevent the intentional alteration of a work that would be harmful to the artists' "honor or reputation,"[140] and to prevent the intentional or grossly negligent destruction of a "work of recognized stature."[141]

VARA contains a number of exceptions that are of particular importance to cultural institutions. Alterations to a work that are caused by intentional or grossly negligent actions, the passage of time or the nature of the materials, conservation or public presentation, are not actionable under VARA.[142] In addition, the attribution provisions of VARA do not apply to reproductions or other uses of the work.[143]

For works created after June 1, 1991, rights under VARA are limited to the life of the artist, and for jointly created works, the life of the last surviving artist. For works created prior to June 1, 1991, to which title has not been transferred by the artist, rights under VARA last for the same period as copyright protection, currently life of the author plus seventy years.[144] Only the artist has the attribution and integrity rights conferred by VARA. These rights cannot be transferred, but they can be waived in writing by the artist or, in the case of joint works, by one of the co-creators.[145] Remedies under VARA are the same as those for copyright infringement.[146] VARA preempts state law to the extent that those statutes provide equivalent rights.[147]

Artworks Integral to the Structure of a Building

VARA also contains special provisions for limited-edition visual artworks, which could on their own create difficulties for owners of buildings in which visual artworks have been integrated (the most common example in this category would be a mural).[148] The law creates options for building owners to remove artworks when they can without damaging them, and limits creators' rights of integrity for destructive removal of building-integrated works created prior to VARA's effective date. However, destructive removal of works created after VARA's effective date[149] may require a written waiver signed by the artist.[150] It may be advisable for art museums to include such "VARA waivers" in installation or commission agreements. The act also required the US Copyright Office to establish a Visual Arts Registry that allows for the submission of statements regarding works installed in buildings.[151]

VARA Violations

Like the Digital Millennium Copyright Act, VARA created some forms of liability not directly related to violations of §106 rights. VARA only applies to a narrowly specified set of visual artworks, but for those works, VARA violations may occur even in the absence of direct infringement. For example, it might be a VARA violation to misattribute a painting on display in a gallery.[152] In one well-known VARA case, the artist Christoph Büchel was commissioned to create a massive work for MassMOCA. When disagreements arose over management of the project, Bruchel sued the museum claiming that under VARA the museum did not have the right to display the unfinished work. Noting that VARA rights are very limited, the court concluded that while the artist might have a valid VARA claim, VARA did not give the artist control over display of an unfinished work. Despite its victory, the museum chose to respect the artist's concerns and closed the exhibit.[153]

COPYRIGHT INFRINGEMENT

The unauthorized exercise of one of the rights covered by copyright by someone who is not the copyright holder constitutes copyright infringement—unless it is allowed by an exception like fair use or the public display exemption.[154] The actual act of unauthorized copying (or other unauthorized exercise of copyrights) is considered "direct infringement." Because some uses are legally permitted regardless of the preferences of the copyright holder, unauthorized use is only established as "infringement" after a final judgment by a federal court.[155]

A copyright holder may bring a civil lawsuit alleging infringement against anyone who engages in unauthorized uses.[156] The copyright must be registered before the lawsuit can be filed, but that registration can occur after the unauthorized use is first detected.[157] A federal prosecutor can also file criminal charges against an alleged infringer, although at minimum, the allegedly infringing acts must be both "willful" and "for the purpose of commercial advantage or private financial gain" before criminal liability can possibly exist.[158]

Sometimes individuals or entities who have not directly infringed themselves may also be liable for copyright infringement. This is known as "secondary liability." Usually direct infringement must be established for secondary liability to be a possibility.[159] One type of secondary liability arises from the basic principle that employers are usually liable for actions employees take in the course of their employment ("*respondeat superior*"). This principle holds true in copyright law, and the law does not usually distinguish between an employee and employer as direct infringers. This is one form of "vicarious liability." For example, in *Basic Books v. Kinko's Graphics*, direct copying was done by employees, but the lawsuit was brought against the company.[160] When an employee's actions are blatantly illegal, courts sometimes refuse to hold the employer liable, under the theory that such actions could not possibly have been part of the employee's job. Thus, a cultural institution might not be held liable for an employee hypothetically selling unauthorized reproductions off the loading dock.

Courts also extend the vicarious liability concept further: individuals or entities that have the "right and ability" to control the actions of an infringer, and who benefit from the infringement, may be held liable as vicarious infringers.[161] The clearest vicarious liability cases of this type have often involved companies that lease space to independent businesses that sell counterfeit audio or video recordings, with the space provider held liable for failing to stop the counterfeit sales.[162]

Courts sometimes impose vicarious liability when they think an individual or organization *should have known* that an activity was infringing, even when the vicariously liable party did not actually know about the infringement.[163] While the idea of "should have known" liability can be unnerving in the copyright context, it may be helpful to note that similar standards apply to activities as basic as floor mopping. Most cultural institutions that are taking normal care with their employee relationships are not likely to be caught unaware.

An organization can also be liable for a third party's direct infringement if the organization knowingly encouraged or enabled the infringement. This is known as "contributory liability."[164] For example, courts have sometimes found that linking to a site known to contain infringing content is contributory infringement, even though linking to legitimate content is not usually a copyright issue.[165]

It is important to note another basic principle of the law: individuals and organizations are not usually liable for the actions of unrelated third parties when there is no ongoing relationship.[166] Thus, an institution that provides access to a collection or provides legal copies of materials to a visitor is not usually liable if that visitor ultimately misuses those materials when there is no ongoing ability to control the uses.

Sometimes cultural institutions accept additional limitations on use of materials as a condition of access to the materials. These limitations are usually created via contracts; contracts themselves can create limitations on use of materials even after copyrights have expired. While not copyright violations or infringement, there may be violations of contracts, which can give rise to potential lawsuits. These can also present more pragmatic issues such as disruption of business and/or donor relationships.

The Digital Millennium Copyright Act

The Digital Millennium Copyright Act (DMCA) created protections for organizations that host user-generated content—often referred to as the DMCA "Safe Harbor."[167] There are requirements that must be followed to qualify for the Safe Harbor, including following specific "notice and takedown" procedures.[168] Content curated by the hosting organization is not covered by the Safe Harbor, even if it originated outside the organization. It is vital for cultural institutions to remain cognizant of DMCA protections when posting content on the websites that they host and/or link to from its sites.

The DMCA also created some forms of liability not directly related to §106 copyright rights; for example, unauthorized decryption of a media disc may violate the DMCA's "anticircumvention" provisions.[169] Courts are split as to whether a copyright violation has to occur before DMCA liability arises, although most have concluded that DMCA violations may exist in the absence of direct infringement.[170] For example, it might be a DMCA violation to circumvent "region encoding" on a DVD, even if just in order to (legally) watch it.

ENFORCEMENT MECHANISMS

A common way for copyright holders to enforce their copyrights is by sending a letter (often via an attorney) that lays out an alleged infringement, and often includes a proposed course of action. Such letters are often referred to as "cease and desist" letters. While these letters are sometimes phrased aggressively, they do not usually constitute formal legal action, and may present an opportunity to resolve an issue quickly and painlessly.

In part because of a provision of the DMCA, another form of initial allegation of infringement, the "takedown notice," has grown in recent years.[171] Although DMCA "notice and takedown" procedures only apply by statute to a limited subset of online content, the *form* of the takedown notice sometimes appears in other situations.

Not all cease and desist letters or takedown notices are based on valid allegations of infringement. Sometimes individuals are uninformed about the scope of their rights as copyright holders or creators, and sometimes cease and desist letters and takedown notices are misused to stifle criticism or to intentionally make overbroad assertions of rights.[172] Cultural institutions are advised to consult with legal counsel about letters or notices alleging copyright infringement, as appropriate institutional responses vary widely in individual cases.

It is important to note that copyright holders may initiate a civil suit alleging infringement even without an initial nonlawsuit salvo such as a cease and desist letter or takedown notice. In that case, the plaintiff will file the lawsuit in federal court and the parties affected will receive notice via formal legal channels.

Even before an actual lawsuit is filed accusing infringement, organizations or individuals may choose to file their own lawsuit, which would allege noninfringement. One form of such a defensive lawsuit is an action for a "declaratory judgment." Documentary filmmakers have found declaratory judgments helpful when their films include primary documents of uncertain rights status. With a declaration that use of these materials is likely a fair use, it can be easier to get a film insured for distribution.

When a lawsuit is filed, it may still end without any court rulings if the parties "settle," or agree to terms that resolve the legal dispute. A judge may have to approve some settlements. If the lawsuit progresses, it may be concluded fairly quickly (often via dismissal or "summary judgment"), or it may continue through the full legal process to a ruling (and possibly appeals). In either case, litigation will impose costs related to legal representation and time taken from other activities. However, litigation may present benefits such as the formal resolution of a previously unsettled issue of law.

As a practical matter, suing for copyright infringement is quite expensive because the lawsuit must be filed in federal court and can often involve complex legal arguments. In one recent case involving the unpermitted use of celebrity photos to illustrate celebrity gossip blogs, the court found copyright infringement but assessed only a total of $10,880—an amount equal to what the court determined to be the reasonable license fees due the plaintiff.[173] As a result, most copyright infringement claims are settled by stopping the allegedly infringing use and possibly the payment of a "retroactive" license fee to compensate for the unpermitted use. Proposals have been floated as part of copyright reform to create a copyright "small claims" court to make it easier and more efficient to prosecute copyright infringement claims.

REMEDIES

In a criminal prosecution, proven infringers may face imprisonment, fines, or both.[174] In a civil suit, a prevailing plaintiff may be awarded an injunction.[175] In some cases, infringing copies must be destroyed, usually at the expense of the losing defendant.[176] Prevailing plaintiffs may also be awarded damages for harm suffered. These may be actual damages (e.g., proven monetary losses, etc.) or statutory damages of between $750 and $30,000 per infringement. At the discretion of the court, statutory damages may be reduced to as little as $200 per infringement, for cases where a defendant was "not aware and had not reason to believe: they were infringing, or increased as high as $150,000 per infringement, for cases where the defendant's infringement is found to be willful.[177]

Importantly, the law instructs judges to waive statutory damages when the infringer is an employee of or is itself "a nonprofit educational institution, library, or archives" that was making copies *and* "believed and had reasonable grounds for believing that his or her use of the copyrighted work was a fair use."[178] Related costs and attorneys' fees may be available to any party (plaintiff or defendant) who prevails in a copyright lawsuit.[179] Thus, while the risks and costs of litigation are not minimal, it may sometimes be worthwhile financially for a cultural institution to pursue a principled case to completion.

TRADITIONAL KNOWLEDGE AND CULTURAL EXPRESSIONS[180]

The historical practices of many American cultural institutions and legal systems have reflected European traditions. These systems reflect certain assumptions and cultural norms about the nature of property, ownership, science, art, and knowledge—but these assumptions and norms are not universal. Although legal structures and cultural institution practices have evolved to appreciate and respect the traditions of other cultural and political groups, there are many ways current systems and practices can improve to address and even explore past or ongoing injustice.

The "economic incentive" theory of IP law that is dominant in Anglo-American legal systems—and heavily influences many other legal systems internationally—is structured to incentivize and favor *innovations* and *new* cultural production.[181] Good policy reasons exist for ensuring that legal protections for past inventions and existing expressive works end at some point; knowledge, innovation, and creativity depend on and spring from the innovations and creations that have come before. While the Anglo-American tradition favors "personal" ownership for "new" creators, and recognizes long-existing works or knowledge as belonging to a "public domain" that anyone can use, many indigenous cultures have different understandings of property and ownership.

In practice, the work of innovators, artists, and other IP owners who are members of dominant cultural groups is often recognized as "new" and deserving of legal ownership, even when based on the longstanding traditions or practices of indigenous or marginalized cultural groups. These legal defaults have often produced economic benefit to "innovators" at the expense of others, and even when the authorship of creators from marginalized groups has been recognized, economic and other social forces have often resulted in legal ownership (and economic benefits) lodging elsewhere than with the creators. For example, the history of popular music in the United States is quite often one of exploitation of African American practices and traditions in ways that conferred legal "ownership" on individuals and entities who did not share that background. Subsequently, that legal ownership has often been exercised to bar further reuse or development of forms and practices, even from the individuals or groups from whom they originate.[182] Cultural institutions increasingly recognize and acknowledge these historical and present-day tensions.

Traditional knowledge is also often leveraged in pursuit of new patentable inventions in biomedical research. International agreements and national laws in a variety of nations address this issue, often barring patentability of certain types of biological materials or traditional knowledge.[183] The implementation of these laws and agreements can be less than consistent, and their provisions are not always satisfactory to parties on many sides of the issues, so advocacy continues on the national and international stage. This may be a significant issue for natural history collections, botanical gardens, and zoological parks.

The law also often does not formally acknowledge indigenous or marginalized groups' internally established rules, or internally recognized group or individual rights related to cultural knowledge, practices, and objects. Organizations and individuals may, intentionally or unintentionally, lack awareness of these norms. This can result in exploitation or disrespectful treatment of cultural objects, arts, and experiences of indigenous and marginalized groups. For example, feathered headdresses are often treated as generic decorative elements in popular culture, although specific forms and styles have deep cultural and spiritual meanings for specific American Indian groups.

Often, respecting the norms of other cultural groups may conflict with fundamental principles and purposes for cultural institutions. Scholarship or inquiry related to a culture in which women are not allowed to handle certain objects, or not in certain contexts, would conflict with values of egalitarian inquiry, and limiting access for women could create legal liability for unequal treatment. Multiple groups with conflicting norms and principles may lay claim to an item from a collection. Flexibility and innovative thinking may sometimes resolve tensions, as may compromises. At other times, tensions will not be resolvable in ways that satisfy all parties that claim an interest.

Cultural institutions have few clear legal obligations with respect to IP of or by exploited individuals or groups, and may sometimes be required to act in relation to legal ownership in ways that can perpetuate exploitation. However, there is growing recognition in the field that professional ethics require consideration and/or acknowledgment of these issues. Missteps increasingly attract public attention and sometimes backlash, while consultation and collaboration with creators, their heirs, and members of indigenous and marginalized groups can develop positive relationships and outcomes for all parties.

HUMAN REMAINS

Most societies recognize human remains as deserving special treatment, and the Anglo-American legal tradition is no exception. However, in practice, remains of individuals from populations indigenous to colonized areas have often been treated less as subjects of veneration and more as objects of scientific inquiry. Ties to extant cultural groups have been minimized or ignored.[184] Since many museums have significant holdings of human remains and related funerary objects, many are already well aware of the major legal, policy, and professional ethics developments on these topics in the last twenty-five years.

TAKING RESPONSIBILITY; CONNECTING WITH COMMUNITIES

Fashion brand Paul Frank was able to create a positive outcome from a misstep in September 2012. Use of American Indian "headdresses" and other stereotypes in some marketing attracted negative publicity, but their quick response to apologize and take action to avoid reoccurrences quickly improved the situation.[1] Ultimately, Paul Frank created a new program to feature the works of American Indian artists that benefited the artists and created positive publicity for the company.[2]

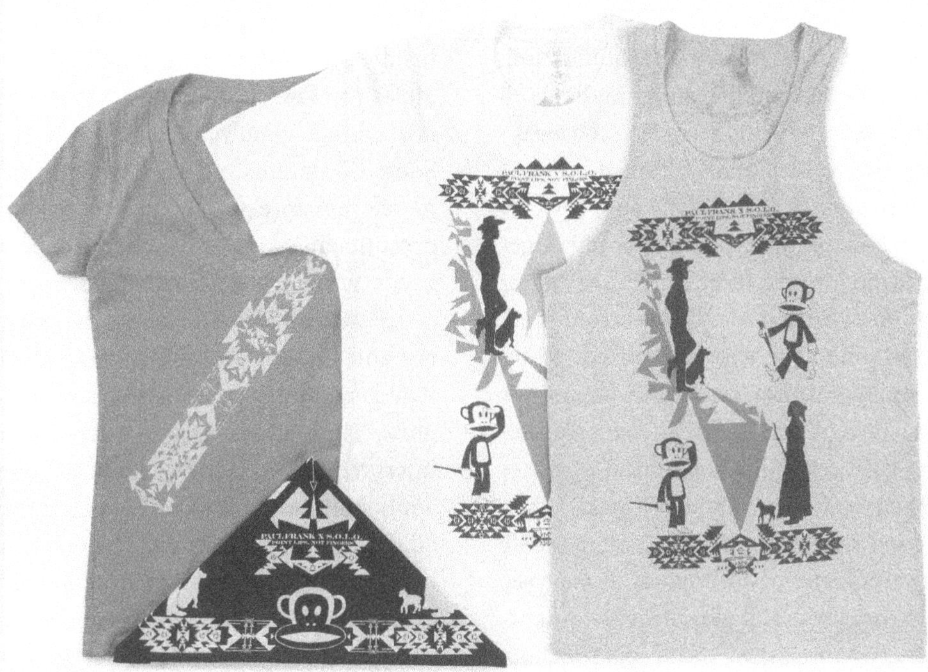

FIGURE 1.6
Merchandise from the controversial Paul Frank line in 2012.

NOTES

1. Adrienne Keene, "Paul Frank Powwow Party Update: Am I Dreaming?" Native Appropriations, September 14, 2012, http://nativeappropriations.com/2012/09/paul-frank-powwow-party-update-am-i-dreaming.html.
2. Susan Montoya Bryan, "Paul Frank teams up with Native American artists," Yahoo! News, August 16, 2013, 6:47 p.m., http://news.yahoo.com/paul-frank-teams-native-american-artists-202540914.html.

The Native American Graves Protection and Repatriation Act of 1990[185] requires museums to work to repatriate human remains, funerary and sacred objects, and objects of cultural patrimony to lineal descendants or culturally affiliated tribes. This legislation also imposes specific requirements for the treatment of remains and cultural items associated with human remains newly found on tribal or federal lands.[186] Many states have passed similar legislation and some international agreements also address similar issues. The founding of the Smithsonian's National Museum of the American Indian was a significant catalyst for honest public conversation about these issues, which continue arguably as a core part of the mission of that museum. There are ethnographic and anthropology museums all over the world that grapple with these same concerns.

Identification and repatriation of human remains and cultural items present many challenges for cultural institutions. In addition to the costs of investigation and administrative work, there can be difficulties when identification of remains or objects is contested, when more than one federally recognized group claims ties to remains or objects,[187] and for groups that lack federal recognition of tribal status. Sometimes, emerging legal standards and ethical practices come at the expense of science and research. When a skeleton has been repatriated, it may be impossible to apply new technologies or techniques of analysis, even when new investigations may benefit present-day descendants.

International repatriation of remains and cultural objects remains a more contentious area for a number of reasons. While some museums have undertaken great efforts to repatriate materials across international boundaries, international law is less clear in its requirements (and its application in various international jurisdictions less predictable). Ongoing geopolitical tensions or conflict can also make repatriation more difficult or even undesirable for all parties.[188]

INTERNATIONAL INTELLECTUAL PROPERTY RIGHTS

The international context of copyright is critically important in several ways. First, while copyright law is fundamentally domestic, the laws of most countries are influenced extensively by the obligations countries have to one another under the terms of various multinational treaties. Second, activities that raise copyright questions routinely cross national borders, giving rise to issues under the laws of multiple countries. Third, although a given situation may implicate multiple countries, for most questions and events arising in each country, one would ordinarily apply the law of that country. For example, if a book is first created and sold in France, one would apply French copyright law to analyze those facts. Once the book is shipped and used in the United States, however, one would apply US law to the importation and to the uses that occur inside US borders. In general, when in the United States (or France, or almost any country), apply the law of that country. That is only a generalization. Some US statutes and court rulings include references to relevant foreign law, but those developments are exceptional, taking us back to the general rule for most needs: when in the United States, apply US law.

In the United States, copyright law, along with patent and most trademark law, are statutory creatures that generally start with the laws enacted by Congress. The statutes apply nationwide and are in turn interpreted by the courts. Judicial rulings technically apply only in the area of the country where the specific court has jurisdiction. The practical reality is that many rulings are influential nationwide, even if not exactly binding. Cases arising under federal copyright and patent laws must be brought to the federal courts, so only occasionally will a state court rule on such a matter. Conversely, trademarks are a combination of federal and state law, but most of the interesting and important cases arise under federal law. Other legal doctrines such as right of publicity, contract law, and defamation are almost entirely state law. This overview reinforces a key point: the law varies with geography. Some law exists or applies differently in different states within the United States. The law can also change dramatically from one country to the next.

There may be no such thing as "international copyright law" per se, but there is plenty of law in the form of international treaties and agreements that shapes domestic laws of copyright and other forms of

IP. Some of the leading international instruments on copyright law include:

- Berne Convention for the Protection of Literary and Artistic Works (1886)[189]
- Universal Copyright Convention (1952)[190]
- WIPO Copyright Treaty (1996)[191]
- WIPO Phonograms and Performances Treaty (1996)[192]

Patent and trademark law are the subject of various other international agreements, including:

- Paris Convention for the Protection of Industrial Property (1883)[193]
- Madrid Agreement Concerning the International Registration of Marks (1891)[194]

Many of these agreements were first negotiated decades ago but are often revisited at diplomatic conferences and revised in response to changing needs. All the agreements listed above are administered by the World IP Organization, an agency of the United Nations that is headquartered in Geneva, Switzerland.

Important in a different respect is the World Trade Organization (WTO). The WTO agreement includes a set of Trade Related Aspects of IP (TRIPs) provisions. Like the agreements listed above, TRIPs sets required standards for domestic laws and introduces an enforcement mechanism. Only since the conclusion of WTO negotiations in 1994 have countries been able to bring some form of action against one another, alleging that a country has not met its obligations under international IP agreements. The WTO can issue orders demanding that a country revise its law and can impose trade sanctions and other penalties for noncompliance.

As the role of the WTO suggests, one of the most important functions of international treaties is to influence the shape of domestic law. The international system is not making law that is binding on a particular museum, artist, or any other party. But the system is pressuring nations to revise their laws to meet international substantive standards. The following aspects of US copyright law are the direct result of US membership in copyright treaties:

- revising the duration law from a period of years to a term based on the life of the author
- elimination of formalities, such as the copyright notice and registration, as a precondition to protection
- restoration of protection for foreign copyrights that had entered the public domain
- adding limited moral rights
- prohibitions against circumvention of technological protection measures
- prohibitions against the removal of copyright management information

The theory behind these substantive standards is the quest to "harmonize" the laws so that they will be more predictable for business transactions occurring across national borders. Many fundamental aspects of copyright, such as the standards for securing rights and a minimum duration, have been largely harmonized. Other aspects, especially the important principles of fair use and other exceptions,[195] are almost entirely devoid of harmonization.[196] Any harmonization on any piece of copyright is only a generalization; the details of domestic law vary greatly. The practical bottom line is that copyright laws of different countries may be somewhat predictable, but when doing business in another country, you may need to research its specific laws.

In addition to harmonization, another important objective of international agreements is the mutual protection of copyrighted works. The Berne Convention and other agreements introduce the concept of "national treatment," which requires each member country to offer at least the same level of protection to works that originate in other countries as the member offers to its domestic works. The United States, France, and Japan are members of Berne, along with approximately 160 other countries. Each Berne country must protect copyrighted works that come from any other member countries on at least the same terms that the country offers to its own copyrighted works.

Consider the practical consequences of this overview of international copyright principles. You are an artist based in a country that is part of Berne and TRIPs. Because of the requirements of Berne, your country has dropped all formalities for copyright protection. You, therefore, instantly get copyright protection for your artistic work, and due to international harmonization, you get that protection for the duration of your life, plus at least fifty years. The United States and many other countries have gone further and extended the term to life plus seventy years. That instant protection is valid in all Berne countries, which comprise nearly all the countries of the world. You may never have given copyright a single thought, but all that legal protection and the right to enforce copyrights around the world is yours whether you wanted it or not. At its core, that is the role and function of the international system.

The artist in this hypothetical is in a position of strength under the law. However, the right to enforce a copyright is not the same as the ability. Tracking infringers and bringing lawsuits is an expensive and nuanced business. The artist is nevertheless in a position of strength to make decisions about how to act. The artist, as the copyright owner, is also in a position of strength to determine whether and on what terms to engage in licensing or selling works in different countries, all with considerable confidence that the copyright is valid. For the museum, publisher, educator, researcher, or anyone else who wants to reproduce or use the artwork, the international system is a reminder that copyright law in the United States (and most other countries) applies to works that come from the United States and all other treaty countries.

NOTES

1. 17 U.S.C. § 102 (a).

2. 17 U.S.C. § 106.

3. 17 U.S.C. § 102(a).

4. 17 U.S.C. § 102(b).

5. *Gund, Inc. v. Applause, Inc.*, 809 F. Supp. 304 (S.D.N.Y. 1993).

6. 17 U.S.C. §§ 1 et seq.

7. U.S. Const. art. I, § 8, cl. 8.

8. 17 U.S.C. § 102(a).

9. See, for example, *Feist Publications, Inc. v. Rural Telephone Service Co.*, 499 U.S. 340, 345 (1991). "To be sure, the requisite level of creativity is extremely low; even a slight amount will suffice."

10. 17 U.S.C. § 302(a).

11. 17 U.S.C. § 105.

12. These exclusions have developed as a matter of case law that were then codified to statute, which is conceptually different from US government works.

13. *Feist Publications, Inc. v. Rural Telephone Service Co.*, 499 U.S. at 344–45, 349. "The most fundamental axiom of copyright law is that '[n]o author may copyright his ideas or the facts he narrates,'"quoting *Harper & Row Publishers, Inc. v. Nation Enterprises*, 471 U.S. 539, 556 (1985).

14. Ibid. at 350.

15. Ibid. at 362–63.

16. 17 U.S.C. § 106.

17. Ibid.

18. 17 U.S.C. § 204.

19. 17 U.S.C. § 205.

20. 17 U.S.C. § 201(d).

21. 17 U.S.C. § 201(a).

22. Ibid.

23. 17 U.S.C. § 201(b).

24. Ibid.

25. Cultural institutions must also be aware of different state-by-state employment provisions. For example, under current California law, a copyright "work-for-hire" provision in an independent contractor agreement that actually creates an employment relationship and subjects the employer to state employment laws. For that reason when a California citizen is hired as an independent contractor, work-for-hire language is replaced by assignment language in the contract.

26. See, for example, *Golan v. Holder*, 132 S.Ct. 873 (2012).

27. Noted by the inclusion of one or more of the following: ©, author, year, etc.

28. 17 U.S.C. § 302(a).

29. 17 U.S.C. §§ 408, 412.

30. For current US works.

31. 17 U.S.C. § 302(a).

32. 17 U.S.C. § 302(b).

33. Note, however, that this approach is not universal. Many countries calculate copyright duration for works for hire with the same single or joint authorship concept of "life plus a term of years" rather than having an option for measure from the date of publication or creation. This can make it very difficult to identify copyright durations because corporate works are often anonymous vis-a-vis the individual author; even if named, the individual author's biographical information can be difficult to find.

34. 17 U.S.C. § 105.

35. Archivist Carl Malamud has encountered copyright claims to legal codes from a number of US state governments. For example, see "The Oregon Question: What is the copyright status of primary legal materials governing the actions of the citizens of Oregon?" Public .Resource.Org, accessed March 13, 2018, https://public .resource.org/oregon.gov/index.html.

36. For example, see Walter G. Lehmann, "Wake of the Flood: Public Records, Copyright and Fair use in Documentary Film," *Landslide*, accessed April 20, 2018, https://www.americanbar.org/publications/landslide/2016-17/july-august/wake-flood-public-records-copyright-and-fair-use-documentary-film.html.

37. The evolving complications in duration law and the factors that can determine the outcome are examined in Kenneth D. Crews, "Copyright Duration and the Progressive Degeneration of a Constitutional Doctrine," *Syracuse Law Review* 55 (2005): 189–250, http://papers .ssrn.com/sol3/papers.cfm?abstract_id=1656604.

38. Uruguay Round Agreements Act, Pub. L. 103–465, 108 Stat. 4809 (1994).

39. 17 U.S.C. § 102(a).

40. 17 U.S.C. § 102(b).

41. See, for example, *Feist Publications, Inc. v. Rural Telephone Service Co.*, 499 U.S. at 340; United States Copyright Office, *Circular 34: Multiple Works* (revised September 2017), http://www.copyright.gov/circs/circ34 .pdf.

42. 17 U.S.C. § 101 (defining "publication").

43. *Estate of Martin Luther King, Jr., Inc. v. CBS, Inc.*, 194 F.3d 1211, 1217 (11th Cir. 1999). King's holding was limited; the court disclaimed any opinion on the merits and simply stated that summary judgment was inappropriate as there *was* a genuine issue of material fact regarding whether there had been general publication. It was sent back down to the trial court, then the case settled. As Nimmer quoted in the case, "'Publication' is a legal word denoting a process much more esoteric than is suggested by the lay definition of the term."

44. 17 U.S.C. § 114.

45. See generally Peter Jaszi and Nick Lewis, *Protection for Pre-1972 Sound Recordings under State Law and Its Impact on Use by Nonprofit Institutions: A 10-State Analysis*, Washington College of Law, American University (September 2009), http://www.clir.org/pubs/reports/pub146.

46. *Flo and Eddie, Inc. v. Sirrius XM Radio*, No. SC16-1161 (Fla. October 26, 2017), *Flo & Eddie, Inc. v Sirius XM Radio, Inc.* 2016 NY Slip Op 08480. Decided on December 20, 2016, Court of Appeals Stein, J., and *Flo & Eddie, Inc. v. Pandora Media, Inc.*, S240649. (9th Cir. No. 15-55287; 851 F.3d 950; Central District of California; No. 2:14-cv-07648 -PSG-RZ.).

47. See generally Jeffery A. Abrahamson, "Tuning Up for a New Musical Age: Sound Recording Copyright Protection in a Digital Environment," *AIPLA Quarterly Journal* 25, no. 2 (1997): 181.

48. *Bridgeport Music, Inc. v. Dimension Films*, 410 F.3d 792 (6th Cir. 2005).

49. 17 U.S.C. § 107.

50. Some rights holders share their works intentionally through voluntary terms of use, Creative Commons licensing, etc. See chapter 7, Creative Commons Licensing, for a more detailed discussion.

51. 17 U.S.C. § 107.

52. See, for example, *Cariou v. Prince*, 714 F.3d 694 (2d 2013).

53. See, for example, *Campbell v. Acuff-Rose Music, Inc.*, 510 U.S. 569 (1994).

54. See chapter 7, "New Frontiers in Fair Use and Open Access" for a more detailed discussion of recent applications of fair use by cultural institutions.

55. *Sony Corp. of America v. Universal City Studios, Inc.*, 464 U.S. 417, 445 (1984).

56. A recent case that further defines fair use is *Barcroft Media, Ltd. v. Coed Media Group, LLC.*, in which the use of copyrighted images of celebrities in connection with blog posts about the celebrity were found to not be a fair use and the only damages the plaintiff could recover would be a retroactive licensing fee. *Barcroft Media, Ltd. v. Coed Media Group, LLC.*, F. Supp.3d. (S.D.N.Y. 2017).

57. 17 U.S.C. § 108.

58. United States Copyright Office, "Revising Section 108: Copyright Exceptions for Libraries and Archives," accessed March 14, 2018, https://www.copyright.gov/policy/section108/discussion-document.pdf.

59. 17 U.S.C. § 110(1).

60. 17 U.S.C. § 110(2).

61. 17 U.S.C. § 113.

62. *Ets-Hokin v. Skyy Spirits, Inc.* 225 Ets-Hokin 1068 (9th Cir. 2000).

63. 37 C.F.R. § 202.11.

64. 17 U.S.C. § 120.

65. *The Rock & Roll Hall of Fame and Museum, Inc., et al., Plaintiffs v. Gentile Productions, et al., Defendants*, 71 F. Supp.2d 755 (1999).

66. 17 U.S.C. § 121.

67. *Sony Corp. of America v. Universal City Studios, Inc.*, 464 U.S. 417, 455 n. 40 (1984).

68. See, for example, *Authors Guild v. HathiTrust* (2nd Cir. 2014) (26–31).

69. "Library Copyright Alliance Welcomes Introduction of Marrakesh Treaty Implementation Act, S. 2559," Library Copyright Alliance, accessed April 20, 2018, http://www.librarycopyrightalliance.org/storage/documents/Marrakesh_Act_PR_final.pdf and "ARL Urges US to Ratify Marrakesh Treaty, Improve Access to Publications for Visually Impaired," Association of Research Libraries, accessed April 20, 2018, http://www.arl.org/news/arl-news/4489-arl-urges-us-to-ratify-marrakesh-treaty-improve-access-to-publications-for-visually-impaired#.Wqqvwmrwa00.

70. 17 U.S.C. §109(a).

71. 17 U.S.C. §109(c).

72. 15 U.S.C. § 1127 (defining "trademark").

73. 15 U.S.C. § 1115.

74. *Bristol-Myers Squibb Co. v. McNeil-P.P.C., Inc.*, 973 F.2d 1033 (2nd Cir. 1992); See generally *Champions Golf Club, Inc. v. The Champions Golf Club, Inc.*, 78 F.3d 1111 (6th Cir. 1996). For example, the word "Pepsi" is a fanciful word that had no English meaning until used by a carbonated beverage maker. By contrast "Jones Soda" could describe any soda made by a person named Jones, or in a location associated with the name Jones, but has been registered, and through usage has come to be a strong mark for a specific brand of soft drink.

75. 15 U.S.C. § 1115(a); see, for example, *Dollcraft Co. v. Nancy Ann Storybook Dolls*, 94 F.Supp. 1 (N.D.Cal. 1950).

76. 15 U.S.C. § 1064.

77. The decision to trademark is often a business one, but should take into account the business cost of enforcement needed to protect the mark. Formal trademark registration for programs or exhibits can be problematic because institutions then have to police the use for the registration term. It is often simpler to not register the mark, but much will depend on the business decision of commercialization of the trademark or protecting its use by others.

78. *Mattel, Inc. v. Walking Mountain Productions*, 353 F.3d 792 (9th Cir. 2003) ("Food Chain Barbie" photo series was copyright fair use); *Mattel, Inc. v. MCA Records, Inc.*, 296 F.3d 894 (9th Cir. 2002) ("Barbie Girl" song was trademark fair use).

79. 35 U.S.C. § 101–102 (defining "patent").

80. 35 U.S.C. § 154(a)(2).

81. Even for nature or science museums, the patent is usually controlled by the funding provider for the work, which is typically the US government. Thus, patent is a minimal issue.

82. 18 U.S.C. § 1839 (defining "trade secret").

83. See generally Robert Sprague, "Orwell was an Optimist: The Evolution of Privacy in the United States and its De-Evolution for American Employees," *John Marshall Law Review* 42, No. 1 (2008); Kevin L. Vick andJean-Paul Jassy, "Why a Federal Right of Publicity Statute is Necessary," *Communications Lawyer* 28, no. 2 (August 2011); Brian Angelo Lee, "Making Sense of 'Moral Rights' in Intellectual Property," *Temple Law Review* 84 (2011).

84. *Gertz v. Robert Welch, Inc.*, 418 U.S. 323 (1974).

85. *Olmstead v. United States*, 277 U.S. 438 (1928).

86. Restatement (Second) of Torts §§ 652B-E (1977); W. Prosser, *Law of Torts*, pp. 637–39 (2d ed. 1955). See, for example, *Phillips v. Smalley Maintenance Services, Inc.*, 435 So.2d 705 (1983); Disa Sim, "The Right to Solitude in the United States and Singapore: A Call for a Fundamental Reordering," *Loyola of Los Angeles Entertainment Law Review* 22 (2002): 443, 445.

87. Restatement (Second) of Torts § 652B (1977).

88. See, for example, *Galella v. Onassis*, 487 F.2d 986 (2nd Cir. 1973); *Wilson v. Layne*, 526 U.S. 603 (1999).

89. See, for example, *Doe v. Roe*, 638 So.2d 826 (1994); *Smith v. Doss*, 251 Ala. 250 (1948).

90. See, for example, *Cox Broadcasting Corp. v. Cohn*, 420 U.S. 469 (1975); *Chaney v. Fayette County Pub. Sch. Dist.*, 977 F. Supp. 2d 1308 (N.D. Ga. 2013).

91. Restatement (Second) of Torts § 652E (1977).

92. See, for example, *Alahverdian v. Grebinski*, 2014 U.S. Dist. LEXIS 68347 (S.D. Ohio 2014).

93. See, for example, *Pavesich v. New England Life Ins. Co.*, 69 L.R.A. 101 (1905).

94. Emily Doskow, "Defamation Law Made Simple," NOLO: Law for All, accessed March 14, 2018, http://www.nolo.com/legal-encyclopedia/defamation-law-made-simple-29718.html.

95. Restatement (Second) of Torts § 558 (1977).

96. Restatement (Second) of Torts § 559 (1977).

97. Restatement (Second) of Torts § 581A (1977).

98. Restatement (Second) of Torts § 566 (1977).

99. *Haelan Laboratories, Inc. v. Topps Chewing Gum Inc.*, 202 F.2d 866, 868 (2d Cir. 1953), in which Judge Jerome Frank coined the term "right of publicity."

100. "Right of Publicity State-by-State," Rothman's Roadmap to the Right of Publicity, accessed April 20, 2018, https://www.rightofpublicityroadmap.com/.

101. § 6:3. Introduction to the law of the states—Right of publicity.

102. 15 U.S.C. § 1125.

103. See, for example, *Waits v. Frito-Lay, Inc.*, 978 F.2d 1093 (9th Cir. 1992); *ETW Corp. v. Jireh Publishing, Inc.*, 332 F.3d 915 (6th Cir. 2003).

104. *Shaw Family Archives, Ltd. v. CMG Worldwide, Inc.*, 434 F.Supp.2d 203 (S.D.N.Y. 2006); *Price v. Hal Roach Studios, Inc.*, 400 F. Supp. 836 (S.D.N.Y. 1975) (right to publicity included in right to privacy).

105. Fla. Stat. Ann. § 540.08(5) (West 2007).

106. Ohio Rev. Code Ann. § 2741.02 (West 2009).

107. Indiana Code IC 32-36-1-8.

108. Cal. Civ. Code § 3344.1(f) (West 2012). See "Special Filings: Successor in Interest," California Business Portal, accessed March 14, 2018, https://specialfilings.sos.ca.gov/sii.

109. *Gionfriddo v. Major League Baseball*, 94 Cal.App.4th 400 (2001).

110. Frank Ryan and Matt Ganas, "Rights or Publicity in Sports-Media," Syracuse Law Review, accessed April 20, 2018, http://lawreview.syr.edu/wp-content/uploads/2017/03/Vol-67.2_Ryan.pdf.

111. Peter Colin Jr. "Elvis and Prince: Personality Rights Guidance for Dead Celebrities and the Lawyers and Legislatures Who Protect Them," *Northeastern University Law Review*, accessed April 20, 2018, http://nulawreview.org/extralegalrecent/2017/5/8/elvis-and-prince.

112. See Restatement (Third) of Unfair Competition, § 47.

113. Moral rights originated with the French legal concept of *le droit moral*. Economic rights are protected through the legal concept of *droit de suite*, which allows artists to profit from the resale of their work. For a discussion of moral rights, see Marie C. Malaro, *A Legal Primer on*

Managing Museum Collections, 2nd ed. (Washington, DC: Smithsonian Books, 1995), 184.

114. Moral rights are based on "a belief that an artist in the process of creation injects his spirit into the work and that the artist's personality, as well as the integrity of the work, should therefore be protected and preserved." *Carter v. Helmsley-Spear, Inc.*, 71 F.3d 77, 81 (2d Cir. 1995).

115. RayMing Chang, "Revisiting the Visual Artists Rights Act of 1990: A Follow-up Survey About Awareness and Waiver," *Texas Intellectual Property Law Journal* 13, no. 2 (Winter 2005): 129.

116. Ibid. Proof of Facts 3d 1 § 4, *Proof of Infringement of the Visual Artists Rights Act of 1990*, (2003) (this concept is sometimes referred to as the "right of exposure").

117. *Caslon Analytics Note Moral Rights Cases*, Australia, May 2006, www.caslon.com/au/mrcasenote.htm.

118. Stephen E. Weil, "Copyrights and Wrongs," *Museum News*, July/August 1993, 40.

119. US courts may still review applicable foreign laws as necessary.

120. The US Constitution authorizes Congress to enact legislation "to promote the progress of science and useful arts, by securing for limited times to authors and inventors the exclusive right to their respective writings and discoveries." U.S. Const. art. I, § 8, cl. 8.

121. The fair use doctrine. 17 U.S.C. § 107.

122. Marie C. Malaro, *A Legal Primer on Managing Museum Collections*, 2nd ed. (Washington, DC: Smithsonian Books, 1995), 151.

123. For example, as a "work for hire" pursuant to 17 U.S.C. § 201(b), or through assignment or license under 17 U.S.C. § 203.

124. 17 U.S.C. § 202.

125. 17 U.S.C. § 109(b). For a discussion of the right of display, see Marie C. Malaro, *A Legal Primer on Managing Museum Collections*, 2nd ed. (Washington, DC: Smithsonian Books, 1995), 168n28.

126. 17 U.S.C. § 106A(e) and (d).

127. 17 U.S.C. § 106A(a).

128. *Gilliam v. American Broadcasting Companies*, 538 F.2d 14, 24–25 (2d 1976).

129. Visual Artists Rights Act (VARA) of 1990, 17 U.S.C. § 106A.

130. 17 U.S.C. § 101 (defining "work of visual art").

131. 17 U.S.C. § 106A.

132. In 1958, an Alexander Calder black-and-white mobile, which was donated to the Pittsburgh Airport, was repainted green and gold, locked into place, and motorized contrary to the artist's intentions. David M. Spatt, "Moral Rights Survive the Sale and the Southern District," *OSLA Arts & Law* (1996), http://www.artslaw.org/moral.htm. In 1980, the Bank of Tokyo commissioned and then removed an Isamu Noguchi sculpture from its Manhattan lobby. In 1981, the General Services Administration removed Richard Serra's *Tilted Arc* from the Federal Plaza in New York City (Spatt, "Moral Rights"). In 1966, Maryland commissioned William Smith to create nine murals highlighting the state's history. He installed but altered the central panel and then refused to remove his name from the piece (Cynthia Esworthy, "A Guide to the Visual Artists Rights Act," Harvard Law School, www.law.harvard.edu/faculty/martin/art_law/esworthy.htm). For other pre-VARA cases, see generally US Copyright Office, "Waiver of Moral Rights in Visual Artworks Executive Summary" (October 24, 1996), www.copyright.gov/reports/exsum.html.

133. The states were California, Connecticut, Louisiana, Maine, Massachusetts, Pennsylvania, New Jersey, New Mexico, New York, and Rhode Island. RayMing Chang, "Revisiting the Visual Artists Rights Act of 1990: A Follow-up Survey About Awareness and Waiver," *Texas Intellectual Property Law Journal* 13, no. 2 (Winter 2005): 129.

134. The Visual Artists Rights Act (VARA), Pub. L. 101-650, 104 Stat. 5132, Dec. 1, 1990, codified in part at 17 U.S.C. §§ 106A et. seq.

135. 17 U.S.C. § 101 (defining "work of visual art").

136. In *Pollara v. Seymour*, the court held that a banner commissioned by a legal group was an advertisement because the group determined the content, and the banner promoted a lobbying message and was displayed next to the group's information table. *Pollara v. Seymour*, 344 F.3d 265 (2nd Cir. 2003).

137. In *Carter v. Helmsley-Spear, Inc.*, the Court of Appeals overturned the trial court ruling, holding that the work in question was actually a work for hire that was not covered by VARA because, among other reasons, the artists were paid a weekly salary and received employment benefits. 71 F.3d 77 (2d Cir. 1996). For a detailed discussion of this case, see William M. Landes, "What has the Visual Artists Rights Act of 1990 Accomplished?" John M. Olin Law & Economics Working Paper, No. 123 (2d Series), University of Chicago Law School.

138. William M. Landes, "What has the Visual Artists Rights Act of 1990 Accomplished?" John M. Olin Law & Economics Working Paper, No. 123 (2d Series), University of Chicago Law School (citing *Flack v. Friends of Queen Catherine Inc.*, 139 F. Supp. 2d 526, 534 (S.D.N.Y. 2001).

139. 17 U.S.C. § 106A(a)(1) and (2).

140. *Noland v. Janssen, et al.*, Southern District of New York; No. 1:17-cv-05452 (2017).

141. 17 U.S.C. § 106A(a)(3)(A) and (B). For a discussion of the meaning of the terms "honor" and "reputation," which are derived from European concepts of moral rights, see William M. Landes, "What has the Visual Artists Rights Act of 1990 Accomplished?" John M. Olin Law & Economics Working Paper, No. 123 (2d Series), University of Chicago Law School. "Recognized stature" refers to society's interest in protecting important works of art. In *Martin v. City of Indianapolis*, the city demolished a sculpture without giving prior notice to the artist. The court allowed the use of newspaper articles and letters about the sculpture to conclude that the work was one of "recognized stature." *Martin v. City of Indianapolis.* 928 F. Supp. 625 (S.D. Ind. 1997), affirmed 192 F. 3d 608 (7th Cir. 1999).

142. 17 U.S.C § 106A(c)(1)(2) and (3). For a discussion of negligence, see William M. Landes, "What has the Visual Artists Rights Act of 1990 Accomplished?" John M. Olin Law & Economics Working Paper, No. 123 (2d Series), University of Chicago Law School. See also Martin, 892 F. Supp. 625 (S.D. Ind. 1997). In *Pavia v. 1120 Avenue of the Americas*, the court denied a claim under VARA because the alleged alteration had occurred prior to the effective date of the act. The court denied a claim under VARA based on the ongoing display of the altered work, saying that VARA does not cover display rights. However, the court allowed a claim based on New York's Artists Rights Act, which does cover display rights and is not preempted by VARA. *Pavia v. 1120 Avenue of the Americas Associates*, 901 F.Supp. 620 (S.D.N.Y. 1995). In *Pfaff v. Denver Art Museum*, an artist claimed that the Denver Art Museum damaged her work when it improperly dismantled it after an exhibit. 94 Civ. 9271. (JSM), 1995 WL 393489 (S.D.N.Y. June 22, 1995). See Marie C. Malaro, *A Legal Primer on Managing Museum Collections*, 2nd ed. (Washington, DC: Smithsonian Books, 1995), 187n351.

143. 17 U.S.C. § 106A(c)(3). For example, an artist cannot base a VARA claim on damage to reputation as the result of a dimly lit gallery, or a poor-quality photo of the work in a pamphlet or website. See William M. Landes, "What has the Visual Artists Rights Act of 1990 Accomplished?" John M. Olin Law & Economics Working Paper, No. 123 (2d Series), University of Chicago Law School. In *Peker v. Masters Collection*, an artist who objected to the way that his work was being reproduced by a licensee brought claims under both VARA and the Copyright Act. The court dismissed the VARA on the grounds that the modification was to the reproductions and not to the artist's original work. The court did find for the artist based on the copyright claim of unauthorized reproduction. 96 F. Supp.2d 216 (E.D.N.Y. 2000). In *Berrios Nogueras v. Home Depot*, the court denied a claim under VARA for reproduction of an artist's work in brochures and advertisements, stating that the rights of attribution and integrity do not apply to reproductions of an otherwise protected work when used in connection with works specifically excluded from the definition of "works of visual art." 330 F. Supp. 2d 48 (D.P.R. 2004).

144. 17 U.S.C. § 106A(d).

145. 17 U.S.C. § 106A(e). For sample VARA waiver forms, see Marie C. Malaro, *A Legal Primer on Managing Museum Collections*, 2nd ed. (Washington, DC: Smithsonian Books, 1995), 196–97.

146. 17 U.S.C. § 501(a) includes VARA violations among the actions that infringe a copyright. The Copyright Act allows for enhanced damages for willful or intentional violations. In *Martin v. City of Indianapolis*, the court held that although the destruction of the artist's sculpture had been intentional, the defendant's actions were careless rather than willful. 982 F. Supp. 625 (S.D. Ind. 1997).

147. 17 U.S.C. § 301(f). See RayMing Chang, "Revisiting the Visual Artists Rights Act of 1990: A Follow-up Survey About Awareness and Waiver," *Texas Intellectual Property*

Law Journal 13, no. 2 (Winter 2005): 137. In *Pavia v. 1120 Avenue of the Americas Associates*, the court addressed the question of preemption with respect to a provision of the New York Artist's Rights Act. 901 F. Supp. 620 (S.D.N.Y. 1995).

148. 17 U.S.C. § 106A. If the work cannot be removed from a building without damage, the building owner must obtain a written waiver from the artist. If the work can be removed without damage, the building owner must notify the artist and provide an opportunity for the artist to remove the work at her own expense. No waiver is required for works installed with the artist's consent, prior to June 1, 1991. 17 U.S.C. § 113(d)(1) and (2).

149. Colloquially known as the "5Pointz Case," this case is a prime example of the implication of VARA on visual arts when a 2017 jury determined a developer violated VARA by whitewashing graffiti murals in Queens. *Cohen et al. v. G&M Realty L.P. et al.*, No. 1:13-cv-05612 (E.D.N.Y.).

150. 17 U.S.C. § 113(d).

151. 17 U.S.C. § 113(d)(3). See 37 CFR 201 for procedures. As of October 31, 2007, only three such statements have been recorded.

152. 17 U.S.C. § 106(a).

153. *Massachusetts Museum of Contemporary Art Foundation v. Büchel*, No. 08-2199 (1st Cir. Jan. 27, 2010) https://caselaw.findlaw.com/us-1st-circuit/1500091.html

154. 17 U.S.C. § 501(a).

155. Copyright law is the exclusive domain of the federal government per 17 U.S.C. § 301.

156. 17 U.S.C. § 501(b).

157. 17 U.S.C. § 411.

158. 17 U.S.C. § 506(a).

159. See *A&M Records, Inc. v. Napster, Inc.*, 239 F.3d 1004, 1013 n.2 (2001).

160. In this case, the company was held to have infringed. See *Basic Books v. Kinko's Graphics*, 758 F.Supp. 1522 (S.D.N.Y. 1991).

161. See *MGM Studios, Inc. v. Grokster, Ltd.*, 545 U.S. 913 (2005) at 930.

162. See, for example, *Fonovisa, Inc. v. Cherry Auction, Inc.*, 76 F.3d 259 (9th Cir. 1996) (swap meet); *Arista Records, Inc. v. Flea World*, 356 F. Supp. 2d 411 (D.N.J. 2005) (flea market).

163. See *A&M Records, Inc. v. Napster, Inc.*, 239 F.3d 1004 (9th Cir. 2001).

164. See *MGM Studios, Inc. v. Grokster, Ltd.*, 545 U.S. 913 (2005) at 930.

165. See, for example, *Intellectual Reserve, Inc. v. Utah Lighthouse Ministry Inc.*, 75 F. Supp. 2d 1290 (D. Utah 1999) and *Online Policy Group v. Diebold, Inc.*, 337 F. Supp. 2d 1195, 1202 n.12 (N.D. Cal. 2004).

166. See *Sony Corp. of America v. Universal City Studios, Inc.*, 464 U.S. 417 (1984).

167. 17 U.S.C. § 512(c).

168. 17 U.S.C. § 512(c)(3).

169. 17 U.S.C. § 1201; *Universal City Studios, Inc. v. Reimerdes*, 111 F. Supp. 2d 294 (S.D.N.Y., 2000), aff'd, 273 F.3d 429 (2d Cir. 2001).

170. See *Chamberlain Group, Inc. v. Skylink Technologies, Inc.*, 381 F. 3d 1178 (Fed. Cir. 2004); *MDY Industries, LLC v. Blizzard Entertainment, Inc.*, 629 F.3d 928 (9th Cir. 2010); *Universal City Studios v. Reimerdes*, 111 F. Supp. 2d 294 (S.D.N.Y., 2000).

171. 17 U.S.C. § 512(c).

172. For example, see Jon Healey, "The Guardian uses copyright to shush a critic of its cultural criticism," *Los Angeles Times*, June 11, 2015, http://www.latimes.com/opinion/opinion-la/la-ol-the-guardian-copyright-takedown-africa-video-20150610-story.html.

173. In a recent case, the court rejected a subsequent claim for the recovery of attorneys' fees incurred in bringing the lawsuit. *Barcroft Media, Ltd. v. Coed Media Group, LLC.*, F. Supp.3d. (S.D.N.Y. 2017).

174. 18 U.S.C. § 2319.

175. 17 U.S.C. § 502.

176. 17 U.S.C. § 503.

177. 17 U.S.C. § 504(b) (c).

178. 17 U.S.C. § 504(c)(2)(ii).

179. 17 U.S.C. § 505.

180. "Protection of Traditional Cultural Expressions and Traditional Knowledge–Gap Analyses," World Intellectual Property Organization, accessed March 14, 2018, http://www.wipo.int/tk/en/igc/gap-analyses.html.

181. See, for example, U.S. Const. art. I, § 8, cl. 8. "[t]o promote the Progress of Science and useful Arts."

182. James Boyle, *The Public Domain: Enclosing the Commons of the Mind* (New Haven: Yale University Press, 2008), 129; see also Candace Hines, "Black Musical Traditions and Copyright Law: Historical Tensions," *Michigan Journal of Race & Law* 10 (2005): 463, 464.

183. See "Declaration on the TRIPS Agreement and Public Health," adopted on November 14, 2001, World Trade Organization Ministerial Conference, Doha, November 9–14, 2001.

184. See Patty Gerstenblith, "Identity and Cultural Property: The Protection of Cultural Property in the United States," *Boston University Law Review* 75, No. 559 (1995): 578.

185. 25 U.S.C. §§ 3001 et seq.

186. 25 U.S.C. §§ 3002.

187. See discussion of the discovery of human ancestor remains that have variously been referred to as Kennewick or Richland Man, found in July 1996. Anne Laure Bandle, Andrea Wallace, Marc-André Renold, "Case Kennewick Man—Bonnichsen v. United States," Platform ArThemis, Art-Law Centre, University of Geneva (July 2013), accessed March 14, 2018, https://plone.unige.ch/art-adr/cases-affaires/kennewick-man-2013-bonnichsen-v-united-states/case-note-kennewick-man.

188. See discussion of the Taliban destruction of cultural artifacts and the desires and actions of local scholars and curators to remove or hide the items counter to the desires of international protection organizations, in Kwame Anthony Appiah, "Whose Culture Is It?," *The New York Review of Books*, Februry 9, 2006, http://www.nybooks.com/articles/archives/2006/feb/09/whose-culture-is-it/.

189. Berne Convention for the Protection of Literary and Artistic Works, World Intellectual Property Organization, September 9, 1886, amended on September 28, 1979, 828 U.N.T.S. 221, http://www.wipo.int/treaties/en/text.jsp?file_id=283698.

190. Universal Copyright Convention, September 6, 1952, revised on July 24, 1971, 25 U.S.T. 1241 (1975), http://portal.unesco.org/en/ev.php-URL_ID=15381&URL_DO=DO_TOPIC&URL_SECTION=201.html.

191. WIPO Copyright Treaty, World Intellectual Property Organization, adopted on December 20, 1996, 36 I.L.M. 65, http://www.wipo.int/treaties/en/text.jsp?file_id=295166.

192. WIPO Performances and Phonograms Treaty (WPPT), World Intellectual Property Organization, adopted on December 20, 1996, CRNR/DC/95, http://www.wipo.int/treaties/en/text.jsp?file_id=295578.

193. Paris Convention for the Protection of Industrial Property, World Intellectual Property Organization, March 20, 1883, amended on September 28, 1979, 24 U.S.T. 2140, http://www.wipo.int/treaties/en/text.jsp?file_id=288514.

194. Madrid Agreement Concerning the International Registration of Marks, World Intellectual Property Organization, April 14, 1891, amended on September 28, 1979, http://www.wipo.int/wipolex/en/wipo_treaties/text.jsp?file_id=283530.

195. Berne and TRIPs address copyright exceptions only briefly, and each of those agreements authorizes countries to make copyright exceptions, subject to compliance with the "three-step test." The version of the three-step text from the TRIPs agreement is at Article 13: "Members shall confine limitations or exceptions to exclusive rights to certain special cases which do not conflict with a normal exploitation of the work and do not unreasonably prejudice the legitimate interests of the right holder."

196. In an important change of direction, WIPO has in recent years begun to bring details about copyright exceptions into the treaty language. In 2013, WIPO adopted the "Marrakesh Treaty to Facilitate Access to Published Works for Persons Who Are Blind, Visually Impaired or Otherwise Print Disabled" that calls for countries to enact statutory exceptions to meet the needs of persons who are blind or have impairments. Under consideration are issues related to exceptions for libraries and to support education. "Marrakesh Treaty to Facilitate Access to Published Works for Persons Who Are Blind, Visually Impaired or Otherwise Print Disabled," World Intellectual Property Organization, June 27, 2013, http://www.wipo.int/treaties/en/ip/marrakesh/.

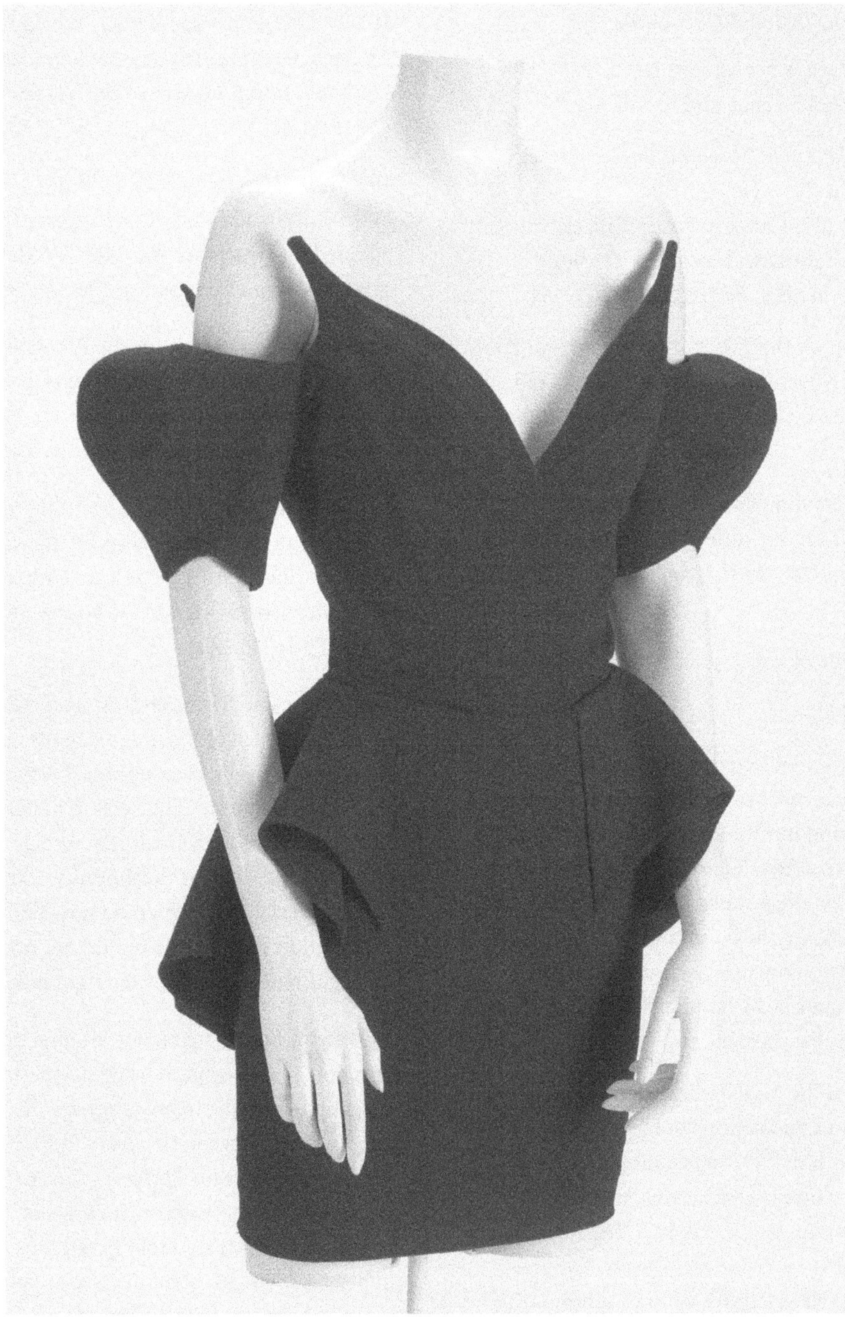

2

Institutional Intellectual Property Policies

JOHN FFRENCH, WALTER G. LEHMANN, MELISSA LEVINE, MICHELLE GALLAGHER ROBERTS, NANCY SIMS, AND ANNE M. YOUNG

INTELLECTUAL PROPERTY POLICIES

As leaders in the knowledge-based economy, cultural institutions are intrinsically involved in the creation and distribution of Intellectual Property (IP) assets. Cultural institutions routinely create and use IP as part of every functional aspect of their daily activities—from collections management to human resources, to fundraising and retail sales. This knowledge is the cultural institution's intellectual capital. Today, IP assets of cultural institutions "have an economic component that makes them valuable in a financial, as well as in an aesthetic, historical, or scientific sense."[1] Cultural institutions also routinely use IP assets created and owned by others. The use of IP assets of others can raise significant liability concerns. As a result, it is imperative for cultural institutions to develop comprehensive IP policies to provide oversight and guidance with respect to the institutions' day-to-day practices and procedures regarding the creation and use of IP. Armed with an understanding of the varying types of IP, cultural institutions' IP policies provide a set of guidelines to help leverage IP assets and manage the risks associated with their use.[2]

OWNERSHIP AND THE DEVELOPMENT OF IP POLICIES

There is a long-standing tradition in the United States of treating *scholarly* works as though they belong to their authors, with little regard for the default rules of copyright and other IP laws under which ownership of all employee works vest in the employer.[3] For many years, these informal practices governed the treatment of almost all IP in research institutions—faculty members were deemed to be the owners of the IP they created. However, both industry developments and legal changes began to make ownership of IP a higher profile issue within research and education contexts, and formal institutional policies addressing details of ownership began to develop in response.

One major spur for the development of institutional IP policies was the Bayh-Dole Act, which primarily addressed patents.[4] Aligning with established principles of IP law, early institutional ownership policies, therefore, often formalized an assumption that the university owned and would be in charge of decision making around patents. This was in opposition to the long-standing practice of treating copyrights as if they belonged to academic authors. Additionally, later federal legislation created separate incentives for academic institutions to have specific copyright-oriented policies.[5] Thus, by the 1990s and early 2000s, many academic institutions had separate policies surrounding copyright and patent ownership, often treating the two types of IP quite differently.

Institutional copyright policies in academic settings often confirm that employees (i.e., professors) who produce scholarship, such as books, papers, and presentations, in the course of their employment own the copyright in those materials. In some cases, the institution is entitled to use the work for certain limited institutional purposes pursuant to a license granted by the employee. The exact legal mechanisms of these policies vary, though the specific wording of a policy can have real legal impact.[6]

Employees who are not scholars are often not granted such ownership by institutional policies—although distinguishing between scholars and "nonscholars" is often a matter of both policy and practice within institutions and departments. Ownership of nonemployee student work (both copyright and patent) is sometimes addressed by policies, which vary widely, with most defaulting to students owning their own works, but with institutions able to require certain permissions as conditions of enrollment. And, since most students are not employees, the legal "hook" on which to hang institutional ownership rights is weaker. Similarly, cultural institutions may or may not be part of a broader university setting for the governance of the IP their employees create. Therefore, separate, yet similar IP policies may be required by cultural institutions. It is increasingly being recommended by professional organizations to develop policies to govern and address the ownership of IP by employees, independent contractors, collaborators, and even volunteers and visitors.

USE POLICIES

Academic institutions often have one or more campus policies that address appropriate uses of copyrighted materials, but often these policies are a bit fractured. Student conduct rules, employment contracts, "acceptable use" policies related to campus information technology, and other rules and regulations may all address appropriate uses of copyrighted materials. It is less common for academic or research institutions to have a policy that addresses appropriate uses in a specific and isolated way, although recent legislation has provided incentives for institutions to take a more active role in communicating about this with their users.[7]

Many research libraries employ policies to address IP issues created by the libraries' basic services, such as copying, interlibrary loan, and other library services. However, the rapid evolution of services and activities provided by these cultural institutions toward efforts that often involve large-scale copying and public sharing of those copies raises issues that existing policies may not address.

CASE STUDY

CRAFTING AN IP POLICY

Anne M. Young

The Indianapolis Museum of Art, Inc. DBA Newfields (Newfields) Intellectual Property (IP) and Open Access (OA) Policy is intended to:

- foster awareness among Newfields staff of the importance of IP
- clearly define the ownership rights of Newfields and staff in relation to IP
- direct Newfields staff on the use of IP owned by Newfields and promote consistency in its use across Newfields
- provide guidance to Newfields staff regarding the use of external materials to limit the risks of infringement on third-party IP rights.

Initially prepared in 2001, the IP and OA policy is now reviewed and updated every two years. The first iteration of the policy to adopt an OA element was finalized in 2012 when a comprehensive update was undertaken for the first time since 2007. The 2012 IP Policy Task Force was led by the rights and reproductions department and included approximately fifteen other staff members from across museum divisions.[1] Subsequent updates have been completed with representatives from the same departments, but only required one formal meeting and a handful of emails to review and amend the policy, primarily to update legal language and make minor edits to reflect changes in internal practices and procedures.

The IP and OA policy applies to all Newfields staff: part-time or full-time, temporary or regular, interns and fellows, volunteers, and members of the board of governors. Further, the policy is incorporated by reference into the agreements with all contract or freelance workers, work-for-hire agreements, commissioned artists, and researchers.

The policy addresses Newfields' ownership and use(s) of IP created by Newfields, IP created by Newfields in conjunction with a third party, and IP created solely by a third party. Where Newfields is the contracted party, Newfields only reuses the IP with prior permission or in accordance with a licensing agreement.

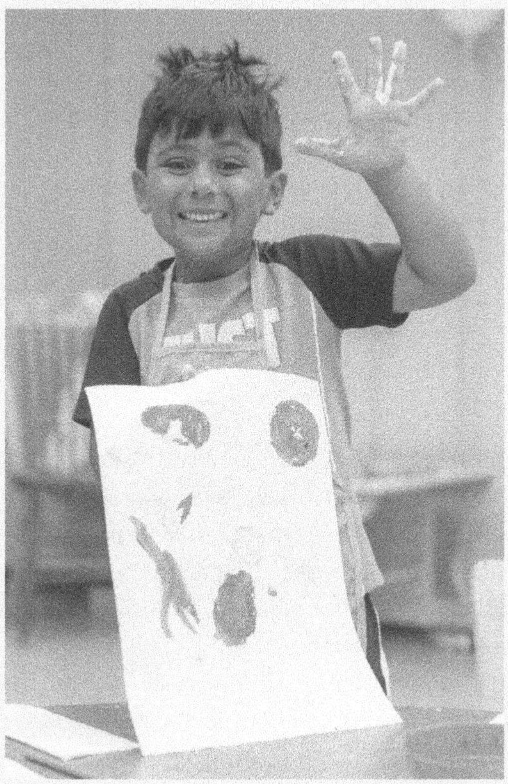

FIGURE 2.1
Students enrolled in summer camps at Newfields retain their IP rights to the works they create.

The IP policy details the ownership possibilities of IP created by the following:

- Newfields staff during the course of their employment at Newfields
- Newfields staff outside their contract of employment
- volunteers, researchers, freelancers, commissioned/contracted parties, and other work-for-hire parties creating copyrightable material for Newfields
- those participating in Newfields-funded projects or research
- collaborators
- guests

The 2014 review of the IP and OA policy led to the development of formal procedures should Newfields discover that its IP has been infringed or if Newfields has purportedly infringed any third-party IP rights. The notice and claims will be reviewed by the Rights and Reproductions Department in conjunction with other department(s) as needed and, when applicable, with the advice of legal counsel. To aid in any infringement procedures, a template cease and desist letter and takedown notice were developed should the need for their use arise.[2]

NOTES

1. The following departments had representatives on the task force: conservation, curatorial, design, human resources, library and archives, marketing and public affairs, photography, publishing, registration, retail, and technology.
2. Direct quotes and information drawn from Newfields, *Intellectual Property and Open Access Policy* (Indianapolis: 2018).

OPEN ACCESS POLICIES

Open Access (OA) is a movement within research communities toward providing free online public access to (and in many definitions, public reuse rights for) published scholarly research. It arises from (i) idealistic principles about free access to knowledge, (ii) practical recognition that the marginal costs of distribution of research are greatly reduced online, (iii) pragmatic interest in the more rapid exchange and critique of ideas that can occur in online environments, and (iv) recognition by funders that paying for future access to publications they have backed is an ineffective use of resources.

In many fields, OA is not a widely accepted school of thought, while in others, almost all publication is open. Institutions that derive benefit from OA, primarily public research institutions and research funding organizations, have developed policies to spur access to published research.

Currently, almost all European public research institutions have OA policies created by law or institutional leadership. The adoption of institutional policies in the United States has been less systematic due to greater independence of individual institutions, more distributed institutional governance structures, the great variation of attitudes toward OA,

CASE STUDY

DEFINING USES OF IP

Anne M. Young

"Newfields staff must respect and honor Newfields and third-party rights, trademarks, trade secrets, and confidential information during the course of their employment." Once ownership, creation, and types of IP were defined in Newfields' IP policy, the uses were separated into three distinct categories: Newfields-Created IP, Third-Party-Created IP, and Public Access.

Newfields-Created IP

Images of Newfields, images of objects in the collections, or any textual materials relating to the collection must not be used in any media to assert or imply that Newfields endorses any commercial product or enterprise, concurs with the opinions expressed, or confirms the accuracy of any text used with these images or materials. Use of Newfields' name, logo, trademark, and any other marks or names commonly associated with Newfields by outside clients may only be granted permission by Newfields. Newfields staff may use Newfields' name, logo, trademark, and any other marks or names commonly associated with Newfields during the course of their work and in describing their relationship with Newfields. Newfields' trade secrets in information, concepts, plans, designs, ideas, technology, potential inventions, and other confidential information and agreements are important assets that must be protected and may not be used in contexts that may negatively impact upon Newfields.

Third-Party-Created IP

Newfields Library and Archives staff may make copies of published or unpublished works from the collections for Newfields staff, commissioned/contracted parties, and guests for noncommercial personal use, research, or private study subject to internal procedures and licensing agreements. Newfields staff, commissioned/contracted parties, and guests who wish to make copies of or use third-party works of art, records, books, films, software, etc. for any purposes beyond these uses must obtain the appropriate permissions from the rights holder(s). In cases where ownership of rights cannot be established or where rights cannot be traced (orphan works), Newfields staff, commissioned/contracted parties, and guests must follow previously established procedures for the use of these materials. Newfields endeavors to secure third-party permissions for funding bodies, sponsors, and other partners in accordance with contractual obligations. Use of third-party software and databases is subject to the appropriate commercial and open-source licensing agreements and IT Conditions of Use.

Public Access

Newfields aims to provide free online public access to works in its collections under open-access principles subject to copyright restrictions, compliance with third-party rights, and the contractual obligations of funding bodies, sponsors, and other partners. To this end, Newfields facilitates and encourages public access and use of its materials for scholarly research, educational projects, outreach programs, promotion of Newfields' collections and activities, and to foster exploration of art, design, and the natural environment. Permission for use of Newfields materials under open access principles is given on a nonexclusive basis and should include an attribution credit to Newfields in all reproductions.

Further, Newfields' IP Policy supports the utilization of the fair use doctrine, recognizing that it is a privilege to grant various reproduction permissions and respects the rights of others to do the same. Central to any claims of fair use is an analysis of the four factors set out in the Copyright Act.[1] Newfields also recognizes its responsibility to properly credit content created by third parties. Newfields

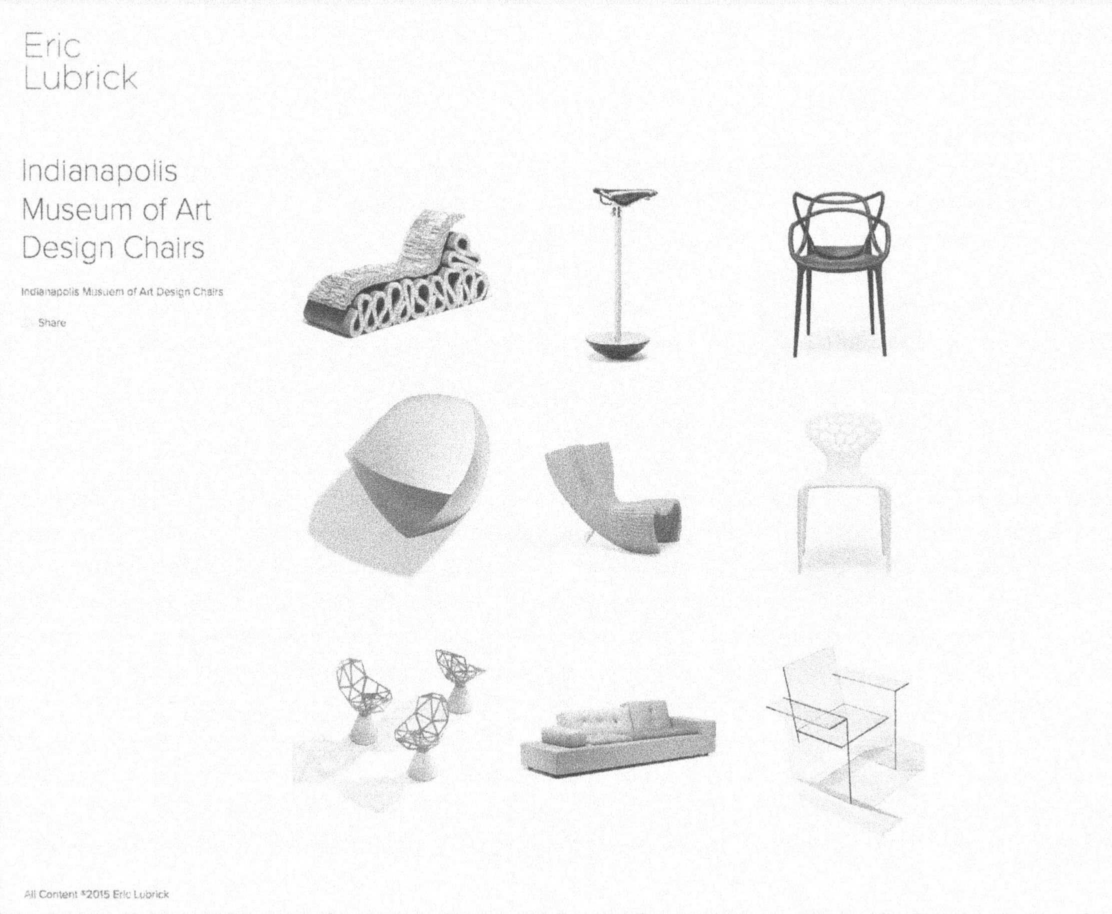

FIGURE 2.2
Sample page from a staff member's personal website crediting the Indianapolis Museum of Art at Newfields for images created as part of their work at the museum.

strives to clearly identify all rights ownership in its own published content, except where it is impossible for reasons of practicality.

In addition, the development of a mechanism to permit staff to utilize the materials they created or co-created during their term of employment in personal portfolios was central to the development of Newfields' IP and OA policy.[2] It was vital for staff, particularly the photographers, designers, and other "creative-team" members, to be able to repurpose their work product for inclusion in their personal portfolios, with certain limited exceptions.

Provisions were developed to guide personal portfolio use by staff:

1. Content used in online portfolios must link back to the appropriate page(s) of Newfields' website, when possible, to provide more context to the exhibitions and/or collection pieces.
2. Materials created in relation to exhibitions that were not organized by Newfields may not be used in online personal portfolios.
3. The use of any media containing works of art in Newfields' collection must be reviewed by the Rights and Reproductions Department to ensure compliance with any use restrictions imposed by copyright or any lender/donor requirements.
4. All content must include the appropriate credit line(s) in the provided format.[3]

NOTES

1. 17 U.S.C. § 107. See chapters 1, 5, and 7, Fair Use, for a more detailed discussion.
2. It is important to note that Newfields owns the copyright and related rights in all works, performances, data, databases, software, and designs ("work product") created by Newfields staff during the course of their employment with Newfields.
3. Direct quotes and information drawn from: Newfields, *Intellectual Property and Open Access Policy* (Indianapolis: 2018).

and to some degree the nature of US copyright laws, particularly presumptions about ownership of IP. However, many institutions have now adopted OA policies, usually as a matter of faculty governance. The most common model of policy, originally developed at MIT, involves authors licensing some of their copyrights back to the institution for the purposes of providing OA.[8] Most such policies also allow authors to unconditionally opt out. The effect of such policies is twofold: they enable institutions to provide access to publications produced by their employees via institutional or other scholarly repositories, and they enable employees to negotiate with publishers regarding specific rights.

A wide variety of OA policies have also been adopted by funders of academic research. Most prominently in the United States, the National Institutes of Health began requiring in 2007 that published journal articles resulting from research they had funded be deposited in a central online archive, PubMed Central, within twelve months after publication.[9] The White House Office of Science and Technology Policy requires[10] that most other major federal research-granting agencies develop OA policies for both publications and data.[11] Agencies are developing a variety of approaches to this requirement. Many

CASE STUDY

DEVELOPING AN INSTITUTIONAL REPOSITORY

Anne M. Young

The update of Newfields' IP and OA policy in 2012 included the creation of an Institutional Repository (IR)[1] for which each staff member grants Newfields a nonexclusive, irrevocable, worldwide license to make available their scholarly products that reference or utilize Newfields materials.

Scholarly products are made available through the IR only for the purposes of personal study, teaching, research, and scholarship.[2] Submission to the IR is not required for scholarly products completed before the adoption of the policy, "products for which the staff member entered into an incompatible licensing agreement," or "materials produced that do not reference or utilize Newfields materials." Staff compliance with the OA policy requires the submission of these scholarly products to the IR (Newfields retains the right to waive the nonexclusive license).[3]

The creation of Newfields' OA policy and the adoption of the IR aim to:

- improve the management of Newfields' IP
- better disseminate the scholarly products of Newfields staff and improve Newfields' reputation as a leader in the field
- encourage staff to use alternative publishing platforms that support more sustainable forms of scholarly communication
- provide a formal process to submit copies of scholarly products to the IR
- retain and organize scholarly products related to Newfields' collections[4]

NOTES

1. The IR is accessed via the document management system of Newfields.
2. Staff members do not give up their exclusive rights, but rather grant Newfields permission to include and make available the products in the IR.
3. Any product that has been waived for submission should still be submitted to the IR. The product will be kept for archival purposes, but will not be made available to the public. A citation will appear in searches and may have a link to the product (possibly on the publisher's website), but the full text will not be made available to the public.
4. Direct quotes and information drawn from Newfields, *Intellectual Property and Open Access Policy* (Indianapolis: 2018).

private research funders are also developing OA requirements for recipients of their grant funding.[12] Thus, it is important for cultural institutions to be conscious of contractual obligations and/or restrictions that may be imposed when accepting an award from a granting organization.

PHOTOGRAPHY POLICIES

With changes in technology and the rise of social media, as well as movements toward OA policies, it is important that cultural institutions review their photography policies, particularly as new technologies emerge. The public's desire to access cultural institutions' collections, share their experiences with others, and the ubiquitous presence of smartphones increasingly challenges policies that at one time served to protect the interests of revenue streams or to protect the interest of collection objects, creators, and donors.

A photography policy governs how and under what circumstances items in a cultural institution's

CASE STUDY

OA AT YALE UNIVERSITY

John ffrench

In May 2011, Yale University announced a groundbreaking new policy for access to digital representations of works in the public domain. Yale's policy represents a departure from preceding efforts premised on material and permission fees, and now provides that no license is required for, nor any limitations imposed upon, the use of digital images of works in the public domain.[1]

Yale University's Open Access Policy provides license-free and royalty-free access to digital images of public domain materials in all Yale collections. OA materials may be requested and used by anyone for any purpose. Yale's policy was unique when launched in 2011 in that its scope was not restricted by collection or use. Use of Yale's digital representations of works in the public domain is *not* limited to scholarly purposes. Any use of public domain material is permitted, including commercial applications.[2]

The Yale policy grew out of the changing landscape as more and more cultural institutions crossed the digital divide in the 1990s, as institutions switched to digital workflows, models, and motivations for creating and distributing images of cultural works changed. The College Art Association statement in the 1990s noted that imaging fees had a profound effect on scholarship and argued for fair use more broadly.[3] While it did not specifically address works in the public domain, the 2004 Mellon Foundation study, "Reproduction Charging Models & Rights Policy for Digital Images in American Art Museums," found by and large that imaging rights models were not profitable and perhaps antagonistic, and recommended that museums review their priorities in providing imaging services.[4] The Max Planck Institute's report "Best Practices for Access to Images: Recommendations for Scholarly Use and Publishing," published in 2009, was a set of even-handed recommendations directed at cultural heritage institutions and scholars alike. It drew attention to the distinction between physical property and intellectual property, and recommended OA for educational purposes and waiver of reproduction fees for scholarly use.[5]

Prior to OA, the Yale University Art Gallery (YUAG) maintained a sliding scale of material and permission fees depending on the nature of the request, but in 2008 began to provide images for education and scholarly use free of any charge across the board.[6] As all departments of Yale crossed the digital divide, it was imperative to share with each other in order to share with the world.

> The museum community now has two decades of the experience of "being digital" to look back on, and it is fairly clear that digital networks and online access to collections has not substantially changed image-licensing revenue—as was anticipated by many in the early 1990s. What has happened, but has received much less attention, is that the potential for fulfilling mission in research, education, and general creativity has greatly increased because of those same developments—digital networks and online access. In the end, all of the directors of Yale collections came down on the side of research, education and creativity. The greater risk was thought not to be loss of future revenue, but diminution of mission capacity by continuing to place obstacles like small images at low resolution, with forms to fill and fees to pay where they might very easily be removed.[7]

Following a series of meetings, both on campus and with other cultural institutions around the United States, the directors of the Yale cultural institutions issued a joint memo in support of an OA policy in the fall of 2010, which led to the university-wide endorsement of an OA policy for works in Yale collections in the public domain. The directors' memo outlined four drivers for the adoption of a university-wide OA policy:

1. The university itself:
   "Yale's mission is to advance, disseminate, and preserve knowledge. We strive to educate leaders in the service of society." The directors noted that limiting access to its collections in the digital world would serve only to circumscribe the quality of research, education, and creative endeavors that are the core of the university's mission. YUAG's director (1998–2018), Jock Reynolds, also stressed the importance of ensuring access to public domain works in support of creativity, noting that the process of new works building on and transforming past works is not an insignificant model of cultural evolution.
2. Thought leadership:
   The directors recognized that academic and cultural heritage communities were ready to embrace new policies, and that Yale had an opportunity to be a leader in this effort.
3. Financial considerations:
   The directors acknowledged that the cost of managing intellectual property, maintaining payment structures, and enforcing contractual restrictions almost always outweighs actual revenue.
4. Legal considerations:
   The directors acknowledged that digitizing public domain content may not in and of itself add enough unique creative value to warrant an attempt to copyright; that enforcing copyright is costly; and that attempts to restrict access to public domain cultural heritage material through licensing provisions may be neither legally enforceable nor ethically prudent.

At the outset, an OA Working Group was formed on campus to identify, address, and work through issues related to interpretation and implementation of the policy. Most issues boiled down to the large size and diversity of Yale's campus and collections. Differences in practice are as inevitable as differences in resources and collection materials themselves. It was necessary to reach a consensus in order to move forward as a unit.

One area where departmental practices differed was in service charges. There are costs associated with fulfilling requests for new or original digitization. Yale's policy allows for these fees—for materials or service, not for intellectual property rights—to be assessed according to the practice of the specific collection. Having already all but eliminated reproduction fees prior to the announcement of the policy, the YUAG and the Yale Center for British Art moved toward the elimination of as many other costs and administrative barriers as possible, including, in most cases, fees for new photography.

The policy does not preclude the use of other distribution channels that may serve specific collections. Many Yale repositories have agreements in place with vendors and licensing agencies. While these are not forbidden, these relationships must be reexamined for consistency.[8]

The often-cited fear of seeing collection images adorned on shower curtains or toilet paper has not, to Yale's knowledge, materialized. Yet, if this did or does occur, particularly with a well-produced reproduction, would it really be such a bad thing? Yale has seen a positive increase in individuals looking to its collections as a resource, and Yale has become a role model for other institutions considering a move toward OA. In turn, OA benefits Yale overall and its individual departments by bringing further attention to its objects and collections.

NOTES

1. Yale University, "Open Access to Digital Representations of Works in the Public Domain from Museum, Library, and Archive Collections at Yale University, accessed March 12, 2018, http://web.library.yale.edu/sites/default/files/files/faq_oatodigitalrepresentations_pdworks_21mar2012.pdf.
2. Ibid.
3. Phyllis Pray Bober, "Standards and Guidelines: Copyrights and Permissions in Scholarly and Educational Publishing," College Art Association, accessed September 21, 2014, http://www.collegeart.org/standards-and-guidelines/guidelines/educationsl-publishing-permissions.
4. Simon Tanner, *Reproduction Charging Models & Rights Policy for Digital Images in American Art Museums: A Mellon Foundation Study* (August 2004), http://www.kdcs.kcl.ac.uk/fileadmin/documents/USMuseum_SimonTanner.pdf.
5. Max Planck Institute for the History of Science, *Best Practices for Access to Images: Recommendations for Scholarly Use and Publishing* (January 5, 2009), accessed March 12, 2018 http://www.mpiwg-berlin.mpg.de/PDF/MPIWGBestPracticesRecommendations.pdf.
6. Melissa Fournier, *Opening Access to Works in the Public Domain at Yale University* (February 14, 2012): 7, https://www.diglib.org/yale-center-for-british-art-releases-thousands-of-public-domain-images/.
7. Ken Hamma, September 15, 2011 (5:35 p.m.), comment on Tyler Green, "The Copyright Revolution at US Art Museums," *Modern Art Notes: Art-focused Journalism* (blog), September 15, 2011, https://web.archive.org/web/20160518061413/http://blogs.artinfo.com/modernartnotes/2011/09/the-copyright-revolution-at-us-art-museums/.
8. As an example, the YUAG maintains third-party agreements with Artstor/ITHAKA, and for the first year after the Open Access policy debuted, with Art Resource, Scala, and DNP Art Communications Co., Ltd.

collection can be photographed and who can take the photographs. It also addresses what the creator (photographer) can or cannot do with the resulting images. Most often this policy involves visitors taking images in a gallery, but it can also include nonaffiliated researchers taking their own images while interacting with an object in storage or a camera crew shooting on the institution's property.

Increasingly, visitors are walking in the door carrying at least one camera, increasingly in the form of a smartphone.[13] It is more important than ever for cultural institutions to create a well-thought-out policy that considers potential risks, the needs of their collections, and its patrons. At its simplest, a photography policy stated within a broader IP policy could read: "Photography and filming by visitors is permitted for private, noncommercial use only in specified gallery spaces. Resulting photographs may not be published, sold, reproduced, distributed, or otherwise commercially exploited."[14]

A rights and reproductions specialist should consider the nature of the cultural institution's collections and properties when drafting a photography policy. These policies should be weighed within the broader scope of the institution and its IP policy (if one exists). There is no one "right" answer; rather, the policy should be tailored to each institution. The goals of a photography policy and an institution's priorities and ambitions should be considered when determining if a policy will be more open or more restrictive.

In the last ten to fifteen years, many cultural institutions have rethought the nature of their photography policies in light of OA, the prevalence of camera phones, and social media platforms.[15] Many cultural institutions have relaxed their policies about personal photography and accepted the futility of trying to police visitors with camera phones. Instead, they now try to harness the potential social media impact. Simultaneously, others have reconfirmed their restrictions.[16] The primary arguments for more restrictive policies have been based on concerns related to IP, conservation and preservation of objects, the effect on revenue streams, visitor experience, and security. More liberal policies cite the power of allowing the consumer broader freedom and access.[17] What is perhaps most important when writing a photography policy is determining who on staff maintains the policy and has the power to change it as attitudes and technologies evolve.[18]

The first step in developing a photography policy is to gather all staff with a vested interest in the topic. These representatives will vary at any given institution but could include staff from the following departments: senior management and administration, rights and reproductions, retail, social media, special events, marketing and public relations, visitor services and security (including gallery attendants and docents), conservation, registration, and exhibitions. Each will bring a unique perspective and interaction with the institution's various constituents, objects, and buildings.

Questions to consider when crafting a photography policy:

1. Is there a current policy?
2. Review the current policy.
   a. Where does it appear on the institution's website and is it easily found? [19]
   b. Is the language formal (policy) or informal (FAQ)?
   c. Does it still match the institutional mission and brand?
3. Who "owns" the current policy?[20]
   a. Whose voices should be heard in updating it, if needed? Stakeholders may include curatorial, visitor services, rights and reproductions, legal, conservation, and security.
4. How can staff training support the policy?
   a. Do guards, educators, visitor services staff (who will have to communicate it to visitors) understand the policy and its rationale? The verbal communication of the policy by staff should mirror and not contradict the written policies.

CASE STUDY

CASE STUDY: VISITOR PHOTOGRAPHY AND SOCIAL MEDIA

Anne M. Young

In 2013 Carolina A. Miranda noted, "As a culture, we increasingly communicate in images."[1] Visitor photography facilitates this communication through images and social media. As a particular benefit to temporary exhibitions, visitors who share images on social media rally awareness and excitement for these limited-time-only experiences.

The Indianapolis Museum of Art at Newfields began experimenting with permitting visitor photography in temporary exhibitions when it opened "Ai Weiwei: According to What?" April 5–July 21, 2013, as the first exhibition in which Newfields actively promoted visitor photography. Given how active Ai Weiwei is himself on social media and sharing images, this exhibition was the perfect opportunity to allow visitors to photograph and share their images for personal use. Through this exhibition, it became clear that permitting visitor photography can enhance the experiences of the audience while directing attention to the collections, programs, and exhibitions that Newfields presents.[2]

Newfields has worked closely with lenders and copyright holders on more recent exhibitions to obtain approval to permit visitor photography.[3] Central to obtaining these approvals has been Newfields' ability to cite increased visitor engagement via the number of posts, shares, and likes on a variety of social media outlets. To further this engagement, Newfields actively informs its visitors that photography is allowed within these spaces and encourages them to share their images on the social media platform of their choice with the provided exhibition hashtag.

NOTES

1. Carolina A. Miranda, "Why Can't We Take Pictures in Art Museums?" *ARTnews*, May 13, 2013, http://www.artnews.com/2013/05/13/photography-in-art-museums/.
2. The hashtag #whoisaiweiwei, created by the Indianapolis Museum of Art at Newfields for the exhibition, returned more than 190 images on Instagram alone.
3. Since 2013, Newfields actively coordinates approval to allow visitor photography from all exhibition lenders and collaborators.

5. Are visitors and staff happy with the current policy?
6. Do visitors follow the policy?
7. Examine the visitor experience (both for those photographing and those not):
   a. What aspects would be enhanced by allowing photography?
   b. How might it detract?[21]
8. What are the conservation issues?
   a. Are there light level and flash exposure concerns?
   b. Is the institution willing to risk damage from visitor photography?
9. How are the institution's spaces laid out? Are there areas of congestion where visitors taking photographs would cause safety or other concerns?

10. What are the security issues?
    a. Can the policy be enforced?
    b. Are there crowd flow issues that personal photography exacerbates?
11. What ability does the institution have to enforce the current or a new policy?
12. Is the policy consistently applied across the institution?
    a. Website, gallery, and loan policies should ideally all be in synch.
13. Consider branding and marketing.
    a. Will "spreadable media," passed on, reused, adapted, and remixed,[22] enhance and expand the institution's message?
14. Does the institution have a social media presence? Can visitors' posts and hashtags on social media be harnessed to further the institution's goals?[23]
15. Does the collection primarily fall into the public domain?
16. For works protected by copyright, is the museum responsible for preventing infringement or is informing visitors about the issues and risks sufficient?
17. What photography restrictions have been imposed by lenders, donors, artists, etc.? Will the institution ask for a variance from these restrictions?
    a. Will all photography in a space be restricted, or will photography be permitted on a piece-by-piece indication (e.g., the inclusion of an icon for "no photography" added to the bottom of the wall label for works that cannot be photographed by visitors)?
18. Are there exhibit areas that might call for a more restrictive policy because of IP, conservation, or other concerns?
19. Are there specific pieces of the collection that need to have a more restrictive policy? If so, how is that enforced?
20. Will separate policies address public spaces versus those not generally open to the public but made accessible to researchers?
21. Will researchers be allowed to take their own publication-quality images?
    a. What kind of equipment can they use?
    b. How much advance notice do they need to provide?
    c. What level of supervision will they require?
    d. What format will be required for attribution and credit lines?
    e. Is their future use of the resulting images restricted? If so, how?
22. What are the institutional IP policy issues and concerns?
    a. Is there a need to protect an income stream?
23. Will film crews be allowed into the institution or onto the property?
    a. What kind of equipment can they use?
    b. What level of supervision will they require?
    c. What type of credit will the institution require?

Crafting the policy is only part of the process. Introducing the policy to the public is as important as drafting it thoughtfully. Cultural institutions must also communicate these policies to staff and visitors in clear, easy-to-understand ways. The policy (or a brief version of it) should be prominently displayed throughout the institution and on its website to inform the public of the photography allowed in public spaces. Any space within the museum that varies from the general policy should also be clearly marked.[24] Restating the policy on any forms or contracts that researchers complete for access to the collection is also recommended. Importantly, staff who interact with the public should be thoroughly informed of the policy and how to politely enforce it. Recurrent training with frontline staff will be vital to the integration and success of an institution's photography policy.

IP AUDITS

While cataloguing and caring for tangible assets is second nature for most cultural institutions, the proper management of intangible assets is often less intuitive. It is just as important—perhaps more so in some situations—for cultural institutions to keep careful track of the extent, quality, and use of their intangible assets,

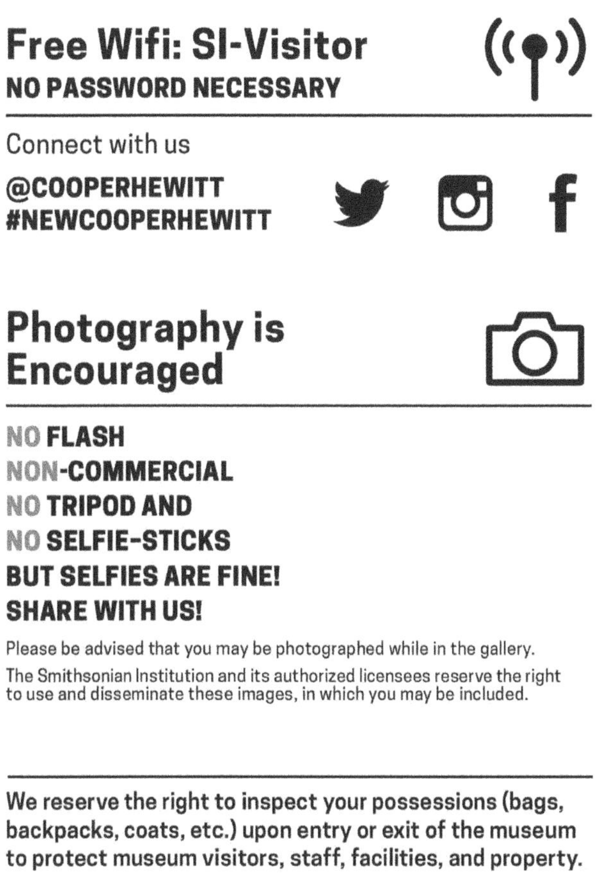

FIGURE 2.3
The Cooper Hewitt, Smithsonian National Design Museum signage clearly communicates what is and is not permitted while photographing in its gallery spaces.

as well as to have processes and procedures in place to create, inventory, perfect, and use the IP rights associated with those assets. Why? Because the creation and use of IP brings with it both risks and rewards. Cultural institutions have a fiduciary duty to minimize the former and maximize the latter, and in order to properly manage its own IP rights and those of others, cultural institutions must first know what those IP assets are.

What Is an IP Audit?

An IP audit is a consistent, continuous process of self-evaluation with the following goals:

1. Assess the IP assets for which the institution is responsible.
2. Manage those assets to further the institution's mission, values, and goals.
3. Implement strategies to minimize the risks associated with the use of those assets.[25]

An IP audit is more than just a catalogue of IP—it can be an important part of strategic planning and risk assessment. The frequency and comprehensiveness of an IP audit should be governed by the institution's IP policy that outlines how the IP assets of an institution are assessed. Properly done, an IP audit will enable the cultural institution to provide adequate protection for its IP assets while ensuring that it is not infringing on the IP rights of others. An IP audit will also help the institution leverage its intellectual capital in support of its public purpose. Although establishing asset value or identifying potential revenue sources may be byproducts of an IP audit, under normal circumstances these are not the primary reasons to perform an IP audit. As John Falk and Beverly Sheppard have noted: "Understanding how to manage and exploit IP assets, be they tangible assets like collections or buildings, or intangible assets such as the ideas and theories that derive from museum scholarship or expertise, should be important parts of any museum's business model."[26]

When to Undertake an IP Audit?

There is never a bad time to begin an IP audit. Establishment of a new management team, development of a new initiative, or preparing a response to a claim or pending litigation may influence the decision to start an IP audit. An IP audit can be conducted in conjunction with an accreditation process—many of the same policies and practices can be reviewed with an eye toward compliance with both cultural institutions' professional standards and IP laws.[27]

An IP audit manages potential risks, so it is best to be proactive and initiate an IP audit as soon as sufficient resources can be allocated to the task. Preferably, the IP audit should be an ongoing process integrated with other routine institutional functions. In an ideal situation the IP audit is conducted on an institution-wide basis. However, it can be scaled to meet immediate needs and available resources. The institution's IP can be subdivided into the interests associated with the collection and the interests associated with the management and operation of the institution. These in turn can be subdivided by department or project. Each subaudit can be conducted simultaneously or piecemeal. Organizing and completing the IP audit as a series of discrete subaudits will make the process more manageable and less taxing on staff and resources.

For example, a collections-based IP audit could be conducted in coordination with a general inventory of the collection, which may complement ongoing provenance research and enhance scholarship and knowledge of the collections. Similarly, an operational IP audit can be conducted in coordination with strategic planning initiatives, which will assist in exercising proper stewardship of culturally created content and intellectual capital and will support ongoing branding and marketing efforts.

Who Conducts the IP Audit?

The size of the IP audit team depends on the nature and scope of the audit. Since an IP audit is inherently a legal assessment of IP rights, it should ideally be conducted by a team including legal counsel with expertise in IP laws applicable to cultural institutions and a representative from each applicable department. If possible, the team should also include personnel with sufficient knowledge of both the institution's IP assets and the applicable IP laws, including relevant international laws, treaties, and conventions.

Unlike commercial entities, cultural institutions hold their IP assets in trust for the benefit of the public. As a result, in addition to knowledge of applicable laws, the attorney or staff conducting the IP audit must also be familiar with applicable professional and ethical codes and the institution's own internal policies and procedures. If confidentiality is a concern, the IP audit team should be organized to maintain confidentiality and preserve attorney-client and work product privileges.

How to Conduct an IP Audit

To ensure that the IP audit is conducted efficiently and effectively, a plan defining the areas of inquiry, scope, schedule, areas of responsibility, procedures, and form of the final report should be prepared in advance. The plan may include an initial list of documents to be reviewed and personnel to be interviewed, which will likely be revised as the audit proceeds. The IP audit plan will serve as a template to guide the execution of the audit and the final results. The IP audit plan should focus on the identification of four key areas:

1. IP assets
2. IP problems
3. defects in IP title or protection
4. unprotected IP assets

To accomplish this, the IP audit team will gather and review a wide range of information about the institution and its assets. To organize the inquiry, it may be helpful to develop a checklist and catalogue the identified IP assets on a departmental basis. The database should include commentary on the status of each identified asset and any applicable IP rights. Emphasis will usually be on copyrights, trademarks, and personal rights of privacy and publicity. However, potential patent and trade secret rights should not be overlooked.[28]

Members of the IP audit team should then review all documents that pertain to the creation, exploitation, or protection of the institution's IP rights. At a minimum this will require a review of employment contracts and independent contractor agreements;[29] funding agreements, including grants, sponsorships, terms of restricted gifts, and other relevant financial instruments; documents pertaining to permanent and temporary asset transfers, including purchase and sale, loan, licensing, and publishing agreements; service and maintenance contracts; and all other contractual agreements that may potentially affect the institution's IP assets. A search of certain databases—including those from the US Copyright Office, the

US Patent and Trademark Office, and certain state offices—may be warranted in some situations, such as to assess the nature and status of the institution's trademarks.

Where standard form agreements are used, such as most employment contracts, review of the basic terms pertaining to IP protection may be sufficient.[30] However, care should be taken to note any customized changes to these standard provisions. Due to the often sizable collections maintained by cultural institutions, the IP audit will likely exclude the review of most individual collection objects. Nevertheless, a general review of collections management policies and procedures, as well as certain specified objects or portions of the collection, may be warranted depending on the desired scope of the IP audit.

The IP Audit Report

Finally, the IP audit results should be formalized in a written report. Commercial practice advises that an IP audit written report should be prepared in such a way that it remains confidential, subject to the attorney-client privilege[31] and not discoverable. However, in the context of cultural institutions, such precautions will depend on a variety of factors. Since many cultural institutions operate in the public trust, it may be considered necessary, or perhaps even ethical, to make the report public or available upon request. Cultural institutions are well advised to consult with legal counsel regarding the confidentiality of the report before it is compiled.

The IP audit report should explain in detail the process and scope of the audit, as well as its findings and recommendations. It should clearly identify any asset that is either unprotected or appears to be entitled to more protection than that it currently enjoys.[32] The IP audit report should also identify any problems with the museum's management of its IP, such as contract revisions or defects in title to certain assets. An executive summary of the IP audit report's findings and conclusions can be a helpful addition to the IP audit report.

It is not unusual for an IP audit to disclose issues involving content ownership, IP formalities, contract management, and organizational policies. Typical IP audit findings may include:

- oral or defective written independent contractor work-for-hire agreements
- inadequate procedures for overseeing compliance with IP terms in grants, contracts, and licensing agreements
- decentralized and inconsistent administration of contracts and agreements
- nonexistent, outdated, or inadequate institutional IP policies
- lack of formal trademark clearance and registration for key assets such as the institution name, titles of exhibitions or programs, and other source identifiers important to the institution's brand
- inconsistent or nonexistent copyright registration practices for collections management, scholarship, publications, and other works

The IP audit may include recommendations for addressing these findings, including establishing consistent copyright and trademark clearance and registration procedures, centralized contract administration, and comprehensive policies on the creation and use of IP.

A well-executed IP audit provides a detailed inventory and analysis of a cultural institution's existing intellectual capital at the time the IP audit was conducted. However, the creation and use of IP is never static. As a result, the IP audit should be reviewed regularly and updated as necessary to reflect changes in the creation and use of an institution's own intangible assets and those of others. Conducting and maintaining an IP audit is an important part of collections management. To effectively manage the IP rights associated with intangible assets, cultural institutions need to know which assets they are responsible for. Armed with an accurate, up-to-date IP audit, a cultural institution can more effectively manage its intangible assets and the associated IP rights to further its mission, minimize risks, and enhance its reputation.

CASE STUDY

CONDUCTING AN IP AUDIT

Anne M. Young

Every five years Newfields undertakes an audit of its IP assets. As defined in Newfields' Intellectual Property Audit, this is intended to:

- record and quantify the museum's current IP assets by department
- determine the current registration protection status of the IP assets
- recommend the applicable IP assets for formal registered protection
- provide guidelines to museum staff for the storage, retention, and formal registration of IP assets[1]

Conducted through communication with representatives from each department of the museum, Newfields' most recent IP audit took approximately eighteen months to complete.[2] Beginning in May 2012, each representative was asked to provide a list of potential IP assets created by their respective departments. From these lists of potential IP, comprehensive lists of the museum's current IP assets were methodically categorized. Within each department the findings were broadly divided and organized by four types of IP: copyright, trademark, trade secret, and patent.

Through March 2013, the assets were then quantified, using approximations when exact numbers were unavailable or impracticable. For most departments, the quantifications spanned the five years since the last IP audit was completed in 2007. The quantification of IP assets aids in identifying the departments that produce the highest volume of the museum's IP assets. Overall, there were 761,102 IP assets reported in the 2012–2013 audit, which was a significant increase from the 133,798 assets reported in 2007.[3]

Once the IP assets were identified and quantified, recommendations were established regarding which assets merit formal legal protection. The need for formal legal protection was based on balancing the costs to pursuing formal registration with the benefits of formal legal protection. The recommendations were divided by IP type and compiled as part of the final IP audit report.

The IP audit process was completed with the creation of the report structured to include the impetus behind Newfields conducting an IP audit, the process and scope of the audit, quantifications (overall numbers as well as the breakdowns by department), and recommendations by IP type for potential formal registrations as well as plans for future audits. As part of the finalization of the report, the IP audit was scheduled to be conducted every five years in order to accurately reflect changes in Newfields' IP assets, which will help the museum more effectively manage and protect its assets to further its mission and minimize institutional risk.[4]

NOTES

1. Newfields, *Intellectual Property and Open Access Policy* (Indianapolis: 2018), 6.
2. Early research for the IP audit began in February 2012 when the 2012 Indianapolis Museum of Art IP Policy Task Force was convened to update the IP and Open Access Policy.
3. The increase in quantified IP assets between the 2007 and the 2012–2013 audits is a result of not all departments being reviewed and/or reporting assets in 2007. In 2012–2013, a more comprehensive approach was taken in an attempt to quantify assets produced by all departments. While every attempt was made to collect data from all departments, due to time and staff constraints, not every department was able to contribute to the IP Audit by the time of its finalization in 2013.
4. At the time of writing the *Handbook's* second edition in 2018, Newfields was just preparing to undertake its next IP audit of the institution.

NOTES

1. Diane Zorich, "Developing Intellectual Property Policies: A How-To Guide for Museums," Canadian Heritage Information Network (CHIN) (2003): 18, https://www.canada.ca/en/heritage-information-network/services/intellectual-property-copyright/guide-developing-intellectual-property-policies.html.

2. Institutional policies may reflect the law, but may also establish internal organizational rules that may either alter established law or provide guidance where the law is not clear. Institutional policies may reflect that cultural institution's particular practice, or may reflect policies and practices of professional or community-wide associations, such as the American Alliance of Museums, American Association for State and Local History, Art Libraries Society of North America, Society of American Archivists, etc.

3. See chapter 1, The Copyright Holder, for a more detailed discussion about works for hire and employee created works.

4. Also referred to as the Patent and Trademark Law Amendments Act, the Bayh-Dole Act dealt with the ownership of inventions arising from federal funding.

5. The TEACH Act of 2002 provides some specific allowances for use of copyrighted materials in distance education, but requires that the institution "institute policies regarding copyright" to qualify as TEACH Act users. Many institutions found the provisions of the TEACH Act far too limited for effective distance education, so only some created or updated copyright policies in response. Technology, Education and Copyright Harmonization (TEACH) Act of 2002, § 13301, Pub. L. No. 107–273 (codified at 17 U.S.C. §§ 101, 110, 112, 801 [Supp. 2004]).

6. This case was primarily concerned with the specific wording of Stanford's policy on ownership, and a contract a researcher had signed with Roche. In the court's interpretation, the Stanford policy under which the researcher "agree[d] to assign" ownership of patents to the university was superseded by the Roche agreement providing that the researcher "will assign and do[es] hereby assign" ownership. The former was understood to be a promise of a future transfer of ownership, whereas the latter included the actual act. Many institutions revised policy language in response. *Board of Trustees of the Leland Stanford Junior University v. Roche Molecular Systems, Inc.*, 131 S. Ct. 2188 (2011).

7. The Higher Education Opportunity Act of 2008 conditions receipt of quite a bit of federal funding on universities making yearly disclosures to students about campus use policies and copyright law; making plans to "effectively combat" unauthorized use of copyrighted materials; and making plans to "offer alternatives to illegal downloading." As is evidenced by these provisions, the main focus of this piece of legislation was the perceived high levels of infringement of commercial entertainment materials by college students. The law does little to incentivize communication or policy formation around copyright issues for employees, or even students in the course of their academics. Higher Education Opportunity Act, Pub. L. No. 110-315 (codified in scattered sections of 20 U.S.C.) (2008).

8. Massachusetts Institute of Technology, MIT Faculty Open Access Policy (Cambridge, MA: Scholarly Publishing @ MIT Libraries: 2009), http://libraries.mit.edu/scholarly/mit-open-access/open-access-at-mit/mit-open-access-policy/.

9. Omnibus Appropriations Act of 2009, Pub. L. No. 111-8 § 217 ("The Director of the National Institutes of Health [NIH] shall require in the current fiscal year and thereafter that all investigators funded by the NIH submit or have submitted for them to the National Library of Medicine's PubMed Central an electronic version of their final, peer-reviewed manuscripts upon acceptance for publication, to be made publicly available no later than 12 months after the official date of publication: *Provided*, That the NIH shall implement the public access policy in a manner consistent with copyright law.")

10. National Institutes of Health, "Upcoming Changes to Public Access Policy Reporting Requirements and Related NIH Efforts to Enhance Compliance," US Department of Health and Human Services, November 16, 2012, http://grants.nih.gov/grants/guide/notice-files/NOT-OD-12-160.html.

11. Director John P. Holdren to Heads of Executive Departments and Agencies, memorandum, February 22, 2013, "Increasing Access to the Result of Federally Funded Scientific Research," Office of Science and

Technology Policy, https://obamawhitehouse.archives.gov/blog/2016/02/22/increasing-access-results-federally-funded-science.

12. For example, the Bill & Melinda Gates Foundation implemented a new OA policy effective January 1, 2015, which mandates all published research funded by the foundation (excluding books) must be published under the Creative Commons 4.0 Generic License (CC BY 4.0) or an equivalent license. "Bill & Melinda Gate Foundation Open Access Policy," Bill & Melinda Gates Foundation, accessed March 8, 2018, http://www.gatesfoundation.org/How-We-Work/General-Information/Open-Access-Policy.

13. A recent Pew Research project found that 56 percent of adults purchased a smartphone in 2013 and 80 percent of "young adults" own a smartphone. Aaron Smith, "Smartphone Ownership 2013," Pew Research Internet Project (June 5, 2013), http://www.pewinternet.org/2013/06/05/smartphone-ownership-2013/.

14. Newfields, *Intellectual Property and Open Access Policy* (Indianapolis: 2018): 6.

15. Stephanie G. Johnson, "Visitor Photography Policy: An Exploration of Current Trends and Considerations Across American Museums" (master's research project, University of Oregon, June 4, 2014), 11, https://scholarsbank.uoregon.edu/xmlui/handle/1794/17940.

16. See, for example, "May I take photographs?" The Frick Collection, accessed March 11, 2018, http://www.frick.org/visit/museum/may-i-take-photographs.

17. See, for example, "Visitor Policies," Minneapolis Institute of Arts, accessed March 11, 2018, http://new.artsmia.org/visit/policies-guidelines/.

18. For example, in early 2015 cultural institutions found themselves faced with how to address the new piece of equipment that many visitors were suddenly bringing into gallery spaces. Selfie sticks were suddenly at the forefront of discussions to revisions in visitor photography policies. William Grimes, "Museum Rules: Talk Softly, and Carry No Selfie Stick," *New York Times*, February 14, 2015, http://www.nytimes.com/2015/02/15/us/museum-rules-talk-softly-and-carry-no-selfie-stick.html?_r=0.

19. Many museums include this topic on a Visit/FAQs page. For example, see "Things to Know," Newfields, accessed March 11, 2018, https://discovernewfields.org/visit#things-to-know.

20. Nina Simon addresses this issue in the final paragraph of "Museum Photo Policies Should Be as Open as Possible." Nina Simon, "Museum Photo Policies Should Be as Open as Possible," Museum 2.0 (blog), August 20, 2009, http://museumtwo.blogspot.com/2009/08/museum-photo-policies-should-be-as-open.html.

21. For example, when reviewing and updating its visitor photography policy in 2012, The Sixth Floor Museum at Dealey Plaza chose to continue its no-photography restriction in its permanent exhibition, while lifting the restriction in other areas of the museum. This decision was made primarily out of concern for preserving the visitor experience in the core exhibition. Due to the exhibit's tight spaces and somber subject matter, there was concern that allowing personal photography could impede traffic flow, as well as cause disruptions to what many visitors find a deeply emotional experience. The museum plans a study and review of this policy in 2018–2019.

22. Nina Simon summarizes the conclusions of Henry Jenkins's expansive white paper, "If it Doesn't Spread, It's Dead," in "Museum Photo Policies Should Be as Open as Possible." Nina Simon, "Museum Photo Policies Should Be as Open as Possible," Museum 2.0 (blog), August 20, 2009, http://museumtwo.blogspot.com/2009/08/museum-photo-policies-should-be-as-open.html. (summarizing Henry Jenkins, "If It Doesn't Spread, It's Dead (Part One): Media Viruses and Memes," Confessions of an Aca-Fan (Blog), February 11, 2009, http://henryjenkins.org/2009/02/if_it_doesnt_spread_its_dead_p.html).

23. For example see, W. Ryan Dodge and Laura Haapio-Kirk, "The Sharypic PhotoWall at the Royal Ontario Museum: An experiment in real-time crowdsourcing," *Electronic Visualization and the Arts (EVA 2013),* accessed March 31, 2018, https://ewic.bcs.org/content/ConWebDoc/51038.

24. Often traveling and temporary exhibitions have different restrictions than items in a permanent collection.

25. Rina Elster Pantalony, World Intellectual Property Organization, *Managing Intellectual Property for Museums* (2013), 22, http://www.wipo.int/edocs/pubdocs/en/copyright/1001/wipo_pub_1001.pdf.

26. John H. Falk and Beverly K. Sheppard, *Thriving in the Knowledge Age: New Business Models for Museums and Other Cultural Institutions* (2006), 129.

27. The documents and other materials compiled and submitted as part of the accreditation or reaccreditation process for the American Alliance of Museums can serve as a useful resource for conducting the IP audit. These materials provide an overview of the collections and provide insight into the museum's policies and practices.

28. See chapter 1 for a detailed discussion of these IP types.

29. Reminder: most employment relationships are "employment at will" and where no formal, written employment agreement exists the IP ownership will depend upon whether the work was created within or outside of the scope of the employee's job duties.

30. For example, confidentiality, nondisclosure, and noncompete clauses.

31. A document is protected by the attorney-client privilege when it is prepared by an attorney acting in a legal capacity for a client. (The lawyer acting in another capacity, such as serving on the institution's board, for example, may not be sufficient to raise the attorney-client privilege.)

32. For example, a museum may use a name or slogan that may be federally registerable, or a museum may own a registered trademark that should be more consciously utilized and protected against infringing uses.

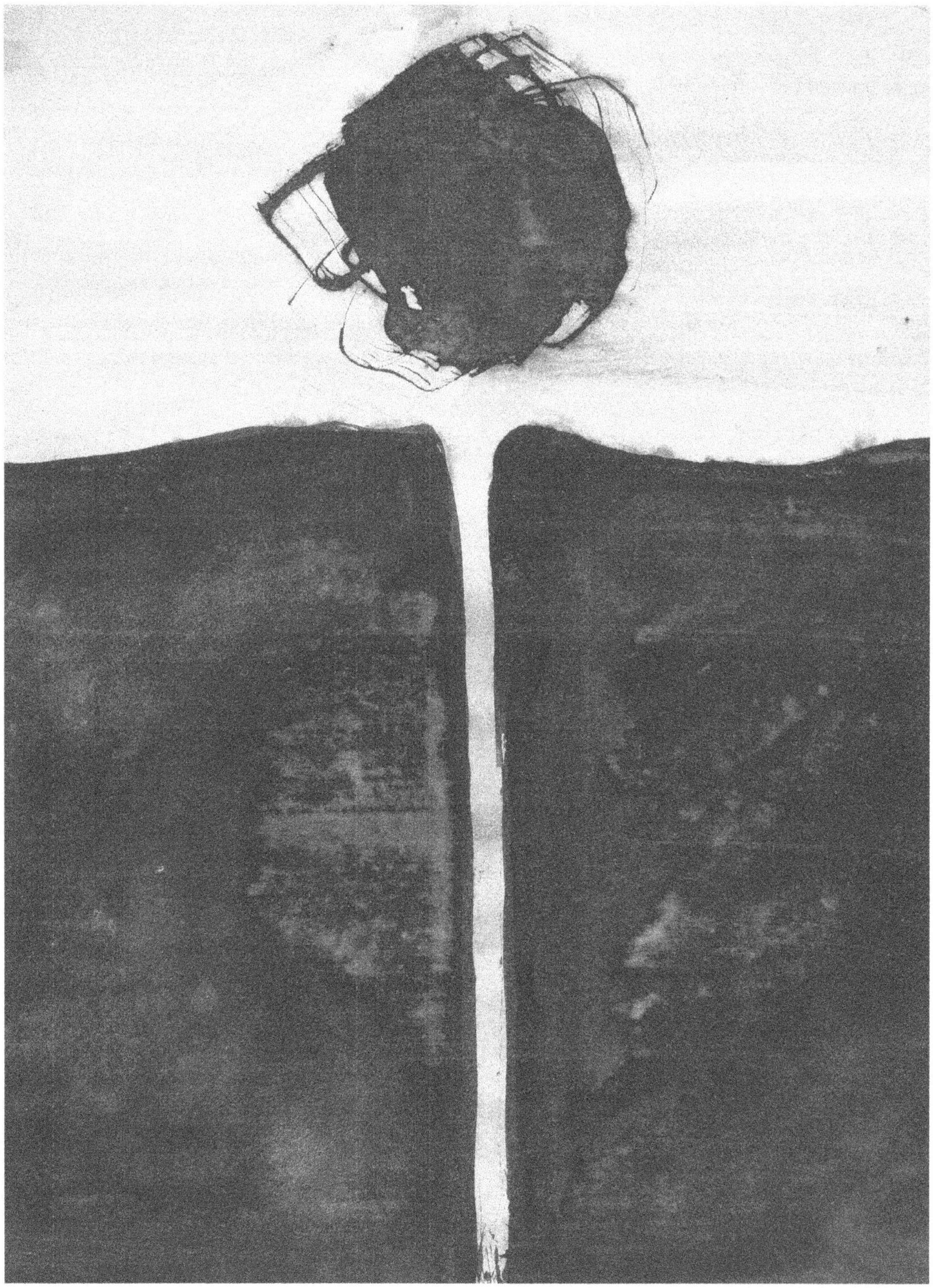

3

Rights Issues for the Collection

MEGAN P. BRYANT, CHERIE C. CHEN, JOHN FFRENCH, SOFÍA GALARZA LIU, MICHELLE GALLAGHER ROBERTS, DEBORAH WYTHE, AND ANNE M. YOUNG

Building a strong foundation in rights management skills begins with knowing how to identify the rights issues related to each object in an institution's collection. This includes determining if a work is protected by copyright and how to find the copyright holder, as well as understanding when other issues—such as moral, privacy, and publicity rights—may come into play. Once the rights research and analysis has been completed, the resulting information must be properly documented and shared within the institution. In cases where a rights holder has been identified, an institution may attempt to obtain a license to guide how a work can be reproduced for a wide range of purposes. This chapter covers these basic rights management topics and provides practical guidance on the steps to identify rights issues and rights holders, explains the process for requesting a license, and concludes with some suggested best practices for record keeping.

DETERMINING COPYRIGHT STATUS

Determining whether a work in the collection is still under copyright can be a complicated task even for the experienced rights and reproductions specialist. Due to the many revisions to US copyright law, the rules for calculating copyright terms are based on a maze of specific factors ranging from when the work was created, the life dates and nationality of the creator, and the type of work, to whether the work has been published and where and when it was published.[1] An invaluable resource developed by Peter B. Hirtle of the Copyright Information Center at the Cornell University Library helps navigate these complicated rules. First published in 1999, Hirtle's chart, "Copyright Term and the Public Domain in the United States," is available for reference online and updated annually.[2] The chart covers five broad categories for determination of copyright status and notes exceptions, conditions, and special cases for each of the following:

- Never Published, Never Registered Works
- Works Registered or First Published in the United States
- Works First Published Outside the United States by Foreign Nationals or US Citizens Living Abroad
- Sound Recordings
- Architectural Works[3]

Armed with resources like Hirtle's chart and basic information about the creator, the date of creation and the publication status[4] of the work, a researcher can often identify whether the work is still under copyright protection in the United States or is in the public domain.[5]

As a practical matter, the simplest approach for an institution will be to start by determining broadly at the creator level what the likely copyright status is for all works by a particular creator in the collection before delving deeper into the unique factors affecting the status of individual works. While broadly categorizing works by an artist can be efficient, it is important to remember that copyright is determined on a per-object basis. Thus, it is possible for different works by the same creator to have different copyright statuses. For example, some Dorothea Lange photographs, such as those in the famous *Migrant Mother* series that were captured while on assignment for the Farm Security Administration, are in the public domain as US federal government works, whereas the photographs in which she retained the copyright will remain under copyright protection until January 1, 2036.[6]

Some general rules of thumb can be followed in making broad copyright determinations for individual creators of literary and artistic works:[7]

- Assume all works by the creator are unpublished or unregistered until research on individual works concludes otherwise, at which point consult Hirtle's chart to calculate the term for registered or published works.
- Works by living creators or creators who died within the past seventy years are under copyright for the life of the creator plus seventy years.[8]
- Works by anonymous creators or creators whose death date is unknown, and works made for hire,[9] are under copyright for 120 years from the date of creation.[10]

Additionally, researchers should also be aware that a single work may have multiple creators and copyrights. For example, a silent film would include the rights in the film and the rights in the accompanying sheet music. Review all the component parts of the broader work being assessed to determine if there is more than one creator and rights owner. Then follow the general rules of thumb above to make the copyright status determination for the creator of each component part.

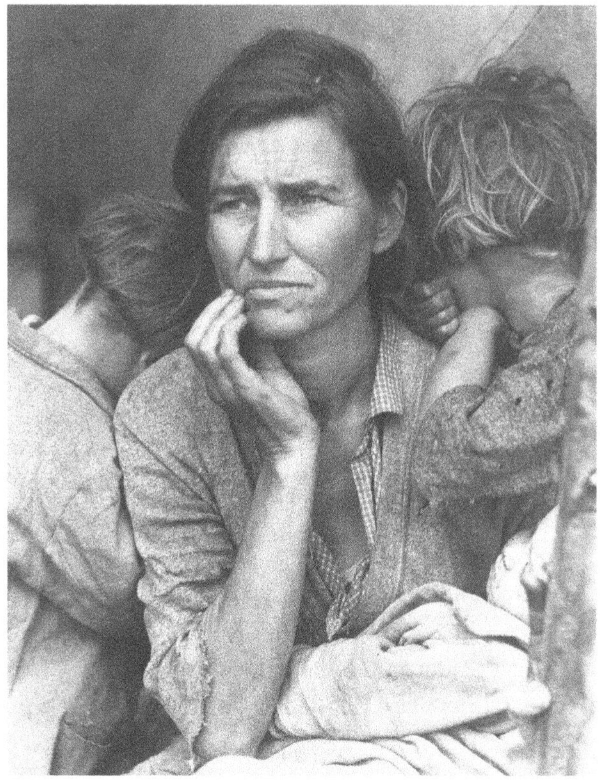

FIGURE 3.1
One of the images from Lange's *Migrant Mother* series.

PUBLICATION AND REGISTRATION

It may appear conservative to begin with a blanket assumption that all works by an author or artist are unpublished and unregistered since this approach will likely result in assigning copyright protection to many pre-1989 works that have fallen into the public domain due to failure to comply with formalities—such as publication without a notice or copyright renewal.[11] However, it can be challenging and time-consuming to determine with certainty whether an individual work has been published or registered, when and where it was *first* published, whether it was published with or without a copyright notice, and whether the registration was renewed. The older the work, the more difficult it may be to answer these questions. Sometimes the availability (or lack thereof) of detailed information about either the creator or the work can turn the task of determining copyright status into a frustrating and laborious research project.

Many institutions simply do not have the staff or budget to conduct detailed research into the publication and registration status of every potentially copyrighted work in its collection. Particularly for archival material collections that are often measured in linear feet, determining the copyright status for individual items can be impractical.[12] Instead, it is more likely that further research is undertaken on an as-needed basis, such as prior to reproducing a work in a publication or for the promotion and marketing of an exhibition.

Researching Registration Status

- Records for works registered since January 1, 1978, are searchable electronically on the US Copyright Office website.[13]
- Pre-1978 copyright registrations are currently only searchable in person using the copyright card catalogue at the Library of Congress, or, for an hourly fee, the Copyright Office staff will search the records on your behalf.[14] Detailed information about searching the card catalogue can be found in Circular 23 issued by the Copyright Office.[15]
- The Copyright Office published compilations of registration records from 1891 through 1977 in 660 volumes of *The Catalog of Copyright Entries* (CCEs). While CCEs only provide an abbreviated record of the registrations, these volumes have been digitized and are available for reference online at the Internet Archive.[16] The CCEs are organized by year and category or class of work (i.e., music, motion pictures, books, or works of art). Circular 23 also includes tips for using the CCEs.[17]

Determining Publication Status

- As discussed in chapter 1, "publication," as defined under US copyright law, generally refers to the act of a work being distributed to the public through sale or other transfer of ownership, or by rental, lease, or lending.[18] The ultimate goal in researching publication status is to determine not just that the work has been published, but when the work was *first* published and whether that first publication included a copyright notice.[19] A cultural institution's curatorial and accession files are often the primary internal documents to review for such bibliographic and provenance information, but collection catalogues and catalogues raisonnés can also provide useful information. Further review of the collection database (or the object itself) is also recommended to see if a copyright notice is inscribed on the object, a review that is especially relevant for materials held in library and archive collections. Absent any detailed information in institutional files or publications, query the relevant curatorial or acquiring department(s) staff to confirm that no additional information is available in-house. Search for and consult external publications about the creator, especially catalogues raisonnés, to check for publication history. This is most easily accomplished if the researcher has access to university libraries where subject-specific collections often exist, such as art history, science, or law. If that option is not available, there may be alternate means of reviewing the information. Many academic and research institutions have partnered with the HathiTrust[20] and Google Books[21] to digitize large portions of their library holdings. Millions of books are now available for online search through these mass digitization projects. For instance, in HathiTrust books identified as being in the public domain are accessible to anyone for reading. Further, rights holders often grant permission to HathiTrust to "open" works and make them readable by anyone for free; rights holders may either place their work in the public domain or select a Creative Commons license.[22]
- Conduct a broad online search for reproductions of the work, bibliographic information, or any other leads about the history of the work. In general, online information about sale or publication history from unknown sources should be vetted by internal experts before relying upon it to make a determination of publication status.

It is entirely possible that despite undertaking best efforts based on an institution's available resources, the research results prove inconclusive in confirming either registration or publication status. In these cases, the institution can either fall back on the assumption that the work is unpublished and unregistered, or consult with legal counsel and institutional leadership on a reasonable position to take based on the available facts and risk profile of the institution. All research efforts and the rationale behind the final registration and publication determinations should be documented in the institution's files to demonstrate due diligence if a use is challenged in the future.

PUBLIC DOMAIN

Once the copyright term for a work expires, it enters the public domain and the former copyright holder can no longer legally control its reproduction, distribution, performance, etc. Determining that a work is in the public domain is simply one possible outcome of undertaking the copyright status analysis as previously described. If a work is no longer under copyright following these rules, then the work is considered to be in the public domain in the United States.

Contrary to popular belief, there is no rule that states works older than *X* number of years are in the public domain. Consider, for example, that unpublished anonymous works are protected for 120 years in the United States from the date of creation. That means unpublished anonymous works created in the late nineteenth century are still protected as of the early twenty-first century! However, there are two distinct categories of works that are easily identifiable as being in the public domain:

- works registered or first published in the United States before 1923[23]
- works created by employees of the US federal government within the scope of their employment[24]

ORPHAN WORKS

The term "orphan works" is commonly used to refer to works still believed to be protected by copyright, but the rights holder(s) either cannot be determined or, if identified, cannot be located despite best efforts. Thus, it is impossible to obtain permission to use an orphan work. If an institution uses an orphaned work, it assumes the risk of an infringement claim if the rights holder(s) later come forward. Orphan work status is not an official copyright category under US law, although in 2004 with roundtable meetings and notices of inquiry, the US Copyright Office has attempted to address this issue.[25] The most recent roundtable was held March 10–11, 2014, at which comments from the

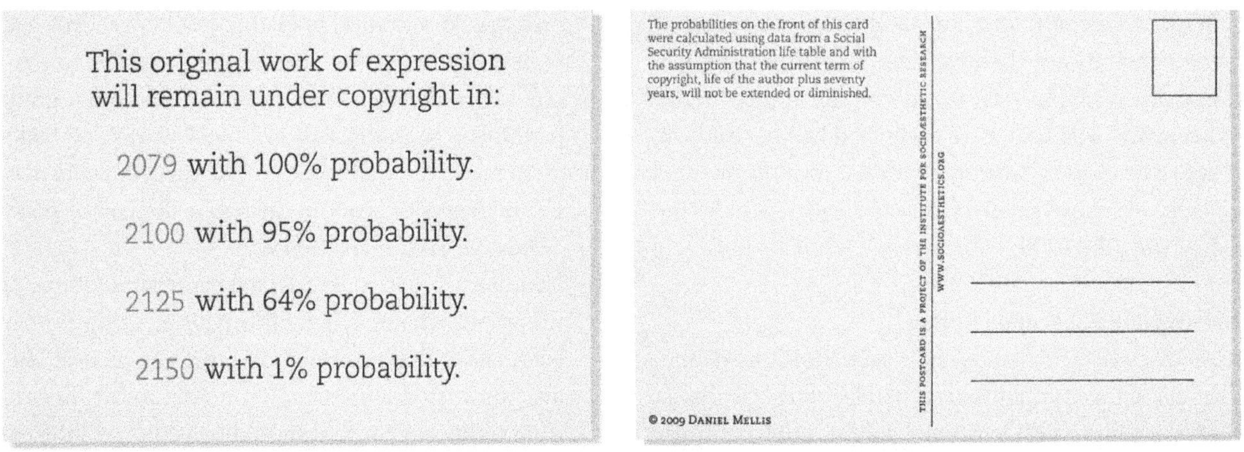

FIGURE 3.2
An artist's postcard intended to predict when this individual work will still be under copyright. The original expression of this postcard was registered with the US Copyright Office with registration number VA0001672722.

CASE STUDY

DETERMINING "PUBLISHED"

In the fall of 2017, the Museum Intellectual Property group received the following query from Sionan Guenther of the Rhode Island School of Design (RISD) Museum: "Does anyone have contact information for the Estate of Kazimir Malevich (1879–1935)? We would like to include a couple of his works from around 1925 (just missing 1923!) in an upcoming publication and want to be as safe as possible."

As a perfect example of listserv collegiality, Tom Morgan of M+ quickly replied: "My understanding is that these works would be very comfortably in the public domain, in terms of artists copyright, so that the only rights you might need to take care of would be photographers copyright in respect of the photographs of the works, where such copyright is asserted."

To which RISD Museum responded: "We believe that the two pieces we hope to include in our project may have been published in the U.S. in 1925 which I believe would put them under copyright until 2021 because of the 1998 Copyright Term Extension Act but I would love to be wrong about this!"

Insight for this particular situation was provided by none other than Peter Hirtle himself:

> I am far from an expert on Russian copyright, but here is how I think things work. The first thing you need to answer is how the works were published in the U.S. in 1925. If the works were published with a copyright notice and Malevich's copyright was renewed in 1953 (28 years after initial publication), then the works would still be protected in the U.S. If the works were published without a copyright notice, or the copyright was not renewed, or publication occurred through public sale of the original paintings, then the works would be in the public domain in the US. That is because copyright could only be restored by 17 U.S.C. § 104A if the works were still protected by copyright in Russia on 1 January 1996. At that time, Russia had a life + 50 year term for copyright, so Malevich's works would have been in the public domain in Russia. Copyright could not be restored in the US. It could only exist if it had never been lost.[1]

This discussion is a perfect example of how determining publication status is not always cut-and-dried. And it further illustrates many of the issues that should be considered when attempting to determine if a work has been "published," not least of which is the valuable nature of conferring with colleagues.

NOTE

1. Excerpts from Museum Intellectual Property group communication, "Museum IP Estate of Kazimir Malevich," September 19, 2017.

public were solicited in order to advise Congress on possible next steps for pending legislation. Cultural institutions and their associated professional organizations have responded with proposals for a "safe harbor"—limited protection against damages—and statements of best practices to use orphan works if a reasonable due diligence search does not find the rights holder.[26] Ultimately, though, Congress must pass legislation to codify an orphan works approach, and this has failed to happen as of 2018.

PUBLIC DOMAIN DAY

The entry of works into the public domain is a true reason to celebrate! January 1 of every year, due to the expiration of copyright protections, thousands of works enter the public domain:

> "the realm of material—ideas, images, sounds, discoveries, facts, text—that is unprotected by intellectual property rights and free for all to use or build upon."[1] Each year, the corpus of works that are in the public domain increases and new works can be referenced and built upon without having to seek the approval of the creator. This means that anyone can use the work and that no one owns it.[2]

There are, of course, caveats to the entrance of works into the public domain each year. Due to various extensions and changes in copyright law by Congress, there are works in the United States that will not enter the public domain until 2057, which one may have expected to otherwise enter in 2018.[3] It is important to note that unpublished and unregistered works created before 1978 will still enter the public domain in their given year.

NOTES

1. "About Us," Duke Law: Center for the Study of the Public Domain, accessed March 13, 2018, https://law.duke.edu/cspd/publicdomainday/.
2. Copyright in a work may enter the public domain if the creator or other owner publicly forfeits his or her rights and declares it to be in the public domain; additionally, Creative Commons licenses may grant the public similar rights by private contract.
3. "Public Domain Day," Duke Law: Center for the Study of the Public Domain, accessed March 13, 2018, https://law.duke.edu/cspd/publicdomainday/.

While the United States has yet to pass any legislation, some localities, like the European Union and the United Kingdom, have formalized processes to enable cultural institutions to utilize orphan works with mitigated risk. The EU Orphan Works Directive, issued in October 2012, states that after the completion of a diligent query for the rights holder(s), cultural institutions in the European Union may display and digitize orphan works for noncommercial uses.[27] Taking this a step further, in October 2014 the United Kingdom established a licensing system for the use of orphan works by which end users may apply to the UK Intellectual Property Office and pay a market-rate fee for the use.[28] Collected fees and corresponding licenses, both pending and granted, are maintained by the office for payment in the future should a rights holder come forward.[29] New processes like these protect the risk assumed by cultural institutions by the dissemination of orphan works, allow these works to be shared more broadly with the public, and provide a means of credit and restitution should a rights holder become known in the future.

By contrast, many cultural institutions in the United States have adopted an informal orphan works solution by conducting a diligent and reasonable search before deciding to use an orphan work on a case-by-

TEST YOUR COPYRIGHT TERMS KNOWLEDGE[1]

Megan P. Bryant and Cherie C. Chen

Grab a copy of Hirtle's chart[2] and calculate when copyright for these works expire:

1. A painting was created in 1965 by a living artist. The work is unpublished.[3]
2. A sculpture was created in 1980 by an artist who died in 2001. The work is unpublished.[4]
3. A corporate work was created in 1942. The work is unpublished.[5]
4. A drawing was created in 1922 by an artist who died in 1950. The work was first published in the United States in 1971 with a copyright notice.[6]
5. A home movie was created in 1963 by a filmmaker who died in 1970. The work was first published in the United States in 1963 with a copyright notice and the copyright registration was renewed.[7]
6. A photograph was created in 1910 by a photographer who died in 1949. The work was first published in the United States in 1915 with a copyright notice.[8]
7. A work was created sometime in the 1950s and first published in the United States in 1960.[9]

NOTES

1. See notes after each question for the answer.
2. Peter B. Hirtle, "Copyright Term and the Public Domain in the United States," Cornell University: Copyright Information Center, last modified January 1, 2018, https://copyright.cornell.edu/publicdomain.
3. Answer: Copyrighted for the life of the artist plus 70 years
4. Answer: Copyrighted for the life of the artist plus 70 years, or 2071.
5. Answer: Copyrighted for 120 years from the date of creation, or 2062.
6. Answer: Copyrighted for 95 years after publication date, or 2066.
7. Answer: Copyrighted for 95 years after publication date, or 2058.
8. Answer: In the public domain due to first publication before 1923.
9. Answer: It depends! If published without a notice, the work is in the public domain. If published with a notice, but copyright registration was not renewed in the last year of copyright (1988), the work is in the public domain. If published with a notice and copyright registration was renewed, the work is copyrighted for 95 years after publication date, or 2055.

case basis, under a good faith belief that the rights holder(s) cannot be identified or located. While doing so may expose the institution to legal risk, the use of orphan works is often in support of the scholarly and educational missions of the institution, for the benefit of the public. Furthermore, this use of orphan works may be considered a fair use especially with regard to the lack of potential for market damage; if there is no known rights holder, the practical risk of a claim is likely minimal.

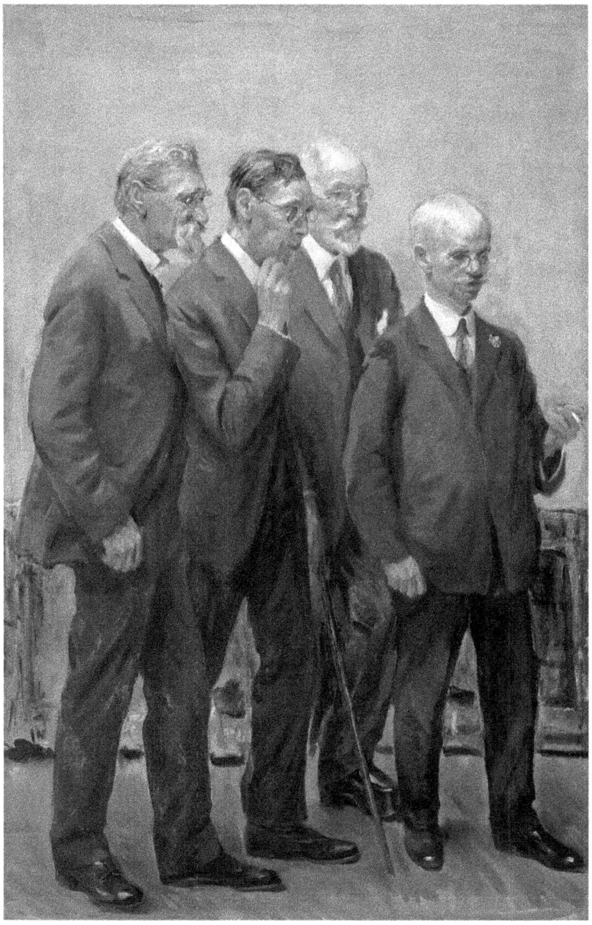

FIGURE 3.3
The Art Jury is a piece considered to be an orphan work in the Indianapolis Museum of Art at Newfields' collection.

While museums have not developed standardized best practices or defined what constitutes due diligence efforts, in 2009 the Society of American Archivists (SAA) issued their "Orphan Works: Statement of Best Practices" for libraries and archives that "describes what professional archivists consider to be best practices regarding reasonable efforts to identify and locate rights holders."[30] Many of the steps outlined in the SAA statement for identifying and locating rights holders of unpublished materials and orphan works are equally applicable to researching the rights holders of clearly authored and published works.

More recently, the "Statement of Best Practices in Fair Use of Collections Containing Orphan Works for Libraries, Archives, and Other Memory Institutions" was coordinated and issued in 2014 by the Program on Information Justice and Intellectual Property, American University's Washington College of Law and Center for Media & Social Impact, School of Communication, as well as by the Berkeley Digital Library Copyright Project at the University of California, Berkeley, School of Law. This statement outlines further steps for cultural institutions whose collections contain orphan works, whether the specific objects are clearly identified or are part of larger unknown collections.

IDENTIFYING AND FINDING RIGHTS HOLDERS

Today, those engaged in rights clearance projects are greatly aided by internet search tools and the ubiquity of websites, which often make finding contact information for living authors and artists as simple as a single online search. When this fails or when other complexities come into play—for example, common names, name changes, uncertainty about who controls an estate, works made by multiple creators, or in connection with a publisher—strong research skills and a knowledge of relevant resources are critical.

Workflow and Resources for a Rights Clearance Project

1. Copyright Notice
   First, look at the work and determine if there are any copyright notices (e.g., Copyright © 2018, Jane Smith). Absence of a copyright notice does not mean the work is unprotected by US copyright laws.
2. Background Research
   Use the information found by examining the work to do a basic search on the author or artist. Is the individual still alive? If not, when and where did the creator die? How and when did the institution acquire the work?

   If the individual is no longer alive, heirs or other representatives of the estate likely will be the rights holder(s). Begin by searching for an obituary or other information about any remaining family. Research may point to a spouse or children who have information about or control of an estate.

When reaching out to heirs and assigns of the creator to ascertain whether they hold rights, keep in mind that it is not uncommon for individuals to have very little knowledge about copyright or the transfer of rights. As part of the research and identification process, it may be helpful to develop a standard form letter, with input and review from legal counsel, that explains to the rights holder(s) the rights requested and provides a basic overview without providing legal advice about copyright.

3. Check Institutional Records
If the work was acquired directly from the creator, contact information may be readily available in a collections management system or paper records available for reference from a registrar, curator, archivist, or librarian. There may even be a transfer of copyright in the original acquisition paperwork (purchase agreement, deed of gift, commission contract, etc.). These resources may also provide contact information for a gallery representative, studio, family descendants, or the donor. Even if the contact information is out of date, it may still provide valuable clues that will aid in later searches.
4. Check Aggregate Databases
Copyright collectives and licensing agencies serve as representatives for authors, artists, and performers as well as their estates. While numerous licensing agencies exist across industries, some of the most active, and most commonly referenced by cultural institutions, include:[31]
    - literary works:
        - Access © (Copyright)[32]
        - Authors' Licensing and Collecting Society[33]
        - Copyright Clearance Center (CCC)[34]
        - The Authors Registry[35]
        - The Copyright Licensing Agency (CLA)[36]
    - musical works and sound recordings:
        - Amazon Digital Music Store[37]
        - American Society of Composers, Authors & Publishers (ASCAP)[38]
        - Broadcast Music, Inc. (BMI)[39]
        - Harry Fox Agency[40]
        - iTunes[41]
        - SESAC[42]
    - visual arts works:
        - Artists Rights Society (ARS)[43]
        - Bridgeman Copyright[44]
        - The Design and Artists Copyright Society (DACS)[45]

These organizations negotiate uses and permissions and collect licensing fees on behalf of the represented individuals and estates. Furthermore, they act as agents for affiliated societies and copyright collectives worldwide. The organizations' websites provide extensive lists of the authors, artists, performers, and estates they represent.[46] These organizations will also sometimes have contact information for nonmember estates.

In addition to licensing agencies, there are multiple organizations and resources for cultural institutions to reference:

- Writers Artists and Their Copyright Holders, the WATCH File, is a joint undertaking between the Harry Ransom Center of The University of Texas at Austin and the Library at the University of Reading in England. The WATCH File database contains contact information for, or pointers to, intermediaries for writers, artists, and others in creative fields, as well as representing galleries, estates, and other rights organizations. Established in 1994 with a focus on authors and their manuscripts, the WATCH File has expanded into one of the largest databases of contact information for copyright holders in the United States and United Kingdom and now includes information for more than twenty-six thousand individuals and estates.[47]
- The Library of Congress Prints & Photographs Division's Rights and Restrictions Information[48] page provides rights information for the selected creators of works in the Prints & Photographs Division collections. The entries include

a rights analysis of works along with contact information for rights holders when available.

- For works registered with the US Copyright Office, the online registration database may include contact information in the Copyright Claimant or Rights & Reproductions fields.
- For film and video, the National Archives and Records Administration's Source and Permission Contact List[49] can be a good starting point for rights research.

5. Mine the Web
If the aforementioned searches do not lead directly to contact information, deeper searches will potentially bear fruit. A simple internet search on the name of the creator name is often the place to start.[50] More and more creative individuals maintain their own websites and provide contact information or an online contact form. Refining the search slightly by including qualifiers such as artist, photographer, or printmaker will help filter out some of the search results. Estates often have established foundations, whose management responsibilities include associated IP rights.[51] Furthermore, it is not uncommon for a gallery or publisher to act as a representative by signing on behalf of the creator and/or forwarding an inquiry to the appropriate individual directly.[52] Additionally, cultural institutions sometimes own both physical materials and the IP rights. These relationships will not always be obvious or readily discoverable, but may be found as part of the institution's rights and reproductions website information. Further investigations via email or telephone inquiry may lead a researcher in the right direction.

When these searches are unsuccessful or inconclusive, more commercial websites and databases may lead to individuals who can assist in finding a rights holder.[53] These can range from sites maintained by professional organizations to focused research databases and museum websites. For example, with a general idea of where the creator lives (and if they do not have a common name), people-finder websites such as Spokeo[54] can be extraordinarily helpful and well worth the cost of an annual subscription. Likewise, subscription-based genealogical resources, such as Ancestry.com,[55] may prove to be useful tools.

6. Confer with Colleagues
As more and more cultural institutions undertake rights clearance projects, a growing community of rights and reproductions specialists has amassed significant knowledge of rights holders and their contact information. An inquiry to these colleagues after preliminary research is completed can often produce leads.

- The Museum Intellectual Property group serves as "a resource for the sharing of contact information for artists, foundations, estates or agencies for various Intellectual Property permissions." The more than two hundred members serve as an up-to-the minute resource for finding contacts, sharing information about orphan works, and learning about current IP issues.[56]
- Members of the Museum Computer Network (MCN)[57] have access to an Intellectual Property Special Interest Group.[58] Traffic on the MCN listserv tends more to IP news and notes and less toward contact information searches.
- The ImageMuse group facilitates discussions on "cultural heritage imaging, DAM and publishing."[59] With more than eight hundred members, ImageMuse is a crossroad of information for rights and reproductions specialists who can also gain insight from other cultural institution photographers, digital asset managers, and publishing specialists who contribute to a range of discussions on everything from color management, specific equipment recommendations, and workflows in DAMS and publishing to IIIF integrations, IP considerations, and more.[60]
- The Collections Stewardship Professional Network of the American Alliance of Museums (CSAAM)[61] provides members with access

to general IP and rights contact information through the Rights and Reproductions Professional Practices Committee and communications on the CSAAM listserv. While the discussions on the CSAAM listserv cover all manner of registration and collections management topics, IP concerns and questions about best practices and sharing of rights holder information are also prevalent.

- The Intellectual Property Rights Committee of the Visual Resources Association (VRA-IPR)[62] provides members with similar access to general IP and rights contact information through the VRA listserv. While like the CSAAM listserv in that it covers a variety of topics, rights and reproductions specialists may find the VRA-IPR of particular interest due to the overlap of rights topics with management of digital files and other topics of collection accessibility.

One of the most difficult issues facing rights researchers is reaching out to international creators and estates, particularly if there is a language barrier.[63] If an initial search is unsuccessful, colleagues at a national or regional museum may be willing to assist, either in providing contact resources or even in helping to approach the rights holder.

7. Evaluate Priorities

Overall, the first steps in this section are straightforward. If, after a careful and exhaustive search, these resources do not return a definitive rights holder and associated contact information, it is important to review the next steps and prioritize on a case-by-case basis. Is the cultural institution conducting a general copyright clearance project? If so, consider setting aside more difficult individuals and estates for more in-depth research at a later time. If, however, clearance is required for a specific, time-sensitive publication, exhibition, marketing, or website end use, creative research skills may be necessary. Information gleaned from colleagues and from museum, gallery, and newspaper sites; clues in publications and ephemera found in library or archive holdings; and suggestions from individuals who might have had contact with the creator will all need to be gathered and studied. In the case of some rights holders, the search will end with no clear answer. In those cases a discussion should be held with legal counsel and institutional leadership about the potential risk, including whether the institution should treat the work as an orphan or apply the fair use analysis to any use of the works.

NONEXCLUSIVE LICENSING AGREEMENTS

When the copyright holder for a work has been identified and contact information is available, it is advisable for a cultural institution to request a broad nonexclusive license to reproduce the work for a range of purposes. Unlike permissions for one-time specific uses, a broad nonexclusive license can allow an institution to reproduce a work on an ongoing basis for any of the uses covered by the license, ideally for the entire duration of the term of copyright. Having a long-term licensing agreement on file saves an institution time and resources in the long run by eliminating the need to make repeated requests for permission for any of the covered uses. It can provide clarity with respect to permitted uses by clearly spelling out what the institution can or cannot do with the copyrighted work, ranging from educational and promotional materials to retail merchandise.[64] In addition to the institution's own uses, the licensing agreement may also include limited authority to sublicense the image—that is, to approve uses by third parties who contact the institution for image and copyright permission.

It is important to note that a grant of a nonexclusive license is not a transfer or surrender of any rights by the copyright holder. A licensing agreement simply bestows limited rights to the institution, and the copyright holder retains the ability to grant the same permission(s) to others and to exercise all of the rights of a copyright owner under the law. Nevertheless, some rights holders may be hesitant to grant a broad nonexclusive license and will prefer to be contacted for permission for each requested use, which allows them to maintain greater control over uses as well as the ability to charge separate license fees, if they choose. Typically, rights holders represented by copyright collectives or licensing agencies are the least likely to agree to broad nonexclusive licensing agreements.

There are several ways an institution may obtain or request a broad nonexclusive license:

1. Negotiate with Purchase or Donation
   An institution's best opportunity for securing a broad nonexclusive license is to negotiate for one as part of the acquisition of the work. Try to make the license a condition of the purchase agreement if the work is being purchased directly from the creator or a representative of the creator or creator's estate (e.g., a gallery or an heir). For gifts from the creator or their representative, it may be simplest to enclose the licensing agreement with the deed of gift. Donors typically prefer to grant a license rather than assign copyright in the work as part of the gift. It is also best to request the license while the donor's attention is focused on the institution.
2. Request License upon Acquisition
   If the representative or donor is not the creator or has no connection to the copyright holder, it will not be possible to make the license a condition of purchase or part of the deed of gift. In such cases, assuming contact information for the rights holder is available, the institution should make it a practice to request a license as soon as the work is acquired.
3. Request License as Part of Ongoing Project or as Needed
   Since seeking nonexclusive licensing agreements as part of the acquisition process is a relatively new endeavor at many cultural institutions, large portions of the collection (works acquired before instituting a license request policy) will not be covered by an agreement completed for acquisitions of new works. Depending on available staffing and resources as well as the size of the collection, an institution could tackle the backlog by undertaking a comprehensive license request project. Institutions can prioritize certain works or creators, or they may choose to start at the beginning of the collection (however that is defined) and systematically work their way through by first identifying rights holders and then by sending out nonexclusive licensing agreements. Institutions with more limited resources can request agreements on an as-needed basis. An exhibition, publication, publicity, or marketing request could spur the institution to research and contact a rights holder. When contacting a rights holder about current work(s) in its collection, the institution may also attempt to secure an agreement covering all the works acquired in the future by the same creator in the collection in case circumstances change and the rights holder is no longer reachable in the future.

ELEMENTS OF A NONEXCLUSIVE LICENSING AGREEMENT

While the specific wording inevitably varies from institution to institution, there are some standard elements that should be included with any nonexclusive licensing agreement.[65]

Introductory Cover Letter

a. includes an explanation of how the agreement aids the institution in the fulfillment of its mission
b. may also outline how requests that are not covered by the agreement will be handled (e.g., forwarded to the rights holder or a new agreement is drafted)
c. reference to relevant gift or acquisition policies for the institution

Requested Permissions (License)

d. Identifies how the cultural institution may reproduce and use copyrighted materials, which may include some or all the following:
   i. institutional websites and other electronic media
   ii. editorial content, press, marketing, publication, and exhibition activities

CASE STUDY

BROOKLYN MUSEUM COPYRIGHT PROJECT

Deborah Wythe

In 2008, as the Brooklyn Museum geared up to release its collection on its website, the digital lab and technology staff working on the project realized that a huge problem was on the horizon: none of the more than 150,000 objects in the collection had rights information recorded in the collections database. Broken down into the steps below, the project has resulted in both a mission-driven online transparency that shares known rights information with online visitors and a repeatable, ongoing rights clearance process.[1] The digital lab, which also houses the museum's rights and reproductions and picture research staff, has assumed responsibility of this process.

Education and Research on Rights and Plan Development

- Drawing in very broad strokes, a series of rights categories and accompanying text for the website were written and reviewed by legal counsel. A nonexclusive license, including a standard cover letter, was drafted and approved by counsel.

Standardize Object Rights Types

- In the Rights and Reproductions module of the museum's collections management system, The Museum System (TMS), Object Rights Types were created and standardized. Employing targeted searches, objects were identified and grouped into packages for batch assignment of Object Rights Types. A quarterly rights audit finds new objects and changes in dates or creator names. The database is then updated as needed.

Website Collection Pages

- As part of the website collections page design, TMS Object Rights Types drive online output, including image size, rights statements, and pop-up text with explanatory notes. Updates to TMS are automatically reflected on the website nightly.

Copyright Interns

- An intern (usually one per year) researches artists and seeks nonexclusive licenses, tracks their work in an Access database, records contact information, updates TMS, and maintains the master file of licenses.[2] A standardized workflow and detailed manual facilitates a smooth transition from one intern to the next, with minimal training. Detailed tracking from research through license acquisition allows staff and interns to identify artists and estates that require follow-up.[3] Inquiries go out over the signature of a permanent staff member to ensure continuity and that a permanent staff member is responsible for more complex situations, such as orphaned works.

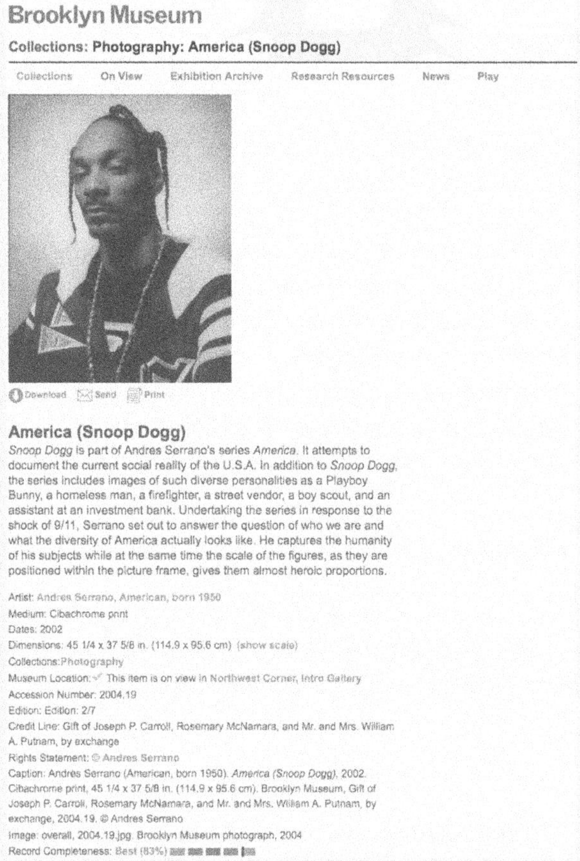
Brooklyn Museum

Collections: Photography: America (Snoop Dogg)

Collections On View Exhibition Archive Research Resources News Play

Download Send Print

America (Snoop Dogg)

Snoop Dogg is part of Andres Serrano's series *America*. It attempts to document the current social reality of the U.S.A. In addition to *Snoop Dogg*, the series includes images of such diverse personalities as a Playboy Bunny, a homeless man, a firefighter, a street vendor, a boy scout, and an assistant at an investment bank. Undertaking the series in response to the shock of 9/11, Serrano set out to answer the question of who we are and what the diversity of America actually looks like. He captures the humanity of his subjects while at the same time the scale of the figures, as they are positioned within the picture frame, gives them almost heroic proportions.

Artist: Andres Serrano, American, born 1950
Medium: Cibachrome print
Dates: 2002
Dimensions: 45 1/4 x 37 5/8 in. (114.9 x 95.6 cm) (show scale)
Collections:Photography
Museum Location: This item is on view in Northwest Corner, Intro Gallery
Accession Number: 2004.19
Edition: Edition: 2/7
Credit Line: Gift of Joseph P. Carroll, Rosemary McNamara, and Mr. and Mrs. William A. Putnam, by exchange
Rights Statement: © Andres Serrano
Caption: Andres Serrano (American, born 1950). *America (Snoop Dogg)*, 2002. Cibachrome print, 45 1/4 x 37 5/8 in. (114.9 x 95.6 cm). Brooklyn Museum, Gift of Joseph P. Carroll, Rosemary McNamara, and Mr. and Mrs. William A. Putnam, by exchange, 2004.19. © Andres Serrano
Image: overall, 2004.19.jpg. Brooklyn Museum photograph, 2004
Record Completeness: Best (83%)

FIGURE 3.4
Sample collection object page from the Brooklyn Museum website.

Curatorial Assistance

- As part of the acquisition process, curatorial staff is required to identify and reach out to rights holders, with the goal of acquiring a nonexclusive license. Digital lab staff train the curatorial assistants and serve as the repository for the signed licenses acquired.

Staff Education and Buy-In

- Rights data from TMS also appears in the museum's digital asset management system (DAMS), which is available on all staff workstations. Three fields appear: the Object Rights Type, Rights Statement, and Restrictions. Staff members using images for museum publications of all kinds are asked to check these fields and reach out to the Digital Lab with any questions.

NOTES

1. Deborah Wythe, "Working Guidelines for the Copyright Project," BKM Tech., last modified January 14, 2010, http://www.brooklynmuseum.org/community/blogosphere/2010/01/14/working-guidelines-for-the-copyright-project/.
2. Arlene Yu, "Little Images, Big Art," BKM Tech, last modified Jan. 14, 2010, http://www.brooklynmuseum.org/community/blogosphere/2010/01/14/little-images-big-art/.
3. While some licenses are returned immediately, others may require repeated contact over a period of months or years before the return and completion of an agreement.

iii. scholarly research and educational programming
iv. extension of agreed-upon permissions to third parties[66]
v. right to display and migrate to new or different formats for time-based media[67]
vi. extension of permissions to apply to works acquired in the future[68]

Terms and Conditions

e. terms to govern the uses outlined in the requested permissions, which may include some or all the following:
   i. modifications to reproductions of the work (e.g., resizing the image file or cropping to a detail of the work)
   ii. credit line and notices
   iii. ownership
   iv. representations and warranties regarding non-infringement
   v. indemnification
   vi. limitation of liability
   vii. rights reserved by rights holder
   viii. duration and termination[69]

Object List

f. inventory of the works that the agreement covers, ideally coupled with a general statement that the agreement covers future acquisitions to reduce paperwork and the potential of continually contacting the rights holder to review updated or new agreements

Contact Information

g. area for the rights holder or authorized representative to include current and complete contact information should the institution need to contact them in the future

Area to Sign and Agree to Agreement

h. depending on institutional practice and advice of legal counsel, may or may not include space for the institution to countersign the agreement;[70] space for the cultural institution (or licensee) to sign is needed if the institution is required to perform any actions under the agreement

COPYRIGHT ASSIGNMENT

For a variety of reasons, a copyright holder may choose to transfer or assign copyright to an institution instead of granting a nonexclusive license. This transfer of rights is referred to as a copyright assignment. For a copyright assignment to be valid, the assignment of copyright in the work must be explicitly stated in writing. A deed of gift that states the donor transfers "all rights" or "all rights, title, and interest" to the donee, without specifically mentioning copyright may not effectively assign copyright in the work to a cultural institution.[71] While many institutions interpret older deeds of gift that list "all rights" to include copyright, barring any additional documentation as to the donor's intent, would probably not hold up if challenged in court. For this reason a well-drafted deed of gift should include language stating that the donor transfers "all rights *including copyright*" to the donee.

There are many pros and cons to copyright assignment. If an institution has specific works in the collection for which external reproduction requests are frequently made, a copyright assignment may be desirable since it eliminates the need to repeatedly contact a rights holder to obtain permissions. Retail products are also easier to produce when the copyright is held by the institution. Licensing is easier and the need to pay royalties to a rights holder may not be required.[72] Managing the rights for an artist or for specific works can also be a revenue-generating endeavor for the institution depending on demand. The downside is that every time a request is made to reproduce the work, it becomes the responsibility of the institution to field requests and grant or deny permissions. If the institution owns the copyright for multiple creators, managing the rights can become an arduous task that is both time and cost intensive. This is especially true in cases where an institution owns the rights but not necessarily all the copies of the work such as for photographs or editioned graphics. Taking on the responsibility for

CASE STUDY

NEW MEXICO MUSEUM OF ART

Michelle Gallagher Roberts

At the New Mexico Museum of Art (NMMA), nonexclusive licensing agreements are sent along with Deeds of Gift or Purchase Agreements to artists donating their own work or when the museum purchases an artwork directly from the artist. For works acquired before NMMA instituted this practice, rights holders are contacted on an as-needed basis. When NMMA does contact an individual for a license, agreements are sent for everything by that artist currently in the collection. The agreements spell out what the museum can or cannot do with the image while the artist is alive.[1]

Additionally, the museum requests that all copyrights for unique works of art (paintings, drawings, etc.) transfer to the museum upon the artist's death. This is a win-win for NMMA and the artists. It allows artists to benefit from their creative endeavors during their lifetime but also ensures their legacy will be overseen by a cultural institution after their passing. Furthermore, this transfer can greatly reduce the chance of the artist's works becoming orphaned after their deaths. The museum owns all rights associated with the works and can use them to further its mission. Significantly, most artists who have been asked to transfer their copyright in this manner have agreed.[2] Most artists sign and return the form without comment, but for the few that ask, it opens a dialogue with museum staff about the artist's intentions and plans for their copyrights and gets them to think about the future.

NOTES

1. The standard license allows the museum to use the artwork for all standard museum purposes (including educational materials, publicity, books, exhibition catalogues, etc. to distribute two-dimensional reproductions to the public in connection with standard museum activities (including printed materials, films, televisions, DVDs, and internet websites) without limit and without monetary compensation. It also allows the museum to sublicense the specific rights granted to third parties.
2. Roughly 97 percent of artists asked to transfer copyrights upon their death have agreed.

a creator's entire oeuvre is a large endeavor and should not be accepted lightly.

Due to the staff resources required to manage copyright assignments, many institutions find it preferable to enter into nonexclusive licensing agreements with the copyright holders for works in their institution's collections. The advantage to this approach is that it grants the institution only the rights needed to fulfill its institutional mission without the additional workload of managing permissions for outside users' requests.

COMMISSIONING WORKS

In addition to acquiring existing works for collections by gift or purchase, cultural institutions often commission new works either for temporary exhibition or for acquisition by the permanent collection. Vital to the creation of these new works is the execution of a well-planned commission contract that not only governs the production of the work but makes provisions for future uses of the IP inherent in the work, both by the creator and the commissioning institution.[73]

CASE STUDY

HOW NOT TO DONATE COPYRIGHT TO AN INSTITUTION

A well-loved artist passed away several years ago. Her estate was large and consisted of both works created by her and the artwork she collected. The distribution of her estate was handled by a bank, with numerous lawyers assisting. A museum in her community was named as a beneficiary in the estate, and was very generously given first choice of items from the estate for its permanent collection. Along with thirteen other individuals, foundations, and museums, this museum was also listed as a beneficiary to any residuals of the estate.

All fourteen listed beneficiaries were notified that as a part of the estate disbursement they would all share equally in the copyright of the artist's works. Each beneficiary received 1/14th of the copyright in each work. The beneficiaries are spread over the country and have nothing in common besides being named in the artist's will. Barring a huge effort to organize, such factors could discourage the artwork from ever being reproduced. While current copyright law would allow for any one of the fourteen beneficiaries to grant nonexclusive licenses, licensees may not feel comfortable receiving a license from only one owner. The beneficiary granting permission would also need to distribute any fees they receive on a pro rata basis to the others, creating an additional burden.

This estate is essentially the opposite of orphaned works. It has too many rights holders. While this was a well-meaning gesture on the part of the artist, it would have been much more practical and effective to name a single person or institution as beneficiary of all her copyrights. While some artists are very informed and current on IP issues, others still lack basic knowledge of real-world applications.

The commission contract should clearly delineate which party retains copyright to the resultant work. Is it the creator or the institution? If the creator retains copyright to the work, it is recommended that the commission agreement include a nonexclusive license back to the commissioning institution that governs its future use(s) of the work. The contract should also specify the agreed-upon credit to the work in any resulting reproductions for publications, subsequent exhibitions of the work, or installations produced as a result of the broader commissioning agreement. Furthermore, this license should detail the ownership of rights in the resultant image or video materials, and, if applicable, a license back to the creator for their own use of the institution's images or videos. For example, in the case of an artist performing or creating a site-specific work that is visually documented by the commissioning institution, the contract should clearly state if the resulting images or videos are the final means through which the artwork is experienced and include all required credits to both the artwork and image or video production.

Additionally, when executing a commission contract, cultural institutions should include provisions governing the destruction, removal, or dismantling of the work in accordance with VARA.[74] Particularly for commissions that are site specific, intended to be temporary, or subject to unforeseen damage (by nature or man), outlining the rights of both the commissioned party and the commissioning institution are vital.[75] Language related to VARA may include the following: "Pursuant to the Visual Artists Right Act of 1990, Artist hereby specifically waives any and all rights that may be granted under such law with respect to destruction of the art work and acknowledges understanding that the installation to be produced under this Agreement may . . . be dismantled and destroyed after installation unless Artist has received or can remove the installation from the premises by [insert date]."[76]

UNDERLYING RIGHTS

Occasionally, a work in a cultural institution's collection (the "core work") may depict another work of art (the "work depicted") that is still under copyright. The term "underlying rights" is used to refer to the additional layer of copyright for the work depicted. A simple example is a photograph in the collection (core work) that shows a mural on a building (work depicted). The mural is another work of art with its own copyright, separate from the copyright in the photograph. Photographs of exhibition installations often have underlying rights since installation views typically depict multiple works.

When reproducing works with underlying rights, permission for the work depicted may also need to be obtained depending on how visible or recognizable it is in the core work, or on whether the appearance of the work depicted is really incidental in the core work. This is a judgment call to be made on a case-by-case basis depending on the specific image and the institution's risk tolerance level. Fair use for the reproduction of the work depicted may be a reasonable conclusion if the work depicted is incidental rather than the focus of the image.

ARCHITECTURAL PHOTOGRAPHY

Architectural photography is another area where underlying rights may exist. If a building depicted in a photograph[77] qualifies for copyright protection under the 1990 Architectural Works Copyright Protection Act, then permission to reproduce the photograph may also be required from the rights holder in the architectural work, *unless* the building "is located in or ordinarily visible from a public place."[78] However, copyright aside, some structures may be protected by trademark or private property rights. Using images of architectural works for commercial purposes may violate these other aspects of IP law and should be carefully reviewed in consultation with legal counsel.

PRIVACY RIGHTS AND THE COLLECTION

The right of privacy applies only to living people. As such, privacy rights will arise most frequently with collections of photographs, videos, or archives containing material from the last century.

As previously discussed in chapter 1, there are four basic forms of privacy rights:[79]

1. unreasonable intrusion on personal solitude
2. public disclosure of true but embarrassing private facts
3. false light
4. appropriation of name and likeness

Privacy rights should be evaluated whenever an institution wishes to reproduce collection materials (e.g., a photograph) that depict a known or potentially living person.[80] Unfortunately, there is no simple formula to determine whether privacy rights may be violated by a particular use since, like fair use, the specific use is an important factor, as is the nature of the work. Asking the following questions will help to identify the potential risks:

1. For what purposes does the institution wish to reproduce the work? Limited distribution uses (printed catalogues) carry less risk than those with wider distribution (website). Advertising and other promotional uses, including social media, might arguably be considered appropriation for commercial use. Reproduction of the work as a book cover and in retail merchandise should be carefully considered if permission from the person depicted cannot be obtained.

CASE STUDY

DETERMINING UNDERLYING RIGHTS

Cherie C. Chen and Anne M. Young

The following is an example of a photograph with underlying rights. This photograph by Manuel Álvarez Bravo is the core work, whereas Pablo Picasso's *The Acrobat*, shown in the photograph, is the work depicted. How clearly is the work depicted shown in this photograph? In this case, the work depicted is easily recognizable despite the lower left portion being obstructed from view by the seated Frida Kahlo and is not incidental to the image.

Typically, unless there is a clear fair use argument for the underlying work, in cases where the underlying work is visible and reasonably identifiable in the image or via caption information, it is advisable to clear the use.

Additionally, this core work by Bravo raises potential right of publicity issues that a rights and reproductions specialist should be cognizant of when assessing works. Depending on the image use and the applicable publicity rights law in the state, Kahlo's publicity rights may need to be cleared in addition to the more obvious copyright considerations of Bravo and Picasso.

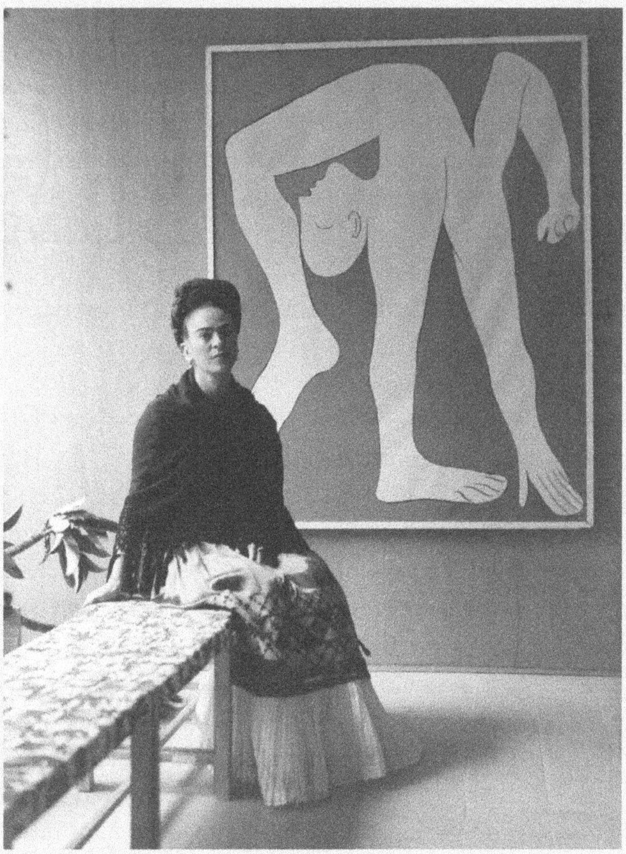

FIGURE 3.5
Core work by Manuel Álvarez Bravo. Work depicted by Pablo Picasso. Individual depicted is Frida Kahlo.

2. What is the context in which the person(s) is depicted? If the person was photographed in a public place, then at least there is no invasion of privacy (intrusion). Relatedly, was the person looking at the camera and potentially aware of being photographed? Is the person depicted in a situation in which disclosure would be found to be offensive, or could cause embarrassment, humiliation, and damage to reputation?[81]
3. Is the person clearly identifiable? Look beyond whether the face is shown or obscured, and consider if the person can be identified given the context and other information about the work, including the title and date. A privacy claim can be made even if just one person can identify the depicted person.[82] This is true in defamation law, where publication to one person is sufficient to make a claim.[83]
4. Has the work been published previously? Unpublished works require greater scrutiny since the institution would be the first to expose and distribute the work to the public.
5. Did the artist obtain a model release from the person depicted? Some artists make it part of their practice to do so, and the existing release might cover the institution's use of the image. If not, can the institution obtain a release directly?[84] Note that releases for minors should be signed by a parent or legal guardian (i.e., not Uncle Bob or a teacher), as some young minors do not have the capacity to consent on their own behalf. It is important to note that under many state laws, minors can "disaffirm" an agreement they enter into at any time up to and for a reasonable time after attaining the age of majority (usually eighteen years). This is another reason why parents should sign as well as the minor, as this will make the agreement as enforceable as possible under various state laws.
6. Finally, is there another image with fewer or no privacy issues that can serve the same purpose?

While privacy concerns typically focus on visual material that depict people, claims may also arise from reproducing nonpictorial material such as personal letters or oral histories[85]—often unpublished—held by libraries and archives.[86] Institutions should consider whether the publication or display of the materials may disclose embarrassing private facts about the correspondents or potentially give rise to defamation claims.[87]

PUBLICITY RIGHTS AND THE COLLECTION

The right of privacy typically ends at death; some institutions will agree to keep materials closed for a period after a donor's death as a condition of a gift.[88] In contrast, publicity rights may continue well after death and are governed by laws that vary from state to state.[89] Similar to the privacy tort of appropriation,[90] the right of publicity protects against the unauthorized use of an individual's name, voice, or likeness for commercial purposes. An institution is most likely to encounter publicity rights issues in its retail operation if it produces merchandise such as postcards or posters with collection images depicting living people (or deceased individuals in some states). However, the use of such images for other routine activities could also implicate publicity rights, regardless of the cultural institution's nonprofit status. These uses may include:

- paid advertising and promotional material
- fundraising and sponsorship material
- social media posts
- invitations
- publication cover art

Absent explicit permission or a release agreement from the person(s) depicted in the image, or from the estate or other owner of a deceased person's publicity rights, the institution should consider how "reasonable persons" would view the use—commercial or as press/commentary? If the image is of a famous person, is the institution implying endorsement by the celebrity or gaining by association in some way? Is the institution using the celebrity's image to fund-raise? Is the celebrity or their estate known to be litigious? Celebrities make their living in part from product endorse-

THE IMPORTANCE OF MODEL RELEASES

A museum's publication marketing coordinator received an angry email from the mother of a high school senior whose photograph by a well-known artist was published by the museum in a monograph. The photograph was released for book publicity purposes and was subsequently reproduced in a national magazine. The mother demanded proof that the artist and the museum had permission to publish her child's photograph. The artist routinely obtained model releases and was able to forward a copy of the release to the museum. The signed release, which specified publication and promotional rights, stated that the student was eighteen (not a minor). In this case, the student-signed release was valid, and the matter was dropped.

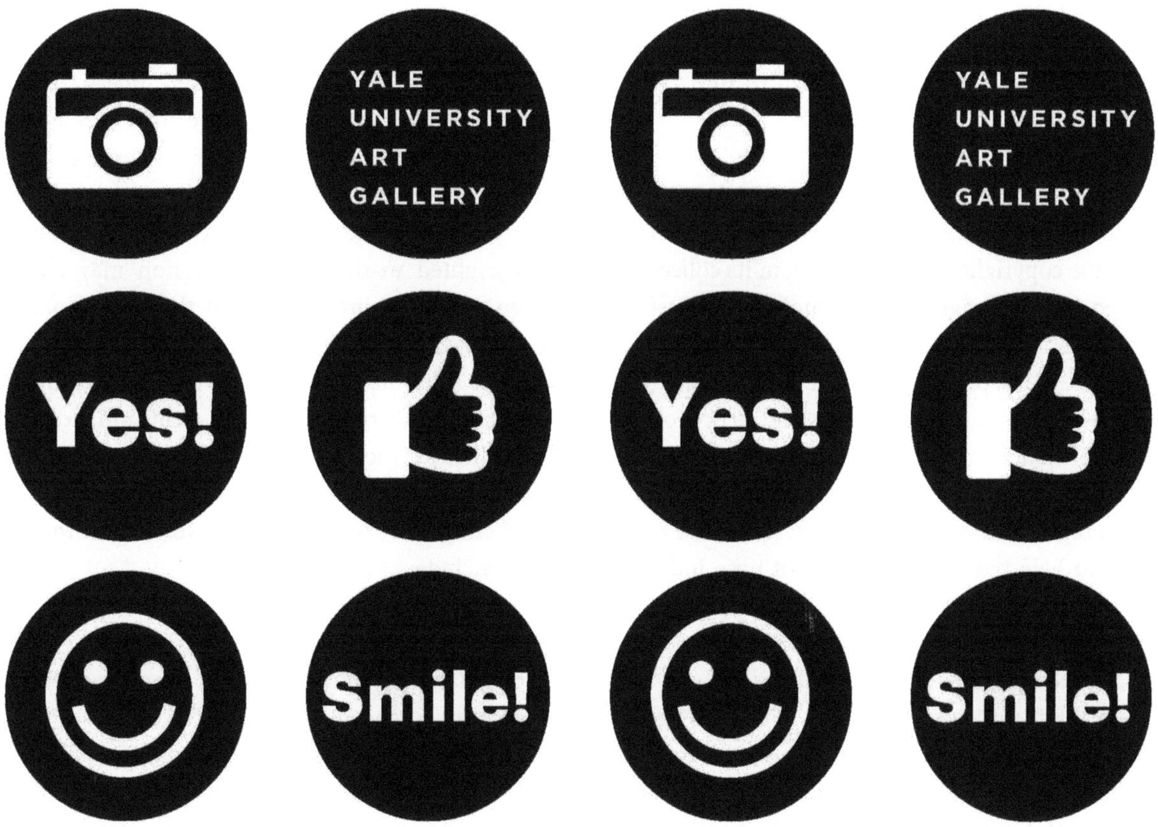

FIGURE 3.6
Yale University Art Gallery uses stickers to quickly identify children at events whose parent or legal guardian has completed the permission forms agreeing to photographs being taken. In this way, the photographer has a better sense of who can or cannot be photographed and the sticker is not too obtrusive if it appears in photographs.

ments, and an institution may inadvertently create conflicts by implying a celebrity endorses a competing brand—for example, by putting the celebrity's image on a promotional banner with an exhibition sponsor's logo, when in fact the celebrity represents the sponsor's competitor.

One way to avoid running afoul of publicity rights protections is to ask for one-time permission or to obtain a release agreement for commercial uses of collection images depicting living people. Perhaps the artist already obtained a release that will cover the institution's use or has contact information for the person depicted. Celebrities can be reached through their agents, and may in fact be supportive of the institution's mission and show that support by agreeing to the use of their likeness. Remember that releases for minors must be signed by a parent or legal guardian. However, teenagers are also encouraged to sign the release, in addition to the parent or legal guardian, since they are considered old enough to understand the consent form.

RECORDING AND SHARING RIGHTS INFORMATION

Once a cultural institution has done the research to determine the copyright status of a work in its collection, identified the copyright holder, and/or successfully obtained a grant of nonexclusive license to reproduce copies of the work, the essential next step is to maintain a comprehensive and easily accessible record of the rights information that has been collected about that object. Barring any confidentiality restrictions, rights information should be shared widely within an organization to help reduce the amount of time independently spent by staff researching rights as well as to aid staff in quickly identifying potential image-use restrictions. Maintaining accurate and updated records may also prevent the accidental misuse of a copyrighted work, save time and money spent on unnecessary requests for permission, and minimizes potential statutory damages if a fair use reproduction undertaken in good faith turns out to be an infringing use.[91]

Rights information can exist in both digital and printed forms. In a museum, the most logical places to record rights information and store original rights documents include: the collection management system (CMS), the digital asset management system (DAMS), and the central object and/or copyright files for the collection. Whereas a CMS and DAMS are best for recording a summary of the *current* rights status for an object in the collection, an organization's central files should serve as a repository for the complete *historical* copyright record for an object or artist. Access to each of these systems and files will likely vary for staff depending on their responsibilities, thus duplication of elements of this information between these records may be necessary and inevitable. In such cases, it is critical to establish procedures to ensure that any updates to rights data are made concurrently—whether by manual or automated means—in all places where the information exists.

Central Object and/or Copyright Files

Copyright status changes over time—artists may grant a license or die; rights are transferred; new research identifies a rights holder for orphan works—and such changes should be documented in the permanent records. Organizations with only a few copyrighted works in the collection may choose to keep copyright information in the central object file (often kept by the registrar or collections manager). On the other hand, collections with large numbers of copyrighted works may elect to create individual copyright files for each artist (often kept by the registration or rights and reproductions departments).

Examples of documentation to keep in the central files include:

- printouts or copies of copyright research
- original grant of nonexclusive license agreements
- correspondence with rights holder
- internal correspondence about usage
- contemporaneous record of fair use analysis
- one-time permissions granted by the copyright holder (ideally aggregated from across the organization)
- if applicable, information about or personal releases from people depicted in the work

- if applicable, information about other copyrighted works that may be depicted in a core work[92]

Collection Management System (CMS)

Since rights information varies from object to object, a CMS with object-level records is ideally suited for recording the rights information unique to an object. Only designated and trained staff should have the authority to update CMS rights data, though all CMS users should have read access.

The exact fields used to record rights information will differ from one CMS system to another, but the recommended data to be captured includes:[93]

- copyright status of the work (e.g., public domain, copyrighted orphan work)[94]
- copyright holder (name of person or organization) and contact information
- copyright notice (exact wording to accompany reproductions of the work)
- publication status (i.e., has it been published, and if so, where, and when)
- summary and highlights of current copyright research or restrictions (e.g., is a license on file, are there additional considerations such as privacy or publicity rights, other potential claimants, and where to go for more details and information)
- date of last copyright research and/or update
- staff member who completed the last copyright research and/or update (particularly important if multiple people are authorized to make updates)

For CMS systems with media components, scans of licenses and other permissions documents may also be uploaded and linked to the corresponding object records for easy retrieval in a digital format.

Digital Asset Management System (DAMS)

A DAMS is a tool for storing, managing, and retrieving digital assets, such as images of collection objects.

EMBEDDING METADATA

Some DAMS are capable of embedding metadata into a digital file when retrieved or exported from the system.[1] Metadata fields can include object tombstone, the related copyright information for the work, and the name and contact information for the creator of the digital file. Embedded metadata is easily read by basic imaging software and enables any user of the file to identify who created the image and to assess whether permission might be necessary to use it. Given the ease of content distribution in the digital age, embedded metadata—while not indelible—can help prevent misuse of copyrighted material since rights information "travels" with the digital file.[2]

NOTES

1. A fundamental concern is maintaining most current information. If embedding is done during (or prior to) ingest, the information in the file will become outdated if the data changes.
2. For detailed information about metadata methods, tools, and standards, see generally Murtha Baca, ed., *Introduction to Metadata*, 2d ed. (Los Angeles, CA: Getty Publications, 2008), http://www.getty.edu/publications/virtuallibrary/0892368969.html.

Ideally, images of collection objects stored in a DAMS are accompanied by basic object tombstone information (core data fields, such as creator, place of origin, title, date, materials or medium, credit, etc.) and rights information at a minimum. If possible, an organization's CMS and DAMS should be integrated so that the DAMS data is linked to the CMS and automatically updated when the object data in the CMS changes. Integration eliminates the need to update the same rights data in multiple places as well as the potential errors a manual update process may introduce. If integrated systems are not possible,[95] the recommended rights data to be directly entered into the DAMS for images of the collection are the same as those listed above for the CMS. Only designated and trained staff should have the authority to update DAMS rights data, though all DAMS users should have read access.

Other Means of Recording and Sharing Rights Information

Not all institutions utilize a CMS or DAMS. In these situations, a simple searchable database or spreadsheet dedicated to tracking rights holders may be the best electronic means for recording and sharing rights information. The recommended rights data to be recorded are the same as those listed above for the CMS. As with the CMS or DAMS, only trained staff should have the authority to update the database or spreadsheet. The database or spreadsheet should be a complement to, and not a substitute for, storing historical copyright information and original documents in the central object and/or copyright files for the collection.

ADDITIONAL CONSIDERATIONS

While there are numerous forms of IP to consider when reproducing images of collection objects, rights and reproductions specialists need to be mindful of additional issues surrounding certain types and uses of works. It is not uncommon to find collection objects that raise the following considerations that cultural institutions must also address:

- rights of indigenous peoples
- contractual restrictions
- sensitive content and restricted materials, including obscenity, violence, and graphic depictions
- documentation of collection materials by freelance photographers or for conservation purposes

Rights of Indigenous Peoples

Rights and reproductions specialists in institutions holding materials—objects and archival collections—created by members of indigenous peoples' groups around the world face complex and developing issues. According to a post in Intellectual Property Watch in August 2013, "World Intellectual Property Organization [WIPO] member states in July [2013] concluded the biennium work of the committee tasked with finding agreement on international legal tools to prevent misappropriation and misuse of genetic resources, traditional knowledge and folklore. Indigenous peoples and local communities are holders of a substantial part of this knowledge, and are demanding that it be protected against misappropriation but also against its use without their consent."[96]

The two areas most likely to affect cultural institutions are traditional knowledge[97] and traditional cultural expression or "expressions of folklore."[98] Works of art, design elements on utilitarian objects, audio, and video of activities and ceremonies have minimal protection under US IP laws, which are based on individual property and authorship, fixation in a tangible medium, and commercial value. However, many indigenous peoples, such as the American Indian sovereign nations, "value communal property, have strong spiritual connections to intellectual property, and have customs and laws that limit access to certain types of information."[99] Many studies have indicated that the current US IP laws "[do] not adequately protect Native American interests in traditional intellectual property."[100]

Thus, cultural institutions must work to strike a balance between mission-based activities such as providing access to collection objects and responsiveness to the sensitivities to the potential IP holders of tradition-based works. In the United States, the 1990 passage of the Native American Graves Protection and

Repatriation Act (NAGPRA) provides legal remedies for control over actual property, including objects created by these peoples and tribes that may be held in the collections of cultural institutions. NAGPRA more specifically addresses the rights of lineal descendants, Indian tribes, and Native Hawaiian organizations to American Indian cultural items, including human remains, funerary objects, sacred objects, and objects of cultural patrimony. Implementation of NAGPRA was assigned as part of the responsibilities of the secretary of the interior.[101] The ongoing work of WIPO may provide further guidance to the management of the IP related to these objects in the future.

Although the United States currently lacks specific legislation in this area, there are certain steps that rights and reproductions specialists with responsibility for the rights considerations within American Indian collections (and by extension, collections of works of indigenous peoples worldwide) may follow:[102]

- Learn about the issues facing indigenous peoples in their works and the current, applicable international IP law.
- Increase institutional involvement in the WIPO process (particularly museums, following the example of libraries and archives).
- Foster a dialogue with the individual source communities affected, both at individual institutions and through professional organizations.
- Work to develop best practices within institutional practices.
- Expand the activities of rights management organizations to cover TCEs and represent the works of indigenous artists.
- Interact with traditional communities as they assert ownership through litigation or mediation.
- Incorporate practices into institutional CMS and DAMS as well as IP policies and practices that reflect those protections in online databases.[103]

Contractual Restrictions

Contractual restrictions may prevent the dissemination of images or information related to collection works, including sensitive information surrounding provenance or conservation research. Purchase, donation, or licensing agreements sometimes include provisions that restrict the publication or other use of collection material for a limited period of time. Such embargoes can exist for a variety of reasons. For example, an artist might wish to reserve first publication rights and prohibit the institution from publishing the works until the artist has had a chance to do so. Archives may contain sensitive information that sellers or donors wish to keep confidential during their lifetime. While uncommon because institutions generally hesitate to acquire works that bear restrictions, these embargoes must be carefully tracked and honored to avoid violations of contractual terms.

Sensitive Content and Restricted Materials

Collections are varied in the breadth and content of the subjects that they encompass, and it is not uncommon to find materials that raise a red flag for their content and lead an institution to exercise caution in their dissemination. This can range from violent or sexually explicit works to works with deeply personal or emotional ties for both the individual(s) from whom the work was acquired as well as the public. While these considerations are not intrinsically linked to underlying IP rights in the works themselves, they must be considered when the works are displayed or reproduced by cultural institutions. Public domain works may still present challenging subject matter that requires careful communication in its presentation to the public.

Obscenity

The decision to share sexually explicit collection materials should be made after careful deliberation and ideally in consultation with legal counsel. Obscenity, including child pornography, is not protected by the First Amendment, and its distribution is punishable under both state and federal law. However, there is no single definition of what constitutes obscenity. The US Supreme Court's 1973 decision in *Miller v. California* established a three-pronged test for obscenity based on whether the:

CASE STUDY

KINSEY INSTITUTE, INDIANA UNIVERSITY

Anne M. Young

An institution's presentation of works containing obscene and/or sexually explicit content—in a physical exhibition space, in a printed publication, or as part of an institution's website—must be approached with care and concern for the end viewer. Clear messaging of the content contained in these works is key to informing viewers prior to their experiencing the works firsthand. For an exhibition, this may include physically separating materials into a different gallery room with clear signage informing the visitor of the sexually explicit or sensitive nature of the content presented in that space. The Kinsey Institute's online art galleries are no stranger to these practices as the trusted source for critical issues in sexuality, gender, and reproduction since 1947.[1] It clearly informs potential visitors before proceeding to the gallery pages themselves, "Age verification: The Kinsey Institute galleries contains imagery that may be inappropriate for audiences under 18 years old. Please verify that you are of legal age before continuing."[2] This messaging is reiterated at its physical gallery space as well as on the institution's website to inform people who are planning a visit.

Similarly, if the decision is made to include images of works containing sexually explicit content online, a disclaimer should ideally be placed before online galleries of collection images are viewed. Further protection of unsuspecting viewers may be the careful selection of detail images that do not show sexually explicit content unless the viewer physically clicks on the image and enlarges to the full work. The Kinsey Institute actively places images of its collection works online for visitors to view. Through all of these uses, straightforward messaging precedes the images from its art, archive, and library collections, for example, "Galleries may contain explicit images." This sentence appears prior to clicking on the next page of the website or the images themselves (often utilizing cropped images that enlarge to the full works revealing the explicit material).[3]

NOTES

1. "Learn our history," Kinsey Institute, Indiana University, accessed March 13, 2018, https://kinseyinstitute.org/about/index.php.
2. "Online art galleries," Kinsey Institute, Indiana University, accessed March 13, 2018, https://kinseyinstitute.org/collections/art-artifacts-photographs/interrupt.php.
3. For example, see "The Shape of Us," Kinsey Institute, Indiana University, accessed March 13, 2018, https://kinseyinstitute.org/collections/art-artifacts-photographs/shape-of-us.php.

1. "average person, applying contemporary community standards would find that the work, taken as a whole, appeals to the prurient interest"
2. "work depicts or describes, in a patently offensive way, sexual conduct specifically defined by applicable state law"
3. "work, taken as a whole, lacks serious literary, artistic, political, or scientific value."[104]

This "contemporary community standards" approach essentially means that what is considered obscene can vary from state to state and evolve over the years. In deciding to disseminate sexually explicit material as part of its mission-related work, an institution's leadership should understand the risks it is taking given the wide diversity of community opinions about such material. It should also consider beforehand—and be prepared to defend—whether the works have serious artistic, historic, or cultural value.

Violence and Graphic Materials

Depictions of violence are inherently sensitive subjects. When there are depictions of violence that are part of the collective historical memory of a people or country, they can have an even larger impact in their presentation to and use by the public. While it is not uncommon to find museums dedicated in whole to subjects that are sensitive overall,[105] it is almost more common to find these types of materials interspersed with broader library and archive collections. In such instances, the materials may remain largely unknown and anonymous in their depictions.

CASE STUDY

THE ZAPRUDER FILM

Megan P. Bryant

Perhaps the most well-known home movie ever filmed, the Zapruder film, is a twenty-six-second, silent, 8mm color home movie of the November 1963 assassination of President John F. Kennedy, taken by Dallas businessman and assassination eyewitness Abraham Zapruder. The Zapruder film is the only known complete visual record of the assassination and a vitally important piece of history. Since 1999, The Sixth Floor Museum at Dealey Plaza (TSFM) has owned the copyright to the film by direct assignment from Zapruder's heirs.[1] More than fifty years later, the Kennedy assassination continues to evoke strong emotions, and TSFM is ethically committed to avoiding exploitation of the trauma and violence of the event documented in the Zapruder film. Management of the film's copyright is intrinsically tied to the ethical concerns and respect for Zapruder's wishes for its use and dissemination. He was haunted by the assassination that he inadvertently captured, and just days after the event expressed a desire that the film be presented to the public in a manner that was "consonant with good taste and dignity."[2] Since Zapruder's death in 1970, his heirs have striven to balance the interests of "respect for the sensitive nature of the film's images and an appropriate response to the public's demand for access to the film."[3]

TSFM is committed to ensuring that all TSFM-sanctioned uses of the film are appropriate and in keeping with the spirit of the family's wishes. However, these intangible concerns can be difficult to codify in policy and procedure versus the more straightforward management of the copyright assignment. Practices and thinking have evolved as TSFM has grown more knowledgeable and comfortable in its

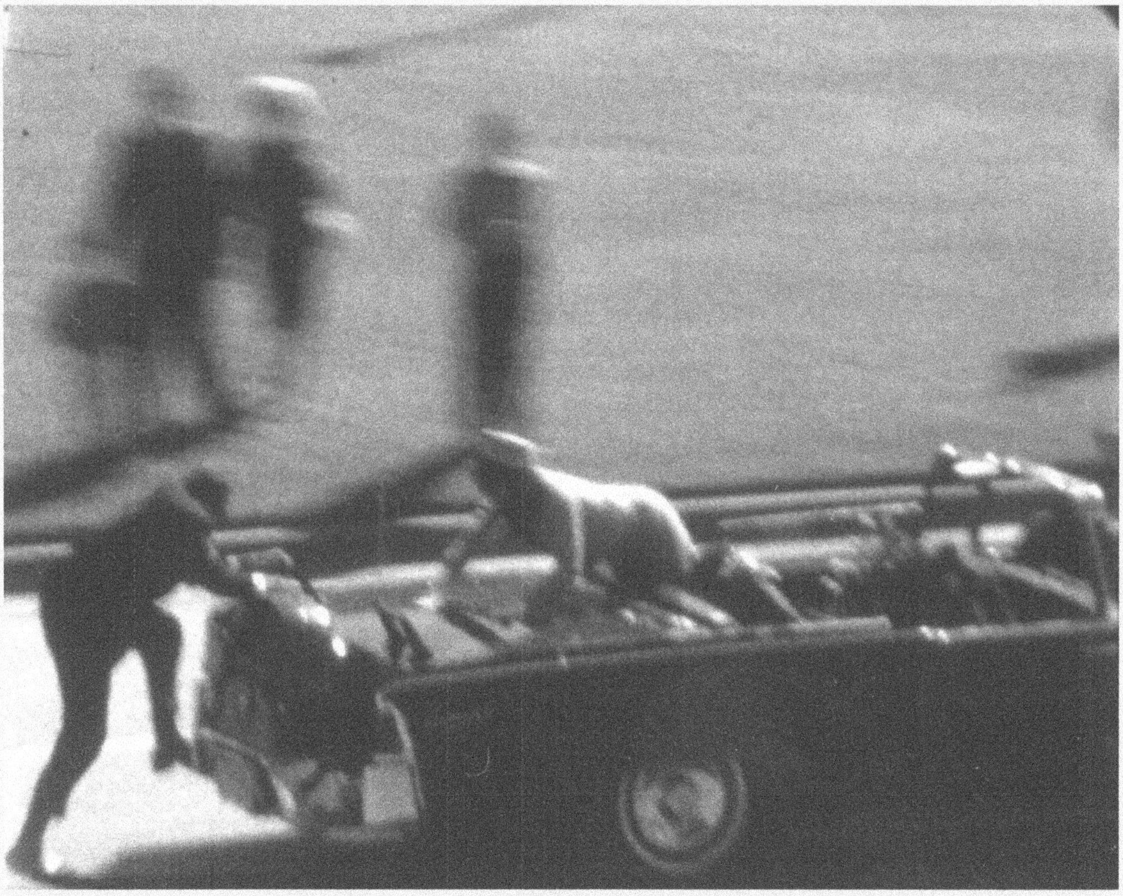

FIGURE 3.7
Footage capturing the November 1963 assassination of President John F. Kennedy.

role as custodian, as rapid technological advancements have changed the way images are accessed, and as the assassination itself moves further into history.

The Zapruder film does not appear in its entirety in TSFM's permanent exhibition.[4] The film was shown in whole for the first time at TSFM in a 2007 temporary exhibit about home movies of the Kennedys' November 1963 visit to Texas.[5] After much discussion, the curatorial staff chose to make it a conscious visitor choice to view the film. The Zapruder content was physically sectioned off from the rest of the exhibit. Once in the space, visitors had to opt to view the film by pressing a play button—whereas the other home movies in the exhibit played automatically. A brief advisory statement was also placed near the entry to the Zapruder section: "The Sixth Floor Museum advises visitors that the footage on view in this area depicts the graphic assassination of President John F. Kennedy. This footage, taken by Abraham Zapruder, includes the fatal shot to the President's head, and is shown in its entirety. Caution is strongly advised for young children or sensitive visitors. Thank you."[6]

Shortly after the opening of this exhibit, TSFM launched its first online collections database in 2008. While there was no question that the Zapruder film would be included, concerns about the content again prompted the inclusion of an advisory statement embedded at the beginning of the video. When TSFM redesigned its online collections a few years later, the ubiquity of multiple versions of the Zapruder film on YouTube[7]—as well as the presence of many other depictions of violence on the internet—had essentially desensitized most online audiences to the violence in the film. The new online collection pages launched in 2011; the film now appears on TSFM's website without any precautionary warning.[8]

While TSFM's philosophy on the presentation of the Zapruder film online and in exhibitions has evolved, one thing has remained constant: a strict, no-exceptions prohibition on promotional, advertising, or retail merchandising use of the film. This policy applies not only to uses the museum might consider making, but extends to proposed uses by outside parties. TSFM does not use the film or images from the film to promote the museum in any way, nor does it use the film in products developed for retail.[9]

There is understandably a great deal of outside interest in and use of the Zapruder film by documentary and film producers, researchers, authors, and publishers, and its sensitive content must be considered in TSFM's licensing practices for external uses. The film is frequently licensed for documentaries and publications, and TSFM makes a point to not get involved in an editorial review of content in these cases. However, TSFM does limit certain uses—typically proposed entertainment or commercial purposes for which there is no apparent historical context.[10] TSFM also considers the context when approached with requests to use the film in works of fiction, which usually involves a review of plot treatments or overviews, scripts, and sometimes rough cuts for film projects. While TSFM does not seek to make judgments or editorial reviews on content, it does try to ensure that proposed uses of the film align with the museum's concerns regarding respectful treatment of the film and that it is not solely being used for sensationalistic purposes.[11]

NOTES

1. Prior to this, the film had a somewhat complicated ownership history. In the days immediately following the assassination, Zapruder sold first all print, then all motion picture rights to the film to Time Inc./*LIFE* magazine. In 1975, shortly after an unauthorized airing of a bootleg copy of the film on Geraldo Rivera's *Good Night America* talk show, Time Inc. transferred the copyright back to the Zapruder family. The family maintained ownership of both the camera-original film and its copyright until 1998, when the camera-original film was declared an "assassination record" under the JFK Assassination Records Collection Act of 1992, and was officially transferred to the JFK Assassination Records Collection at the National Archives. The family retained ownership of the copyright, which they assigned to TSFM in 1999. Thus, while TSFM owns the copyright to the film, the physical film itself is owned by the US government.

2. Letter of Agreement, November 25, 1963, from Abraham Zapruder to C. D. Jackson, Publisher, *LIFE* magazine.
3. Statement issued by Zapruder family, January 26, 2000.
4. For various reasons (including concerns about the graphic content and the licensing costs), the original exhibit developers in 1988–1989 decided to only include selected still frames from the film in appropriate locations throughout the exhibit. Developed more than ten years prior to the copyright assignment to the museum, these elements have not changed.
5. "Filming Kennedy: Home Movies from Dallas," The Sixth Floor Museum, 411 Elm Street, Dallas, TX, 75202, November 2007—October 2008.
6. Including the Zapruder film in this exhibit involved an additional layer of sensitivity. There is a rarely seen early segment of the home movie, filmed days prior to the assassination, with images of Zapruder's young grandsons playing in the backyard. Because the exhibit focused on how regular citizens had captured historic events on their family home movies of ordinary events, TSFM curators wanted to include this section of the film in the exhibit—but not before obtaining the consent of the Zapruder family, and specifically the two grandsons seen in the clip.
7. It was around this same time that the video-sharing website (first launched in 2005) really started to expand, and the Zapruder film began appearing in greater and greater numbers on the site. For a point of reference, a September 25, 2014, YouTube search resulted in approximately forty-two thousand results for "Zapruder film" and the same search done March 13, 2018, resulted in more than fifty-six thousand results.
8. "Abraham Zapruder Film," The Sixth Floor Museum at Dealey Plaza: Collections, accessed March 13, 2018, http://eMuseum.jfk.org/view/objects/asitem/items@:32274.
9. Some examples of external requests for promotional use of the Zapruder film that TSFM has declined include: trailer for a major motion picture, television ad campaign for automaker, signage for bus tours, and a poster promoting book sales.
10. For example, in 2010, the museum was approached by a popular first-person shooter video game franchise with a request to include the Zapruder film in a new version of the game. While the company pushed the request hard, it was quickly determined that such a use of the film would be in direct contradiction to the spirit of dignity and respect that TSFM and the Zapruders practiced in regard to presentation of the film, and the request was declined. Other examples of requests declined due to lack of historical context include: appearance in opening credits for a television series and several for use in different music videos.
11. All revenue earned from licensing of the Zapruder film is restricted for use for collections acquisitions or care and support of collections. This reinvestment of monies earned from the film back into the museum's collections is intended as a further step in protecting the integrity of the film, while also allowing for the needs and rights of the public in their demand for access to and use of the Zapruder film.

Freelance Photography of the Collection

Even in institutions with professional photography staff, occasions may arise when a contract photographer must be hired to undertake a project. In institutions without dedicated imaging staff, this process will be the rule rather than the exception. Protecting the institution's investment in these images and streamlining future use of them requires attention to several details in the contract, beyond the normal clauses about scope, technical specifications, and deadlines.

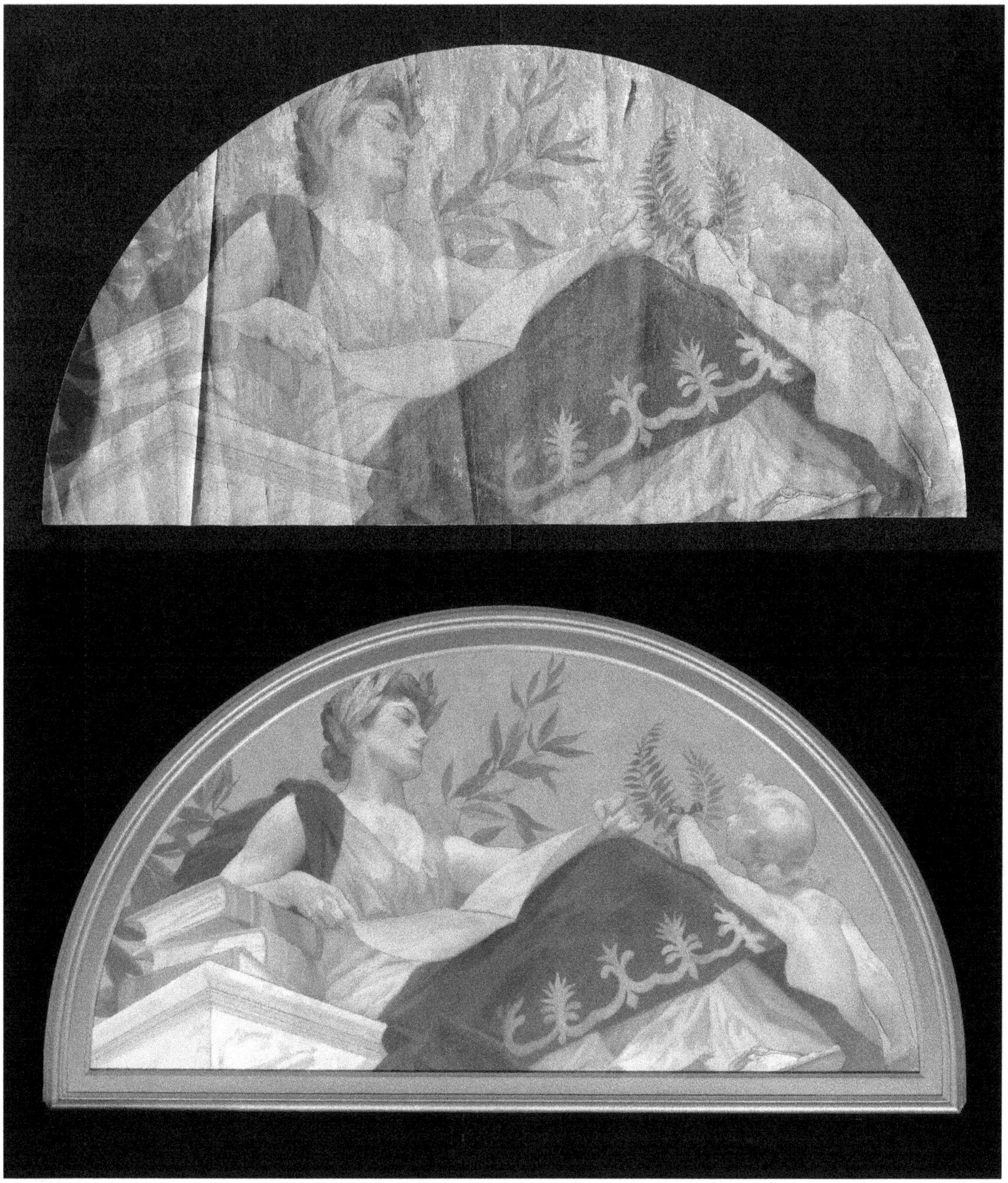

FIGURE 3.8
Top image taken before treatment on October 1, 2008, and bottom image taken after treatment of the work.

Except in certain, very specific cases, work by nonemployees does not qualify as "work for hire" under copyright law.[106] Thus, copyright in images created by a contract photographer would be held by the contractor unless explicitly transferred in writing to the hiring organization.

When hiring a contract or freelance photographer, consider including wording in the contract that would transfer all rights to the institution.[107] If the photographer is not willing to agree to a full transfer, clarify the rights being assigned to the institution in a formal nonexclusive license, ensuring that the institution will have free use of the images for every future purpose that might be envisioned. Photographers often wish to include images from a shoot in their own online portfolio as a promotional tool. This use and any other requests should also be expressly addressed in the contract or license.[108]

If the works being photographed are works on long-term loan or on loan to the permanent collection,[109] the situation may be slightly less clear in terms of who should best hold copyright to the images. Does the cultural institution wish to manage rights to those images in perpetuity, even after the works have been returned to the lender? If not, then include a nonexclusive license as part of the contract, spelling out the specific uses allowed.

Conservation and Documentation Considerations

Conservators routinely document the treatment process of collection objects. These images often are taken to highlight characteristics of the object such as cracking or lifting of a paint surface and may include areas filled but not yet retouched. While there is no question that members of the community find conservation images very interesting and engaging, particularly if an explanation is included, to an average viewer these images can lead to a misunderstanding of the object or even to the belief the cultural institution is not properly caring for the collection. The release of conservation images and treatment reports out of context should therefore be carefully considered. This might be addressed by including descriptive text in the image metadata (for example, "before treatment" or "after treatment") or caption ("conservation treatment view showing before-treatment condition of object").

For example, figure 3.8 shows a Yale University Art Gallery painting that was photographed during and after conservation treatment. While images such as these aid the conservator in understanding the surface and condition of the work, without proper contextualization, the public may view such an image and make presumptions about the care or condition of works at a particular cultural institution.

Balancing the standard documentary practices of conservators and the privacy of creators is also a concern. A creator, donor, or lender might not want his or her work to be placed on view or have images reproduced of it that do not show it at its best condition. Whether these records may be made public should ideally be addressed in the applicable donor, commission, or loan agreement. Similarly, cultural institutions with archaeology or anthropology programs should consider policies on the disclosure of images and documentation relating to field work. While some sites are well-known and well protected, in other instances concerns over the potential for looting may limit disclosure of documentation that would point to the exact site.

CONCLUSION

By the conclusion of this chapter, a rights and reproductions specialist should now have the tools to assess and identify the varied rights issues present in their institution's collection materials. The following chapters will outline current licensing practices and procedures, building upon the legal overview of IP issues described thus far. With a greater understanding of the IP issues applicable to their collection, a rights and reproductions specialist is now prepared to undertake licensing for various institutional uses, to leverage content with distribution partners, and to effectively communicate the IP in its collection to the public.

NOTES

1. See chapter 1, Duration of Copyright, for a more detailed discussion.

2. Peter B. Hirtle, "Copyright Term and the Public Domain in the United States," Cornell University: Copyright Information Center, last modified January 1, 2018, https://copyright.cornell.edu/publicdomain.

3. Ibid.

4. See chapter 1, Publication, for the definition of publication under the copyright law.

5. There is no single, uniform, international copyright law or term for the entire world. Instead, under the rule of

national treatment, US law should be applied to activities taking place in the United States regardless of a work's country of origin. Although the activities of cultural institutions may cross national boundaries, it is beyond the scope of this publication to cover how to determine whether a work is still under copyright outside of the United States. See chapter 1, International IP Rights, for more information.

6. The Oakland Museum of California holds rights to Lange's non-FSA images. See "Dorothea Lange Archive," Oakland Museum of California, accessed March 13, 2018, http://museumca.org/collection/dorothea-lange-archive.

7. Copyright term is calculated differently for sound recordings and architectural works. See 17 U.S.C. §§ 302, 303, 304. These are also addressed in Hirtle's chart.

8. 17 U.S.C. § 302(a). Copyright runs through the end of the day on December 31 of the seventieth year. 17 U.S.C. § 305. For example, copyright to works by an artist who died in 1955 will pass into the public domain on January 1, 2026.

9. See chapter 1, The Copyright Holder, for definition of works made for hire.

10. 17 U.S.C. § 302(c).

11. See chapter 1, Publication, for a discussion of these formalities.

12. Rather than specific copyright notices, the utilization of broad statements on use restrictions are advised for informing staff and outside users. Sample statement from the Indianapolis Museum of Art Archives at Newfields: "Unpublished manuscripts are protected by copyright. Permission to publish, quote, or reproduce must be secured from the repository and the copyright holder."

13. Note: this may be a good option if the institution has a small number of items to research for a specific end use. The process can be time and cost intensive to have the Copyright Office complete the research on your behalf. "Public Catalog: Copyright Catalog (1978 to present)," United States Copyright Office, accessed March 13, 2018, http://cocatalog.loc.gov/cgi-bin/Pwebrecon.cgi?DB=local&PAGE=First.

14. Ibid.

15. United States Copyright Office, *Circular 23: The Copyright Card Catalog and the Online Files of the Copyright Office* (revised December 2015), http://www.copyright.gov/circs/circ23.pdf.

16. "Copyright Records," Library of Congress: FEDLINK – United States Federal Collection, accessed March 13, 2018, https://archive.org/details/copyrightrecords.

17. United States Copyright Office, *Circular 23: The Copyright Card Catalog and the Online Files of the Copyright Office* (revised December 2015), http://www.copyright.gov/circs/circ23.pdf.

18. 17 U.S.C. § 101 (defining "publication").

19. While any publication without copyright notice, not just the first publication, might potentially affect the copyright status, for the purposes of these broad determinations only first publication is considered. It is important to keep in mind that first publication is relevant to the copyright term and the timing of required copyright renewals, if applicable. Any pre-1964 publication is useful to narrowing the range of the renewal deadline.

20. "Our Partnership," HathiTrust Digital Library, accessed March 13, 2018, http://www.hathitrust.org/partnership.

21. "Library Partners," Google Books, accessed March 13, 2018, http://www.google.com/intl/en/googlebooks/library/partners.html.

22. See chapter 5, HathiTrust, for a more detailed discussion.

23. Peter B. Hirtle, "Copyright Term and the Public Domain in the United States," Cornell University: Copyright Information Center, last modified January 1, 2018, https://copyright.cornell.edu/publicdomain.

24. 17 U.S.C. § 105.

25. "Orphan Works," United States Copyright Office, accessed March 13, 2018, http://copyright.gov/orphan/.

26. See, for example, Society of American Archivists, *Orphan Works: Statement of Best Practices* (January 12, 2009; rev. June 17, 2009), https://www2.archivists.org/sites/all/files/OrphanWorks-June2009.pdf.

27. "Directive 2012/28/EU of the European Parliament and the Council of 25 October 2012 on Certain Permitted Uses of Orphan Works," accessed March 13, 2018, http://ec.europa.eu/internal_market/copyright/orphan_works/index_en.htm.

28. Orphan works licenses are only eligible for use in the United Kingdom for up to seven years, but may be renewed. See "Apply for an orphan works license," *GOV.UK*, accessed March 13, 2018, https://www.gov.uk/guidance/copyright-orphan-works#apply-for-an-orphan-works-licence.

29. Department for Business, Innovation & Skills, Intellectual Property Office and Baroness Neville-Rolfe DBE CMG, "UK Opens Access to 91 Million Orphan Works," October 29, 2014 press release, accessed March 13, 2018, https://www.gov.uk/government/news/uk-opens-access-to-91-million-orphan-works.

30. Society of American Archivists, *Orphan Works: Statement of Best Practices* (January 12, 2009; rev. June 17, 2009), https://www2.archivists.org/sites/all/files/OrphanWorks-June2009.pdf.

31. This list is not meant to be all inclusive; for a more comprehensive overview see Appendix C: References and Resources. Another extensive list of global agencies can be found at "List of Copyright Collection Societies," Wikipedia, accessed March 13, 2018, http://en.wikipedia.org/wiki/List_of_copyright_collection_societies.

32. Access ©, accessed March 13, 2018, http://www.accesscopyright.ca/.

33. Authors' Licensing and Collecting Society, accessed March 13, 2018, http://www.alcs.co.uk/.

34. Copyright Clearance Center, accessed March 13, 2018, http://www.copyright.com/.

35. The Authors Registry, accessed March 13, 2018, http://www.authorsregistry.org/.

36. The Copyright Licensing Agency, accessed March 13, 2018, http://www.cla.co.uk/.

37. Amazon Digital Music Store, accessed March 13, 2018, https://www.amazon.com/MP3-Music-Download/b?ie=UTF8&node=163856011.

38. The American Society of Composers, Authors and Publishers, accessed March 13, 2018, http://www.ascap.com/.

39. BMI, accessed March 13, 2018, http://www.bmi.com/.

40. Harry Fox Agency, accessed March 13, 2018, https://www.harryfox.com/.

41. iTunes, accessed March 13, 2018, http://www.apple.com/itunes/.

42. SESAC, accessed March 13, 2018, http://www.sesac.com/.

43. In July 2018 artists previously represented by Visual Artists and Galleries Association (VAGA) joined the ARS membership roster. Artists Rights Society, accessed July 26, 2018, http://www.arsny.com/.

44. Bridgeman Copyright, Bridgeman Images, accessed March 13, 2018, http://www.bridgemanimages.com/en-US/bridgeman-copyright-service.

45. The Design and Artists Copyright Society, accessed March 13, 2018, http://www.dacs.org.uk/.

46. It is important to note that many of these websites, including ARS, are not indexed by Web crawlers at this point. A search by name on a Web search engine will *not* return a licensing agency record.

47. Writers Artists and their Copyright Holders, Harry Ransom Center: The University of Texas at Austin, accessed March 13, 2018, http://norman.hrc.utexas.edu/watch/. For more information, see About WATCH, Harry Ransom Center: The University of Texas at Austin, accessed March 13, 2018, http://norman.hrc.utexas.edu/watch/about.cfm.

48. "Rights and Restrictions Information," The Library of Congress: Prints & Photographs Reading Room, accessed March 13, 2018, https://www.loc.gov/rr/print/res/index.html.

49. "Source and Permission Contact List," National Archives, accessed March 13, 2018, http://www.archives.gov/research/order/film-sources-contact-list.html.

50. Personal preference of the rights and reproductions specialist will dictate the search engine utilized; the authors of this *Handbook* do not advocate the use of one over another.

51. For example, see "Rights & Reproductions, Roy Lichtenstein Foundation, accessed March 13, 2018, http://lichtensteinfoundation.org/rights-reproductions/.

52. With the caveat that it can be difficult to know whether a legal, contractual relationship actually exists: Does the gallery actually have the right to sign for the artist? It is important to include language in your license so that the person signing warrants that they have this right. When galleries close down, it can also be very difficult to learn where representation, especially of estates, now resides.

53. See Appendix C: References and Resources for additional websites and databases.

54. Spokeo, accessed March 13, 2018, http://www.spokeo.com/.

55. Ancestry, accessed March 13, 2018, https://www.ancestry.com/.

56. "Museum Intellectual Property," Groups.io, accessed June 12, 2018, https://groups.io/g/musip.

57. Museum Computer Network, accessed March 13, 2018, http://mcn.edu.

58. Intellectual Property SIG, Museum Computer Network, accessed March 13, 2018, http://mcn.edu/community/special-interest-groups-sigs/intellectual-property-sig/.

59. "About," ImageMuse, accessed March 31, 2018, http://www.imagemuse.org/.

60. "ImageMuse," Groups.io, accessed June 12, 2018, https://imagemuse.groups.io/g/main.

61. Collections Stewardship Professional Network of the American Alliance of Museums, accessed March 13, 2018, https://www.collectionsstewardship.org/.

62. Intellectual Property Rights Committee (IPR), Visual Resources Association, accessed March 13, 2018, http://vraweb.org/about/committees/intellectual-property-rights-committee-ipr/.

63. Maintaining an institutional list of colleagues who are fluent in other languages can be a useful resource to leverage when translation services may be required to negotiate with international rights holders.

64. Retail commercial uses are often limited, or the license may specifically exclude retail and make reference to the need for a separate agreement for such uses. See chapter 4, Retail and Commercial Products, for a detailed discussion.

65. See Appendix B: Document and Contract Templates for sample agreements that illustrate differently formatted agreements from varying institutions.

66. Extension may be limited to institutions borrowing the work(s) or to fewer uses than those granted to the institution.

67. Depending on institutional practice, time-based media works may also be referred to as variable art.

68. It is possible such a grant of rights for unspecified works may be challenged legally because at the time of the grant of rights, it was not known to which works a license might apply.

69. Duration for the full copyright term is preferable. Ideally, the license should avoid any explicit limits on the length of time of use. This way, the work may be used for the full copyright term or until the copyright holder revokes the permission. Absent any specific term for the license, the grant of rights will extend to the full term of copyright.

70. Only exclusive grants of rights must be signed by both parties. For a basic nonexclusive licensing agreement, it is sufficient for only the licensor (the rights holder) to sign. However, the licensee (the cultural institution) should sign if the licensee also has obligations under the license. It is still good policy to have both parties sign nonexclusive licensing agreements so as to avoid any questions about the agreement in the future.

71. When a purported rights holder transfers all the rights they have or may have in the work (if any), without any warranty of ownership of such rights, it is often referred to as a "quitclaim." In a broadly drafted quitclaim, the grantor is not specifying what rights they actually have. Rather, the person or entity is merely assigning all rights they may possibly have, and it is possible they do not own copyright or have other IP rights in the work. Rights and reproductions specialists need to carefully interpret these broad quitclaim statements before relying on them. Copyright and contract laws require that all transfers of rights ownership be in writing and be specific. In order to determine whether it is reasonable to rely on statements

with this general language, it would be necessary to review other facts that would indicate the intention of the parties. As a practical matter, if it appears the parties did intend to transfer both the physical and IP rights in the work, then a conclusion to that effect seems reasonable.

72. This is dependent on the agreement made with the rights holder at the time of the assignment.

73. See Appendix B: Document and Contract Templates for sample commission contract.

74. Visual Artists Rights Act, 17 U.S.C. § 106A. See chapter 1, Visual Artists Rights Act, for a more detailed discussion.

75. Also, some states (such as California) have artist rights laws that are in addition to and not preempted by federal law. In California, some artist rights cannot be waived.

76. Indianapolis Museum of Art at Newfields, "The Visual Artists' Rights Act of 1990," *Artist Agreement for Commissioned Artwork.*

77. Depiction may also take the form of other visual representations such as a drawing, painting, or video.

78. 17 U.S.C. § 120.

79. It is important to note that publicity is a form of privacy rights in some jurisdictions and may apply postmortem.

80. Unless the person depicted is a public figure, it is often not possible to know for sure whether the person is still living. In such cases, simply consider the date of the work and the estimated age of the person when the picture was taken, then extrapolate the age of the person in present time. For example, a teenager depicted in a 1960 photograph is probably in their mid-seventies by the year 2018 and therefore likely to be still living.

81. For example, in July 2014, a Yankees fan caught napping on camera by ESPN filed a defamation lawsuit against the broadcaster and Major League Baseball for subjecting him to mockery and emotional distress. ESPN has denied the charges, but the case serves as an example of how a seemingly innocuous situation could trigger a privacy claim. "Sleeping Yankees Fan Sues ESPN for Defamation," The Smoking Gun, last modified July 7, 2014, http://www.thesmokinggun.com/documents/sleeping-fan-sues-Yankees-ESPN-576321.

82. See, e.g., Cal. Civ. Code § 3344(b)(1) (West 2014).

83. Indiana follows the Restatement (Second) of Torts § 652D, which states that invasion of privacy requires "publicity" to be given to the matter. The Indiana Supreme Court has held that communication to a small group of people or one person is *not enough* to satisfy the "publicity" requirement and bring a privacy claim.

84. See Appendix B: Document and Contract Templates for a sample release.

85. See Appendix B: Document and Contract Templates for a sample oral history release.

86. This may also include materials related to medical records and doctor-patient confidentialities.

87. Real-life hidden perils: before it published a personal letter held in an artist archive, an institution requested permission from the living author to do so. The author declined to grant permission, as publishing the letter would have disclosed the embarrassing fact that she ate something that was prohibited by her religion.

88. See generally Joseph L. Sax, *Playing Darts with a Rembrandt: Public and Private Rights in Cultural Treasures.* Ann Arbor: The University of Michigan Press, 2001.

89. The duration of postmortem rights varies by state. In California, for example, postmortem rights last for seventy years for famous people. Cal. Civ. Code § 3344.1(g) (West 2014).

90. See chapter 1, Rights of Privacy, for a more detailed discussion. See, for example, Cal. Civ. Code § 3344 (West 2014).

91. See chapter 1, Remedies, for a more detailed discussion.

92. See chapter 3, Underlying Rights, for a discussion of core works and works depicted.

93. To be clear, the recorded rights information should be substantially about the main object in the collection, the core work. A core work may be a photograph that depicts other copyrighted work, works depicted. Rights information about works depicted in a core work should be clearly labeled and recorded as an additional restriction or claimant in a summary field.

94. Copyright status and publication status may be recorded using a picklist of values. See Maureen Whalen, "Developing a Rights Metadata Dictionary for Digital Surrogates," *Journal of Library Metadata* 9 (2009): 15–35.

95. This likely applies to organizations that do not have object-level CMS records for their entire collection. Large archives, for example, may only be recorded in the CMS as a collection or at a box level. In such cases, the DAMS, with its images and records of individual objects, may be the only object-level record of the work.

96. Catherine Saez, "Interviews: What Protection of Traditional Knowledge Means To Indigenous Peoples," Intellectual Property Watch, last modified August 20, 2013, http://www.ip-watch.org/2013/08/20/interviews-what-protection-of-traditional-knowledge-means-to-indigenous-peoples/.

97. Traditional knowledge is knowledge, know-how, skills, and practices that are developed, sustained, and passed on from generation to generation within a community, often forming part of its cultural or spiritual identity. "Traditional Knowledge," World Intellectual Property Organization, accessed March 13, 2018, http://www.wipo.int/tk/en/tk/.

98. Traditional cultural expressions, also called "expressions of folklore," may include music, dance, art, designs, names, signs and symbols, performances, ceremonies, architectural forms, handicrafts and narratives, or many other artistic or cultural expressions. "Traditional Cultural Expressions, (TCE)" World Intellectual Property Organization, accessed March 13, 2018, http://www.wipo.int/tk/en/folklore/.

99. Patricia M. Lord, "Unrepatriatable: Native American Intellectual Property and Museum Digital Publication" (master's thesis, John F. Kennedy University, June 18, 2014), 26–27, https://www.academia.edu/7770593/Unrepatriatable_Native_American_Intellectual_Property_and_Museum_Digital_Publication.

100. Ibid., 86.

101. Native American Graves Protection and Repatriation Act, Pub. L. 101-601, 104 Stat. 3048 (1990) (codified as amended in scattered sections of 25 U.S.C. and 18 U.S.C.). National NAGPRA, National Park Service: U.S. Department of the Interior, accessed March 13, 2018, http://www.nps.gov/nagpra/.

102. Patricia M. Lord, "Unrepatriatable: Native American Intellectual Property and Museum Digital Publication" (master's thesis, John F. Kennedy University, June 18, 2014), 83–98, https://www.academia.edu/7770593/Unrepatriatable_Native_American_Intellectual_Property_and_Museum_Digital_Publication.

103. Including a recommendation to customize data formatting so that name and tribal affiliation are given weight as creator and, when the maker is unknown, indicate that fact rather than omitting it. Ibid., 90–91.

104. *Miller v. California*, 413 U.S. 15, 24 (1973).

105. For example, see the National September 11 Memorial & Museum, accessed March 13, 2018, https://www.911memorial.org/ and the United States Holocaust Memorial Museum, accessed March 13, 2018, https://www.ushmm.org/.

106. 17 U.S.C. § 101(1). A "work made for hire" is defined as "a work prepared by an employee within the scope of his or her employment; or (2) a work specially ordered or commissioned for use as a contribution to a collective work, as a part of a motion picture or other audiovisual work, as a translation, as a supplementary work, as a compilation, as an instructional text, as a test, as answer material for a test, or as an atlas, if the parties expressly agree in a written instrument signed by them that the work shall be considered a work made for hire."

107. See Appendix B: Document and Contract Templates for sample agreements. Best approach: (1) state that the work is a work for hire, but (2) if the work is not deemed a work for hire, all rights are hereby assigned and transferred.

108. See chapter 2, Case Study: Crafting an IP Policy, for a more detailed discussion about the IP ownership in contractor, volunteer, and intern situations, any of which may contribute to creating new photography for a cultural institution.

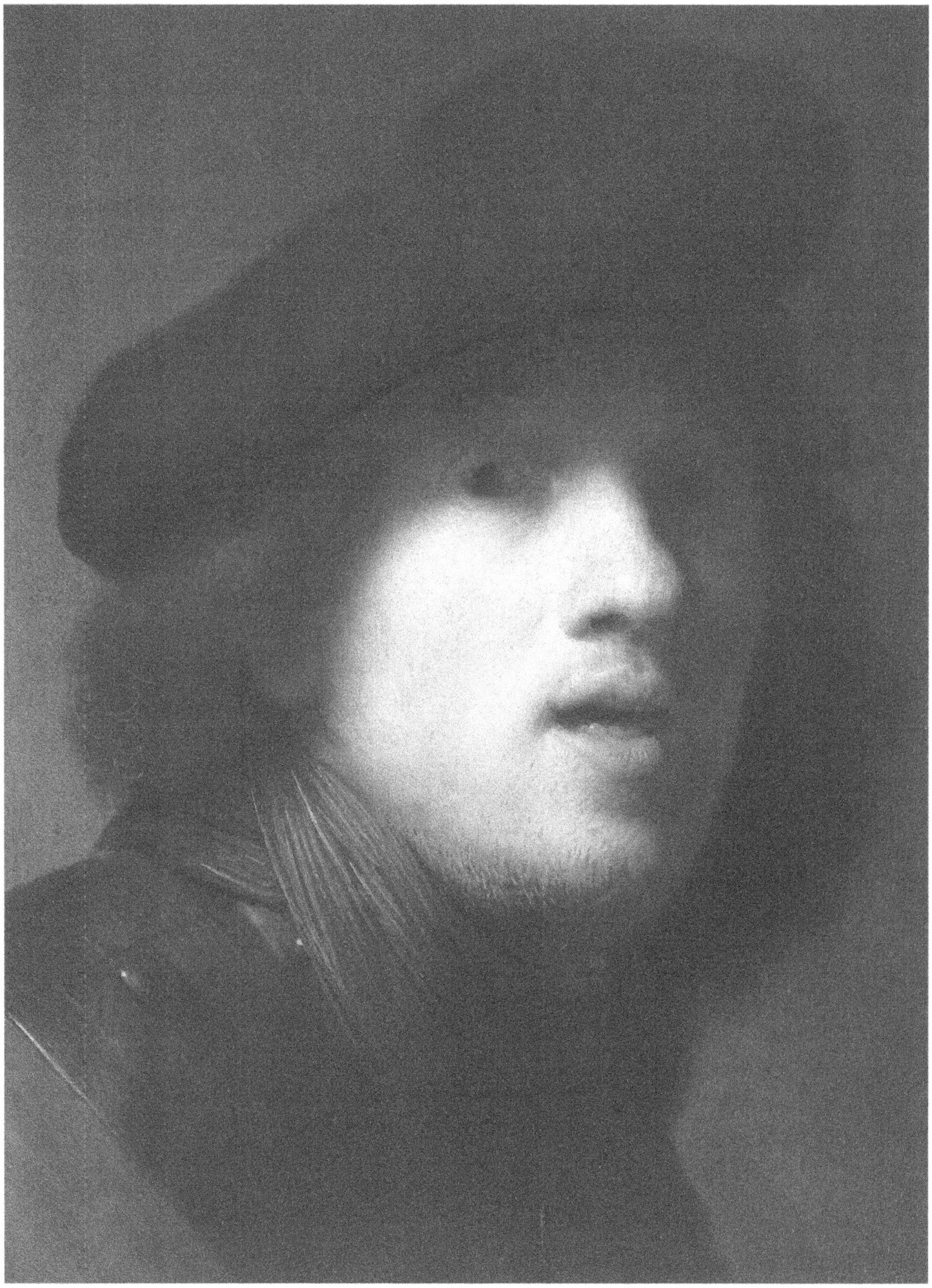

4

Institutional Uses

MEGAN P. BRYANT, CHERIE C. CHEN, JOHN FFRENCH, SOFÍA GALARZA LIU, MICHELLE GALLAGHER ROBERTS, NAOMI LEIBOWITZ, NANCY SIMS, DEBORAH WYTHE, AND ANNE M. YOUNG

Cultural institutions routinely reproduce and distribute copyrighted or other rights-protected[1] materials in their mission-related activities. Familiar institutional uses range from publishing catalogues or collection websites, marketing and promotion materials, educational outreach, and public programs, to the creation of retail products. Digital platforms such as blogs, social media, email blasts, videos, and smartphone apps have also become common dissemination and communications tools. Permission from rights holders—whether for a one-time use related to a specific project or for an ongoing use such as on an institution's website—may be necessary before using the material at hand. How an institution uses the materials in its collection is an important aspect of the permissions process. This chapter outlines the permissions process, provides resources for obtaining materials from third parties, and discusses the rights issues for some typical institutional uses.

THE PERMISSIONS PROCESS: RIGHTS ANALYSIS

When considering materials[2] for use in any of an institution's many possible projects, begin by assessing the intellectual property (IP) issues related to each work. The permission process requires attention to every layer of rights in the work. Multiple clearances for a single work may be necessary depending on the intended use, who owns the object, who controls rights to the work, and who provides the image. Use the questions listed below as a checklist for identifying the potential rights to be cleared:

- Is the *work itself* protected by copyright?[3]
  - If yes, does the institution already have a nonexclusive license from the copyright holder to reproduce the work for the intended use?
  - If yes, could the intended use potentially qualify as a fair use?
- Are there any *underlying rights* in the work?
- Is the *image* of the work protected by copyright?[4]
- Does the institution need an image of the work? If the work depicts an individual, do rights of privacy and publicity apply?[5]
- Are any trademarks involved?[6]
- If the work is a loan, are there any lender restrictions outlined in the loan agreement?
- If using music, video, or film, does the institution need public performance, display, publishing, or sync rights?
- Are there any additional considerations as previously discussed that may prohibit the use?[7]

THE PERMISSIONS PROCESS: REQUESTING RIGHTS

Permission must be obtained from the rights holder when the rights analysis finds that a work is protected by copyright[8] but the cultural institution does not have a license to reproduce it *and* has determined that the proposed use does not appear to fall within

RIGHTS ANALYSIS: WORKS ENTERING THE PUBLIC DOMAIN

Michelle Gallagher Roberts

American photographer Alfred Stieglitz died July 13, 1946. As of January 1, 2016, many works by Stieglitz may have entered the public domain as seventy years had passed since his death. However, some of his works may still be protected by copyright given when the individual objects were published, and if the copyright was registered, renewed, etc. Nevertheless, the Georgia O'Keeffe Museum, the rights holder for both Alfred Stieglitz and Georgia O'Keeffe has taken the following stance regarding the copyright of Stieglitz's works:

> It is our belief, guided by the advice of legal counsel, that the works of Alfred Stieglitz are now in the public domain. In keeping with our values as an educational organization committed to access and scholarship, and being mindful of the best use of our limited resources, we do not wish to continue claiming or enforcing control over the usage of Stieglitz photographs. We will continue to actively manage and license the usage of works by Georgia O'Keeffe, as well as related uses of her name, through copyright and trademark. This may include enforcing our rights if we feel that images of Georgia O'Keeffe made by Alfred Stieglitz are used in a way that is judged inappropriate or disrespectful.[1]

This shows the complicated nature of public domain and enforcing rights. Intellectual rights are often layered, and each use must be evaluated.

NOTE

1. Georgia O'Keeffe Museum, personal communication with the author, April 2, 2018.

the scope of fair use based on the institution's level of risk-taking. If the work is part of the permanent collection, the institution may request either a broad nonexclusive license or a one-time permission for the specific use. The decision to proceed with a broad or specific request depends on a number of factors, some of which are listed below.

Reasons to proceed with a broad nonexclusive license request:

- The institution has a good relationship with the rights holder
- The rights holder has previously granted one-time permission when requested, but the institution has not yet attempted to request a broad license agreement
- The institution owns multiple works by the rights holder and can use this opportunity to obtain a broad license for all the works in its collection
- Project schedule allows plenty of time to prepare and negotiate a broad license

Reasons to request one-time permission:

- Rights holder previously indicated preference to handle requests on a case-by-case basis
- Rights holder is represented by a licensing agency, such as ARS, ASCAP, or BMI

- Rights holder charges a fee for each use
- Project schedule requires a quick response

A request for one-time permission may be made by email, mail, fax, or even by telephone,[9] and is usually more abbreviated in format compared to a broad nonexclusive license request.[10] Providing a simple, "human readable" or "plain language" permission letter is a useful starting point for rights requests of this type,[11] particularly when dealing with artists and individuals who may find complex legal documents off-putting or confusing. A one-time request letter should include the following elements:[12]

- brief description of the institution and its mission
- identifying information about the work, including a reference image if available
- description of the specific project:
  - What is the project?
  - When and where does it take place?
- detailed information about how the work may be reproduced or used by the institution,[13] and for how long, in connection with the project (e.g., print publication, website, publicity, etc.)
- how the institution plans to credit the work in its materials unless the copyright holder requests alternate wording
- deadline for a response from the rights holder

Once the request has been sent, keep track of the process and plan ahead to follow up after a reasonable interval. Note that a rights holder has no legal obligation to respond to a permission request. A nonresponse does not mean "yes," and it can require diligence, perseverance, and time to obtain an answer. In a best-case scenario, the rights holder responds with approval for all of the requested uses without charging any fees or imposing additional terms and conditions. At worst, permission is denied, in which case the institution may not reproduce the work unless the institution believes in good faith it is exercising fair use or another limitation to the exclusive rights of copyright appropriate under the particular situation and facts.

A rights holder may also respond with their own license agreement, impose additional terms and conditions,[14] or charge a fee. Licensing agencies and institutional rights holders commonly issue "boilerplate" agreements that cover every possible aspect of use, which should be reviewed carefully. Alterations to clauses may need to be negotiated and revised to meet the institution's needs. Be sure to follow the appropriate internal procurement or legal procedures for contract approval. Once an agreement is finalized, carefully adhere to any special terms and conditions. Finally, remember to document the permission granted (or denied) in the institution's files and/or CMS.[15]

The general request process described above may be repeated as needed to obtain permission from additional rights holders, such as the rights holder in any *underlying work* depicted or the copyright holder in the *image* of the work. A similar process may also be followed to request other types of permissions, including privacy or publicity rights from the individual(s) depicted. If, after careful review,[16] it is decided that using an image in a particular way may infringe on the individual's privacy or publicity rights, permission should be sought. In such cases, it is advisable to enclose a personal release form[17] with the request letter for their signature. The release form may be tailored to the specific project or worded generally to give the institution broader permission.

An institution can occasionally obtain a personal release in anticipation of future uses of an image. For works by living artists, make it a part of the acquisition process to request copies of any model releases the artist may have obtained or ask the artist to sign the release if the work is a self-portrait. For event or site photography taken by the institution, work in tandem with the photographer to identify individuals who are recognizable in the images and approach them for a release during the shoot. Plan ahead for scheduled shoots—if the institution wants to photograph a school group visit, provide the teacher with releases for the children to bring home for a parent's signature in advance of the school visit. Use of images of children is of particular importance to many institutions given their educational missions, yet parents may feel strongly about the use of their child's image for marketing purposes. Clear communication, via a release form sent home in advance, of an institution's intent to photograph the children and use their images may minimize problems in the future if images are later used for program documentation, publicity, or marketing purposes.

THE PERMISSIONS PROCESS: CONTRACTUAL LIMITATIONS

Copyright status is determined by law and applied on a work-by-work basis.[18] However, if a contract has been signed between two parties, the terms of that contract take precedence over IP law. For example, if an institution borrows a work for an exhibition and the loan agreement stipulates that permission from the lender is required before reproducing an image of the work, then the institution may not use the work without the lender's permission—even if the work itself is in the public domain or the use falls under fair use,[19] without risking a breach of the agreement. Loan agreements should be reviewed carefully for rights and reproductions restrictions—which are often buried in the fine print—that specify how images of the work may be used for the borrower's purposes. If an intended use is not allowed under the loan agreement, the institution will have to request special permission from the lender. Beware that loan agreements may also stipulate that the borrower must use images supplied directly by the lender for any reproductions versus using images supplied by a third party or permitting the borrowing institution to photograph the works themselves.

The process for requesting lender permissions does not differ much from the process for clearing rights, except that the permissions will always be limited to a specific project—say for publication or exhibition—for a set period of time. Start by reviewing the loan agreement terms and check the lender's website. Many institutional lenders provide detailed information in their loan documents or on their websites about how to request rights and images, how long the process takes, and the fees, if applicable, for various uses. Many larger institutions even offer online shopping sites for images or online request forms that further expedite the process. As with rights permission requests, it is important to provide several key pieces of information in a lender request:

- identifying information about the work, including a reference image if available
- mention that the work will be on loan, as that may affect how the request is processed by the lender and whether fees are assessed
- description of the specific project
    - What is the project?
    - When and where does it take place?
- detailed information about how the work may be reproduced or used by the institution, and for how long, in connection with the project (e.g., print publication, website, publicity, etc.)[20]
- request for the exact collection credit line to be used with any reproductions
- deadline for a response from the lender

Expect to receive a license agreement from the lender with detailed terms and conditions that should be reviewed carefully. Follow internal procedures for contract approval, adhere to the terms, and document the permissions granted. Note that license agreements, like loan agreements, are also contracts that may "trump" copyright law. If the license agreement limits the use of the image for a specific purpose, such as a publication, the institution may not reuse the image for another purpose, such as on a gallery graphic, without requesting additional permission—even if the work is in the public domain or if it is potentially a fair use.

TEST YOUR RIGHTS ANALYSIS SKILLS[1]

Cherie C. Chen

What rights need to be obtained in the following scenarios?

1. Photograph in the permanent collection taken by a living artist in 1979 for use in a catalogue. The institution does not have a broad nonexclusive license for the work.[2]

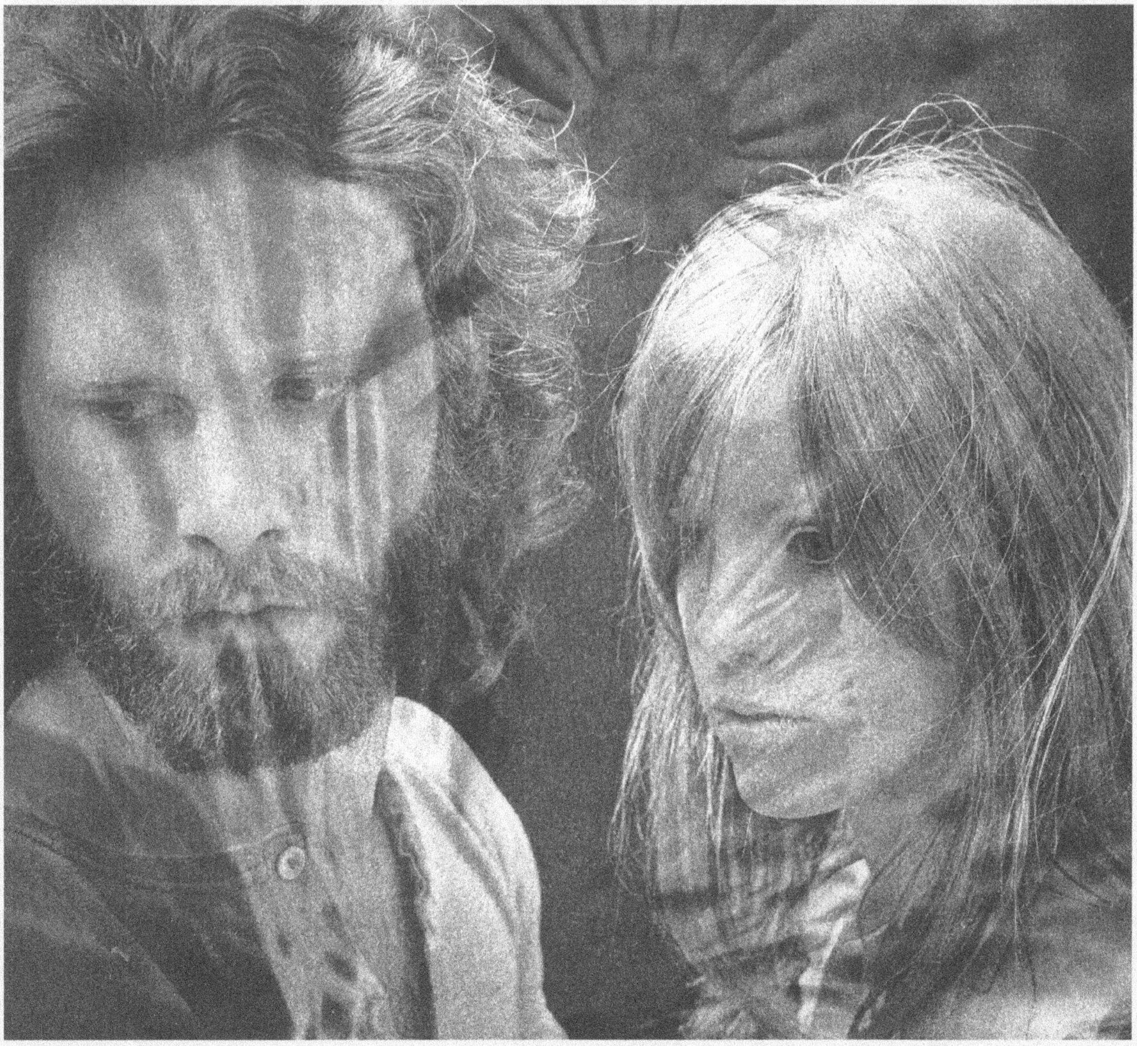

FIGURE 4.1
1969 photograph of Jim Morrison and Pamela Courson taken by Edmund Teske.

2. Image of a public domain painting on loan for an exhibition to be used on the borrower's website.[3]
3. Recent photograph taken by a freelance photographer of a visitor in the galleries for use in a newspaper ad for the institution. The institution needs a digital file of the photograph.[4]
4. Image of a copyrighted drawing owned by another institution for use as a comparative illustration on a gallery label. The drawing is not a loan.[5]
5. Video work in the permanent collection by a deceased artist represented by ARS for display in an exhibition. The institution does not have a license on file for the work.[6]
6. The photograph in figure 4.1 for use as a retail postcard by the owner institution. The institution has a broad license on file from the copyright holder for noncommercial uses.[7]

NOTES

1. See notes after each question for the answer.
2. Answer: Copyright permission from the artist.
3. Answer: Lender permission, if the loan agreement specifies that rights and/or images must be requested for the use.
4. Answer: Copyright permission and the image from the freelance photographer. (This assumes the image was not originally taken as a "work for hire" where copyright was assigned to the institution.) Privacy/publicity rights from the visitor depicted in the photograph.
5. Answer: Permission from the owner, if the institution needs an image of the work or previously licensed the image for a different use. The intended use may be considered fair use by the institution, thus copyright permission is not needed.
6. Answer: Copyright permission from ARS to display and/or publicly perform the video in the exhibition.
7. Answer: Copyright permission from the photographer's estate, since the license on file only covers noncommercial use. Depending on the state in which the institution operates, publicity rights from the estate of Jim Morrison (d. 1971) and possibly from the estate of Pamela Courson (d. 1974). Consult with legal counsel.

THE PERMISSIONS PROCESS: MUSIC

Music licensing can be complicated and confusing since two separate copyrights may exist in a single work—in the composition and in the sound recording—and it is not intuitive which rights may need to be cleared for various uses of music.[21] Without diving into the intricacies of the law, which is beyond the scope of this publication, some common institutional uses are described below along with the permission required for each. Consult with legal counsel for any uses of copyrighted music beyond the common ones listed here.

Cultural institutions often seek to augment the visitor experience with related background audio or general musical selections. It is not uncommon to find ambient music playing within public spaces, such as a retail shop, café, or restaurant. An institution may also offer live music performances or wish to enhance an exhibition by playing music in the galleries to evoke a mood or time period. To play or perform music to the visiting public in these scenarios, cultural institutions generally need a license from one of the performing rights organizations (PROs)—ASCAP,[22] BMI,[23] or SESAC[24]—that represent the composers and/or publishers of musical works. PROs offer one-time or blanket licenses, which provide the most flexibility and are often renewed annually. The type of license to obtain will depend on the institution's needs and budget. In some cases, the institution may need to license from all three agencies to offer the selection of music that it wants.

On the other hand, using music as a component of audio and/or video materials such as audio guides, promotional, or educational videos may require a different type of permission called a synchronization (or "sync," for short) license. In these instances, the PROs may be able to provide contact information for the copyright holder in the musical work, but the PROs do not directly offer sync licenses. Songs have to be licensed directly from the individual composer or publisher, usually for a negotiated fee. Cultural institutions with limited budgets should explore various music sharing sites that offer original compositions (often by lower-profile artists), many of which simply require attribution in exchange for free use or a nominal fee.[25] When clearing music for a specific use, attribution is a common requirement of the license. For instance, licensing individual songs for an audio guide or video may require a credit to appear on the final screen of the production.

FAIR USE

Fair use should play an important role in many institutional uses of collection items.[26] While the practices of many cultural institutions tend to be permission oriented, there are times when permissions may simply not be necessary. Even when users have sought permission for a use in the past, there is nothing to prevent them from reconsidering the situation as a possible fair use in the future, especially in response to developing fair use case law. And because the case law contains many fine distinctions, it is understandable for similar users to feel differently about the applicability of fair use, even in similar situations based upon varying interpretations of the copyright law.

Cultural institutions sometimes fail to consider that there are also risks in not relying on fair use or other statutory exceptions to the rights of copyright holders. Never relying on fair use for digitization and sharing of copyrighted works means that an organization's collections will be less available to the public and of less use to students, researchers, and others than they could be. Never relying on fair use can also result in unnecessary expenditures and "permissions creep," where more and more often permissions are expected, often for increasingly minimal uses. Both granting and seeking permissions impose costs on an organization, and reliance on permissions can impose limitations on free speech and expression. Cultural institutions have good reason to be concerned about the erosion of fair use and to consider how appropriately relying on fair use in some situations—even in the face of risk—may be of public benefit.

One heartening consideration for employees of a "nonprofit educational institution, library, or archives," or the institutions themselves, is that copyright law includes a provision that may limit monetary damages if the institutional user made a reasonable guess at fair use—even if a court later concludes they were incorrect.[27]

SOURCING MATERIALS

Sources for materials—images, music, video, and the like[28]—will often become clear during the permissions process discussed earlier in this chapter. In many cases, both materials and permissions may be obtained in a single request. Once the project checklist of requested materials is complete,[29] a careful review will help in mapping out the image acquisition process, and having the relevant project information on hand will smooth the request submissions.

Key Considerations:

- Which works are in the institution's own collection?
- Are publication-quality images on file (digital or analog formats)?
  - Are existing images acceptable to the project curator?
  - Will new photography need to be scheduled?
- Are specific works requested from known collections, institutions, galleries, or directly from artists?
- Which artists and/or institutions are represented by a licensing agency or image resource company?
- Are images based on a generic description requested ("image of pyramids at Giza"), in which case use of a stock photography site may be advantageous?
- Which works are in the public domain?[30]

Entering requests into a spreadsheet or database will allow greater control of the many threads of the workflow over potentially months of active work and project follow-up. Diligent tracking and organization will ultimately ensure that all rights are cleared, images and descriptive data (including caption and credit information) are acquired and approved, invoices are paid, complimentary copies are sent out, and the inevitable post-project questions easily answered. During the entire process of rights and materials acquisition, information will be gathered for captions and credits. Establishing a standard format for recording and tracking this information is a critical function that can be addressed with good record keeping.

As previously discussed, detailed information is normally required by sources when requesting rights and image file materials. As much information as possible should be included in the initial request to avoid extra back-and-forth.[31] At a minimum, be prepared to provide the following:

- publication/project title
- author/curator
- publisher/organization
- expected release date (publication date, exhibition dates, etc.)
- print run/term of use
- language(s)
- edition(s)
- format (print, web, e-book, etc.)
- materials delivery deadline
- desired image file size
- layout information (cover, interior, etc.)

Sourcing Materials Directly from Institutions, Collectors, and Creators

Images of works owned by institutions are generally easiest to find and acquire. Many museums make collections databases available online, provide images and approved metadata, and often have trained rights and reproductions specialists to assist those placing requests.[32] A growing number of institutions are adopting open access policies, allowing free use of their images of works in the public domain and providing publication-ready images for download,[33] so it is always wise to investigate that first.[34] Also, it is possible that images of objects on loan may be provided at no or a reduced charge (e.g., for publicity purposes) as part of the loan agreement, so it is important to note a piece is being loaned when placing the request.

Objects owned by collectors present a slightly more complex process. In some cases, the collector is able to provide a high-resolution image and contact information for the image rights holder (the photographer) or an assurance that the collector has the right to authorize reproduction of the image. If the work was acquired from a gallery or directly from the artist, both of whom may maintain archives of images, a file of the image may be acquired from one of those sources. If neither of these sources has an image, or an image of sufficient quality, then a contract photographer may need to be sought out who can shoot the work at the collector's home or storage facility.[35]

Artists present a similar situation: they or their galleries may have a comprehensive archive of images of their work, or they may have minimal visual documentation. However, since rights permission will have to be acquired, a question about images as part of that

WORKING WITH CONTRACT PHOTOGRAPHERS

John ffrench and Deborah Wythe

While many cultural institutions have an internal photography department or photographer who can take photographs of works, people, and events, there are cases where an institution will need to hire a photographer to work on a project. This may arise because staff members do not have time or the proper expertise or because the location of the shoot makes sending a staff member impractical.

When contracting a photographer, be sure to execute a detailed written agreement that ensures the cultural institution has the necessary usage rights, and that both parties are protected in the unfortunate event that something is damaged during a shoot. Verbal agreement transactions are not advised.

Identifying and Supervising a Contract Photographer

It is helpful to retain contact information, résumés, and portfolios for freelance photographers; these will often come in "over the transom," but the best resource is typically colleague recommendations. When faced with contracting a photographer in a remote location, a query to colleagues or other cultural institutions within proximity will likely lead to a professional with the right skills. Private collectors may already have a photographer who they use and trust. Review the photographer's website to see if they have undertaken a similar project before and has the skills and equipment required.

Once a cultural institution has approached the contractor and has a reasonable estimate outlined, contract negotiations will ensue.[1] In addition to standard items such as cost, scope, deliverables, and deadline, make sure to discuss quality control in detail, including what will constitute a completed image and who has the authority to sign off on it (ideally the cultural institution hiring the contractor). Providing sample images and detailed technical requirements to the photographer along with metadata templates will alleviate headaches and downtime when the project starts.

Questions the Contract Should Address

- Who retains the rights to the photographs being taken?

  Exclusive Rights: Ideally the museum retains all rights to the images, but this can come at a greater cost. Consider whether the works are in the permanent collection, for which obtaining full rights is useful, or whether they are loaned objects, for which there is no need for the institution to take on the burden of administering rights once the project is complete.

  Nonexclusive Rights: The photographer retains copyright in the images, but grants the institution a broad nonexclusive license to use the images for any institutional purposes in all media in perpetuity. The photographer is also free to use the images and license them to others.

Limited Rights: The photographer may specify that the permissions are for a specific project and assess a separate fee and permissions for any future uses.

- Future use by the photographer: A photographer may request to use images for self-promotion, but be aware that there may be added restrictions. For loaned items or works under copyright, text should be included indicating that it is the photographer's responsibility to obtain permission for any uses and indemnify the cultural institution against future claims.
- How will the images be credited?

  Devise a credit line that acknowledges both the institution and photographer's role (e.g., City Museum photograph; Janet Doe, photographer).

Risk Assessment

Many cultural institutions require that all contractors submit to a background check prior to being hired, which serves to limit liability for the institution. If a background check is a requirement of employment, plan ample time for this process to be completed. If the photographer is someone the institution will work with often, inquire if they can be set up as a vendor in the business office system to eliminate the need for creating new forms each time they are hired and also speed up the payment process for invoices.

If the photographer is going to work with artwork from the collection or at a collector's home, shooting art that will be on loan to the museum, clarify whose insurance covers the object if an accident occurs. Most museums require photographers to have a certificate of insurance of a minimum specified amount on file.

NOTE

1. See Appendix B: Document and Contract Templates, for a sample contract.

process will be the first step leading to the best image. Negotiating the tricky shoals of acquiring a publication quality image will come into play here: snapshots taken for documentation may not be high enough quality for publication. The image researcher or rights and reproductions specialist may need to dig deeper (or hire a photographer) to acquire better images.

COLLECTIVE IMAGE RESOURCES

A wide variety of online image databases exist, from highly developed commercial entities to scholarly databases to community-sourced collections. In most cases, rights are provided as part of the image or subscription purchase process or are specified so that the user can follow up. A selection follows.[36]

- *Artstor Digital Library*[37]
  One of the earliest online image databases, founded in 2004, Artstor provides more than two million images to subscribing members, primarily universities and special libraries.[38] It originally began as an aggregator of digitized slide libraries, but more recently has been adding content directly from museum collections.[39] Artstor's Images for Academic Publishing (IAP) makes selected images available for scholarly use at no cost.[40] Independent scholars who are not affiliated with an Artstor-subscribing institution may register for access to IAP images.[41]
- *Wikimedia Commons*[42]
  The Commons currently provides more than forty-five million images, all in the public domain and freely available for download.[43] Images can be uploaded by anyone in the community (caveat: a wide variety in quality of images and data), but high-quality images may be found there. The WikiProject Museums is working to improve metadata inclusion and consistency.[44] Cultural institutions, including museums, are contributing content to the Commons to achieve a wider reach.[45] Images and/or pointers to collections' websites may be found in Wikimedia Commons.[46]
- *Flickr*[47]
  The photo-sharing site Flickr and its offshoot Flickr Commons make billions of images available and (often) downloadable under a variety of rights profiles.[48] Rights holders generally supply contact information in their profile so that image researchers can reach out to acquire images and rights. Search capability is fairly rudimentary, but the advanced search does allow researchers to specify images with a Creative Commons license. The Commons, a project that started with a large contribution by the Library of Congress in 2008, provides access to images in publicly held photograph collections,[49] all with a "no known restrictions" status.[50]

STOCK AGENCIES

A wide variety of stock agencies provide access to images and an expedited rights clearance process. These services come at a price, of course, though a not-for-profit discount can often be negotiated. Large stock agencies cover topics from current events to fine art and everything in between, offering detailed search capability, instant download, subscriptions media, and rights for images, film, video, and music. Smaller, more specialized agencies may represent a narrower field of interest. Some cultural institutions are moving to outsource rights and reproductions activities to specific agencies, so image researchers may find requests redirected to a non-museum resource for collection images. Furthermore, stock agencies typically differentiate between royalty-free images, which can be licensed for multiple uses based on single payment, and rights-managed images, which provide a license for a single use and require additional payments for each new use. It is important to remember that while some stock agencies will expedite the rights clearance and/or complete the rights clearance themselves, many do not and only serve to provide the image files, leaving rights clearance to be completed separately.

Some of the stock agencies that may be used by cultural institutions for projects include:[51]

- Fine art images and historic photographs:
  - Alinari[52]
  - Art Resource[53]
  - Bridgeman Images[54]
  - Davis Art Images[55]
  - Granger Historical Picture Archive[56]
  - Scholars Resource[57]
- Standard stock photographs and videos:
  - AP Images[58]
  - Getty Images[59]
  - iStock[60]
  - Masterfile[61]
  - Science Photo Library[62]
  - Shutterstock[63]
  - Superstock[64]
  - T3Media[65]
- Motion picture film still and marketing photographs:
  - CineMaterial[66]
  - MovieStillsDB[67]
  - Photofest[68]

ATTRIBUTION

In general, in the United States, both the existence of any kind of attribution, and the specific form that attribution takes, is more a matter of cultural norms and expectations than a statutory legal requirement. It may sometimes be a legal requirement of licensing agreements or other contracts, yet in many situations the most relevant standards are not law, but the expectations of particular groups of users. For example, academic users have a multitude of different citation formats that vary by academic discipline; none are more "correct" than any other, except by the expectations of the venue in which they are being used. Cultural institutions, as is appropriate for stewards of cultural resources, will want to provide attribution of materials they reproduce and encourage attribution by others, regardless of specific legal circumstances.

There is one major exception to the general principle that US statutory law is little concerned with specifics of attribution, and it is of great importance to cultural institutions: VARA[69] gives creators of certain kinds of visual artworks[70] some rights beyond those usually granted to copyright holders. Under VARA, artists have a legal right of attribution (and the right to *non*-attribution or disavowal), a right to control modification of their work and some other rights, all of which are separate from the ownership of the copyright.[71] Some kinds of uses may also separately raise attribution issues where laws around trademark, business competition, and even fraud may be applicable.[72] However, even when there is a statutory element to attribution requirements, the form of attribution is usually not legally determined.

Forms of attribution may be specified in a contract or license, but otherwise the specific form of attribution can be adapted as appropriate for various institutional uses. An item record in an online collection object page will appropriately have far more extensive attribution information than can fit in a limited-character social media post. It can be useful for institutions to develop caption and credit templates that outline for both internal and external users what information is required (e.g., creator name, title and date of the work, and institutional credit) versus what information can be removed in cases of space restraints (e.g., creator life dates, medium, or measurements for a work).

INSTITUTIONAL USES

Cultural institutions seek to promote a greater understanding of cultural heritage through the dissemination of objects in not only exhibitions or publications, but also through a variety of educational programs and public-facing materials. While the broad steps for clearing permissions and sourcing materials can be consistently applied across institutional uses—identify materials, assess rights, find the source(s), and clear any necessary rights—there are nuances in different potential reproductions. What follows is a more in-depth discussion of licensing for common uses: publications, educational materials, marketing and promotion, social media, retail and commercial products, and institutional websites.

PUBLICATIONS

Scholarly publications are a vital part of cultural institutions' educational missions. Publications may accompany a specific exhibition, but can also relate to permanent collections, major gifts, institutional history, or the specific research focus of a staff member. In obtaining rights for images in catalogues, the rights and reproductions specialist must consider multiple levels of clearance. In addition to the process discussed previously in this chapter, the following must be considered:

1. Are there permissions that may be required for the underlying work that appears in the image?
2. Permission from the photographer or cultural institution that documented the work.
3. If clearing images for a catalogue coinciding with a temporary exhibition inclusive of loaned works, the image rights holder may also be the lender. It

would be prudent to check loan forms for information on image rights associated with those works.

4. Permission from the lender of the work, if required separately from the loan agreement.
5. Is there a completed nonexclusive license on file that makes further clearance unnecessary?

Contacting the Rights Holder

Sending information up front with the permission request will save time in the process and reduce the likelihood of delayed processing of the reproduction request. When you are clearing rights for a work or image for use in a publication, be prepared to provide the following information (at a minimum):

- title
- author
- short description of the publication
- publisher
- print run
- page count
- publication distribution
- anticipated publication date
- size the image will be reproduced relative to the page (e.g., quarter, half, or whole)
- black-and-white or color reproduction
- image reproduced in whole or with details

During the process of clearing rights and obtaining files, be sure to do the following:

- Negotiate rates. A nonprofit institution might not pay the same fees as for-profit publishers.
- Acquire all caption information, photograph credits, and copyright notices that will need to be included with the reproduction.
- If obtaining an image file as part of the permission request, check the image resolution. This responsibility may lie with another staff member, but understanding the general image quality being sought will make for a more efficient quality review. A good starting point of reference would be to seek an uncompressed TIFF 16 bit file with a resolution of 300 pixels per inch. For example, for a print publication size of 8 × 10 inches, the pixel dimensions would be 2,400 × 3,000.[73]
- Note and follow any contractual obligations: providing color proofs for approval prior to publication, sending complimentary copies after publication, etc.

Digital Publications

Digital publications provide the opportunity for additional content, like videos, external sources, and conservation views and treatments, to be included. While cultural institutions can aggregate data and media in new ways with digital publications, the need for licensing and image credits is largely still the same as with print counterparts, but terms and conditions, fees, and length of licenses are vastly inconsistent. As there is a shift at cultural institutions to creating born-digital publications, it is important to consider whether it makes sense to produce both print and digital versions of a publication, or only one or the other. This is important for rights and reproductions specialists, as it is a more efficient use of time and staff resources to license for both a print and digital version at the outset than to have to relicense for a digital counterpart at a later date. For instance, would a digital publication highlight interactive aspects of video or performance art in a digital platform that could only be reproduced via still images in a traditional print publication, possibly requiring extra levels of licensing? Formatting constraints of some digital publishing platforms should also be considered. There may be situations where the design and placement of caption, credit, and copyright information is dictated by the tools and not the preferred ideal location of the designers, authors, or publishers.

Key considerations for digital publication licensing include:

- term lengths
- image and video screen resolutions

CASE STUDY

LICENSING AND TERM LENGTHS IN A DIGITAL-ONLY CATALOGUE

Anne M. Young

In working on *Graphite*, the Indianapolis Museum of Art at Newfields' first digital-only exhibition catalogue, published in 2013, one of the biggest challenges faced was consistency in term lengths. All licensing permissions were sought for a term either in perpetuity or for ten years; less than ten years (several rights holders only wanted to license for five years) is a relatively short time to have to renew licenses. This was particularly important in this project, for which there is no print counterpart. In the end, all licenses were obtained for a ten-year minimum, including licenses from ARS, VAGA, and Art Resource. After the ten-year period, the licenses will be renewed for the content not licensed in perpetuity. If this is not a possibility, the previous version will be archived as the first edition of the publication and a subsequent edition will be released minus the content that could not be renewed.

FIGURE 4.2
Judith Braun video excerpt capturing the installation of her site-specific piece from the *Graphite* digital exhibition catalogue.

- availability and protection from download by end users
- multiple platforms with differing formats
- distribution modes
- type of digital publication: app, ePub, website, etc.
- print counterpart or not

EDUCATIONAL MATERIALS

The production of educational materials can be spurred by the development of an upcoming exhibition or may be developed in conjunction with longer-term permanent collection installations. Simply placing collection or borrowed works on display does little to promote visitor interaction or foster a deeper understanding of what is being viewed. Rather, display coupled with interpretive materials provides opportunities for engaged context, interaction, and learning for visitors of all ages.

Whichever is the driving force behind these educational materials, it is important for cultural institutions to remember that the sourcing of materials for educational purposes still has the potential to incur fees for use and/or obtaining image or video files of a high enough quality to produce the desired material(s). While fair use may apply in many instances, the need to obtain a file of a high enough quality may necessitate paying fees. As discussed with publications, assessing the quality of the file is important but can

FILE SIZE GUIDELINES

Anne M. Young

To ease quality review, Newfields' photography department developed the following minimum size guidelines to give to its image researchers and rights and reproductions specialists, with the caveat that these guidelines are subject to change as technologies evolve.

iPad or Tablet Use:

- Screen resolution or about 1024 pixels on the long side is preferred. If utilizing newer iPads or tablets with capacities for higher resolutions, that is, 4k screens, then 2048 pixels on the long side is preferred.

Videos:

- 5 x 7 inches at 300 dpi or about 2300 pixels on the long side is preferred. If presenting videos on screens with the capacity for higher resolutions a larger file size may be preferred.

Labels:

- 5 x 7 inches at 300 dpi or about 2300 pixels on the long side is preferred.

Didactics and Wall Murals:

- 8 x 10 inches at 300 dpi or about 3000 pixels on the long side is preferred.

Remember, these size guidelines are the minimum recommended, but try to ask for the largest original file. The bigger the file size the better.

be more of a challenge with the variety of educational materials being produced today.

New means of interaction allow visitors to engage and learn in ways beyond traditional presentations (labels, didactics, tours, etc.) utilized by cultural institutions for decades. If there are plans to sell or utilize the materials outside the confines of the physical cultural institution building (e.g., video online as well as in the gallery or an app that is downloadable, free or for a fee, to personal devices), some rights holders may believe this constitutes a promotional or marketing use outside of fair use and will seek a licensing fee. Furthermore, the ability to integrate technology-based learning tools into exhibition spaces allows cultural institutions to include much greater amounts of interpretive content without the confines of available wall or display case space. Educational materials in cultural institutions today come in a variety of formats and may include any or all of the following: labels, didactics, audio guides, videos, iPad or tablet apps, interactive activity spaces, docent or self-led tours, classes and camps, institutional website features, and exhibition brochures.

TRADITIONAL MARKETING AND PROMOTION USES

Marketing and promotional materials related to cultural institutions' exhibitions, publications, collections, and programs help to generate awareness of an institution and its resources. Traditional marketing materials include different types of collateral pieces designed to advertise various museum activities—brochures, flyers, billboards, posters, calendars, postcards, etc. These promotional materials would not be terribly effective without images, so it is only natural that marketing and public relations staff seek to use collection or visitor images in their efforts to promote a cultural institution's activities.

As with the other uses outlined in this chapter, it is important to ensure that the appropriate rights are obtained when using images in marketing materials. This is especially important, as it is less likely that image use for advertising or promotional activities would be considered "fair use."[74] If the work pictured in the image to be used in marketing materials is protected by copyright, there are several levels of rights clearance permissions that should be considered:

- rights holder of the work pictured
- photographer of the image
- owner of the work pictured (if the work is not owned by the institution)

Under most circumstances, best practice would be to request marketing and promotional rights at the same time that rights for a publication, exhibition, or program are being negotiated, centralizing all rights clearances in one document.

When working with living creators or their estates, institutions need to be aware that they are not a homogenous group. Every person or group will have a different opinion and approach to the use of their creative work depending on the situation. If permission is granted, the use may be conditioned on stipulations regarding how the work can be presented (e.g., no details allowed or must have a white border). Alternatively, permission may be flatly refused. A word of caution about publicity and/or privacy concerns: the appropriation of the image of a specific person for marketing purposes without that person's permission could be problematic because individuals and estates vary in how they wish to have their work or themselves publicized. Some are very relaxed about uses by cultural institutions, like museum exhibits, while others are very proactive in controlling all aspects of their persona and work. Therefore, if a cultural institution is utilizing an individual's likeness for promotional activities, it is vital that all identifiable individuals grant permission for such use of their image.[75]

SOCIAL MEDIA

Social media has become an increasingly integral part of cultural institutions' marketing and digital initiatives. Given the ever-changing nature of these platforms, this section provides general guidelines, policies, and suggested best practices for the management of IP on social media outlets in general.

Understanding Terms of Use

Almost all social media sites require users to agree to some set of terms of use or terms of service (TOS). It is very common for the TOS on user-generated content sites to include most (if not all) of the following clauses:

- Users promise they are only uploading content to that which they themselves have created, and/or,
- Users promise they are only uploading content for which they have permission (few sites explicitly recognize that users may have rights that arise from something other than creation or permission, though some do acknowledge fair use and other statutory exceptions).
- Users promise that content they upload does not violate any rights of privacy or publicity, and does not defame, libel, or otherwise harm third parties.
- Users grant a license (usually quite broad) to the social media service to use and share the content that users upload.
- Users promise to indemnify the service should any legal disputes arise.

Typically, the average user of a social media site pays little to no attention to these terms, and only some users think critically about fair use or permission. When a cultural institution uses social media, it is worth more active contemplation of the specific TOS of each outlet. The enforceability of TOS for users merely browsing a site is a matter of legal debate, but TOS to which you have actively agreed (i.e., by clicking "I agree" or a similar mechanism) are more likely to be legally binding.[76]

Overall, sharing on social media is not unlike sharing on a cultural institution's website—thumbnails and detail images may be fair use much of the time. Sharing public domain and open-licensed images, or images where the only extant rights belong to the organization, present few problems. Sharing larger or higher resolution images or videos may be covered by existing nonexclusive licenses, dependent of course, on the license language and terms. Probably the most important difference between use on an institutional website and use on social media is that the institution will almost always be granting a license *to the social media service provider*. This is an area where a cultural institution's existing licenses from rights holders or other limitations (e.g., contractual restrictions) on the use of content may prove a barrier to posting on some or all outlets.

Another difference between use on a cultural institution's website and the use of the same or similar content on social media is that social media often has a broader reach and spread, so there is a higher chance that unexpected parties may see and object to the social media use. The notice-and-takedown provisions of the DMCA mean that if a rights holder takes issue with a cultural institution's use, the likeliest outcome is simply that the post will be taken down from the social media site.[77] Remember, even if a post is taken down, it likely does not go away. The internet remembers and users quickly repost or screenshot posts that may later be removed if/when a post is flagged by a DMCA action. However, it is worth noting that the DMCA takedown process limits the liability for the provider of the site, not necessarily for users. Theoretically a rights holder can take separate legal action against a user instead of, or after following, the takedown process.[78]

For particularly problematic social media uses—where the rights holders for a particular image are notoriously litigious, or where questions surround the applicability of fair use or licenses—one option for reducing or limiting risk is to share *links* rather than *copies* of images. For example, if the institution has a license to share the image on its website but not to post on other sites, a social media post with text and a link to the licensed use on the website could be the solution. (Note: Some social media services copy images from websites anytime you share a link. There is not much you can do about that. If you are particularly risk averse, avoid those tools altogether.)

Potential outlets:[79]

- Facebook
- Flickr
- Google+
- Instagram
- Pinterest
- Snapchat
- SoundCloud
- Tumblr
- Twitter
- YouTube
- Vimeo
- WordPress

Social Media Policies and Best Practices

Cultural institutions posting on social media outlets should consider developing a social media policy to govern posts by the institution and by the institution's employees.[80] Often staff representatives from human resources, marketing, and communications will lead the policy development with consultation from legal counsel as well as photography or media staff. While a rights and reproductions specialist may not be the driving staff member to develop and write such a policy, it is advised that they be part of the panel reviewing and providing feedback on a draft version prior to finalization. While a separate social media policy is not necessarily a requirement, it can work in tandem with a cultural institution's other guiding documents, such as an employee handbook, ethics policy, and intellectual property policy. A benefit of a separate social media policy is that it provides staff guidance on how social media is utilized by the cultural institution, as well as how staff members should present themselves online when posting content related to activities at the cultural institution (i.e., behind the scenes, installations, events, exciting news, etc.).

Guidelines cultural institutions should consider when posting on social media outlets include:

- Include full caption and copyright information when possible.[81]
- Provide context and content for the image or video being posted.
- Link back to relevant object, exhibition, publication, event, etc. information on the cultural institution's main website.
- Take note of automatic cropping or resizing when posting to outlets.
  - Add borders or padding to the images in case of automatic cropping occurs to reduce the chance of the work within the image being cropped or resized by the post.

RETAIL AND COMMERCIAL PRODUCTS

For many cultural institutions, it is important that a rights and reproductions specialist work closely with retail development staff to assess pieces in the institution's collection that may still be under copyright and that will need to be cleared prior to the creation of new products for sale. Retail development of commercial products to sell to the public is a unique opportunity for cultural institutions to not only give visitors a memento of their visit, but to create a lasting memory and identification with the brand. Products available for sale can, with effective marketing, strengthen brand identity and leverage the strengths of a cultural institution, its services, building(s), and collection(s).

Central to the development of any products will be an analysis of rights clearances, including the complete caption, credit, and copyright information. Especially for commercial products, the inclusion of complete crediting information is almost always a prerequisite for final approval, and its omission will likely result in the denial of a product development request. Furthermore, rights negotiations will often hinge not only on copyright clearance and caption placement, but also licensing the use of any third-party logos or trademarks associated with a particular artist, manufacturer, or other brand that may be included, or are planned to be included, on the final product. A key difference to many rights negotiations for retail and commercial products versus the uses already outlined are the negotiations and payment structures for royalties paid to the rights holders. Royalties may be the

CASE STUDY

COMMERCIAL PROVISIONS IN A COMMISSION CONTRACT

Anne M. Young

In addition to strengthening the institutional brand, retail products are often developed as targeted support for upcoming exhibitions, new publications, recent acquisitions, and/or commissions. For instance, when Newfields commissions works, the following nonexclusive license language is part of the broader commission contract and includes a provision allowing the institution to create commercial products in association with the commissioned work and its exhibition at Newfields (emphasis added):

> Artist retains copyright in the Work. Artist grants Newfields a nonexclusive license and agrees to permit Newfields to photograph the Work and use the resulting photographic materials without restrictions or royalties paid to Artist by Newfields, for archival, promotional, marketing, website, educational, **commercial, and such other purposes as Newfields determines in perpetuity**. Such photographic materials are the property of Newfields.

While not explicitly required by the language in Newfields' commission contract, to maintain the institution's relationship with the artists it collaborates with, the retail staff sends artists and their rights holder(s) designs of what is proposed for retail development. Once approved, copies of the products are provided to the artists and their rights holders for their records.

only form of fee assessed for licensing the creation of a product, or royalties may be in addition to a licensing fee that is already paid.[82]

Having permission or the rights to create retail or commercial products is only part of the equation for determining whether it is the correct course of action for the institution, especially when dealing with art. Many artists have very clear visions and philosophies about the commercialization of their work. While an institution might have the legal right to do something, countering an artist's stated or implied wish is a decision that must be weighed carefully. It becomes even more problematic when an artist is deceased and cannot be consulted. The cultural institution must act in the best interest of not only themselves but also the artist and their legacy.

When embarking on creating retail or commercial products, it is important to ensure that any product created cannot be mistaken for an original work by the artist. For example, posters of prints or photographs should be of a dramatically different size from the original so as to avoid being passed off by less-than-scrupulous people as originals. Additionally, copyright symbols and credit lines should be clearly visible and not easily removed.

INSTITUTIONAL WEBSITES

Online presentation of a cultural institution's collections offers a twofold opportunity: to feature and interpret objects within an online context and to present the entire collection and its accompanying catalogue data as a whole, providing website visitors with the chance to delve deeply into the institution's holdings. Technology and staff input will be different for these two approaches—the first drawing on curatorial and editorial staff for content and web designers for custom pages, the second depending on collections, photography, and rights and reproductions staff in collaboration with web database programmers. The rights issues are somewhat different as well.

Thumbnail File Sizes and Fair Use

In 2011, responding to a growing need for industry-wide best practices, the Association of Art Museum Directors (AAMD) published their *Policy on the Use of "Thumbnail" Digital Images in Museum Online Initiatives*.[83] This policy asserted that the "use of thumbnail images in the museum's collections image database, promotional materials to identify works in a museum's collection, and online scholarly publications are fair uses under applicable provisions of the United States copyright law."[84] Prior to the release of this policy, many institutions were either paying heavy licensing fees to post collection images online and/or were prevented from posting images online out of fear of potential lawsuits for not formally licensing and paying for such use. This AAMD policy served as a major voice in the field at the time and for the five years it was in existence for the fair use of images and established what many viewed as a "standard" for thumbnail image sizes. For the purposes of the 2011 policy, AAMD defined thumbnails as images smaller than or equal to 250 × 300 pixels.[85] Though institutions must still make their own fair use assessments and risk evaluations before posting any images online at or above AAMD's previous recommended minimum pixel dimensions, this first AAMD fair use policy brought to the fore the necessity of an institutional online presence, of which collection object pages are a growing, née necessary, part.[86]

Website Feature Pages

Special-focus website pages (e.g., an introduction to an upcoming exhibition, a description of a curatorial department, or information on an institutional program) typically include a limited number of images at full size, along with explanatory and/or interpretive text.[87] Institutional blogs, while often more informal, have a similar profile. Image choices may include collection objects, staff snapshots, "comparative" images from other collections or published sources, audio or video clips, and interactive features. As such, rights clearance for website pages has much in common with the image and rights acquisition process and considerations as for a publication.

As discussed previously, a standard nonexclusive license should normally include language that allows for these types of use.[88] If a restriction has been placed on website use by any of the rights holders, then negotiations must ensue if the use is not determined to be a fair use. Permissions and licensing for website uses often come with a limited term in years; if the featured page is going to be maintained long-term, a system needs to be put in place to track these licenses and either renew or revert to a thumbnail image, or establish a fair use justification.

Rights for upcoming and current exhibition pages should ideally be negotiated as part of exhibition and catalogue development, with terms in place for catalogue, website, and publicity use as part of the loan paperwork for incoming works, through licenses for comparative and didactic images, and in the nonexclusive licenses acquired for collection objects.

Collection Pages

Online database access to collections provides unprecedented global reach for cultural institutions. Even the wealthiest museums of the past were unable to make the full extent of their collections accessible via print publications; now it is, if not a given, at least a main goal to have a "Collections" tab with search-and-browse capabilities, object by object and across collection areas. Object pages normally include basic (tombstone) data and, ideally, one or more images. Some museums include additional content, such as extended descriptions, related documents, audiovisual materials, user-generated comments, and keyword tags.

For most cultural institutions, at least some portion of their collections are protected by copyright, so ideally a mechanism is built into the collections pages to reflect each object's rights status. In addition,

ONLINE IMAGE USE SURVEY

Michelle Gallagher Roberts

In December 2014, the *Handbook* contributors conducted an online survey asking volunteers to respond to a series of questions about their cultural institutions' standards and practices related to digital images in online applications, including collection databases and blogs.[1] Respondents were asked to list their institutions' maximum height, width, and resolution for each of the aforementioned uses.

For online collection databases, 67 percent of respondents had an established standard. The median standard was 900 × 1024 pixels (height x width) at 150 ppi. Median was a more revealing metric since there were several extreme outliers on the survey that skewed the averages. For images on blogs, only 31.4 percent of institutions have established standards. The median standard was 850 × 1000 pixels (height x width) at 72 ppi.

In early 2018, a new survey was conducted to gauge the current trends in the field and changes occurring since the original survey.[2] A total of eighty-six respondents answered ten questions related to online image use.

For online collection databases, 54.65 percent of respondents currently have a standard file size. The largest median standard was 1000 × 600 pixels (height × width) at 300 ppi. The smallest median standard was 300 × 300 pixels (height x width) at 72 ppi. The number of respondents that do not have a standard file size for their online collection databases is 27.91 percent. For blogs, only 24.71 percent of respondents have a standard file size. The largest median standard was 1000 × 1000 pixels (height × width) at 300 ppi. The smallest median standard was 475 × 475 pixels (height x width) at 186 ppi.

32.8 percent of respondents have changed their standard files sizes in the last five years. Some of the reasons given were related to technological changes, an increased acceptance of fair use, and a willingness to take greater risks by using larger file sizes, and increased public expectations.

Currently, 48.24 percent of respondents are using an in-house created guideline for online image use. The number of respondents currently using *Guidelines for The Use of Copyrighted Materials and Works of Art By Art Museums* (which replaced the Association of Art Museum Directors' (AAMD) *Policy on the Use of "Thumbnail" Digital Images in Museum Online Initiatives* as a guideline), is 30.59 percent, followed by 29.41 percent of respondents using College Art Associations' *Code of Best Practices in Fair Use for the Visual Arts.* An additional 29.41 percent do not follow a specific guideline.

NOTES

1. See Appendix C: References and Resources, for the complete 2014 survey results.
2. See Appendix C: References and Resources, for the complete 2018 survey results.

images themselves may be protected by copyright, requiring either rights clearance or a statement of the institutional policy on use of images created by staff (or contractors). If this information is incorporated as part of the data retained in the institution's CMS and/or DAMS,[89] the information on collection pages may be automated to reflect the status of each object and image, and to update that status seamlessly when a nonexclusive license is acquired.

Institutions are faced with the still ongoing question of "what size is a thumbnail?" although the former AAMD policy defining thumbnails as 250 × 300 pixels provided a starting point of reference for thumbnail file sizes for institutions just beginning to put their collection images online. These small thumbnails will serve identification purposes adequately, but those institutions that are able (barring an internal risk and liability assessment) to provide larger images on their collection pages—possibly even zoomable—can enhance public access to the collection objects. A decision must also be made whether to allow image downloads and, if so, at what resolution. For many reasons, institutions may choose to limit downloading of some or all of its images, either by providing only lower resolution surrogates or by implementing technologies that limit the downloading of viewable images. It is worth noting that many users may be able to circumvent technologies that limit downloading of viewable images, so these technological restrictions should not be relied upon for total control, and care should be taken to avoid promising absolute control and download restrictions to third parties. Similarly, if high-resolution images are made available online for download, the institution will need to assess what it considers "high resolution" and whether the downloadable files are JPEG or TIFF format. Once again, acquiring nonexclusive licenses for collection objects that are protected by copyright becomes a highly desirable part of the workflow. It is wise to avoid citing specific image standards in the license; changing web design standards, improved web technology, connection speeds, and user demand for higher-resolution images have caused image standards to continue to evolve and become larger in recent years.

CASE STUDY

RETHINKING INSTITUTIONAL COLLECTION PAGES

Anne M. Young

In 2014, the Indianapolis Museum of Art at Newfields redesigned its online collection pages, which included a concerted effort to focus on the numerous images of the works in the collection.[1] The initial landing page places imagery foremost to the visitor, providing a minimalistic design and highlighting a rotating selection of images from the collection that are either in the public domain or have a completed nonexclusive licensing agreement on file for copyrighted works.

Once visitors enter a search term—artist, title, accession number, etc.—they are directed to the object page that places the imagery at the top of the page. The primary image is designated within Newfields' DAMS and below the primary image are secondary views (if available) of the object, which may include verso, side, or various season and time-of-day shots (for outdoor works). Further emphasizing the images is the ability for almost all of those presented in the online collection pages to be enlarged using the zooming tools on the right side of the screen. From the images, the visitor scrolls down the page to find related media (if available) and then the object information, which includes copyright information, if known and recorded in the CMS.

To make images the central focus of the collection pages, an in-depth review of the rights information recorded within the CMS was necessary. This included developing an efficient way to quickly attach rights records for "low hanging fruit" of works that were easily identified as either public domain or having no known rights holder. Once a series of export and import templates were developed, more than forty-four thousand rights records with one of these two designations were added to the object records within the catalogue module of the CMS within less than two months.

The rights and reproductions department worked first to identify subgroups of the collection, such as European and American art before 1800, which could be easily exported as a single group and have a public domain record attached to all the records without having to complete an object-by-object review for date of creation, artist life dates, etc. Similarly, a review of works identified only as being created in mid-twentieth century, but without a known creator identified or specific date were labeled as orphan works—where researchers assumed copyright existed, but could not identify a rights holder—and designated as "no known rights holder." The more time-consuming review was the analysis of subgroups that span both public domain and copyright works. This required a careful review of all works to assess their rights status and, if under copyright with a known rights holder, to record that information as a separate rights record from public domain or no known rights holder.

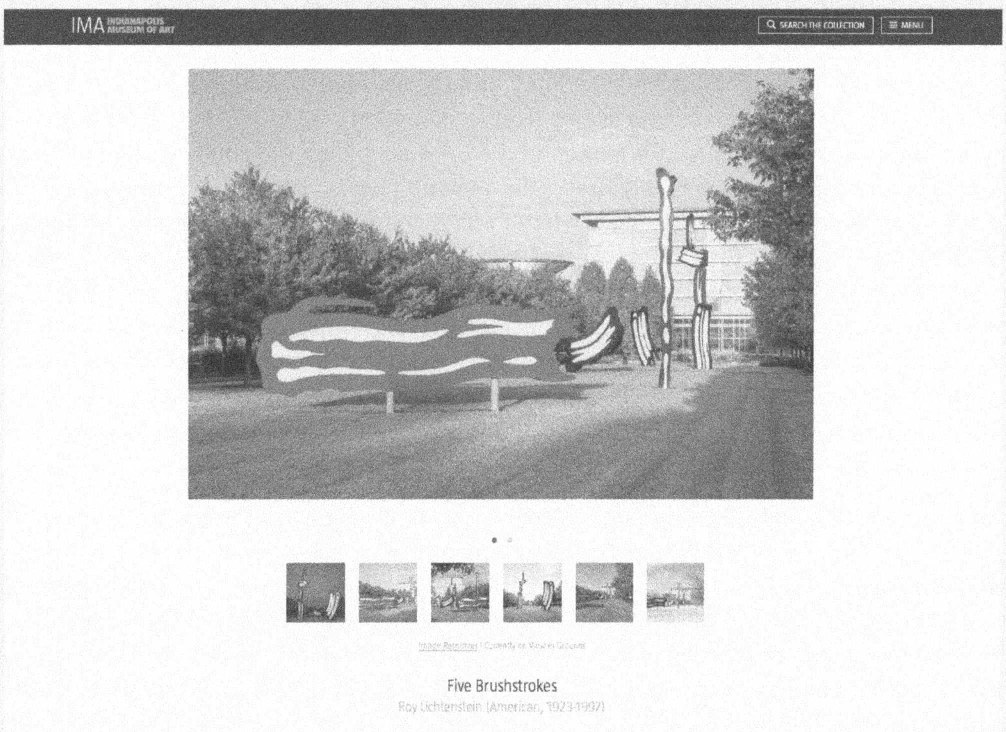

FIGURE 4.3
The online collection page for Roy Lichtenstein's *Five Brushstrokes*, illustrating the zoom capabilities of the new design.

Parallel to the addition of rights information to the CMS was the determination of what information and image file sizes would be available online. Eventually, it was determined that all images would allow zooming with the exception of works by artists whose rights are managed by ARS and VAGA, which would have thumbnail images no larger than 600 pixels on the long side. In addition to restricting the zooming feature for ARS and VAGA works, right click is disabled to reduce easy download of the image; when the visitor clicks on the image, a copyright notice box appears. The redesign was an opportunity to communicate copyright to visitors by adding language that explains why the image is not available at a larger size and include links back to ARS, VAGA, and the Image Resources section of Newfields' website.

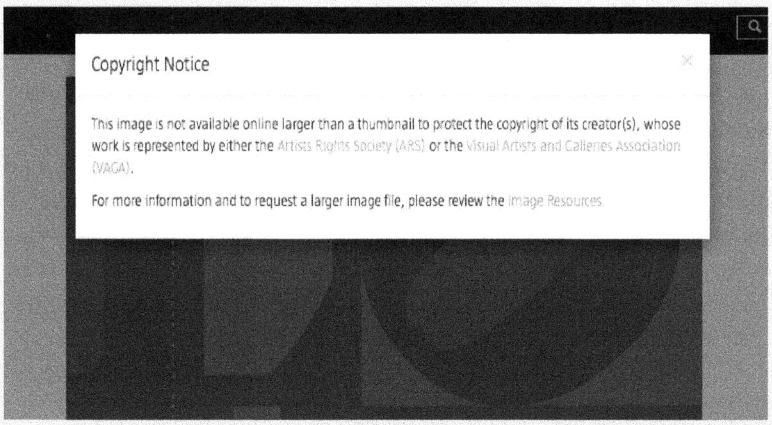

FIGURE 4.4
The Copyright Notice box that now appears over ARS- and VAGA-represented works when a visitor clicks on the image.

Finally, the collection page redesign was the impetus to move forward with offering direct download of Open Access (OA) public domain image files. The combination of a DAMS with improved image file naming and more complete rights information in the CMS simplified the ability to identify public domain works with publication-quality, high-resolution image files available. This combination of information then pushes to the collection pages where high-resolution JPEG files are available for instant download; an arrow appears on the right side of the screen beneath the zooming tools to indicate the works with OA download available. Newfields simply requires the downloader to select the type of use: personal, scholarly, or commercial. If personal is selected, no further information is captured and the file is immediately available to download. For scholarly and commercial uses, Newfields requires that a short form be completed before the download is enabled. This is not to deny or approve a use, but rather to capture information about where and how images of works are reproduced. Once the form is completed, the image file can be downloaded.

While this iteration of Newfields' online collection pages is relatively recent, technology is ever-changing. As of 2018, Newfields was undertaking a review of its collection pages to reconsider them for the future as part of an overall research and discovery portal for online visitors to learn about not only individual objects, but to include cross-reference to bibliographic data, archival information, past exhibition histories, provenance, conservation, and more. A review of the current OA practices and how those can be improved and expanded will be part of the new collection pages when they are launched in the future.

NOTE

1. "Collections," Newfields, accessed March 23, 2018, https://discovernewfields.org/collections.

CONCLUSION

This chapter touches on only a few of the most common institutional uses of rights-protected materials. Future advances in technology, such as virtual reality and augmented reality, will inevitably create new and exciting ways for cultural institutions to share and distribute their collections. Image display standards and practices are also certain to change over time. No matter what shape and format these new uses take, rights and reproductions specialists can rely on the principles and processes described in this chapter to obtain any necessary permission(s). Before using rights-protected materials, always analyze the IP issues, consider whether fair use applies, request and negotiate necessary rights, document the permissions, and provide attribution when using the materials. Through diligent and consistent practice, the rights and reproductions specialist plays an important role by protecting the institution from copyright infringement or breach-of-contract claims, as well as the potential damage to reputation that may result from claims.

NOTES

1. See chapter 3: Rights Issues for the Collections, for a more detailed discussion of identifying the various IP issues related to collections.

2. "Materials" as discussed in this chapter broadly means a wide variety of content used by cultural institutions, although the examples within focus on images of collection objects. Materials may be created by the cultural institution or provided by external sources. In addition to images of collection objects, they commonly include photographs of an institution's buildings or site; photographs or audio/video recordings of visitors, staff, or performers; music; film; text; and so on.

3. 17 U.S.C. § 102.

4. 17 U.S.C. § 103. See chapter 1, What Makes a Work "Original"?, for more information about the *Bridgeman Art Library v. Corel Corp.* 1999 case.

5. See, for example, Ind. Code § 32-36-1-7 (2015); Cal. Civ. Code § 3344.

6. See generally 15 U.S.C. § § 1051 et seq. For example, The Children's Museum of Indianapolis encounters licensing the use of popular toy manufacturer names and products lines for its traveling exhibitions, like "Hot Wheels™: Race to Win™" for which the marketing materials all include some combination of the following symbols: TM, ®, and/or this statement: "Hot Wheels and associated trademarks are owned and used under license from Mattel, Inc. © 2015 Mattel, Inc. All Rights Reserved." "Book a Traveling Exhibit," The Children's Museum of Indianapolis, accessed March 23, 2018, https://www.childrensmuseum.org/about/traveling-exhibits.

7. These additional considerations may include donor restrictions in deeds of gift, rights of indigenous peoples, sensitive or graphic content, or conservation considerations. See chapter 3: Rights Issues for the Collections, for a more detailed discussion.

8. 7 U.S.C. § 102.

9. Written permissions, on paper or in email, are strongly suggested, but in cases where only verbal permission is possible, be sure to document the conversation in writing for the institution's project or rights files. If a verbal license is all that can be obtained, it is at least *something* (possibly for low-risk uses). It is highly recommended to document the verbal license in a contemporaneous written record (paper or email) in case the institution has to prove that the license existed (in addition to its scope, term, etc.). In many cases institutions might rely on more informal documentation of permissions, including confirmations through email exchanges. With any form of permission documentation, it is a question of risk management and guidance by legal counsel. This may also affect relations with external contractors. For example, a contractor working on a project (an author using images or a producer using material in a documentary) relying on the institution to clear rights may be used to more formal documentation and may (justifiably) insist on indemnification if the cultural institution clearing the rights is relying on more informal communications.

10. See chapter 3, Nonexclusive Licensing Agreements, for a more detailed discussion.

11. Before sending out a request, check to see if an online form is available from the institutions that hold the work(s) in their collections; this may be a required part of the process, since it allows rights and reproductions specialists to gather all necessary information in one step.

12. See Appendix B: Document and Contract Templates for sample request letters.

13. When drafting such a document, though, keep in mind that "scope creep" is a very real phenomenon. Make sure that any possible use within the context of the project is included in the text.

14. Some common examples include image size restrictions, supplying free copies of the materials in which the work is reproduced, limitations on how long the work may be used, etc.

15. See chapter 3, Best Practices for Recording and Sharing Rights Information, for a more detailed discussion.

16. See chapter 1, Privacy and Publicity, and chapter 3, Privacy Rights and the Collection and Publicity Rights and the Collection, for more detailed discussions. Analysis of the type of use is critical in assessing risk and the need to seek permission. Not every use of a person's image will infringe on privacy or publicity rights.

17. See Appendix B: Document and Contract Templates for sample release forms and request letters.

18. 17 U.S.C. § 102.

19. 17 U.S.C. § 107.

20. Again, keep in mind "scope creep" and make sure to include all potential uses of the work. Some lenders may prefer to handle uses on a case-by-case basis, but many others will grant broad noncommercial rights (educational, publicity, or archival) for uses related to the exhibition loan up front.

21. AAM members might wish to reference "Learning Music Licensing" by Elizabeth T. Russell and the "Information Center Fact Sheet: Museum Licensing for Museums."

22. "Music Users," ASCAP, accessed March 23, 2018, https://www.ascap.com/music-users. ASCAP is the American Society of Composers, Authors and Publishers. 17 U.S.C. § 107.

23. "Music Users," BMI, accessed March 23, 2018, https://www.bmi.com/licensing. BMI is Broadcast Music, Inc. 17 U.S.C. § 107.

24. "Obtain a SESAC License," SESAC, accessed March 23, 2018, https://www.sesac.com/Licensing/obtainlicense.aspx . 17 U.S.C. § 107.

25. For instance, cultural institutions might utilize sites like AudioJungle or Stockmusic.net that provide minimally priced licenses for individual tracks. While neither offers free music, AudioJungle does have two license options: $5 per song for limited use and $40 per song for unlimited use. Stockmusic.net offers a single "media producer license" for $39.95, which is very similar to the unlimited use license from AudioJungle. AudioJungle, accessed March 23, 2018, https://audiojungle.net/. Stockmusic.net, accessed March 23, 2018, http://www.stockmusic.net/.

26. See chapter 1, Fair Use, and chapter 7, Fair Use Codes, Guidelines, and Statements for a more detailed discussion.

27. 17 U.S.C. § 504(c)(2)(ii). See chapter 1: What is Intellectual Property?, for a more detailed discussion.

28. Since images form the bulk of rights and reproductions requests, that term will be used in this section to represent all materials types, except in cases where specific information about other media is relevant.

29. Image researchers often deal with requests from a wide variety of authors with varied skills and experience in this area, so a clear guide to the background information needed to acquire images smoothly can be a useful tool. When images were originally found in publications, a copy of the title page, image page, and credits page will save effort. A link to online images is a must.

30. Peter B. Hirtle, "Copyright Term and the Public Domain in the United States," Copyright Information Center, last modified January 1, 2018, https://copyright.cornell.edu/publicdomain.

31. Many image sources have an online form with prompts for the relevant data, another way to avoid extra steps in the request process.

32. See, for example, "Rights and Reproductions," Chicago History Museum, accessed March 23, 2018, https://www.chicagohistory.org/rights-reproductions/.

33. See, for example, "NGA Images," National Gallery of Art, accessed March 23, 2018, https://images.nga.gov/en/page/show_home_page.html; "Digital Collections," Yale University Library, accessed March 23, 2018, http://web.library.yale.

edu/digital-collections; "Image Resources," Newfields, accessed March 23, 2018, https://discovernewfields.org/research/image-resources; "Open Content Program," The Getty, accessed March 23, 2018, http://www.getty.edu/about/whatwedo/opencontent.html; and "Search the Collection," Los Angeles County Museum of Art, accessed March 23, 2018, https://collections.lacma.org/.

34. See chapter 7, What Open Access Makes Possible, for a more detailed discussion about institutions with Open Access.

35. See chapter 3, Freelance Photography of the Collection, for a more detailed discussion.

36. This list is not meant to be all inclusive; for a more comprehensive overview see Appendix C: References and Resources.

37. "Artstor Digital Library," Artstor, accessed March 22, 2018, http://www.artstor.org/content/artstor-digital-library-features-benefits

38. "Artstor Digital Library: Features & Benefits," Artstor, accessed March 22, 2018, http://www.artstor.org/content/artstor-digital-library-features-benefits.

39. Ibid.

40. See chapter 5, Images for Academic Publishing, for a more detailed discussion. "Initiatives: Images for Academic Publishing (IAP)," Artstor, accessed March 5, 2018, http://www.artstor.org/content/collaborations.

41. Ibid.

42. Wikimedia Commons, accessed March 22, 2018, https://commons.wikimedia.org/wiki/Main_Page.

43. "Commons: Welcome," Wikimedia Commons, accessed March 22, 2018, http://commons.wikimedia.org/wiki/Commons:Welcome.

44. "Commons: WikiProject Museums," Wikimedia Commons, accessed April 5, 2015, https://commons.wikimedia.org/wiki/Commons:WikiProject_Museums.

45. See, for example, the Brooklyn Museum's contributions: "Category: Media Contributed by the Brooklyn Museum," Wikimedia Commons, accessed March 23, 2018, https://commons.wikimedia.org/wiki/Category:Media_contributed_by_the_Brooklyn_Museum.

46. See chapter 7: Case Study: The MET, Creative Commons, and Wikipedia, for a more detailed discussion about museum contributions to Wikimedia Commons.

47. Flickr, accessed March 22, 2018, https://www.flickr.com/.

48. "The Commons," Flickr, accessed March 22, 2018, https://www.flickr.com/commons/.

49. See chapter 5, Flickr, for a more detailed discussion. "The Library of Congress," Flickr, accessed March 22, 2018, https://www.flickr.com/photos/library_of_congress/.

50. That useful status was coined by the Library of Congress and was very quickly adopted in the cultural heritage community, beyond Flickr Commons. "Copyright and Other Restrictions That Apply to Publication/Distribution of Images: Assessing the Risk of Using a P&P Image," The Library of Congress: Prints & Photographs Reading Room, accessed March 22, 2018, http://www.loc.gov/rr/print/195_copr.html#noknown.

51. This list is not meant to be all inclusive; for a more comprehensive overview, see Appendix C: References and Resources.

52. Alinari, accessed March 23, 2018, https://www.alinari.it/.

53. Art Resource, accessed March 23, 2018, http://www.artres.com/.

54. Bridgeman Images, accessed March 23, 2018, http://www.bridgemanimages.com/en-US/.

55. Davis, accessed March 23, 2018, https://www.davisart.com/.

56. Granger Historical Picture Archive, accessed March 23, 2018, https://www.granger.com/.

57. Scholars Resource, accessed March 23, 2018, https://www.scholarsresource.com/.

58. AP Images, accessed March 23, 2018, http://www.apimages.com/.

59. Getty Images, accessed March 23, 2018, https://www.gettyimages.com/.

60. iStock by Getty Images, accessed March 23, 2018, https://www.istockphoto.com/.

61. Masterfile, accessed March 23, 2018, https://www.masterfile.com/.

62. Science Photo Library, accessed March 23, 2018, http://www.sciencephoto.com/

63. Shutterstock, accessed March 23, 2018, https://www.shutterstock.com/home.

64. Superstock, accessed March 23, 2018, https://www.superstock.com/.

65. T3 Media, accessed March 23, 2018, http://dev.t3media.com/.

66. CineMaterial, accessed March 23, 2018, https://www.cinematerial.com/.

67. MovieStillsDB, accessed March 23, 2018, https://www.moviestillsdb.com/.

68. Photofest Digital, accessed March 23, 2018, http://www.photofestnyc.com/index.html.

69. See chapter 1, Visual Artists Rights Act, for a more detailed discussion.

70. Specifically "works of visual art" as defined in 17 U.S.C. § 101.

71. 17 U.S.C. § 106A.

72. For example, there have been several cases affirming a right under trademark law for an artist to not have unapproved versions of their work credited to them and/or to not have their work credited to someone else. See, for example, *Gilliam, et al., v. American Broadcasting Companies, Inc.*, 538 F.2d 14 (2d Cir 1976); *Dastar Corp. v. Twentieth Century Fox Film Corp.*, 539 U.S. 23 (2003).

73. The image review process can be subjective in many ways to identify a "good" file but using size guidelines in addition to assessing the overall image quality can aid in making the determination. Another consideration for printed publications is acquiring a TIFF over a JPEG file. A JPEG is a compressed file with limited color reproduction capabilities.

74. 17 U.S.C. § 107.

75. See chapter 1, Privacy and Publicity, for a more detailed discussion.

76. For discussion on this, see Allison S. Brehm and Cathy D. Lee, "Click Here to Accept the Terms of Service," *Communications Lawyer* 31 (2015).

77. See generally 17 U.S.C. § 512.

78. 17 U.S.C. § 512(b)(1).

79. Outlets as of March 2018.

80. See Appendix B: Document and Contract Templates for sample social media policies and guidelines.

81. To accommodate restrictions in different outlets, a reduced or partial caption may need to be used. Additionally, caption and copyright information may be embedded in a bar at the bottom of the image file or through detailed metadata attached to the file. In some cases, cultural institutions may also use a second post or tweet as the means of conveying the relevant credit or copyright information or link the image back to the institution's website where full caption and credit information is present.

82. Royalties may be calculated either way according to institutional and/or rights holder preference; some may prefer to pay an up-front royalty calculated on retail price multiplied by quantity to be produced, as opposed to a royalty based on actual sales.

83. In 2016, AAMD revoked the *Policy on the Use of "Thumbnail" Digital Images in Museum Online Initiatives* due to evolutions in technology that made this policy obsolete and necessitated more nuanced guidelines. In response, AAMD released their *Guidelines for the Use of Copyrighted Materials and Works of Art by Art Museums.* See chapter 7, Fair Use Codes, Guidelines, and Statements, for a more detailed discussion of these Guidelines.

84. Association of Art Museum Directors, *AAMD Policy on the Use of "Thumbnail" Digital Images in Museum Online Initiatives* (New York, 2011), 4.

85. Ibid., 3.

86. See chapter 7, Fair Use Codes, Guidelines, and Statements, for a detailed discussion of AAMD's most recent fair use guidelines.

87. See, for example, Thomas Hart Benton's feature at the Metropolitan Museum of Art, "MetCollects," The Metropolitan Museum of Art, accessed March 23, 2018, https://www.metmuseum.org/art/online-features/metcollects/benton-murals; the "Killer Heels" exhibition at the Brooklyn Museum, "Exhibitions: Killer Heels: The Art of the High-Heeled Shoe," Brooklyn Museum, accessed March 23, 2018, https://www.brooklynmuseum.org/exhibitions/heels/; and the Photography Collection at the MFA Boston, "Photography," Museum of Fine Arts Boston, accessed March 23, 2018, http://www.mfa.org/collections/photography.

88. See chapter 3, Nonexclusive Licensing Agreements, for a more detailed discussion.

89. See chapter 3, Best Practices for Recording and Sharing Rights Information, for a more detailed discussion.

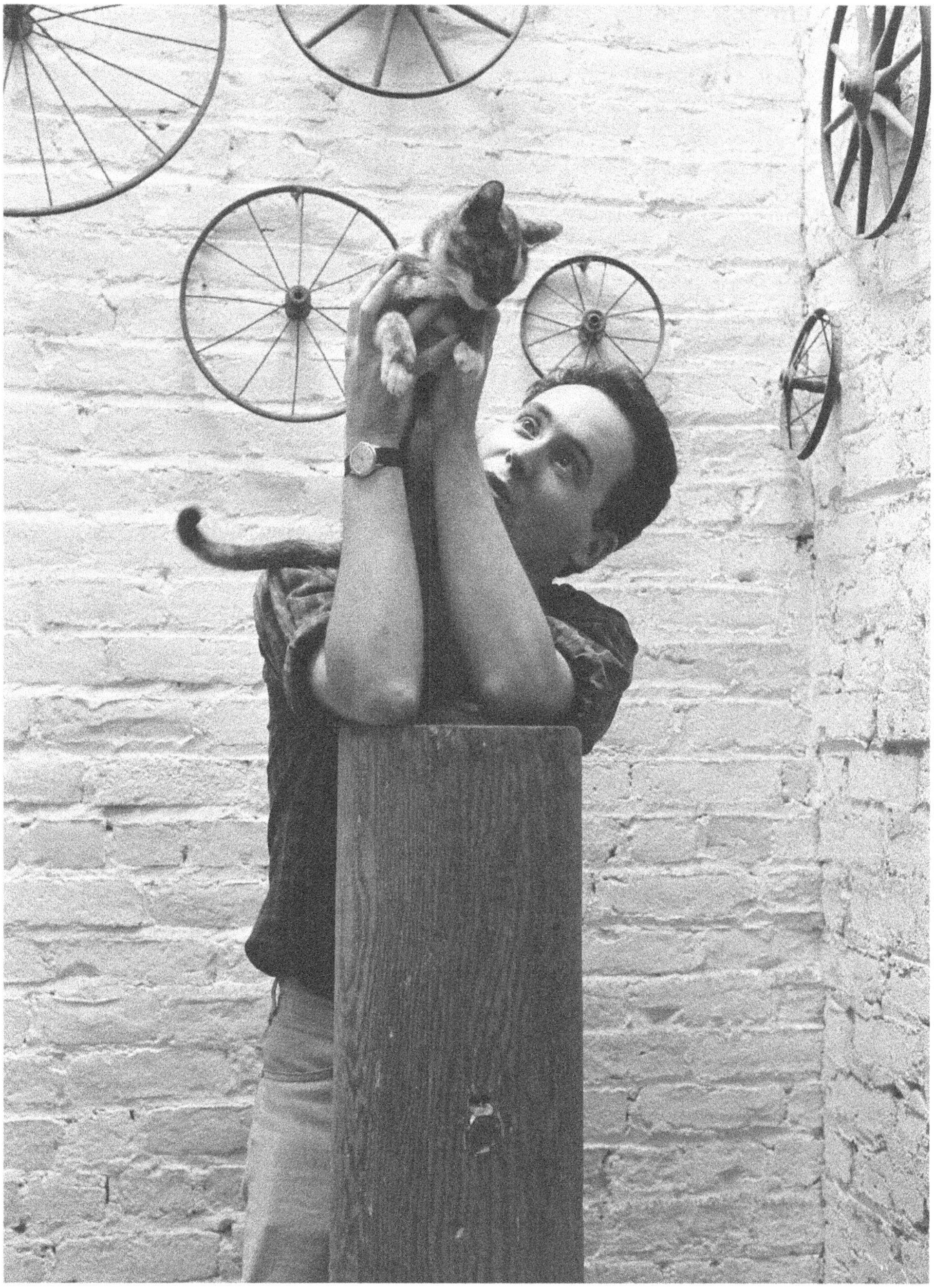

5

Leveraging Content with Distribution Partners

JOHN FFRENCH, MELISSA LEVINE, NANCY SIMS, DEBORAH WYTHE, AND ANNE M. YOUNG

Once cultural institutions have established practices for institutional uses of content, it is time to explore external possibilities. While cultural institution websites often serve as a primary mechanism for delivering information and images about collections objects and related content, there are times when it is advantageous to partner with external organizations to increase community outreach and to enable a greater number of users to discover the available content. Whether for broader collection visibility for scholarly purposes or as a means of generating revenue, there are a multitude of distribution partners[1] available that each offer different opportunities. Often, cultural institutions will find that working with more than one partner will fill a multitude of institutional needs for exposure to different audiences and end goals (e.g., open scholarship, increased access to data, or possible revenue generation), but it requires a careful review of institutional priorities, risk, and liability to determine which partners to work with and how much content to share. It is inadvisable, and possibly irresponsible, for institutions to rely on distribution partners to perform core mission activities.[2] A good relationship with a distribution partner should expand the institutional audience, reach, and impact and not serve as a replacement for interactions with the institution itself.

Cultural institutions would like to think that they know their audiences the best, including what they are looking for and whether they know where to find it, but this is not always the case. Researchers and casual visitors may be simply looking for works by a particular author or artist, within a genre, or for a particular subject in a general internet search. In these cases, third parties may help to fulfill researcher needs more efficiently or be able to point them back to the institution's website. While some distribution partners require a fee for cultural institutions to participate in their services, or charge the end user a licensing fee for individual uses, many are simply interested in aggregating content (for which it is not uncommon to charge the end user a licensing or subscription fee for access to the content, which in turn supports the business model rather than returning directly to the institution that contributed the content).

This chapter outlines several of the more common distribution partners a cultural institution may want to consider partnering with to leverage content related to collection media, be it images, videos, books, archival materials, or data.[3] Cultural institutions' relationships with distribution partners may be motivated by the desire to generate revenue or expand noncommercial purposes. When investigating potential partners to work with, it is important to fully understand what the working relationship covers and whether the agreement will be exclusive or nonexclusive, the latter of which is the preferred option in nearly every case, as it will not limit the institution from partnering with multiple external distributors.

CONSIDERING DISTRIBUTION PARTNERS

The first question a cultural institution must ask itself is quite simply, Why do this? The answer is twofold: support of its mission and potential revenue generation. By sharing collection media, cultural institutions foster the exploration of cultural heritage and promote the interests of their collections by furthering awareness and research.[4] For some cultural institutions, it can also be a source of revenue. It is important for institutions to balance these interests when determining where to distribute media and if, when, and how they will receive revenue.

Key considerations:

- The distribution partner should enable the cultural institution to further its mission, either directly or indirectly.
- The partnership should not be contrary to the ethics policy of the cultural institution.
- The partnership should not compromise the reputation of the cultural institution and, in appropriate cases, should enhance it.
- The partnership should produce sufficient benefit for the cultural institution within its strategic objectives, and it should not be a detriment to the wider public interest for/of the collection.
- The benefits of any working agreement must outweigh any risk of disadvantage for the cultural institution through an association with the third party.

Consider whether the distribution partner supports the cultural institution as the authoritative and primary resource for content about its collections.

Furthermore, cultural institutions must carefully assess the risk and liability of contributing content through third-party distributors. Any decision made or partnership entered into should be in line with the broader institutional stance for the risk and liability it would assume for the presentation of any of the same content on its own website or other internal uses. Central to this assessment is the identification of the staff member(s) with the authority to make the decision to share content externally and therefore bind the institution to the agreement(s) with third-party distribution partners or agree to the distributors' terms of service/terms of use on behalf of the institution.[5] Institutions should also take careful note of which party is responsible for completing the rights clearance for the content presented on the third-party site. While some agreements assign responsibility for rights clearance to the distribution partner, other agreements require the contributing cultural institution to perform rights clearance prior to contributing content.[6]

Finally, cultural institutions should carefully review the process for physically delivering the content and its related metadata to the distribution partners. Providing content to multiple third parties should be a seamless experience for the cultural institution, completed through either the utilization of a cultural institution's or distribution partner's API,[7] FTP delivery, or the exchange of physical external hard drives. Ideally, files can be exported and formatted once from an institution's CMS and/or DAMS and provided to multiple partners with minimal, if any, changes. If distribution does not occur through an API, thought should be given to if the data should be reviewed and updated on some periodic basis. Over time, rights status or attribution may change. These changes may be important to end users.

POTENTIAL DISTRIBUTION PARTNERS (NONREVENUE GENERATING)[8]

Artstor

Artstor Digital Library

The Artstor Digital Library[9] is a nonprofit resource that makes available to nonprofit subscribers more than two million digital images, videos, and QTVRs in the arts, architecture, humanities, and sciences for noncommercial, educational, and scholarly uses. Artstor, the nonprofit corporation that makes available the Artstor Digital Library, was created by the Andrew W. Mellon Foundation in 2002 in response to the need of higher education institutions to access high-quality digital images for teaching and education,

CASE STUDY

THE IMPORTANCE OF PARTNERING WITH THIRD-PARTY DISTRIBUTORS

Anne M. Young in conversation with James Shulman, former president of Artstor, and Christine Kuan, former chief curator of Artsy, in 2015.

Anne Young (AY): Why is it important for cultural institutions (museums, libraries, archives, etc.) to provide content (image, video, and audio files) to external distributors?

James Shulman (JS): Institutions that want their collections to be better known, studied, and understood can do so by reaching people where they are. Digital distribution makes it possible for an institution to use various channels to carry out different parts of their mission.

Christine Kuan (CK): The central purpose of cultural institutions is to preserve cultural objects and to educate the public about history and culture through their collections, exhibitions, and programs. The internet today is one of the most powerful mediums, second only to the onsite visitor experience and engagement with the authentic objects, for accomplishing the missions of cultural institutions. In 2015, the Musée du Louvre is projected to reach twelve million visitors, and museums around the world are enjoying unprecedented visitor numbers. The increasing ability for the public to access rich information about cultural heritage online is critical to people feeling excited about visiting museums, seeing the original objects, learning about them, and developing a long-term relationship with museums and culture that will be instrumental to the future preservation of those cultural objects.

AY: Why should cultural institutions contribute to different external distributors?

JS: Distributing through different channels reaches different audiences. Lending institutional *imprimatur* is an act that reflects back on the contributor, so generally it makes sense to support distributors with which the contributor shares an affinity of missions. As we all know, these missions are complex and multifaceted, so having a range of ways of promoting the collection can align with various needs of the institution.

CK: Simply placing images of exhibitions and collections on a single institutional website (or single online outlet) fails to take advantage of the nature of the internet, which is designed for the sharing and easy distribution and discovery of content. Distributing high-quality information about cultural objects over multiple channels is one of the important ways to achieve widespread public understanding of cultural objects and our global heritage, and therefore can lead to the long-term protection of cultural objects by integrating these objects into the fabric of popular culture (along with music, fashion, film, etc.) and inviting future generations to engage with and care about cultural institutions and their collections.

AY: What do you view as the differences, advantages, and/or disadvantages of providing content to different distributors (i.e., differences between Artstor, Artsy, Bridgeman, and the Google Cultural Institute)?

JS: Artstor allows contributors to reach and serve an educational audience. The content is going to be used by teachers, students, and scholars—a very focused and contained universe of users. This environment enables the distribution of very large image files and images of works under copyright for very particular purposes. Promoting a museum or artist's collections through this channel helps to support knowledge of collections and legacies in an important community. Different degrees of distribution can and should be enabled to serve contributors' needs. For this reason, Artstor works with cultural heritage institutions in a range of ways—to make available high-quality images free of charge for scholarly publication through its

Images for Academic Publishing (IAP) program, and helps museums and other institutions make content freely available through the Digital Public Library of America (DPLA).

CK: Each of these commercial and noncommercial platforms and services has different objectives: some are to serve strictly educational purposes, some are to provide licensing services, some reach the public, and some, like Artsy, are a hybrid platform serving both commercial and noncommercial needs for the art community. The main advantages of utilizing these platforms are to augment the impact and reach of the institution (and in some cases generate revenue through licensing images, for example). In most cases, institutions that have digitized their collections for licensing purposes can easily deploy those images and metadata to other outlets like Artstor, Google Cultural Institute, Artsy, and more, without creating additional work for the staff, but exponentially increasing the reach and impact of those digital assets and of the museum. One issue that has delayed or prevented many museums from widely sharing their digital collections is the fear of losing out on image licensing revenue. I think the larger question is whether a focus on licensing revenue might be costing the museum in other ways—less brand recognition, less public visibility, less educational impact, fewer onsite visitors, fewer scholarly publications (e.g., scholars may choose images that are more easily accessible or free), and less engagement with people who do not have physical access to art museums, art libraries, and other resources besides the web.

AY: What direction do you see image licensing and distribution moving in the future?

JS: Approaches to distribution may well become more unbundled for individual institutions—a museum may well want to make some content completely open and free and widely used. Other content they might want to (or need to) constrain with licenses. As tools and the use of data standards enable easier flows, institutions should not have to work as hard as they do today to get into different channels. For Artstor, aggregating deep and high-quality pools of content to help educational users will continue to be important, but so will our work on asset management tools and data standards that help institutions let content flow where it wants to flow.

CK: Image access, licensing, and distribution will become increasingly varied, and there will be thousands of channels for users to access the content they need for both commercial and noncommercial purposes.

AY: What role does Open Access play in in this move? Or does it?

JS: Content that can be made openly available should be promoted widely. The web is getting pretty noisy, and getting open content into places where people can find and appreciate it will be a priority in the coming years. Artstor does not believe in a "one-size-fits-all" model of aggregation, and seeks to harmonize with and support the distribution desires of the content contributor. By serving as a Digital Public Library of America (DPLA) hub, Artstor is able make open content more widely discoverable.

CK: While many major museums and institutions have adopted Open Access policies (such as The J. Paul Getty Trust, National Gallery of Art, Yale University, Rijksmuseum, etc.), most museums have not. Many of us working in cultural heritage have hoped that many more museums would adopt Open Access policies, but in reality, the change has been slow to take hold. However, the public and the internet have already made these institutional policy decisions about access somewhat obsolete in the sense that practically everyone visiting a museum today has a phone with a camera that takes decent pictures. And regardless of whether visitors are permitted to or not, they are taking photos of cultural objects and posting them to the web. So in essence, museums that are not actively distributing their high-quality authoritative data through the open web are ceding the creation and distribution of their collections and exhibitions to their visitors. Eventually, I think most museums will want to play a proactive role in disseminating their high-quality information on the web and enabling the public to look to them for providing that service and that knowledge. Ultimately, it is in the long-term interest of the museum to be the primary, most accessible, and free public resource for images and information about their own collections.

AY: Why does the existing ("old") model of image licensing need to change? Or does it?

JS: Elements of the "old" model that cost museums more money to manage than they produce in net revenue are difficult to justify. And participating in networked access can help overcome perceptions of "hoarding" that some communities feel toward collecting institutions, and support those institutions in better achieving their missions. Museums also can benefit from recognizing that not all content has to be shared in the same way, and museums know best the delicate balance of interested constituencies as they evolve their policies in a digital age.

CK: Image licensing was created to facilitate the creation of print publications and is now out of sync with contemporary publishing needs. Today, nearly all art publishing is in worldwide distribution, in color, and should be eventually available online (even if it is initially only slated for print publication). The concept of licensing images according to number of "copies," size on the page, cover image versus interior image, or black-and-white versus color, is simply absurd on the web, where in order for a post to be "successful" it needs to be "reposted" hundreds, if not thousands, of times and digital images are already higher quality than what can possibly be achieved in a print publication. Image licensing models should change if cultural institutions (and artists) want scholarly publishing in print and online to thrive. Licensing models have little impact on public behavior and only impact scholars, curators, and institutions who are working within a network of relationships and must abide by those licensing rules.

AY: Should cultural institutions still be "gatekeepers" of images?

JS: As a practical matter, cultural institutions continue to act as "gatekeepers" of images in their collections, and serve important missions and public interests in doing so, both broadening access to images and promoting useful, accurate information for education and scholarship (such as accurate color information and provenance details). Their roles are clearly evolving, but they continue to be very important.

CK: Cultural institutions should be the primary resource for authoritative, high-quality images and information about their collections. Rather than thinking of institutions as "gatekeepers," institutions should be seen as resources of culture for the public. Institutions are sources of knowledge about their collections; therefore, institutions should be the most accessible providers of that knowledge.

AY: What does this mean in the digital and online world?

JS: The "gatekeepers" can support research and education with respect to images of works in their care by promoting appropriate levels of access to these images as well as offering high-quality data (such as accurate color renderings and metadata reflecting the most current scholarship on a work). In the absence of this facilitation of online access, users will find a great deal of images and information regarding particular works online, but much of it can be misleading.

CK: It has been demonstrated across various arts industries that "gatekeeping" in the digital realm is nearly impossible, and only through legal action can one control the distribution of content. In most cases, for digital images, the cost of pursuing legal action would exceed the amount of money one would recoup.

AY: How does providing content to external distributors further engage visitors and viewers both onsite and offsite? Or does it?

JS: The best thing that a digital surrogate can do is to awaken interest in the object. Digital images can teach people about collections and create new interest in art and cultures—and in doing so enhance all of our collective visual vocabularies. In the end, if we have more people who know about and care about our collective cultural heritage, many good effects will follow.

CK: We have seen many museums and cultural institutions thrive as a result of greater online visibility. The Van Gogh Museum did a study many years ago that showed by providing rich information about the exhibition online visitors spent much longer in the physical exhibition than visitors who had not read about the exhibition online beforehand. Similarly, we are seeing huge numbers of museum visitors to art museums whose collections and exhibitions are widely accessible on the web. In contrast, many museums that make very little of their collection and few of their exhibitions accessible on the web have little visitor number growth. In short, I think museums have yet to fully harness the power of the internet to their advantage. I think a willingness to experiment with new platforms and new ideas will be key to museums figuring out how to best deploy their incredible holdings to serve their missions and the public.

at a time when digital files began to take precedence over traditional slide libraries.[10] Artstor was founded with the mission "to use digital technology to enhance scholarship, teaching, and learning in the arts and associated fields."[11] Since creating the Artstor Digital Library, Artstor has developed various other services to allow institutions to more broadly share their content, such as Shared Shelf Commons[12] and Open Artstor,[13] which are discussed separately in this chapter. In 2016, Artstor and ITHAKA announced an alliance between the two organizations that brought Artstor under the ITHAKA umbrella to bring together their "complementary efforts: Artstor has supported the visual, where JSTOR has emphasized textual materials. Artstor has supported teaching and learning primarily, while JSTOR has been an indispensable part of research."[14]

Cultural institutions, artists, and scholars can provide Artstor with images, videos, and related metadata of their collections to be made available through the digital library free of charge.[15] The Artstor Digital Library currently makes available content from almost three hundred "of the world's leading museums, photo archives, scholars and artists."[16] Content made available through the Artstor Digital Library can be used to enrich teaching and study at a variety of grade levels ranging from grade school to doctoral research, and in numerous subjects from the more obvious art and history to architecture, anthropology, music, literature, religion, and more.[17]

A subscription to the Artstor Digital Library allows users at the subscribing institution to use the content in the digital library for broad noncommercial, educational, and scholarly purposes.[18] Users can access the Artstor Digital Library anywhere on the grounds or campus, remotely through internet protocol (IP) authentication, and, once the user has set up a user name and password, remotely for 120 days from outside the institution's IP range, to enable distance learning.[19] In limited cases, access may be limited to onsite access at a subscribing organization's library,[20] but overall access is unlimited to the number of individual and simultaneous authorized users that can utilize the Artstor Digital Library from the organization at any given time.[21]

Cultural institutions contributing content to the Artstor Digital Library complete an agreement to contribute a specified number of images over an agreed-upon timeframe. For instance, in 2011, the Indianapolis Museum of Art at Newfields expanded its agreement with Artstor to contribute a minimum of ten thousand images from its collection to the digital library over a five-year period. Media files and their related metadata can be provided to Artstor in a variety of ways. Most commonly, contributors deliver content to Artstor by uploading it to an external hard drive, or by allowing Artstor to harvest the content via an OAI server or through the use of APIs. Artstor staff reviews the metadata and maps it to the Artstor data schema. Furthermore, Artstor staff performs legal review on each work and assesses whether any rights need to be cleared prior to its presentation to Artstor Digital Library users. It is key that cultural institutions do not have to complete this rights clearance themselves before providing the content to Artstor, as this means that media files and the related metadata can be exported and sent with minimal formatting and review for rights considerations. This makes for a much quicker process for the institutions that may not have the time or the staff to undertake a detailed rights assessment prior to sending content.

Images for Academic Publishing

Introduced in 2007 at the request of The Metropolitan Museum of Art, the Images for Academic Publishing (IAP) service was developed to "address the challenges of scholarly publishing in the digital age by providing free images for academic publications through an automated Web-based service."[22] IAP has since expanded to include eleven collections and more than twenty-seven thousand images.[23] Any contributor to the Artstor Digital Library may opt to participate in IAP, thereby further promoting and enabling scholarly publishing.[24] Each contributor can identify specific terms and conditions (e.g., print run not in excess of X number of copies) for the use of images from their collections in IAP.

IAP makes these "publication-quality images [available] for use in scholarly publications free of charge" to any member of the general public requesting access.[25] Artstor Digital Library subscribers can access IAP directly through the digital library's interface. Nonsubscribers can simply request from Artstor a free password account to access, research, and download images from within IAP. Users may still need to obtain permission from the copyright owner in the underlying work represented in the image prior to use in a publication.[26] Depending on the file size required for the end publication, images are made available to users in the following standard options:

- quarter page (TIFF file: 1200 × 1500 pixels, 300 dpi) at approximately 5MB
- half page (TIFF file: 1500 × 2100 pixels, 300 dpi) at approximately 10MB
- full page (TIFF File: 2400 × 3000 pixels, 300 dpi) at approximately 20MB

Open Artstor

Launched in 2013, Open Artstor is a web-based initiative hosted by Artstor that allows contributors to make their images and metadata available to the general public.[27] Open Artstor operates on the principles of Open Access and is freely accessible to anyone, with no account required. Artstor describes the Open Artstor initiative as "working with leading museums, libraries, and archives, we aggregate art and cultural heritage collections to support their efforts to share digital content broadly with the public."[28] The first collaboration of Open Artstor was with the launch of the Digital Public Library of America (DPLA),[29] through which Artstor made thousands of public domain images and metadata freely accessible to everyone with access to an internet connection.[30]

JSTOR Forum

Building upon Artstor's joining forces with ITHAKA, JSTOR Forum is the next generation of Artstor's Shared Shelf Commons, that allows institutions to manage and distribute educational and scholarly images to increase their discoverability and usage.[31] Libraries and museums will be able to use JSTOR Forum's text and media management software to upload and manage content, which can then be delivered to end users in a variety of ways, including through the Artstor Digital Library, DPLA, or Omeka sites,[32] currently under development as of 2018. ITHAKA president Kevin Guthrie notes: "JSTOR Forum becomes the mechanism for those users and their institutions to load, manage, and make discoverable their own material alongside some of the most highly used scholarly content in the world."[33]

Artsy

Launched in October 2012, Artsy[34] explains its mission as "mak[ing] all the world's art accessible to anyone with an Internet connection. We are a platform for collecting and discovering art."[35] Since its launch, Artsy has partnered with galleries, art fairs, auctions, museums, cultural institutions, foundations, and artist estates to reach a global audience of more than 2.2 million unique art lovers per month.[36] Through these partnerships, Artsy's database has expanded to more than eight hundred thousand art, design, and architecture images that include both historic and contemporary art images.[37]

Artsy provides a number of services to both commercial galleries and cultural institutions.[38] For galleries and institutions, Artsy serves as a platform for collectors to discover and purchase limited-edition artworks through its e-commerce platform, including the promotion of a variety of art fairs.[39] For cultural institutions, Artsy promotes collection objects, exhibitions, and programs through a unique page tailored for each institution.[40] Artsy also makes open access images freely downloadable provided by institutions that have open access policies, such as the J. Paul Getty Museum and the National Gallery of Art, Washington, DC. Furthermore, Artsy features a unique breadth of reach to host benefit auctions for partner institutions by utilizing cutting-edge web and mobile technologies.[41]

As with many other third-party distributors, cultural institutions providing content to Artsy complete an agreement prior to contributing any images or accept the terms of use of the website. The agreed-upon image files and their related metadata are provided to Artsy either by direct upload to their CMS or, if it is a large volume of content, via an external hard drive. The metadata sent to Artsy is formatted in a CSV file containing tombstone information about the works being contributed. Artsy staff reviews the image files, metadata, and any third-party rights that Artsy may need to clear prior to the presentation of the images. Again, Artsy being responsible for clearing any rights makes the partnership simpler for any contributing cultural institution.

The Art Genome Project

Artsy is powered by The Art Genome Project, which analyzes and identifies unique characteristics that are present within and connect works of art with one another. The Art Genome Project is ongoing and to date has identified more than one thousand characteristics, which Artsy refers to as "genes." These "genes" range from art historical movements or styles, to medium, subject matter, formal visual qualities, technique, and geographic regions.[42]

The process of identifying and mapping these "genes" is referred to as "genoming," which is completed by Artsy's team of art historians as well as soliciting input from contributors.[43] The process of "genoming" connects artworks and artists across history through their assigned characteristics, and the resulting associations enable experts and nonexperts alike to browse art serendipitously.[44] This results in endless opportunities for discovery and learning, connecting works being made today to works with similar attributes, including art made decades or even hundreds of years ago.[45]

Artsy Education

A year after it publicly launched, Artsy introduced Artsy Education in October 2013.[46] Artsy Education provides students and educators with a host of free tools, not the least of which is more than twenty-six thousand images of art and architecture available for free high-resolution download from Artsy's database.[47] Typically limited to public domain works, the addition of a cultural institution's images to Artsy Education is predicated on a separate agreement that the institution can always opt out of in the future. To make it easier for users to identify the works that are part of Artsy Education and to know if they can download the file or not, a "Download Image" button will appear beside the image if it is available in this capacity. These images are also searchable with the term "Downloadable Images" on Artsy. Coupled with the download, Artsy Education also offers a growing repository of text posts that provide art historical references and comparison with contemporary works in a manner that is easily understood by everyone, whether they are versed in art history or not.[48]

Artsy regularly partners with institutions to promote art education, including a partnership with ten New York City high schools as part of a new NYC Department of Education digital literacy program called "Digital Ready." Artsy also partnered with the Robert Rauschenberg Foundation to launch the Emerging Curator Competition in 2014. College and university students from seventy-eight cities across five continents submitted exhibition proposals using Artsy's blogging tools and database of images.[49] The winning student mounted a physical exhibition with works from the Rauschenberg Foundation loan bank.

Bridgeman Education

A division of Bridgeman Images,[50] Bridgeman Education[51] is another online image resource for educational users.[52] Bridgeman Education provides a database of images for research and teaching, derived from contributions provided by museums, galleries, contemporary artists, and private collections.[53] These images are provided on a flat-rate annual subscription fee basis to educators working from grade school through the university level, as well as to their students and researchers.[54]

Bridgeman Education is a service that cultural institutions already contributing to Bridgeman Images may opt to be a part of, and participants can always withdraw their images at any time. Cultural institutions do not receive any revenue from providing their content to Bridgeman Education.

Digital Public Library of America

The Digital Public Library of America (DPLA)[55] is a public nonprofit portal and platform for sharing content broadly and openly.[56] With an extremely broad scope of collections, DPLA aggregates art images, historical documents, scientific data, and more. DPLA seeks to make the content of US research institutions, libraries, archives, and museums freely and publicly available to anyone, anywhere, anytime through a single online access point.[57]

DPLA works with a network of content and service "hubs" to aggregate content, primarily that which is already available online, through their own sites, providing a single access point for users.[58] "DPLA content hubs are large libraries, museums, archives, or other digital repositories that maintain a one-to-one relationship with the DPLA."[59] Slightly different are the service hubs that are collaborative at the state or regional level and collect metadata from several different cultural institutions and provide it to the DPLA through a single portal.[60] Cultural institutions that wish to have their content included in the DPLA will usually have to work with a regional service hub to develop a partnership with one of the larger content hubs. Once materials have been incorporated, end users are able to discover online materials and view thumbnails within the DPLA site but are routed to the original online collection of the partner organization to view full-size images and complete information about materials. Since DPLA has an active and growing user base, it can be a good option for making content easily discoverable to more users while still providing traffic to a cultural institution's own online resources.

DPLA includes records for individual images with a wide variety of rights statuses: public domain, open licensed, or subject to active copyrights, but shared

CASE STUDY

CONTRIBUTING TO DPLA THROUGH A CONTENT HUB

Anne M. Young

As part of its two-year Digital Hubs Pilot Project (2011–2013), the DPLA introduced several large digital content hubs, including Artstor, HathiTrust Digital Library, The J. Paul Getty Trust, the National Archives and Records Administration, and the Smithsonian Institution.[1] In 2013, the Indianapolis Museum of Art at Newfields became one of six museum contributors to use the Artstor content hub to facilitate content contribution to the DPLA.[2] As part of the collaboration between Artstor and the DPLA, metadata records, small thumbnail images, a link to the original contributing museum's own website, and a link to the corresponding images and records on an Open Artstor landing page are made available to DPLA users on the DPLA site. The Open Artstor landing page contains a larger thumbnail version of the image, a link to the high-resolution version of the image, a copy of the contributing institution's logo, and a link to the contributing museum's webpage.[3]

"We are enormously grateful for this partnership with Artstor and its partner museums," remarked Dan Cohen, former DPLA executive director. "Our vision for the Digital Public Library of America has always been one of open access to the full range of human expression, including visual culture, and Artstor's contribution adds vital works of art to our growing, networked collection."[4]

Increasing Newfields' reach by participating in DPLA was simplified by its existing collaboration with Artstor. All technical aspects of contributing content to DPLA were handled by Artstor. Newfields was simply required to enter into a short agreement to confirm the terms of its participation in DPLA and to identify the content that would be provided by Artstor to DPLA. In the end, Newfields decided that all clearly identifiable public domain content would be shared through the DPLA. As part of its agreement with Artstor, and pursuant to DPLA policy, Newfields was required to confirm that all of the metadata was provided to DPLA under a CC Zero license. In the future, as Newfields contributes more content to the Artstor Digital Library, it can make additional public domain images and associated metadata available to the public at large through DPLA.

NOTES

1. For a complete list of the content hubs, see "Our Hubs," Digital Public Library of America, accessed March 22, 2018, https://pro.dp.la/hubs/our-hubs.
2. The original six contributing museums were the Dallas Museum of Art, the Indianapolis Museum of Art at Newfields, the National Gallery of Art (paintings from the Samuel H. Kress Collection), the Walters Art Museum, the Yale Center for British Art, and the Yale University Art Gallery. "Artstor to help launch the Digital Public Library of America," Artstor Blog: Images and Ideas for Teaching and Scholarship, March 28, 2013, https://Artstor.wordpress.com/2013/03/28/Artstor-to-help-launch-the-digital-public-library-of-america/.
3. See chapter 5, Open Artstor, for more information.
4. Ibid.

online with permission or through a copyright exception. DPLA requires that all *metadata* be provided under a Creative Commons "CC Zero" Public Domain Dedication.[61] In other words, contributing cultural institutions waive all copyrights, database rights, and other related or neighboring rights in the metadata at the time it is shared with DPLA.[62] Within the United States, there are very few copyright rights in metadata to begin with, and DPLA is committed to sharing metadata in order to "promote innovation in the development of applications and tools that use and rely on this metadata."[63]

Curated exhibits are developed from the DPLA aggregated collections, and DPLA has also developed new interactive tools for exploring its collections.[64] In addition, because the metadata are open and an API is provided, third-party developers are encouraged to explore the data and collections in exciting new ways.[65]

In addition to its portal and platform aggregation activities, DPLA engages in related public interest projects.[66] DPLA has become engaged in projects to develop better communications about copyright and related rights statuses with end users, to collaborate with schools to develop educational uses of its aggregated content, and to connect public librarians with training and infrastructure resources to support local digitization.[67]

Google Cultural Institute

Google Arts & Culture

Google Arts & Culture,[68] created by the Google Cultural Institute, brings together images from cultural institutions and world landmarks, as well as other items of cultural significance, within a single, searchable portal that is accessible to global online users.[69] Comprised of two main projects, the Art Project and World Wonders Project, Google Arts & Culture is a unique distribution partner for cultural institutions.[70] Google Arts & Culture not only offers a broad audience for collection materials, but is also able to offer a suite of innovative technological tools to present interactive experiences to end users. This includes advanced capturing tools to re-create the experience of walking in museum galleries, exploring archaeological sites across the globe, and extreme high-definition images that allow viewers to explore the minutiae of two-dimensional works.[71]

Art Project

One of the earliest initiatives of the Google Cultural Institute, the Art Project[72] has partnered with more than one thousand museums and collections worldwide to make images of six million objects available.[73] First launched in February 2011 with just seventeen museums from nine countries, the Art Project greatly expanded with its second iteration in April 2012 and has continued to add partners since, ranging from institutions that contributed just a few images through those that contributed thousands.[74] Images are high resolution and object data follows metadata standards based on the information provided by the contributing institution, with a structured search capability on the site. The Art Project provides cultural institutions with the opportunity to expand its audiences worldwide and thereby increase exposure to the collections. As Douglas Druick, former director of The Art Institute of Chicago stated: "By sharing works of art in this way, all it will do is increase the interest in visual works of art and the desire to come to institutions like the Art Institute."[75]

Initial steps for participating in the Google Art Project include intensive contract negotiations under a nondisclosure agreement.[76] Once the agreement is in place, the selection of works of art and images takes place. A decision must be made by the cultural institution whether to include only works in the public domain, to clear permissions to the works with the rights holder, potentially via a nonexclusive licensing agreement, or to include works that are protected by copyright. Google does not undertake any rights clearance for the works represented within the Art Project, so the inclusion of any copyrighted works is the onus of the contributing cultural institution, which also bears the liability for any suits arising out of the use. Depending on the works selected and the utilization of the institution's CMS and/or DAMS, this may be labor intensive and time consuming. The data must be exported to a format defined by Google staff[77] and the fields mapped to the Art Project data schema through Google's CMS portal.[78] Images are uploaded separately to the Art Project site and linked with the associated data (any problems mapping to the data records must be dealt with or the works will not appear online).

Art Project: Street View

The Art Project also includes Street View[79] panoramas that provide online visitors with a sense of walking through the partnering cultural institutions.[80] As part of the review process of the images, designated staff of the cultural institution can link works represented in the galleries to the image file and data of the work provided to the objects pages in the Art Project. There is also the capacity to block out or blur images of works of art protected by copyright or with other concerns that may restrict their inclusion (i.e., rights of privacy or publicity, loaned objects, or other creator/donor restrictions).

Captures for the Street View can take from one to several days. Technicians arrive with all equipment and work with museum staff on setting up a walk-through path and then planning out the multiple shots needed to create panoramic views. Once the shoot is complete, Google staff will process the image captures and return the panoramas to the cultural institution for review and approval (or rejection as the case may be). At that point, each image must be evaluated by museum staff for rights issues and the works protected by copyright obscured or a nonexclusive license obtained. The museum may also choose to link the works on the wall to the item records in the main Google Art Project set.

Art Project Gigapixels

While all images in the Art Project are capable of being zoomed in upon to the extent possible, select works are photographed by Google staff using specialized photographic equipment that create gigapixel[81] images with exceptionally high-detailed zooming (i.e., individual brushstrokes and cracking in paint layers become readily visible).[82] Cultural institutions considering a gigapixel capture of a work or works in its collection should note that Google retains the copyright to the final images created from the multiple captures that are stitched together to form the whole. Google does not claim any rights to the underlying work, only to the technology and specialized process of image creation utilized in creating the gigapixel images. Typically, the cultural institution is granted a free-of-charge and royalty-free nonexclusive license to utilize the image after a predetermined embargo period following the initial release of the gigapixel within the Art Project.

While a cultural institution may impose additional considerations (e.g., significance of the work to the collection, donor, or copyright restrictions) for the work selected for the gigapixel capture, Google does require the following to integrate the capture into the Art Project:

- The work must be part of the collection images submitted to the Art Project.
- The work has to be on view in the gallery to integrate with Street View captures.
- The work has to be able to be shot vertically.
- Due to the vertical shoot requirement, Google prefers capturing two-dimensional works.

After a work is selected for the gigapixel treatment and a visit scheduled, Google's gigapixel team arrives with specialized photographic equipment. Unlike the equipment used to conduct the Street View captures, the gigapixel equipment includes numerous elements including lighting and an extensive array of cords running among all of the equipment.[83] Once this is all set up to evenly light the piece, the captures follow a similar process to the Street View filming with multiple shots from various viewpoints and with the

CASE STUDY

STREET VIEW FILMING

Anne M. Young

After the launch of the collection works in the Art Project, the Indianapolis Museum of Art at Newfields began discussions with Google about increasing access to the collection by Street View filming. While it sounds like a simple prospect—film the galleries, stitch the images together, and publish online—the actual process took over a year to complete and launch.

Street View filming in the galleries and on the grounds did not include the following:

- works with lender or donor restrictions
- copyrighted works, *unless* Newfields owns the copyright or cleared the permissions[1]
- temporary exhibitions or rotations, *unless* a collection would not be otherwise represented

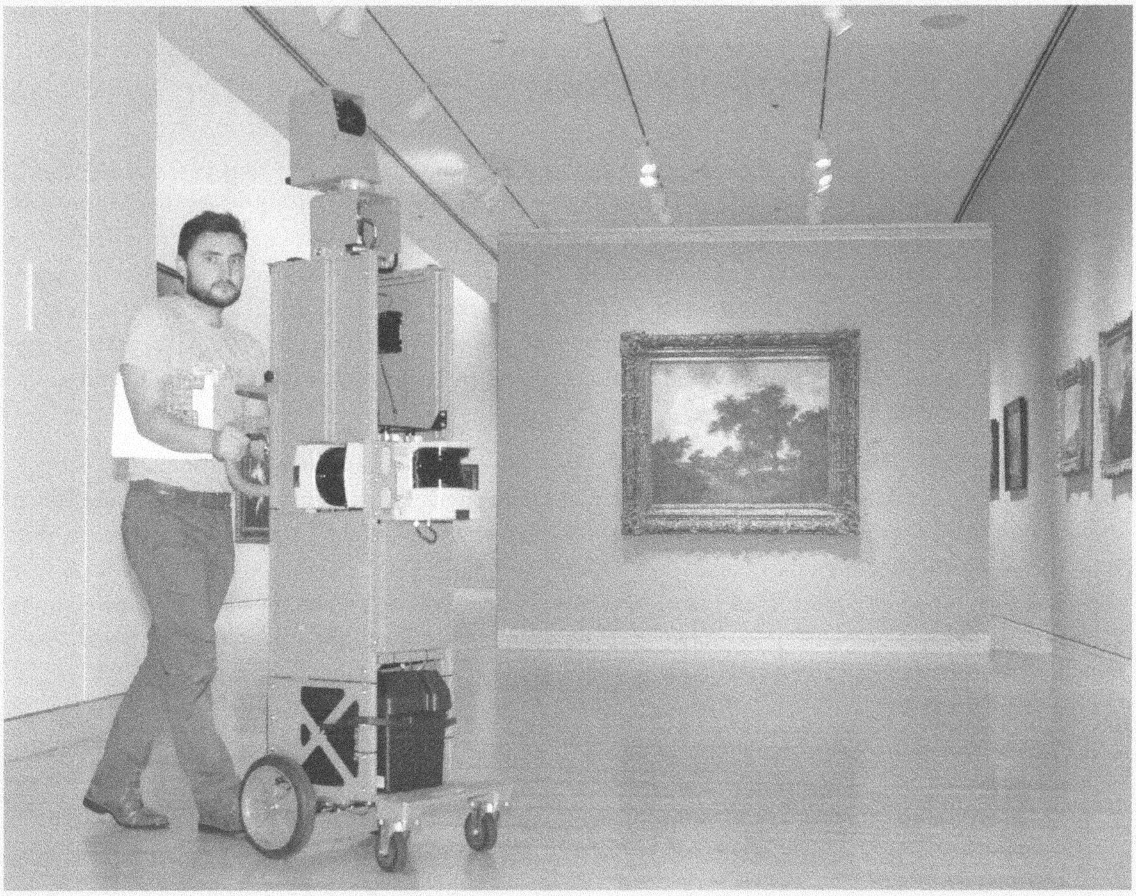

FIGURE 5.1
Google staff walking the European galleries

Prior to Google's arrival, staff walked the museum galleries and garden with maps marking the locations of works with potential restrictions that could prohibit their inclusion. These works were then assessed with input from curatorial and registration staff to determine those for which rights clearance would be pursued. In the end, temporary exhibitions were not filmed, unless it meant a collection was not represented.[2] The decision was also made to clear permissions for several copyrighted artists (otherwise the Contemporary galleries would not have been represented at all); most of those contacted approved the inclusion of their works in the Street View. By and large, the only rights holders not pursued were those affiliated with ARS and VAGA.[3] The exception to this was Robert Irwin's *Light and Space III* that is integrally tied to the museum's architecture, which was ultimately approved for inclusion and appears in almost half of the captures.

Armed with the annotated gallery maps, Google's capture team spent two days in October 2012 filming the museum galleries. Interestingly, Google does not refer to the equipment as a camera; rather, it is "an imaging device for indoors." The entire device is contained on a trolley operated by a car battery, with no cords, no track to lay down, and no external lights. Furthermore, no one could be in the galleries while the captures were done; as one of their operators explained "if you can see it, it can see you!"

Google spent the next ten months processing the captures and in August 2013 presented Newfields with 998 images; 30 were rejected for less-than-optimal image quality and representation of the collection work(s). Rights and reproductions staff then reviewed each remaining image to identify the works that could not be included due to lender or copyright restrictions. Once identified, these were manually blurred in every image they appeared in, which ultimately resulted in over 2,100 individual blurs. The final step to approving the indoor view captures was to connect the 209 collection images Newfields shared in 2011 to their physical locations in the galleries. This Street View launched to users in December 2013.[4]

Google returned to Newfields in 2016 to capture new views of the museum galleries, historic properties (Lilly House and Miller House), and the Garden. Many spaces were not filmed the first time Street Views were captured and in many others there were notable changes to installations that further spurred the desire to update Newfields' Street View. The filming undertook a similar process as was completed with the first captures, and as of 2018 Newfields was finalizing its review of the new images for any needed blurs and linking to individual collection items prior to the updated Street View being launched to users later.

NOTES

1. It is important to note that it was Newfields' stance that the terms of the agreement with Google went beyond the rights granted to Newfields by rights holders who completed the standard nonexclusive licensing agreement. Thus, any copyrighted works included in the Street View were cleared separately from any previously completed nonexclusive licensing agreements.
2. Notably, the Textile and Fashion exhibitions were filmed, but not all of the print exhibitions were filmed, as prints were on view in several galleries.

3. ARS- and VAGA-represented artists were not approached by and large because the standard response from these representatives is to decline inclusion of the works in the Google Cultural Institute. Overall, Newfields determined it was not worth the staff time to pursue these works, where there was no compelling or specific reason to include them (e.g., works part of the building architecture or a key collection object), when the overarching answer would be "no" to their inclusion.
4. "Indianapolis Museum of Art at Newfields," Google Arts & Culture," accessed March 22, 2018, https://artsandculture.google.com/partner/indianapolis-museum-of-art.

finished image eventually processed and loaded into the Art Project.

Access to the gallery will be restricted during the shoot, since all gallery lights will need to be turned off and windows covered to prevent ambient light leaking into the gallery (in cases where this is not possible, the shoot will likely have to take place at night). Furthermore, limited access to adjacent gallery spaces is required as any vibrations in the flooring or walls can create errors in the capture process. Because the individual captures are of such small areas of the work, the slightest tremor can change the registration and leveling of the equipment and necessitate the shoot starting over. The overall process of the gigapixel capture can take the better part of a day (or night) to complete a single work; the larger the work, the longer the capture time. As a result of the lengthy time commitment, Google has typically completed only one gigapixel capture per contributing cultural institution.

Open Gallery

A new initiative of the Google Cultural Institute, Open Gallery,[84] provides cultural institutions with a set of free tools to create curated exhibitions online.[85] Available by invitation only, Open Gallery provides cultural institutions with the Google technology that powers the various projects in the Cultural Institute to publish stories around their imagery through additional text, audio, and video content.[86] Open Gallery can utilize images and metadata previously uploaded to the Art Project, including Street View images, or new content and metadata can be uploaded with the curation tools. Once the content is put into the curation tools, the exhibition can be configured and published by the cultural institution itself.

World Wonders Project

Utilizing Street View technologies, the World Wonders Project[87] brings heritage sites across the world to the online environment. By combining Street View filming with three-dimensional modeling and other Google technologies, online visitors can virtually explore sites like Stonehenge, the Palace of Versailles, Pompeii's archaeological dig locations, and natural phenomena such as the Great Barrier Reef as if they were physically present. This immersive experience makes the World Wonders Project a unique tool for educators to expose students to these cultural sites.[88] Any cultural institution interested in partnering with Google for the World Wonders Project will undergo a similar contract review and Street View filming experience as outlined previously in the Art Project.

Flickr

Flickr[89] serves as a useful tool for cultural institutions to highlight both collection and noncollection imagery. Images uploaded to Flickr can be made available for the general public to download at a variety of size options at no charge. Access to images may also be restricted and made available only for "private" viewing.[90]

Additionally, The Commons on Flickr is another avenue to make content publicly accessible.[91] The Commons started in 2008 as a pilot project through which Flickr partnered with the Library of Congress to bring together and catalogue its public photographic archive for use by everyone.[92] A variety of cultural institutions, including several libraries as well as museums, now contribute to The Commons, in which users can contribute information and knowledge through tagging and commenting on the image collections presented.[93] Almost one hundred cultural institutions now make their content available through The Commons.

When cultural institutions contribute images to The Commons, each provides its own rights statement to govern the resultant use(s) of the images, typically linking back to the institution's own website information. For example, when the Library of Congress began its contribution to The Commons, it utilized the Flickr API to upload the image files and basic descriptions, including the rights statement, in batches rather than one at a time.[94]

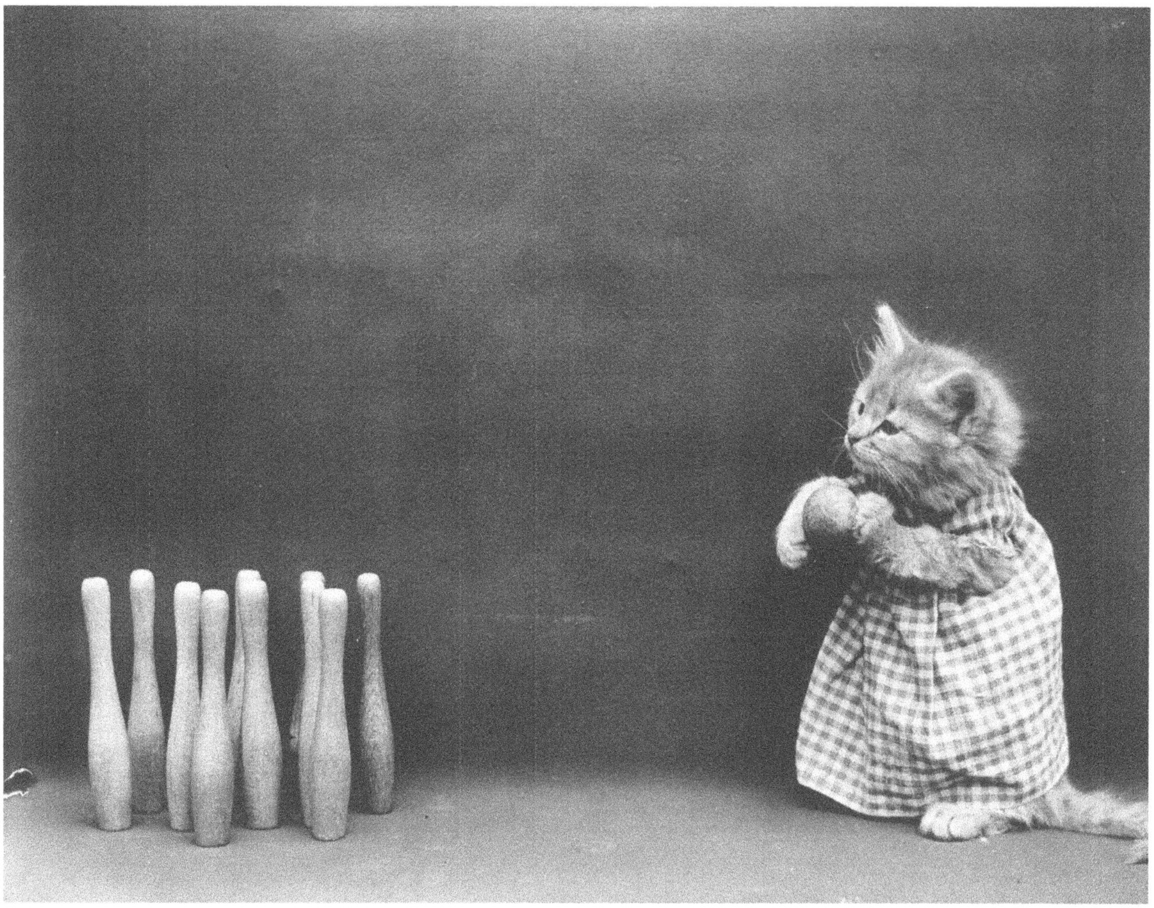

FIGURE 5.2.
An image from The Library of Congress that was posted as part of their commemoration of the 10th anniversary of their sharing images in The Commons on Flickr.

HathiTrust Digital Library

The HathiTrust Digital Library[95] describes itself as "a partnership of academic and research institutions, offering a collection of millions of titles digitized from libraries around the world."[96] You can browse the collections and develop personal study collections. Anyone may read books or other print materials in the collection online, provided a given item is in the public domain (with download of public domain works available to member institutions) or if permission is granted to make a copyrighted work accessible to the general public.[97] HathiTrust offers a simple, standard permission form for rights holders that includes a menu of Creative Commons license options that helps copyright holders to indicate the level of sharing they desire.[98]

"HathiTrust began in 2008 as a collaboration of the universities of the Committee on Institutional Cooperation and the University of California system to establish a repository to archive and share their digitized collections. HathiTrust has quickly expanded to include additional partners and to provide those partners with an easy means to archive their digital content."[99] The initial focus is on preserving and providing access to book and journal content digitized from partner library collections. "The partners aim to build a comprehensive archive of published literature from around the world and develop shared strategies for managing and developing their digital and print holdings in a collaborative way."[100]

"The primary communities that HathiTrust serves are the members (faculty, students, and users) of its partner libraries, but the materials in HathiTrust are available to all to the extent permitted by law and contracts, providing the published record as a public good to users around the world."[101] Cultural institutions are presented with a wealth of research opportunities by HathiTrust collections.[102] Currently, the focus is on text material rather than images per se, but public domain books may provide important images for research and exhibitions.[103] Cultural institutions with a backlist of books that are out of print may find that HathiTrust contains scans of those books—if they are subject to copyright, one may only see the catalogue information (not the work itself). That said, HathiTrust works with scholarly publishers and rights holders to identify works that could be made openly accessible with permission.[104] This is a great way to support a cultural institution's research and education mission where the necessary rights are available. A basic permission form is on the website, which can be used for simple arrangements.[105] A more complex situation that, for example, involves a large number of works or the need for more formal warranty and indemnification might require a more involved agreement.

Wikimedia Commons

Wikipedia, "the free encyclopedia that anyone can edit," is one of the largest resources, with arguably the largest reach, of any encyclopedic information source online.[106] With millions of articles in just about any language imaginable, this ever-growing resource is often one of the first places people turn to when researching. The Wikimedia Foundation, Wikipedia's not-for-profit parent organization, hosts many other related sites,[107] including Wikimedia Commons,[108] a valuable resource for extending the reach of image collections.[109] Anyone can upload images to the Commons, provided they are the sole copyright holder, if they have received permission from the relevant rights holder, or if the work is in the public domain. The images can be made available broadly pursuant to one of several Creative Commons licenses.[110] Currently, more than forty-five million images are available in Wikimedia Commons.[111] The advantage of contributing images directly to the Commons is twofold: full and correct object and image data[112] can be made available, including a link back to the institution's online collections pages, and an approved color correct image can be provided.

Content from cultural institutions is welcomed in both Wikipedia and Wikimedia Commons, although it is important for individuals working on behalf of an institution to make that relationship clear. For first-time users, reaching out to an experienced Wikipedian, such as a member of the GLAM-Wiki initiative,[113] is critical, since the community standards are robust and errors, or perceived errors, will quickly come under discussion by alert editors.[114]

Once images are on Wikimedia Commons, they are accessible for inclusion in Wikipedia articles (where their use is tracked) and can be downloaded and used for those purposes specified in the applicable license. While upload size is not restricted, providing even modest-size image files may result in requests to reproduce (even though further permission is not required under the licenses) and possibly orders for higher-resolution files.

Community projects often arise in Wikimedia Commons, with enthusiasts in specific areas reaching out to collaborate with cultural institutions to upload targeted collections for use in enhancing articles. Working with specialists can bring lesser-known parts of the collection to greater visibility.[115] Some examples include WikiAfrica,[116] Wikipedia: Wikipedia Loves Art,[117] WikiPop,[118] and Wikipedia: WikiProject Public art/TheArtistResearchProject/TonySmith.[119]

POTENTIAL DISTRIBUTION PARTNERS (REVENUE GENERATING)[120]

There are several third-party distribution partners who largely work to represent the interests of cultural institutions by managing image distribution and rights for a usage fee. While several institutions now work exclusively with third-party distributors to alleviate the volume of external requests coming directly to the institution for image access and rights, many still handle requests internally and see these partnerships as a further means of bringing attention to the collections as well as a means of revenue generation.

Individual contracts vary with each company, and cultural institutions working with some of the image distribution partners discussed below can expect to receive a portion of the licensing and use fees collected by the distributor in return for representation of their works. In most cases, the royalties are paid out quarterly and typically can range anywhere from 35 to 60 percent of the overall fees assessed. Generally, these companies have standard, boilerplate contracts they prefer to work with, but often the cultural institutions can negotiate restrictions or additional use approvals required, prior to licensing a requested use.

Stock Photography Agencies

Subsets of distribution partners that are revenue generating for cultural institutions are stock photography agencies such as Art Resource[121] and Getty Images.[122] While some individuals may be happy to search for images at their source or on aggregating websites such as Wikimedia Commons, Flickr, or the Google Art Project, image researchers also depend on commercial licensing and stock photography agencies whose online search engines and data sets are tuned to serve their specific requirements—by orientation, color, rights, image type, and category—to name just a few options. The convenience of one-stop shopping, click-through licenses, subscriptions, credit card payments, and, in some instances, precleared rights serve to justify the fees charged by these businesses. For many users, licensing through stock agencies is the only option for obtaining a needed image due to the nature of their use (commercial, scholarly, and nonscholarly publication, etc.) or the need to avoid the sometimes laborious process of searching through smaller sites, working through a variety of permissions and payment requirements.

Cultural institutions may choose to partner with these agencies to make images available to worldwide audiences and to reduce the staff effort and paperwork of processing image orders; in return, royalties are received.[123] As previously discussed, with nonrevenue-generating distribution partners, completing an agreement for contributing images and data is standard with stock agencies, where it is also preferable that it be a nonexclusive agreement. Specific categories of use may be highlighted that require individual permission; a cultural institution may, for example, automatically allow editorial use by publishers, but require that agency staff reach out for permission for a commercial use such as a book cover, advertisement, or product development. Selection of images is made in collaboration with the distribution partner contact person, who may have very specific requests, depending on

CASE STUDY

EASTMAN JOHNSON'S *A RIDE FOR LIBERTY— THE FUGITIVE SLAVES*

Deborah Wythe

The Brooklyn Museum has been contributing images to Wikimedia Commons since 2010, when a staff-developed bot (automatic uploader) added more than four thousand images to the Commons. Since then, additional images have been added via projects and seeding efforts, for a total of more than ten thousand images. A look at Eastman Johnson's *A Ride for Liberty—The Fugitive Slaves* from the Brooklyn Museum collection on Wikimedia Commons reveals some of the challenges and advantages of participation with this image distribution partner.[1]

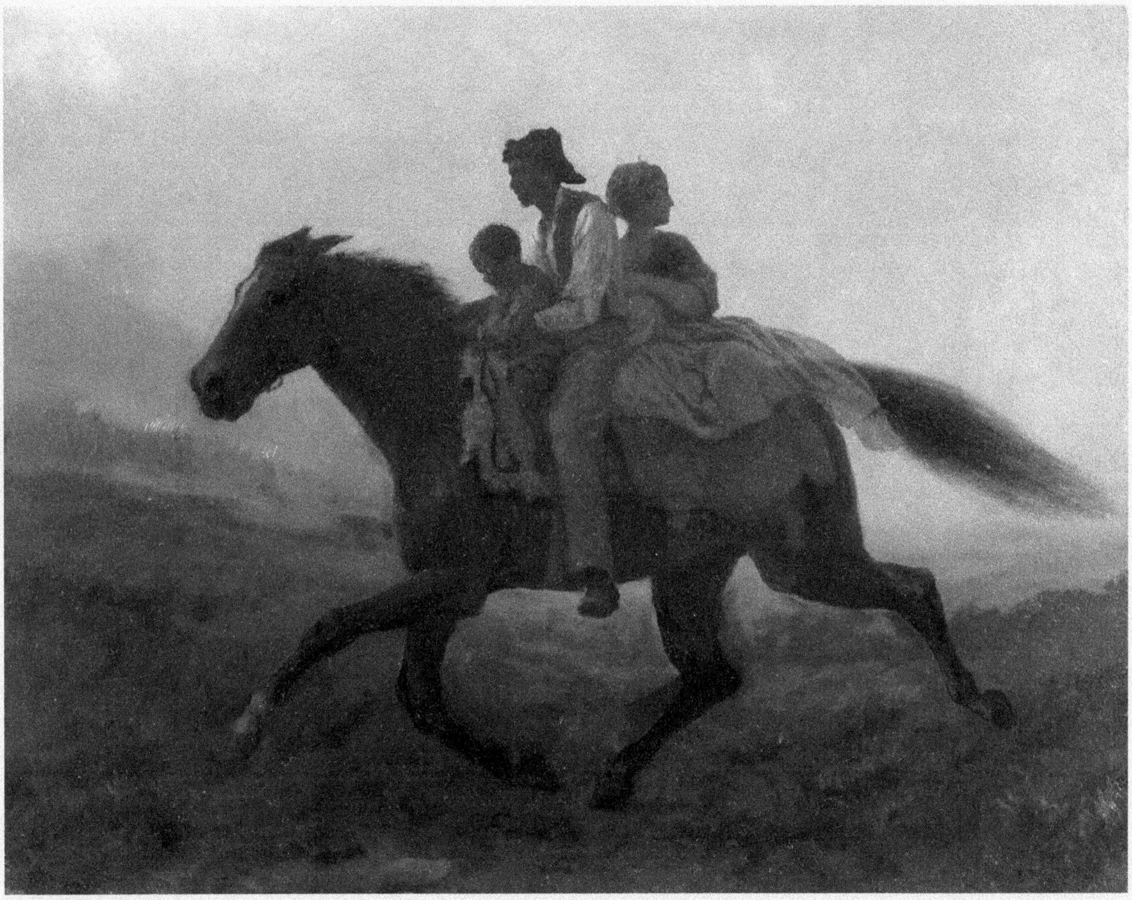

FIGURE 5.3
The primary image file of Eastman Johnson's *A Ride for Liberty—The Fugitive* Slaves from the Brooklyn Museum.

Five versions of Johnson's work, which is one of the most popular and reproduced images in the Brooklyn Museum's collection, appear in Wikimedia Commons—with highly variable color.[2] Two files were uploaded as part of the Wikipedia Loves Art[3] project in 2009, the third is a scan from a book, the fourth is a high-resolution "scrape" of the museum's image from Google's Art Project, and the fifth is a mid-sized image (approximately 1,500 pixels on the long side) contributed by the Brooklyn Museum. All have accurate caption and credit information, thanks to the museum's online catalogue, and all link back to that resource. Savvy users should be able to detect and select the museum-generated image file for their purposes. An image search on Google for this work results in hundreds of images with highly variable color, underlining the importance of providing the best image, but acknowledging that control of images is ultimately impossible. Ideally, the cultural institution where an object resides should be the authoritative resource for image files and data about its works.

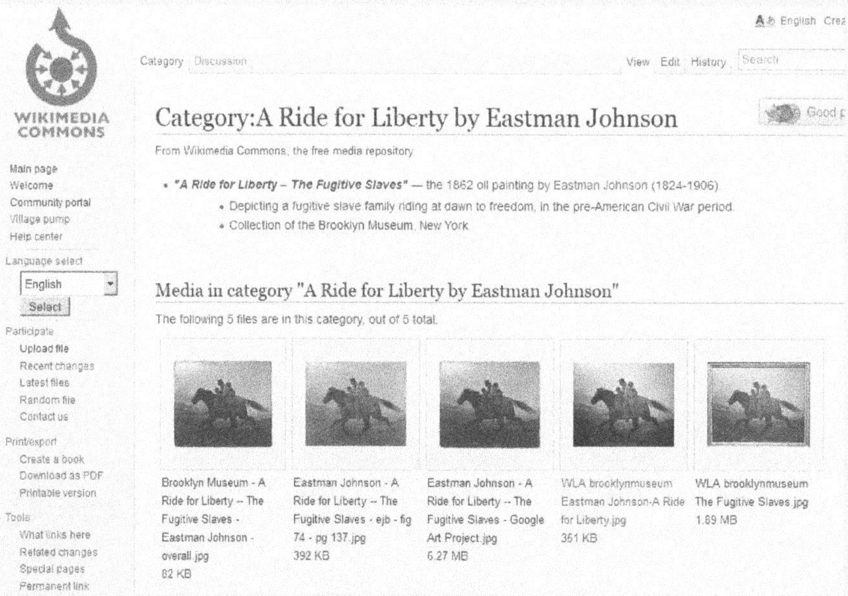

FIGURE 5.4
The tonal variation is readily visible among the five versions of Johnson's work that appear in Wikimedia Commons.

The two versions of the museum's image file have been used in twenty-five articles in sixteen languages; several additional articles utilize the scanned image. *A Ride for Liberty—The Fugitive Slaves* illustrates articles ranging from expected entries about Eastman Johnson and slavery topics to wide-ranging articles about a related painting by Johnson, *The Girl I left Behind Me,*[4] a pseudoscientific description of the mental illness Drapetomanie,[5] and an entry on songs of the Underground Railway.[6]

NOTES

1. "File: Brooklyn Museum – A Ride for Liberty -- The Fugitive Slaves – Eastman Johnson – overall.jpg," Wikimedia Commons, accessed March 22, 2018, https://commons.wikimedia.org/wiki/File:Brooklyn_Museum_-_A_Ride_for_Liberty_--_The_Fugitive_Slaves_-_Eastman_Johnson_-_overall.jpg.

2. "Category: A Ride for Liberty by Eastman Johnson," Wikimedia Commons, accessed March 22, 2018, https://commons.wikimedia.org/wiki/Category:A_Ride_for_Liberty_by_Eastman_Johnson.
3. "Wikipedia: Wikipedia Loves Art," Wikipedia, accessed March 22, 2018, https://en.wikipedia.org/wiki/Wikipedia:Wikipedia_Loves_Art.
4. "The Girl I Left Behind Me," Wikipedia, accessed March 22, 2018, https://de.wikipedia.org/wiki/The_Girl_I_left_behind_me.
5. "Drapetomanie," Wikipedia, accessed March 22, 2018, https://nl.wikipedia.org/wiki/Drapetomanie.
6. "Songs of the Underground Railroad," Wikipedia, accessed March 22, 2018, https://en.wikipedia.org/wiki/Songs_of_the_Underground_Railroad.

their gaps and the cultural institution's strengths. For example, stock photography options may be an opportunity for a cultural institution to leverage not only images of collection objects but also noncollection images of their buildings and/or grounds.

Art Resource

Founded in 1968, Art Resource[124] is the world's largest fine art stock photography archive, with searchable fine art images from a variety of cultural institutions, available for licensing to all media.[125] Art Resource provides end users with access to more than three million transparencies and black-and-white photographs of paintings, sculptures, architecture, and other art forms.[126] All images that are contributed to Art Resource are cross-referenced by their metadata: subject, title, artist, period, place, and medium. Furthermore, the subject indexing follows similar headings as are found in larger stock agencies like Getty Images, including topics ranging from architecture, animals, and religions to sports, water, and weapons.[127]

Art Resource represents a number of major European archives of art and architecture, including Scala Fine Arts and Fratelli Alinari of Florence, Bildarchiv Preussischer Kulturbesitz, the Erich Lessing Culture and Fine Arts Archive of Vienna, and the photographic holdings of the Victoria and Albert Museum, the Werner Forman Archive of London. Art Resource is also the exclusive North American representative of all the institutions that are part of the Réunion des Musées Nationaux. While Art Resource hosts images for a variety of cultural institutions, it also functions as the official rights and permissions representative for numerous major museums and archives.[128]

Bridgeman Images

Founded in 1972, Bridgeman Images[129] (formerly Bridgeman Art Library) is based in London and maintains offices in New York, Paris, and Berlin.[130] Bridgeman Images specializes in fine art images, working with museums, galleries, private collections, artists, and estates to provide a central resource of fine art images and archival footage made accessible for reproduction to creative professionals.[131] More than seventy museums, libraries, and other collections make content available through Bridgeman.[132] The collections, while heavily weighted toward British institutions, do have an international reach. Similar to other stock agencies, Bridgeman Images provides an extensive list of keywords for each image, complete object data, and links back to the cultural institution's website. Bridgeman Images also administers the copyright for artists and estates through the Bridgeman Copyright Artists[133] and offers the Bridgeman Print on Demand service that provides users with reproduction prints and

CHECKLIST FOR LICENSING WITH A STOCK PHOTOGRAPHY AGENCY[1]

Deborah Wythe

Placing images with distribution partners, particularly stock photography agencies, involves entering into the commercial environment and requires careful thought to the details of the contract. Most aspects will be negotiable, but the following should be examined before signing are:

- *Goals of the Relationship*

  Some common goals might be expanding reach into new markets, increasing revenue, publicizing the collection to customers who prefer using a single source for images, or relieving pressure on rights and reproductions specialists.

- *Impact of Goals on Other Mission-Driven Activities*

  If the institution is considering or has implemented OA, selling images through a commercial vendor may have repercussions.[2] Will directing clients solely to an outside source affect relationships?

- *Exclusive or Nonexclusive Contract*

  An exclusive contract—essentially outsourcing all image sales—will likely bring a larger return. Be sure to clarify what rights the cultural institution retains for using for its own purposes under such a contract. A nonexclusive contract allows the cultural institution to continue licensing at will, providing discounts or gratis images to colleagues, and other institutions pursuing joint projects such as catalogues and exhibitions, or pursuing commercial projects without having to split royalty fees.

- *Approvals*

  Distribution partners, including stock photography agencies, typically allow image providers to set approval levels, allowing or requiring prior approval for editorial use, merchandise, advertising, and the like. Learning what terms the partner uses and how they are defined is critical. When approvals are required, a quick turnaround is important: commercial clients do not like to wait.

- *Rights*

  Both the distribution partner and the cultural institution should evaluate rights status. Prior to providing images, it is important to ensure that there are no donor, ownership, image, or copyright restrictions. Clearance for a specific use is typically undertaken by the end user; the distribution partner may provide assistance in that process and in evaluating personality rights. For artists represented by a licensing agency such as ARS, the partner may hold a subscription allowing them to display and distribute the images.

- *Cost to Users*

  While most stock photography agencies have a standard fee schedule, images do not fall under a "one-size-fits-all" cost model: discounts are typically allowed for scholarly and not-for-profit users. The distribution partner will evaluate what constitutes "scholarly" by assessing the profit model of the publisher or governing organization.

- *Royalties*

  The cultural institution provides the publication-quality image files and descriptive metadata. In return, a royalty fee split or percentage of sales is negotiated and becomes part of the contract. This will vary depending on the contract terms, but may range anywhere from 35 to 50 percent back to the cultural institution.

- *General Terms*

  Review terms such as duration, geographic reach, and the like to ensure that all are clear. How long will the agreement be in effect? What are the procedures for cancelling or extending? If the cultural institution needs to remove an image or provide corrected metadata, what are the procedures and what is the turnaround? Worldwide distribution or only in selected geographic markets?

NOTES

1. Input for this section was provided by representatives from Bridgeman Images and the former stock agency Corbis in response to a brief email query; personal communication with the author, March 20, 2015.
2. See chapter 2, Case Study: OA at Yale University, for a more detailed discussion.

a variety of other products ranging from $4 to $400.[134] And, as previously discussed, Bridgeman Education offers a subscription service for students, teachers, and researchers.[135]

Cultural institutions contributing to Bridgeman Images make their content available for scholarly, editorial, and commercial uses.[136] For their contributions, cultural institutions receive 50 percent of any reproduction fees that are assessed.[137] Additionally, the contributing institutions have the ability to decide which, if any, user requests for their content are sent back to them by Bridgeman Images for review and approval (or denial). Bridgeman Images clears copyright for the presentation of contributed content online and directs users back to rights holders to clear specific requests. Thus, contributing institutions can send a representative selection of their collections without having to complete a rights analysis first.

Davis Art

Operating several subsets, Davis Art[138] offers access to its collections through subscription services.[139] Davis Art Images has a mission to serve the art education community from K–12 through college.[140] Collections include Davis Digital,[141] Davis Art Images,[142] and SchoolArts Magazine.[143] Davis Digital provides both educators and students with access to e-books, e-portfolios, and a curriculum builder from any device with an internet connection.[144] Similarly, SchoolArts Magazine is a subscription-based national art education magazine covering all grade levels and providing professional support to arts educators.[145]

Davis Art Images provides more than thirty-five thousand fine art images to subscribers through three categories: Digital Fine Art Images, the Art Institute of Chicago, and the purchase of individual images through Scholars Resource. Davis Digital Art Images includes the ability for users to add keywords to images, create groupings for specific lessons, build curricula, and make these directly available to students. Davis Art Images has also partnered with Scholars Resource to make the individual images contributed to them available for purchase and download, thus broadening the reach of cultural institutions that have contributed to Davis Art Images.[146]

DNP Art Communications Co., Ltd.

DNP Art Communications Co., Ltd. (DNP),[147] is the result of the merging of three companies in Japan—DNP Archives.Com Co., Ltd., Trans Art Inc., and Maison de DNP Ginza Co., Ltd. DNP provides total solutions from planning to production, manufacturing, sales, and administration over a wide range of businesses in the fields of fine arts and graphic design, including publishing, licensing, and goods development. The primary interest is in Asian arts, though other cultures are also represented.[148]

Cultural institutions can provide images to DNP via FTP or physical media along with XML or similar object metadata templates. DNP seeks and clears permissions in all cases so the contributing institution does not bear that responsibility. Furthermore, DNP contacts the institution each time they receive a request for final review and approval. The initial agreement to contribute is straightforward and provides contributors with a 50 percent commission on all sales, which is paid quarterly.

Getty Images

Founded in 1995, Getty Images[149] was the first stock photography agency to license images online; effectively changing the entire licensing industry model. Today, Getty Images is one of the leading distributors of image, video, music, and multimedia products.[150] Image content is divided into two categories: Creative and Editorial.[151] Creative content includes images available in a variety of subcategories: royalty free, rights managed, and archival images.[152] Editorial collections include sports, entertainment, news, archival, and fashion images.[153] Getty Images works with more than one hundred distribution partnerships worldwide to leverage the content available to its fullest extent.[154] Additionally, since 2016, Getty Images has been the exclusive access point for the former Corbis images collection.[155] While not all of the images formerly available from Corbis have transferred to Getty Images for licensing and distribution, the vast majority have, which makes relicensing Corbis content now possible with Getty Images.

Cultural institutions that choose to contribute content to Getty Images will be able to select the collection and noncollection images they contribute and outline any use restrictions for the images. This includes the opportunity to review and approve or deny specific types of requests. Prior to providing images to Getty Images, the cultural institution will complete a standard contributor agreement, which by default asks that the images be provided on an exclusive basis, but is open for amendment to be a nonexclusive contract so as to not conflict with any other partnerships the cultural institution may have already entered or may consider in the future. Getty Images guarantees all royalty payments, which typically range from 20 to 40 percent of the license fee to contributing institutions (meaning that if a license is unpaid, the contributor still receives its percentage of the fees while Getty Images will endeavor to receive the payment). Furthermore, Getty Images takes on the assessment of all legal issues, including rights clearance of contributed content, as well as the promotion and marketing of the image collection that is contributed.

Scala Archives

The Scala Archives[156] was founded in 1953 as a means of professionally photographing works of art and architecture and making the images available for publications and other commercial endeavors. It has since grown in scope, and today the Scala Picture Library includes more than three hundred thousand images available as high-resolution files covering all periods of Western art from antiquity to the present. The broader Scala Archives serves as the representative of several additional image collections from cultural institutions and professional photography and film company archives, amounting to millions of additional images that can be researched and licensed through their staff.[157]

To further increase distribution, the Scala Archives have partnered with Art Resource since 1999 to be the European representative of the US collections it has partnered with (and vice versa: users in the United States can license Scala Archives images through Art Resource). With a staff of trained art historians available to research all manner of requests, from paintings by specific artists to works that illustrate a given idea or theme, Scala images are utilized in book and magazine publications, prints, merchandising, television, film, and publicity.[158]

Scholars Resource

Scholars Resource[159] provides educational access to their image library via site licenses.[160] To this end, Scholars Resource strictly licenses images via site licenses to educational institutions for noncommercial teaching and research purposes only; images are not licensed to individuals or commercial entities. Notably, all images from Scholars Resource are licensed in perpetuity so end users do not have to complete the site license agreement repeatedly.[161] The content available spans every period of art history and is coupled with standardized metadata delivered with each image file. With its focus on the educational curriculum, Scholars Resource's textbook sets provide digital access to images in many art history textbooks, and curated image sets provide teaching resources for specific art historical eras and topics.[162]

Contributions to Scholars Resource are from cultural institutions directly as well as through the aggregation of content from other image distributors, including Bridgeman Education and Davis Art Images. Any cultural institution to one of these latter partners has the opportunity to approve the extension of their images and data to Scholars Resource.

REVENUE GENERATION AND OPEN ACCESS

If a cultural institution decides to go the Open Access (OA) route for image distribution, the question should be asked of whether it will still receive fees from third-party distributors and continue the working relationship. An institution may find itself in the position of giving something away for free while a third party is charging a licensing fee and sending the institution a check for its percentage of the sales. Institutions that work with third-party distribution partners and also operate under an OA policy should consider whether they wish to maintain their relationships, particularly if there is the potential of a mixed message that may be perceived by the public. There is no right or wrong answer, and each institution should study its own situation.

REVENUE GENERATION WITH OPEN AND PUBLIC DOMAIN CONTENT

Several cultural institutions continue to explore open licenses as opportunities for revenue generation. While open licenses have many similarities to traditional licenses of collection materials, they offer the opportunity to rethink more traditional licensing models.[163] For many cultural organizations, traditional licensing may still be a steady source of revenue generation (via reproductions, merchandising, and more), even if that revenue is just compensation for staff services rendered to provide the materials. Open licenses are different from traditional cultural institution practices with public domain materials in a key way: institutions have often been able to exercise de facto "ownership" of public domain materials in their collections because those materials are unique items to which the institutions can control access. Open licensing, by contrast, involves intentionally *not* trying to control access to or use of materials.

However, open licensed materials often can and do spread much further than limited-access materials. Thus, they often provide surprising opportunities for their creators and sharers to generate revenues, just by reaching newer and broader audiences.

Some common revenue-generation opportunities related to open-licensed content include:

- *Sales of Original Copies*
  Many readers are willing to pay for electronic or print copies of original works, even when they are openly licensed. A number of books, both fiction and nonfiction, have been published with open licenses, and there is some evidence that open electronic copies may actively drive sales.[164] In addition,

CASE STUDY

CONSIDERING WHEN NOT TO USE THIRD-PARTY IMAGE DISTRIBUTION

John ffrench

For several years the Yale University Art Gallery (YUAG) worked with Art Resource, Scala, and DNP Communications Co. Initially, the primary reasons for working with these distribution partners was to broaden the outreach of its collections. However, the relationships were also seen as a revenue stream that helped to offset the costs of digitizing collection objects through the licensing of images for scholarly and commercial purposes.

In the summer of 2011, Yale University adopted its Open Access policy[1] and the YUAG became an active participant. At that time, open access was still new for the Gallery, which did not have an efficient means of quickly delivering images. The decision was made to continue operating under the original agreements that granted each distribution partner the right to supply digital files for selling, leasing, or licensing images for reproduction in return for a percentage of fees realized.

Since that time, the Gallery improved its ability to deliver images of public domain objects to users directly from its website. When reviewing the quarterly income statements from each company, it was found that the majority of the images licensed were for works in the public domain. While recognizing that the companies did help bring visibility to collections that may not have otherwise been found, and that they provide a valuable service, the Gallery felt it was inappropriate to continue receiving income for sales generated on works that are offered for free directly through its own website. Therefore, in the summer of 2014, the YUAG decided to terminate its contracts with the aforementioned organizations.

NOTE

1. For more information, see chapter 2, Yale University Open Access Policy, and "Open Access to Digital Representations of Works in the Public Domain from Museum, Library, and Archive Collections at Yale University," Yale Digital Collections Center, May 5, 2011, http://web.library.yale.edu/sites/default/files/files/faq_oatodigitalrepresentations_pdworks_21mar2012.pdf.

popular books released with open licenses have been rapidly translated into other languages,[165] broadening readership still more.

- *Sales of Higher-Quality Versions*
  Already a familiar practice to many cultural institutions sharing lower-quality versions of a work online can create demand for higher-quality copies provided for a fee.
- *Sales of Merchandise*
  Another familiar practice for many cultural institutions selling attractive merchandise related to an open licensed work can produce revenue.[166]
- *Donations*
  Again a familiar practice for many cultural institutions open licensed content can make more people aware of the work that your organization is doing;

they may be interested in supporting that work with donations of money or time.

In addition to direct opportunities for revenue generation, open-licensed content can be a way to achieve public service missions (such as through open educational materials) and can provide options for exciting new collaborations and crowd-sourcing projects (such as Wikipedia Loves Art). Open licenses can only be granted by copyright holders or their agents, so cultural institutions are most likely to be able to apply them only to materials produced by the organization, or materials in which the organization has been given the copyright. However, a few cultural institutions have also invested in actively encouraging creators to openly license their own works, if only for noncommercial purposes, because of the public benefits.

CONCLUSION

Contributing content to third-party distribution partners is not a decision to be taken lightly or made quickly by cultural institutions. With all potential opportunities, cultural institutions should carefully assess the agreement that will be established with the distribution partner. Furthermore, they must remain cognizant that no one solution will fit all institutions. The decision begins with an assessment of whether an institution will work with distribution partners, and if so, which ones. The assessment should be completed with an analysis of the internal practices, risk, and liability that the cultural institution is comfortable assuming. As practices for licensing, charging fees, and Open Access policies continue to evolve, cultural institutions will likely see changes in the ways they either expand or cease collaborations with distribution partners. Finally, cultural institutions should remain aware that potential revenue generation is distinct from the benefit of reaching new audiences and continuing to serve existing ones.

NOTES

1. For the purposes of this chapter, a "distribution partner" is used to describe any company, service, or entity that a cultural institution may work with to share content related to collection works. The legal relationship between a cultural institution and a distribution partner may not be a legal "partnership" in each instance, but the term is being used generically here for the sake of simplicity.

2. It is critical to maintain this balance, particularly for cultural institutions that may utilize distribution partners as a means of completing the bulk of external requests the institution receives as a means of outsourcing part or all the responsibilities of rights and reproductions specialists.

3. The distribution partners discussed in this chapter are some, but not all, of the options available to cultural institutions.

4. See generally "Principles," OpenGLAM, accessed March 22, 2018, https://openglam.org/principles/.

5. See chapter 4, Assessing Risk, for more information.

6. Increasingly, many models (e.g., Flickr, Google, Shared Shelf Commons, DPLA, etc.) are moving toward the contributing institution clearing the rights, with the distributor acting as an "online service provider." For instance, institutions contributing to the Google Cultural Institute must complete the rights clearance for any content prior to its submission. See "Google Terms of Service," Google, last modified October 25, 2017, https://www.google.com/intl/en/policies/terms/.

7. An API (Application Programming Interface) provides a set of programming tools to search for and download images and metadata in bulk, without any effort on the part of the source institution beyond providing a password or key for access. In addition, if the recipient has the resources, the API can be utilized to keep images and data up to date via automated repeat "calls."

8. This list is not meant to be inclusive of all the distribution partners available.

9. "Artstor Digital Library," Artstor, accessed March 22, 2018, http://www.artstor.org/content/artstor-digital-library-features-benefits.

10. "Mission & History," Artstor, accessed March 22, 2018, http://www.artstor.org/mission.

11. Ibid.

12. See chapter 5, Shared Shelf Commons, for more information.

13. See chapter 5, Open Artstor, for more information.

14. "Artstor and ITHAKA will Join Forces," Artstor press release, January 28, 2016, http://www.artstor.org/press-release/artstor-and-ithaka-will-join-forces.

15. "Artstor Digital Library: Features & Benefits," Artstor, accessed March 22, 2018, http://www.artstor.org/content/artstor-digital-library-features-benefits.

16. Ibid.

17. "Teaching Resources: Subject Guides," Artstor, accessed March 5, 2018, http://www.artstor.org/content/subject-guides.

18. "Artstor Terms and Conditions of Use," Artstor, accessed March 22, 2018, http://www.artstor.org/artstor-terms.

19. "Trial Access," Artstor, accessed March 5, 2018, http://www.artstor.org/trial.

20. This is specifically the case with subscriptions that allow members of the general public to access the Artstor Digital Library through public libraries, in order to ensure that members of the general public cannot use the images outside the library for commercial or other purposes not related to scholarship and education.

21. Users at a subscribing institution authorized to access Artstor Digital Library content consist of (as applicable): (a) individuals officially affiliated with an institution (such as staff, volunteer staff, faculty, enrolled students, affiliated researchers, card holders, and members); (b) individuals not officially affiliated with an institution but who have an educational or scholarly or similar association with it (such as visiting researchers, lecturers, and substitute teachers); and (c) individuals physically present in the facilities of the institution ("walk-in users"). Individuals who do not have an official or unofficial affiliation with the institution (such as alumni or persons whose only association to the institution is that they pay fees to use the physical facilities or services (such as users of a college or museum library), or who, through an agreement with licensee, may access licensee's computer terminals), may only access the Artstor Digital Library as walk-in users. This limitation on the types of users that can access the Artstor Digital Library is meant to ensure that access to the library is only extended to those who would be using the service for noncommercial, educational and scholarly purposes. Ibid.

22. "Initiatives: Images for Academic Publishing (IAP)," Artstor, accessed March 5, 2018, http://www.artstor.org/content/collaborations. For additional information on IAP, see James Shulman, "Sustainable Free: Lessons Learned from the Launch of a Free Service Supporting Publishing in Art History," https://dspace.library.uu.nl/handle/1874/300769.

23. Institutions contributing to IAP as of 2018: The Metropolitan Museum of Art: Brooklyn Museum Costumes, Mellink Archive of Bryn Mawr College, Dallas Museum of Art, Getty Research Institute: Photo Archives, Getty Research Institute: Study of Photographs of Tapestries, Indianapolis Museum of Art at Newfields, Northwestern University Library: Ramon Casas sketchbooks, Princeton University Art Museum, The Walters Art Museum, and Yale University Art Gallery. "Images for Academic Publishing," Artstor, accessed March 22, 2018, https://support.artstor.org/?article=images-for-academic-publishing.

24. Ibid.

25. Ibid.

26. Ibid.

27. "Artstor Terms and Conditions of Use," Artstor, updated March 5, 2018, http://www.artstor.org/artstor-terms.

28. "Lincoln's Inn, the Chapel, and Old Hall, London," Yale Center for British Art, Open Artstor, accessed March 22, 2018, http://search.openlibrary.artstor.org/object/AYCBAIG_10313605219.

29. See chapter 5, Digital Public Library of America, for more information.

30. Artstor, "Artstor to help launch the Digital Public Library of America," Artstor Blog: Images and Ideas for Teaching and Scholarship, March 28, 2013, https://Artstor.wordpress.com/2013/03/28/Artstor-to-help-launch-the-digital-public-library-of-america/.

31. "NEW: JSTOR Forum: Make your local collections more discoverable," JSTOR, accessed March 22, 108, https://about.jstor.org/l/introducing-jstor-forum/.

32. "Introducing JSTOR Forum: A new tool for managing and distributing collections," JSTOR, accessed March 22, 2018, https://about.jstor.org/news/introducing-jstor-forum-new-tool-managing-distributing-collections/.

33. Ibid.

34. Artsy, accessed March 5, 2018, https://www.artsy.net/.

35. "About Artsy," Artsy, accessed March 5, 2018, https://www.artsy.net/about.

36. "Artsy for Museums; Audience," Artsy, accessed March 5, 2018, https://www.artsy.net/institution-partnerships/audience.

37. "Artsy for Museums: Education," Artsy, accessed March 5, 2018, https://www.artsy.net/institution-partnerships/education.

38. See generally "Artsy for Galleries," Artsy, accessed March 5, 2018, https://www.artsy.net/gallery-partnerships; "Artsy for Museums," Artsy, accessed March 5, 2018, https://www.artsy.net/institution-partnerships.

39. Ibid.

40. "Artsy for Museums," Artsy, accessed March 5, 2018, https://www.artsy.net/institution-partnerships.

41. Ibid.

42. "The Art Genome Project," Artsy, accessed March 22, 2018, https://www.artsy.net/about/the-art-genome-project.

43. Ibid.

44. Ibid.

45. Ibid.

46. "Artsy 2013," Artsy, accessed March 22, 2018, http://2013.artsy.net.

47. Artsy Education, "What else does Artsy offer? Additional Features for You," Artsy, accessed March 22, 2018, https://www.artsy.net/post/artsyed-what-else-does-artsy-offer-additional-features.

48. Ibid.

49. "Artsy for Museums," Artsy, accessed March 22, 2013, https://www.artsy.net/institution-partnerships/audience.

50. See chapter 5, Bridgeman Images, for more information.

51. Bridgeman Education, accessed March 22, 2018, https://www.bridgemaneducation.com/.

52. "About Us," Bridgeman Education, accessed March 22, 2018, https://www.bridgemaneducation.com/en/about-us.

53. Ibid.

54. Fees are based on the size of school or institution and the individual status of the person requesting access: teacher or student. Ibid.

55. Digital Public Library of America, accessed March 22, 2018, https://dp.la/.

56. "About DPLA," Digital Public Library of America, accessed March 22, 2018, https://dp.la/about.

57. Ibid.

58. "Hub Network," Digital Public Library of America, accessed March 22, 2018, https://pro.dp.la/hubs.

59. Content hubs can provide the DPLA with a large volume of metadata records (typically more than 150,000) that are linked to digital media (images, texts, etc.) and for which they commit to maintaining. "Become a Hub," Digital Public Library of America, accessed March 22, 2018, https://pro.dp.la/prospective-hubs/become-a-hub.

60. "Becoming a Service Hub," Digital Public Library of America, accessed March 22, 2018, https://pro.dp.la/prospective-hubs/becoming-a-service-hub. For a full list of current service hubs, see "Our Hubs," Digital Public Library of America, accessed March 22, 2018, https://pro.dp.la/hubs/our-hubs.

61. "The Digital Public Library of America Policy Statement on Metadata," Digital Public Library of America, accessed March 22, 2018, https://pro.dp.la/hubs/metadata-application-profile.

62. It should be noted that patent and trademark rights are not affected by attaching a CC Zero license, nor are the rights that other people may have in the work or in how the work is used, such as publicity or privacy rights. Ibid.

63. Ibid.

64. "Exhibitions," Digital Public Library of America, accessed March 22, 2018, https://dp.la/exhibitions.

65. "Developers," Digital Public Library of America, accessed March 9, 2015, https://pro.dp.la/developers.

66. "Projects," Digital Public Library of America, accessed March 22, 2018, https://pro.dp.la/projects.

67. Ibid.

68. "Google Arts & Culture," Google, accessed March 22, 2018, https://artsandculture.google.com/.

69. "About Google Cultural Institute," Google Cultural Institute, accessed March 22, 2018, https://www.google.com/culturalinstitute/about/.

70. Ibid.

71. Ibid.

72. "Google Arts & Culture," Google, accessed March 22, 2018, https://artsandculture.google.com/

73. Amit Sood, "From self-portraits to street art: 1,000 museums at your fingertips," Google Blog, January 21, 2016, https://blog.google/topics/arts-culture/from-self-portraits-to-street-art-1000/.

74. "Our History," Google Cultural Institute, accessed March 22, 2018, https://www.google.com/culturalinstitute/about/partners/.

75. Caryn Rousseau, "Google Art Project premiers upgrades in Chicago," The San Diego Union-Tribune, updated April 3, 2012, http://www.sandiegouniontribune.com/sdut-google-art-project-premieres-upgrades-in-chicago-2012apr03-story.html.

76. Google holds cultural institutions that are considering partnering with the Art Project (or other part of the Cultural Institute) to a nondisclosure agreement by which they cannot discuss or release any information about the upcoming partnership prior to its launch by Google.

77. If available, a collections website API is extremely helpful in this process.

78. Contributing institutions can edit, update, add, or delete any content directly through Google's CMS at any time.

79. "Street View," Google, accessed March 22, 2018, https://www.google.com/streetview/.

80. For example, visitors can explore the Isabella Stewart Gardner Museum's three floors: "Isabella Stewart Gardner Museum," Google Arts & Culture," accessed March 22, 2018, https://artsandculture.google.com/partner/isabella-stewart-gardner-museum.

81. "Art Project Gigapixels," Google Arts & Cultural, accessed March 22, 2018, https://artsandculture.google.com/usergallery/art-project-gigapixels/DAJiOwFKTTbQLQ.

82. For example, *Virgin and Child*, after 1454, at the Museum of Fine Arts, Houston was captured with the Gigapixel technology. "Virgin and Child," Google Arts & Cultural, accessed March 22, 2018, https://artsandculture.google.com/asset/virgin-and-child/hQFbxk_b423Q-g?hl=en.

83. The Tate detailed the experience in the blog post: James Davis, "Google Art Project: Behind the Scenes: Glowy Night at the Museum," Tate (blog), February 11, 2011, http://www.tate.org.uk/context-comment/blogs/google-art-project-behind-scenes-0.

84. "Google Open Gallery," Google Arts & Culture, accessed March 22, 2018, https://artsandculture.google.com/opengalleryinfo.

85. Ibid.

86. Ibid.

87. "World Wonders Project," Google Cultural Institute, accessed March 22, 2018, https://www.google.com/culturalinstitute/about/wonders/.

88. Ibid.

89. Flickr, accessed March 22, 2018, https://www.flickr.com/.

90. In April 2018, Flickr announced it had agreed to be acquired by SmugMug. At the time of publication it is still to be determined what changes this will mean to the platform and its use by cultural institutions. "Together is Where Photographers Belong! SmugMug + Flickr," Flickr Blog, accessed April 20, 2018.

91. "The Commons," Flickr, accessed March 22, 2018, https://www.flickr.com/commons.

92. "The Library of Congress," Flickr, accessed March 22, 2018, https://www.flickr.com/photos/library_of_congress/.

93. A full list of participating institutions can be found at "The Commons: Participating Institutions," Flickr, accessed March 22, 2018, https://www.flickr.com/commons/institutions/.

94. Library of Congress Photos on Flickr: Frequently Asked Questions: Technical Information, accessed March 22, 2018, http://www.loc.gov/rr/print/flickr_pilot_faq.html#why.

95. HathiTrust Digital Library, accessed March 22, 2018, http://www.hathitrust.org/.

96. "About," HathiTrust, accessed March 22, 2018, http://www.hathitrust.org/about.

97. "Searching, Reading, Building Collections, and Accessibility," HathiTrust, accessed March 22, 2018, http://www.hathitrust.org/access.

98. "Rights Holder Creative Commons Declaration Form," HathiTrust, accessed March 22, 2018, https://www.hathitrust.org/creative_commons_declaration_form

99. "Our Partnership," HathiTrust, accessed March 22, 2018, https://www.hathitrust.org/partnership.

100. Ibid.

101. Ibid.

102. "Features and Benefits," HathiTrust, accessed March 3022, 2018, https://www.hathitrust.org/features_benefits.

103. "Our Partnership," HathiTrust, accessed March 22, 2018, https://www.hathitrust.org/partnership.

104. "Features and Benefits," HathiTrust, accessed March 22, 2018, https://www.hathitrust.org/features_benefits.

105. "Rights Holder Creative Commons Declaration Form," HathiTrust, accessed March 22, 2018, https://www.hathitrust.org/creative_commons_declaration_form.

106. "Main Page," Wikipedia, accessed March 22, 2018, https://en.wikipedia.org/wiki/Main_Page.

107. "Wikimedia Foundation," Wikipedia, accessed March 22, 2018, https://en.wikipedia.org/wiki/Wikimedia_Foundation.

108. Wikimedia Commons, accessed March 22, 2018, https://commons.wikimedia.org/wiki/Main_Page.

109. "Commons: Welcome," Wikimedia Commons, accessed March 22, 2018, http://commons.wikimedia.org/wiki/Commons:Welcome.

110. "Commons: Copyright Tags," Wikimedia Commons, accessed March 22, 2018, https://commons.wikimedia.org/wiki/Commons:Copyright_tags.

111. "Commons: Welcome," Wikimedia Commons, accessed March 22, 2018, http://commons.wikimedia.org/wiki/Commons:Welcome..

112. The image data structure allows for inclusion of fields that match museum standards remarkably well, allowing tombstone information to be mapped to logical fields.

113. GLAM includes galleries, libraries, archives, and museums. "GLAM Wiki," Wikipedia, accessed March 22, 2018, https://en.wikipedia.org/wiki/Wikipedia:GLAM.

114. Wikipedia and Wikimedia content are entirely user generated, and anyone can edit, question, or remove content. For example, if an image is uploaded of a work that may not be in the public domain, it will likely be flagged for removal by an alert user. A discussion will ensue, in which the person who uploaded the image either provides additional information supporting their position, resulting in the flag being removed, or concedes the point and the image is taken down.

115. A list of Commons partnerships is available at "Commons: Partnerships," Wikimedia Commons, accessed March 22, 2018, https://commons.wikimedia.org/wiki/Commons:Partnerships/en.

116. "WikiAfrica," Wikipedia, accessed March 22, 2018, https://en.wikipedia.org/wiki/WikiAfrica.

117. "Wikipedia: Wikipedia Loves Art," Wikipedia, accessed March 22, 2018, https://en.wikipedia.org/wiki/Wikipedia:Wikipedia_Loves_Art.

118. "WikiPop," Brooklyn Museum, accessed March 22, 2018, https://www.brooklynmuseum.org/community/blogosphere/tag/wikipop/.

119. "Wikipedia: WikiProject Public art/TheArtistResearchProject/TonySmith," Wikipedia,

accessed March 22, 2018, http://en.wikipedia.org/wiki/Wikipedia:WikiProject_Public_art/TheArtistResearchProject/TonySmith.

120. This list is not meant to be inclusive of all the distribution partners available.

121. Art Resource, accessed March 22, 2018, http://www.artres.com.

122. Getty Images, accessed March 22, 2018, https://www.gettyimages.com/.

123. It is important for cultural institutions to be aware that many stock photography agencies seek to enforce copyrights in images of two-dimensional public domain works. See chapter 1, What Makes a Work "Original"?, for more information about the *Bridgeman Art Library v. Corel Corp.* 1999 case.

124. Art Resource, accessed March 22, 2018, http://www.artres.com/.

125. Ibid.

126. "About Us," Art Resource, accessed March 22, 2018, http://www.artres.com/C.aspx?VP3=CMS3&VF=ARTHO1_4_VForm&Flash=1&FRM=AboutUs_MainMenuContent:ARTHO1_6.

127. Ibid.

128. "Famous Museums, Monuments & Archives," Art Resource, accessed March 5, 2018, http://www.artres.com/C.aspx?VP3=CMS3&VF=ARTHO1_7.

129. Bridgeman Images, accessed March 22, 2018, http://www.bridgemanimages.com/en-US/.

130. "About Bridgeman," Bridgeman Images, accessed March 22, 2018, http://www.bridgemanimages.com/en-US/about-bridgeman/US.

131. Ibid.

132. "Museums," Bridgeman Images, accessed March 8, 2018, http://www.bridgemanimages.com/en-US/collections/museums-and-collections/museum/.

133. BACS represents the copyright of artists and their estates similar to ARS. "Bridgeman Copyright Artists," Bridgeman Images, accessed March 5, 2018, http://www.bridgemanimages.com/en-US/collections/bridgeman-copyright-artists/.

134. Bridgeman Images are made available for print on demand, which contributing institutions can opt in or out of at any time. "Bridgeman Art is in Demand this Christmas," Bridgeman Images, accessed March 5, 2018, http://www.bridgemanimages.com/en-GB/about-bridgeman/news/bridgeman-art-is-in-demand-this-christmas.

135. Bridgeman Education, accessed March 5, 2018, https://www.bridgemaneducation.com/en/. See chapter 5, Bridgeman Education, for more detailed information.

136. "About Bridgeman," Bridgeman Images, accessed March 5, 2018, http://www.bridgemanimages.com/en-US/about-bridgeman/US.

137. Ibid.

138. Davis, accessed March 5, 2018, https://www.davisart.com/.

139. "Subscribe to *SchoolArts* / Renew Your Subscription," Davis, accessed March 22, 2018, https://www.davisart.com/Promotions/SchoolArts/Subscribe.aspx.

140. "Divisions," Davis, accessed March 22, 2018, https://www.davisart.com/Promotions/AboutUs/Divisions.aspx.

141. "Davis Digital," Davis, accessed March 22, 2018, https://www.davisart.com/Promotions/Davis-Digital/Davis-Digital.aspx.

142. "Davis Art Images," Davis, accessed March 22, 2018, https://www.davisart.com/Promotions/Fine-Art-Images/Fine-Art-Images.aspx.

143. "SchoolArts Magazine," Davis, accessed March 5, 2018, https://www.davisart.com/Promotions/SchoolArts/Default.aspx.

144. "Davis Digital," Davis, accessed March 22, 2018, https://www.davisart.com/Promotions/Davis-Digital/Davis-Digital.aspx.

145. "SchoolArts Magazine," Davis, accessed March 22, 2018, https://www.davisart.com/Promotions/SchoolArts/Default.aspx.

146. "Davis Digital," Davis, accessed March 22, 2018, https://www.davisart.com/Promotions/Davis-Digital/Davis-Digital.aspx.

147. DNP Art Communications Co., Ltd., accessed March 5, 2018, http://dnpartcom.jp/en.

148. "About Us (English)," DNP Art Communications Co., Ltd., accessed March 5, 2018, http://dnpartcom.jp/en/.

149. Getty Images, accessed March 5, 2018, https://www.gettyimages.com/.

150. "About Us," Getty Images, accessed March 5, 2018, http://press.gettyimages.com/about-us/.

151. Getty Images, accessed March 5, 2018, https://www.gettyimages.com/.

152. "Creative Images," Getty Images, accessed March 5, 2018, https://www.gettyimages.com/creativeimages.

153. "Editorial Images," Getty Images, accessed March 5, 2018, https://www.gettyimages.com/editorialimages.

154. "Editorial Collections," Getty Images, accessed March 22, 2018, https://www.gettyimages.com/editorial-images/collections.

155. Tom Seymour, "Bill Gates sells Corbis to Getty via Chinese Consortium," British Journal of Photography, January 25, 2016, http://www.bjp-online.com/2016/01/bill-gates-sells-corbis-to-getty-via-chinese-consortium/.

156. Scala Archives, accessed March 22, 2018, http://www.scalarchives.com/.

157. "About Us? SCALA Archives in 10 Points," Scala Archives, accessed March 22, 2018, http://www.scalarchives.com/web/presentazione.asp.

158. Ibid.

159. Scholars Resource, accessed March 22, 2018, https://www.scholarsresource.com/.

160. Ibid.

161. "What Sets Scholars Resources Apart?," Scholars Resource, accessed March 22, 2018, https://www.scholarsresource.com/content/benefits.

162. "Textbook Sets," Scholars Resource, accessed March 22, 2018, http://www.scholarsresource.com/browse/textbooks.

163. An open license can be defined as "one which grants permission to access, re-use and redistribute a work with few or no restrictions." "Guide to Open Licensing," Open Definitions, accessed March 22, 2018, http://opendefinition.org/guide/.

164. John Hilton III and David Wiley, "Free: Why Authors Are Giving Books Away on the Internet," *TechTrends* 54, no. 2 (March 1, 2010): 43–49. doi:10.1007/s11528-010-0381-8.

165. For example, see Cory Doctorow's blog post announcing a German translation of his novel *Little Brother*. Cory Doctorow, "Little Brother German Fan-Translation," *Craphound* (blog), November 23, 2008, http://craphound.com/?p=2145.

166. For example, animator Nina Paley sells merchandise related to her film *Sita Sings the Blues*, which is available under a CC0 Public Domain Dedication. "Home," Sita Sings the Blues, accessed March 22, 2018, http://sitasingstheblues.com/.

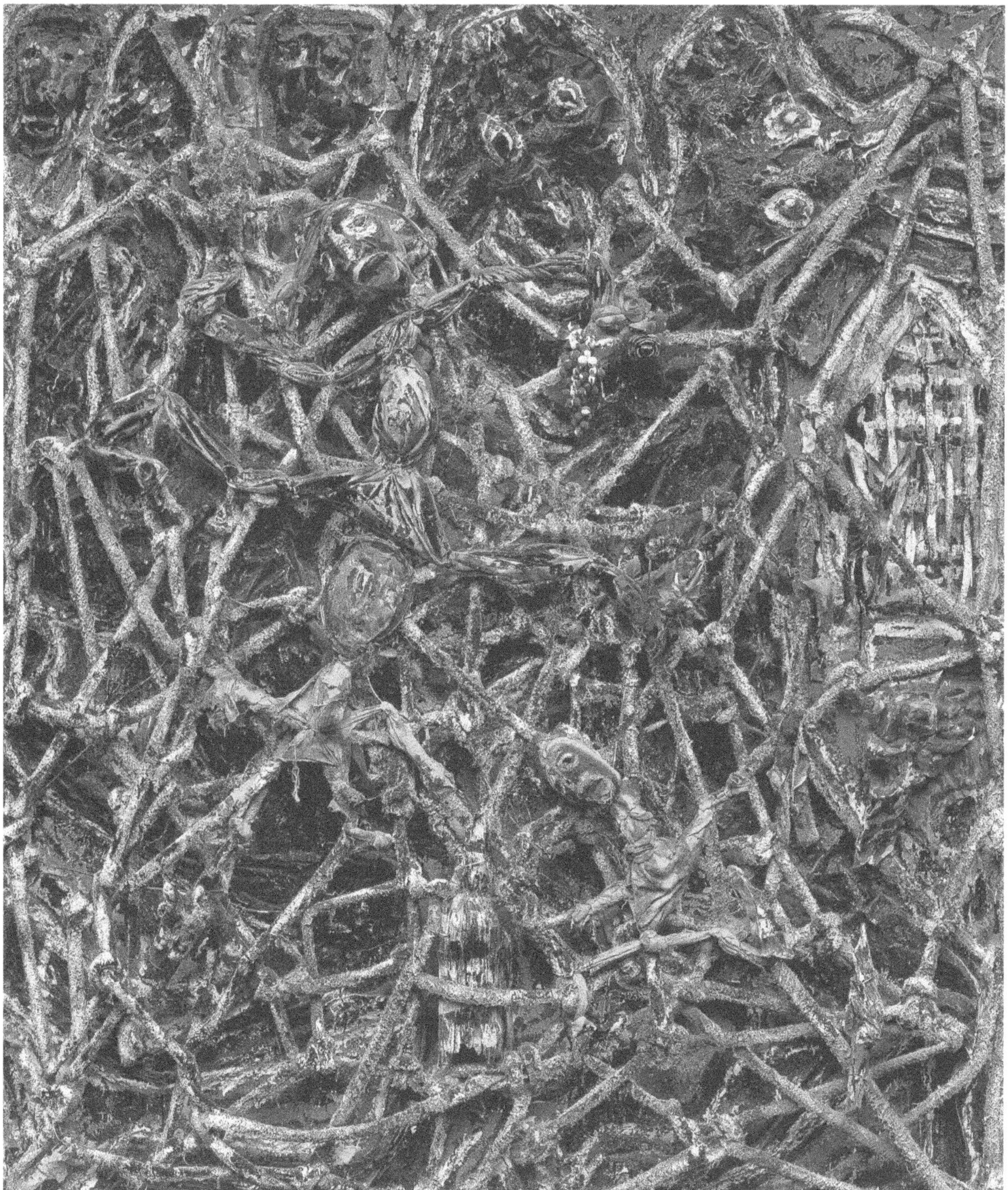

6

External Uses

MEGAN P. BRYANT, CHERIE C. CHEN, JOHN FFRENCH, MELISSA LEVINE, SOFÍA GALARZA LIU, MICHELLE GALLAGHER ROBERTS, NANCY SIMS, DEBORAH WYTHE, AND ANNE M. YOUNG

Cultural institutions spend vast amounts of time and resources developing procedures for institutional uses of intellectual property (IP) in or related to its collections, but the day-to-day focus of rights and reproductions specialists' work often centers on responding to external requests to use collection materials. This may involve everything from licensing images, video, and audio media of the collection to fielding requests to conducting a location shoot in the institution's building(s) or on its grounds. This chapter outlines the policies a cultural institution can adopt to govern external uses and provides practical step-by-step guidelines for processing the inquiries rights and reproductions specialists receive every day.

ACCESS TO IMAGES AND REPRODUCTIONS OF COLLECTION MATERIALS FOR EXTERNAL USES

Cultural institutions frequently receive external requests to reproduce images, videos, text, or audio recordings related to works in their collections. Third parties may seek to use these materials in a wide variety of commercial and noncommercial applications including, but not limited to, textbooks, exhibition catalogues, journals, television programs, films, brochures, billboards, websites, social media, calendars, apps, dissertations, and newspapers. Establishing formal procedures to handle external reproduction requests results in efficiency and consistency, as well as adherence to institutional policies, and aids in the documented use of collection materials. Providing image files for external reproduction purposes is one of the key ways that cultural institutions share their collections with the public; it is not uncommon to track external image request statistics in similar ways that attendance figures are tracked.

There are several approaches to granting access to images (or other materials) related to the collection:

1. licensing when the institution holds the copyright, or when the institution has a nonexclusive license from the rights holder that permits sublicensing
2. providing access to the images when requestor has permission of the copyright holder
3. providing access, either completely open or restricted to a specified use, to only images of public domain works
4. providing access to images of all works; rights clearance is the responsibility of the requestor[1]

An institution can utilize one or more of these approaches depending on the rights status of its collection, and there are pros and cons to every method. The first three hold the least amount of risk for the institution but can leave large sections of the collection inaccessible if much of the collection remains under copyright. The fourth approach allows an institution to grant access to images of all works in its collection.[2] However, since the responsibility to clear all applicable third-party rights rests entirely on the requestor, this should be clearly spelled out in the contract or agreement that governs the use of the provided media.[3] If an institution takes this approach, any liability associated with the third-party use should be transferred to the requestor via the terms of use in a written contract or agreement.

INFORMATION ABOUT THE REQUEST PROCESS

No matter which approach a cultural institution chooses to utilize when granting access to collection materials, it is important to provide some general information about the request process to the public so that a request can be handled efficiently. Ideally, this information is posted on an institution's website for easy reference,[4] though it could also be communicated upon request. It should include the types of uses that will be considered by the institution as well as practical details about the information the institution needs from requestors to process their order. Here are some recommended items to include on an information page:

- definitions for varying types of use (e.g., scholarly, commercial, personal, etc.)
- time frame for submitting a request (e.g., "at least six weeks prior to date needed")
- information required when submitting a request (e.g., full contact and usage details)
- link to an image request form or online submission template
- fees and payment process, if applicable
- credit line requirements
- number of gratis copies for the institution required
- party responsible for rights clearance

DEVELOPING A REQUEST FORM

Processing external requests can be streamlined by utilizing a form that collects all the necessary information required to assess and fulfill the request.[5] This form may be a Word or PDF document that the institution sends to the requestor to complete and return, or it may be available online so that it can be directly submitted.

Key information to capture on the request form:

- name of work/object in collection
- name of artist or maker
- unique identifier (e.g., accession or catalogue number)
- intended usage (catalogue, T-shirt, movie, etc.)
- project title
- author
- publisher
- expected release date
- print run, language(s), editions, formats (print, web, e-book, etc.)
- geographic distribution/territory
- reproduction size (e.g., cover, half-page, etc.)
- requestor's full contact information, including email address, phone number, and mailing address

Many institutions offer image request forms that allow information to be submitted directly via the institution's website.[6] Online forms can streamline and automate the request procedure both for the requestor and for the institution.

REPRODUCTION FEES

Reproduction fees vary from institution to institution for a variety of reasons.[7] Sometimes the governing body of an institution will influence the setting of fees, with private nonprofits having more flexibility than a governmental agency. Some cultural institutions consider supplying image files as a public service and part of their mission, and thus charge reduced fees (or waive them entirely) for educational uses. Others may need to consider the staff resources that go into processing requests—for instance, the cost of new photography or scanning—and thus structure their fees to recover those costs. While licensing can serve as a source of revenue, previous studies conducted by the Mellon Foundation have found that most cultural institutions do not make a significant profit against expenditures in their licensing activities.[8] It is helpful for potential requestors if the institution's fee schedule or, at minimum, an explanation of how fees are calculated, is posted on its website. Supplying this information up front will save time negotiating rates after the request has been submitted and will also negate any claims of capriciousness or unfair treatment.

When creating a fee schedule, it may be helpful to survey similar and local institutions to ensure general uniformity in fee categories, while the exact fee amounts should be determined based on the institution's budget needs and philosophical approach. Noncommercial uses such as scholarly publications or catalogue raisonnés will often fall under a reduced-rate category, whereas commercial uses such as coffee table books and calendars will not.[9] Just because a requestor is a nonprofit does not automatically make all its reproductions noncommercial. Consider the size of the print run and the publisher when determining what is commercial and what is noncommercial. Is a textbook with a run of 250,000 copies really a scholarly

CASE STUDY

SPECIAL TREATMENT OF LICENSING REVENUE AT THE SIXTH FLOOR MUSEUM

Megan P. Bryant

The Sixth Floor Museum at Dealey Plaza (TSFM) holds an extensive collection of film, video, audio, and images that constitute the primary visual record of the assassination of President John F. Kennedy and its aftermath. TSFM is in the unique position of owning the copyright to most of these holdings and has thus been able to respond to the high demand for external use of its collections with an active licensing program. While interest in TSFM images and licensing activity levels can be quite varied on a year-to-year basis and is often influenced by significant anniversary years, the generated revenue from licensing fees often surpasses the museum's production expenses to fulfill those requests.

TSFM has approached its licensing program with the philosophy that any revenue earned from licensing collection images that exceeds administrative costs is directed back into support of the collections. This philosophy was enacted into policy in 2010 with the establishment of TSFM's Board Designated Collections/Licensing Fund to capture revenues generated by the licensing of historic images, film, and footage owned and administered by TSFM. The policy directs that expenditures from the fund must be for the acquisition, care, or support of the museum's collections. The policy is stated in brief in the museum's Collections Management Policy and Ethics Policy, while the separate Collections/Licensing Fund Policy and Procedures provides details and guidelines. In general, this approach is similar to the ethical standards regarding the appropriate use of funds generated from the sale of deaccessioned collections. While the collection objects themselves are not sold, the revenue is tied closely to the reproduction and use of collection items. This budgetary designation of revenue from image use is a reinvestment in the museum's mission by directing the funds back to support the collections. This approach is not necessarily feasible for all cultural institutions, as revenue generated from licensing may not exceed the expenses involved. However, it is a practice worth considering in cases where there may be net income.

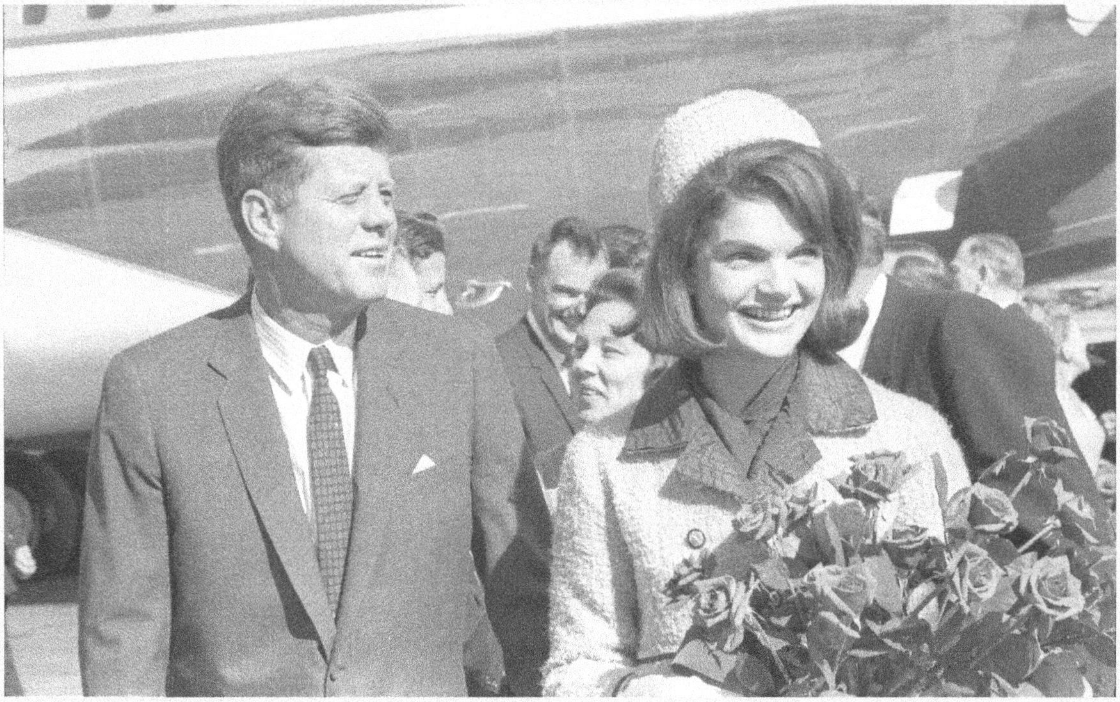

FIGURE 6.1
One of the photographs for which TSFM holds the copyright, showing President and Mrs. Kennedy arriving at Dallas Love Field Airport on November 22, 1963.

TSFM's Collections/Licensing Fund is neither substantial nor predictable enough for the museum to rely on in perpetuity, as the generated revenue depends entirely on the interest of paying external constituents. However, in the years since it was established,[1] the fund has allowed the museum to do things it would not otherwise have accomplished through the general operating budget. These expenditures included: successfully acquiring certain important, high-profile artifacts related to the Kennedy assassination at auction and by direct purchase from collectors; funding the initial setup of an online collections database; and digitizing select film and video collections.

TSFM's Collections/Licensing Fund evolved from the unusual circumstances of this history museum managing the rights to a collection of images and recordings that a persistent audience finds of interest. Applying the same ethical considerations that guide museums on the handling of funds generated by deaccessions seemed a natural direction for TSFM to take when establishing the Fund parameters.

NOTE

1. This period included 2013, the fiftieth anniversary of the Kennedy assassination, a time of unusually numerous licensing requests and contracts.

request? Sometimes an additional fee is assessed for cover uses of an image since it can be considered more promotional or decorative than an interior use.

Electronic books (e-books) and website uses are causing many institutions to reexamine their fee schedules since they do not have a traditional print run and do not fit neatly into established procedures. One way of handling e-books is to equate downloads to print runs. An institution can count downloads in addition to a traditional print run or as a part of it (if a printed copy is also being produced). However, duration or term length of use may be a more efficient means of measure. An institution could allow an unlimited number of downloads as long as they occur within a set time period. Time limits are the most useful and applicable when it comes to websites. While there are few standards for determining duration and term lengths, the length used most often is a two- to five-year limit before additional permissions are required.[10] Licensing in perpetuity may be an option for a cultural institution, particularly given the difficulty that can arise with having to track licenses with a time limit.

PRODUCT DEVELOPMENT AND ROYALTIES

A cultural institution owning both the copyright to the objects in its collection and the photographic images of these works can enter into licensing agreements with product development companies. Often under these circumstances, an institution will waive any up-front image or licensing fees (as applicable) in exchange for recurring royalties. It is critical that an institution clearly understands the terms of the commercial licensing agreement.[11] Some questions to consider:

- Does the contract bestow any exclusivity to the licensing company?
- What is the final product?
- Who will own the copyright to the final product?
- What are the terms of the contract?
- What are each party's responsibilities?
- Does the cultural institution have final approval of the product?
- What is the agreed-upon schedule for approvals and deliverables?
- What is the payment schedule?
- Under what circumstances can the contract be canceled?
- Will use of the images be assignable by the external user to third parties?
- Will the external user be able to create derivative uses?
- Will the institution take on additional liability under the contract?

A cultural institution that owns the object—but not some or all the rights to the work or images of the work—may license images to an external user provided that all other rights holders have consented. This consent must be in writing and is typically through a written agreement between the rights holder and the institution. The institution would need to get the rights holder to agree to the terms of the arrangement and either become a party to the contract with the product development company or sign a separate agreement with the institution giving it permission to enter into the agreement with the product development company on his or her behalf. Depending on the terms of the underlying agreement (including any revenue-sharing provisions), the institution can then typically license these images.

PROCESSING EXTERNAL REQUESTS

Depending on the institution's approach to licensing images, the following questions need to be answered internally:

1. Does the request meet the institution's policy on permitted uses?
2. What rights to license the image does the institution hold?
3. Is the work in the public domain?

CASE STUDY: RECONSIDERING REPRODUCTION FEES

Anne M. Young

Beginning first in 2012 and again in 2015, the Indianapolis Museum of Art at Newfields undertook systematic reviews of the rights and reproductions fees assessed for external requests. These reviews were driven by the need to balance increasing access to collection materials while still maintaining an income stream. It was quickly determined that while some level of income generation was desired, it would no longer be the main goal. The main goal would be the dissemination of information and images of the collection to reach the widest audience possible and foster scholarly endeavors.

With the first review in 2012, reproduction fees for most uses were either significantly reduced or completely eliminated. Image preparation fees were retained and often still apply when new photography is required to fulfill a request that had waived reproduction fees. Additionally, the number of gratis copies requested was reduced from asking for three to five copies to simply one. Tangible results were readily visible with the overall fee reduction, which resulted in additional requests, increased staff workload, and—most surprisingly—increased revenue. In many cases, requestors were happy to pay the image preparation fee, often for more works than initially requested, as the cost for the new photography was significantly lower than paying for both new photography and reproduction fees and allowed the requestor to source more images. Furthermore, seeking only a single gratis copy increased the number actually received; previously it was not uncommon to receive fewer copies than requested or none at all.

Building upon the success of the 2012 changes, research continued into various types of open access (OA) models that would further the institution's goals and mission. Central to the consideration of an OA model was the ability to capture information about where and when collection images are reproduced. This information is sought not to control the use of the images or charge fees, but to retain a bibliography of how and where collection objects are reproduced. The 2015 online collection pages redesign included the functionality for the direct download of OA images.[1]

Prior to the OA launch, the fee structure was benchmarked by two legal interns against the fee structures at other museums, libraries, and archives. It was then revised to reflect the new OA model, including raising the threshold for when reproduction fees may apply for images not provided via OA.[2] For non-OA images, if a high-resolution image file is available, no reproduction fee is assessed for research, teaching, or scholarly uses under 10,000 copies or for up to a 10-year term (almost all of these types of requests fall well under these thresholds). This update maintained the policy that a fee will be assessed for these types of requests only if a new scan or photography is required.

After both revisions, Newfields has seen increased uses of its collection materials. Because the image preparation fee is often the only fee assessed, more collection works are undergoing new photography, which means more collection objects are digitized, more images are now available via OA, and more works are reproduced by external users.

NOTES

1. See chapter 5, Case Study: Rethinking Online Collection Pages, for a more detailed discussion.
2. "Rights & Reproductions Fee Schedule," Newfields, accessed March 21, 2018, https://discovernewfields.org/application/files/8315/0733/2356/RR_FeeSchedule_Newfields_2017.pdf.

4. If the work is under copyright, is there a nonexclusive license for the photographic representation and/or underlying work that permits sublicensing it to a third party for the requested use?
5. If the work depicts sensitive content, does the request meet the institution's policy about distribution of such materials?

Once it is determined that the image can be licensed, the rights and reproductions specialist generates a contract or agreement that includes the conditions under which institutional permission is granted to the requestor. This will be a legally binding agreement, and the template should be developed in consultation with legal counsel.[12] As long as the agreement does not require alteration of the institution's template, each new request and contract should not need to be reviewed by legal counsel.[13]

The details specific to each request (as captured in the request form submitted by the requestor) should be clearly outlined in the agreement, which may include some or all the following:

- exact use(s) of the image(s) being granted
- object attribution
- how the institution will be credited
- whether cropping, text overlay, or color manipulation of the image are allowed
- whether color proofs are required for approval prior to printing (if applicable)
- the approval process for the use of details, colored ink, or colored stock
- number of print runs, downloads, editions, or time limits (years) of use allowed before additional permissions are required
- number of gratis copies, or copies at cost, of the publication that must be supplied to the institution[14]
- licensing fees, if applicable
- whether advertising uses of the image are allowed
- whether the image may be used on any covers without further permission
- any applicable term of use
- any applicable geographic territory distribution limits
- whether the digital file must be deleted after a set time period[15]
- if the image will be reproduced digitally, what resolution or size must be used
- what, if any, image file will be supplied by the holding institution

The agreement should be signed and dated by the requestor and countersigned by the rights and reproductions specialist or other authorized staff member as determined by the institution's policy.[16] It is advisable to send the image files only after the agreement has been completed and any applicable fees paid.

A STEP-BY-STEP GUIDE TO PROCESSING EXTERNAL REQUESTS

Anne M. Young

Having step-by-step guidelines in place for how to process an external request ensures standard procedures are followed. These guidelines are also useful when new staff are hired or in cases where alternate staff members are required to assist the rights and reproductions specialist. The following are general recommendations for the overall process and should be tailored to the specific needs, staff workflows, and rights and reproductions practices at the cultural institution.

When an external request is received, first assess it to ensure all required information (e.g., contact information, image requirements, and intended publication or project use) is present to allow the rights and reproductions specialist to process what is sought. If the request *does not* contain all the required information, contact the requestor and ask that they fill out an image request form, either for the first time or more completely. It is also recommended that the institution's fee schedule and any requirements for reproducing works be included with the communication. The following is an example of the text that might be sent to the requestor:

> Thank you for your recent inquiry to obtain an image(s) from [insert institution name]. In order to more fully assess your needs, please complete the attached image request form. Our fee schedule and requirements for reproducing works from the collection are also attached for your review. Upon receipt of the completed form, we will be able to let you know if/when we will be able to supply you with the requested image(s). If you have any questions, please do not hesitate to contact us.

If/when the request *does* contain all the required information, the rights and reproductions specialist can do the following:

- Review work(s) being requested for any rights concerns. If an artist's work(s) are under copyright, follow the institution's practice for licensing images of copyrighted works and either provide files for which the institution has approval from the rights holder to sublicense or direct the requestor to the rights holder or licensing agency to obtain permission for their use.
- Review current photography available of the work(s) requested. If available, review the files that may be located within the institution's DAMS. If a digital image file is not available in the DAMS, consult with photography and imaging staff to complete an image quality check. This will be done to determine if another digital file exists that can be used and/or if a usable transparency is available. If there is no usable digital image file or transparency, new photography of the work will need to be scheduled.
- Review what fees might be assessed based upon the cultural institution's fee schedule. Be sure to note if the intended use is scholarly or commercial, including the print run or term length being sought, both of which may have a bearing on the reproduction fees that may or may not apply for the given use. Furthermore, if the image requested requires either a transparency to be scanned or new photography to be conducted, an image preparation fee may need to be assessed.

After the assessment of the submitted request, contact the requestor to notify them of any copyright concerns, the current photography available, estimated image delivery date, and any associated fees that may apply. The following is an example of the text that might be sent to the requestor:

> Thank you for completing the image request form. We will be able to supply you with the image(s) by [insert date]. As far as fees go, due to your use and low print run, we can waive any reproduction fee. We will have to assess our image preparation fee of $X USD [plus $X rush fee, if applicable] to [scan and prepare a digital file of the existing transparency or complete new photography] of this work. Let me know if this fee meets your approval, and we will schedule the preparation, contract, and invoice. If you have any questions, do not hesitate to contact us.

Once this communication is sent, the rights and reproductions specialist is in a holding pattern waiting for the requestor to advise if/how they would like to proceed based upon the aforementioned information.

If all of the conditions are amenable and the request will be fulfilled, prepare the contract/agreement and invoice (if applicable) for the use. Retain a copy of the drafted contract and invoice should they need to be re-sent to the requestor. At this point in the process, it can be helpful to utilize a project management system, such as Basecamp,[1] or other database or spreadsheet system, such as Access or Excel, if a cultural institution does not have a CMS or DAMS that can track and record the variety of steps when processing external requests. Thus, project management systems can facilitate tracking the progress of the request by noting when:

- the contract and invoice (if applicable) are sent
- the contract is completed
- payment (if applicable) is received
- requests are completed, denied, and/or abandoned

Once prepared, send the contract and invoice (if applicable) to the requestor to review and sign. The following are examples of the text that might be sent to the requestor:

> **With an invoice:** Attached is the contract and invoice for your use of the image(s) from [insert institution name]. Please review, sign, and return the contract. Payment information for the invoice is included with the contract. If you have questions about the invoice, please contact [insert name and email address]. Once we have received the contract and payment, the image will be sent to you by the date requested. Please note that the contract does ask for [X] copies of the publication when it is produced. If you have any questions, please do not hesitate to contact us.
>
> **Without an invoice:** Attached is the contract for your use of the image(s) from [insert institution name]. Please review, sign, and return the contract. Once we have received the contract, the image will be sent to you by the date requested. Please note that the contract does ask for [X] copies of the publication when it is produced. If you have any questions, please do not hesitate to contact us.

Once the contract is completed by both parties, send the requestor a copy for their records and retain a copy to be filed with the request. The following is an example of the text that might be sent to the requestor: "Attached is a copy of the completed image use contract for your records. If you have any questions, please do not hesitate to contact us."

Concurrent with the contract and invoice process, any needed image preparation can be scheduled and completed. Similarly, it is helpful to utilize a project management system and/or a DAM to streamline and track the requests for image preparation, any new photography, and sending the requested image file(s). This will allow the entire request to be tracked by both the rights and reproductions specialist and the imaging or photography staff involved in the fulfillment of the requested images. Send the file(s) as close to the due date as possible to allow adequate time for contract paperwork to be completed prior to the image file being sent. Additionally, if fees are assessed it is recommended that the image file is not sent until confirmation of payment. Following these guidelines will result in less time spent trying to track down payments and unreturned contracts. For these reasons, it is important that all parties involved are aware of the agreed-upon timelines and any fees being assessed so that files are not sent to the external requestor prior to the completion of these elements.

Finally, the cultural institution should retain both digital and hard copies of the following materials related to the request (filed by institution or individual):[2]

- image request form (and/or request email, letter, etc.)
- contract/agreement for image use (if applicable)
- invoice (if applicable)
- pertinent e-mail communication(s) with requestor concerning the request for or use of the image materials

NOTES

1. Basecamp, accessed March 21, 2018, https://basecamp.com.
2. Long-term retention of these documents should be based upon the cultural institution's practices for archiving materials and documents. For example, Newfields retains external request documents for up to ten years within the rights and reproductions department files; files older than ten years are transferred to the institutional archive.

OPEN ACCESS FOR EXTERNAL USES

Open access (OA)[17] sits on the opposite end of the licensing spectrum from handling external use requests on a case-by-case basis. A growing number of cultural institutions worldwide have announced OA initiatives that offer free downloads of high-resolution public domain collection images for a range of preapproved uses.[18] Problematically, OA programs vary from institution to institution, with no consistent definition of what constitutes "open access" among them. Some institutions limit uses of the downloadable OA files to noncommercial purposes, essentially only semi-open access, whereas others offer unrestricted use, including commercial ones. Thus, it is important to read and understand the specific terms and conditions for the individual institutions when using OA images from different sources.[19]

A cultural institution planning to offer OA should work to clearly communicate its terms and conditions and decide how best to deliver the image files given its resources. A separate microsite or website can be created to provide OA information and downloads,[20] or the institution can integrate the policy information within its existing online request pages and offer downloads from its online collection pages.[21] Whichever format is chosen, the institution should visibly label the OA content and provide cross-references on its website to help viewers find the OA images. It may also be helpful to communicate how the external requestor can request additional content that is not yet included as part of the OA distribution (either larger file sizes or perhaps a work for which an image does not currently exist).[22]

Beyond the exact mechanisms of content delivery, there are a host of other decisions to make regarding the parameters of an OA program:

- **Usage restrictions:** Will the institution permit noncommercial uses only, unrestricted uses, or something in between? If uses will be limited, be sure to provide clear definitions of the types approved.
- **Object attribution and collection credit line:** Will these be required? Whether required or merely recommended, it is helpful to supply attribution and credit line information with the downloaded image to assist those who want to identify the work

or credit the collection from which the image was sourced. A credit line can be as simple as: "Image courtesy of [insert institution name]," where the institution is identified without claiming any rights to the materials.

- **Gratis copies:** Will these be requested? A cultural institution making the shift to OA must understand and accept that it will receive fewer gratis copies for its records and library, which may be a concern for its curators. One way to address this concern is to ask users of OA content to send a gratis copy of whatever is produced for its institutional records, while making it clear that this is not a condition of use, but rather a courtesy back to the institution.[23]
- **Data collection:** Does the institution want to track download statistics? Should users be required to provide any information about who they are and how the content will be utilized? Some OA advocates consider any data collection to be a barrier to true OA, while others believe the curatorial responsibility to maintain the collection bibliography should take precedence.[24] If the decision is made to collect data, an institution may wish to capture more or less information depending upon the intended use. For instance, knowing more complete information about a scholarly publication is likely to be more valuable for the institution than collecting similar information about the personal use of an image used as a computer screen background.[25]
- **File specifications:** What size files should be provided? A single size or multiple sizes optimized for different uses? Consider that an extremely large, high-resolution file may be unwieldy for lecture or classroom use. Should the user be able to request image resizing or additional content (perhaps a work for which an image does not currently exist), and would fees apply for those added services? The institution may also wish to consider embedding metadata in the downloadable files.
- **FAQ:** In addition to revising its terms and conditions and its existing online request materials, an institution may wish to prepare a FAQ in advance to address specific questions.[26]

Finally, collection images offered under OA should be carefully reviewed by the institution and be free of:

- **Third-party copyright restrictions:** The work depicted should be in the public domain, or rights in the work must be held by the institution. Rights in any images of the work should be held by the institution (e.g., not by a contract photographer who retained rights).
- **Privacy/publicity restrictions:** If the original work is a photograph and depicts a person, are there any potential privacy or publicity issues with offering the image under the contemplated OA terms and conditions? This is of greater concern when the images may be used for any purpose, including commercial use. Institutions offering unrestricted OA images may want to individually review these images to determine if the individual depicted is likely to be deceased.[27]
- **Contractual restrictions:** If the original work was donated to the institution (or its purchase was funded by donors), are gift credit lines mandated in the gift agreements? If so, the institution may need to require attribution for any third-party uses and exclude the work from OA. Deeds of gift must be reviewed for these and any other restrictions, which should be noted in the rights records in the institution's CMS, before images of donated works are added to OA.

LICENSING AND LOCATION SHOOTS

Many cultural institutions are in the fortunate position of being able to leverage their building(s) and ground(s) for licensing and location shoots as an alternate means of revenue generation.[28] A location shoot may take the form of major motion pictures, television shows, documentaries, and print or television commercials. An institution seeking to formalize a program to leverage its building or grounds for location shoots should first research similar institutions with a program already in place. Being able to compare with an institution within the same geographic region will greatly aid in developing an hourly or daily fee range

CASE STUDY

PUBLIC DOMAIN AND OA AT THE YALE UNIVERSITY ART GALLERY

John ffrench

It's your cultural heritage.

Rip. Mix. Burn.

Remember Apple's slogan when they launched the iMac range in 2001? "Rip, mix, burn. After all, it's your music." While seen by some as advocating piracy, Apple was aiming to put consumers' music in their hands and to give them the freedom to be creative. In his keynote speech at the 2006 Museum Computer Network (MCN) conference, Ken Hamma urged the museum community to open up and share, to provide access[1]—that doing something was clearly the better alternative to doing nothing. Today's OA policies provide the public direct access to work in the public domain freely and unrestricted, allowing for creativity.

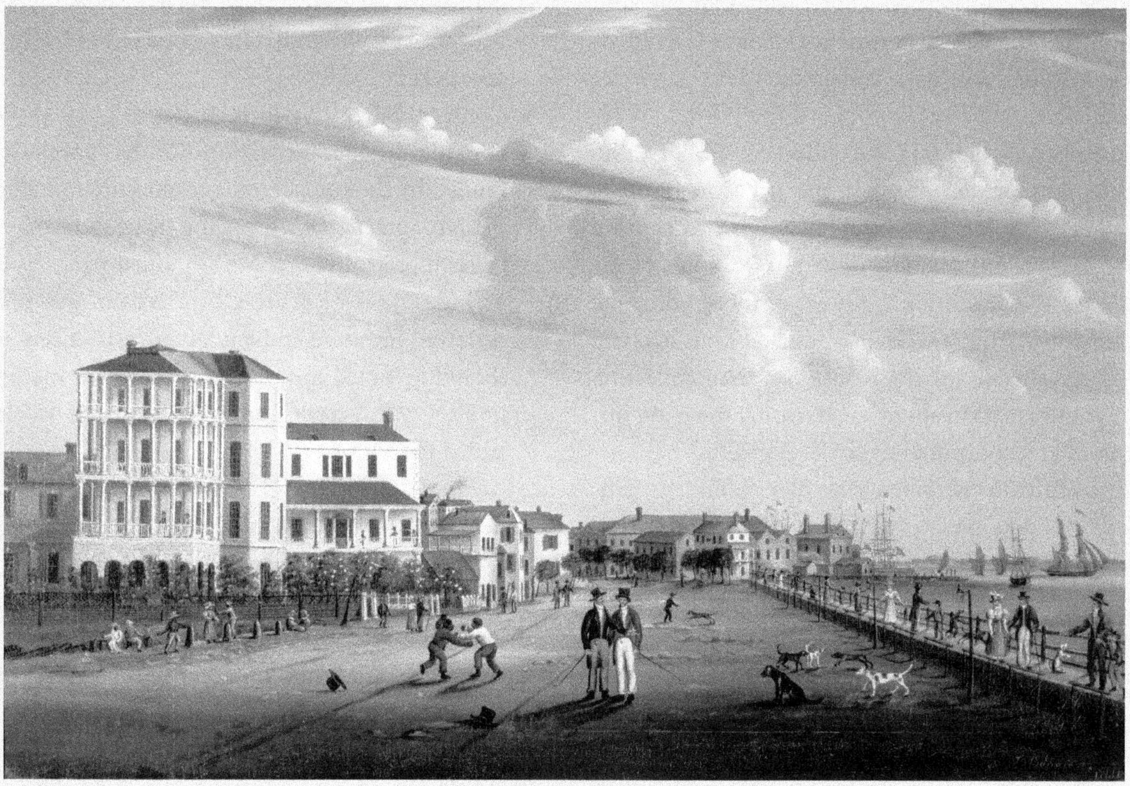

FIGURE 6.2
Work from the YUAG collection that was manipulated in a reproduction as permitted via YUAG's OA program.

In the fall of 2014, a freelance image researcher working with Penguin Books wrote to express interest in reproducing a Yale University Art Gallery (YUAG) OA image on the cover of a novel. However, the researcher wished to manipulate the image for the book cover design by cropping it as well as digitally introducing new elements and removing others. The image in question was a painting dated 1831 by Samuel Barnard entitled, *View along the East Battery, Charleston.* The image fit the general era and scenes within the book, but Penguin Books wanted to remove two of the key figures in the painting and replace them with the central characters in the story.

YUAG did not need to be contacted to approve this requested use, given that the work is in the public domain and the image is available under Yale's OA policy. Yale believes cultural heritage materials should be freely available to the public, and while the primary goal of its OA policy is to enable scholarship about its collections, the commercial creative reuse of material should not necessarily be prohibited either.[2] When deciding to adopt an OA policy, the YUAG was particularly interested in seeing how people might creatively reuse or reimagine works in its collection. This was the first known case where Yale was directly contacted about the use.

Institutions contemplating OA must be willing to accept that it will reach beyond the primary bounds of scholarly work. The sticking point in these cases may well be determining how best to cite the original work. The suggestion made to Penguin Books in this case was to credit the work as: "Altered image based on original work in the collection of the Yale University Art Gallery."

NOTES

1. Ken Hamma, "Investing for the Public," 2006 Museum Computer Network Conference, last modified September 7, 2006, http://mcn.edu/conferences/past-conferences/.
2. See chapter 2, Case Study: OA at Yale University, for more information about the adoption of OA at YUAG.

for location shoots (e.g., an institution in a major metropolitan city can command a higher hourly rate than an institution in a more rural setting).

Secondly, a cross-departmental committee should be established to review any applications for licensing and location shoots for aesthetics, appropriateness, economics, and potential legal issues.[29] Members of this committee should at the very least include representatives from rights and reproductions, marketing, collections management staff (including registration and conservation), and other departments that may be impacted by the potential shoot (e.g., curatorial, gardens, or grounds staff). When reviewing the shoot application, the committee should consider factors such as the appropriateness of the project's association with the institution, scheduling and logistical restrictions, conservation concerns, and availability of staff and resources to oversee the shoot.[30]

If a shoot is provisionally approved by the committee, negotiations with the requestor will ensue for the terms of the contract, including but not limited to the rights of both parties to use the resulting media, utilization of any branding or trademarks of the licensing institution, and the hourly rate for the location shoot fee. The institution should utilize a standard written contract to be executed prior to commencement of a shoot, which includes an express license and warranty for use of the cultural institution's intellectual property and indemnification of the institution by the requestor against any third-party infringement claims, including but not limited to copyrights, trademarks, privacy, and publicity.[31] Credit lines, copyright notices, and trademark notices are typically required and specified where relevant. Unlike processing an external request to reproduce an image or text, fees for a location shoot can be more variable and subject to a number of factors, including the duration of the shoot, the nature of the project, the type of media, the print run/distribution, and the prominence of the cultural institution's name and/or location in the end product. Additional expenses may be billed separately and generally include, but are not limited to, staffing, insurance, parking, and security costs.

Rights and reproductions specialists should be involved with all discussions for potential location shoots to advise the requestor of any third-party rights that may need to be cleared prior to the shoot. Furthermore, it can be useful for the specialist to be on hand the day(s) of the shoot to review any spaces or works that may be unexpectedly included in the shoot.[32] After the shoot takes place, the institution must follow

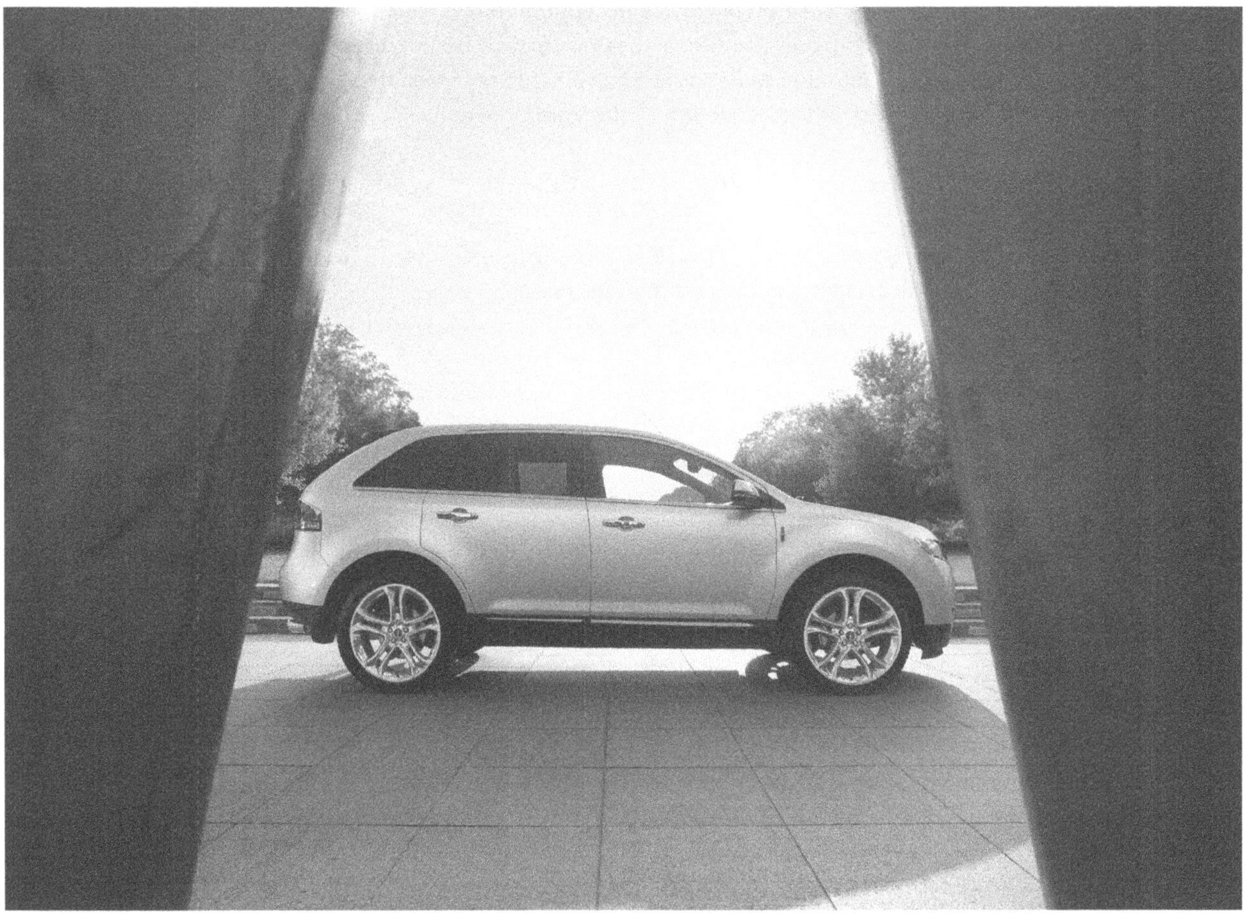

FIGURE 6.3
Commercial location shoot for Lincoln MKX on the Sutphin Mall at Newfields.

through with the requestor to review and approve the final work product. This is the opportunity for the rights and reproductions specialist to ensure that any works visible with potential rights to clear have been identified and that the cultural institution is properly acknowledged and credited.

POINTS OF CONSIDERATION FOR LOCATION SHOOT REQUESTS

1. What areas of the institution will be impacted?
   a. public areas (gardens, grounds, or common areas of the institution)?
   b. other visitors?
   c. collection items?
   d. exhibition spaces?
2. How can the institution mitigate any negative impacts (if needed)?
3. What staffing will be required before, during, and after the shoot?
   a. security?
   b. collection staff?
   c. rights and reproduction specialists?
4. Will staff appear in the final product?
   a. Do individual staff members agree to the use of their likeness?
5. What type and limits of insurance will the institution require?
   a. property damage?
   b. liability?
   c. fine arts?
6. Who will carry the insurance?
   a. the requestor?
   b. the institution?
7. What equipment and crew will be required during the shoot?
   a. What will be the intensity and duration of the lights?
   b. How many cameras, tripods, track, drones, sound booms, etc. will be needed?
   c. How many people will be onsite during the shoot?
   d. How many people and how much equipment can safely be in the space?
8. Will the final product give the appearance that the institution is endorsing it?
   a. Does that violate any institutional policies?
   b. Does the institution want that type of exposure?
   c. Can the institution harness the exposure for its own benefit?
9. Are there other issues that must be addressed by the requestor?
   a. copyright of surrounding objects?
   b. rights of privacy or publicity of any visible visitors?
   c. the institution's own trademarks (if applicable)?
   d. any institutional security concerns?
10. What fees will the institution charge?
    a. staff time? overtime if necessary?
    b. space rental fees?
    c. photography pass?
    d. one-time fee?
    e. hourly fee?
11. Does the institution want or require preapproval of script or final approval of product?
12. How will the institution be credited, if at all?
13. Can the institution use the final product for its own uses?

ADDITIONAL PHOTOGRAPHY SHOOT POLICIES

In addition to licensing for location shoots, many cultural institutions also need to develop policies for less formal photography shoots. These may involve shoots for everything from engagements and weddings to family portraits and high school senior pictures. Particularly for institutions with gardens and grounds that are popular destination spots for visitors, a written photography shoot policy serves as a powerful tool to protect the grounds and any collection works on display.[33] Additionally, this type of policy allows the cultural institution to control the number of photography and video shoots being conducted at one time to minimize disruptions to scheduled events and general visitors to the institution.

When developing a photography policy, the cultural institution must first decide if shoots will be restricted to its exterior spaces or if they will also be permitted in its interior locations, including galleries.

For example, while Newfields will work with location shoot requests to facilitate interior shoots, wedding or family photography is only permitted outdoors. Like location shoots, a policy for these photography shoots may be another source of revenue for the institution by requiring photographers to obtain a pass prior to their shoot, which may allow access for a specific set of hours, a single day, or for an entire year.[34]

It is important that a rights and reproductions specialist be involved in the development and implementation of a photography policy. The specialist will be able to advise photographers if areas are off-limits for shoots, as well as provide guidance for the use of the resultant imagery (e.g., providing wedding images to a client from the shoot on the institution's grounds is appropriate, but utilizing an image from the shoot where the institution is clearly visible on the photographer's business card is not appropriate). At no time should the resultant imagery be used in a way by the photographer that implies the cultural institution endorses or is a co-creator in some way of the images. Additionally, the rights and reproductions specialist will be able to alert photographers to collections works on the institution's grounds that may be protected by copyright and should not be photographed for the purposes of reproduction or publication.

Personal Visitor Photography

With the development of digital cameras and, especially, with the increasing sophistication and ubiquity of cell phone cameras,[35] not to mention the ongoing development of new imaging technologies and apps, cultural institutions face a rapidly changing landscape with respect to visitor photography policies. In the past, it was relatively easy to restrict the use of analog cameras, which required a tripod and flash to obtain a reasonable image in a gallery setting. Many cultural institutions, particularly museums, previously required photographers to apply for a camera pass, if they did not restrict photography entirely. Today, nearly every visitor has a cell phone in their pocket or hand, and requiring guards to enforce no-photography policies has arguably become untenable.

Beginning with Nina Simon's 2009 Museums 2.0 post, "Museum Photo Policies Should be as Open as Possible,"[36] which makes the case against restricting visitor photography, the topic has spread to the mainstream media, with articles on both sides of the issue.[37] It is clear from these articles, as well as an informal survey of a variety of US museum and library websites, that allowing noncommercial visitor photography is becoming the standard rather than the exception. While photography in special or temporary exhibitions is still often restricted, there is a growing movement to include language allowing visitor photography in outgoing loan agreements or to request that lenders lift bans on photography for incoming loans. A clear, understandable policy enhances the visitor experience and avoids conflict in cases where restrictions must be applied.[38]

COMMUNICATING ABOUT COPYRIGHT TO THE PUBLIC

Museums and archives have long had some practices around rights, use, and permissions issues that do not entirely match up with the provisions of copyright law. Most cultural institutions today are working to improve both their documentation and their public communications about rights issues. These improvements provide greater clarity for individuals requesting to use collection materials and, when materials are shared online, provide greater clarity to the public.

One area of problematic inconsistency in the past has been how cultural institutions worked with and communicated about materials that are either possibly or definitely in the public domain.[39] If a work is in the public domain, there is no right under US statutory law for the holding institution to either give or withhold permission for its use.[40] An obligation to obtain permission from the holding institution can be created via a contract, as with a contractual agreement that researchers sign to gain access to a collection. Such an obligation is only binding on those who have agreed to it.

Regardless of the lack of statutory support, it has been common practice for many organizations to provide permission to use public domain materials. These practices have carried over into freely available online image collections, where clearly public domain materials often are accompanied by a statement such as "Permission to use this image must be obtained in writing from XYZ Museum," or even "All Rights Reserved, PQR County Historical Society." While consonant with common practices of assisting researchers and other users in obtaining licenses or permissions, such statements (and any purported "permission" to use public domain materials) serve to muddy the waters of the public domain. On the other hand, statements that a work "is in the public domain" may be inaccurate, given the difficulties of determining that with certainty in various jurisdictions.[41]

Cultural institutions are working to improve on these practices in a number of ways. One way is the development of practices and procedures for reviewing works in hopes of concretely determining a public domain status. The HathiTrust Digital Library has led efforts to develop tools for reviewing book-like materials,[42] and other projects are addressing other materials in cultural institutions.[43] Another area of focus is developing consistent language to communicate that a work is believed to be in the public domain—"no known rights restrictions" is one such option. Large intercultural sharing organizations that serve as aggregators such as Europeana[44] and the DPLA[45] are spearheading projects to develop widely applicable standards.[46]

When an individual does seek "permission" to use public domain collection materials, many cultural institutions have developed alternative language that clarifies that the institution is not a rights holder to the underlying work (and depending on institutional practice disclaims any rights to the images of the work). Often, such statements affirm that the institution does not believe itself to be a rights holder and has no objections to a particular proposed use. These statements may also include a disclaimer that the institution is not certifying the work to be in the public domain (unless the institution has been able to concretely determine the object's rights status).

Providing "non-permission" statements about works is *not* incompatible with charging fees for use of materials (it is difficult to impose any conditions of use on materials that are freely available online; most organizations that wish to charge fees limit the public availability of high-quality images and charge use or preparation fees at the time of inquiry). There is not yet consistent "non-permissions" language for such fees, but some commonly used descriptions are "use fees," "access fees," "overhead charges," and "image preparation fees." It is also possible to encourage citation of the cultural institution as the holding institution without implying that citation is required by copyright law, which can be as simple as including one or more suggested credit lines (e.g., "Courtesy of the ABC Archive").

A different carryover of these past practices has been the sharing of public domain works via Creative Commons licenses.[47] Sometimes cultural organizations use Creative Commons licenses to share multiple image materials of a public domain work in which the organization itself may own a copyright—for example, museum-created photographs of a Roman marble sculpture. In these cases, the Creative Commons license is appropriate, since it is being used for a work (the image created by the institution) in which there may be an extant copyright.[48]

Communicating the copyright status of works to the public, shared via permissions to the cultural institution from a rights holder, is often less complex than communicating the status of public domain materials in the institution's collection to the public. Usually, the rights holder conveys their expectation about how such information should be shared or credited, and the cultural institution complies. For example, Newfields asks that public domain collection images downloaded from its website be credited: "Courtesy of the Indianapolis Museum of Art at Newfields" and indicates additional caption (tombstone) information about the work is provided with the image files and, if/when applicable, image use contracts.[49]

Another area where the practices of cultural institutions are evolving is in the general tenor of public communications about rights issues. Many institutions today are working to improve communications about how the public may make legitimate uses of materials even where a copyright may exist. At the same time, institutions strive to balance respect for the rights holder's interests, permissions, risk management, and overarching imperative to be responsible stewards for collections consistent with institutional mission. The rights of creators and other rights holders exist in tandem with exceptions allowing use in a variety of situations, including fair use. Instead of focusing on what people cannot or may not do, or on legal risks of use, some institutions are working to convey information about what people *may* do. For example, in addition to including language near self-service copiers and scanners encouraging users to avoid infringement, some libraries and archives are also including resources for users to learn about fair use and other copyright exceptions.[50] Since this is a significant departure from past practices in some situations, it may be perceived as undermining or eroding copyright in general. However, copyright law encourages creation *because* the public benefits from creation.

CONCLUSION

While the number of external requests a cultural institution might receive for the use of its collection materials is likely countless, this chapter outlines the most common situations that a rights and reproductions specialist will encounter daily. Similar to leveraging content with distribution partners, cultural institutions must balance the potential of revenue generation from external uses with the increased visibility of the collection and the ability to reach new audiences. As technology and practices evolve, rights and reproductions specialists will have to remain flexible to the ever-changing types of requests and modes of fulfilling them. By and large, the days of shipping transparencies back and forth between the institution and requestor are over; digital technologies are simultaneously streamlining and increasing external requests for collection materials.

NOTES

1. Some institutions will provide works that are protected by copyright if the requestor signs an agreement regarding how the images will be used, for example stating that they will not publish the image without first obtaining permission from the copyright holder. The decision to provide access to all works should be made in consultation with the institution's legal counsel.

2. Exceptions to this might be in the case of sensitive images that may include images of violence, objects covered by NAGPRA, or images of religious ceremonies. Native American Graves Protection Act and Repatriation Act, 25 U.S.C. § § 3001 et seq.

3. See Appendix B: Document and Contract Templates for sample use agreements.

4. For example, see "Ordering and Reproducing Images from the J. Paul Getty Museum's Collection," J. Paul Getty Museum, accessed March 21, 2018, http://www.getty.edu/legal/image_request/index.html.

5. See Appendix B: Document and Contract Templates for sample external request forms.

6. For example, see "Rights and Reproductions Request Form," The Sixth Floor Museum at Dealey Plaza, accessed February 23, 2018, https://www.jfk.org/the-collections/rights-reproductions-request-form/.

7. See Appendix B: Document and Contract Templates for examples of reproduction fee structures.

8. See Tanner, Simon. *Reproduction charging models & rights policy for digital images in American art museums: A Mellon Foundation study*, KDCS Digital Consultancy, 2004; and Kelly, Kristin, "Images of Works of Art in Museum Collections: The Experience of Open Access." *A Study of Eleven Museums. Prepared for the Andrew W. Mellon Foundation* (2013).

9. See chapter 4, Retail and Commercial Products section, for a more detailed discussion.

10. It is generally common to run into term limits with licensing agencies, but less frequently with other cultural institutions.

11. Like all contracts, it is important they be reviewed by knowledgeable legal advisors.

12. See Appendix B: Document and Contract Templates for sample contracts.

13. However, whether an unmodified template can be used without further legal review is a determination typically made by legal counsel.

14. An institution may consider accepting digital excerpts or PDF copies in place of a printed gratis copy, which may be cost prohibitive for the external requestor to provide.

15. Increasingly, external requestors retain the digital files licensed from cultural institutions, which can make the enforceability of a term requiring its deletion impractical. Conversely, a cultural institution may ask external requestors to utilize the digital file that most truly represents the work represented, which may often be a more recently created file.

16. Some institutions' web request forms also serve as a click-through agreement. Terms and conditions are provided to the requestor when the form is accessed, and the requestor must agree to the terms to submit the online request. This process thus eliminates the need to send contracts back and forth for signatures.

17. May also be referred to as "Open Content."

18. See Appendix C: References and Resources for a list of OA programs at cultural institutions as of March 2018.

19. See chapter 7, Open Access Case Studies, for examples of various OA programs.

20. For example, see "NGA Images," National Gallery of Art, accessed March 21, 2018, https://images.nga.gov/en/page/show_home_page.html.

21. For example, see "Open Content Program," The Getty, accessed March 21, 2018, http://www.getty.edu/about/whatwedo/opencontent.html.

22. For example, a reference from the rights and reproductions pages of an institution's site should direct visitors to OA content, such as: "Many images of public domain works are available for free download from the Indianapolis Museum of Art at Newfields' collection pages. Simply look for the download icon to access a high resolution JPG file and begin using the image for any purpose." "Image Resources," Newfields, accessed March 21, 2018, https://discovernewfields.org/research/image-resources.

23. An institution might ask for gratis copies by utilizing language such as this: "While there are no restrictions or conditions for the use of downloadable public domain images, Newfields would appreciate receiving a gratis copy of publications containing collection works in order to retain the record of how image reproductions are utilized." This phrase could then be followed by the address of where to send gratis copies. Ibid.

24. For example, Getty users are asked to provide additional information only for publication uses.

25. See Newfields, NGA and Getty websites for different approaches to data collection.

26. For example, see the Getty's Open Content FAQ, accessed March 21, 2018, http://www.getty.edu/about/whatwedo/opencontentfaq.html.

27. It is true that by the time most photographic works fall into the public domain, any persons depicted are likely already deceased. However, some public domain works—such as FSA photographs—are not that old and may in fact depict living people. At the Getty, public domain photographs of people are only released for Open Content if the work was created more than eighty years ago. If the photograph depicts a famous person, the person must have been deceased for more than seventy years.

28. For example, see "Location Shoots," Guggenheim Museum, accessed March 21, 2018, https://www.guggenheim.org/location-shoots and "Newfields Licensing and Location Shoots," Newfields, accessed March 21, 2018, https://discovernewfields.org/photography-policy/newfields-licensing-and-location-shoots.

29. See Appendix B: Document and Contract Templates for sample location shoot applications.

30. Ideally, a location shoot is submitted within the time frame requested by the cultural institution (often several weeks or even months in advance of the proposed shoot), but in cases where a quicker review and answer is required, a smaller version of the committee may be able to assess if the request is appropriate based on the institution's outlined policy for types of location shoots considered.

31. See Appendix B: Document and Contract Templates for sample contracts.

32. This is particularly important as changes to the works on view may occur between a scouting trip and the shoot itself, as well as changes to the angle of shots that may capture additional works not originally planned for inclusion in the shoot. See Appendix B: Document and Contract Templates for guidelines and staff process samples for overseeing a location shoot.

33. The overall considerations for photography shoot policies are like those reviewed for developing location shoot policies. See chapter 6, Points of Consideration for Location Shoot Requests, for a more detailed discussion.

34. For example, Newfields requires photographers to purchase a one-day pass (fifty dollars) in order to bring clients to the Garden. Management of passes for limited hours was too cumbersome for staff to oversee and is not an option. "Photography and Video Shoots," Newfields, accessed March 21, 2018, https://discovernewfields.org/photography-policy.

35. The first cell phone camera was released in 2000; by 2012, 41-megapixel cameras were available. Simon Hill, "From J-Phone to Lumia 1020: A Complete History of the Camera Phone," last modified August 11, 2013, http://www.digitaltrends.com/mobile/camera-phone-history/.

36. Nina Simon, "Museum Photo Policies Should Be as Open as Possible," Museum 2.0 (blog), August 20, 2009, http://museumtwo.blogspot.com/2009/08/museum-photo-policies-should-be-as-open.html.

37. See generally Carolina A. Miranda, "Why Can't We Take Pictures in Art Museums?" *ARTnews*, last modified May 13, 2013. http://www.artnews.com/2013/05/13/photography-in-art-museums/; "Ten Reasons Why You Shouldn't Take Photos in Museums," The Everywhereist (blog), January 20, 2010, http://www.everywhereist.com/ten-reasons-why-you-shouldnt-take-photos-in-museums; Rupert Christiansen, "Should We Ban Photography in Museums and Galleries?" *Telegraph*, last modified March 8, 2014, http://www.telegraph.co.uk/culture/museums/10682442/Should-we-ban-photography-in-museums-and-galleries.html; Rebecca Atkinson, "Should Museums Allow People to Take Photographs in Galleries?" *Museums Journal* (blog), July 30, 2012, http://www.museumsassociation.org/museums-journal/news/30072012-poll-should-museums-allow-photography; William Grimes, "Talk Softly and Carry No Selfie Stick," *New York Times*, last modified February 14, 2015, http://www.nytimes.com/2015/02/15/us/museum-rules-talk-softly-and-carry-no-selfie-stick.html?_r=2; Jason, Horejs, "Debate: Should Visitors be Allowed to Photograph Artwork in Galleries, Museums and Art Shows?" *Red Dot Blog*, March 16, 2015, http://reddotblog.com/debate-should-visitors-be-allowed-to-photograph-artwork-in-galleries-museums-and-art-shows/ and reposted September 25, 2017, http://reddotblog.com/debate-should-visitors-be-allowed-to-photograph-artwork-in-galleries-museums-and-art-shows-2/.

38. See chapter 2, Photography Policies, for a more detailed discussion of the IP policy implications and theory behind the development of a photography policy.

39. Since copyright terms vary with jurisdiction, works may sometimes be in the public domain in one country and not in others—hence, some works may be "possibly" in the public domain. Other works in the collections of cultural organizations, however, are of such great age that there is no possibility of an extant copyright or may be ineligible for copyright protection.

40. It is important to note that this permission for use is in regard to the underlying work in an image material. In many cases, an institution is providing access to the high-resolution image file, which the institution may rely upon as a source of revenue, and then limiting its use. In cases such as this, the institution is not only giving permission but also selling a product—the image. It should also be reiterated that in many parts of the world, the digital image may still hold copyright.

41. If the external user plans to use the material outside the jurisdiction of the United States, where the work may or may not be in the public domain, and where fair use or fair dealing may or may not apply, the inclusion of a disclaimer stating the cultural institution believes the work is in the public domain in the United States is vital. This disclaimer should also note that the end user is responsible for any rights clearances that may arise outside of the United States.

42. "Our Digital Library," HathiTrust, accessed March 21, 2018, https://www.hathitrust.org/digital_library.

43. One such project to follow is the recently announced joint venture of DPLA, Europeana, and Creative Commons. Emily Gore, "The principles for establishing international & interoperable rights statements," May 11, 2015, DPLA Blog, accessed March 21, 2018, http://dp.la/info/2015/05/11/the-principles-for-establishing-international-interoperable-rights-statements/.

44. "Available Rights Statements," Europeana, accessed March 21, 2018, http://pro.europeana.eu/share-your-data/rights-statement-guidelines/available-rights-statements.

45. "Getting It Right on Rights," Digital Public Library of America, accessed March 21, 2018, http://dp.la/info/about/projects/getting-it-right-on-rights/.

46. See chapter 7, RightsStatements.org, for a more detailed discussion.

47. For more information, see "CC0—'No Rights Reserved,'" Creative Commons, accessed March 21, 2018, https://creativecommons.org/share-your-work/public-domain/cc0/.

48. See chapter 7, Creative Commons, for a more detailed discussion.

49. "Image Resources," Newfields, accessed March 21, 2018, https://discovernewfields.org/research/image-resources.

50. In any communication about rights to the public, legal counsel should be consulted to limit the liability of the cultural institution from being implicated in potential infringement claims (e.g., a rights holder claiming infringement by a third party of the content provided by the institution, where the third party states "The 'X' institution said it was all right."

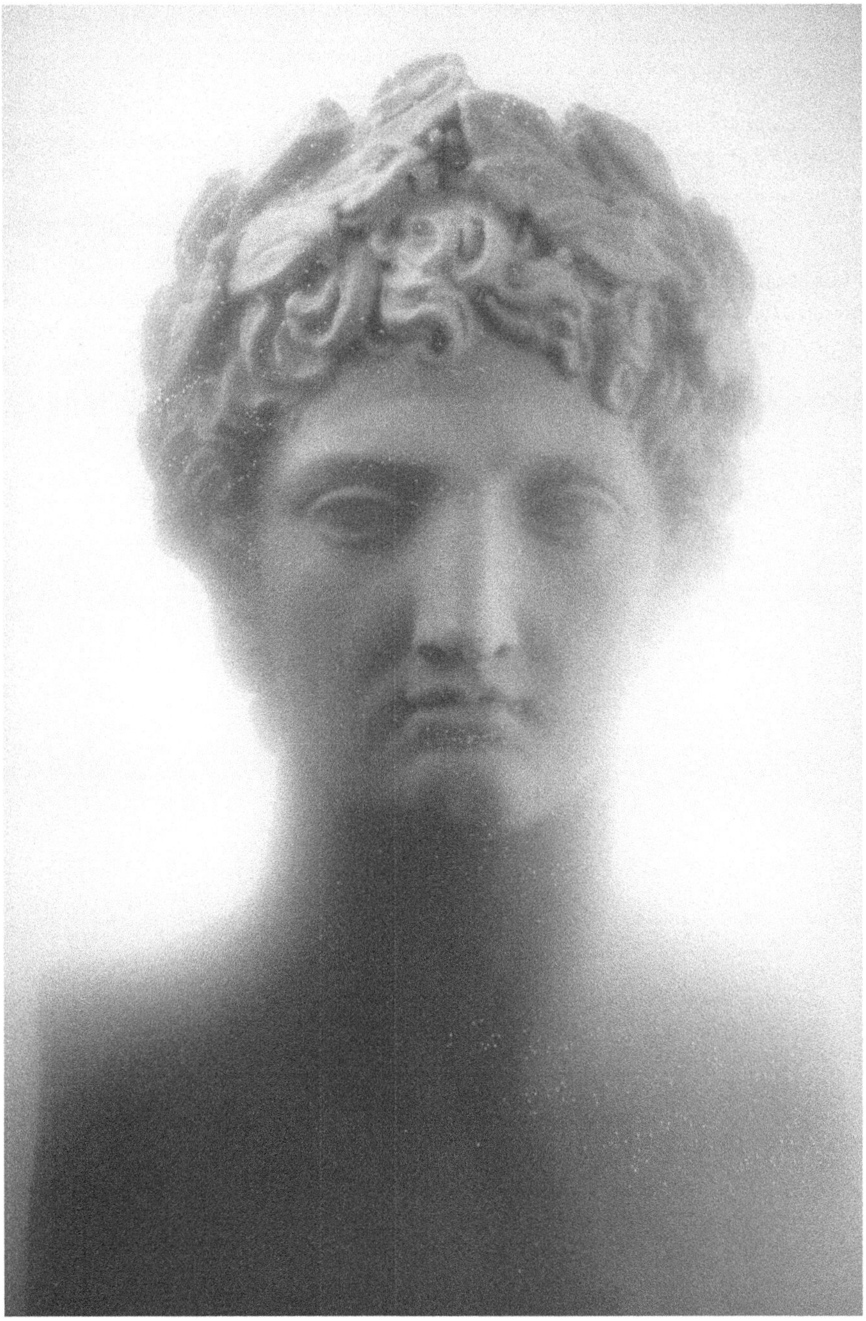

7

New Frontiers in Fair Use and Open Access

JOHN FFRENCH, WALTER G. LEHMANN, DEBORAH WYTHE, AND ANNE M. YOUNG

Advancements in technology not only bring new considerations for types of materials to license, but also the means and practices by which rights and reproductions specialists undertake day-to-day activities. Notably, the utilization of fair use codes or guidelines and the increased adoption of Open Access (OA) policies, both of which have increased substantially since the early 2000s, are incrementally shifting the culture of licensing everything or abandoning projects because of rights restrictions toward one of assessing fair use opportunities. While earlier chapters discussed the fundamentals of fair use and adopting OA within the scope of copyright law, this chapter more closely examines some of the unique projects and activities that are made possible when cultural institutions embrace either or both fair use and OA.

PUTTING FAIR USE INTO ACTION

As of 2018, there are numerous codes or guidelines in existence that are meant to serve as guideposts to creators and cultural institutions seeking to navigate the use of rights-protected materials. Many of these have grown from predecessors in the fields of academics and documentary filmmakers, which have been at the forefront of using materials under fair use and their dissemination with OA. As the utilization of fair use gains increased acceptance and the willingness among cultural institutions to undertake fair use analyses balanced with the associated real and/or perceived risks of infringement, the true winners are the scholars, researchers, students, artists, and the general public who benefit as more cultural heritage is made available to be built upon now and by future generations.

Given that opinions and legal precedents vary widely, some individuals and institutions find fair use[1] intimidating or too unpredictable, and may choose not to rely on it. However, the statutory language indicates that fair use is intended to enable (among other things) educational and critical uses,[2] and many developments in the case law over the last twenty-five to thirty years strongly favor nonprofit, educational, artistic, and other transformative uses.[3] Examples of fair use may include, but are not limited to online collections, documentary films, exhibition catalogues, scholarly articles, blogs, educational materials, collection handbooks, social media posts, fundraising by development and advancement teams, digitizing archival, museum, and library collections, and many othe uses not listed here may be a fair use after reviewing the four factors for a specific case.[4]

The US Copyright Office has a list of copyright fair use cases that can be helpful in determining whether a particular use may be considered "fair use." The "Copyright Fair Use Index" is a searchable collection of fair use cases that is intended to aid in understanding the types of uses the courts have determined are fair use—and those that are not.[5] The Index includes cases from multiple federal jurisdictions, each summarized in a standard format, which includes the key facts of the case, the relevant question(s) of law addressed, the court's fair use analysis, and its decision. Cases included in the index are

FAIR USE/FAIR DEALING WEEK

Held annually since 2014, "Fair Use Week," began as an outgrowth idea to celebrate the Association of Research Libraries release of its *Code of Best Practices in Fair Use for Academic and Research Libraries.* After the success of the first Fair Use Week held at Harvard University, the Association of Research

Fair Use Fundamentals

fair use week

Copyright law is a carefully balanced system meant to encourage creativity as well as cultural and scientific progress. The law encourages authors by giving them limited control over certain uses of their works, and it encourages everyone (including authors) to use existing cultural and scientific material without permission, under certain circumstances, to engage in a wide variety of vital activities. Many parts of the law favor the freedom to use culture, but by far and away the most flexible, powerful, and universal user's right is fair use. As you'll see below: fair use is a right, fair use is vitally important, fair use is for everyone, and fair uses are everywhere.

Fair Use is a Right

Some people think fair use is a minor exception or a marginal carve-out from the expansive protection for authors, but **fair use is a fundamental right.**

the notorious r.b.g.

Thanks to Justice Ruth Bader Ginsburg, the Supreme Court said fair use is a **"First Amendment Safeguard".**

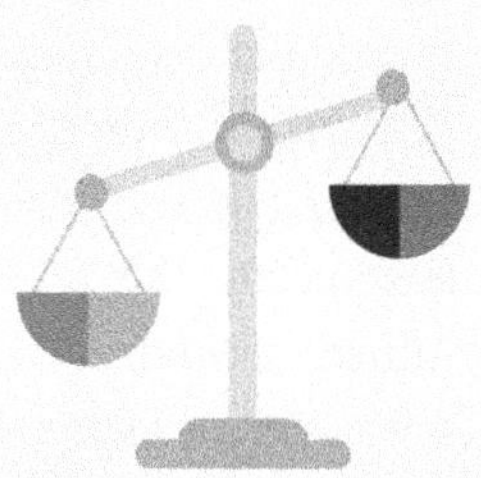

Like the First Amendment itself, fair use is **broad, flexible, and responsive to change.** That's why fair use supports the constitutional purpose of copyright: **to "promote the progress of science and the useful arts".**

Fair Use is Vitally Important

to the economy

Experts estimate that industries reliant on fair use contributed $2.4 trillion to the U.S. economy in 2008–2009, or approximately 17 percent of the US GDP.[1] In comparison:

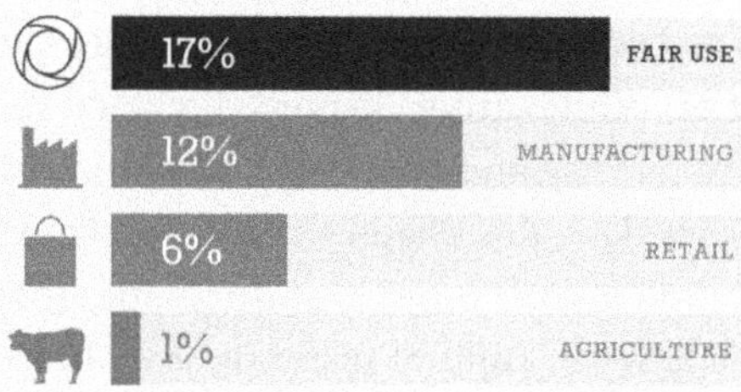

to innovation

Fair use enables new technologies and advancements, including new products like DVRs and search engines.

to creativity

Without fair use, there would be no parody, no critique and commentary, no transformative mash-ups, and no homage or pastiche.

THE DAILY SHOW WITH JON STEWART

to scholarship

Imagine trying to prove your brilliant theory about Ernest Hemingway without quoting Hemingway?

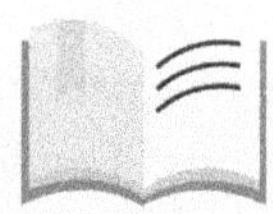

1. CCIA, Fair Use in the US Economy, http://www.ccianet.org/wp content/uploads/library/CCIA-FairUseintheUSEconomy-2011.pdf
2. US BEA Statistics, hhp://www.bea.gov/industry/gdpbyind_data.htm

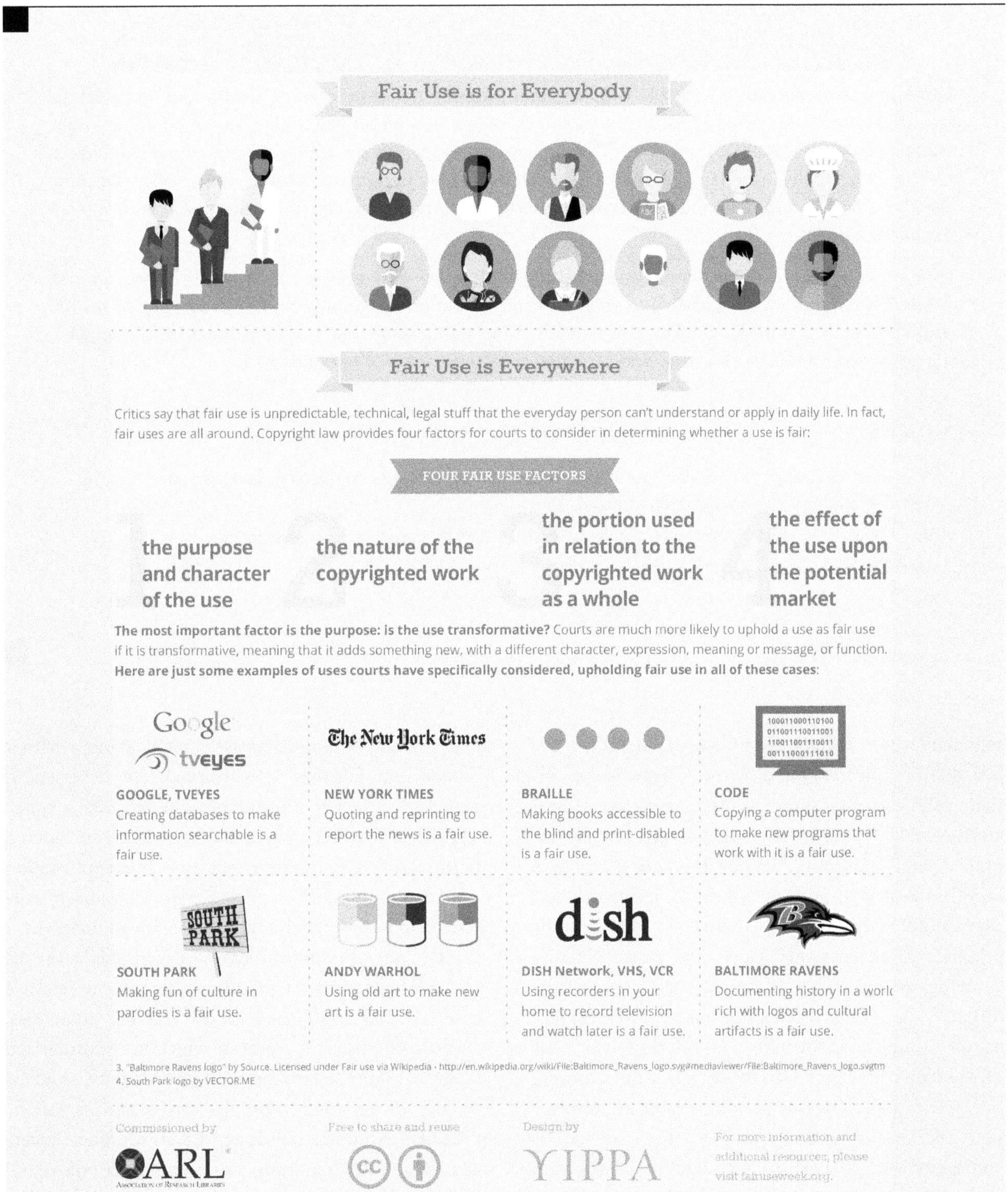

FIGURE 7.1
The Fair Use Fundamentals infographic presents what people can do with fair use in an approachable format.

Libraries partnered with Harvard to organize and promote the annual week celebrating advances in fair use in the United States and fair dealing in Canada and other jurisdictions.[1] As noted in materials explaining Fair Use/Fair Dealing Week: "While fair use and fair dealing are employed on a daily basis by students, faculty, librarians, journalists, and all users of copyrighted material, Fair Use/Fair Dealing Week is a time to promote and discuss the opportunities presented, celebrate successful stories, and explain the doctrines."[2]

Numerous activities, publications, and teaching tools have now evolved as a result of this annual event. One of the most accessible to those seeking to better understand and employ fair use or fair dealing in their activities is the Fair Use Fundamentals infographic that "explains what fair use is, why it is important, who uses fair use, and provides some examples of fair use."[3]

NOTES

1. Kyle K. Courtney, "About Fair Use Week," Copyright at Harvard Library Blog, accessed May 3, 2018, https://blogs.harvard.edu/copyrightosc/about-fair-use-week/.
2. "About," Fair Use/Fair Dealing Week, accessed May 3, 2018, http://fairuseweek.org/about/.
3. Ibid.

searchable by a variety of key words, including the jurisdiction and the type of work. Categories potentially relevant to cultural institutions include "film/audiovisual," "painting/drawing/graphic," "photograph," and "sculpture." While the Index can be a useful tool, it is important to keep in mind that fair use is a judicially applied balancing test. Fact patterns and judicial analysis vary widely and are continually evolving, so the ability to draw bright lines can be difficult. Therefore, while it does not provide explicit answers, cultural institutions can reference the tools of the Copyright Fair Use Index when determining the level of risk they may be comfortable assuming.

While the admonition to "seek legal advice" is commonplace, establishing an ongoing relationship with an attorney versed in copyright law and the application of fair use in the cultural context can be empowering. When questions regarding fair use arise, the attorney can be called on to review the proposed use and provide an informal assessment about whether reliance on fair use is warranted. An experienced copyright attorney should be able to give a quick analysis of whether a particular use may be considered fair use. In some situations, such as a book publication or a documentary film, once the work is substantially complete an informal analysis is often followed by a formal "fair use opinion letter," which details the attorney's legal analysis, including references to relevant case law and established industry codes, guidelines, and/or statements (several of which are summarized below). A fair use legal opinion letter may be required as part of an application for errors and omissions ("E&O") insurance coverage.[6] E&O insurance coverage (which is a common requirement in publishing and film and television distribution agreements) can be an effective way to address potential risks that may arise from clearing rights, including reasonable reliance on fair use.

FAIR USE CODES, GUIDELINES, AND STATEMENTS

Seeking out such guiding principles, or developing them independently, may be useful for cultural institutions considering the applicability of fair use to specific projects or for long-term planning. A number of "best practices" guidelines have been developed over the years. Some pertain to particular industries, such as documentary filmmaking, while others address particular types of works, such as the application of fair use in the visual arts. While such guidelines are not substitutes for legal advice on specific situations, they provide rights and reproductions specialists with useful insight into the principles and practices that have become common in certain industries and user communities. Many of the guidelines listed below were developed after lengthy input from both copyright creators and users in the respective industry or community. Others were developed by professional associations in response to particular problems, such as the use of "thumbnail" images online by art museums, or to address the application of fair use more broadly, such as those recently developed by the College Art Association to address fair use in the visual arts and by the Association of Art Museum Directors with respect to fair use in art museums. These guidelines can be useful starting points to assess whether it may be reasonable to rely on fair use in a particular situation, with the caveat that these codes, guidelines, and statements may not accurately reflect the current state of the continually evolving fair use case law.

Tracking the evolution and growing number of codes, guidelines, and statements with related applicability to cultural institutions can be tricky business, particularly as many, if not all, could in theory have applicability to a use or project at a cultural institution. Several of these with direct applicability to the collections held by libraries, archives, and museums are discussed in greater detail below,[7] but some of the earliest "flags in the sand" that rights and reproductions specialists should be aware of, if the need to use them arises, include:

- 2005–*Documentary Filmmakers' Statement of Best Practices in Fair Use*[8]
  Association of Independent Video and Filmmakers, Independent Feature Project, International Documentary Association, National Alliance for Media Arts and Culture, and Women in Film and Video
- 2008–*Code of Best Practices in Fair Use for Online Video*[9]
  American University: Washington College of Law: Program on Information Justice and Intellectual Property
- 2011–*Code of Best Practices in Fair Use for Poetry*[10]
  The Poetry Foundation's Harriet Monroe Poetry Institute and American University School of Communication

Since 2011, the development, endorsement, increased support, and use of fair use codes, guidelines, and statements have increased exponentially, particularly those with potential applicability to the practices of rights and reproductions specialists in cultural institutions.

2011—*Policy on the Use of "Thumbnail" Digital Images in Museum Online Initiatives*[11]

Association of Art Museum Directors

The 2011 Association of Art Museum Directors' (AAMD) *Policy on the Use of "Thumbnail" Digital Images in Museum Online Initiatives* was a prime example of an organization considering all the relevant background and laying out general guiding principles for the application of fair use in a fairly narrow range of situations.[12] Highlighting how strongly the museum community felt in need of guidance in 2011, many museums quickly adjusted the size of the thumbnail images on their websites based on the "maximum size" outlined in the AAMD policy as less than 300 pixels on the long side. However, as technologies have evolved, the concept of a "thumbnail" changed, and professional discussions ensued, AAMD found this policy in dire need of updating to stay current, and in 2016 this policy was revoked with AAMD's release of its new *Guidelines for the Use of Copyrighted Materials and Works of Art by Art Museums* (discussed in greater detail below).

2012—*Code of Best Practices in Fair Use for Academic and Research Libraries*[13]

Association of Research Libraries

The 2012 *Code of Best Practices in Fair Use for Academic and Research Libraries* was developed by the Association of Research Libraries in partnership with the Center for Social Media and the Washington College of Law at American University is intended to be "a clear and easy-to-use statement of fair and reasonable approaches to fair use developed by and for librarians who support academic inquiry and higher education."[14] It addresses the use of copyrighted material digitized for student use; approaches to video; online presentation of special collections; and archiving websites.

Eight recurring situations for fair use applications are addressed in the code:

1. using digital technologies to supply library materials in support of teaching and learning
2. using selections of materials to publicize library activities and create exhibitions, both physical and virtual
3. preserving at-risk items through digitization
4. increasing access to materials in archival and special collections through the development of digital collections
5. supporting disabled individuals via reproducing materials
6. maintaining the integrity of materials in institutional repositories
7. creating databases for non-consumptive research
8. collecting and making available materials posted on the web[15]

2013—*Statement on the Fair Use of Images for Teaching, Research, and Study*[16]

Visual Resources Association

The 2013 Visual Resources Association (VRA) *Statement on the Fair Use of Images for Teaching, Research, and Study* identifies six ways in which still visual images may be used under fair use:

1. preservation (storing images for repeated use in a teaching context and transferring images to new formats)
2. use of images for teaching purposes
3. use of images (both large, high-resolution images, and thumbnails) on course websites and in other online study materials
4. adaptations of images for teaching and classroom work by students
5. sharing images among educational and cultural institutions to facilitate teaching and study
6. reproduction of images in theses[17]

In addition to outlining ways in which fair use applies in these areas, the statement also provides a useful history of the fair use of visual images in academic works. The VRA statement was and still is a vital tool for those working at a variety of cultural institutions to understand ways in which images may be utilized without seeking licenses for every use.

2014—*Statement of Best Practices in Fair Use of Collections Containing Orphan Works*[18]

Center for Media and Social Impact

Fair use can be particularly important in enabling the use of orphan works in collections. Most helpful is the fact that no rights holders can be identified, which may strengthen a traditional fair use analysis. As noted in the Center for Media and Social Impact's Statement of Best Practices in Fair Use of Collections Containing Orphan Works, it is difficult to argue market harm in the absence of an owner for a work.[19] However, legitimately concluding that there is no identifiable rights holder for a work may involve extensive research to complete an investigation, and even then, mistakes could be made. There is no explicit protection in the law for a user who thinks that a work is an orphan work and no formal legal definition of orphan works. There is always some level of risk in the use of potentially copyrighted works without permission.[20]

2015—*Code of Best Practices in Fair Use for the Visual Arts*[21]

College Art Association

When the College Art Association (CAA) released its *Code of Best Practices in Fair Use for the Visual Arts* cultural institutions almost immediately took notice.

While a number of fair use codes, guidelines, and statements existed before the CAA released the code, it is unique in that it provides visual-arts professionals with a set of principles addressing best practices in the fair use of copyrighted materials. It describes how fair use can be invoked and implemented when using copyrighted materials in scholarship, teaching, museums, archives, and in the creation of art. The Code addresses the following five questions:

1. **Analytic Writing**
   When may scholars and other writers about art invoke fair use to quote, excerpt, or reproduce copyrighted works?
2. **Teaching about Art**
   When may teachers invoke fair use in using copyrighted works to support formal instruction in a range of settings, including online and distance teaching?
3. **Making Art**
   Under what circumstances may artists invoke fair use to incorporate copyrighted material into new artworks in any medium?
4. **Museum Uses**
   When may museums and their staffs invoke fair use in using copyrighted works—including images and text as well as time-based and born-digital materials—when organizing exhibitions, developing educational materials (within the museum and online), publishing catalogues, and other related activities?
5. **Online Access to Archival and Special Collections**
   When may such institutions and their staffs invoke fair use to create digital preservation copies and/or enable digital access to copyrighted materials in their collections?[22]

2016—*Guidelines for the Use of Copyrighted Materials and Works of Art by Art Museums*[23]

Association of Art Museum Directors

Initially released in 2016, with subsequent updates and additions, on October 11, 2017, the AAMD released the most-updated version of their report, *Guidelines for the Use of Copyrighted Materials and Works of Art by Art Museums.* After the release of the CAA's *Code of Best Practices in Fair Use for the Visual Arts,* it became clear that AAMD's former *Policy on the Use of "Thumbnail" Digital Images in Museum Online Initiatives* had become outdated and a more robust document was needed to build upon the "Museum Uses" section of the CAA code and provide more specific guidance to art museums in particular. "With an ever-evolving technological world and legal landscape, art museums need and want guidance with respect to how they can fulfill their missions while respecting the rights of authors, artists and copyright holders. Any such guidance should acknowledge the right to use copyrighted materials and works of art without undue restriction or limitation, so long as such uses are legally and ethically sound."[24]

AAMD designed the guidelines to specifically serve as a resource and educational tool for staff of AAMD-member art museums as well as other art and non-art museums that may choose to follow these recommendations using several common areas of museum reproductions. The guidelines describe six categories of specific examples in which art museums may utilize fair use or in some cases seek a "courtesy clearance" to maintain institutional relationships with rights holders. These categories, each of which is discussed in terms of the four factors for balancing and making a fair use analysis, include the following common art museum uses:

1. Online Collections
2. Publications
3. Promotional, Marketing, and Advertising Materials
4. Fundraising
5. Archives and Other Special Collections
6. Onsite Uses

The guidelines conclude with an essay on fair use and the four factors.[25] Users of the guidelines can take comfort in knowing their counterpart professional organizations are adopting similar stances in the use of images, and that a large organization, the American Alliance of Museums, supports the statement.

FAIR USE IN PUBLISHING

Putting its code into practice, the CAA's publication, *The Art Bulletin,* now encourages transparency in the copyright status of the artworks and image reproductions that appear within the journal. Notably, *The Art Bulletin* does not require all images submitted by article authors to be accompanied by specific licenses or contracts. Instead, the journal provides flexibility to its authors with the option to credit images "Artworks published under fair use." Furthermore, the colophon of *The Art Bulletin* provides readers with a detailed description of how to interpret the copyright notices and credit lines they will encounter in articles:

> In order to provide clear information to readers, rights holders, and subsequent users of images, CAA has established conventions for describing the copyright status of the works we publish:
>
> Artwork in the public domain
>
> Artwork copyright © Name
>
> Photograph copyright © Name
>
> Photograph provided by [name of photographer, image bank, or other provider]
>
> Artwork published under fair use
>
> Photograph by Name (where copyright is not asserted by the provider)
>
> Photograph by the author[1]

A major academic publisher embracing CAA's Code, Yale University Press (YUP), now provides its authors with the "Yale University Press Guidelines for Authors re Fair Use of Art Images in Scholarly Art and Architecture Monographs," which empowers authors to utilize fair use when reproducing images.[2] This document from Yale outlines the fair use factors authors should consider when assessing each image for publication as well as outlining how images may be used under a fair use or a fair dealing defense. Specifically, YUP requires attribution to the images, that the images be fundamental to commentary in the publication, and stresses reproduction sizes relative to the full page that will be best used under fair use, typically not more than one-quarter of the page but may be reconsidered on a case-by-case basis.[3]

As more publishers and cultural institutions follow in the steps of CAA and YUP, it will only further benefit future researchers, creators, authors, and end users from the access to increased content. Cultural institutions will equally see increased distribution, utilization, and reach through additional reproductions of works within their collections.

NOTES

1. College Art Association, *The Art Bulletin,* vol. 99, no. 3, September 2017.
2. Janet Landay, "A CAA Road Trip,"CAA News Today, October 18, 2016, http://www.collegeart.org/news/?s=monographs.
3. Yale University Press, *Yale University Press Guidelines for Authors re Fair Use of Art Images in Scholarly Art and Architecture Monographs,* last revised February 10, 2016.

SIMPLIFYING AND STANDARDIZING

Complexities of copyright law can make navigating licensing, fair use, open access, and general uses of materials an utterly confusing maze of legalese, court decisions, and conflicting statements. Despite some of the inherent confusion, rights and reproductions specialists need not fret—organizations that work with creators as well as cultural institutions are working to streamline, simplify, and standardize the language and processes surrounding copyright, licensing, and use of materials. Fundamentally, these organizations are working to establish the use of voluntary "proactive" licenses that grant permission to use a given work for certain specified purposes (or for all purposes) without having to obtain the permission from the copyright holder (typically the creator) in each instance.

For instance, a Creative Commons license notice affixed to the work designates that the work may be used for the purposes and in the manner specified in the applicable license selected. This allows the copyright holder to make the work freely available for the uses specified in the license. By doing so, the copyright holder is giving up control over the work and making it available for use by others subject only to the limitations and restrictions included in the selected license. For copyright holders, including libraries, museums, and other cultural institutions, who want to encourage the use of their copyrighted works, the use of such proactive licenses may be a viable option. For users, such pro-active licenses relieve them of often burdensome clearance efforts. When relying on such pro-active licenses, however, cultural institutions and individuals should be sure to document the particular notice on which they are relying as part of licensing and use clearance records.

CREATIVE COMMONS

"One goal of Creative Commons is to increase the amount of openly licensed creativity in 'the commons'—the body of work freely available for legal use, sharing, repurposing, and remixing."[26] While individuals have been utilizing Creative Commons licenses to make their "creative content available for any member of the public to use,"[27] it is a type of licensing that cultural institutions may also adopt. Creative Commons licenses provide a variety of flexible options to enable the use of works owned by a cultural institution by proactively granting permissions to anyone to make use of the work without payment. Almost all Creative Commons licenses require attribution as a condition of use (referred to in Creative Commons licenses as BY); cultural organizations may want to provide some suggestions on the form of that attribution—for example, is an individual author to be credited, the organization, or both?

Other options offered by Creative Commons licenses include a limitation to noncommercial use (referred to in Creative Commons licenses as NC), a limitation on use that permits no derivative works to be made of the work (referred to in Creative Commons licenses as ND) and a requirement that any works created using the licensed work also themselves be licensed under the same terms as the original work (referred to in Creative Commons licenses as SA or the Share Alike option). Note that all versions of Creative Commons licenses explicitly preserve statutory exceptions and limitations to copyright law—so, for example, even if the No Derivatives limitation is applied to the licenses, derivative works considered to be fair uses are still allowed. Each of the above licensing options can be deployed in a variety of combinations with others.[28] Institutions will have to make their own decisions as to what combination of license terms best serve their needs.

A cultural institution can also waive all rights to a work via a Creative Commons Zero (CC0) waiver.[29] This enables the broadest possible use of a work and places absolutely no limits on reuse. Note that this license can only be used when the institution is itself the copyright holder or agent of the rights holder and has the authority to waive those rights.

Using a Creative Commons license requires no centralized registration or certification; it is easily accomplished by placing language or symbols on a work that indicate the intended Creative Commons license.[30] It can also be accomplished through use of the machine-readable Creative Commons Rights Expression Language, which is generally preferred for online materials to enable identification by web crawlers.[31]

The use of Creative Commons licenses are not appropriate for works that are definitively known to have no copyright or where copyright has expired, also known as works explicitly in the public domain in all jurisdictions worldwide. Specifically, works that are known to be in the public domain should be labeled as such using the Creative Commons Public Domain Mark.[32] The Creative Commons Zero (CC0) license may also be applied to cases where the works are believed to be in the public domain in the United States but may not be definitely known to be public domain throughout the world (e.g., see *Case Study: The Met, Creative Commons, and Wikipedia* where the CC0 license rather than the Public Domain Mark was applied to the digital reproductions of works in The Met collection).

RIGHTSSTATEMENTS.ORG

As many rights and reproductions specialists who work with digital collections know, ambiguous or meaningless rights statements can cause confusion and limit the downstream use of materials. Unfortunately, "there is no global approach to rights statements that works for a broad set of institutions, leading to a confusing proliferation of terms."[33] Despite this ominous state of affairs, cultural institutions need not fear, "RightsStatements.org establishes the vocabulary that every organization can use to talk to their audiences about copyright and related rights in a meaningful way."[34]

RightsStatements.org is a joint project of the DPLA and Europeana that provides a set of standardized rights statements that can be used to communicate the copyright and re-use status of digital objects to the public.[35] RightsStatements.org features twelve rights statements that are meant to be used in conjunction with Creative Commons licenses that describe rights

CASE STUDY

THE MET, CREATIVE COMMONS, AND WIKIPEDIA

Deborah Wythe

In February 2017, The Metropolitan Museum of Art (The Met) made images of all of its public domain works—some 375,000 images of 200,000 works of art—available to the public under a Creative Commons Zero (CC0) license.[1] A strong commitment to Open Access (OA), this initiative supports using, sharing, and remixing the images and provides a filter on the MetMuseum.org Collections pages that allows users to specify works in the public domain and easily download images as well as catalogue metadata.[2]

Recognizing that visits to The Met website will always lag behind web behemoths, the museum established partnerships with Wikimedia, Artstor, the Digital Public Library of America (DPLA), and Pinterest.[3] A year's work by the museum's Wikimedian-in-residence, Richard Knipel, led to clear documentation of the power of both OA and broader visibility via multiple platforms, in particular Wikimedia and Wikipedia. Statistics document strong interest in the images and use beyond the art-history-centered approach one might expect from an art museum collection. One example is cited as follows:

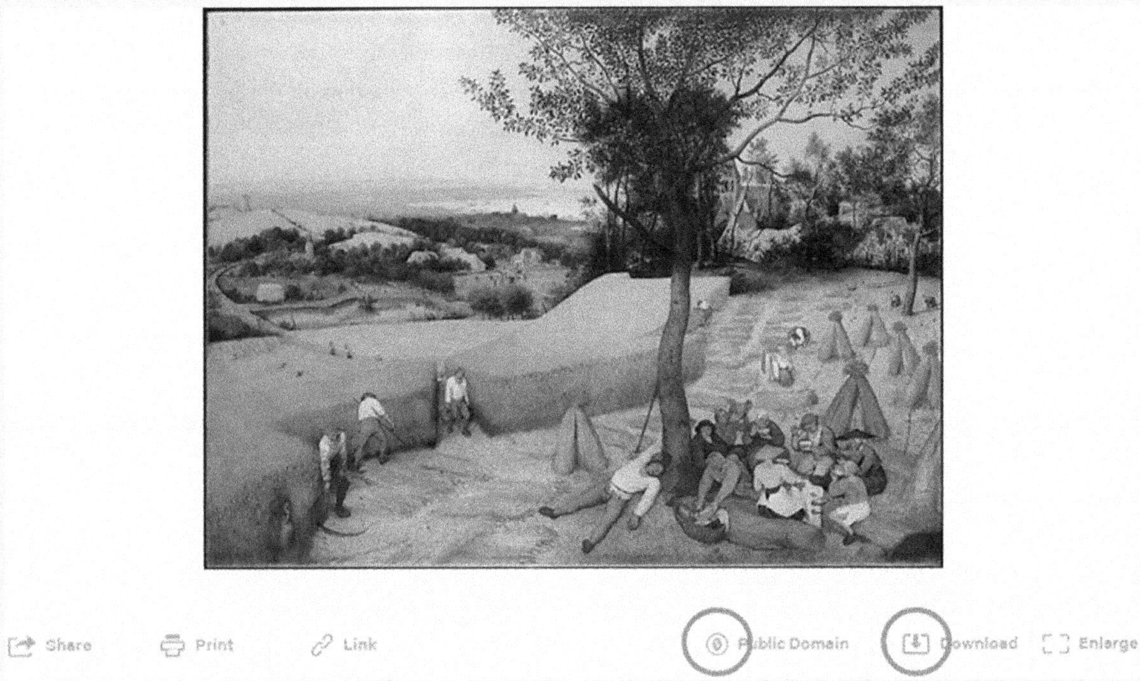

FIGURE 7.2
The Creative Commons license designation and download functionality are readily visible below the image itself.

> Jacques Louis David's *Death of Socrates* is presented only in English on metmuseum.org, where it is viewed an average of 2,700 times a month (Q4 2017). The Wikipedia article about the same artwork exists in 28 languages in addition to English, including Arabic, Chinese, French, Spanish, and Turkish. The article in English is viewed an average of 11,800 times a month; the other 28 versions are viewed an additional 19,010 times a month (Q4 2017).[4]

Recognition of these positive effects has led The Met to conclude that visits to the museum's website do not equate with success and that metrics must also include The Met objects on other platforms. The Wikimedian-in-residence staff position should become a permanent part of the Met's program. And that partnerships like the Wikimedia project should be managed and expanded as an ongoing part of The Met's digital initiatives.[5]

NOTES

1. "CC0—'No Rights Reserved,'" Creative Commons, accessed May 5, 2018, https://creativecommons.org/about/cc0.
2. *The Harvesters*, MetMuseum.org Collection, accessed May 6, 2018, https://www.metmuseum.org/art/collection/search/435809?sortBy=Relevance&ft=wheat+field&offset=0&rpp=20&pos=9.

3. Loic Tallon, "Introducing Open Access at The Met," *Digital Underground Met Blog,* February 7, 2017, https://www.metmuseum.org/blogs/digital-underground/2017/open-access-at-the-met.
4. Loic Tallon, "Creating Access beyond metmuseum.org: The Met Collection on Wikipedia," *Now at The Met Blog,* February 7, 2018, https://www.metmuseum.org/blogs/now-at-the-met/2018/open-access-at-the-met-year-one.
5. Ibid.

status for an international audience. It creates three categories of statements to be used with cultural heritage materials, including some terms for use specifically in the EU.[36]

The "In Copyright" category outlines five rights statements for use with digital objects that are in copyright:

1. In Copyright
2. In Copyright—EU Orphan Work
3. In Copyright—Educational Uses Permitted
4. In Copyright—Non-Commercial Use Permitted
5. In Copyright—Rights-Holder(s) Unlocatable or Unidentifiable[37]

The "No Copyright" category outlines four rights statements for use with works that are not in copyright, but where the copyright status has only been determined for a specific jurisdiction or where there may be other restrictions aside from copyright that prevent free use of the materials:

1. No Copyright—Contractual Restrictions
2. No Copyright—Non-Commercial Use Only
3. No Copyright—Other Known Legal Restrictions
4. No Copyright—United States[38]

The "Other" category outlines three rights statements for use when the copyright status for specific objects has not been determined, for one reason or another:

1. Copyright Not Evaluated
2. Copyright Undetermined
3. No Known Copyright[39]

The goal of these twelve rights statements is to provide cultural heritage institutions with simple and standardized terms to summarize the copyright status of works in their collection and how those works may be used. Following DPLA and Europeana's lead in drafting simple, standardized terms that help metadata contributors more effectively communicate copyright and reuse status of digital objects, cultural institutions can now utilize the tools and statements available in RightsStatement.org, which went live in 2016, to provide greater clarity to end users of their content.[40]

COPYRIGHT CORTEX

Further centralizing and standardizing access to reference materials and practical resources is the Copyright Cortex, an online, open access resource project launched in June 2017.[41] "The Copyright Cortex is an online resource dedicated to copyright and digital cultural heritage. It was developed to provide libraries, museums and other memory institutions with information and expert commentary on how copyright law

CASE STUDY

NEW YORK PUBLIC LIBRARY

Anne M. Young

In 2016, the New York Public Library (NYPL) released more than 180,000 digitized unique and rare works available as high-resolution downloads with the empowering statement: "No permission required, no hoops to jump through: just go forth and reuse!"[1] NYPL Digital Collections website now includes easy to find filters that enable users to more quickly find restriction-free content and quickly download the public domain content, which to date has grown to more than 222,500 items.[2] Opening access to these materials was further enabled and refined by the use of tools, such as Creative Commons CC0 license and RightsStatements.org, to standardize and simplify the language that end users find when encountering collection objects and further promote the reuse of collection materials. Other cultural institutions can follow the lead of NYPL to make images and metadata of its library, archive, and other collection objects available with greater clarity for how their materials may be reused.

NOTES

1. Shana Kimball, "Free for All: NYPL Enhances Public Domain Collections for Sharing and Reuse," *NYPL Labs, Spotlight on the Public Domain,* January 5, 2016, https://www.nypl.org/blog/2016/01/05/share-public-domain-collections.
2. "About NYPL Digital Collections," *The New York Public Library Digital Collections,* accessed May 9, 2018, https://digitalcollections.nypl.org/about.

affects the creation and management of digital cultural heritage."[42]

The main feature of the Copyright Cortex is as a catalogue that centralizes materials from across the globe that are related to copyright and digital cultural heritage. These materials, including guidelines, policy documents, case studies, and scholarly publications, are broadly organized into three categories:

1. Research
   Materials in this section include research in copyright law, policy and practices in cultural contexts, and a range of additional topics from orphan works to digital surrogates.[43]
2. Tools & Resources
   Materials in this section cover a variety of resources rights and reproductions specialists at cultural institutions may find useful, including public domain calculators, videos, conference presentations on open culture, and a variety of other practical guides.[44]
3. Policy & Evidence
   Materials in this section are focused on documentation for government and legislative changes around copyright issues internationally. A large number of materials come from the UK Intellectual Property Office and the European Commission.[45]

The secondary feature of Copyright Cortex, although not any less important, is the open access book, *Copyright and Digital Cultural Heritage*, referred to as Copyright 101. Copyright 101 is available to be downloaded or read as individual sections online. It provides readers with an introduction to copyright law, specifically focusing on the impact of copyright in international contexts for access to and use of cultural heritage.[46]

Copyright Cortex is an ongoing project with new content and functions being added through links to the original materials, when possible. When launched, it was noted that "the Copyright Cortex could be a useful source of examples of risk analysis and management strategies" for cultural institutions that may be considering utilizing fair use and/or making their collections more widely available online through an open access program.[47] As this resource continues to add materials and expand its resources it will be a useful tool for rights and reproductions specialists to reference when making decisions about the use of materials in the collections of their cultural institutions.

WHAT OPEN ACCESS MAKES POSSIBLE

Open Access (OA) is an ever-growing area for cultural institutions. OA, open content, open source, and other variations on the theme of "open" are becoming more prevalent among galleries, libraries, archives, and museums that are endeavoring to provide broader public access to their collection materials. While the adoption of a formal OA policy[48] or the introduction of OA or open content image and video files provided directly from a cultural institution's website[49] are growing in number, there are several inconsistencies in delivery and formatting that rights and reproductions specialists should be aware of when seeking to reuse content. For instance, images may be available for free on an institutional website that may be available at a cost on a commercial site such as Art Resource or Bridgeman Images. It is worth careful examination to determine whether a collection is truly "open"—some cultural institutions use language like "free" and "open" to describe publicly available collections, while simultaneously imposing limitations on their use. Sometimes the limitations lack legal basis (e.g., a limited Creative Commons license on a scan of a public domain work), but they still convey information about the expectations of the organization providing access, and may contain valid limits on use (i.e., contractual restrictions from a donor or lender to the cultural institution).

Yet, rights and reproductions specialists need not fret. While these inconsistencies exist, the more exciting news is that the numbers continue to grow. At the time of authoring this chapter, more than three hundred international cultural institutions with some level of "open" data and content have been organized by Andrea Wallace and Douglas McCarthy in their "Survey of GLAM open access policies."[50] This informal survey organizes the institutions by country and "examines how GLAMs make data—whether digital objects, metadata or text—available for reuse."[51] Beneficially, the survey defines OA according to Open Knowledge International's spectrum for OA licenses and rights statements, which at its simplest definition reads: "Open data and content can be freely used, modified, and shared by anyone for any purpose."[52] Rights and reproductions specialists can find useful information in this survey when researching content for use with a specific project or to be used as a means to argue the importance of developing a new OA policy and developing a delivery mechanism for open content delivery at their own cultural institution.

A selection of international cultural institutions utilizing image reproductions, fair use, fair dealing, and/or OA principles are discussed below.

Rijksmuseum Rijksstudo

Launched October 30, 2012, with 125,000 digital images, the Rijksstudio gives visitors virtual access to works of art from the Rijksmuseum, museum of the Netherlands.[53] Innovative when launched and still at the forefront of presenting collection images, the Rijksstudio makes a large part of the museum's collection available free of charge to all. It was and is unique in the high-resolution images made available coupled with the encouraged interaction by the public to create

CASE STUDY

THE RIJKSSTUDIO AWARD

Anne M. Young

The Rijksmuseum awarded the Rijksstudio Award for the third time in 2017. For this competition, the public was invited to "draw inspiration from the Rijksmuseum collection, download images from Rijksstudio and use them to create their own artwork."[1] First launched in 2014, the Rijksstudio Award competition takes place biannually and places the Rijksmuseum "firmly in a leading position in the world of digital image culture and open design."[2]

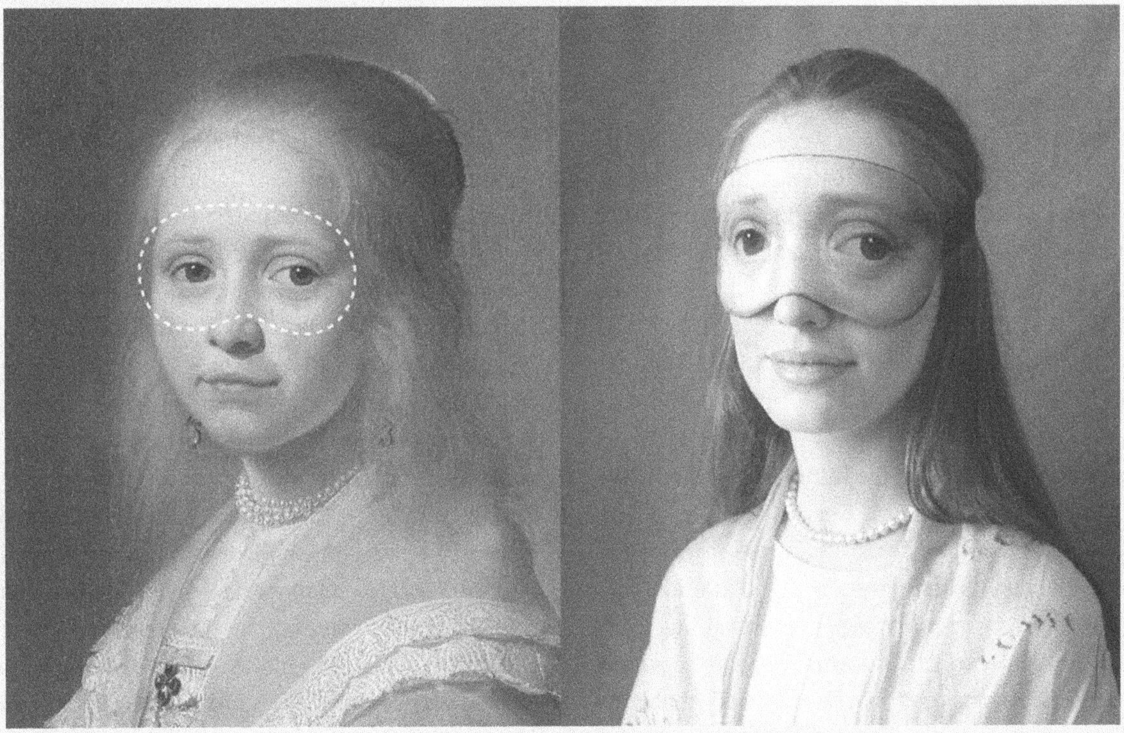

FIGURE 7.3
The 2017 Rijksstudio Award winner, *Masterpieces Never Sleep* by Lesha Limonov (right), inspired by Johannes Cornelisz Verspronck's *Portrait of a Girl Dressed in Blue* (left).

NOTES

1. "2017 International Rijksstudio Award: And the winner is...," Rijksmuseum, accessed May 11, 2018, https://www.rijksmuseum.nl/en/rijksstudio-award.
2. "Entry open for Rijksstudio 2017 Award: Public invited to make their own masterpieces inspired by the Rijksmuseum's collection," Rijksmuseum, September 13, 2016, https://www.rijksmuseum.nl/en/press/press-releases/entry-open-for-rijksstudio-2017-award.

a closer connection with the Rijksmuseum's collections.[54] "With Rijksstudio everyone can use the images from the Rijksmuseum's collection free of charge to discover, collect, share, touch, 'like' and edit."[55]

Further enabling engagement by the public, the Rijksmuseum redesigned Rijksstudio and launched a new Rijskmuseum app in January 2018. Today, Rijksstudio presents more than 325,000 works of art from the Rijksmuseum collection and "presents personal collections compiled by users, together with stories from the Rijksmuseum in the same simple and mobile-first visual template."[56]

Auckland War Memorial Museum

Expanding the reach of Open Access beyond North American and European institutions, the Auckland War Memorial Museum in New Zealand joined the international initiative among museums and cultural institutions "to digitise and upload public domain works to the internet free of charge and without restrictions, with the aim of generating new study, sparking creativity, and providing inspiration to people across the globe."[57] Importantly, the Auckland Museum approaches its three hundred thousand images of collection objects as "open by default" to be downloaded and reused for any purpose imaginable. "Open by default" is an important way that other cultural institutions can adopt when approaching open access to images of collections work. For the Auckland Museum this "means that images of collection objects for which no copyright exists, or where copyright has expired, we allow reuse for any purpose, including commercial, as long as Auckland Museum is identified as the source."[58]

Toward this end, the Auckland Museum utilized both Creative Commons licenses and RightsStatements.org rights statements to share high-resolution images. Images have either a CC-BY license or a No Known Copyright Restrictions rights statement attached, which allows anyone throughout the world that is familiar with Creative Commons and RightsStatements.org to know how they can utilize images from the Auckland Museum. By attaching Creative Commons licenses the Auckland Museum is seeing new and broader uses of its collection images, such as Wikipedia articles where they may not have intuitively seen connections, but where other members of the public can draw inspiration and use the content to highlight different articles.[59]

SMK Open

Statens Museum for Kunst (SMK) in Denmark launched the project SMK Open in 2016 with the aim of making the SMK collection available to everyone. SMK Open builds upon the success of a variety of predecessors in making collections available via Open Access, including those in the United States and the Netherlands. A common finding among cultural institutions, museums in particular, with Open Access is that "far more people use the collections when they can actively select, reuse, remix and share the works—including people who would not otherwise use the museums."[60] SMK Open builds upon this concept to make art accessible, including not only images and metadata about the works, but also supplementary materials such as film, articles, exhibition histories, and conservation X-ray photographs.[61] SMK Open encourages everyone in the world to access, download, and use public domain works, referred to as copyright-free. Further broadening the conversation between the museum and visitors by not only encouraging use of the materials, but to also comment on works, provide information they might have, and engage in conversations with staff about the art.[62]

To date, SMK Open contains more than twenty-five thousand images, a number which is continually growing as older representations of works are replaced with new high-resolution image files.[63] The downloadable image files are limited to those in which the copyright to the artworks has expired and moved into the public domain. These images are designated "'Public Doman' to clearly signify that they are no longer subject to copyright. They belong to the public—to you."[64] Even more helpful than the "Public Domain"

CASE STUDY

DISPLAY AT YOUR OWN RISK

Anne M. Young

Display At Your Own Risk (DAYOR) examines the limitations of access to digital surrogates (digital images) of works in the collections of cultural institutions globally.[1] DAYOR strengthens the argument for cultural institutions to develop Open Access policies and procedures for end users to access image reproductions of works in their collections. Envisioned as an open source exhibition research project, DAYOR is intended for public use beyond the documentation it created and gallery exhibition that was presented on June 8, 2016.[2] The exhibition was curated from the online collection of internationally renowned cultural institutions that make images of collection works available online. For the exhibition, these digital surrogates were printed to the original dimensions of the work itself (i.e., the digital file of the Mona Lisa painting was printed to the original dimensions of the painting itself).[3] In this way, the exhibition drew attention to the wide variety of creating digital representations of collection works, including the variant image qualities and file sizes made available by cultural institutions.

As many cultural institutions have grappled with control of the representation of their collection objects verses making the image files of public domain works available through open access, DAYOR highlights that it is truly to the benefit of cultural institutions to create and share the authoritative representation of works. Otherwise, digital surrogates of a lesser quality may (will) be promulgated and used as a potentially poor substitute to the high-resolution digital file the cultural institution may be able to provide directly.[4]

DAYOR considered the "meaning of concepts such as access, transparency and user engagement in an age where digital collections are becoming increasingly relevant." And almost more importantly, DAYOR explored the issue that was at the very heart of the US case *Bridgeman v. Corel*, in which it was found that two-dimensional photographic reproductions of works of art do not imbue a new copyright to the creator of the photograph.[5] This tension persists among many cultural institutions today that continue to claim a copyright to images, the digital surrogates, of works in their collections that they view as new assets. Through projects like DAYOR, cultural institutions can view tangible benefits to not claiming a copyright to the images they create of collection works, making those images available through Open Access programs, and enabling future reuse by new generations of creators.

NOTES

1. Display At Your Own Risk, accessed May 11, 2018, http://displayatyourownrisk.org/.
2. "About," Display At Your Own Risk, accessed May 11, 2018, http://displayatyourownrisk.org/about-dayor/.
3. Ibid.
4. Ibid.
5. See chapter 1, What Makes a Work "Original?" for a more detailed discussion of *Bridgeman Art Library v. Corel Corp.*

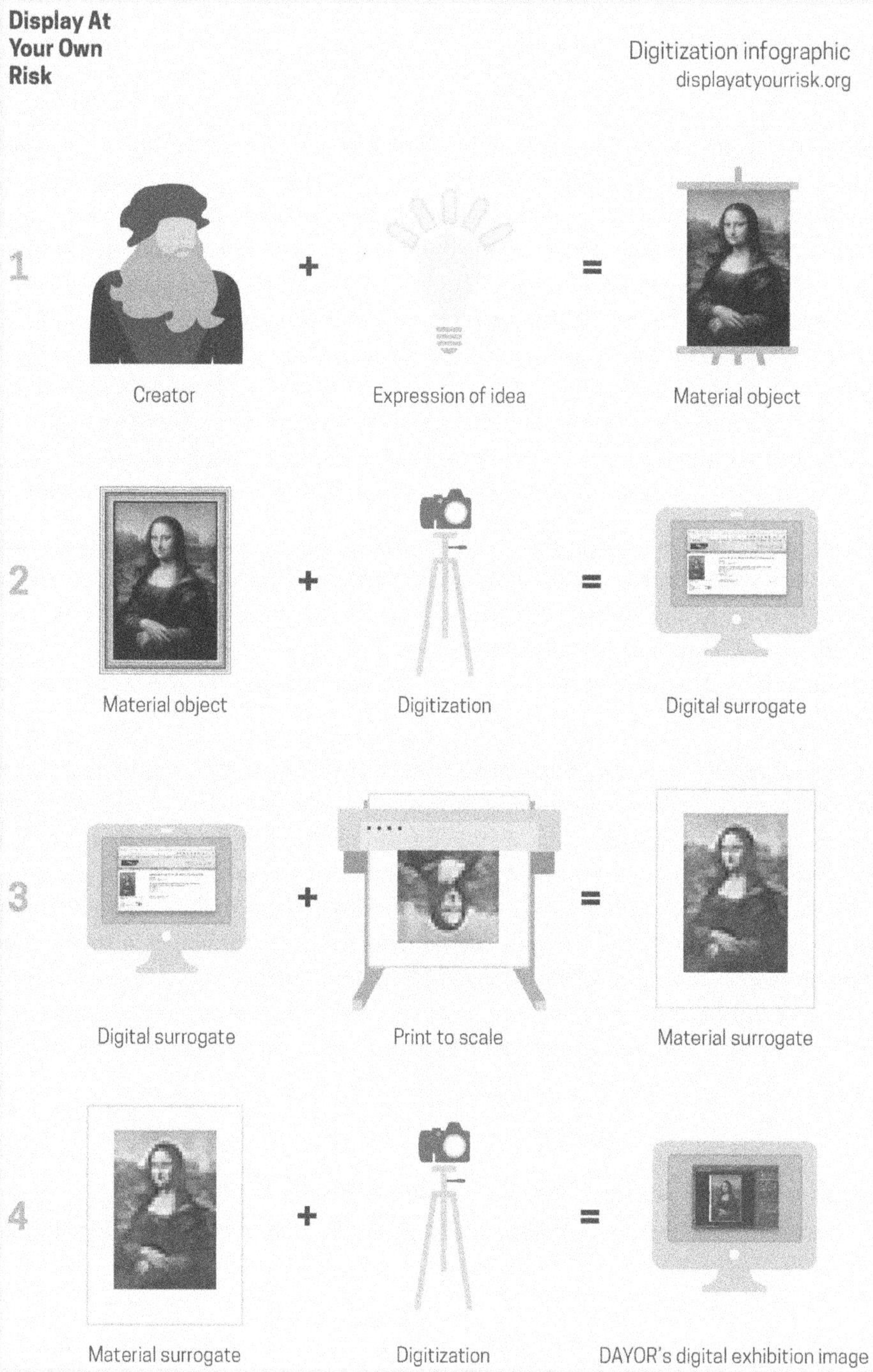

FIGURE 7.4
Digitization infographic that walks users through the process cultural institutions undertake to provide digital image files of collection objects.

designation on the image files, is the information that SMK provides to users by identifying potential uses, as well as guidelines that users may want to consider when using the public domain materials. While not required by SMK to use downloaded image files, the guidelines suggest the following:

- Give credit where credit is due
- Protect the reputation of the artist and museum
- Show respect for the original work
- Share knowledge
- Preserve Public Domain marks and notices[65]

Overall, SMK Open is just one part of SMK's endeavors to make image reproductions of its artworks publicly available, to encourage reuse, and provide guidelines for that reuse. SMK broadens its reach through partnerships such as Wiki labs and Europeana, which, respectively, write and publish articles on artists, artworks, and styles in Wikipedia and creates a digital art collection build from cultural institutions in twenty-eight European countries.[66]

CONCLUSION

While there is no definitive black-and-white answer for the utilization of fair use per US copyright law, tools like the aforementioned codes, guidelines, and statements should provide a measure of guidance to rights and reproductions specialists at cultural institutions and individual creators considering the application of fair use, or fair dealing, in their work(s). Future generations will likely see an increased adoption of fair use, fair dealing, and OA for the preservation, dissemination, and utilization of the shared cultural heritage cared for by archives, libraries, galleries, and museums.

NOTES

1. See chapters 1 and 4, Fair Use, for a more detailed discussion.

2. "[T]he fair use of a copyrighted work [. . .] for purposes such as criticism, comment, news reporting, teaching (including multiple copies for classroom use), scholarship, or research, is not an infringement of copyright." 17 U.S.C. § 107.

3. See chapter 1, Appropriation Art, for a discussion of the following examples: *Blanch v. Koons*, 467 F.3d 244 (2d Cir. 2006) and *Cariou v. Prince*, 714 F.3d 694 (2d Cir. 2013).

4. Additional examples of fair use are outlined in the examples of fair use collected by documentary filmmakers and within the Association of Art Museum Directors' *Guidelines for the Use of Copyrighted Materials and Works of Art by Art Museums,* which has a lengthy section on specific examples of fair use. See Center for Media and Social Impact, *Examples of Successful Fair Use in Documentary Film*, accessed May 3, 2018, http://cmsimpact.org/resource/examples-of-successful-fair-use-in-documentary-film/.

5. *U.S. Copyright Office Fair Use Index*, accessed May 3, 2018, https://www.copyright.gov/fls/fl102.html.

6. For a discussion of the role of the lawyer in fair use see J. Garon, The Lawyer's Role in Promoting Fair Use, https://papers.ssrn.com/sol3/papers.cfm?abstract_id=2750462.

7. This list is not meant to be all inclusive; for a more comprehensive overview see Appendix C: References and Resources.

8. Association of Independent Video and Filmmakers, Independent Feature Project, International Documentary Association, National Alliance for Media Arts and Culture, and Women in Film and Video, "Documentary Filmmakers' Statement of Best Practices in Fair Use," Center for Media & Social Impact (June 2005), http://www.cmsimpact.org/sites/default/files/fair_use_final.pdf.

9. American University: Washington College of Law: Program on Information Justice and Intellectual Property, "Code of Best Practices in Fair Use for Online Video," Center for Social Media (June 2008), http://www.cmsimpact.org/sites/default/files/online_best_practices_in_fair_use.pdf.

10. Patricia Aufderheide, Katharine Coles, Peter Jaszi, and Jennifer Urban, "Code of Best Practices in Fair Use for Poetry," Center for Media & Social Impact (January 2011), http://www.cmsimpact.org/sites/default/files/documents/pages/fairusepoetrybooklet_singlepg_3.pdf.

11. Association of Art Museum Directors, *AAMD Policy on the Use of "Thumbnail" Digital Images in Museum Online Initiatives* (New York, 2011).

12. See chapter 4, File Sizes, Fair Use and AAMD, for a more detailed discussion.

13. Association of Research Libraries, "Code of Best Practices in Fair Use for Academic and Research Libraries," Association of Research Libraries (January 2012), http://www.arl.org/storage/documents/publications/code-of-best-practices-fair-use.pdf.

14. Association of Research Libraries, *Code of Best Practices in Fair Use*, accessed May 3, 2018, http://www.arl.org/focus-areas/copyright-ip/fair-use/code-of-best-practices.

15. Ibid.

16. Visual Resources Association, "Statement on the Fair Use of Images for Teaching, Research, and Study, August 30, 2013, http://vraweb.org/vra-fair-use-statement/.

17. Ibid.

18. Patricia Aufderheide, David R. Hansen, Meredith Jacob, Peter Jaszi, and Jennifer M. Urban, "Statement of Best Practices in Fair Use of Collections Containing Orphan Works," Center for Media & Social Impact (2014), http://www.cmsimpact.org/sites/default/files/documents/orphanworks-dec14.pdf.

19. Ibid.

20. Ibid.

21. College Art Association, "Code of Best Practices in Fair Use for the Visual Arts," February 2015, http://www.collegeart.org/pdf/fair-use/best-practices-fair-use-visual-arts.pdf.

22. Ibid.

23. Association of Art Museum Directors, *Guidelines for the Use of Copyright Materials and Works of Art by Art Museums.* New York: October 11, 2017.

24. Ibid.

25. Ibid.

26. "Use & remix," *Creative Commons,* accessed May 5, 2018, https://creativecommons.org/use-remix/.

27. Ibid.

28. "About the Licenses," Creative Commons, accessed May 5, 2018, http://creativecommons.org/licenses/.

29. "CC0—'No Rights Reserved,'" Creative Commons, accessed May 5, 2018, https://creativecommons.org/about/cc0.

30. Examples from a variety of media forms and distribution channels are available at "Marking Your Work with a CC License," CC Wiki, accessed May 5, 20185, https://wiki.creativecommons.org/Marking_your_work_with_a_CC_license.

31. "CC REL," CC Wiki, May 5, 2018, https://wiki.creativecommons.org/Ccrel.

32. "Public Domain Mark ," Creative Commons, accessed May 5, 2018, https://creativecommons.org/share-your-work/public-domain/pdm.

33. "About RightsStatements.org," RightsStatements.org, accessed May 8, 2018, http://rightsstatements.org/en/about.html.

34. Ibid.

35. Ibid.

36. "Three Categories of Rights Statements," RightsStatements.org, accessed May 8, 2018, http://rightsstatements.org/page/1.0/?language=en.

37. "Rights statements for in copyright objects," RightsStatements.org, accessed May 8, 2018, http://rightsstatements.org/page/1.0/?language=en#rights-statements-for-in-copyright-objects.

38. "Rights statements for objects that are not in copyright," RighstStatements.org, accessed May 8, 2018, http://rightsstatements.org/page/1.0/?language=en#rights-statements-for-objects-that-are-not-in-copyright.

39. "Other rights statements," RightsStatements.org, accessed May 8, 2018, http://rightsstatements.org/page/1.0/?language=en#other-rights-statements.

40. "Use by cultural heritage institutions," RightsStatements.org, accessed May 8, 2018, http://rightsstatements.org/en/documentation/#use-by-cultural-heritage-institutions.

41. Ronan Deazley, "The British Library hosts launch of The Copyright Cortex, *Europeana Pro*, June 20, 2017, https://pro.europeana.eu/post/the-british-library-launches-the-copyright-cortex.

42. "About the Copyright Cortex." *Copyright Cortex*, accessed May 11, 2018, https://copyrightcortex.org/about.

43. "Research," *Copyright Cortex*, accessed May 11, 2018, https://copyrightcortex.org/research.

44. "Tools & Resources," *Copyright Cortex"* accessed May 11, 2018, https://copyrightcortex.org/tools-resources.

45. "Policy & Evidence," *Copyright Cortex*, accessed May 11, 2018, https://copyrightcortex.org/policy-evidence.

46. "About the Copyright Cortex." *Copyright Cortex*, accessed May 11, 2018, https://copyrightcortex.org/about.

47. Victoria Stobo, "The Copyright Cortex: Launch Event," *CREATe*, July 24, 2017, https://www.create.ac.uk/blog/2017/07/24/copyright-cortex-british-library/.

48. See chapter 2 for a more detailed discussion of Open Access policies.

49. See chapter 6 for a more detailed discussion of enabling Open Access or open content images.

50. Andrea Wallace and Douglas McCarthy, *Survey of GLAM open access policies [2.0]*, accessed May 14, 2018, https://docs.google.com/spreadsheets/d/1WPS-KJptUJ-o8SXtg00llcxq0IKJu8eO6Ege_GrLaNc/edit#gid=1216556120.

51. Andrea Wallace and Douglas McCarthy, "About this Survey," *Survey of GLAM open access policies [2.0]*, accessed May 14, 2018, https://docs.google.com/document/d/15U__Z50WCUM_OWQ9HKLvLMlkcMoCN68FLVl9OKJQ8yY/edit.

52. For more detail about Open Knowledge International's definition for OA see "The Open Definition," accessed May 14, 2018, https://opendefinition.org/.

53. Peter Gorgels, "Rijksstudio: Make Your Own Masterpiece!," *Museums and the Web 2013*, January 28, 2013, https://mw2013.museumsandtheweb.com/paper/rijksstudio-make-your-own-masterpiece/.

54. Ibid.

55. "2017 International Rijksstudio Award: And the winner is. . . ," *Rijksmuseum*, accessed May 11, 2018, https://www.rijksmuseum.nl/en/rijksstudio-award.

56. Peter Gorgels, "Rijksmuseum Mobile First: Rijksstudio Redesign And The New Rijksmuseum App," *Museums and the Web 2018*, January 14, 2018, https://mw18.mwconf.org/paper/rijksmuseum-mobile-first-redesign-rijksstudio-the-new-rijksmuseum-app/.

57. Sarah Powell, "300,000 open images and counting . . . ," *Auckland War Memorial Museum Blog*, July 14, 2017, http://www.aucklandmuseum.com/discover/stories/blog/2017/300,000-open-images-and-counting.

58. Ibid.

59. Sarah Powell, "Enriching our Online Collections—Managing image rights for digital surrogates," *Auckland War Memorial Museum*, October 22, 2016, http://www.aucklandmuseum.com/discover/stories/blog/2016/enriching-our-online-collections-rights-management.

60. "SMK Open," *Statens Museum for Kunst*, accessed May 11, 2018, http://www.smk.dk/en/about-smk/camp00/.

61. Ibid.

62. Ibid.

63. "Free download of artworks," *Statens Museum for Kunst*, accessed May 11, 2018, http://www.smk.dk/en/use-of-images-and-text/free-download-of-artworks/.

64. Ibid.

65. Ibid.

66. "SMK Open," *Statens Museum for Kunst*, accessed May 11, 2018, http://www.smk.dk/en/about-smk/camp00/.

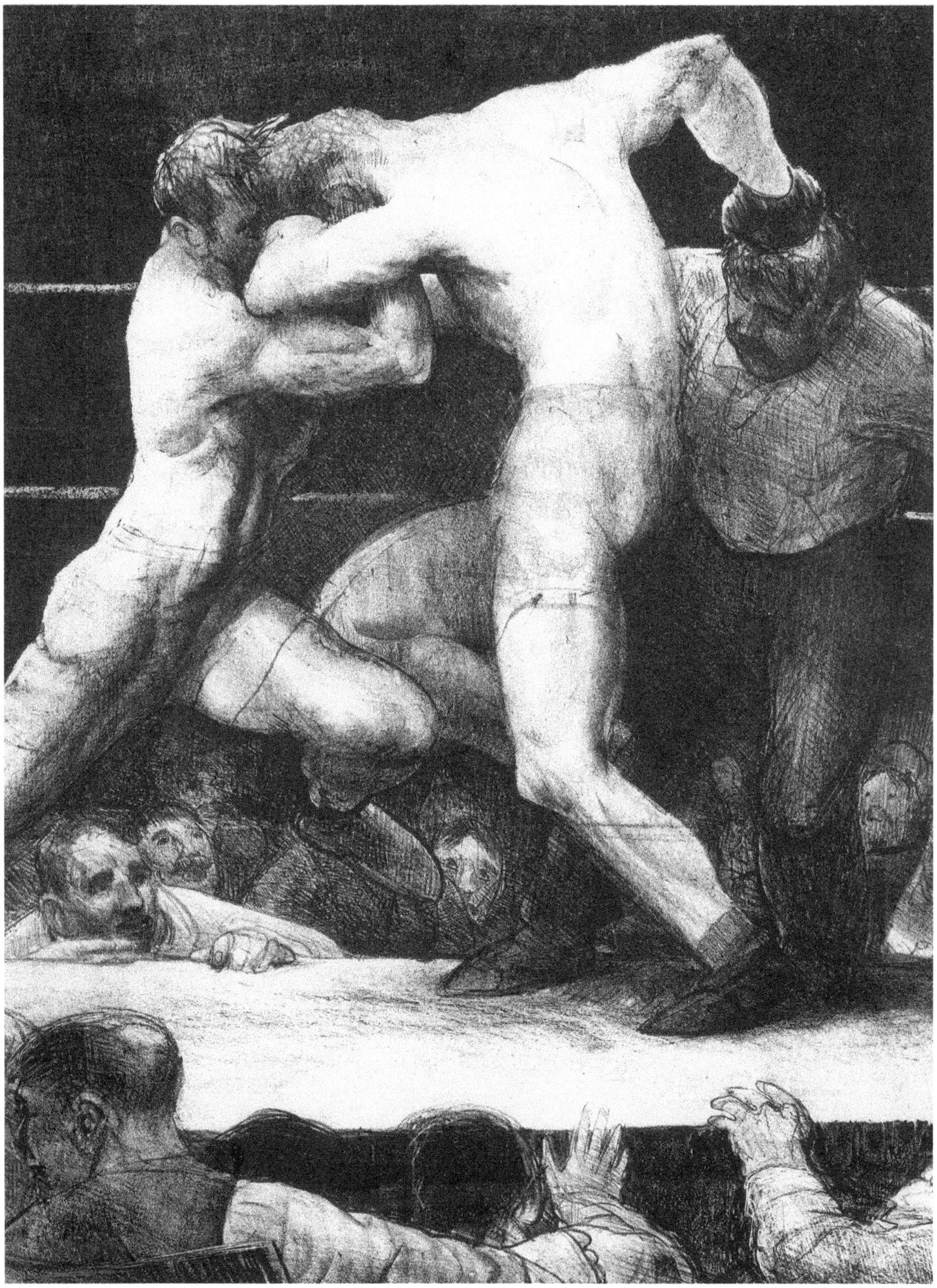

Appendix A

International Treaties, Federal Legal Materials, and Court Decisions

Note: Legal materials listed below are not intended as a comprehensive list of all relevant resources, but are included because of reference within and relevance to the main text of the *Handbook.*

INTERNATIONAL TREATIES

- **Agreement on Trade-Related Aspects of Intellectual Property Rights (TRIPs Agreement), World Trade Organization (WTO)**
  https://www.wto.org/english/tratop_e/trips_e/intel2_e.htm
- **Berne Convention for the Protection of Literary and Artistic Works, World Intellectual Property Organization (WIPO)**
  http://www.wipo.int/treaties/en/text.jsp?file_id=283698
- **Madrid Agreement Concerning the International Registration of Marks, WIPO**
  http://www.wipo.int/wipolex/en/wipo_treaties/text.jsp?file_id=283530
- **Marrakesh Treaty to Facilitate Access to Published Works for Persons Who Are Blind, Visually Impaired or Otherwise Print Disabled, WIPO**
  http://www.wipo.int/treaties/en/ip/marrakesh/
- **Paris Convention for the Protection of Industrial Property, WIPO**
  http://www.wipo.int/treaties/en/text.jsp?file_id=288514
- **Universal Copyright Convention (UCC), United Nations Educational, Scientific and Cultural Organization (UNESCO)**
  http://portal.unesco.org/en/ev.php-URL_ID=15381&URL_DO=DO_TOPIC&URL_SECTION=201.html
- **WIPO Copyright Treaty, WIPO**
  http://www.wipo.int/treaties/en/ip/wct/
- **WIPO Performances and Phonograms Treaty, WIPO**
  http://www.wipo.int/treaties/en/ip/wppt/

UNITED STATES FEDERAL LAW

US Constitution, Article I § 8, cl. 8

U.S. Code

- **Title 15. Commerce and Trade; Chapter 22. Trademarks**
  - § 1064. Cancellation of registration
  - § 1115. Registration on principal register as evidence of exclusive right to use mark; defenses Effective: November 2, 2002
  - § 1125. False designations of origin, false descriptions, and dilution forbidden Effective: October 5, 2012
  - § 1127. Construction and definitions; intent of chapter Effective: October 6, 2006
- **Title 17. Copyrights**
  - Chapter 1. Subject Matter and Scope of Copyright
    - § 101. Definitions Effective: December 9, 2010
    - § 102. Subject matter of copyright: In general
    - § 103. Subject matter of copyright: Compilations and derivative works
    - § 105. Subject matter of copyright: United States Government works
    - § 106. Exclusive rights in copyrighted works
    - § 106A. Rights of certain authors to attribution and integrity
    - § 107. Limitations on exclusive rights: Fair use
    - § 108. Limitations on exclusive rights: Reproduction by libraries and archives
    - § 109. Limitations on exclusive rights: Effect of transfer of particular copy or phonorecord Effective: October 13, 2008

- ▫ § 110. Limitations on exclusive rights: Exemption of certain performances and displays Effective: April 27, 2005
- ▫ § 112. Limitations on exclusive rights: Ephemeral recordings
- ▫ § 113. Scope of exclusive rights in pictorial, graphic, and sculptural works
- ▫ § 114. Scope of exclusive rights in sound recordings Effective: December 9, 2010
- ▫ § 117. Limitations on exclusive rights: Computer programs Effective October 28, 1998
- ▫ § 120. Scope of exclusive rights in architectural works Effective December 1, 1990
- ▫ § 121. Limitations on exclusive rights: Reproduction for blind or other people with disabilities Effective: December 3, 2004

▫ Chapter 2. Copyright Ownership and Transfer
- ▫ § 201. Ownership of copyright
- ▫ § 202. Ownership of copyright as distinct from ownership of material object
- ▫ § 203. Termination of transfers and licenses granted by the author Effective: November 2, 2002
- ▫ § 204. Execution of transfers of copyright ownership
- ▫ § 205. Recordation of transfers and other documents

▫ Chapter 3. Duration of Copyright
- ▫ § 301. Preemption with respect to other laws Effective: October 27, 1998
- ▫ § 302. Duration of copyright: Works created on or after January 1, 1997 Effective: October 27, 1998
- ▫ § 303. Duration of copyright: Works created but not published or copyrighted before January 1, 1978 Effective: December 9, 2010
- ▫ § 304. Duration of copyright: Subsisting copyrights Effective: November 2, 2002
- ▫ § 305. Duration of copyright: Terminal date

▫ Chapter 4. Copyright Notice, Deposit, and Registration
- ▫ § 408. Copyright registration in general Effective: April 27, 2005
- ▫ § 411. Registration and civil infringement actions Effective: October 13, 2008
- ▫ § 412. Registration as prerequisite to certain remedies for infringement Effective: October 13, 2008

▫ Chapter 5. Copyright Infringement and Remedies
- ▫ § 501. Infringement of copyright Effective: November 2, 2002
- ▫ § 502. Remedies for infringement: Injunctions
- ▫ § 503. Remedies for infringement: Impounding and disposition of infringing articles Effective: December 9, 2010
- ▫ § 504. Remedies for infringement: Damages and profits Effective: December 9, 2010
- ▫ § 505. Remedies for infringement: Costs and attorney›s fees
- ▫ § 506. Criminal offenses Effective: October 13, 2008
- ▫ § 512. Limitations on liability relating to material online Effective: December 9, 2010

▫ Chapter 12. Copyright Protection and Management Systems
- ▫ § 1201. Circumvention of copyright protection systems Effective: November 29, 1999
- ▫ § 1202. Integrity of copyright management information: November 29, 1999

- **Title 18. Crimes and Criminal Procedure; Part I—Crimes**
  - ▫ Chapter 90. Protection of Trade secrets
    - ▫ § 1839. Definitions Effective: October 11, 1996
  - ▫ Chapter 113. Stolen Property
    - ▫ § 2319. Criminal infringement of a copyright Effective: October 13, 2008
- **Title 25. Indians**
  - ▫ Chapter 32. Native American Graves Protection and Repatriation
    - ▫ § 3001. Definitions
    - ▫ § 3002. Ownership
- **Title 35. Patents; Part II—Patentability of Inventions and Grant of Patents**
  - ▫ Chapter 10. Patentability of Inventions
    - ▫ § 101. Inventions patentable
    - ▫ § 102. Conditions for patentability; novelty
  - ▫ Chapter 14. Issue of Patent
    - ▫ § 154. Contents and term of patent; provisional rights
  - ▫ Chapter 18. Patent Rights in Inventions Made With Federal Assistance
    - ▫ §§ 200–211 (Codified versions of Bayh-Dole University and Small Business Patent Procedures Act, Pub.L. 96–517, § 6(a), Dec. 12, 1980, 94 Stat. 3019; An Act to amend the patent and trademark laws, PL 96–517, December 12, 1980, 94 Stat 3015)

Note: All statutory references, unless otherwise noted, are to the version in effect at the time this edition of the *Handbook* was written in 2018.

US CODE OF FEDERAL REGULATIONS

- Title 37. Patents, Trademarks, and Copyrights; Chapter II. Copyright Office, Library of Congress; Subchapter A. Copyright Office and Procedures; Part 202. Preregistration and Registration of Claims to Copyright
  - § 202.11 Architectural works

US STATUTES

- Bayh-Dole University and Small Business Patent Procedures Act, Pub. L. 96–517, § 6(a), 94 Stat. 3019, Dec. 12, 1980; codified at 18 U.S.C §§200-211.
- Native American Graves Protection and Repatriation Act, Pub. L. 101-601, 104 Stat. 3048, Nov. 16, 1990; codified as amended in scattered sections of 25 U.S.C. and 18 U.S.C.
- President John F. Kennedy Assassination Records Collection Act of 1992, Pub.L. 102-526, 106 Stat. 3443, Oct. 26, 1992; codified at 44 U.S.C. §2107.
- Visual Artists Rights Act (VARA), Pub. L. 101-650, 104 Stat. 5132, Dec. 1, 1990; codified in part at 17 U.S.C. §§ 106A et. seq.
- Uruguay Round Agreements Act, Pub. L. 103-465, 108 Stat. 4809, Dec. 8, 1994; codified in scattered sections of 19 U.S.C.
- Technology, Education and Copyright Harmonization (TEACH) Act of 2002. Passed via 21st Century Department of Justice Appropriations Authorization Act Pub. L. 107–273, November 2, 2002, 116 Stat 1758; codified at 17 U.S.C. §§ 101, 110, 112, 801.
- Higher Education Opportunity Act, Pub. L. 110-315, 122 Stat. 3078, Aug. 14, 2008; codified in scattered sections of 20 U.S.C.
- Omnibus Appropriations Act of 2009, Pub. L. 111-8, § 217, 123 Stat. 524, Mar. 11, 2009; codified at 42 U.S.C. § 282c. (Enacting open access requirements for NIH-funded research)
- LANHAM ACT

US SUPREME COURT CASES

- *Bd. Of Tr. of Stanford Junior Univ. v. Roche Molecular Sys, Inc.*, 53 U.S. __/131 S.Ct. 2188 (2011)
- *Campbell v. Acuff-Rose Music, Inc.*, 510 U.S. 569 (1994)
- *Community For Creative Non–Violence v. James Earl Reid*, 490 U.S. 730 (1989)
- *Cox Broadcasting Corporation et al., Appellants, v. Martin Cohn*, 420 U.S. 469 (1975)
- *Feist Publications, Inc. v. Rural Telephone Service Company, Inc.*, 499 U.S. 340 (1991)
- *Gertz v. Robert Welch, Inc.*, 418 U.S. 323 (1974)
- *Golan v. Holder*, 565 U.S. ___ /132 S.Ct. 873 (2012)
- *Miller v. California*, 413 U.S. 15 (1973)
- *MGM Studios Inc. v. Grokster, Ltd.*, 545 U.S. 913 (2005)
- *Olmstead et al. v. United States.*, 277 U.S. 438 (1928)
- *Sony Corporation of America v. Universal City Studios, Inc.*, 464 U.S. 417 (1984)
- *Wilson v. Layne*, 526 U.S. 603 (1999)

US FEDERAL COURTS OF APPEAL

- ***First Circuit***
  - *Mass. Museum of Contemporary Art Found., Inc. v. Büchel*, 593 F. 3d 38 (2010)
- ***Second Circuit***
  - *Authors Guild, Inc. v. HathiTrust*, 755 F.3d87 (2d Cir. 2014)
  - *Bill Graham Archives v. Dorling Kindersley Ltd.*, 448 F.3d 605 (2006)
  - *Blanch v. Koons*, 467 F.3d 244 (2006)
  - *Bristol-Myers Squibb Company v. McNeil-Ppc Inc.*, 973 F.2d 1033 (1992)
  - *Cariou v. Prince*, 714 F.3d 694 (2013)
  - *Carter v. Helmsley-Spear, Inc.*, 71 F.3d 77 (1995), cert. denied 116 S. Ct. 1824 (1996)
  - *Galella v. Onassis*, 487 F.2d 986 (1973)
  - *Haelan Laboratories, Inc. v. Topps Chewing Gum, Inc.*, 202 F.2d 866 (1953)
  - *Pollara v. Seymour*, 344 F.3d 265 (2003)
  - *Rogers v. Koons*, 960 F.2d 301 (1992)
- ***Third Circuit***
  - *Arista Records, Inc. v. Flea World, Inc.*, 356 F.Supp.2d 411 (2005)
- ***Sixth Circuit***
  - *Bridgeport Music, Inc. v. Dimension Films*, 410 F.3d 792 (2005)
  - *Champions Golf Club, Inc. v. The Champions Golf Club, Inc.*, 78 F.3d 1111 (1996)
  - *ETW Corporation v. Jireh Publishing, Inc.*, 332 F.3d 915 (2003)
- ***Seventh Circuit***
  - *Martin v. City of Indianapolis*, 192 F.3d 608 (1999)
- ***Ninth Circuit***
  - *A&M Records v. Napster, Inc.*, 239 F.3d 1004 (2001)
  - *Ets-Hokin v. Skyy Spirits, Inc.*, 225 F.3d 1068 (2000)

  - *Fonovisa, Inc. v. Cherry Auction, Inc.*, 76 F.3d 259 (1996)
  - *Mattel, Inc. v. MCA Records, Inc.*, 296 F.3d 894 (2002)
  - *Mattel, Inc. v. Walking Mountain Productions*, 353 F.3d 792 (2003)
  - *MDY Industries, LLC v. Blizzard Entertainment, Inc.*, 629 F.3d 928 (2010)
  - *Milton H. Greene Archives, Inc. v. Marilyn Monroe LLC*, 692 F.3d 983 (9th Cir. 2012)
  - *Waits v. Frito-Lay, Inc.*, 978 F.2d 1093 (1992)
- ***Eleventh Circuit***
  - *Estate Of Martin Luther King, Jr., Inc. v. CBS, Inc.*, 194 F.3d 1211 (1999)
  - *Peter Letterese And Associates, Inc. v. World Inst. Of Scientology Enters*, 533 F.3d 1287 (2008)
- ***Federal Circuit***
  - *The Chamberlain Group, Inc. v. Skylink Technologies, Inc.*, 381 F.3d 1178 (2004)

US DISTRICT COURTS

- ***Alahverdian v. Grebinski***
  Southern District of Ohio, Western Division; Case No. 3:13-cv-00132 (2014)
- ***Basic Books, Inc. v. Kinko's Graphics Corp.***
  Southern District of New York; No. 89 CIV. 2807 (CBM) (1991)
- ***Berrios Nogueras v. Home Depot***
  District of Puerto Rico; CIVIL NO. 02-2069 (RLA) (2004)
- ***The Bridgeman Art Library, Ltd. V. Corel Corporation***
  Southern District of New York; 36 F.Supp.2d 191 (1999)
- ***Cariou v. Prince***
  Southern District of New York; 784 F.Supp.2d 337 (2011)
- ***Chaney v. Fayette County Pub. Sch. Dist.***
  Northern District of Georgia, Newnan Division; No. 3:13-Cv-89-Tcb (2013)
- ***Cohen et al. v. G&M Realty L.P. et al.***
  Eastern District of New York; No. 1:13-cv-05612 (2013)
- ***Dollcraft Co. Et Al. v. Nancy Ann Storybook Dolls, Inc.***
  Northern District of California, Southern Division; 94 F.Supp. 1 (1950)
- ***Flack v. Friends Of Queen Catherine, Inc.***
  Southern District of New York; 139 F.Supp.2d 526 (2001)
- ***Fraley v. Facebook, Inc.***
  Northern District of California, San Francisco Division; No. C 11-1726 RS (2012)
- ***Graham v. Prince***
  Southern District of New York; 265 F.Supp. 3d 366 (2017)
- ***Gund, Inc. v. Applause, Inc.***
  Southern District of New York; 809 F.Supp. 304 (1993)
- ***Intellectual Reserve, Inc. v. Utah Lighthouse Ministry, Inc.***
  District of Utah, Central Division; No. 2:99-CV-808C (1999)
- ***Martin v. City of Indianapolis***
  Southern District of Indiana, Indianapolis Division; No. IP 96-0330-C-B/S (1997)
- ***Mass. Museum of Contemporary Art Found., Inc. v. Büchel***
  District of Massachusetts; No. C.A. No. 07-30089-MAP (2008)
- ***Noland v. Janssen, et al.***
  Southern District of New York; No. 1:17-cv-05452 (2017)
- ***Online Policy Group v. Diebold, Inc.***
  Northern District of California, San Jose Division; No. C 03-04913 JF (2004)
- ***Pavia v. 1120 Ave. of the Americas Association.***
  Southern District of New York; No. 95 Civ. 1302 (RWS) (1995)
- ***Peker v. Masters Collection***
  Eastern District of New York; No. 98 CV 0672 (2000)
- ***Pfaff v. Denver Art Museum***
  Southern District of New York; No. 94 Civ. 9271 (JSM) (1995)
- ***Price v. Hal Roach Studios, Inc***
  Southern District of New York; 400 F.Supp. 836 (1975)
- ***Shaw Family Archives v. CMG Worldwide, Inc***
  Southern District of New York; 434 F.Supp.2d 203 (2006)
- ***Universal City Studios, Inc. v. Reimerdes***
  Southern District of New York; 111 F.Supp.2d 294 (2000)

US STATE LAWS

- **California Civil Code §3344.1.**
  Deceased personality's name, voice, signature, photograph, or likeness; unauthorized use; damages and profits from use; protected uses; persons entitled to exercise rights; successors in interest or licensees; registration of claim
- **California Civil Code §3344.**
  Use of another's name, voice, signature, photograph, or likeness for advertising or selling or soliciting purposes
- **Florida Statutes Annotated § 540.08**
  Unauthorized publication of name or likeness
- **Florida Statutes Annotated § 540.08**
  Unauthorized publication of name or likeness

- **Annotated Indiana Code 32-36-1-7**
  "Right of publicity" defined
- **Annotated Indiana Code 32-36-1-8**
  Use of personality's right of publicity
  Formerly cited as IN ST 32-13-1-8
- **New York Civil Rights Law § 50, NY CIV RTS § 50**
  Right of privacy
- **Ohio Revised Code Annotated R.C. § 2741.02**
  Use of individual's persona for commercial purpose
- **Ohio Revised Code Annotated R.C. § 2741.02**
  Use of individual's persona for commercial purpose
- **Ohio's Revised Code § 2741.02**
  Use of individual's persona for commercial purpose

Note: All statutory references, unless otherwise noted, are to the version in effect at the time this edition of the *Handbook* was written in 2018.

US STATE COURT OPINIONS

- ***Comedy III Productions, Inc. v. Gary Saderup, Inc.***
  Supreme Court of California; 106 Ca. Rptr. 2d 126; Apr. 30, 2001.
- ***Jane Doe v. John Roe, as father and next friend of A, B, and C, minor children***
  Supreme Court of Alabama; 638 So.2d 826; 1921382; March 4, 1994.
- ***Gionfriddo v. Major League Baseball***
  Cailfornia Court of Appeals; 94 Cal. App. 4th 400 (2001)
- ***Pavesich v. New England Life Ins. Co.***
  Supreme Court of Georgia. No. 69 L.R.A. 101; March 3, 1905.
- ***Phillips v. Smalley Maintenance Services, Inc.***
  Supreme Court of Alabama; No. 435 So.2d 705 CER 24; June 3, 1983.
- ***Smith et al. v. Doss***
  Supreme Court of Alabama; 251 Ala. 250 (1948)

US LEGAL COMMENTARY

- **The Rights of Publicity and Privacy (2d ed), J. Thomas**
  - Chapter 6. Legal Sources Defining the Rights of Publicity and Privacy: State Common Law (Database updated 2018)
- **Restatement (Third) of Unfair Competition (1995), American Law Institute**
  - Chapter 4. Appropriation of Trade Values > Topic 3-Right of Publicity > § 47 Use for Purposes of Trade
- **Restatement (Second) of Torts (1977), American Law Institute**
  - Division 5. Defamation > Chapter 24. Invasions of Interest in Reputation
    - Topic 1. Elements of a Cause of Action for Defamation
      - § 558 Elements Stated
    - Topic 2. Defamatory Communications
      - § 559 Defamatory Communication Defined
    - Topic 3. Types of Defamatory Communication
      - § 566 Expressions of Opinion
    - Topic 9. Truth
      - § 581A True Statements
  - Division 6A. Privacy > Chapter 28A. Invasion of Privacy
    - § 652B Intrusion upon Seclusion
    - § 652C Appropriation of Name or Likeness
    - § 652D Publicity Given to Private Life
    - § 652E Publicity Placing Person in False Light

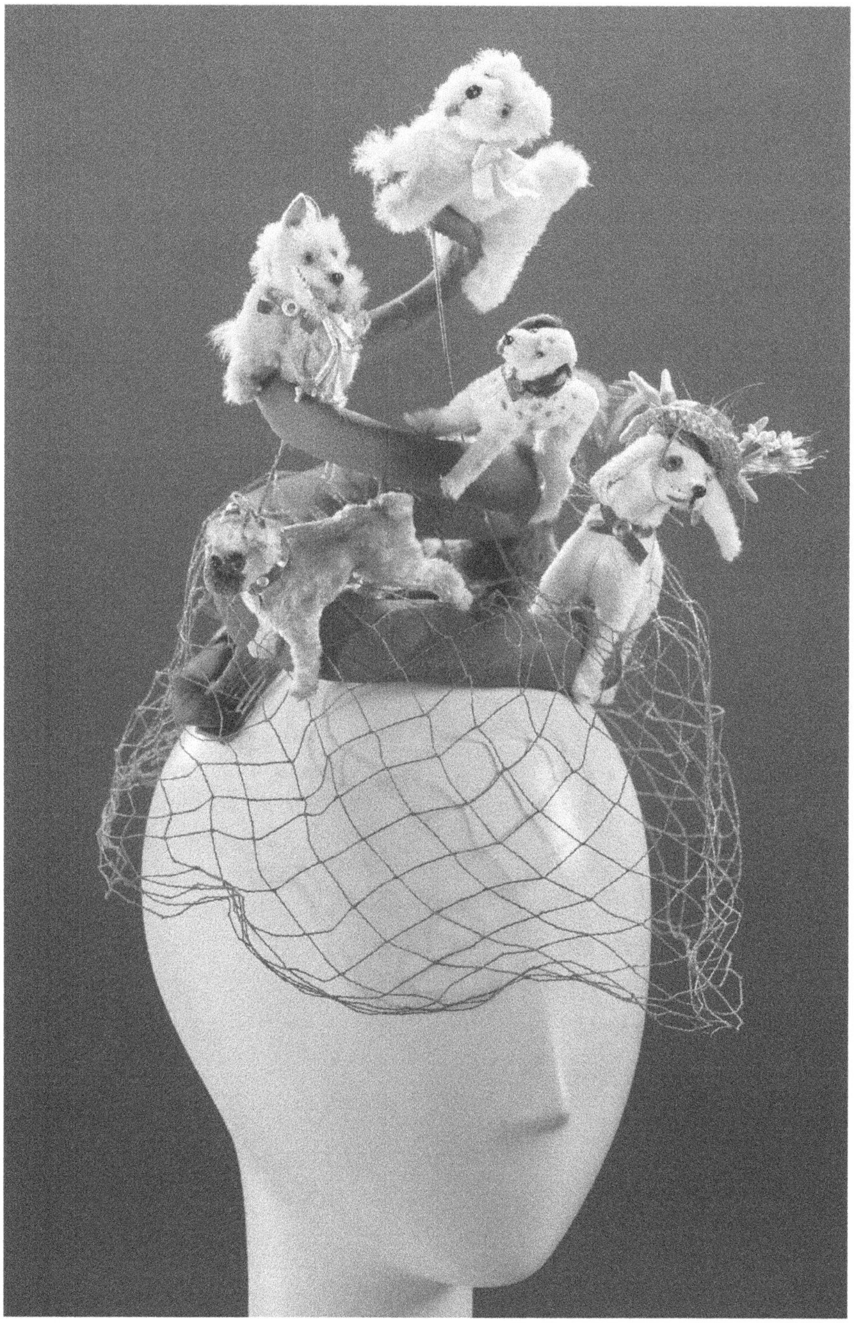

Appendix B

Document and Contract Templates

DISCLAIMER

The sample documents and contract templates in this appendix are included for general reference purposes only and should not be construed to provide legal advice. Readers should determine for themselves if these documents are appropriate for their specific use, are free to modify them to suit their needs, and should seek professional legal advice where appropriate. The authors expressly disclaim any representations, express or implied, as to the currency or accuracy of the templates and whether they are appropriate for use.

CONTRACTORS AND VENDORS

EXTERNAL REPRODUCTION REQUESTS

GENERAL DOCUMENTS FOR USES OF IP

LOCATION SHOOT PHOTOGRAPHY AND FILMING

NONEXCLUSIVE LICENSING AGREEMENTS

RELEASE FORMS

Deborah Wythe
Digital Collections and Services

[date]

[photographer]
[address]

Dear :

You are hereby commissioned by the Brooklyn Museum (the "Museum") to create photographs ("the Images") of the following works of art.

[project description]

1. In creating or furnishing the Photographs, you and any associates retained by you shall be acting as independent contractors and not as agents or employees of the Museum.

2. You agree to deliver to the Museum, not later than [date], a minimum of [##] photographs conforming to the following technical specifications:
TIFF file, Adobe RGB (1998) color, minimum of 9x12 inches @ 400 ppi (3600x4800 pixels)

3. The Museum shall pay to you, in consideration hereof, a fee not to exceed $[####], inclusive of all expenses. Payment will be made within 30 days of receipt by the Museum of an invoice, which may be issued on or after the Museum's acceptance of the deliverables specified above.

4. Photographic credit for the Images shall include the following information: [credit]. While the Museum customarily includes photographic credit when it reproduces shots such as the Images and requests that outside agencies do so as well, any failure for such credit to appear in connection with the Photographs shall not constitute a breach of this agreement.

6. The Museum may terminate this Agreement without cause at any time, immediately upon notice. In such event, you will be paid for services actually rendered as of the termination date.

7. The Museum intends to reproduce the Images in a catalogue (the "Catalogue") related to an exhibition (the "Exhibition") that will feature the Objects. You retain copyright to the Images, but hereby agree not to reproduce, distribute or license them to a third party without permission from the Museum until after the publication of the Catalog and closing of the Exhibition at the Museum.

8. You grant to the Museum, as of the date written above, a fully paid up, non-exclusive right and license (the "License") to reproduce the Images for the life of their copyright and any renewals or extensions thereof, in any media whether now known or invented after the date hereof, and to display, transmit,

Brooklyn Museum
200 Eastern Parkway, Brooklyn, NY 11238-6052
T 718-501-6311 F 718-501-6145
Deborah.Wythe@brooklynmuseum.org

publish, distribute, prepare derivative works of and otherwise use the Images throughout the world as follows:

1) in educational materials related to the Museum's collection and programs (including, for example, posters, postcards, teaching materials, web sites, social networks, catalogues and similar publications, some of which may be offered through Museum's stores); and

2) in publicity and informational materials about the Museum's collection and programs (including, for example, press releases, web sites, social networks, annual reports, promotional flyers, email, posters or films, and membership solicitations).

You agree that the License expressly authorizes the Museum to sublicense the specific rights granted herein to third parties as necessary (in the discretion of the Museum) to fulfill its mission. For all other rights, you understand that the Museum shall seek permission from you and that it will direct inquiring third parties to do the same.

This License is binding on your heirs, administrators, executors, successors and assigns.

9. You acknowledge that copyright to the Objects is held by [the artist/artist's estate] and therefore any future use of the Images requires that you obtain the permission of [the artist/the estate]. You hereby agree to defend, indemnify and hold the Museum harmless against any damages or losses (including reasonable attorney's fees) arising from any third-party claims relating to your use of the Images.

10. This Agreement shall constitute the entire agreement between you and the Museum, and may be altered only by subsequent written agreement. This Agreement shall be governed by the laws of the State of New York and any dispute hereunder shall be solely resolved in the state or federal courts located in New York, New York.

If the foregoing terms are acceptable to you, please sign and return to me one copy of this letter, retaining the second copy for your records.

For the BROOKLYN MUSEUM

By:__________________________________
Deborah Wythe
Head of Digital Collections and Services

AGREED & ACCEPTED:

____
[name] Date

____
Social Security # or EIN

Sarah DeSantis
Digital Collections & Services

Dear :

You are hereby commissioned by the Brooklyn Museum ("the Museum") to create photographs of the following [work(s) of art]/[performance(s)]/[public program(s)] :

1. You acknowledge the Museum to be the sole, exclusive and perpetual owner of the Photographs throughout the world, which ownership shall entitle the Museum, among other things, to all right, title, and interest in and to the copyrights in and to the Photographs throughout the world, including, without limitation, the right to reproduce, transform, alter or adapt the Photographs and to create derivative works based on the Photographs. You and the Museum expressly agree that the Photographs shall be considered a "work made-for-hire" as that term is used in United States copyright law. To the extent that you may be deemed to have any right, title or interest in the Photographs under United States law, including any copyrights, you hereby assign all such right, title and interest to the Museum. You hereby waive any and all "artist'srights"you may have pursuant to any state or federal statutes regarding the Photographs.

2. In creating or furnishing the Photographs, you and any associates retained by you shall be acting as independent contractors and not as agents or employees of the Museum.

3. You agree to deliver to the Museum, not later than , a minimum of photographs conforming to the following technical specifications:

- Selects: 400 ppi TIFF files @ 4800 pixels on the long side, Adobe RGB (1998) color
- Full set: 400 ppi uncompressed JPG files @ 4800 pixels on the long side, Adobe RGB (1998) color

A link to download files must be sent to contract.photographer@brooklynmuseum.org for processing.

4. The Museum shall pay to you, in consideration hereof, a fee not to exceed [$], inclusive of all expenses. Payment will be made within 30 days of receipt by the Museum of an invoice, which may be issued on or after the Museum's acceptance of the deliverables specified above.

5. You agree that you shall not reproduce or authorize the reproduction, publication or use of the Photographs without the prior written consent of the Museum. The final decision as to whether to publish the Photographs, in whole, in part or at all, lies within the sole and absolute discretion of the Museum. You may include reasonable selections of the Photographs in a reasonable and customary manner in your professional portfolio, for presentation purposes only. Any other use of the Photographs requires the Museums express prior written consent. You are solely responsible for obtaining all consents, permissions or waivers that may be necessary from any third party for any use you make of the Photographs.

Brooklyn Museum
200 Eastern Parkway, Brooklyn, NY 11238-6052
T 718-501-6345 F 718-501-6145
Sarah.DeSantis@brooklynmuseum.org

6. Photographic credit for the Photographs, shall read as follows:
(Brooklyn Museum photograph:)
While the Museum customarily includes photographic credit when it reproduces shots such as the Photographs and requests that outside agencies do so as well, any failure for such credit to appear in connection with the Photographs shall not constitute a breach of this agreement.

7. The Museum may terminate this Agreement without cause at any time, immediately upon notice. In such event, you will be paid for services actually rendered as of the termination date.

8. This Agreement shall constitute the entire agreement between you and the Museum, and may be altered only by subsequent written agreement. This Agreement shall be governed by the laws of the State of New York and any dispute hereunder shall be solely resolved in the state or federal courts located in New York, New York.

If the foregoing terms are acceptable to you, please sign and return to me one copy of this letter, retaining the second copy for your records.

For the BROOKLYN MUSEUM

By:____

By:____
Sarah DeSantis
Digital Collections & Services

AGREED & ACCEPTED:

____
Date

____
Social Security # or EIN

Name
Department

[date]

[address block]

Dear:

You are hereby commissioned by the Brooklyn Museum (the "Museum") to create a 3-4 minute video ("Video") [meaning the finished, edited product and any footage created in the process of producing the finished video] of the following:

- Project description

1. You acknowledge the Museum to be the sole, exclusive and perpetual owner of the Video throughout the world, which ownership shall entitle the Museum, among other things, to all right, title, and interest in and to the copyrights in and to the Video throughout the world, including, without limitation, the right to reproduce, transform, alter or adapt the Video and to create derivative works based on the Video. You and the Museum expressly agree that the Video shall be considered a "work made-for-hire" as that term is used in United States copyright law. To the extent that you may be deemed to have any right, title or interest in the Video under United States law, including any copyrights, you hereby assign all such right, title and interest to the Museum. You hereby waive any and all "artist's rights" you may have pursuant to any state or federal statutes regarding the Video.

2. In creating or furnishing the Video, you and any associates retained by you shall be acting as independent contractors and not as agents or employees of the Museum.

3. You agree to deliver to the Museum, not later than [deadline], a minimum of 3 minutes conforming to the following technical specifications:

- **Final finished video should be delivered as H.264.mov for web hosting.**
- **Final finished video and raw footage created as part of the project should be delivered PRORES.**

4. The Museum shall pay to you, in consideration hereof, a fee not to exceed [$] inclusive of all expenses. Payment will be made within 30 days of receipt by the Museum of an invoice, which may be issued on or after the Museum's acceptance of the deliverables specified above.

Brooklyn Museum
200 Eastern Parkway, Brooklyn, NY 11238-6052
T 718-501-6201 F 718-501-6129
Email address

5. You agree that you shall not reproduce or authorize the reproduction, publication or use of the Video without the prior written consent of the Museum. The final decision as to whether to publish the Video, in whole, in part or at all, lies within the sole and absolute discretion of the Museum. You may include reasonable selections of the Video in a reasonable and customary manner in your professional portfolio, for presentation purposes only. Any other use of the Video requires the Museum's express prior written consent. You are solely responsible for obtaining all consents, permissions or waivers that may be necessary from any third party for any use you make of the Video.

6. Credit for the Video, shall read as follows:
Brooklyn Museum video ([name], videographer)
While the Museum customarily includes credit when it reproduces products such as the Video and requests that outside agencies do so as well, any failure for such credit to appear in connection with the Video shall not constitute a breach of this agreement.

7. The Museum may terminate this Agreement without cause at any time, immediately upon notice. In such event, you will be paid for services actually rendered as of the termination date.

8. This Agreement shall constitute the entire agreement between you and the Museum, and may be altered only by subsequent written agreement. This Agreement shall be governed by the laws of the State of New York and any dispute hereunder shall be solely resolved in the state or federal courts located in New York, New York.

If the foregoing terms are acceptable to you, please sign and return to me one copy of this letter, retaining the second copy for your records.

For the BROOKLYN MUSEUM

By:____________________________
Name
Department

By:____________________________
Deborah Wythe
Head of Digital Collections and Services

AGREED & ACCEPTED:

____
Name Date

____
Social Security # or EIN

Page: 2
Date

THE SIXTH FLOOR MUSEUM
AT DEALEY PLAZA

PHOTOGRAPHER AGREEMENT

This Photographer Agreement ("Agreement") is entered into and effective as of this ______ day of ________________, 20______ ("Effective Date"), by and between the undersigned Photographer ("Photographer") and the Dallas County Historical Foundation d/b/a The Sixth Floor Museum at Dealey Plaza ("Museum"), a Texas non-profit corporation.

This Agreement, and the rights and obligations of the parties hereto, shall be governed by and construed and enforced in accordance with the laws of the State of Texas, without regard to its principles of conflict of laws. Any suit or proceeding hereunder shall be brought only in Dallas County, Texas, and each party consents to the personal jurisdiction and venue of the courts, state and federal, located therein.

The undersigned Photographer hereby sells, assigns, transfers, conveys and delivers to Museum all of Photographer's right, title and interest (including copyright rights) in and to the photographs described below (the "Photographs"), and in and to any copyright registrations and renewals and extensions that may be granted thereon, together with the rights to duplicate, reproduce, copy, license, create derivative works, or otherwise utilize the Photographs, and together with the right of Photographer to recover for damages and profits for past and future infringements thereof.

Description of Photographs and Deliverables:
(include description and approximate number of images, as well as media/format in which they are to be provided)

For and in consideration of this Agreement, the Museum will pay, within thirty (30) days after receipt of the Photographs as described above, the Photographer the amount of $__________. This is a one-time compensation for Photographer's services and Photographer understands that this will comprise Photographer's complete and sole payment.

Wherefore the parties below execute and acknowledge this Agreement.

Photographer

Name: ______________________________

Company: ______________________________

Address: ______________________________

City, State, Zip: ______________________________

Phone: ______________________________

Email: ______________________________

Signature: ______________________________

Date: ______________________________

Museum

DALLAS COUNTY HISTORICAL FOUNDATION d/b/a

THE SIXTH FLOOR MUSEUM AT DEALEY PLAZA

411 Elm Street

Dallas, TX 75202

Signature: ______________________________

Date: ______________________________

CONTRACT PHOTOGRAPHY

Photographers name/address/phone/web/e-mail

(sample contract prepared by external photographer)

ESTIMATE

REFERENCE#

CLIENT: Museum Name   Contact: Primary contact person who will approve images/billing

Dates of Photography:

ASSIGNMENT DESCRIPTION

Description: (brief description of project/objects)

Estimated Time Onsite for planning: (hours of intended access)

USAGE SPECIFICATIONS: Photographer retains image copyright. Client (Museum Name) is licensed non-exclusive usage rights for archive and all forms of publication in perpetuity. All use requires accompanied photo credit: "Photographers name/credit line".

PRICE SCHEDULE:

Estimated Price:

Description	Unit	Qty	Total
Photographer's fee (per half day)	$amount	# of ½ days	$
Assistant fee (per half day)	$amount	# of ½ days	$
Digital Processing (per image)	$amount	# of images	$
Delivery (disk/drive, shipping)	$amount	# of media	$
Total:			$

Conditions of Transaction:

1. The Client is licensed the above usage specifications in accord with the conditions stated herein. Photographer request acknowledged printed with images, which reads: 'photo credit: Photographers name'
2. Usage specifications above convert to copyright license only upon receipt of full payment.
3. Invoices are payable on receipt.
4. If you order the performance of any services required to complete the above described assignment, that act constitutes your acceptance by conduct of the terms of this estimate in their entirety, whether signed by you or not.

SUBMITTED BY: (Photographers Name)   Date:

ACCEPTED BY: (Museum contact or Business office)   Date:

Requirements for Incoming Certificate of Insurance
For Vendors, Contractors working at the INSTITUTION NAME XX

It is suggested that this document be shared with the vendors insurance carrier and the COI is sent directly from the carrier to the INSTITUTION NAME XX.

A. COMMERCIAL GENERAL LIABILITY
Bodily Injury and Property Damage
$2,000,000 combined single limit per occurrence
$2,000,000 general Aggregate
$1,000,000 products/completed operations aggregate
Personal and Advertising Injury
$1,000,000 per occurrence
Policy must contain contractual liability coverage
B. WORKERS COMPENSATION
STATE NAME Statutory Limits
Employer's Liability
$100,000 Each Accident
$500,000 Disease Policy Limit
$500,000 Disease Each Employee
C. UMBRELLA/EXCESS LIABILITY
$5,000,000 excess of primary per occurrence
$5,000,000 excess of liability aggregate

D. PROFESSIONAL LEGAL LIABILITY (if appropriate)
$1,000,000 per claim
$1,000,000 aggregate

E. INSTITUTION NAME XX must be shown as Additional Insured on all liability policies
- Additional insured status must apply to ongoing operations as well as products and completed operations

F. All insurance carriers must be rated A or better by AM Best

G. Thirty Days notice of cancellation is required on all policies

H. A description of the service provided and anticipated dates on campus must be shown on the certificate of insurance

I. All certificates must be sent to:
Institution contact name, address, phone, and e-mail.

All exclusions added by endorsement must be indicated

Certificate must be signed by an authorized representative

NEWFIELDS

CONTRACT FOR IMAGE USE PERMISSION

APPLICANT: x
x
ADDRESS: x
x
TELEPHONE: x
E-MAIL: x

FOR AND IN CONSIDERATION OF the mutual undertakings herein, agreed to and to be performed in Indianapolis, Indiana, Licensee ("you") and Indianapolis Museum of Art, Inc. DBA Newfields ("Newfields") agree as follows:

IMAGES REQUESTED: 1. x
2. x

CREDIT LINE: 1. Indianapolis Museum of Art at Newfields,
2. Indianapolis Museum of Art at Newfields,
THE CREDIT LINE IS REQUIRED WITH PUBLICATION IN THE FORM WE PROVIDE ABOVE.

USE REQUESTED:
Title: *x*
Description of Use: *x*
Month & Year of Use: *x*
Publisher/Distributor Name: *x*

IMAGE REQUIREMENTS:
☐ In Color ☐ In Whole
☐ In Black & White ☐ In Detail

REPRODUCTION WILL BE FOR:
☐ Scholarly Purposes
☐ Commercial Purposes
☐ Personal / Study Purposes

PRINT RUN/TERM: *x*

ADDITIONAL PROVISIONS (if any): one-time, non-exclusive use: English language, worldwide distribution.

Newfields grants you permission to make and use reproductions of the image(s) described above from the collections of Newfields, subject to the following terms and conditions, and including the *Regulations for Reproducing Images from Newfields* ("Regulations").

1. **NON-WAIVER.** No Action, other than an express written waiver signed by Newfields, may be construed as a waiver of any clause of this contract. A waiver of a specific clause of this contract will not be considered a waiver of any other clause or term.
2. **SEVERABILITY.** Should any of the paragraphs of this Contract or in the Regulations be found unenforceable, the other paragraphs will be unaffected and will remain in full force and effect.
3. **GOVERNING LAW.** This contract will be governed and interpreted by Indiana law.
4. **ARBITRATION.** Any and all disputes arising out of, under or in connection with this agreement, including without limitations, the validity, interpretation, performance and breach hereof, will be settled by arbitration in Indianapolis, Indiana, pursuant to the rules of the American Arbitration Association. Judgment upon any award rendered may be entered in the highest court, state, or federal, of the forum having jurisdiction. If you breach any of the terms in this contract or in the regulations and force us to demand payment, you agree to pay a reasonable legal fee as determined by the arbitrator and will pay in full all disbursements and the cost of arbitration.
5. **AMENDMENT.** This contract constitutes the entire agreement between the parties and supersedes all prior written or oral agreements. This contract may be amended only in writing clearly setting forth any amendment and signed by both parties to this contract.

INVOICE NO: to follow

Image Preparation Fee: x
Reproduction Fee: x
File Delivery: x
TOTAL SUM: x
NEWFIELDS PAYMENT OPTIONS CAN BE FOUND AT THE END OF THIS DOCUMENT.

Please sign and return this contract to: Rights & Reproductions Department, Newfields, 4000 Michigan Road, Indianapolis, IN 46208

YOU DO NOT HAVE PERMISSION TO REPRODUCE UNTIL THIS DOCUMENT IS COUNTERSIGNED AND PAYMENT OF ANY APPLICABLE FEES HAS BEEN RECEIVED BY NEWFIELDS.

Applicant's Signature Terms and conditions agreed to (date)

Authorizing Official, Newfields Permission Granted (date)

THIS IS AN IMPORTANT DOCUMENT. PLEASE READ COMPLETELY. YOUR SIGNATURE OBLIGATES YOU TO ABIDE BY EACH TERM AND CONDITION DETAILED IN THIS CONTRACT AND THE "REGULATIONS FOR REPRODUCING IMAGES FROM NEWFIELDS."

4000 MICHIGAN ROAD · INDIANAPOLIS, IN 46208 · 317-923-1331 · DISCOVER**NEWFIELDS**.ORG

REGULATIONS FOR REPRODUCING IMAGES FROM NEWFIELDS

GENERAL CONDITIONS:

1. All communications connected with the reproduction of photographs and videos from Newfields should be addressed to the Rights and Reproductions Department, Newfields, 4000 Michigan Road, Indianapolis, IN 46208; telephone (317) 923-1331, ext. 171; email: permissions@discovernewfields.org.
2. Written permission to reproduce must be obtained before publication.
3. Requests for permission to reproduce photographs and videos from Newfields will be considered not only when application is made by the publisher or agent, but also when made from authors who do not have a publisher identified.
4. Authors, educators, and researchers obtaining image files for study purposes is permitted.
5. Permission to reproduce and the fee payable (if applicable) cover only the specific occasion and use detailed in the application. Any and all reprints, further editions, re-employment of the image files or additional use of any kind must be preceded by a new application and is not covered by the original fee or permission to reproduce. Line drawings and adaptations made from photographs may not be published and objects illustrated in the photographs may not be reproduced without permission. Unless otherwise specified by Newfields, permission to reproduce covers worldwide distribution, in one language, in monochrome or color.
6. All supplied files remain the property of Newfields. Image files will not be supplied on approval or sold outright.
7. Minimum specifications for digital files are 300 dpi x the size of the reproduction. Reproductions from low resolution files (less than 300 dpi) are prohibited, with exceptions made on a case-by-case basis for the news media and publications with limited circulation.
8. The image area of the picture, or the area within the outline of a sculpture, or backdrop to the sculpture with shadows, scale indications, etc., may not be masked out, cut down, superimposed with type matter, or in any way defaced or altered.
9. Application to reproduce a detail from a work will be considered only upon receipt of a sketch or marked-up photograph showing the area to be reproduced. The caption must include the word "detail." Permission may also require the full image reproduction elsewhere in the same publication.
10. Application for permission to reproduce works of art in advertising, a promotional context, or as an integral part of a commercial product must include a layout and a full description of the proposed use, including the context in which the reproduction will be used, together with details of intended distribution/circulation. In the case of an adaptation, a prototype must be submitted for approval before production may proceed.
11. Digital scans or reproductions may not be made by outside companies or photographers for commercial purposes without the prior written consent of Newfields. Permission will be granted on condition that all digital files and copyright are forwarded and assigned to Newfields after being used for the permitted purpose. The outside photographer or publisher may retain a reasonable number of prints for portfolio or archival use.
12. Newfields does not supply images of works in its collection to companies or individuals operating a photograph rental and/or sales service. Applicants will be required to represent as a pre-condition for permission to reproduce that no such use will be made of any material obtained from Newfields pursuant to any application hereunder.
13. Reproduction from printed or other non-photographic materials, or from photographic materials not supplied directly by Newfields, is strictly prohibited. See paragraph 11 for regulations concerning outside commercial photographers.
14. All final reproductions, unless specifically stipulated in writing by Newfields, must be smaller than the original work of art, except sculpture.
15. Applicants will be responsible for the safekeeping of all digital files. Any unauthorized use of digital files, by any person or entity, will render applicant responsible and liable to Newfields for appropriate compensation and other costs, regardless of whether applicant has profited from or is responsible for such unauthorized use.
16. Newfields reserves the right, in its sole discretion, to refuse permission for further applications from a publisher or other applicant, if, in its opinion, the standard of reproduction has not been of acceptable quality.
17. Newfields' policy is not to grant an exclusive right to reproduce any photograph or video from Newfields. Newfields will not assume any responsibility for duplication of subjects or reproduction of the same work of art by other applicants or persons not authorized to reproduce said work. Newfields assumes no responsibility for claims against the applicant or Newfields by third parties, and applicants agree to indemnify Newfields and hold it harmless against any and all such claims and costs, including copyright infringement claims arising out of applicant's reproduction of the work of art in question.
18. ***On the publishing date, one copy must be forwarded to Newfields for archival and other purposes.***
19. Newfields reserves the right to limit the number of reproductions of Newfields-owned works of art in any single publication or film, if it appears that their number is disproportionate in relation to those from other sources.

COPYRIGHT AND CREDIT LINE:

1. Newfields makes no warranties or representations and assumes no responsibility whatsoever for any claims, royalties or fees demanded by an artist, his agent, estate or by any other party in connection with the reproduction of works of art in the collections of Newfields. Additionally, the applicant agrees to indemnify Newfields and hold it harmless against any and all such claims, demands and/or actions, including the costs thereof, arising as a result of the applicant's reproduction of images from Newfields
2. A credit line acknowledgment, as supplied by Newfields, including, but not limited to, copyright notice, the donor's name or the specific collection, must appear in immediate proximity to the reproduction or in the section within the publication devoted to acknowledgments, as specified by Newfields. ***Abbreviations are not permitted without prior approval of Newfields.***

FEES:

1. Permission to reproduce is premised and conditioned upon payment of all applicable preparation, reproduction, and shipping fees within thirty (30) days of receipt of the relevant invoice and may not be deferred until the date of publication.. Fees are based on the images sent out by request and are not conditioned on whether the images are used in a publication. Failure to pay the required fees means that permission has not been granted. ***When paid, the receipted invoice, together with executed contract, constitutes permission for reproduction. Images will not be released until payment has been received.*** Fees are formulated by Newfields in its sole discretion. Fees so established apply solely to the specific application upon which they are based and will not serve as future precedent.

4000 MICHIGAN ROAD · INDIANAPOLIS, IN 46208 · 317-923-1331 · DISCOVER**NEWFIELDS**.ORG

New Mexico Museum of Art

Photographic Reproduction Agreement

This agreement is made on ____________________ between the New Mexico Museum of Art, a unit of the Department of Cultural Affairs and ____________________ for permission to publish photographic images of collections owned by the New Mexico Museum of Art under the stated Condition for Reproduction/Publication (see reverse).

The New Mexico Museum of Art gives no exclusive rights to any publisher, author or photographer and assumes no responsibility for duplication of subjects by others and no responsibility for claims by third parties.

This agreement applies to the following images (please use the following as the credit line):

Reproduction Rights Granted by New Mexico Museum of Art			
Title:			
Author:			
Publisher:			
Publication covers:		Advertising use:	
Print Run or Downloads Allowed:			
Term Limit:			
Language(s):			
Distribution Region:			
Digital File Supplied			
Resolution (dpi):			
Image Dimensions:			
Image format:			

The undersigned agrees to abide by all stated conditions for reproduction/publication of photographic images from the New Mexico Museum of Art.

______________________________ ______________________

Author/Publisher Date

______________________________ ______________________

New Mexico Museum of Art Representative Date

Conditions For Reproduction/Publication

1. Written permission to reproduce or publish photographic images must be secured from the New Mexico Museum of Art. Permission is granted for use **one time, one edition at the designated print run only**. All other rights, including those of further reproduction or publication, are reserved in full by the New Mexico Museum of Art. Possession of a Museum image does not constitute permission to use or publish it.
2. Requests for alterations or variations to the image such as cropping, overprinting or bleeding to edge of any reproduction must be made in writing to the New Mexico Museum of Art. Details must be identified as such.
3. All efforts should be made to make photographic reproductions as faithful and accurate to the originals as possible. Before publication of any reproduction, the New Mexico Museum of Art reserves the right to require a proof for final approval.
4. The New Mexico Museum of Art requires and will furnish the exact citation (credit line) to accompany each reproduction.
5. The credit line as specified is **MANDATORY**.
    i. With printed matter, it is preferred that the credit line appear on the same or facing page as the illustrations with other "Sources of Illustrations". Crediting of each individual item is necessary in all cases.
    ii. With films, filmstrips, and video use, it is preferred that the credit line be included with the other "Source of Illustrations". In manuals that accompany filmstrips give credit at the point where the illustration is discussed.
    iii. With exhibitions, it is preferred the credit be shown within exhibition area.
6. Publisher shall furnish the New Mexico Museum of Art without charge two (2) copies of each publication or book in which reproduction appears.
7. Orders will not be processed until payment is received in full; the New Mexico Museum of Art is not responsible for foreign banking fees. The granting of rights is contingent upon payment of fees.
8. Checks must be made payable to the New Mexico Museum of Art. Credit cards cannot be accepted.
9. The New Mexico Museum of Art gives no exclusive rights to any publisher, author or photographer and assumes no responsibility for duplication of subjects by others.
10. It is the responsibility of the applicant to secure the rights to reproduce the requested images from the appropriate copyright holders.
11. In the event that any additional uses of the image(s), not currently listed on the front, are planned additional permission must be obtained in advance.
12. Web images must not exceed 600 pixels on the longest edge.

NON-EXCLUSIVE LICENSE AGREEMENT

[for broadcast productions]

ATTACHMENT A	
Licensee Contact:	
Licensee:	
Licensee's Work:	
Licensor's Work(s):	
Term:	
Primary Territory:	
Market:	
License Fees:	
Effective Date:	
Special Restriction:	No advertising or promotional use (including in-context promo) of the material is permitted per Museum policy (see Paragraph 9)

Licensor Signature Date Licensee Signature Date

NON-EXCLUSIVE LICENSE AGREEMENT

[for broadcast productions]

This Non-Exclusive License Agreement ("Agreement") is entered into and effective as of the date set forth on Attachment A hereto ("Effective Date"), which attachment is herein incorporated by reference, between Dallas County Historical Foundation d/b/a The Sixth Floor Museum at Dealey Plaza, a Texas non-profit corporation, having an address of 411 Elm Street, Dallas, TX 75202-3308 (hereinafter "Licensor"), and the Licensee whose name appears on Attachment A (hereinafter "Licensee"). All capitalized terms not specifically defined herein shall have the meaning ascribed to them in the Attachment A.

In consideration of the mutual promises and agreements contained herein, and other good and valuable consideration, the receipt and sufficiency of which is hereby acknowledged, the parties hereby agree as follows:

1. Definitions:

"Licensor's Works" shall mean and refer to the Works set forth in Attachment A, which attachment is herein incorporated by reference.

"Licensee's Work" shall mean and refer to one or more master video tapes created by or for the Licensee which incorporates Licensor's Works, in whole or in part, for telecast under program name and description set forth in Attachment A.

"Primary Territory" shall mean and refer to the Primary Territory set forth in Attachment A.

"Market" shall mean and refer to the Market(s) set forth in Attachment A.

"Affiliates" shall mean and refer to agents of Licensee necessary for Licensee to exhibit and distribute Licensee's Work during the term of the Agreement and within the Primary Territory.

In the case of Licensee's Work, a **"Release"** shall mean and refer to unlimited exhibition and distribution of Licensee's Work in the Market, subject to the terms and conditions set forth in Section 3 herein.

2. Copyright Ownership in the Work.

Licensor warrants that Licensor is the claimant of the copyright in Licensor's Works identified as *[IDENTIFY SPECIFIC WORK(S)]* in Attachment A. Licensor represents that it has the power and authority to grant the licenses herein provided.

3. License Authorizations; Licensee's Work.

3.01 Master Video Authorization.

Licensor hereby grants to Licensee the nonexclusive license to incorporate Licensor's Works into Licensee's Work.

3.02 Release Authorization for Licensee's Work.

Subject to the terms of this Agreement, Licensor further grants to Licensee and Licensee's Affiliates a limited, non-exclusive license to Release the Licensee's Work in the Market during the Term only as set forth in Attachment A.

4. Copyright Notice.

Authorization to Release the Licensee's Work is expressly conditioned upon the use and display of a copyright notice in connection with Licensee's Work in the following form:

[INSERT PROPER COPYRIGHT NOTICE/CREDIT LINE(S) FOR LICENSOR'S WORK(S)]

Said notice shall be displayed in the end credits of Licensee's Work and during each Release of Licensee's Work.

5. Museum Copy.

Licensee shall provide Licensor with a DVD copy of Licensee's Work within thirty (30) days of the first release of Licensee's Work for in-house educational uses and for the purpose of keeping such copy in Licensor's archive ("Museum Copy"). Licensor shall not make any commercial use of the Museum Copy.

6. License Fee.

As a condition precedent to any Release of Licensee's Work, the Licensee shall pay the Licensor the non-refundable License Fee(s) set forth in Attachment A by check, credit card, or wire transfer payable to the "Sixth Floor Museum at Dealey Plaza," within thirty (30) days of the execution of the Agreement.

7. Special Conditions. *[APPLIES TO ZAPRUDER AND NIX FILMS ONLY]*

The licenses granted herein are expressly conditioned upon, and Licensee hereby agrees, (i) that the Licensee shall not use the Licensor's Works in a manner which is sensational; (ii) that the purpose of Licensee's Work is to examine the physical evidence involved in the assassination of President John F. Kennedy; and (iii) that the Licensee shall not (other than for historic or scientific inquiry, illustration, or study) punctuate or emphasize the episodes of violence contained in the Licensor's Works, particularly those parts of the Licensor's Works which depict and follow the depiction of a bullet striking President John F. Kennedy. A good faith determination by the Licensor of Licensee's compliance with these special conditions shall be conclusive and binding on Licensee.

8. Reservation of Rights.

All right, title, and interest in and to Licensor's Works is expressly retained by the Licensor. The parties expressly agree that nothing herein contained shall constitute them the agent or joint author of the other party. Licensee shall take reasonable steps necessary to protect the copyright in Licensor's Works in connection with Licensee's Work. All right, title, and interest in and to Licensee's Work, excluding Licensor's Works, is expressly retained by Licensee.

9. Excerpting Prohibited.

This Agreement shall not be construed to extend to Licensee any license or authorization to copy, publish, or otherwise use Licensor's Works, in whole or in part, or Licensee's Work which includes Licensor's Works, in whole or in part, separately from the use provided in this Agreement, and Licensee shall not use or authorize others to use Licensor's Works, in whole or in part, or Licensee's Work, which includes Licensor's Works, in whole or in part, for advertising, promotion, publicity, or merchandising or any other purpose not expressly provided for in this Agreement.

10. Third Party Rights.

Licensee expressly acknowledges that Licensor does not purport to convey or license the rights of any other party, if any, in or to derivations or copies of Licensor's Works in which any other party may have an interest.

11. Indemnification.

Licensee hereby agrees to indemnify, protect, defend and hold harmless Licensor from and for any and all claims, demands, actions, proceedings and costs (including attorney's fees and expenses and court costs) which Licensor incurs for or by reason of Licensee's Work and Licensee's exploitation, distribution, and/or use thereof, including the Releases.

12. Assignment.

The licenses granted herein are not assignable by the Licensee, except with Licensor's prior express written consent. The licenses granted herein shall terminate and are void ab initio upon assignment, except with Licensor's prior express written consent.

13. Integration.

This Agreement, including Attachment A, constitutes the entire agreement between parties and supersedes any previous written or oral agreements with regard to the subject matter hereof.

14. Governing Law.

This Agreement, and the rights and obligations of the parties hereto, shall be governed by and construed and enforced in accordance with the laws of the State of Texas, without regard to its principles of conflict of laws. Any suit or proceeding hereunder shall be brought **ONLY** in Dallas County, Texas, and each party consents to the personal jurisdiction of the courts, state and federal, located therein. Licensee agrees to waive any objection that the state or federal courts of Dallas County, Texas, are an inconvenient forum.

15. Breach by Licensee.

In the event of a breach of this Agreement by Licensee, the licenses granted herein shall automatically terminate and the Licensee shall reimburse the Licensor for any and all costs (including but not limited to attorney's fees and expenses and court and/or arbitration costs) incurred by the Licensor for the purposes of obtaining remedy for and as a result of said breach.

16. Waiver.

No amendment or waiver of any provision of this Agreement, nor consent to any departure therefrom, shall be effective unless the same shall be in writing and signed by an authorized representative of each party hereto, and then such waiver or consent shall be effective only in a specific instance and for the specific purpose for which given. No failure on the part of a party hereto to exercise, and no delay in exercising, any right hereunder shall operate as a waiver thereof; nor shall any single or partial exercise of any right hereunder preclude any other or further exercise thereof or the exercise of any other right. The remedies provided in this Agreement are cumulative and not exclusive of any remedies provided by law.

17. Amendment.

No change, termination, waiver, amendment or modification of any of the provisions hereof shall be binding upon the Parties, unless in writing signed by duly authorized representatives of the parties.

18. Dispute Resolution.

Any claim, action, dispute or controversy of any kind arising out of, in connection with, or relating to this Agreement or concerning any aspect of performance by any party under the terms of this Agreement (a "Dispute") shall be resolved by mandatory and binding arbitration administered by the American Arbitration Association (the "AAA") pursuant to the Federal Arbitration Act (Title 9 of the United States Code) in accordance with this Agreement and the then-applicable Commercial Arbitration Rules of the AAA. The parties acknowledge and agree that the transactions evidenced and contemplated hereby involve "commerce" as contemplated in Section 2 of the Federal Arbitration Act. If Title 9 of the United States Code is inapplicable to any such Dispute for any reason, such arbitration shall be conducted pursuant to the Texas General Arbitration Act (V.T.C.A., Civil Practice & Remedies Code Section 171.001, et. seq. Vernon 1997), this Agreement and the then-applicable Commercial Arbitration Rules of the AAA. To the extent that any inconsistency exists between this Agreement and the foregoing statutes or rules, this Agreement shall control. Arbitration proceedings shall be conducted in Dallas, Texas. Notwithstanding the foregoing, either party may (i) exercise any termination rights provided for herein and/or (ii) institute legal proceedings to seek injunctive relief, and such termination rights and injunctive relief are not subject to this mandatory arbitration provision.

19. Notices and Counterparts.

Notices may be sent to the parties at their respective addresses as first above written, or at such new address as each may respectively provide to the other in writing. Facsimile signatures and counterpart signatures shall be binding.

Wherefore the parties below execute and acknowledge this Agreement.

Licensee:

By:____
LICENSEE NAME Date

DALLAS COUNTY HISTORICAL FOUNDATION d/b/a
THE SIXTH FLOOR MUSEUM AT DEALEY PLAZA

By:____
NAME, Executive Director Date

Limited, Non-Exclusive License Agreement

[used primarily for non-commercial projects, such as exhibitions, scholarly presentations, etc.]

This Limited, Non-Exclusive License Agreement ("Agreement") is entered into and effective as of this __ day of ___, *2015* ("Effective Date"), by and between _________ ("Licensee"), and the Dallas County Historical Foundation d/b/a The Sixth Floor Museum at Dealey Plaza ("Licensor").

In consideration of the mutual promises and agreements contained herein, the receipt and sufficiency of which are hereby acknowledged, Licensor hereby agrees to grant Licensee certain limited rights to use *(Collection Object ID Number and Description)* on and subject to the terms and conditions attached hereto, and Licensee hereby agrees to abide by such terms and conditions.

IN WITNESS WHEREOF, the parties have duly caused this Agreement to be executed as of the Effective Date.

Licensor	**Licensee**
DALLAS COUNTY HISTORICAL FOUNDATION d/b/a	*NAME*
THE SIXTH FLOOR MUSEUM AT DEALEY PLAZA	*ORGANIZATION*
411 Elm Street	*ADDRESS*
Dallas, TX 75202	*CITY, STATE ZIP*

By:______________________________	By: (signature)____________________
NAME, Executive Director	Date:__________________________

TERMS AND CONDITIONS

1. **Licensee Request.** Licensee hereby requests the use of *(Collection Object ID Number and Description)*

2. **Licensor's Works**. Licensor shall provide the Licensee with an appropriately formatted file *[SPECIFY LICENSOR'S WORKS]* for the material identified in section 1, above.

3. **Limited, Non-Exclusive License.** Licensor hereby grants to Licensee a limited, non-exclusive, non-transferable license to use the Licensor's Works for the limited purpose of *[DESCRIBE SPECIFIC USAGE]*. This license does not include any right to display (other than as described above), sub-license, transfer, publish, broadcast, copy or sell any the Licensor's Works or create derivative works from the Licensor's Work ("Non-licensed Activities"), and Licensee hereby agrees not to use the Licensor's Works for any Non-licensed Activity or any other purpose not specifically licensed by this Agreement. Any and all rights in and to the Licensor's Works and any other rights held by Licensor not specifically licensed herein are expressly reserved to Licensor and not included in this limited, non-exclusive license, whether identified or not as Non-licensed Activities.

4. **Reproduction and Handling Fee / Or License Fee.** *[If applicable, indicate appropriate fees]*

5. **Unlawful Copying.** Licensee warrants that Licensee shall not copy or allow others to copy, and shall not, except as expressly provided for herein, otherwise use the Licensor's Works or any portions thereof.

6. **Copyright Notice.** Whenever any of the Licensor's Work is displayed under the authority herein provided, a notice of copyright shall be affixed in a manner and location as to give reasonable notice of the claim of copyright. The notice shall appear in the following form:

   [INSERT PROPER COPYRIGHT NOTICE/CREDIT LINE(S) FOR LICENSOR'S WORK(S)]

7. **Excerpting Prohibited.** This Agreement shall not be construed to extend to Licensee any license or authorization to use the Licensor's Work in whole or in part for advertising, promotion, publicity or merchandising or any other purpose not expressly provided for in this Agreement.

8. **Copyright Ownership.** Licensor warrants that it is the claimant of the copyright in the Licensor's Work and represents that it can grant the license herein provided.

9. **Disputes.** This Agreement shall be governed by, and construed in accordance with, the laws of the State of Texas. In the event of a breach of this Agreement by Licensee, Licensee shall reimburse Licensor for any and all costs (including but not limited to attorney's fees and expenses and court costs) incurred by Licensor for the purposes of obtaining a remedy for said breach and Licensee shall delete the Licensor's Works, including any unauthorized copies of Licensor's Work, in its possession or under its control. No waiver or purported waiver of any breach shall be construed as a continuing or permanent waiver of said breach. The authorization granted herein shall not be assignable and shall terminate automatically in the event of Licensee's breach of or noncompliance with any provision of this Agreement. This Agreement may be modified only in writing executed by both parties. This Agreement constitutes the entire agreement between the parties concerning the subject matter of this Agreement and there are no other understandings, written or oral, on the subject matter hereof.

Licensee's Acceptance of Terms and Conditions:______________________________

(signature)

NON-EXCLUSIVE LICENSE AGREEMENT
[for print and digital publications]

ATTACHMENT A	
Licensee Contact(s):	
Licensee Name and Address:	
Licensee's Work:	
Licensor's Work(s):	
Print Run:	
Term:	
Primary Territory:	
Languages:	
Use:	
License Fee:	
Licensor Signature Date	Licensee Signature Date

NON-EXCLUSIVE LICENSE AGREEMENT

[for print and digital publications]

This Non-Exclusive License Agreement ("Agreement") is entered into and effective as of this _XX_ day of, 20XX ("Effective Date"), by and between Dallas County Historical Foundation d/b/a The Sixth Floor Museum at Dealey Plaza ("Licensor"), a Texas non-profit corporation, having an address of 411 Elm Street, Dallas TX 75202-3308, and the Licensee whose name appears on Attachment A ("Licensee"). All capitalized terms not specifically defined herein shall have the meaning ascribed to them in Attachment A attached hereto and incorporated herein for all purposes.

TERMS AND CONDITIONS

1. Non-Exclusive License.

Subject to the terms and conditions of this Agreement, Licensor hereby grants to Licensee a limited, non-exclusive license to (i) incorporate the Licensor's Work into Licensee's Work and (ii) to reproduce Licensor's Works as part of Licensee's Work in the aggregate not to exceed the number of copies in the Print Run. All other or further license or authorization is hereby reserved to Licensor, and all other derivative use is expressly prohibited. Licensee shall not print any copies of Licensee's Work in excess of the Print Run.

2. License Fee.

Licensee shall pay to Licensor the non-refundable sum of *$XXXX* as a condition of permissions granted herein by credit card or check payable to "The Sixth Floor Museum at Dealey Plaza" and said fee shall be paid within thirty (30) days of the execution of the Agreement. No authorization shall be effective absent receipt of such payment.

3. Copyright Notice.

Whenever any portion of Licensor's Works is displayed or published under the authority herein provided, a notice of copyright shall be affixed in a manner and location as to give reasonable notice of the claim of copyright. The notice for each of Licensor's Works shall read as follows:

[INSERT PROPER COPYRIGHT NOTICE/CREDIT LINE(S) FOR LICENSOR'S WORK(S)]

4. Records and Audit.

Licensee shall maintain accurate books and records and shall at the Licensor's reasonable request, but not more than twice per year, accurately report to Licensor the number of copies of Licensee's Work which have been printed. Licensor may inspect Licensee's books and records in connection with Licensee's Work to the extent necessary to verify Licensee's report.

5. Museum Copy.

Licensee shall provide Licensor with one (1) copy of Licensee's Work within thirty (30) days of publication for the purpose of keeping such copy in Licensor's library.

6. Out of Print.

If Licensee fails to print any copies of the Licensee's Work during any consecutive five-year period, all authorization to print copies of the Licensee's Work shall automatically terminate.

7. Copy Limit.

If Licensee fails to print in the aggregate the number of copies in the Print Run during the Term, all authorization to print additional copies of the Licensee's Work shall automatically terminate.

8. Special Conditions. *[APPLIES TO ZAPRUDER AND NIX FILMS ONLY]*

The licenses granted herein are expressly conditioned upon the Licensee's acknowledgment and agreement (i) that the Licensee shall not use the Licensor's Work in a manner which is sensational; (ii) that the purpose of Licensee's Work is to examine the physical evidence involved in the assassination of President John F. Kennedy; and (iii) that the Licensee does not intend to and shall not attempt to punctuate or emphasize the episodes of violence contained in the Licensor's Work, particularly those parts of the Licensor's Work which depict and follow the depiction of a bullet striking President John F. Kennedy.

9. Reservation of Rights.

All right, title, and interest in and to Licensor's Works is expressly retained by the Licensor. The parties expressly agree that nothing herein contained shall constitute them the agent or joint author of the other party. Licensee shall take reasonable steps necessary to protect the copyright in Licensor's Works in connection with Licensee's Work. All right, title, and interest in and to Licensee's Work, excluding Licensor's Works, is expressly retained by Licensee.

10. Excerpting Prohibited.

This Agreement shall not be construed to extend to Licensee any license or authorization to copy, publish or otherwise use Licensor's Works, in whole or in part, or Licensee's Work which include Licensor's Works, in whole or in part, separately from the use provided in Paragraph 1, and Licensee shall not use or authorize others to use Licensor's Works, in whole or in part, or Licensee's Work, which include Licensor's Works, in whole or in part, for advertising, promotion, publicity, or merchandising or any other purpose not expressly provided for in this Agreement.

11. Assignment.

The licenses granted herein are not assignable by the Licensee, except with Licensor's prior express written consent. The licenses granted herein shall terminate and are void ab initio upon assignment, except with Licensor's prior express written consent.

12. Integration.

This Agreement, including Attachment A, constitutes the entire agreement between parties and supersedes any previous written or oral agreements with regard to the subject matter hereof.

13. Governing Law.

This Agreement, and the rights and obligations of the parties hereto, shall be governed by and construed and enforced in accordance with the laws of the State of Texas, without regard to its principles of conflict of laws. Any suit or proceeding hereunder shall be brought **ONLY** in Dallas County, Texas, and each party consents to the personal jurisdiction of the courts, state and federal, located therein. Licensee agrees to waive any objection that the state or federal courts of Dallas County, Texas, are an inconvenient forum.

14. Breach by Licensee.

In the unlikely event of a breach of this Agreement by Licensee, the licenses granted herein shall automatically terminate and the Licensee shall reimburse the Licensor for any and all costs (including but not limited to attorney's fees and expenses and court and/or arbitration costs) incurred by the Licensor for the purposes of obtaining remedy for and as a result of said breach.

15. Waiver.

No amendment or waiver of any provision of this Agreement, nor consent to any departure therefrom, shall be effective unless the same shall be in writing and signed by an authorized representative of each party hereto, and then such waiver or consent shall be effective only in a specific instance and for the specific purpose for which given. No failure on the part of a party hereto to exercise, and no delay in exercising, any right hereunder shall operate as a waiver thereof; nor shall any single or partial exercise of any right hereunder preclude any other or further exercise thereof or the exercise of any other right. The remedies provided in this Agreement are cumulative and not exclusive of any remedies provided by law.

16. Amendment.

No change, termination, waiver, amendment or modification of any of the provisions hereof shall be binding upon the Parties, unless in writing signed by duly authorized representatives of the parties.

17. Dispute Resolution.

Any claim, action, dispute or controversy of any kind arising out of, in connection with, or relating to this Agreement or concerning any aspect of performance by any party under the terms of this Agreement (a "Dispute") shall be resolved by mandatory and binding arbitration administered by the American Arbitration Association (the "AAA") pursuant to the Federal Arbitration Act (Title 9 of the United States Code) in accordance with this Agreement and the then-applicable Commercial Arbitration Rules of the AAA. The parties acknowledge and agree that the transactions evidenced and contemplated hereby involve "commerce" as contemplated in Section 2 of the Federal Arbitration Act. If Title 9 of the United States Code is inapplicable to any such Dispute for any reason, such arbitration shall be conducted pursuant to the Texas General Arbitration Act (V.T.C.A., Civil Practice & Remedies Code Section 171.001, et. seq. Vernon 1997), this Agreement and the then-applicable Commercial Arbitration Rules of the AAA. To the extent that any inconsistency exists between this Agreement and the foregoing statutes or rules, this Agreement shall control. Arbitration proceedings shall be conducted in Dallas, Texas. Notwithstanding the foregoing, the fact that arbitration is or may be allowed will not impair the exercise of any termination rights under this Agreement or rights to seek injunctive or other equitable relief.

Wherefore the parties below execute and acknowledge this Agreement.

Licensee:

by:____

LICENSEE NAME Date

Licensor:

by:____

NAME Date

Executive Director, The Sixth Floor Museum at Dealey Plaza

NEWFIELDS

IMAGE REQUEST FORM

Thank you for your recent request for photographic material from Newfields. In order to process your request, we need to determine what kind(s) of photograph(s), reproduction rights, and fees may be involved.

Image requests must be submitted eight weeks prior to the date the material(s) are needed to ensure adequate processing time.

Please fill out the following in as much detail as possible and email to permissions@discovernewfields.org.

CONTACT INFORMATION

Name:

Address:

Telephone: Fax:

E-mail:

Title: Business:

REQUESTED IMAGE(S) **Please attach a separate sheet if you need more room*

Title: Title:

Artist: Artist:

Accession #: Accession #:

PERMISSION IS REQUESTED TO REPRODUCE

☐ In Whole ☐ In Detail ☐ In Color ☐ In Black & White

IMAGE REQUIREMENTS

☐ High Resolution Digital File Size:

☐ Black & White Print Size:

☐ Color Print Size:

FOR REPRODUCTION IN

☐ Book & Journal Interior (print or electronic)

☐ Book & Journal Cover (print or electronic)

☐ Television Broadcast, Film & Video

☐ Exhibition (print or electronic)

☐ All Other Uses (please describe):

☐ Website

☐ Multimedia & Apps

☐ Advertising & Promotion (print or electronic)

☐ Re-Use (no materials furnished)

More on next page

PUBLICATION / PROJECT INFORMATION

Title of Publication / Project:

Author / Director / Producer / Designer:

Publisher:

Number of illustrations:

Approximate Publication / Release Date:

Print Run Quantity or Term Length:

Estimated Price of Publication / Project:

Countries of Distribution:

Language(s) of Publication / Project:

Date Materials Needed By:

ADDITIONAL RELEVANT INFORMATION

New Mexico Museum of Art

REQUEST TO ORDER IMAGES

Applicant Information			
Name:			
Adress:			
Phone:		Fax:	
Email :			
Images being requested (include Museum accession number(s) if possible):			

Purpose of Use				
Print Publications: (please check all applicable)	Book ☐	Periodical ☐	Ebook ☐	Book Cover ☐
Research Only (no publication) ☐	TV, Video/ DVD, Film ☐	Internet ☐	Other - Please Explain:	

Digital File Requirements				
Resolution (dpi):				
Image Dimensions:				
Image format:	tiff ☐	jpg ☐	pdf ☐	bmp ☐

Image Use Specifics	
Project's Proposed Title:	
Author's Name:	
Publisher/Producer:	
Publishing/Release Date:	
Print Run or Download limit:	
Languages:	
Describe how the image(s) will be used:	

This information enables museum staff to locate the image(s) and grant the necessary permission to publish. A signed **Photographic Reproduction Agreement** is required for publication. This Agreement will be sent to you upon approval of your request.

It is the responsibility of the applicant to secure the all necessary rights to reproduce the requested images from the appropriate rights holders.

For more information, call Michelle Gallagher Roberts, Chief Registrar, (505) 476-5066, Fax (505) 476-5076, E-mail: michelle.roberts@state.nm.us

Signature: ______________________________ Date: ____________

Spencer Museum of Art
Application for Reproduction Permission

ARTIST NAME:
TITLE OF WORK:
DATE OF WORK:
ACCESSION NUMBER:

FORMAT:
INTENDED USE:
CONTACT NAME:
ADDRESS:
PHONE:
FAX:
EMAIL:
SPECIAL REQUESTS:

Conditions under which Permission is Granted

1. Permission is only granted for the usage, publication, and edition requested. Separate application must be made for each additional language edition and subsequent edition in the same form.
2. Use of photograph(s) is limited to the publication requested. No other use may be made without additional permission.
3. Reproduction from any photograph or other printed material not supplied by the Spencer Museum of Art is strictly prohibited.
4. Application to reproduce a detail from a work will be considered only upon receipt of a sketch or photograph marked to show the area to be reproduced. The caption must include the word "detail."

5. Unless the application is for a detail, each object must be reproduced in its entirety and the reproduction must not be bled off the page, cropped, or altered in any way.
6. No image, text, or other printing may be superimposed on the reproduction without permission. Reproductions may not be printed in colored ink or on colored stock without permission.
7. The publisher is to provide the Spencer Museum of Art with two complete copies of the publication in which the reproduction appears, without charge. The Museum may order, at the time of printing, any overrun of the reproductions it may desire, to be paid for at cost.
8. The credit line of the object requested must be shown in immediate proximity to the reproduction or in the section within the publication devoted to acknowledgements. If the reproduction is on film, videotape, or other non-printed medium, full credit must be included in the credits and in any accompanying printed materials.

Signatures

APPLICANT SIGNATURE:	______________________________
DATE:	______________
PERMISSION GRANTED ON BEHALF OF THE SPENCER MUSEUM OF ART BY:	______________________________
DATE:	______________

NEWFIELDS

IMAGE / VIDEO USE AGREEMENT

ARTIST and/or: x
REPRESENTATIVE: x
ADDRESS: x
x
TELEPHONE: x
E-MAIL: x

FOR AND IN CONSIDERATION OF the mutual undertakings herein, agreed to and to be performed in Indianapolis, Indiana, Licensee ("you") and Indianapolis Museum of Art, Inc. DBA Newfields ("Newfields") agree as follows:

Do photographic, video, and/or still image materials currently exist? ☐ yes ☐ no

If yes, please indicate format: ______________________________

Do you own copyright? ☐ yes ☐ no If no, do you know who owns the copyright? ☐ yes ☐ no

Please provide name and address of copyright holder: ______________________________

____

____

MATERIAL(S) REQUESTED: ______________________________

______________________________ *(Title of Artworks)*

USE(S) REQUESTED AND AGREED UPON:

The copyright holder will retain copyright of the original artwork. You hereby grant Newfields a non-exclusive and unrestricted license to utilize the existing materials provided by you for archival, educational, promotional, marketing, website, and such other purposes as Newfields will determine in association with the __________ ______________________________ (event) on ______________________ (date).

Any reproduction or subsequent use of the materials will be credited as follows: ______________________

These provisions will govern this Agreement in all respects. Please sign and return this Agreement to the Rights & Reproductions Department, Newfields, 4000 Michigan Road, Indianapolis, IN 46208.

AGREED TO AND ACCEPTED:

By: Date:

Artist and/or Representative

FOR NEWFIELDS:

By: Date:

Newfields Representative

4000 MICHIGAN ROAD · INDIANAPOLIS, IN 46208 · 317-923-1331 · DISCOVER**NEWFIELDS**.ORG

NEWFIELDS

ROYALTY COMMERCIAL IMAGE USE CONTRACT

ARTIST and/or: x

REPRESENTATIVE: x
ADDRESS: x
x

TELEPHONE: x

E-MAIL: x

FOR AND IN CONSIDERATION OF the mutual undertakings herein, agreed to and to be performed in Indianapolis, Indiana, Licensee ("you") and Indianapolis Museum of Art, Inc. DBA Newfields ("Newfields") agree as follows:

IMAGE USE REQUESTED:

[DESCRIPTION OF PROPOSED COMMERCIAL PRODUCT] (See Attached List)
Description:

Approved Sizes (wholesale price ________________ / [COMPANY] website retail price_____): _______
Distribution:

TERM & TERRITORY:

_______ [NUMBER] Years, commencing _________ [START DATE] and ending on _________ [END DATE].

In store in: ____ **[United States/list countries] [and online in United States/list countries/worldwide]**

IMAGE REQUIREMENTS:

1. All images must be reproduced in color in their entirety, no crops, bleeds or details, with a white border of appropriate size.
2. The words "Approved Copy" must be printed at the bottom of each reproduction.

ROYALTY AGREEMENT:

1. An advance in the amount of $____________ will be due on or before ___________________ [DATE].
2. Royalty payments will be due ________based on the calendar __________, along with a report detailing all sales.
3. Royalty payments will be ____% of the wholesale selling price and ____% of the retail selling price, creditable against the advance amount.
4. Royalties will be paid on all quantities sold, less quantities sold to the Indianapolis Museum of Art.
5. Quantities sold to the Indianapolis Museum of Art should be a wholesale less ____%.

ADDITIONAL PROVISIONS

1. **LICENSE.** Newfields grants you a limited non-exclusive license for the terms of this Contract and for no other time.

2. **COPYRIGHT.** You are responsible for obtaining approval on all images that are not in the public domain, and you are responsible for paying any fees. Newfields will make a good faith effort to identify images that require additional approval.
3. **PERMISSION.** Newfields grants you permission to make reproductions of the above described image(s) from the collection of the Indianapolis Museum of Art at Newfields for the use described above, SUBJEC TO THESE TERMS AND CONDITIONS, WHICH INCLUDE APPENDX A: REGULATIONS FOR REPRODUCING IMAGES FROM NEWFIELDS ("Regulations").
4. **PAYMENT.** You are responsible for payment of all applicable material costs, mailing charges, and reproduction fees within thirty (30) days of this date / signature. Reproduction fees are based on the images sent out by request and are not conditioned on whether the images are used.
5. **NON-WAIVER.** No Action, other than an express written waiver signed by Newfields, may be construed as a waiver of any clause of this contract. A waiver of a specific clause of this contract will not be considered a waiver of any other clause or term.
6. **SEVERABILITY.** Should any of the paragraphs of this Contract or in the Regulations be found unenforceable, the other paragraphs will be unaffected and will remain in full force and effect.
7. **GOVERNING LAW.** This contract will be governed and interpreted by Indiana law.
8. **ARBITRATION.** Any and all disputes arising out of, under or in connection with this agreement, including without limitations, the validity, interpretation, performance and breach hereof, will be settled by arbitration in Indianapolis, Indiana, pursuant to the rules of the American Arbitration Association. Judgment upon any award rendered may be entered in the highest court, state, or federal, of the forum having jurisdiction. If you breach any of the terms in this contract or in the regulations and force us to demand payment, you agree to pay a reasonable legal fee as determined by the arbitrator and will pay in full all disbursements and the cost of arbitration.
9. **AMENDMENT.** This contract constitutes the entire agreement between the parties and supersedes all prior written or oral agreements. This contract may be amended only in writing clearly setting forth any amendment and signed by both parties to this contract.

Please sign and return this contract to: Director of Retail Services, Newfields, 4000 Michigan Road, Indianapolis, IN 46208

YOU DO NOT HAVE PERMISSION TO REPRODUCE UNTIL THIS DOCUMENT IS COUNTERSIGNED BY NEWFIELDS.

For the Licensee | Terms and conditions agreed to (date)

Authorizing Official, Newfields | Permission Granted (date)

THIS IS AN IMPORTANT DOCUMENT. PLEASE READ COMPLETELY. YOUR SIGNATURE OBLIGATES YOU TO ABIDE BY EACH TERM AND CONDITION DETAILED IN THIS CONTRACT AND THE "REGULATIONS FOR REPRODUCING IMAGES FROM NEWFIELDS."

4000 MICHIGAN ROAD · INDIANAPOLIS, IN 46208 · 317-923-1331 · DISCOVER**NEWFIELDS**.ORG

REGULATIONS FOR REPRODUCING IMAGES FROM NEWFIELDS

GENERAL CONDITIONS:

1. All communications connected with the reproduction of photographs and videos from Newfields should be addressed to the Rights and Reproductions Department, Newfields, 4000 Michigan Road, Indianapolis, IN 46208; telephone (317) 923-1331, ext. 171; email: permissions@discovernewfields.org.
2. Written permission to reproduce must be obtained before publication.
3. Requests for permission to reproduce photographs and videos from Newfields will be considered not only when application is made by the publisher or agent, but also when made from authors who do not have a publisher identified.
4. Authors, educators, and researchers obtaining image files for study purposes is permitted.
5. Permission to reproduce and the fee payable (if applicable) cover only the specific occasion and use detailed in the application. Any and all reprints, further editions, re-employment of the image files or additional use of any kind must be preceded by a new application and is not covered by the original fee or permission to reproduce. Line drawings and adaptations made from photographs may not be published and objects illustrated in the photographs may not be reproduced without permission. Unless otherwise specified by Newfields, permission to reproduce covers worldwide distribution, in one language, in monochrome or color.
6. All supplied files remain the property of Newfields. Image files will not be supplied on approval or sold outright.
7. Minimum specifications for digital files are 300 dpi x the size of the reproduction. Reproductions from low resolution files (less than 300 dpi) are prohibited, with exceptions made on a case-by-case basis for the news media and publications with limited circulation.
8. The image area of the picture, or the area within the outline of a sculpture, or backdrop to the sculpture with shadows, scale indications, etc., may not be masked out, cut down, superimposed with type matter, or in any way defaced or altered.
9. Application to reproduce a detail from a work will be considered only upon receipt of a sketch or marked-up photograph showing the area to be reproduced. The caption must include the word "detail." Permission may also require the full image reproduction elsewhere in the same publication.
10. Application for permission to reproduce works of art in advertising, a promotional context, or as an integral part of a commercial product must include a layout and a full description of the proposed use, including the context in which the reproduction will be used, together with details of intended distribution/circulation. In the case of an adaptation, a prototype must be submitted for approval before production may proceed.
11. Digital scans or reproductions may not be made by outside companies or photographers for commercial purposes without the prior written consent of Newfields. Permission will be granted on condition that all digital files and copyright are forwarded and assigned to Newfields after being used for the permitted purpose. The outside photographer or publisher may retain a reasonable number of prints for portfolio or archival use.
12. Newfields does not supply images of works in its collection to companies or individuals operating a photograph rental and/or sales service. Applicants will be required to represent as a pre-condition for permission to reproduce that no such use will be made of any material obtained from Newfields pursuant to any application hereunder.
13. Reproduction from printed or other non-photographic materials, or from photographic materials not supplied directly by Newfields, is strictly prohibited. See paragraph 11 for regulations concerning outside commercial photographers.
14. All final reproductions, unless specifically stipulated in writing by Newfields, must be smaller than the original work of art, except sculpture.
15. Applicants will be responsible for the safekeeping of all digital files. Any unauthorized use of digital files, by any person or entity, will render applicant responsible and liable to Newfields for appropriate compensation and other costs, regardless of whether applicant has profited from or is responsible for such unauthorized use.
16. Newfields reserves the right, in its sole discretion, to refuse permission for further applications from a publisher or other applicant, if, in its opinion, the standard of reproduction has not been of acceptable quality.
17. Newfields' policy is not to grant an exclusive right to reproduce any photograph or video from Newfields. Newfields will not assume any responsibility for duplication of subjects or reproduction of the same work of art by other applicants or persons not authorized to reproduce said work. Newfields assumes no responsibility for claims against the applicant or Newfields by third parties, and applicants agree to indemnify Newfields and hold it harmless against any and all such claims and costs, including copyright infringement claims arising out of applicant's reproduction of the work of art in question.
18. ***On the publishing date, one copy must be forwarded to Newfields for archival and other purposes.***
19. Newfields reserves the right to limit the number of reproductions of Newfields-owned works of art in any single publication or film, if it appears that their number is disproportionate in relation to those from other sources.

COPYRIGHT AND CREDIT LINE:

1. Newfields makes no warranties or representations and assumes no responsibility whatsoever for any claims, royalties or fees demanded by an artist, his agent, estate or by any other party in connection with the reproduction of works of art in the collections of Newfields. Additionally, the applicant agrees to indemnify Newfields and hold it harmless against any and all such claims, demands and/or actions, including the costs thereof, arising as a result of the applicant's reproduction of images from Newfields
2. A credit line acknowledgment, as supplied by Newfields, including, but not limited to, copyright notice, the donor's name or the specific collection, must appear in immediate proximity to the reproduction or in the section within the publication devoted to acknowledgments, as specified by Newfields. ***Abbreviations are not permitted without prior approval of Newfields.***

FEES:

1. Permission to reproduce is premised and conditioned upon payment of all applicable preparation, reproduction, and shipping fees within thirty (30) days of receipt of the relevant invoice and may not be deferred until the date of publication.. Fees are based on the images sent out by request and are not conditioned on whether the images are used in a publication. Failure to pay the required fees means that permission has not been granted. ***When paid, the receipted invoice, together with executed contract, constitutes permission for reproduction. Images will not be released until payment has been received.*** Fees are formulated by Newfields in its sole discretion. Fees so established apply solely to the specific application upon which they are based and will not serve as future precedent.

4000 MICHIGAN ROAD · INDIANAPOLIS, IN 46208 · 317-923-1331 · DISCOVERNEWFIELDS.ORG

NEWFIELDS

VIDEO PRODUCTION CONTRACT

ARTIST and/or: x
REPRESENTATIVE: x
ADDRESS: x
x
TELEPHONE: x
E-MAIL: x

FOR AND IN CONSIDERATION OF the mutual undertakings herein, agreed to and to be performed in Indianapolis, Indiana, Licensee ("you") and Indianapolis Museum of Art, Inc. DBA Newfields ("Newfields") agree as follows:

TERMS OF PRODUCTION:

Does the artwork and/or video currently exist? ☐ yes ☐ no

If yes, please indicate format: ______________________________

Is the artwork a performance and/or site-specific piece? ☐ yes ☐ no

If yes, will the resulting video be the final means through which the artwork is experienced? ☐ yes ☐ no

You have editorial input on the video. Newfields retains final editorial and branding control. The Artist and/or Representative retains copyright of the video content. Newfields retains copyright of the final produced video.

USE PROVISIONS:

You grant Newfields a non-exclusive and unrestricted license to create new video stills, video excerpts, and electronic media and to utilize these as well as existing video stills, video excerpts, and electronic media materials provided by you without royalties paid to you by Newfields, unless previously negotiated, for archival, educational, promotional, marketing, website, commercial, and such other purposes as Newfields will determine. Newfields grants you these same aforementioned permissions to use the Newfields-created video. Unless otherwise requested and agreed upon in writing, Newfields will provide you with one copy of the video when it is produced.

Any reproduction or subsequent use of these materials as a result of this Contract will be credited as follows:

© artist name, title of work, year

Video © year, Courtesy of the Indianapolis Museum of Art

These provisions will govern this Agreement in all respects. Please sign and return this Agreement to the Rights & Reproductions Department, Newfields, 4000 Michigan Road, Indianapolis, IN 46208.

AGREED TO AND ACCEPTED:

By: ______________________________ Date: ______________

Artist and/or Representative

FOR NEWFIELDS:

By: ______________________________ Date: ______________

Newfields Representative

4000 MICHIGAN ROAD · INDIANAPOLIS, IN 46208 · 317-923-1331 · DISCOVER**NEWFIELDS**.ORG

THE SIXTH FLOOR MUSEUM
AT DEALEY PLAZA

SPEAKER AGREEMENT

This Agreement is made as of **(DATE)** (the "Effective Date") by and between **The Sixth Floor Museum at Dealey Plaza,** with offices based at 411 Elm Street, Dallas, Texas 75202-3308 ("TSFM") and **(SPEAKER NAME)** ("Speaker").

(SPEAKER) RESPONSIBILITIES:

1.1 The Speaker agrees to participate in a public program hosted by The Sixth Floor Museum at Dealey Plaza on **(DATE)** at **(TIME)**.

1.2 The Speaker agrees to provide an up-to-date bio and headshot for promotional purposes.

1.3 The Speaker agrees to be available for media and press interviews to promote the public program described above, pending his/her schedule.

1.4 The Speaker agrees to notify The Sixth Floor Museum at Dealey Plaza by **(DATE)** if he/she needs to reschedule his/her participation in the program on the dates set forth above.

1.5 The Speaker agrees to obtain any necessary permissions to use images, video or audio recordings included in Speaker's AV presentation from the appropriate copyright owners. Permission must allow the images, film or audio used within the presentation to be video recorded and distributed via TSFM's standard digital media outlets, including but not limited to: jfk.org, YouTube and Facebook.

THE SIXTH FLOOR MUSEUM AT DEALEY PLAZA (TSFM) RESPONSIBILITIES:

2.1 TSFM agrees to provide round-trip airfare from **(AIRPORT)** to Dallas, TX, and ground transportation for the Speaker.

2.2 TSFM agrees to provide hotel accommodations from **(DATE)** through **(DATE)** at **(HOTEL NAME)** for the Speaker.

2.3 TSFM agrees to write and distribute a press release and printed and electronic invitations announcing the public program and to promote the program on its website and social media accounts.

2.4 TSFM agrees to reimburse the Speaker for meals up to $70 per day (with submission of receipt). Note: TSFM cannot reimburse the Speaker for alcoholic beverages.

MISCELLANEOUS:

3.1 The extent and application of each provision of this Agreement is no greater than reasonably necessary for the protection of the interests of the Speaker and TSFM. This Agreement, together with the Speaker Release, sets forth the entire agreement and understanding of the parties and supersedes all prior agreements, arrangements, and understanding between both parties. If any provision of this Agreement is held to be void or unenforceable by a court of competent jurisdiction, the remainder of this Agreement nevertheless remains in full force and effect.

IN WITNESS WHEREOF, this Agreement is executed as of the Effective Date set forth above.

______________________	______________________
Speaker Signature	*TSFM* Signature
______________________	______________________
Name	Name, Title
______________________	______________________
Date	Date

THE SIXTH FLOOR MUSEUM
AT DEALEY PLAZA

SPEAKER RELEASE

Title/Subject of Presentation: ______________________________

I hereby authorize The Sixth Floor Museum at Dealey Plaza ("the Museum"), its successors, licensees and assigns to record my presentation at the Museum on (Date): ________________.

I further authorize the Museum to reproduce, transcribe, edit, excerpt from and otherwise include material from my presentations in Museum productions and publications and on the Museum's website.

I give, grant, and assign to the Museum and its successors, licensees and assigns all copyrights, legal title, literary rights and other rights in and to such recordings and transcripts of my presentation, and the right to unrestricted use of such recordings and transcripts, unless otherwise specified below.

The Museum program will be available to the public, and may be publicly disseminated, including (but not limited to) publication in all media currently in existence (e.g., print, graphic, film, internet and electronic media) or yet to be developed.

In consideration of my agreement, the Museum will provide me one free copy of my presentation at my request, to be used by me for my personal viewing only.

The Museum may use my name, likeness and biography in printed materials, publicity, promotional outreach, and advertising in connection with my presentation and the Museum's reproductions.

I give these rights freely to the Museum, in consideration of certain mutual promises and agreements, the receipt and sufficiency of which are hereby acknowledged.

Additional Provisions or Restrictions:

Speaker Signature: ______________________ Date: ______________

Name: ______________________

Address: ______________________

____

Phone: ______________________

Email: ______________________

The Sixth Floor Museum at Dealey Plaza Speaker Release | February 2018 Page 1 of 1

NEWFIELDS

Date

Name
Organization
Address
City, State Zip Code

Dear [insert name],

The Indianapolis Museum of Art, Inc. DBA Newfields (Newfields) strictly regulates the photography, video, and use of images of Newfields' artworks, exhibits, entities, and events. Newfields' policies exist in part to meet the requirements of federal copyright law that protects artworks and exhibits displayed at Newfields. To reproduce, publish, or utilize images containing any part of Newfields' exhibits, artworks, entities, or events, the party must receive permission from the Rights and Reproductions Department. A copy of Newfields' **[Image Use Policy or Photography Policy]** is attached to this notice.

It has come to our attention that your use of Newfields' exhibits, artworks, or grounds in a photograph, video, or other image may be in violation of this policy. Further, any commercial use you make of these images of Newfields' exhibits or artworks may violate federal copyright law. (See United States Code, Title 17, Section 106, which exclusively reserves the right to reproduce, distribute copies of, or create derivative works based on the copyrighted work for the copyright holder.) Accordingly, you are advised to **cease and desist** from use of the images of Newfields' exhibits, artworks, entities, or events that may violate the aforementioned Newfields policy.

If you have questions regarding Newfields' policy or are unsure as to whether your use violates this policy, please contact the Rights and Reproductions Department.

Respectfully yours,

Anne M. Young
Manager of Rights and Reproductions

Enclosure:

4000 Michigan Road • Indianapolis, IN 46208 • 317-923-1331 x171 • ayoung@DiscoverNewfields.org

INDIANAPOLIS MUSEUM OF ART · THE GARDEN · LILLY HOUSE · THE VIRGINIA B. FAIRBANKS ART & NATURE PARK · MILLER HOUSE & GARDEN

Accession Number ____________________

New Mexico Museum of Art
COPYRIGHT RELEASE AND ASSIGNMENT

Issue Date:
Name (s):
Address:

Telephone: Fax: Email:

I, , "Assignor," being the owner and holder of all copyright interests in and to the following work(s) of art:

In consideration of the Museum's acceptance and acquisition of the work(s) described above, Assignor hereby releases and assigns to the Museum all Assignor's rights (including copyright and rights of privacy and publicity,) ownership, and claims for the following checked items:

_______ Authoring, editing, facilitating, sound, photography, graphics, animation, publishing, musical composition or arrangement, design, artwork, or layout, including any advertising brochures, video, photographs, films, or computer media relating to the above described work(s).

_______ The use of names, images, faces, voices, performances, sound recordings, photographs, videos or film images relating to the work(s) and in any commercial, advertisement, announcement or publication regarding the work(s).

Assignor further agrees to cooperate with the Museum and to execute all documents necessary to secure, register, and renew such rights. If the work(s) is a "work for hire" within the meaning of the Copyright Act (Title 7 of the United States Code), Assignor agrees that the work(s) shall be considered a work made for hire. In the event the Assignor has employees who are not considered "work for hire" or utilize independent contractors for services relating to the work(s), Assignor agrees to obtain a release and assignment from each such person on a form provided by the Museum. Assignor further waives any moral rights, including rights of attribution and integrity that Assignor may have in the work(s).

Assignor warrants that Assignor's rights in the work(s) have not been previously assigned, mortgaged or otherwise encumbered, and Assignor has full right, power and authority to assign all such rights to the Museum hereunder.

Assignor states that Assignor has read this Release and Assignment prior to its execution, and that Assignor is fully familiar with the content thereof. This release shall be binding upon Assignor and Assignor's heirs, personal representative, successors and assigns.

Assignor hereby waives any right that Assignor may have to inspect and approve the finished product or the advertising copy that may be used in connection therewith of the use to which it may be applied.

Assignor name Assignor signature Date

Please sign and date both copies and return one to Head of Registration & Collections, New Mexico Museum of Art, PO Box 2087, Santa Fe, New Mexico 87504-2087. Rev. 09/2003

NEWFIELDS

Intellectual Property and Open Access Policy

Policy History

- 2018: Updated by the Rights and Reproductions Department
    - Included input from:
        - Newfields Brand Book and Style Guide
- 2017: Updated by the Rights and Reproductions Department
    - Included input from:
        - The 2017 Social Media Policy
- 2014: Updated by the Rights and Reproductions Department
    - Included input from:
        - The 2014 IMA Intellectual Property Policy Task Force
- 2012: Updated by the Rights and Reproductions Department
    - Included input from:
        - The 2012 IMA Intellectual Property Policy Task Force
- 2007: Updated by the IMA Photography Services Department – Rights and Reproductions
- 2001: Prepared by the IMA Photography Services Department – Rights and Reproductions
    - Included input from:
        - The 1997–1998 IMA Copyright Committee
        - The 2001 IMA Intellectual Property and Imaging Policies Committee
        - Guidance from the Director of Collections Support

Future Reviews

- Future reviews and needed updates will take place approximately every two years.
- Next review date: September 2020

Policy Manager

- Rights and Reproductions Department

2

Table of Contents

1. Purpose

The Indianapolis Museum of Art, Inc. DBA Newfields (Newfields) Intellectual Property (IP) and Open Access (OA) Policy is intended to provide guidelines for managing the IP that is created, used, and disseminated by Newfields' staff, which supports the integrity of Newfields' mission statement:

To enrich lives through exceptional experiences with art and nature.

This policy addresses Newfields' usage of original Newfields-created visual resources and text as well as any original visual resources or text gleaned from any other source.

2. Objectives

The IP and OA Policy is intended to:

- Foster an awareness among Newfields staff of the importance of IP;
- Clearly define the ownership rights of Newfields and staff in relation to IP;
- Direct Newfields staff on the use of IP owned by Newfields and promote consistency in its use across Newfields; and
- Provide guidance to Newfields staff regarding the use of external materials to limit the risks of infringement on third-party IP rights.

3. Application to Newfields Staff

The IP and OA Policy applies to all Newfields staff including, but not limited to:

- Part-time or full-time
- Temporary or regular
- Interns and fellows
- Volunteers
- Board of Governors

The IP and OA Policy also applies to:

- Contract or freelance workers
- Work-for-hire agreements and contracts
- Commissioned artists
- Researchers

The policy addresses Newfields' ownership and use(s) of IP such as:

- IP created by Newfields
- IP created in conjunction with a third party
- IP created by a third party

Newfields owns the copyright and related rights in all works, performances, data, databases, software, and designs (work products) created by Newfields staff during the course of their employment with Newfields. Newfields staff may not use materials produced during the course of their Newfields employment to commercially market themselves or otherwise commercially exploit the IP owned by Newfields.[1]

---

[1] For information on how Newfields staff may use IP in personal portfolios, see Appendix B.

4. Types of IP Newfields Creates

The Four Categories of IP

Copyright	Object Collections / Publications / Websites / Public Relations Materials / Media / Manuscripts, Maps, Architectural Drawings, Landscape Drawings / Educational Materials / Public Programs / Software / Databases / Administrative and Cataloguing Materials
Trademark	Newfields and Historic Properties Names and Logos / Exhibition Names / Educational Program Names / Buildings or Architectural Features / Slogans / Retail Store and Café Names / Publication Names / Public Program Names / Domain Names
Patent	Exhibition Setups / Scientific Processes / Designs / Mounts, Hardware, and Techniques / Plant Grafts
Trade Secret	Donor Lists / Marketing Plans / Software Codes / Business Ventures / Exhibition Concepts / Plant Varieties

Relationship between Newfields and IP

Owning the object does not necessarily mean IP rights are owned by Newfields. Additional factors, including the date of IP creation and the type of IP, determine ownership.

Examples of Possible IP Ownership Scenarios

IP Created By:	Object Owned By:	IP Rights Owned By:
Newfields Staff (see page 3)	Newfields	Newfields
Non- Newfields	Newfields	Newfields
Non- Newfields	Newfields	Public Domain
Non- Newfields	Newfields	Non- Newfields

Assessing Newfields' IP Assets

Every five years Newfields undertakes an audit of its IP assets.[2] As defined in Newfields' Intellectual Property Audit, this is intended to:

- Record and quantify Newfields' current IP assets by department;
- Determine the current registered protection status of the IP assets;
- Recommend the applicable IP assets for formal registered protection; and
- Provide guidelines to Newfields staff for the storage, retention, and formal registration of IP assets.[3]

---

[2] Most recently conducted in 2012–13.

[3] Indianapolis Museum of Art Intellectual Property Audit 2012–13

5. Intellectual Property (IP) Policy

a. Ownership of IP

- In cases where Newfields does not retain full rights, Newfields must ensure that it reserves the right to reuse the IP for its own purposes and that its ability to commercially utilize the IP is not unduly restricted.
- Where Newfields is the contracted party and rights have been assigned to the client, Newfields only reuses the IP with prior permission from the client or in accordance with a licensing agreement.
- IP created by Newfields staff during the course of their employment at Newfields:
  - Newfields owns the copyright and related rights in all work products.
  - Newfields retains the right to apply for and register worldwide any patents, trademarks, or trade secrets. As required by the registration process, Newfields will name creators in applications and will become the owner of any IP right that is subsequently granted or registered.
- IP created by Newfields staff outside their contract of employment:
  - Newfields staff own the copyright and related rights in works, performances, data, databases, software, and designs created by them outside the course of their employment, where Newfields collections or facilities are not used.
- IP created by other parties:
  - Newfields ensures that it has appropriate agreements in place with volunteers, researchers, freelancers, commissioned/contracted parties, and other work-for-hire parties to negotiate the right to apply for and register worldwide any patents, trademarks, and trade secrets. Newfields will name creators in application, as required by the registration process. In cases where this is not possible Newfields will review the possibility of shared royalties.
  - Volunteers, researchers, freelancers, commissioned/contracted parties, and other work-for-hire parties assign their copyright and related rights to Newfields in writing as well as waive their moral rights to the IP created. Where this is not appropriate, arrangements are made to ensure that Newfields retains the rights to reproduce the material for its own purposes.
- IP created by parties participating in Newfields-funded projects or research:
  - Newfields negotiates in writing the ownership of copyrights and related rights subsisting in all works, performances, data, databases, software, and designs produced by individuals:
    - participating in Newfields-funded projects or research; or
    - contributing work to Newfields.
  - Newfields negotiates full ownership rights, where appropriate, as well as permission to reuse content for Newfields' own purposes. Newfields explores shared royalty provisions, if applicable.
- IP resulting from collaborations:
  - The ownership of copyright and related rights in all work products resulting from collaborations is negotiated with Newfields in writing. Newfields negotiates full ownership, where appropriate, and permission to reuse content for Newfields' own purposes. If applicable, Newfields explores shared royalty provisions.
- IP created by guests:

- o The copyright and related rights subsisting in works created by guests as a result of their visit to Newfields belongs to the creators of such works.

b. Uses of IP

Newfields staff must respect and honor Newfields and third-party rights, trademarks, trade secrets, and confidential information during the course of their employment.

- Newfields-Created IP:
  - Images of Newfields, images of objects in the collections, or any textual materials relating to collection objects, may not be used in any media to assert or imply that Newfields endorses any commercial product or enterprise, concurs with the opinions expressed in any materials, or confirms the accuracy of any text used with these images or materials. A representative of Public Affairs, and other departments as appropriate, must review the text Newfields allows outside parties to use. Newfields holds the right to regulate all usage of images to ensure accuracy of detail and color.
  - Newfields staff, commissioned/contracted parties, and guests making or using copies of published or unpublished works from the collections are subject to internal procedures, relevant IP law, and the terms of licensing agreements.
  - Use of Newfields' name, logo, trademark, and any other marks or names commonly associated with Newfields by outside clients may only be granted permission by Newfields.
  - Newfields staff may use Newfields' name, logo, trademark, and any other marks or names commonly associated with Newfields during the course of their work and in describing their relationship with Newfields. Newfields staff may not use these for personal gain or private commercial activities.
  - Newfields' trade secrets in information, concepts, plans, designs, ideas, technology, potential inventions, and other confidential information and agreements are important assets that must be protected and may not be used in contexts that may impact negatively upon Newfields.
  - Newfields endeavors to allow use of software it develops during the course of research under open-source licensing agreements, subject to third-party contractual obligations.
  - Photography and filming by guests is permitted for private, noncommercial use only in specified gallery spaces. Resulting photographs may not be published, sold, reproduced, distributed, or otherwise commercially exploited.[4]
  - Newfields does not use contractual terms to prohibit uses of Newfields works where such uses would be permitted under the relevant IP law.

- Third-Party-Created IP:
  - Newfields does not condone any violation of federal or international copyright laws and expects all staff to abide fully by the terms and conditions of these laws. Title 17 of the U.S. Code states, *"It is illegal to make or distribute copies of copyrighted material without the owner's authorization."*[5] Illegal reproductions of works of art,

[4] For more information on Newfields' Photography Policies, see https://discovernewfields.org/photography-policy.

[5] 17 U.S. Code § 106

records, books, films, software, etc. may result in civil damages and criminal penalties.

- Newfields Library and Archives staff may make copies of published or unpublished works from the collections for Newfields staff, commissioned/contracted parties, and guests for noncommercial personal use, research, or private study subject to internal procedures and licensing agreements.
- Newfields staff, commissioned/contracted parties, and guests who wish to make copies of or use third-party works of art, records, books, films, software, etc. for any purposes beyond noncommercial personal use, research, or private study must obtain the appropriate permissions from the rights holder(s).
- In cases where ownership of rights cannot be established or where rights cannot be traced (orphan works), Newfields staff, commissioned/contracted parties, and guests must follow previously established procedures for the use of these materials.
- Newfields endeavors to secure third-party permissions for funding bodies, sponsors, and other partners in accordance with contractual obligations.
- Use of third-party software and databases is subject to the appropriate commercial and open-source licensing agreements and IT Conditions of Use.

c. **Fair Use Doctrine** (17 U.S.C. § 107):

- Fair use is a legal doctrine that provides certain limitations on the exclusive rights of copyright holders. Within copyright law, fair use comprises free speech principles guaranteed by the First Amendment and provides the foundation for Newfields' day-to-day activities in scholarship and education.
- Newfields recognizes that the fair use doctrine was created to allow flexibility in using the work of others within Newfields' mission as an educational, nonprofit entity.
- Newfields further recognizes its responsibility to properly credit content created by third parties. Newfields values the privilege to grant various reproduction permissions to others and respects the rights of others to do the same.
- All contentions of fair use must be analyzed by these four factors as part of a balancing test:
    1. What is the character of the use?
    2. What is the nature of the work to be used?
    3. How much of the work will be used?
    4. What effect would this use have on the market for the original or for permissions if the use were widespread?

d. **Crediting**

Newfields content:

- All uses of Newfields content by third parties require the inclusion of the appropriate credit line and rights ownership information unless the use falls under certain specific provisions in the relevant IP law where such acknowledgment is not required or where it is impossible for reasons of practicality.
    - Newfields clearly identifies the rights ownership of its own published content except where it is impossible for reasons of practicality [See Appendix D].

Third-party content:

- All uses of content for which Newfields is not the rights holder require the use of the appropriate credit line, unless the use falls under certain specific provisions in the relevant IP law where such acknowledgment is not required or where it is impossible for reasons of practicality.

Approved Newfields credit line templates:

- General credit line back to Newfields:
  - Courtesy of Newfields.
  - Reproduced with permission of the Indianapolis Museum of Art at Newfields.
  - Photo by [insert photographer's name], Newfields.
- Specific Credit Information for pieces, exhibitions, and archive materials
  - *Exhibition title in Italics* at the Indianapolis Museum of Art, date range of exhibition. Unless otherwise noted all works © artist name.
  - Indianapolis Museum of Art at Newfields, [insert specific collection/object credit line].
  - Item description, date, Container #, Collection Title, Indianapolis Museum of Art Archives at Newfields.
  - Artist name (nationality, birth year–death year), *Title of Artwork in Italics*, date of artwork, medium, dimensions. Indianapolis Museum of Art at Newfields, credit line, accession number. Copyright notice (if applicable).

Examples of credit lines:

- Photo by Eric Lubrick, Indianapolis Museum of Art.
- *Brian McCutcheon: Out of this World* at the Indianapolis Museum of Art at Newfields, September 9, 2011–March 4, 2012. Unless otherwise noted all works © Brian McCutcheon.
- J. Irwin Miller Illustrated furniture inventory, ca. 1958, FF 78, Miller House and Garden Collection, Indianapolis Museum of Art Archives at Newfields.
- Robert Indiana (American, b. 1928), *Love*, 1970, Cor-ten steel, 144 × 144 × 72 in. Indianapolis Museum of Art at Newfields, Gift of the Friends of the Indianapolis Museum of Art in memory of Henry F. DeBoest. Restoration was made possible by Patricia J. and James E. LaCrosse, 75.174 © Morgan Art Foundation/Artists Rights Society (ARS), New York.

e. Public Access

Newfields aims to provide free online public access to works in its collections under open-access principles subject to copyright restrictions.

- Newfields aims to provide open access to users in compliance with third-party rights and the contractual obligations of funding bodies, sponsors, and other partners.
- To this end, Newfields facilitates and encourages public access and use of Newfields materials for scholarly research, educational projects, outreach programs, promotion of Newfields' collections and activities, and to foster exploration of art, design, and the natural environment.
- Newfields staff and commissioned/contracted parties must take necessary, appropriate measures to ensure that they protect the rights in both Newfields' IP and third-party content.
- Permission for use of Newfields materials under open-access principles is given on a non-

exclusive basis and should include an attribution credit to Newfields in all reproductions.

f. Social Media Policy[6]

Newfields understands and appreciates that social media can be a powerful marketing and communication tool. Newfields also understand that social media can be a fun and rewarding way to share life events and personal opinions with family, friends, and colleagues around the world. However, use of social media also presents certain risks and carries with it certain responsibilities. To assist staff members in making responsible decisions about the use of social media, Newfields has established the Social Media Policy and its guidelines for appropriate use of social media. This Policy applies to all Newfields staff members.

g. Management of Rights Information

Newfields staff and commissioned/contracted parties are responsible for ensuring that they record rights management information associated with rights and assets created and owned by Newfields and third parties, in accordance with internal procedures and legal requirements.

h. Infringement

If Newfields receives notification that its IP rights have been infringed or if Newfields has purportedly infringed any third-party IP rights, it will be reviewed as follows:

1. Immediately notify the Rights and Reproductions Department and other department(s) as needed.
2. When applicable, seek outside legal counsel.
3. Respond to the claim in an appropriate and timely manner.

6. Open Access (OA) Policy

Newfields, incorporated for public benefit, is committed to furthering, promoting, and encouraging the understanding of the visual arts through a dedication to the highest standards in the acquisition, preservation, presentation, and research of its collections as a means of inspiring and educating public audiences.[7] As such, Newfields is committed to disseminating the products of its research and scholarship as widely as possible.

In keeping with the aforementioned, Newfields adopts the following policy:

- Each staff member grants Newfields permission to make available their scholarly products that reference or utilize Newfields materials and to exercise the copyright of those products.
  - Scholarly products are made available through the Institutional Repository (IR) only for the purposes of personal study, teaching, research, and scholarship.
  - The non-exclusive license on the "Acknowledgment of Receipt" grants Newfields permission to include the products in the IR and make them publically available through online reference searches.[8]
  - Specifically, each staff member grants Newfields a nonexclusive, irrevocable,

---

[6] Newfields Social Media Policy and Guidelines (2017).

[7] Indianapolis Museum of Art, Inc. DBA Newfields Articles of Incorporation Article 2 §2.01-2.02 (2011).

[8] Newfields staff members do not lose their exclusive rights, but rather grants Newfields permission to include and make available the products in the IR.

worldwide license to exercise any and all rights under copyright relating to each of his or her scholarly products, in any format or medium, provided they are not sold for profit, and authorize others to do the same.[9]

- Applies to all scholarly products, including but not limited to articles, presentations, and other scholarly products authored or coauthored while a staff member of Newfields.
    - Does not apply to any scholarly products completed before the adoption of this policy, products for which the staff member entered into an incompatible licensing agreement before the adoption of this policy, or materials produced that do not reference or utilize Newfields materials.

- Compliance with the OA Policy requires submission of scholarly products to the IR as developed during the course of their Newfields employment. Although Newfields encourages the submission of all scholarly products, the policy does not require the deposit of any products developed before or after being employed with Newfields, nor does it apply to products developed prior to the adoption of this policy.

- Newfields staff should submit final drafts of scholarly products, rather than published versions, when:
    - A publisher refuses to publish an article due to the OA policy. Newfields staff may request a waiver that exempts them from submission to the IR for that particular work.
    - The final draft should still be deposited into the IR for purposes of archiving. The article may also be "kept in the dark" for a period as the publisher requires prior to being made available to the public. Publishers may permit the article to be submitted to the IR provided that specific conditions or terms are met.

- Staff members are encouraged to negotiate with publishers who do not permit OA agreements to be attached to the publishing contract. Newfields will accommodate certain terms where feasible.

- Newfields retains the authority to waive the nonexclusive license, included in the acknowledgment of receipt at the end of this policy, for a particular article or may delay the application of the license for a specific amount of time upon express request by a Newfields staff member.
    - Newfields also retains the authority to provide other feasible accommodations for the author or publisher when doing so is in the best interest of the parties involved.
    - Each Newfields staff member is encouraged to provide, on or before the date of actual publication, an electronic copy of the final or most recently completed version at no charge to Newfields, when possible.

---

[9] Newfields may allow third parties to transfer or distribute the content held in the repository provided that the content is not used for profit, and that such dissemination furthers education or public knowledge or is used for the public interest. This requirement also prohibits Newfields or others, who access the article through the repository from placing advertisements on any page that displays the article.

- Newfields makes the products available to the public through the IR.[10]

- Adoption of the OA Policy will help Newfields to:
  - Improve the management of Newfields' IP;
  - Better disseminate the scholarly products of Newfields staff and improve Newfields' reputation as a leader in the field;
  - Encourage Newfields staff to use alternative publishing platforms that support more sustainable forms of scholarly communication;
  - Provide a formal process to submit copies of scholarly products to the IR; and
  - Retain and organize scholarly products related to Newfields' collections.

7. Breach of Policy

- Violations of the IP and OA Policy may result in disciplinary action, up to and including termination of employment with Newfields.
- Any such violations are reviewed in accordance with the procedures for Corrective Discipline as outlined in the Newfields Employee Handbook.

[10] Any product that has been waived for submission should still be submitted to the IR. The product will be kept for archival purposes, but will not be made available to the public. A citation will appear in searches and may have a link to the product (possibly on the publisher's website), but the full text will not be made available to the public.

APPENDIX A: Definitions (for the purpose of this policy)

Copyright: A set of exclusive rights granted to the creator of an original work or their assignee for a limited period of time in exchange for public disclosure of the work.

- This includes the right to copy, distribute, and adapt the work. In most jurisdictions copyright arises upon fixation and does not need to be registered.
- Copyright owners have the exclusive statutory right to exercise control over copying and other exploitation of the work for a specific period of time, after which the work is said to enter the public domain. Currently, the U.S. term is the life of the copyright author plus 70 years.
- Uses covered under limitation and exceptions to copyright, such as fair use, do not require permission from the copyright owner. All other uses require permission.
- Copyright owners can license, permanently transfer, or assign their rights to others.

- The five exclusive rights of copyright holders:
  1. To reproduce
  2. To prepare derivative works
  3. To distribute
  4. To perform
  5. To display

Copyright Author: The person(s) who created the copyrighted material. The copyright author initially owns the copyright, but may transfer some or all of the rights, or allow others to exercise those rights.

Copyright Owner/Administrator: The person or institution that owns the copyright to the material and oversees its use(s).

Exclusive License: Permits a copyright author to grant a portion of their rights to a third party. The author would retain the other rights that are not transferred.

Fair Use: A doctrine in U.S. copyright law that allows limited use of copyrighted material without acquiring permission from or payment to the rights holders.

- Examples of when fair use may be asserted:
  - Commentary, criticism, news reporting, research, teaching, library archiving, and scholarship.
- How to determine fair use—the four-factor balancing test (17 U.S.C. § 107):
  1. The purpose and character of the use, including whether such use is of a commercial nature or is for nonprofit educational purposes
  2. The nature of the copyrighted work
  3. The amount and substantiality of the portion used in relation to the copyrighted work as a whole
  4. The effect of the use upon the potential market for, or value of, the copyrighted work

Indianapolis Museum of Art, Inc. DBA Newfields (Newfields): Refers to all aspects of the Newfields, including but not limited to:

- Indianapolis Museum of Art
- Lilly House

- Miller House and Garden
- Newfields campus
- The Garden
- The Toby (Tobias Theater)
- The Virginia B. Fairbanks Art & Nature Park

Infringement: The use by one party of another's intellectual property, either intentionally or unintentionally, without permission. An individual asserting a claim of infringement must demonstrate that their work was copied and that the copy violates one of the rights granted under copyright.

Institutional Repository (IR): Exists to ensure the long-term preservation of materials produced by an institution's employees. Additionally, an IR creates a living curriculum vitae of the institution that records all the scholarly products created by its staff members.

Intellectual Property (IP): A term referring to a number of distinct types of creations of the mind for which a set of exclusive rights are recognized under the corresponding fields of law. Under intellectual property law, owners are granted certain exclusive rights to a variety of intangible assets, such as musical, literary, and artistic works; certain discoveries and inventions; and words, phrases, symbols, and designs. Common types of intellectual property rights include copyrights, trademarks, patents, and trade secrets.

License: A contract in which the owner or administrator of specific intellectual property rights grants permission to another to use that intellectual property for a defined purpose.

Licensing: The process by which a copyright author grants some or all of his or her rights to others and may enter into a contract to permit others to exercise these rights on his or her behalf.

Moral Rights: A subset of the rights of creators of copyrighted visual works of art, including:

- The right of attribution
- The right to have a work published anonymously or pseudonymously
- The right to the integrity of the work

Nonexclusive License: Granted for both commercial and noncommercial purposes and permits more than one individual to retain the same license granted by the copyright author, owner, or administrator.

Open Access (OA): The practice of providing unrestricted access via the Internet to peer-reviewed scholarly journal articles. OA is increasingly being provided to theses, scholarly monographs, and book chapters. OA comes in two degrees:

- Gratis OA: no-cost online access
- Libre OA: is Gratis OA plus some additional usage rights

Open Content: Similar to open access, but usually includes the right to *modify* the work, whereas in scholarly publishing it is usual to keep an article's content intact and to associate it with a fixed author or fixed group of authors.

Open-Source Software: Computer software that is available in source code form: the source code and certain other rights normally reserved for copyright holders are provided under an open-source license that permits users to study, change, improve, and at times also to distribute the software.

Orphan Work: Copyrighted work for which the copyright owner cannot be found or located. In some cases, the name of the copyright author or owner may be known but no further contact information can be established.

Patent: A set of exclusive rights granted by the United States Patent and Trademark Office to an inventor or their assignee for a limited period of time in exchange for the public disclosure of an invention.

Policy Manager: Newfields department that is responsible for ensuring compliance with this policy. It does not remove the responsibility of Newfields staff to comply with the policy. Responsibility for ensuring compliance is defined as:

- Maintaining knowledge of the policy and its requirements;
- Monitoring overall compliance (ensuring compliance at the daily operational level remains the responsibility of department managers); and
- Advising Senior Leadership and the Director of any issues concerning compliance arising from, but not limited to, matters such as resource constraints, administrative practice, and conflicts between requirements.

Public Domain: Works not covered by intellectual property rights at all, if the intellectual property rights have expired, or if the intellectual property rights are forfeited.

Scholarly Product: Includes but is not limited to articles, journals, books, conference materials, presentations, theses, interviews, audio or video recordings, web content, or other electronic communications. May include works that have been coauthored with non-Newfields staff members.

Social Media: Social media is a broad term for websites that integrate technology, social interaction, content creation, and dissemination, including but not limited to: wikis, blogs, photograph and video sharing, podcasts, and social networking sites. Social media platforms may include, but are not limited to: blogs, Facebook, Twitter, YouTube, Flickr, ArtBabble, Tumblr, Instagram, Pinterest, Snapchat, Music.ly, and Livestream.

Software: A collection of computer programs and related data that provides the instructions for telling a computer what to do and how to do it. Refers to one or more computer programs and data held in the storage of the computer for some purposes—a set of *programs, procedures, algorithms,* and its *documentation* concerned with the operation of a data processing system. Program software performs the function of the program it implements, either by directly providing instructions to the computer hardware or by serving as input to another piece of software.

Trademark: A name, logo, slogan, color, or other unique characteristic (mark) used by an individual, institution, or other legal entity to identify to consumers that the products or services with which the trademark appears originate from a unique source, and to distinguish its products or services from those of other entities.

Trade Secret: Information, including but not limited to formulas, practices, designs, or compilations of data, that has economic value from not being known to or readily ascertainable by those who could gain value from its use or disclosure and is the subject of reasonable security measures. In some jurisdictions, such secrets are referred to as confidential information or classified information.

Work-for-Hire: Works made by an employee in the course of employment (i.e., while employed with by Newfields) or one of nine types of specially ordered or commissioned works, in writing, where the employer or commissioning entity, not the employee, is the author of the work product(s) and retains the copyright, unless otherwise negotiated.

Work Products: Includes but is not limited to all works, performances, data, databases, software, and designs created by Newfields staff during the course of their employment with Newfields.

16

APPENDIX B: Types of IP Newfields Creates (may include but is not limited to the following)

Copyright

- Agendas and Minutes
- Analysis Methods and Reports
- Applications
- Art Handling Documents
- Artist, Curatorial, and Historical Files
- Blueprints
- Budgets and Financial Statements
- Checklists
- Conference Papers
- Contracts and Agreements
- Correspondence (print and email)
- Data and Database Contents
- Digital Designs
- Drawings and Models
- Evaluations
- Exhibition Planning Documents
- Floor-Plan Designs
- Formal Letters
- Forms, Passes, and System Logs
- Furniture Colors
- Handbooks
- Handouts and Worksheets
- Information Architectures
- Information Packets
- Installation Methods
- Interactives
- Labels, Didactics, and Wall Panel Copy and Graphics
- Landscapes
- Lectures and Course Content
- Marketing and Promotional Materials (print and digital)
    - Banners, Billboards, and Posters
    - Brochures, Flyers, Handbills, and Rackcards
    - Commercials (Radio and TV)
    - Invitations
    - Newsletters
    - Press Releases
    - Programs
- Media
    - Audio
    - Photography
    - Video
- Maps
- Newsletters

17

- Personnel Assessments and Reports
    - Background Documents
    - Job Descriptions
- Policies and Procedures
- Presentations (including PowerPoints)
- Press Releases
- Programs
- Proposals
- Protocols
- Publications (print and digital)
    - Annual Reports
    - Articles
    - Book Chapters
    - Catalogues
    - Newfields Magazine
    - Monographs
- Research Materials
- Retail Products
- Schedules and Calendars
- Signage (print and digital)
- Software
- Statistics
- Surveys
- Wall Colors and Graphics
- Wayfinding Materials
- Websites and Web Content (text and multimedia)
- Wireframes
- Workshops, Activities, and Classes

Trademarks

(may or may not be formally registered with the United States Patent and Trademark Office)

- ArtBabble
- ArtX
- Conservation Science Laboratory
- Domain Names
- Exhibition, Publication, and Public Program Titles
- Café
- Newfields Lab
- Indianapolis Museum of Art Name
- Miller House and Garden
- Museum Store
- Newfield
- Newfields Name(s)
- Newfields Logo(s)
- Oldfields–Lilly House & Gardens

- Slogans
- TAP Tours
- The Toby
- The Virginia B. Fairbanks Art & Nature Park: 100 Acres
- Westerley

Patents

(may or may not be formally registered with the United States Patent and Trademark Office)

- Algorithms
- Designs for Cases, Hardware, Mounts, and Pedestals
- Exhibition Setups
- Plant Grafts
- Scientific Processes

Trade Secrets

- Donor Information
- Exhibition Concepts
- Lender Information
- Marketing Plans
- Plant Varieties (breeding or genetic diversity)
- Retail Product Design
- Retail Manufacturing Process
- Software Codes

APPENDIX C: Related Newfields Policies

- Art Handling Guidelines
- Budget Policy
- Cell Phone Policy
- Code of Ethics
- Collections Management Policy
- Conflict of Interest
- Contract Review Process
- Exhibition Policy
- Fixed Asset Policy
- Greenhouse Policies
- Indianapolis Museum of Art Archives at Newfields Policy and Procedure Handbook
- Newfields Employee Handbook
- Newfields Image Rights and Reproductions Requirements
- Newfields Licensing and Location Shoots Policy
- Investment Policy
- IT Policy
- Miller House and Garden Licensing and Locations Shoots Policy
- Office Supply Policy
- Onsite Photography Policy
- Operating Reserve Policy
- Procurement Policy
- Rotation Policy
- Security Department Policy
- Social Media Policy and Guidelines
- Time Based Media Policy
- Touch Tour Policy
- Travel Policy
- Vehicle Usage Policy

APPENDIX D: Guidelines for Personal Portfolios

For personal portfolios, Newfields staff may use the content that they have personally created and collaborated on during the course of their employment by adhering to the following provisions:

1. Content used in online portfolios must link back to the appropriate page(s) of Newfields' website, when possible, to provide more context to the exhibitions and/or collection pieces.
2. Materials created in relation to exhibitions that were not organized by Newfields may not be used in online personal portfolios.
3. The use of any media containing works of art in Newfields' collection must be reviewed by the Rights and Reproductions Department to ensure compliance with any use restrictions imposed by copyright or any lender/donor requirements.
4. All content must include the appropriate credit line(s) in the following format:
   - General credit line back to Newfields:
     - Reproduced with permission of Newfields.
   - Caption/credit information for pieces, exhibitions, and archive materials (in reproductions):
     - Artist name (nationality, birth year–death year), *Title of Artwork in Italics*, date of artwork, medium, dimensions. Indianapolis Museum of Art at Newfields, credit line, accession number. Copyright notice (if applicable).
     - *Exhibition title in Italics* at the Indianapolis Museum of Art at Newfields, date range of exhibition. Unless otherwise noted all works © artist name.
     - Item description, date, Container #, Collection Title, Indianapolis Museum of Art Archives at Newfields.

Examples of the credit lines:

- Robert Indiana (American, b. 1928), *Love*, 1970, Cor-ten steel, 144 x 144 x 72 in. Indianapolis Museum of Art at Newfields, Gift of the Friends of the Indianapolis Museum of Art in memory of Henry F. DeBoest. Restoration was made possible by Patricia J. and James E. LaCrosse, 75.174 © Morgan Art Foundation/Artists Rights Society (ARS), New York.
- *Brian McCutcheon: Out of this World* at the Indianapolis Museum of Art at Newfields, September 9, 2011–March 4, 2012. Unless otherwise noted all works © Brian McCutcheon.
- J. Irwin Miller Illustrated furniture inventory, ca. 1958, FF 78, Miller House and Garden Collection, Indianapolis Museum of Art Archives at Newfields.

NEWFIELDS

Institutional Repository (IR) Waiver

Compliance with the Open Access (OA) Policy requires staff to submit scholarly products that reference or utilize Newfields materials and were developed during the course of their employment with Newfields to the Institutional Repository (IR). However, in certain cases, publishers may refuse to publish due to the OA Policy. Staff are encouraged to negotiate when publishers will not permit OA agreements to be attached to the publishing contract. Additionally, there may be other reasons for not submitting scholarly products, including personal choice or not retaining the copyright.

Use this form to waive the previously signed agreement to submit scholarly products to the IR.

Please use a new form for each scholarly product waiver you are requesting and attach a copy of any applicable publisher agreements.

I, ______________________________, request that the following scholarly product not be included in the IR (include full bibliographic citation): ______________________________

____

____

____

____

This scholarly product must be excluded for the following reason(s) (select all that apply):

Publisher agreement prohibits making the scholarly product available in an OA IR.

☐ in perpetuity ☐ temporarily

Has the publisher agreed to delayed access? ☐ yes ☐ no

If yes, the scholarly product will be made available on or after: ______________________________

If no, please be aware this option may be requested from the publisher.

☐ I do not retain the copyright or ownership rights to release the scholarly product to the IR.

☐ Other (please specify): ______________________________

____

I understand that Newfields will make available the bibliographic citation of my scholarly product for archival purposes, which means a search of the IR may reference my work without actually making it available to the public. Furthermore, I understand the bibliographic citation may include an abstract of the scholarly product and hyperlink to the publisher's site, which will be viewable by the public.

Signature: ______________________________ Date: ______________

Authorizing Official, Newfields: ______________________________ Date: ______________

NEWFIELDS

General Summary

This summary is intended to provide a high-level overview and is not intended to cover all topics and areas. Before signing the Acknowledgment below, all parties should read the entirety of the Policy.

The Newfields Intellectual Property (IP) and Open Access (OA) Policy provides guidelines for managing the IP that is created, used, and disseminated by Newfields. This Policy applies to all Newfields staff, including but not limited to employees, interns, fellows, volunteers, the Board of Governors, contract or freelance workers, commissioned artists, and researchers.

This IP Policy addresses ownership of IP, uses of IP, fair use doctrine, crediting, public access, management of rights information, and infringement. In order to adequately represent the rights of creators, all works must be properly credited and attributed. Newfields staff is responsible for following all applicable laws in the use of IP. Additionally, Newfields retains all rights to work product created during the course of employment.

This OA Policy provides for the dissemination of the scholarship and research of Newfields staff. Newfields staff grants Newfields permission to make available their scholarly products that reference or utilize Newfields materials and to exercise the copyright of those products through the Institutional Repository (IR). Exceptions to this Policy may be negotiated on a case-by-case basis.

All Newfields staff should consult and abide by this Policy when creating, using, or disseminating IP, and are encouraged to contact the Rights and Reproductions Department with any questions.

Acknowledgment of Receipt

I acknowledge receipt of Newfields' IP and OA Policy, and understand that it is my responsibility to familiarize myself with its contents and abide by the regulations set forth by this Policy. This Policy may change at any time, with or without notice, and I understand that it is my responsibility to review any changes made by Newfields.

I understand that any violation of this Policy may result in disciplinary action, up to and including termination of my employment with Newfields, and that any such violation will be reviewed by my Department or Division Head, Human Resources, and the Director and CEO of Newfields, in order to determine the severity of the violation. Moreover, I understand that violations of this Policy may also constitute transgressions of the law and may result in legal consequences for me and/or Newfields.

Further, this acknowledgment grants Newfields the right to make my submitted scholarly products available through the IR. This acknowledgment serves as a non-exclusive license that permits Newfields to copy, distribute, and make derivative works, as well as permitting third parties to use, access, copy, distribute, and make derivative works.

____

Employee Signature

____

Printed Name

NEWFIELDS

Potential Infringement Procedures[1]

If Newfields staff becomes aware of a potential (alleged) infringement of third-party IP rights by Newfields, staff will immediately report the incident in writing and submit all relevant information, documentation (including notification and correspondence received from third parties), and evidence to the Rights and Reproductions Department and other relevant department(s) as needed.

1. Investigate and assess Newfields' work(s) and ownership role(s) in the potential infringement:
    a. What is the work(s) involved in the infringement?
    b. Review the ownership of the IP rights:
        i. Are the rights owned by Newfields?
        ii. Are the rights owned by the individual/organization contacting Newfields or another third party?
            - Refer to the rights information in the collection database to aid in this assessment. If information is not available, additional research may be required.
                1. <u>If yes</u>, determine whether a licensing agreement has been completed. If a licensing agreement has not been completed, review the use in conjunction with Newfields' policies.
                2. <u>If no</u>, review the use in conjunction with Newfields' policies on using works in the collection.
        iii. For copyright in particular, determine whether the work is in the public domain:
            - If the work was created before 1923, it is generally considered in the public domain.
            - If the work was created in or after 1923, it could be under the protection of copyright law.
2. Determine how Newfields is using the work:
    a. Importantly, determine if the use falls under the umbrella of "fair use," as described in 17 U.S.C. § 107 by applying the four-factor balancing test as outlined in the IP & OA Policy:
3. Assess the rights claim:
    a. Review any relevant contractual or other legal rights and obligations of Newfields regarding the IP.
    b. Determine if Newfields could be held directly or indirectly liable for the infringing use.
        i. <u>If it is conclusively determined that Newfields has or has not infringed any IP rights, it will:</u>
            1. Draft a letter detailing the conclusion and keep it on file for future record;
            2. Inform the staff member(s) who reported the incident;
            3. If initiated by notification from a third party, respond in writing in a timely manner; and
            4. Depending on the conclusion; continue, resume, or permanently cease the use in question.
        ii. <u>If it cannot be conclusively determined that Newfields has or has not infringed any IP rights, it will:</u>
            1. Draft a report of the incident for review by Senior Leadership and outside counsel. If applicable, that includes the following:
                a. Whether the use has been discontinued;
                b. The results of any investigations conducted;
                c. The potential liabilities Newfields may face; and
                d. Newfields staff opinion regarding the incident, including basis, reasons, and analyses.
        iii. <u>In either situation</u>, work with the rights holder(s) to determine a fair and equitable outcome—whether it is stopping use of the work, providing correct attribution/credit, and/or providing compensation, if necessary.

---

[1] These procedures are not meant to be exhaustive or comprehensive and should not be deemed as legal advice. If at any time the situation merits, seek guidance from an attorney.

If Newfields staff becomes aware of a potential (alleged) infringement of IP rights in which Newfields has a controlling interest, staff will immediately report the incident in writing and submit all relevant information, documents (including notification and correspondence received from third parties), and evidence to the Rights and Reproductions Department and other relevant department(s) as needed.

1. The Rights and Reproductions Department will make a good faith effort to investigate and determine:
   a. The ownership of the IP rights;
   b. Any relevant contractual or other legal rights and obligations of Newfields and the party; and
   c. The nature and scope of the alleged IP use infringement.
2. Based on the investigation and determination conducted, the Rights and Reproductions Department will:
   a. Draft a report of the investigation and determination and keep it on file for future record.
   b. Inform Newfields staff member(s) who reported the infringing use of the determination.
   c. Notify the IP owner, if the rights are not owned by Newfields, of the potential infringement.
   d. Send either a "Cease-and-Desist" letter or a "takedown" notice to the potentially infringing party.
      i. Sending a "Cease-and-Desist" letter:
         1. Include specific information with a description of the IP believed to be infringed, the location of the original or authorized copy, and when and where the infringement appeared.
         2. Explain the IP rights status as Newfields understands it:
            a. <u>If Newfields holds the rights:</u> state that, depending on the kind of infringement taking place, Newfields retains the exclusive rights under 17 U.S.C. § 106 to reproduce; prepare derivative works; distribute copies; and display or publicly perform the work.
            b. <u>If the copyright is not held by Newfields</u>, explain that the potential infringer may be in violation of U.S. Copyright law under Title 17 of the United States Code and Article 1, Section 8, Clause 8 of the U.S. Constitution. Advise the user to contact the artist or representative to license the use or forward a request on their behalf.
         3. Formally request that the infringer cease using the infringing material.
      ii. Sending a "takedown" notice pursuant to 17 U.S.C. § 512 must include:
         1. A physical or electronic signature of an authorized official at or for Newfields.
         2. Identification of the work(s) claimed to have been infringed that is to be removed or access to disabled, including information to permit the service provider to locate the material.
         3. Complete contact information for Newfields to permit the service provider to contact Newfields.
         4. A statement that Newfields believes the use is not authorized by the rights owner, agent, or law.
         5. A statement that the information in the notice is accurate, and under penalty of perjury, the complaining party is authorized to act on behalf of the owner of the allegedly infringed right.
3. Review after two weeks to determine if the infringing material has been removed or the use has ceased.
   a. <u>If rights are owned by Newfields</u>, send a second letter via certified mail, retaining the receipt and a copy of the letter for Newfields' records. Include the words "Second Notice" in the second letter.
   b. <u>If rights are not owned by Newfields</u>, send a letter to the artist or artist's representative notifying them of the potential infringement via certified mail, retaining the receipt and a copy of the letter for Newfields' records. After notifying the rights holder, Newfields will consider its due diligence done.
4. Review after a further two weeks to determine if the infringing material has been removed or the use has ceased. If the infringement has not ceased, the Rights and Reproductions Department and Senior Leadership will assess the situation and, as needed, consult with outside counsel to determine the validity and advisability of legal action.

SAMPLE PERMISSION REQUEST TO LENDER

Re: *Tapestries from the Collection of Louis XIV* (working title)

Dear Sir or Madam,

As you may know, the J. Paul Getty Museum is organizing the exhibition, *Tapestries from the Collection of Louis XIV* (working title), which will be on view at the J. Paul Getty Museum from December 15, 2015 through May 1, 2016. We are also publishing an exhibition catalogue to accompany the exhibition, and I am writing today to request an image of and permission to reproduce the following work from your collection:

> *The Reception of the Envoys from Carthage*, late 1540s/1550s. Dermoyen family (Flemish, active 1529-1544 or 1550 GD) after a design in the style of Giulio Romano (Italian, 1499-1546). Tapestry, Wool and silk, 452.12 x 746.76 cm. San Simeon, California, Hearst San Simeon State Historical Monument, inv. 529-9-93

I understand that our exhibition curator has had preliminary discussions with your Museum regarding the potential loan of this work to our exhibition.

Publication details

- Publisher: Getty Publications
- Title: *Tapestries from the Collection of Louis XIV* (working title)
- Author: Charissa Bremer-David, Jean Vittet, Pascal Bertrand
- Print Run: 4,000 copies (English language)
- eBook: No more than 5% of print run (English language)
- Distribution: World
- Publication Date: Fall 2015
- Usage: Interior, Editorial use
- Size of Reproductions: Full page
- Color/BW: Color

Non-commercial educational and promotional use
In the event that our loan request is later approved, we also request permission to reuse the loan image for possible educational and promotional purposes directly related to the exhibition, which may include:

- Designs for directional signage and gallery graphics at the Museum
- Didactic displays and hand-held gallery guides within the Museum
- Free print and electronic newsletters
- Educational gallery pamphlets
- Our official website and other websites on which we maintain a branded presence
- Press kits and press images relating to the exhibition and publication
- Reception and press preview invitations
- Advertising and sponsorship uses relating to the exhibition
- Free exhibition smart phone/tablet apps
- Educational and promotional videos (not for sale)

If the above uses are agreeable to you, we request either a high resolution RGB digital image, approximately 6 x 9 inches with a resolution of 400 dpi, or a 4 x 5 inch color transparency, as well as a color match print if available.

SAMPLE PERMISSION REQUEST TO LENDER

For the purposes of accurate documentation and crediting, please confirm the full information for the work, including:

- correct title, date, dimensions, medium and inventory number
- credit line exactly as you would like it to appear

Please let me know if you have any questions or require any additional information. I would be grateful for a response at your earliest convenience as we are proceeding with the catalogue on a tight schedule.

Sincerely,

SAMPLE LIMITED COPYRIGHT REQUEST TO LIVING ARTIST

Re: *Messerschmidt and Modernism* at the J. Paul Getty Museum

Dear Mr. Rainer,

As you may know, the J. Paul Getty Museum is organizing an exhibition titled *Messerschmidt and Modernism,* which will be on view at the Getty Center from July 24 to October 14, 2012. We are also planning a full-color related publication, with a text emphasizing the significant relationship between the sculpture of Messerschmidt and later work by 19th-, 20th-, and 21st-century artists. We are pleased to feature works by you in the exhibition and related publication.

I am writing today to request copyright permission to reproduce the following works by you:

1. *Messerschmidt Series,* 1976-77, Eight overpainted photographs, mounted on wood panel. Ronald Lauder Collection.
2. *Face Farce*, 1969, From *Neverkampf*, 12 Fotos/Arnulf Rainer. Front of poster 2. Getty Research Institute Collection.

The following uses are requested:

Catalogue use

- Publisher: Getty Publications
- Working Title: Messerschmidt and Modernism
- Author: Antonia Boström
- Print Run: 2,000 copies (English Language)
- eBook: 100 copies (English Language)
- Distribution: World
- Publication Date: July 2012
- Usage: Interior, Editorial use
- Color/BW: Color

Noncommercial educational and promotional use

We also request permission to use the images for possible educational and promotional purposes directly related to the exhibition, which may include:

- Designs for directional signage and gallery graphics at the Museum
- Didactic displays and hand-held gallery guides within the Museum
- Free print and electronic newsletters
- Educational gallery pamphlets
- Our official website and other websites on which we maintain a branded presence
- Press kits and press images relating to the exhibition and publication
- Reception and press preview invitations
- Advertising and sponsorship uses relating to the exhibition
- Free exhibition smart phone/tablet apps
- Educational and promotional videos (not for sale)

We hope that the permissions will be provided free of charge, given the scholarly and noncommercial nature of the uses. Please be assured that our reproductions meet the highest standards, and we strive to preserve the integrity of the art. We shall credit the images as "© Arnulf Rainer" unless you provide different wording.

SAMPLE LIMITED COPYRIGHT REQUEST TO LIVING ARTIST

I would be grateful for a response at your earliest convenience as we are proceeding urgently on the publication. If our request is acceptable to you, please sign a copy of this letter and return it to my attention at the Museum by fax or simply reply by email to indicate your consent. Please don't hesitate to let me know if you have any questions, and I look forward to hearing from you.

Sincerely,

Signed: ______________________________ Dated: ______________

NEWFIELDS

SOCIAL MEDIA POLICY

The Indianapolis Museum of Art, Inc. DBA Newfields ("Newfields") understands and appreciates that social media can be a powerful marketing and communication tool. Newfields also understand that social media can be a fun and rewarding way to share life events and personal opinions with family, friends, and colleagues around the world. However, use of social media also presents certain risks and carries with it certain responsibilities. To assist staff members in making responsible decisions about the use of social media, Newfields has established the Social Media Policy ("Policy") and its guidelines for appropriate use of social media. This Policy applies to all Newfields staff members.

Overview

Social media is a broad term for websites that integrate technology, social interaction, content creation, and dissemination, including but not limited to: wikis, blogs, photograph and video sharing, podcasts, and social networking sites. Social media platforms may include, but are not limited to: blogs, Facebook, Twitter, YouTube, Flickr, ArtBabble, Tumblr, Instagram, Pinterest, Snapchat, Music.ly, and Livestream.

The same principles and guidelines found in the Employee Handbook, including the Ethics policy and the Discrimination and Harassment Prevention policy, apply to this Policy. Ultimately, staff members are solely responsible for what they post online. Content on Newfields' social media platforms must be consistent with Newfields messaging, inform and engage guests about Newfields and/or the cultural field, and follow protocols outlined in this Policy. All Newfields approved social media platforms are subject to periodic review to ensure conformity with this Policy.

General Guidelines

1. Know and follow the rules. Carefully read the following guidelines, the Newfields Employee Handbook, including the Ethics Policy, and ensure posts and comments are consistent with these policies. Inappropriate posts or comments that may include discriminatory remarks, harassment, threats of violence, and/or similarly inappropriate or unlawful conduct will not be tolerated and may subject a staff member to disciplinary action up to and including termination.
2. Be respectful. Always be fair and courteous to fellow staff members, guests, patrons, suppliers or others who work on behalf of Newfields. Keep in mind that it is more likely to resolve work-related complaints by speaking directly to fellow staff members or by utilizing established chains of command than by posting complaints to a social media platform. Nevertheless, if a post or comment contains complaints or criticism, avoid using statements, photographs, video, or audio that reasonably could be viewed as obscene, threatening, or

intimidating, that disparage guests, donors, lenders, Newfields partners or affiliates, or that might constitute harassment or bullying.

3. Be honest and accurate. Strive to always be honest and accurate when posting information or news, and if a mistake is made, correct it quickly. Be open about any previous posts that have been altered. Remember that the Internet archives almost everything; therefore, even deleted posts and comments can be searched. Never post any information or rumors that are known to be false about Newfields, fellow staff members, guests, donors, partners, or others working on behalf of Newfields.
4. Post only appropriate content. Maintain the confidentiality of Newfields trade secrets as well as private or confidential information. Do not post internal reports, policies, procedures, or other internal business-related confidential communications. Do not create a link from a personal blog, website, or other social media platform to Newfields' website without identifying yourself as a Newfields staff member. Express only personal opinions. Never represent yourself as a Newfields spokesperson. If Newfields is the subject of content being posted or commented on, be clear and open about the fact that you are a staff members and make it clear the views expressed do not represent those of Newfields.
5. Do not post information about unconfirmed or unreleased Newfields events or exhibitions. Consult and confirm with the Marketing and Communications department in advance.
6. Do not post or comment on security (i.e., access to the dock), finances (i.e., artwork values), insurance (i.e., property damage) or other similar confidential information about Newfields, its partners, affiliates, donors, lenders, or third parties.
7. Refrain from using social media while on work time. Do not use Newfields email addresses to register on social networks, blogs, or other online tools utilized for personal use.

Official Newfields Social Media Platforms[1]

All posts and comments on official Newfields social media platforms are prepared and maintained by and/or in conjunction with the Marketing and Communications department.

- Posts and comments reflect Newfields as the author and discuss Newfields projects, programs, collections, or exhibitions.
- Posts, comments, shares, and likes by official Newfields accounts do not equate to endorsement.
- Recognition of donors, partners, or sponsors and the inclusion of sponsorship benefits may be required in accordance with an approved agreement.
- Individual departments and staff members should not create their own "Newfields" accounts on any platform without prior consultation with and approval by the Marketing and Communications department.
- Content from other departments is welcomed and encouraged. Posts should be coordinated with the Marketing and Communications department for inclusion on official Newfields social media platforms.

[1] As of October 2017 these include: ArtBabble, Facebook, Flickr, Instagram, Pinterest, Tumblr, Twitter, and YouTube.

No Retaliation for Reporting Violations

Newfields prohibits taking negative action against any staff member for reporting a possible deviation from this Policy or for cooperating in an investigation. Any staff member who retaliates against another staff member for reporting a possible deviation from this Policy or for cooperating in an investigation will be subject to disciplinary action up to and including termination. If you have question about the Policy, contact a representative from the Marketing and Communications, Rights and Reproductions, or Human Resources department for clarification.

Intellectual Property

All content shared on social media platforms, including text, photographs, and videos, contain Intellectual Property rights. Posts and comments that utilize an image or video should include caption and copyright information when possible.[2] Content on social media platforms are subject to all laws and regulations governing copyright and the utilization of fair use. Adherence to best practices for the use of copyrighted materials is essential to limit liability. Newfields and staff members may be subject to rights infringement penalties as an institution as well as individuals and not as agents of Newfields.[3]

Acknowledgment of Receipt

I acknowledge receipt of Newfields' Social Media Policy, and understand that it is my responsibility to familiarize myself with its contents and abide by the regulations set forth herein. This Policy may change at any time, with or without notice, and I understand that it is my responsibility to review any changes made by Newfields.

I understand that any violation of this Policy may result in disciplinary action, up to and including termination of employment with Newfields. Moreover, I understand that violations of this Policy may also constitute transgressions of the law and may result in legal consequences for me and/or Newfields.

Employee Signature Date

Printed Name

[2] See Newfields' Intellectual Property and Open Access Policy for sample caption formats.
[3] Additional information about copyright and fair use can be found in Newfields' Intellectual Property and Open Access Policy.

SOCIAL MEDIA GUIDELINES

These guidelines apply to Newfields employees who create or contribute to personal social media platforms. Whether you log into Twitter, Instagram and/or Facebook – These guidelines are for you.

- As an employee, you are Newfields' biggest advocate. When posting to your personal social media platform don't forget to tag Newfields.
    - Twitter: @NewfieldsToday
    - Instagram: @newfieldstoday
    - Facebook: /newfieldstoday
- Working at Newfields, we as employees are susceptible to information that requires us to maintain a certain level of confidentiality. Please keep the following things in mind while sharing posts related to Newfields. If you are at all uncertain of the content you would like to post, err on the side of caution and first contact your supervisor or the Newfields Online Content Manager.
    - Values of Objects
    - Donor addresses or contact information
    - Security methods used to protect or install objects or security issues specific to the facility (i.e. number of guards on duty; key procedures)
    - Facility related issues/problems that could impact future loans or Newfields' ability to be insured
    - Details about incoming/outgoing shipments of artwork (including type of vehicle, time of arrival, contents, and packing methods)
    - Damages reports/Incidents reports
- Staff members should always assume that their social media updates can be traced back to their affiliation with Newfields so transparency is always best practice. We encourage staff members to identify as representatives of the Newfields brand.
    - For example, Newfields encourages staff to update job titles on social networks, but keep in mind to mention the fact that you are publishing your own opinions.
- Use social media to educate, inform and inspire. Social media is an effective way to share Newfields' story and is extremely powerful. Use your influence as an employee to lift up your coworkers, volunteers, donors and mission.
- When posting about organization culture, offices, team mates etc. do so with appropriate photos or status updates.
- Be kind, considerate, and compassionate online. Don't use social media to start or fuel arguments or debates. Before you comment on a post, Tweet or publish a selfie, remember that you can't take it back and even if you hit "delete", your content can be saved and shared within seconds.
- Individual departments and staff members should not create their own "Newfields" accounts on any platform without prior consultation with and approval by the Marketing and Communications department.
- Most of all... have fun! Social media is a platform we can share the wonderful place we are lucky to work every single day. As an employee, you are our biggest advocate!

SOCIAL MEDIA POLICY

version 1.0 - July 2017

The Social Media Policy ("Policy") governs the publication of and commentary on all forms of social media by employees of the Yale University Art Gallery ("YUAG" or "the Gallery") and its related programs, vendors, and companies. This Policy applies to:

1) Social media created by or on behalf of YUAG; and
2) Personal online activities undertaken by YUAG employees regarding YUAG
3) Content that directly or indirectly identifies an individual as a YUAG employee, even if the content is not YUAG-related, is done outside of work, and is independent of the scope of the individual's employment.

OVERVIEW

Social media is a broad term for websites that integrate technology, social interaction, content creation, and content dissemination, including but not limited to: wikis, blogs, photo and video sharing, podcasts, and social networking sites. Current YUAG social media activity includes Facebook, Twitter, YouTube, Flickr, Instagram, and SoundCloud.[1]

PUBLISHING ON SITES

All online activities, for blogs or other social media sites, in which the author is identified as a YUAG employee in the posting **OR** discusses YUAG projects, programming, or exhibitions is subject to review by the Communications Department or other relevant departments. Abide by the following guidelines:

- Do not post images or information related to events or exhibitions that have not yet been communicated to the public through public-facing channels or materials (usually through any or all of the following: YUAG website, press release, printed or online calendar, magazine, flyer, email blast). When in doubt, consult and confirm with the involved department in advance.
- Do not post images of "behind the scenes" areas or activities, such as storage areas, packing/crating of artworks, installation, or deliveries. Do not post any images of artworks on loan to YUAG that show the work being packed, installed, etc.; only images of loans in their final, installed positions are permitted. This includes when working at collectors' homes.
- Do not post material that is inaccurate, defamatory, libelous, or invasive of another person's privacy, or that could be considered offensive, discriminatory, or obscene.
- Do not comment on security, finances, or other similar confidential information concerning the Gallery, its partners, affiliates, or third parties.
- When possible, obtain permission before referencing or mentioning another YUAG employee or department, partners and affiliated companies, or third parties.

The Gallery may request that you delete or remove specific posts or comments if it believes taking this action is necessary or advisable.

The Communications Department welcomes your ideas for official posts on its social media accounts. Please submit such suggestions to the Director of Communications.

If you have questions, please contact the Director of Communications, Director of Visual Resources, Registrars or Human Resources for clarification.

---

[1] This list is current as of July 2017.

Newfields Location Shoot Application

Requestor

Company

Address

Telephone **Email**

Requested Location(s)

Is a scouting trip required? ☐ Yes ☐ No

If yes, potential date(s)

Desired date(s) to shoot

Anticipated Equipment List (include light type and wattage)

Do you have special power requirements? ☐ Yes ☐ No

If yes, please explain

Brief description of intended project

NEWFIELDS

4000 Michigan Road, Indianapolis, IN 46208 · 317-923-1331 · discover**newfields**.org · permissions@discovernewfields.org

Location Shoot Application *(continued)*

- 50% deposit of agreed upon fees due when application is approved.
- Remainder due ten days before shoot.
- Certificate of insurance must be on file with the Newfields prior to the intended shoot date(s).
- Photographs and film generated are granted permission for one-time use only as agreed upon in the completed contract.
- **Photographs of museum objects and grounds must not be used to assert or imply Newfields endorses any commercial product or enterprise, concurs with the opinions expressed in, or confirms the accuracy of any text used with these photographs.**

If any individual does not comply with the above conditions, the Newfields reserves the right to deny permission to photograph and may request that the individual leave the premises.

The signature below indicates that (print name) ______________________, understands and fully agrees with the Policies outlined herein and agrees to hold Newfields harmless for any and all damages, injuries, and/or losses that may occur while on Newfields property.

Requestor ______________________ **Date** / /

Please return this document to the Rights & Reproductions Department, Newfields, 4000 Michigan Road, Indianapolis, IN 46208 or permissions@discovernewfields.org.

TO BE COMPLETED BY THE NEWFIELDS STAFF

Application Approved ☐ Yes ☐ No

Comments

Fee Required $	**Deposit Paid** $	**Date** / /
	Remainder Paid $	**Date** / /

NEWFIELDS

4000 Michigan Road, Indianapolis, IN 46208 · 317-923-1331 · discover**newfields**.org · permissions@discovernewfields.org

Photography and Video Shoot Application

FOR AND IN CONSIDERATION OF the mutual undertakings herein, agreed to and to be performed in Indianapolis, Indiana, Photographer ("you") and Newfields ("we") agree as follows:

Photographer(s)

Company

Address

Telephone **Email**

Desired date(s) to photograph

Photography start time(s)

Requested photography location(s) ☐ The Garden ☐ The Virginia B. Fairbanks Art & Nature Park: 100 Acres

Brief description of intended project(s)

If any individual does not comply with the above conditions, Newfields reserves the right to deny permission to photograph and may request that the individual leave the premises.

The signature below indicates that (print name) , understands and fully agrees with the Photography and Video Shoots Guidelines outlined herein and agrees to hold Newfields harmless for any and all damages, injuries, and/or losses that may occur while on Newfields property.

Photographer **Date** / /

Please return this document to Newfields, 4000 Michigan Road, Indianapolis, IN 46208 or photopass@discovernewfields.org.

TO BE COMPLETED BY NEWFIELDS STAFF

Approved ☐ Yes ☐ No **Fee Required $** **Fee Paid $** **Date** / /

Newfields **Date** / /

Comments

NEWFIELDS

4000 Michigan Road, Indianapolis, IN 46208 · 317-923-1331 · discover**newfields**.org · photopass@discovernewfields.org

Photography Shoot Application *(continued)*

CREDIT CARD AUTHORIZATION FORM

Card Holder Name

Billing Address

Credit Card Number | **Expiration Date** | **Security Code**

Type of Card ☐ AMEX ☐ VISA ☐ MASTERCARD **Amount to Charge to Card** $.

I hereby authorize Newfields to process the expenses related to the photography listed above.

Approved by (authorized signer on account)

Please return this document to Newfields, 4000 Michigan Road, Indianapolis, IN 46208 or photopass@discovernewfields.org.

- Payment of fees is due with permit application.
- Single day pass fee of $50 covers two photographers from one company.
- Students may obtain a single day pass for completion of class assignments for free with a copy of their student identification. Maximum of 10 per year.
- The photography generated is granted permission for one-time use only for the original purpose listed on the permit application.
- To ensure a scheduled shoot, submit completed application at least two weeks in advance of the intended date(s) of photography. Passes may also be purchased at the Newfields Welcome Desk.
- Completed applications may be submitted by mail or electronically by e-mailing photopass@discovernewfields.org.
- Newfields reserves the right to request one gratis copy of any publication that includes images of any parts of Newfields or its properties.
- Newfields reserves the right to request reciprocal use, for in-house publications or online dissemination, of images created that include any parts of Newfields or its properties. The photographer shall retain copyright of the images and will be appropriately credited in any Newfields uses of the images.
- **Photographs of museum objects and grounds must not be used to assert or imply Newfields endorses any commercial product or enterprise, concurs with the opinions expressed in, or confirms the accuracy of any text used with these photographs.**

NEWFIELDS

4000 Michigan Road, Indianapolis, IN 46208 · 317-923-1331 · discover**newfields**.org · photopass@discovernewfields.org

NEWFIELDS

LICENSING & LOCATION SHOOT CONTRACT

REQUESTOR: x

COMPANY: x

ADDRESS: x
x

TELEPHONE: x
E-MAIL: x

FOR AND IN CONSIDERATION OF the mutual undertakings herein, agreed to and to be performed in Indianapolis, Indiana, Licensee ("you") and Indianapolis Museum of Art, Inc. DBA Newfields ("Newfields") agree as follows:

Date(s) of photo or video shoot:

Start/End Time(s):

Photo or Video Shoot Location(s):

- ☐ The Garden at Newfields
- ☐ Miller House and Garden
- ☐ Oldfields—Lilly House and Gardens at Newfields
- ☐ The Virginia B. Fairbanks Art & Nature Park: 100 Acres at Newfields
- ☐ Indianapolis Museum of Art Galleries at Newfields (specific galleries, if known):

Description of Approved Project:

Equipment:

Crew:

4000 MICHIGAN ROAD · INDIANAPOLIS, IN 46208 · 317-923-1331 · DISCOVER**NEWFIELDS**.ORG

TERMS & CONDITIONS

1. **LICENSE.** Subject to the terms and conditions in this Contract and in the applicable Licensing & Locations Shoots Policy, Newfields hereby grants you permission to perform a photo or video shoot only for the date(s), time(s), and location(s) described above, and to use the resulting photograph(s) or video footage only for the Approved Project described above. If any individual does not comply with the conditions in this Contract and in the Licensing & Location Shoots Policy, Newfields reserves the right to deny permission to photograph or film and may request that the individual leave the premises.
2. **FINAL APPROVAL.** Newfields reserves the right to request and review the final photograph(s) and video(s) before publication or dissemination. If requested, you will not publish or otherwise disseminate until Newfields gives final approval, which will not be unreasonably withheld.
3. **FEE.** You will pay Newfields a total of $____. A 50% deposit is due upon application approval, and the remaining 50% is due ten days before the first day of the shoot.
4. **COPYRIGHT.** You retain copyright of your photograph(s) and video. If your shoot features any works that are not in the public domain, you shall be responsible for obtaining approval from the copyright owner and for paying any associated licensing fees. Newfields will make a good faith effort to identify images that require additional approval.
5. **TRADEMARK.** This Contract does not give you the right to use Newfields' trademarks, including, but not limited to, the names "Newfields," "Indianapolis Museum of Art," and "Miller House and Garden," for commercial purposes.
6. **CREDIT LINE.** You agree that images and video created in connection with this Contract will be accompanied by the following credit line: Filmed at the ____________________. Courtesy of Newfields.
7. **POLICIES.** By signing this Contract, you acknowledge that you have read the Licensing & Location Shoots Policy. You agree to abide the Licensing & Location Shoots Policy and Newfields staff's instructions and guidelines, which are designed to protect and conserve Newfields collections and property during the course of your shoot.
8. **INSURANCE.** You agree that you will provide or have already provided Newfields with a certificate of liability insurance showing personal liability coverage with a single limit of at least $1,000,000 per occurrence for bodily injury and property damage. Newfields shall be listed as an additional insured on the certificate.
9. **WAIVER.** You agree to hold Newfields harmless for any and all damages, injuries, or losses that may occur while on Newfields property.

Please return this document to the Rights & Reproductions Department, Newfields, 4000 Michigan Road, Indianapolis, Indiana 46208 or permissions@discovernewfields.org.

Photographer/Videographer Signature: ______________________________

Printed Name: ______________________________ **Date:** ____________________

Newfields Representative Signature: ______________________________

Printed Name: ______________________________ **Date:** ____________________

THE SIXTH FLOOR MUSEUM
AT DEALEY PLAZA

FILMING LOCATION AGREEMENT

This is a contractual agreement between **The Dallas County Historical Foundation DBA The Sixth Floor Museum at Dealey Plaza** (*Museum*) and *Client* regarding the utilization of Museum facilities by the *Client*. The undersigned *Client* and *Museum* agree to the Conditions of Use and the stipulations outlined below.

Client: ______________________

Program / Project: ______________________

Date: ______________________

Time: ______________________

Location: ______________________

Fees: ______________________

Damages: Any damage to Museum facilities, as a result of the *Client's* group, will be the responsibility of the *Client*. Any associated costs will be assessed upon conclusion of the event, and are the responsibility of the *Client*.

Payment: Amount is due in full at time of invoice. Fees are non-refundable if event is cancelled less than 48 hours prior to the event date.

Liabilities: The *Client* agrees to hold harmless and indemnify **The Dallas County Historical Foundation DBA The Sixth Floor Museum at Dealey Plaza** and **Dallas County** for any bodily injury or property damage sustained by third parties arising out of the use and clean up of the premises by the *Client*. The *Client* also agrees to indemnify **The Dallas County Historical Foundation DBA The Sixth Floor Museum at Dealey Plaza** and **Dallas County** for damage caused by the negligence of the *Client* to personal property owned by the *Client* and in the care, custody, or control of the *Client*.

Museum hereby grants to *Client* and persons authorized by *Client* (and warrants that *Museum* is entitled to grant to *Client*) the non-exclusive right during the Date and Time to enter upon the Sixth Floor gallery and Seventh Floor and to film, photograph and record any part of the interior, the exterior and the contents of the Sixth Floor gallery and Seventh Floor, excluding exhibit content panels in the gallery, and for such purpose to bring onto and into the Sixth Floor gallery and Seventh Floor such persons and equipment as *Museum* may deem appropriate, subject to the Production Guidelines For Filming/Photography.

All rights in the films, photographs and recordings made and/or taken by *Client* in the Sixth Floor gallery and Seventh Floor shall vest in *Client* and *Client* shall be entitled to assign, license and/or exploit and promote the same by all means and in all media worldwide, but only in connection with the Program/Project described herein.

Client Signature:	______________	*Museum* Signature:	______________
Name:	______________	Name:	______________
Title:	______________	Title:	______________
Date:	______________	Date:	______________

If you received this form via email, please complete, sign and email it back to the sender. Or email it to ***media@jfk.org***.

The Sixth Floor Museum | Filming Location Agreement 01-2018
Page 1 of 1

Newfields Guidelines for Photography and Film

These guidelines are to be provided to the prospective photographer or videographer prior to the day of the shoot when possible. Newfields staff member(s) overseeing a particular shoot will review these guidelines with the photographer or videographer prior to the session and answer any questions.

Lights

- Light-sensitive materials (works on paper, Asian paintings, plastics, photographs, ethnographic works, and textiles) should be photographed or filmed using only existing gallery light. Auxiliary photo lamps and flash may not be used, without approval by Newfields Conservation staff.
- Oil paintings, furniture, and polychrome sculpture may be photographed or filmed using auxiliary photo lamps, provided precautions are taken in the setup of the equipment as detailed below. Scandles lamps are recommended because of their low heat and ultraviolet output. The Newfields Conservation department will lend these lamps to the photographer or videographer when possible.
- In the case of composite artworks (more than one type of material), the most sensitive material determines the acceptable light exposure.
- Newfields Conservation staff will identify when and where additional lighting may or may not be used.

Setup and Breakdown

- Newfields staff will work with the photographer or videographer to design a safe setup of their equipment within the galleries and in relation to the artwork.
- Whenever possible, lamps and other equipment should be set up at least five feet away from any artwork, including display cases and furniture. No equipment is to be placed on top of display cases, platforms, or displayed objects, including furniture.
- Equipment stands should be secured with weights to prevent tipping. Newfields will provide protective barriers and weights when appropriate.
- Furniture pads must be brought by photographer or videographer and used underneath all equipment for shoots taking place within Lilly House or Miller House.
- No collection objects may be moved unless approved and coordinated by Newfields staff.
- All extra or backup equipment (lights, cameras, tripods, storage racks, etc.) must be kept in an area designated by Newfields staff.
- Photographer or videographer is responsible for all equipment clean-up and removal at the completion of the shoot.

Other Guidelines

- Photography and film crews must be accompanied by designated Newfields staff member(s) at all times.
- Care should be taken to avoid damaging floors, walls, and artworks.
- In the case of damage to an artwork, DO NOT TOUCH or attempt to handle the damaged artwork in anyway and immediately notify the Newfields staff member(s) who are present.
- Hair, makeup, and wardrobe must be completed in a designated area outside the galleries.
- The use of liquids, food, open flames, and other materials potentially hazardous to the artworks are strictly forbidden within the galleries, Lilly House, or Miller House.
- Access is limited to the agreed upon area(s), date(s), and time(s).
- Doors may not be propped or held open.

Updated 10/19/2017

Newfields Staff Process for Photography and Film

Before the Shoot

1. When a shoot date/time is requested review EMS for potential conflicts with previously scheduled events in the requested area(s) to photograph or film.
2. Coordinate with relevant Newfields staff to ensure the shoot can take place and all needed Newfields staff is available for the requested date/time. This includes, but is not limited to:
    a. Public Affairs;
    b. Conservation;
    c. Registration;
    d. Curatorial;
    e. Security.
3. Provide the requesting photographer or videographer with the Newfields Guidelines for Photography and Film at least one day prior to the intended shoot date.
4. If needed, book the appropriate location(s) for the shoot in EMS.
5. Request visitor badges for all members of the photography or filming crew from reception.

Day of the Shoot

1. Meet the photographer or videographer and any accompanying crew at the Efroymson Family Entrance Pavilion at the scheduled date and time.
2. Before moving to the requested shoot location(s) the following must be completed:
    a. Provide the crew with their previously created visitor badges;
    b. Review the Newfields Guidelines for Photography and Film;
    c. Introduce all Newfields staff that will be part of the shoot (conservation, registration, etc.).
3. Once at the requested shoot location(s), Newfields staff is responsible for monitoring the following:
    a. Proximity of equipment in relation to artworks (nothing should be closer than 5 feet);
    b. Ensuring proper weights and barriers are used around all equipment to prevent accidents;
    c. Coordinate with conservation to provide sandbags or other weights/barriers if the crew has not brought their own;
    d. Ensure all extra equipment, cords, etc. are kept off to one side, away from artworks, and out of any walking paths where they may pose a danger to passersby;
    e. Ensure no one on the crew touches any artworks;
    f. If models/talent are being used, ensure all wardrobe changes, hair, and makeup are completed in a previously designated location away from any artworks;
    g. In the case of damage, immediately notify conservation, registration, and security – do not allow anyone on the crew to touch the damaged work(s).

General Reminder: At least one Newfields staff member must remain with the crew at all times during the shoot.

After the Shoot

1. Oversee the breakdown of all equipment, ensuring nothing is left behind and reclaiming any Newfields provided sandbags, barriers, etc.
2. Escort the crew back the Efroymson Family Entrance Pavilion.

Updated 10/19/2017

New Mexico Museum of Art

Policy and Procedures for Photography and Filming of Facilities and Objects

The Museum staff is entrusted with the preservation and care of its art collection. If your request to work on the property of the New Mexico Museum of Art is approved, it will also become your responsibility to protect the works of art in the areas where you will be working. Use of the New Mexico Museum of Art collections and facilities for commercial purposes requires written permission.

Proof of adequate liability insurance with a fine arts rider for $1,050,000.00 is also required, as specified by State Risk Management. Permission to use collections and facilities will be withdrawn by the Director if the Museum collections are compromised.

1. The work areas(s) must not become a hazard at any time.
    - A. Be prompt for your appointed time. Many activities aimed at monitoring and caring for the collection and the Museum facilities take place during non-public hours. Time to work in the galleries or grounds is at a premium during these periods.
    - B. Please bring only the minimum number of assistants necessary.
    - C. All equipment, case, and personal belongings can be inspected by Museum Security when you arrive and as you leave. The Museum reserves the right to examine and reject any equipment at any time.
    - D. All equipment, cases, and personal belongings should be staged as far from any art and collections as possible.
    - E. <u>If filming near artwork you must submit a filming script with this request for review</u>, amendment and approval by the Museum. Indicate the areas and objects you wish to film, in what sequence, for how long, approximate number and positions of the camera(s) and lights. Include arrival and unloading time, as well as clean up and re-packing time.
    - F. When filming indoors, if there is an unacceptable warming of the galleries from lights, some of your filming time may be taken up by a "cool-down" period when lights are to be turned off.
    - G. Your staff, equipment and models can never be closer than twelve inches from the collection items at any time, for any reason. They may never touch a collection item at any time.
    - H. Please pick up all trash and leave the area that you film as you found it.
2. A museum staff member must accompany you and crew members on the museum's property. They have the final authority to, at any time:
    - A. Verify your signed agreement to abide by these policies and procedures and check that you have brought proper equipment and fitters.
    - B. Approve what will be filmed and how it will be done.
    - C. Protect any art from dangerous situations and make certain safe conditions are being maintained; stop or postpone filming as they feel necessary.
    - D. Monitor light levels and ultraviolet radiation during filming.
    - E. Monitor temperature and relative humidity inside and maintain them within 8 of the preset levels.
    - F. Assure that any protective barriers, vitrines or glazing are not removed except by prior arrangement with the Museum.
3. The intensity and duration of light and heat on artwork, both those being filmed and those adjacent, must be kept within the lowest practical limits. Many types of objects have important restrictions for how much light and heat they can receive. To assure your compliance, the following procedures must be followed **<u>when filming indoors</u>**:
    - A. Light levels may never exceed 100 FC at any time within the Museum.
    - B. Particularly sensitive museum objects such as works on paper, photographs, or materials and coating prone to discoloration when exposed to light are generally photographed with ambient room and exhibition light. Permission for additional lighting can occasionally be obtained for the use of Kino Flo panels for one minute of total exposure not to exceed 20 FC total intensity.
    - C. Quartz or other incandescent light sources must be reflected into umbrellas. Quartz lamps must be used with separate UV filters such as Rosco UV gels or UV absorbing glass. Bring your own UV filters. Kino Flo panels may be directed towards artwork without the use of umbrellas.

   D. Lamps should be turned on only for the final placement, exposure readings and filming. They should be turned off as soon as filming has ended.
   E. All lamps should be base-steadied with sandbag weights that you supply.
   F. Lamps should be located as far as possible from the object being filmed and far enough from adjacent art so that the lamp cannot cause damage to collection items if a lamp stand should accidentally fall over.
4. Photography with electronic flash exposes the objects to high intensity light for a fraction of a second. This represents an instant increase to a light level one million times greater than acceptable levels. Flash photography is NOT permitted for the general public. Please read the following carefully:
   A. No more than two flash sources can be used.
   B. There can be no more than one flash exposure per minute for collection items,
   C. The two flash sources must be placed as far as possible from the object being photographed and to those adjacent.
   D. The flash sources must be filtered to absorb ultraviolet radiation. Bring separate UV filters to be certain you equipment can comply with this specification.

Use of the Museum's facilities must not result in permanent alteration to grounds or structures. Facilities must be returned to their prior condition after use, and the user will be responsible for all cleaning and repairs, all security costs, and additional staff time if required. Visitor access shall not be disrupted.

Commercial media productions must not distort the purposes or integrity of the Museum and its collections. No object, exhibit, or structure will be used in promotion of a product or service that implies endorsement by the State or the Museum.

Fees will be set by the Museum after review of application. Copyright fees and permissions may apply to certain objects in the Museum's collection. The user will be responsible for acquiring permissions to film copyrighted materials and for any fees.

Director/Producer agrees to hold the undersigned, the Museum, its agents and assignees, and the State of New Mexico harmless from and against any and all costs, fees, expenses and damages, except as may relate to negligence of the undersigned which may arise in connection with Director/Producer use of the property as described herein. Director/Producer shall leave the property in the same or an improved condition as it was prior to Director/Producer's uses hereunder, reasonable wear and tear, force majeure and the use permitted hereunder expected.

I as the director/producer and/or the authorized, financially responsible agent for this request for permission to film/photograph at the New Mexico Museum of Art, agree to follow these conditions and cooperate with Museum staff in order to photograph on (dates) ____________________________

Signature: ______________________________________ Date: ____

Name: ____ Title: ____

Company: ____

Address: ____

Telephone #: ____ Fax #: _______________________________

Email: ____

Authorization for the New Mexico Museum of Art

Name: ____ Date: ____________________________

Title ____

THE SIXTH FLOOR MUSEUM AT DEALEY PLAZA

PRODUCTION GUIDELINES FOR FILMING / PHOTOGRAPHY

Updated September 2017

The Sixth Floor Museum at Dealey Plaza's production guidelines are designed to accommodate your needs while assuring minimal disruption to Museum operations and protecting our artifacts, exhibits and intellectual property rights.

GENERAL INFORMATION

1. All sessions must be coordinated and supervised by the Director of Museum Advancement.
2. The Sixth Floor Museum at Dealey Plaza is a non-profit institution. Museum hours are Monday 12 p.m. to 6 p.m. and Tuesday-Sunday 10 a.m. to 6 p.m. Filming/photography sessions must be conducted before regular business hours, must be scheduled in advance and are typically limited to Monday mornings.
3. B-roll video footage (USB format) and non-historic digital stock images are available upon request.

CREDIT AND USE OF PRODUCT

4. The Museum's official name – The Sixth Floor Museum at Dealey Plaza – must be used in all print, broadcast reports, online postings and/or any other medium.
5. The images taken during the session may not be used for purposes beyond the project described in this form or sold for other uses without the prior written consent of the Museum.

FEES, PERMITS AND LICENSING

6. If applicable, fees may be charged for sessions, including but not limited to commercial photography and documentaries, features or short films. The attached Filming/Photography Registration Form must be completed and returned in advance.
7. To film in Dealey Plaza, contact Dee Castillo, Special Events & Film Coordinator for the City of Dallas Office of Special Events at 214.939.2775 or **dee.castillo@dallascityhall.com** or visit **dallasspecialevents.com**. Traffic control and street closures must be approved by the City of Dallas at your expense. The Dallas Film Commission may be able to offer additional assistance for commercial productions at **dallasfilmcommission.com**. The use of drones to film or photograph Dealey Plaza or the exterior of The Sixth Floor Museum at Dealey Plaza is prohibited.
8. To request use of any of the photographs or films shown in the Museum, contact Rights & Reproductions in writing at **registrar@jfk.org** or online at **jfk.org/the-collections/rights-reproductions-request-form**. A written license agreement from the Museum is required for any such use. Please note, the Museum does not possess the rights to all images but can often refer you to its rightful representative.

CONDITIONS FOR FILMING AND TAPING

9. Due to copyright restrictions, filming or photography of individual photographs on the exhibit panels or of the exhibit films is strictly prohibited. In-context, wide shots of the exhibits are allowed.
10. The historic building has limited electrical outlets. If additional lighting is required, please bring battery-operated lights or extension cords.
11. Due to preservation issues and lender restrictions, certain artifacts may be filmed with available light only.
12. If visitors are inside the Museum during your session, do not block exhibits, windows or video monitors. Disruption of normal visitor use is prohibited. Use of cell phones and walkie-talkies is prohibited during public hours.
13. Food and drinks are prohibited inside the Museum galleries.

14. Museum visitors may not be filmed or interviewed inside the galleries or Visitors Center without prior approval by the Director of Museum Advancement.
15. The sniper's perch on the sixth floor is one of the Museum's most important artifacts and is enclosed in glass to protect the floor and the windows. **We DO NOT open the perch for filming.**
16. We do not open artifact display cases for filming or photography.
17. Filming POV angles looking out the windows near the sniper's perch and on the seventh floor is permitted. Windows may not be opened on either floor.
18. Lasers, lights, ropes, etc. may not be used from any of the windows on the sixth or seventh floors.
19. Special effects, animals, props and modifications to the gallery spaces are prohibited.
20. Live broadcasts are permitted only by prior arrangement. Live broadcasts are not permitted in the galleries during regular operating hours, but may be done in the Visitors Center by prior arrangement.
21. We reserve the right to read all scripts or portions of the script that correspond to the planned filming at the Museum before filming is scheduled.
22. No one outside of Museum staff and board members may represent themselves as being associated with the Museum.
23. The Museum reserves the right to deny a filming/photography request or to stop a filming/photography project at any time if it is deemed necessary for the protection of our artifacts and intellectual property rights or the comfort or safety of our guests.

INDEMNIFICATIONS

24. Media are responsible for obtaining all necessary releases from any parties filmed for use in its project. This includes all proper and necessary releases from a school and the parents of any children under legal age. The media firm agrees to hold harmless and indemnify the Dallas County Historical Foundation d/b/a The Sixth Floor Museum at Dealey Plaza and Dallas County for any claims by third parties arising out of the use of any such images for this project.
25. The media firm agrees to hold harmless and indemnify the Dallas County Historical Foundation d/b/a The Sixth Floor Museum at Dealey Plaza and Dallas County for any claims based on personal injury or property damage resulting from accident or negligence by the media firm and its representatives.

THE SIXTH FLOOR MUSEUM
AT DEALEY PLAZA

FILMING / PHOTOGRAPHY REGISTRATION FORM

I hereby acknowledge that I have read and will abide by the attached Production Guidelines for Filming/Photography at The Sixth Floor Museum at Dealey Plaza.

If you received this form via email, please complete pages 3 and 4, sign and email it back to the sender. Or email to ***media@jfk.org***.

Signature ______________________ Date ____________

Name (print) ______________________

Organization ______________________

Street Address ______________________

City ______________________ State ________ Zip ________

Country (if outside US) ______________________

Phone ______________________ Fax ______________________

Email ______________________

Type of project (check one): ☐ News Feature ☐ Documentary

☐ Other (describe) ______________________

Date(s) and time(s) requested for taping/filming in Museum (include time needed for setup/teardown):

____

Project description, including main themes:

When and where will this footage be shown?

____

# of crew members on-site: ________

Name and email/cell of on-site contact (if different from main contact):

____

Additional Information (optional):

A notice confirming receipt and approval of this request will be emailed to you.

Deborah Wythe
Head, Digital Collections and Services

Date

Name
Address

Dear:

The Brooklyn Museum is honored to have in its collection the following works of art which you created:

[Object information]

We are currently going through a process to make sure our paperwork is complete and find that we do not have a non-exclusive license form on file for your works.

While ownership of a work of art gives the Museum the right to do a variety of things, it does not transfer copyright, which you retain. The non-exclusive license will grant us permission to use images of your work for Museum-related activities.

We look forward to receiving the signed document at your earliest convenience. [Name], our project intern, or I would be happy to assist if you have any questions. Please do not hesitate to contact us.

Sincerely and with many thanks,

Deborah Wythe
Head of Digital Collections and Services
Brooklyn Museum
200 Eastern Parkway
Brooklyn, NY 11238
tel: 718 501 6311
fax: 718 501 6145
deborah.wythe@brooklynmuseum.org

Brooklyn Museum
200 Eastern Parkway, Brooklyn, NY 11238-6052
T 718-501-6311 F 718-501-6145
Deborah.Wythe@brooklynmuseum.org

SAMPLE COVER LETTER FOR NON-EXCLUSIVE LICENSE REQUEST TO LIVING ARTIST

Date

Name
Address
Adresss

Dear __________:

Re: Non-exclusive license to reproduce works for scholarly, educational, or noncommercial purposes

The J. Paul Getty Museum (the "Museum") is very pleased to have recently acquired 3 photographs by you as listed in the attached. The Museum is dedicated to collecting, preserving, exhibiting, and interpreting works of art of the highest quality, as exemplified by your work.

In the ordinary course of our activities, we may wish to reproduce or publish works in our collection to further promote public awareness and understanding of art. We hope you will support our educational mission by granting the Museum a non-exclusive license to allow us to reproduce the photographs in Museum publications, including the Getty's website, and to grant third-party rights to reproduce the work for scholarly, educational, or noncommercial purposes. We would, of course, include a copyright notice in any publication and would refer any requests not covered by the license to you. To be clear, we are not requesting a general right to create and distribute merchandise based on the works (such as T-shirts, mugs, etc.). Please note that by granting this non-exclusive permission, you will not transfer the copyright. You will remain the owner of the copyright and retain the ability to do what you want with the copyright and to grant permission to others.

Many key artists or their estates have agreed to similar limited licenses, which have allowed us to maximize the potential of those works in our collection and to let the public know who the copyright owners are. Please be assured that our reproductions meet the highest standards, and that we strive to preserve the integrity of the art. By granting this license, you will also help encourage scholars and students to study and publish your work.

I have taken the liberty of enclosing a non-exclusive license form so that you may review its terms. If you agree to grant permission, please sign and date it, and return the signed copy in the enclosed envelope.

Thank you in advance for your time, and I look forward to your reply. I may be reached at________ should you have any questions.

Sincerely,

NEWFIELDS

Date

Name
Organization
Address
City, State Zip Code

Dear [insert name],

The Indianapolis Museum of Art, Inc. DBA Newfields (Newfields) is pleased to have [xx] of your work(s) in its permanent collection. In an effort to update the current copyright information files on all objects in our collection, I am contacting you to ask for your assistance in helping us reach this goal.

More importantly, our staff and core of volunteers are continually working to engage our varied audiences in exhibitions, programs, and publications designed to highlight the diverse works in our permanent collection. To this end, we often wish to reproduce images of the works in our collection. Completion of the enclosed non-exclusive licensing agreement will help us understand when we may or may not reproduce images of your work(s) and will streamline the overall permission and use request process.

By completing this form you are in no way transferring ownership of any intellectual property rights to Newfields. You retain all copyright and other intellectual property rights as well as all moral rights. Completing this agreement simply aids our understanding of when we may reproduce images of your work(s).

Enclosed please find our non-exclusive licensing agreement for your work(s). I hope that you will take a moment to review this document and, if you wish, to amend the agreement to suit your needs. Once satisfied, please sign and return the agreement to my attention via mail or email. Newfields will return a counter-signed copy for your files.

Thank you for your time and, should you have any questions or concerns, please do not hesitate to contact me or another member of the Rights and Reproductions Department.

Respectfully yours,

Anne M. Young
Manager of Rights and Reproductions

Enclosures:

- Non-Exclusive Licensing Agreement
- Terms of Reproduction
- Object Report

4000 Michigan Road • Indianapolis, IN 46208 • 317-923-1331 x171 • ayoung@DiscoverNewfields.org

INDIANAPOLIS MUSEUM OF ART · THE GARDEN · LILLY HOUSE · THE VIRGINIA B. FAIRBANKS ART & NATURE PARK · MILLER HOUSE & GARDEN

KU SPENCER MUSEUM OF ART
The University of Kansas

15 August 2015

Dear Ms. Xxxx,

The Spencer Museum of Art at the University of Kansas is proud to own a work by Xxxx Xxxx, listed in the enclosed packet. I have identified you as the copyright holder for this artist; if there is someone else I should contact, please let me know. We are contacting all the copyright holders of works in our collection to request permission to reproduce images of the works for educational and promotional purposes. We collect art to fulfill our educational mission by making artwork like Xxxx Xxxx's available to university students, faculty, and the public. Because the Spencer recognizes and respects intellectual property rights we are committed to fulfill the moral and legal obligations that accompany the use of copyright-protected works. The museum often receives outside requests to reproduce the art we own. As always, we are happy to forward these requests directly to you.

As stated in the Spencer Museum Art's mission statement, "The Spencer strengthens, supports, and contributes to the academic research and teaching of the University of Kansas and is committed to serving communities of learners across Kansas and beyond." The Spencer shares its vast collection through exhibitions, the museum's website, and other on-line resources.

I have enclosed our Standard Non-Exclusive Agreement Form. If you are unable to meet these conditions, please contact me so that we may discuss other arrangements.

In addition to making our collection available on-line, we are also interested in having more information about the artists and artworks in our collection. We would like to take this opportunity to request any biographical information or comments about specific artworks so that we can include this information in our collection database. Please send any information you have that you feel should be included in our records back with your response.

Please sign and return the form at your earliest convenience. Your participation in this educational mission is greatly appreciated. Please do not hesitate to contact me with any questions or concerns you might have.

Sincerely,

Rights and Reproductions
photorr@ku.edu
785-864-6368

1301 Mississippi Street | Lawrence, KS 66045-7500 | (785) 864-4710 | Fax (785) 864-3112 | www.spencerart.ku.edu

NON-EXCLUSIVE LICENSE FOR COPYRIGHT

[Object list]
Artist:
Title, Year:
Medium:
Dimensions: Object Number:

I, the undersigned, acknowledge that the Brooklyn Museum (the "Museum") has in its collection the above referenced work(s) (the "Work'), and that the Museum requests permission as described below concerning the Work for purposes consistent with its charitable and educational mission. I understand that the Museum is a not-for-profit, educational corporation dedicated to the primacy of the visitor experience and committed to excellence in every aspect of its collections and programs. Among the specific goals of the Museum is to serve its diverse public as a dynamic, innovative and welcoming center for learning through the visual arts.

In light of the Museum's charitable and educational mission, and in recognition of the Museum's lawful possession of the Work, I hereby grant to the Museum, as of the date written above, a non-exclusive license (the "License") to reproduce the Work, for the life of its copyright and any renewals or extensions thereof, in any media whether now known or invented after the date hereof (all reproductions, the "Images"), and to display, transmit, publish, distribute, prepare derivative works of and otherwise use the Images throughout the world as follows:

1) in educational materials related to the Museum's collection and programs (including, for example, posters, postcards, teaching materials, web sites, social networks, catalogues and similar publications, some of which may be offered through Museum's stores); and
2) in publicity and informational materials about the Museum's collection and programs (including, for example, press releases, web sites, social networks, annual reports, promotional flyers, email, posters or films, and membership solicitations).

I agree that the License expressly authorizes the Museum to sublicense the specific rights granted herein to third parties as necessary (in the discretion of the Museum) to fulfill its mission. For all other rights, I understand that the Museum shall seek permission from me or my representative and that it will direct inquiring third parties to do the same.

Brooklyn Museum
200 Eastern Parkway, Brooklyn, NY 11238-6052

The License is binding on my heirs, administrators, executors, successors and assigns.

Whenever feasible, the Museum shall include (and cause others to include) the following copyright notice, or one similar to it, in connection with Images:

[proposed © statement]

____

I affirm for the Museum that I am the sole and exclusive owner of the copyright to the Work and therefore able to grant the License, as requested herein.

Signature ______________________________

Printed Name ______________________________

(If not Artist) Relationship to Artist ______________________________

Date ____________________

Mailing address:

____

____

____

SAMPLE

GRANT OF NON-EXCLUSIVE LICENSE

I, ________________________, am the owner or the authorized agent of the owner of the copyright to the following object or objects (the "Works"):

I grant to the J. Paul Getty Museum, an operating program of the J. Paul Getty Trust (collectively, the "Getty"):

1. Permission to reproduce and publish images of the Works in materials, in any and all media now known and hereinafter invented, arising from or relating to exhibitions, the permanent collection, and the Getty Center site. This activity includes reproducing the images in catalogs, gallery pamphlets, announcements, press releases, print and electronic books and other materials that promote exhibitions or the permanent collection, on the Getty's web sites and other web sites on which we maintain a branded presence (subject to appropriate measures to guard against misappropriation and misuse of digital imagery), as well as closed circuit electronic kiosk displays and hand-held gallery guides within the Getty's facilities. It also includes distributing photo materials in traditional or digital formats to the press for print and online publicity, as well as filming and photography by the press for news and feature coverage. The general public may film and photograph the works for personal, non-commercial purposes.

2. Permission to reproduce, publish, and distribute images of the Works in scholarly or educational publications, including, but not limited to, publishing or granting the right to others to publish the images in educational or scholarly books or brochures, journals, pamphlets, transparencies and filmstrips distributed for educational or scholarly uses, and publication of electronic or digital works for educational purposes, such as closed circuit transmissions to support educational programs and educational or editorial pages within a web site (subject to appropriate measures to guard against misappropriation and misuse of digital imagery).

3. Permission to reproduce and publish images of the Works in documentary or educational films and videos.

4. Permission to reproduce the Works and create derivative materials based upon the Works to create high quality postcards, posters, stationery, calendars and other printed matter, and permission to publish and distribute these printed materials. Such printed materials will be consistent in quality with the quality of such materials produced by or for the Museum based on other works in the Museum's collection.

All reproductions of the Works will bear an appropriate copyright notice as indicated below:

Copyright notice: ____________©____
(exact form of copyright notice)

It is understood that this non-exclusive license will <u>not</u> be construed to grant a general right to create and distribute merchandise based on the Works (such as T-shirts, mugs, etc.).

In addition, nothing contained herein shall be construed to limit or restrict in any way the Getty's rights to use copyrighted material in accordance with limitations on copyright holder's exclusive rights set forth in the Copyright Act, as it may be amended from time-to-time, such as fair use.

I confirm that I am authorized and able to grant the permissions given in this non-exclusive license, that in granting these permissions, I have not violated any laws or breached any prior commitments to any third party, and that, to the best of my knowledge, there is no third party who owns or claims to own copyright in the Works or who alleges that my activity or this permission infringes or will infringe his or her intellectual property rights.

Signed: ______________________________________ Dated: ______________________
Owner or authorized agent for the owner of the copyright

Print name: ______________________________________

02/17

SAMPLE

GRANT OF NON-EXCLUSIVE LICENSE FOR AUDIO/VISUAL WORK(S)

I, ________________________________, am the owner or the authorized agent for the owner of the copyright to the following audio or audio/visual work or works (the "A/V Work(s)"):

I grant to the J. Paul Getty Museum, an operating program of the J. Paul Getty Trust (collectively, the "Getty"):

1. Permission to exhibit the A/V Work(s) publicly on the Getty's sites at any time, without securing prior authorization each time; such exhibitions may be defined as display or public performance of the A/V Work(s). This includes the right to reproduce the A/V Work(s), including migration to different technical formats and reproduction in sufficient quantities as necessary in order to preserve, display, transmit, distribute and/or publicly perform the A/V Work(s) in all media now known or hereafter devised. The Getty agrees to follow reasonable and current industry standards to ensure high-quality copies. Permission is also hereby granted to the Getty to use my name, voice, photograph, and likeness in connection with its use of the A/V Work(s).

2. Permission to reproduce and publish still images (if applicable) and clips of up to two (2) minutes in length of the A/V Work(s) in materials arising from or relating to exhibitions, the permanent collection, and the Getty sites. This activity includes reproducing the still images and/or clips in catalogs, gallery pamphlets, announcements, press releases, books and other materials that promote exhibitions or the permanent collection, on the Getty's web sites and other web sites on which the Getty maintains a branded presence, as well as closed circuit electronic kiosk displays and hand-held gallery guides within the Getty's facilities. It also includes distributing the clips and/or still images in traditional or digital formats to the press for print and online publicity, as well as filming and photography by the press for news and feature coverage. The general public may film and photograph the A/V Work(s) for personal, non-commercial purposes.

3. Permission to reproduce, publish, and distribute still images (if applicable) and clips of up to two (2) minutes in length of the A/V Work(s) in scholarly or educational publications, including, but not limited to, publishing or granting the right to others to publish the still images and/or clips in educational or scholarly books or brochures, journals, pamphlets, transparencies and filmstrips distributed for educational or scholarly uses, and publication of electronic or digital works for educational purposes, such as closed circuit transmissions to support educational programs and educational or editorial pages within a web site (subject to appropriate measures to guard against misappropriation and misuse of digital imagery).

4. Permission to lend the A/V Work(s) and/or a copy of the A/V Work(s) to other venues for exhibition in accordance with the Getty's standard policies and procedures, including permission to authorize the borrowing institution to display or publicly perform the A/V Work(s).

All reproductions of the A/V Work(s) will bear an appropriate copyright notice as indicated below *(to be filled in by copyright owner or agent)*:

Copyright notice:____
(exact form of copyright notice)

This non-exclusive license does not grant any general right to create and distribute merchandise based on the A/V Work(s) (such as T-shirts, mugs, etc.). In addition, nothing contained herein shall be construed to limit or restrict in any way the Getty's right to use the A/V Work(s) in accordance with limitations on copyright holders' exclusive rights set forth in the Copyright Act, as it may be amended from time-to-time, such as fair use.

I confirm that I am authorized and able to grant the permissions given in this non-exclusive license, that in granting these permissions, I have not violated any laws or breached any prior commitments to any third party, and that, to the best of my knowledge, there is no third party who owns or claims to own copyright in the A/V Work(s) or who alleges that my activity or this permission infringes or will infringe his or her intellectual property rights, and, the A/V Work(s) do not violate any right to privacy or publicity, or otherwise violate any law or any person's personal or property rights.

Signed: ______________________________________ Dated: ____________________
Owner or authorized agent for the owner of the copyright

02-17

NEWFIELDS

NON-EXCLUSIVE LICENSING AGREEMENT

Please complete and return this document to the Rights & Reproductions Department.

I agree to allow the Indianapolis Museum of Art, Inc. DBA Newfields (Newfields) to reproduce images of work(s) (see attached Object Report) by [insert name] for the following categories of use.

1. Scholarly research, research partnerships and databases, including image distribution partners.
   ☐ yes ☐ no ☐ with the following conditions*
2. Educational projects, editorial content, on-site visitor wayfinding, press review, and publications, including, but not limited to, books, exhibition catalogues, annual reports, and member magazines.
   ☐ yes ☐ no ☐ with the following conditions*
3. Promotion and advertising related to the IMA's programs and mission.
   ☐ yes ☐ no ☐ with the following conditions*
4. In any and all media worldwide, whether now known or later developed.
   ☐ yes ☐ no ☐ with the following conditions*
5. Non-commercial photography by the public while on exhibit (use of flash and photo shoots are restricted).
   ☐ yes ☐ no ☐ with the following conditions*
6. Should the IMA acquire additional work(s) after the date of this agreement, the above uses and following Terms of Reproduction shall also extend to and include such work(s).
   ☐ yes ☐ no ☐ with the following conditions*
7. Extension of the permission(s) agreed upon above to institutions borrowing the work(s).
   ☐ yes ☐ no ☐ with the following conditions*

CONTACT INFORMATION

☐ Artist ☐ Representative

Name:

Company:

Address:

City, State, Zip:

Phone: Fax:

Email:

I agree to the Non-Exclusive Licensing Agreement and Terms of Reproduction:

Artist Signature: **Date:**

Authorizing Official, Newfields: **Date:**

INDIANAPOLIS MUSEUM OF ART · THE GARDEN · LILLY HOUSE · THE VIRGINIA B. FAIRBANKS ART & NATURE PARK · MILLER HOUSE & GARDEN

NEWFIELDS NON-EXCLUSIVE LICENSING AGREEMENT TERMS OF REPRODUCTION

These Terms of Reproduction (Terms) between [insert name] (Artist) and the Indianapolis Museum of Art, Inc. DBA Newfields (Newfields) an Indiana non-profit corporation located at 4000 Michigan Road, Indianapolis, Indiana 46208, regarding the work(s) described in the attached Object Report (the Work) are entered into as of the date signed by both parties.

In consideration of the Artist's desire to increase knowledge and visibility of the Work and Newfields' desire to reproduce the Work for the purposes agreed to in the Non-Exclusive Licensing Agreement, the Parties agree to the following licensing terms:

1. **LICENSE.** Artist hereby grants to Newfields, under all of its rights in and to the Work, a royalty-free, worldwide, non-exclusive license to reproduce; distribute in any media, now known or later developed; publicly perform; and publicly display the Work, solely for the purpose(s) agreed to by the Artist in the Non-Exclusive Licensing Agreement. This license does not transfer copyrights or any other intellectual property and/or moral rights in the Work to Newfields.
2. **MODIFICATION.** Newfields may modify reproductions of the Work, solely to re-size and adapt the Work as appropriate to exercise the rights granted above. Newfields agrees that it will not make substantive changes to the Work without Artist's prior approval.
3. **CREDIT AND NOTICES.** Newfields agrees to place authorship credit on all copies of the Work; provided, however, that Newfields will not be obligated to do so if it deems such placement inappropriate due to artistic considerations. Unless otherwise stated, the copyright notice will appear as:

   "© [insert copyright notice]"

   Newfields agrees not to remove any copyright or other proprietary notices contained in the Work.
4. **OWNERSHIP.** Artist will retain title to the Work and all intellectual property rights subject to the license granted to Newfields in these Terms. Artist reserves all rights not granted under these Terms.
5. **LIMITATION OF LIABILITY.** Under no circumstances will Newfields or Artist be liable to the other party for any damages not expressly contemplated under these Terms, including but not limited to, consequential, special, or incidental.
6. **DURATION.** Unless terminated early pursuant to this Section, these Terms and this Agreement will continue until the end of the U.S. Copyright term in the Work (See, 17 U.S.C. § 302(a), life of the Artist plus seventy (70) years).
7. **TERMINATION.** Artist may terminate this Agreement for a material breach by Newfields of any material obligation of these Terms and this Agreement; provided, however, that prior to such termination, Artist provides Newfields with notice of such breach (including a description of the breach and the actions required to remedy the breach) and Newfields has ninety (90) calendar days to cure the breach. Newfields may terminate this Agreement at any time, for any reason or no reason, upon written notice to the Artist.
8. **SURVIVAL.** Sections 5 and 8 will survive the termination of this Agreement for any reason.
9. **GENERAL**. This Agreement and these Terms may be amended only by a writing clearly setting forth any amendment and signed by both parties. The parties are not independent contractors and partners, joint venturers, agents, or employer/employee of the other. Should any of the provisions of this Agreement be found unenforceable, the other provisions will be unaffected and will remain in full force and effect. These Terms and this Agreement will be governed and interpreted by Indiana law. The parties consent to the exclusive jurisdiction of the courts located in Indiana. These Terms, this Agreement, and all these provisions will be binding upon and inure to the benefit of the parties and their respective permitted successors and assigns.

Accession Number ____________________

New Mexico Museum of Art
NON-EXCLUSIVE COPYRIGHT LICENSE

Issue Date:
Name (s):
Address:

Telephone: Fax: Email:

I, , being the sole and exclusive owner of the copyright or the authorized representative of the rights holder to the following work(s):

in consideration of the acquisition of said work(s) by the New Mexico Museum of Art ("the Museum"), do hereby authorize the Museum to copy or reproduce said work(s) for all standard museum purposes (examples include, but are not limited to, educational materials, publicity and marketing purposes, books, exhibition catalogs, etc.), to distribute two-dimensional reproductions thereof to the public, to transmit or otherwise communicate a display thereof by all means or methods now known or hereafter invented in connection with standard museum activities (examples include, but are not limited to, printed material, film, television, DVD, social media and Internet use) without limit and without monetary compensation. The Museum will not copy or reproduce said work(s) for commercial use. The Museum is expressly authorized to sublicense the specific rights granted herein to third parties as necessary (at the discretion of the Museum) to fulfill its mission. Whenever feasible, the Museum shall include (and cause others to include) a copyright notice in connection with the above images, as prescribed by the Copyright Law of the United States. All copyrights in this work shall transfer to the New Mexico Museum of Art upon my death.

This non-exclusive license, which does not transfer ownership of the copyright to the Museum until my death, shall endure for the entire term of the copyright in and to said work, and shall survive all assignments of copyright according to U.S. Title § 17. Any transfer or assignment of the copyright shall be reported to the Head of Registration & Collections, New Mexico Museum of Art.

Signature of Copyright Holder______________________________ Date __________

Please sign and date both copies and return one to Head of Registration & Collections, New Mexico Museum of Art, PO Box 2087, Santa Fe, NM 87504-2087. Rev. 09/2003

STANDARD USE AGREEMENT

The University of Kansas, Spencer Museum of Art is honored to serve as the caretaker of great art. The following is a list of art held in the Spencer Museum of Art's collection for which you hold the copyright:

Artist Information

List of Artworks

WHEREAS**,** the University of Kansas, Spencer Museum of Art ("the Museum") has in its collection the artwork(s) listed and described above (hereafter "the Work(s)"); and

WHEREAS, the individual and/or representative signing this Standard Use Agreement (hereafter "the Copyright Holder") holds the copyright in the Work(s);

NOW THEREFORE, the parties agree to enter into this Standard Use Agreement (hereafter "the Agreement") to grant certain limited rights to the Museum in the Work(s) and govern the Museum's use of the Work(s) on the terms and conditions set forth in this Agreement.

I. REPRESENTATION AND WARRANTIES

A. The Copyright Holder represents and warrants that he/she has the right and authority to enter into this Agreement and to convey to the Museum the rights that are granted in this Agreement.

B. The Copyright Holder represents and warrants to the Museum that the rights granted in this Agreement will not infringe or misappropriate the copyright or other proprietary rights of any third party.

II. LICENSE TO USE THE WORK(S). With respect to the Work(s) identified in this agreement, the Copyright Holder hereby grants to the Museum a non-exclusive, worldwide, perpetual, royalty-free license for use of the Work(s) by the Museum in the following ways:

A. Reproduce the Work(s) through use of any technology now in existence or hereafter created, including through creation of digital images or other means of capturing the Work(s) in electronic or any other form (hereafter "the Reproductions").

B. Retain the Reproductions, in any format now in existence or hereafter created, in archives or databases maintained by the Museum.

C. Modify or adapt the Reproductions, without changing the context or substantive content; for example, for preservation, archival, translation, quality control, delivery and related purposes.

D. Distribute, display and otherwise make available copies of the Reproductions, as follows:
   i. Distribute, display and use the Reproductions for educational, scholarly and other non-commercial purposes. These uses may include; for example, allowing users to print out or save copies of the Reproductions, and distribute the Reproductions for research and teaching.
   ii. Distribute, display and use the Reproductions in the Museum's publicity materials, such as the Museum register, brochures, website and press releases.
   iii. Distribute and use the Reproductions on the Museum's website, social media accounts, and other websites or sources that host content on behalf of the Museum.

It is understood by both parties that no royalty payments will be made to the Copyright Holder by the Museum. The Museum acknowledges that it may not grant any rights in the Work(s) to any third parties and will refer third parties who have requested permission to reproduce the Works directly to the Copyright Holder to request such permission.

The parties acknowledge that the license granted in this Agreement is not exclusive, and does not give the Museum any ownership of or rights in the Work(s) other than the physical ownership of the Work(s) and right to use the Work(s) as described in this Agreement.

Consented and agreed,

Signature ______________________ Date ______________________

Printed Name ______________________

Name of Organization (if applicable) ______________________

Mailing Address ______________________ Email Address ______________________

Acknowledged and agreed,

____

Sofia Galarza Liu, Head of Collection Management, University of Kansas, Spencer Museum of Art

Yale University Art Gallery

The Yale University Art Gallery (YUAG) a part of Yale University, is a non-profit, educational institution dedicated to the promotion of art scholarship and teaching. In the course of meeting its mission to provide public access to its collections for the purposes of the study of art, the YUAG makes available to the public images and basic information about art works from its collections on its web site and searchable databases available through the Internet.

We are currently going through a process to make sure our paperwork is complete and find that we do not have a non-exclusive license form on file for all of your works in the collection.

While ownership of a work of art gives the YUAG the right to do a variety of things, it does not transfer copyright, which you retain. The non-exclusive license will grant us permission to use images of your work for Museum-related activities only. By signing this license, you grant the YUAG permission on a non-exclusive, worldwide, royalty-free basis, for the duration of the copyright, to reproduce, display, distribute and otherwise use images of your works listed in the attachment (the "Works") in the following ways without specific additional permission:

1. To make large images (i.e., images larger than a thumbnail) of the Works available publicly as part of the YUAG online collections database and the YUAG web site in electronic or digital format (note: Image will not be made available for download)

___ yes ___ no, please contact for written permission in each instance

2. To use images of the Works in YUAG publications (for example, exhibition and collection catalogues, annual reports, calendars of events, and visitor guides)

___ yes ___ no, please contact for written permission in each instance

3. To use images of the Works for Gallery Public Relations purposes of promoting objects or exhibitions (for example, news articles, reviews, and social media)

___ yes ___ no, please contact for written permission in each instance

It is understood that thumbnail images are distributed and made available publicly through the YUAG online collections database, YUAG web site and the Yale Digital Commons for all Works, for basic reference purposes. It is also understood that by granting non-exclusive permission yo do not assign the copyright to the YUAG.

Should the Museum acquire any other of my work(s) after the date of this non-exclusive license, its terms and conditions shall also extend to and include such work(s).

___ yes ___ no, please contact for written permission in each instance

All reproductions of the works will be accompanied by an appropriate copyright notice as indicated below (to be filled in by copyright owner or agent):

Copyright notice: ____

(Exact form of copyright notice)

I confirm that I have the right to permit the Yale University Art Gallery to use the Works as provided in this non-exclusive license and that, to the best of my knowledge, such use will not infringe or violate the rights of any other person or entity.

______________________________Signed: ____________Dated:

Please Print Name: ______________________________

Please provide contact information for additional permission requests and/or questions:

Name:____
Address: ____
Phone: (___) ___________
Email: _________________

Please sign and return this license and the objects list attached to the address below:

Yale University Art Gallery / Rights and Reproductions office
P.O. Box 208271, New Haven, CT 05620

John ffrench
Director of Visual Resources
Yale University Art Gallery
John.ffrench@yale.edu

See Attached for current Works in the Yale University Art Gallery

Updated: April, 2014

SAMPLE

Release Agreement

I, ____, on behalf of myself and/or my minor child, hereby grant to the J. Paul Getty Trust ("Getty"), without condition or further consideration, the exclusive [or non-exclusive] and irrevocable right and license to publish, reproduce, exhibit, and distribute the attached photograph of me and to use my name in connection therewith, in any medium now known or hereafter devised, including, but not limited to, print, video, electronic, and Internet applications, for use by representatives of the J. Paul Getty Trust, and any of its operating programs, for any lawful purpose, including, without limitation, books, web pages, exhibition brochures, and press and promotional materials relating to the Getty's photography collection and/or a specific exhibition. Use of my photograph and name for merchandise such as postcards and posters is specifically excluded from this Release and if such rights are requested, they shall be covered in a separate agreement.

I release the Getty, its trustees, agents, and advisors, from all claims, demands, liabilities, damages, costs and expenses (including attorneys' fees and expenses) that I may now or hereafter have against you or them arising in connection with the rights granted herein.

This Agreement shall be binding upon me and my heirs, personal representatives and assigns, and shall be governed by and construed under the laws of the State of California.

Nothing herein shall be deemed to obligate the Getty to exercise any of the rights, licenses and privileges herein granted.

____ / ______________________

Name (please print) Date

____

Signature

____

Address (please print)

____ / ______________________

City, State, Zip (please print) Phone

The Getty _______________ / _______________ use my name in program credits.

(May) (May not)

SAMPLE

If the photograph includes a minor:

____ / ______________________
Name of Child (please print) Date

____
Signature of Child

____ / ______________________
Name of Parent or Guardian (please print) Date

____
Signature of Parent or Guardian

____
Address (please print)

____ / ______________________
City, State, Zip (please print) Phone

Attach photograph.

NEWFIELDS

PHOTOGRAPHY / VIDEO / AUDIO RELEASE FORM

I hereby grant the Indianapolis Museum of Art, Inc. DBA Newfields ("Newfields") permission to interview me and use my name, voice, signature, photograph, image, and likeness in photograph, video, and audio materials in any and all printed and electronic publications and media applications (including, but not limited to, Newfields' main website and Newfields' external sites on Facebook. Twitter, YouTube, Flickr, ArtBabble, Tumblr, and Instagram).

Additionally, I grant Newfields a non-exclusive license in perpetuity to use the resulting materials for archival, educational, promotional, marketing, website, and such other purposes as Newfields will determine.

I will make no monetary or other claim against Newfields for the use of these materials.

NAME (print full name):______________________________

RELATION TO SUBJECT (if subject is a minor):______________________________

ADDRESS: ______________________________

____

____

TELEPHONE: ______________________________

E-MAIL: ______________________________

SIGNATURE: ______________________________

DATE: ______________________________

REQUESTED BY: ______________________________

PROJECT (exhibition, publication, etc.):______________________________

INTENDED USE(S) IF KNOWN:______________________________

SIGNATURE: ______________________________

DATE: ______________________________

4000 MICHIGAN ROAD · INDIANAPOLIS, IN 46208 · 317-923-1331 · DISCOVERNEWFIELDS.ORG

New Mexico **Museum of Art**

Release and Authorization to Use Likeness

This release and authorization is entered into as of _____________, 2009 by __________ ____________ and the New Mexico Museum of Art, a division of the Department of Cultural Affairs, State of New Mexico.

I, _______________________ hereby grant, free of charge and without remuneration, the New Mexico Museum of Art permission to reproduce my likeness, as depicted on ______ _________________________, in any and all media now and hereafter known, including the internet.

I release and discharge the New Mexico Museum of Art, each of the participating Museums, the Regents, the State of New Mexico, and the officers, agents, and employees of the aforementioned, from any and all claims and demands that may arise out of or in connection with the use of the image, including without limitation any and all claims for libel or violation of any right of publicity or privacy.

I am a legally competent adult and have the right to contract in my own name. I have read this document and fully understand its contents. This release shall be binding upon me and my heirs, legal representatives, and assigns.

____
Name

____
Signature

____
Date

Photograph Release Form

I hereby grant the **New Mexico Museum of Art** permission to use my likeness in a photograph or derivative art form, in any and all publications, including website entries, without payment or any other consideration.

I understand and agree that a scan or digital copy of these images will become the property of the **New Mexico Museum of Art** will not be returned.

I hereby irrevocably authorize the **New Mexico Museum of Art** to edit, alter, copy, exhibit, publish or distribute this photo for any lawful purpose. In addition, I waive the right to inspect or approve the finished product, including written or electronic copy, wherein my likeness appears. Additionally, I waive any right to royalties or other compensation arising or related to the use of the photograph.

I hereby hold harmless and release and forever discharge the **New Mexico Museum of Art** from all claims, demands, and causes of action which I, my heirs, representatives, executors, administrators, or any other persons acting on my behalf or on behalf of my estate have or may have by reason of this authorization.

I am at least 18 years of age and am competent to contract in my own name. I have read this release before signing below and I fully understand the contents, meaning, and impact of this release.

______________________________ ______________

(Signature) (Date)

____

(Printed Name)

If the person signing is under age 18, there must be consent by a parent or guardian, as follows:

I hereby certify that I am the parent or guardian of______________________, named above, and do hereby give my consent without reservation to the foregoing on behalf of this person.

______________________________ ______________

(Parent/Guardian's Signature) (Date)

____

(Parent/Guardian's Printed Name)

THE SIXTH FLOOR MUSEUM
AT DEALEY PLAZA

IMAGE RELEASE

I hereby grant permission to be photographed and/or filmed while visiting or participating in a program at The Sixth Floor Museum at Dealey Plaza. I understand that such photographs and video may be used in promotional materials for the Museum. I recognize that these images may be published in newspapers, magazines, promotional flyers, and/or Museum publications and website (www.jfk.org).

PLEASE PRINT CLEARLY:

Name ______________________________

Street Address ______________________________

City ______________________ State __________ Zip __________

Phone ______________________ Email ______________________

Signature: ______________________ Date: ______________________

If you received this form via email, please complete, sign and email it back to the sender. Or email it to ***media@jfk.org****.*

Questions? Please contact **info@jfk.org**

THE SIXTH FLOOR MUSEUM
AT DEALEY PLAZA

IMAGE RELEASE | MINOR

I hereby grant permission for my child to be photographed and/or filmed while visiting or participating in a program at The Sixth Floor Museum at Dealey Plaza. I understand that such photographs and video may be used in promotional materials for the Museum. I recognize that these images may be published in newspapers, magazines, promotional flyers, and/or Museum publications and website (www.jfk.org).

PLEASE PRINT CLEARLY:

Minor's Name ____________________

Guardian's Name ____________________

Street Address ____________________

City ____________________ State __________ Zip __________

Phone ____________________ Email ____________________

Guardian Signature: ____________________ Date: ____________________

If you received this form via email, please complete, sign and email it back to the sender. Or email it to ***media@jfk.org****.*

Questions? Please contact **info@jfk.org**

YALE
UNIVERSITY
ART
GALLERY

Yale University Art Gallery General Photo Release Form

Date:

Class/Event Title:

I, ___________________________, hereby give the Yale University Art Gallery permission to record my image and use it for educational, promotional, advertising, social media and other purposes that support the mission of the Gallery.

Name:

____
(Please print name clearly)

Phone: (____)______________________ type: cell:____ home:_____ work:_____

E-mail: ____@____________________

Signature:______________________________________ Date:__________________

FOR DEPARTMENT USE

Notes:

YALE
UNIVERSITY
ART
GALLERY

Yale University Art Gallery General Photo Release Form

Date:

School/Event Name:

I, ____________________________, hereby give the Yale University Art Gallery permission to photograph my child/children's (name) ____________________________, __________________________, __________________________ and use the image(s) for educational, promotional, advertising, social media and other purposes that support the mission of the Gallery. *The Yale University Art Gallery will never print a child's name along with a photo.

Child/children's Name:

____

____

____

(Please print name clearly)

Parent/Guardian Name:

____

(Please print name clearly)

Phone: (____)______________________ type: cell:____ home:_____ work:_____

E-mail: ______________________________________@____________________

Parent/Guardian Signature:_______________________________________

Date:____________________

FOR DEPARTMENT USE

Notes:

THE SIXTH FLOOR MUSEUM
AT DEALEY PLAZA

ORAL HISTORY INTERVIEW AGREEMENT

The purpose of The Sixth Floor Museum's Oral History Program is to gather and preserve information by means of video and audio recorded interviews. All or part of your interview will be available to the public, and may be publicly disseminated, including (but not limited to) by publication in all media currently in existence (e.g., print, graphic, film, internet and electronic media) or yet to be developed.

My signature below acknowledges that my interview was recorded and may be used as described above, and that my participation was entirely voluntary. Further, I hereby give, grant, donate and assign to the Dallas County Historical Foundation (the "Sixth Floor Museum") and its successors, licensees and assigns all copyrights, legal title, literary rights, and other rights in and to my interview, and the right to unrestricted use of my interview, unless otherwise specified below. I understand that because of this agreement my interview will belong to The Sixth Floor Museum and not to me or anyone holding under me, and that The Sixth Floor Museum may use my interview as it deems fit, subject to any restriction specified below.

For and in consideration of my agreement, I understand that at my request The Sixth Floor Museum will provide me with $10 and/or one free copy of my interview, to be used by me for my personal viewing only.

Additional Provisions or Restrictions:

Interviewee	**Interviewer**
Name: ______________________	Name: ______________________
Signature: ______________________	Signature: ______________________
Date: ______________________	Date: ______________________

The Sixth Floor Museum is a non-profit organization, operated under the auspices of the Dallas County Historical Foundation.

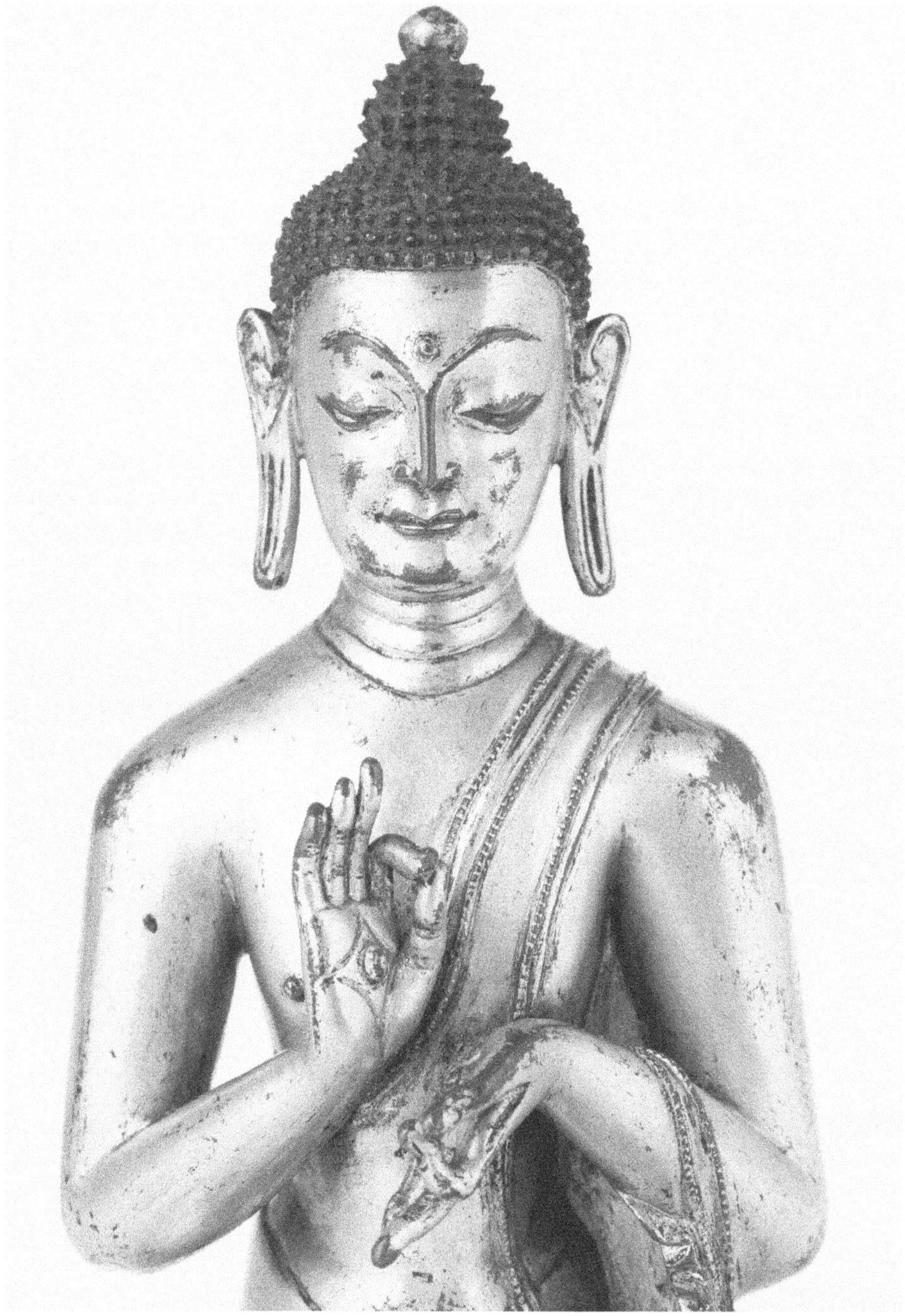

Appendix C

References and Resources

GENERAL INTELLECTUAL PROPERTY RESOURCES

- American Intellectual Property Law Association (AIPLA)
  www.aipla.org/Pages/default.aspx
- Brooklyn Museum Copyright Project
  www.brooklynmuseum.org/community/blogosphere/bloggers/tag/copyright
- Canadian Heritage Information Network (CHIN)
  www.rcip-chin.gc.ca/recherche-search-eng.jsp?No=0&Ne=0&Ntt=intellectual+property&QSo=Search
- Center for Intellectual Property and Innovation, Robert H. McKinney School of Law, Indiana University, Indianapolis
  http://mckinneylaw.iu.edu/ip/
- College Art Association (CAA)
  http://www.collegeart.org/standards-and-guidelines/intellectual-property
- Columbia University Copyright Advisory Office: Copyright Quick Guide
  https://copyright.columbia.edu/basics/copyright-quick-guide.html
- Copyright Advisory Network, American Library Association Office for Information Technology Policy
  http://librarycopyright.net/
- Copyright and Cultural Institutions: Guidelines for Digitization for U.S. Libraries, Archives, and Museums, Peter B. Hirtle, Emily Hudson, Andrew T. Kenyon, 2009
  http://ecommons.cornell.edu/bitstream/1813/14142/2/Hirtle-Copyright_final_RGB_lowres-cover1.pdf (free e-book)
  www.createspace.com/3405063 (to order printed version)
- Copyright for Librarians: the essential handbook from the Berkman Center for Internet and Society
  http://cyber.law.harvard.edu/publications/2013/copyright_for_librarians (free download)
- Copyrightlaws.com
  www.copyrightlaws.com/
- Copyright Term and the Public Domain in the United States (a.k.a. Hirtle's Chart)
  https://copyright.cornell.edu/publicdomain
- Copyright Watch
  www.copyright-watch.org/
- Cornell University Copyright Information Center
  https://copyright.cornell.edu/
- Developing Intellectual Property Policies: A How-To Guide for Museums, Canadian Heritage Information Network (CHIN)
  https://www.canada.ca/en/heritage-information-network/services/intellectual-property-copyright/guide-developing-intellectual-property-policies.html
- Digital Copyright Slider, American Library Association
  http://librarycopyright.net/resources/digitalslider/
- Durationator
  https://www.durationator.com/
- Intellectual Property Issues in Cultural Heritage (IPinCH): Theory, Practice, Policy, Ethics
  www.sfu.ca/ipinch
- Library Digitization Projects and Copyright
  https://www.llrx.com/
- Maryland Intellectual Property Legal Resource Center, University of Maryland
  www.law.umaryland.edu/programs/iplaw/miplrc/
- A Museum Guide to Digital Rights Management, Canadian Heritage Information Network (CHIN)

https://www.canada.ca/en/heritage-information-network/services/intellectual-property-copyright/guide-digital-rights-management.html

- Teaching Copyright, A project of the Electronic Frontier Foundation
www.teachingcopyright.org/
- University of Michigan Copyright Office
www.lib.umich.edu/copyright
- Visual Resources Association (VRA) Intellectual Property Rights (IPR) and Copyright
http://vraweb.org/resources/ipr-and-copyright/
- World Intellectual Property Organization (WIPO)
http://www.wipo.int/portal/en/index.html

PUBLIC DOMAIN AND ORPHAN WORKS

- Best Practices for Access to Images: Recommendations for Scholarly Use and Publishing, Max Planck Institute for the History of Science
https://www.mpiwg-berlin.mpg.de/PDF/MPIWGBestPracticesRecommendations.pdf
- Center for the Study of the Public Domain
https://law.duke.edu/cspd/
- Orphan Works and Mass Digitization, US Copyright Office
http://copyright.gov/orphan/reports/orphan-works2015.pdf
- *The Public Domain: How to Find & Use Copyright-Free Writings, Music, Art & More*, Stephen Fishman, 2014
https://store.nolo.com/products/the-public-domain-publ.html
- Section 108 of the US Copyright Code Spinner
http://librarycopyright.net/resources/spinner/
- Society of American Archivists (SAA) Orphan Works: Statement of Best Practices
https://www2.archivists.org/sites/all/files/OrphanWorks-June2009.pdf
- Standards and Guidelines: Copyrights and Permissions in Scholarly and Educational Publishing, College Art Association
http://www.collegeart.org/standards-and-guidelines/guidelines/educationsl-publishing-permissions
- Statement of Best Practices in Fair Use of Collections Containing Orphan Works for Libraries, Archives, and Other Memory Institutions, Center for Media and Social Impact
http://www.cmsimpact.org/fair-use/best-practices/statement-best-practices-fair-use-orphan-works-libraries-archives

FAIR USE

- Association of Research Libraries (ARL) Code of Best Practices in Fair Use for Academic and Research Libraries
www.arl.org/pp/ppcopyright/codefairuse/code/index.shtml
- Code of Best Practices in Fair Use for Online Video, Center for Social Media, School of Communication, American University
http://www.cmsimpact.org/sites/default/files/online_best_practices_in_fair_use.pdf
- Code of Best Practices in Fair Use for Poetry, Center for Media & Social Impact, School of Communication, and the Program on Information Justice and Intellectual Property, Washington College of Law, American University
http://cmsimpact.org/wp-content/uploads/2016/01/fairusepoetrybooklet_singlepg_3.pdf
- College Art Association, "Code of Best Practices in Fair Use for the Visual Arts"
http://www.collegeart.org/pdf/fair-use/best-practices-fair-use-visual-arts.pdf
- Documentary Filmmakers' Statement of Best Practices in Fair Use, Center for Social Media, School of Communications, American University
www.cmsimpact.org/sites/default/files/fair_use_final.pdf
- Fair Use, Free Speech & Intellectual Property, Center for Media and Social Impact, School of Communications, American University
http://cmsimpact.org/program/fair-use/
- Fair Use Evaluator, American Library Association
http://librarycopyright.net/resources/fairuse/
- The Fair Use Network
http://fairusenetwork.com/
- Guidelines for the Use of Copyrighted Materials and Works of Art by Art Museums, Association of Art Museum Directors
https://www.aamd.org/sites/default/files/document/Guidelines%20for%20the%20Use%20of%20Copyrighted%20Materials.pdf
- *Reclaiming Fair Use: How to Put Balance Back in Copyright*

Patricia Aufderheide and Peter Jaszi, 2011
http://press.uchicago.edu/ucp/books/book/chicago/R/bo11671240.html
- US Copyright Office Fair Use Index
http://copyright.gov/fair-use/index.html
- Visual Resources Association (VRA) Statement on the Fair Use of Images for Teaching, Research, and Study
www.vraweb.org/organization/pdf/VRAFairUseGuidelinesFinal.pdf

COMMONS

- Creative Commons
http://creativecommons.org/
- Flickr Commons
www.flickr.com/commons
- OpenGLAM
http://openglam.org/
- Wikimedia Commons
http://commons.wikimedia.org/wiki/Main_Page

SAMPLE OPEN ACCESS POLICIES

- MIT Faculty Open Access Policy, Scholarly Publishing at MIT Libraries
https://libraries.mit.edu/scholarly/mit-open-access/open-access-at-mit/mit-open-access-policy/
- Yale University Policy: Open Access to Digital Representations of Works in the Public Domain from Museum, Library, and Archive Collections
http://ydc2.yale.edu/sites/default/files/OpenAccessLAMSFinal.pdf

SELECTION OF CULTURAL INSTITUTIONS WITH OPEN ACCESS PROGRAMS[1]

- British Library
https://imagesonline.bl.uk/?service=page&action=show_home_page&language=en
- Brooklyn Museum
http://www.brooklynmuseum.org/opencollection/collections/
- Davidson Art Center at Wesleyan University
http://dac-collection.wesleyan.edu/4DACTION/HANDLECGI/Search?display=POR
- Freer|Sackler Museums, Smithsonian Institution
http://www.asia.si.edu/collections/edan/default.cfm
- Indianapolis Museum of Art at Newfields
https://discovernewfields.org/collections
- J. Paul Getty Museum
http://www.getty.edu/about/opencontent.html
- Library of Congress Prints and Photographs
http://www.loc.gov/pictures/
- Los Angeles County Museum of Art
http://collections.lacma.org/
- Medical Heritage Library
http://www.medicalheritage.org/historical-american-medical-journals/
- Metropolitan Museum of Art
http://www.metmuseum.org/collection
- Museum of New Zealand Te Papa Tongarewa
http://collections.tepapa.govt.nz/
- National Gallery of Art, Washington, DC
https://images.nga.gov/en/page/show_home_page.html
- National Library of the Netherlands Manuscripts
http://manuscripts.kb.nl/
- New York Public Library
http://digitalcollections.nypl.org/
- Rijksmuseum
https://www.rijksmuseum.nl/en/rijksstudio
- Statens Museum for Kunst (National Gallery of Denmark)
http://www.smk.dk/en/use-of-images-and-text/free-download-of-artworks/
- Victoria and Albert Museum
http://collections.vam.ac.uk/
- Walters Art Museum
http://art.thewalters.org/
- Yale Center for British Art
http://britishart.yale.edu/collections
- Yale University Art Gallery
http://artgallery.yale.edu/collection/search

COPYRIGHT HOLDERS AND COPYRIGHT REGISTRATION

- Accessible Registries of Rights Information and Orphan Works (ARROW)
http://www.dlib.org/dlib/january12/caroli/01caroli.html
- Artists Rights Society (ARS)
www.arsny.com/
- Bridgeman Copyright
http://www.bridgemanimages.com/en-US/bridgeman-copyright-service

Canadian Artists Representation Copyright Collective (CARCC)
www.carcc.ca/main-E.html

- Canadian Copyrights Database
http://strategis.ic.gc.ca/app/cipo/copyrights/displaySearch.do?language=eng
- The Catalog of Copyright Entries
http://onlinebooks.library.upenn.edu/cce/
- Catalogue Raisonné Scholars Association
https://www.catalogueraisonne.org/
- College Art Association (CAA) Obituaries
www.collegeart.org/news/category/obituaries/
- Copyright Renewal Database, Stanford University Libraries
http://collections.stanford.edu/copyrightrenewals/bin/page?forward=home
- The Design and Artists Copyright Society (DACS)
https://www.dacs.org.uk/home
- International Foundation for Art Research Catalogues Raisonnés
www.ifar.org/cat_rais.php
- Library of Congress, Rights and Restrictions
www.loc.gov/rr/print/res/rights.html
- National Archives and Records Administration's Source and Permissions Contact List
http://www.archives.gov/research/order/film-sources-contact-list.html
- US Copyright Office, Copyright Information Center
www.copyright.gov/
- US Social Security Death Index, 1935–2014
http://search.ancestry.com/search/db.aspx?dbid=3693
- Writers, Artists and Their Copyright Holders (The WATCH File)
http://tyler.hrc.utexas.edu/index.cfm

VISUAL WORKS IMAGE RESOURCES AND LICENSING

- Art Resource
www.artres.com
- Artstor Images for Academic Publishing
http://www.artstor.org/content/collaborations
- Bridgeman Education
http://www.bridgemaneducation.com/en/
- Bridgeman Images
http://www.bridgemanimages.com/en-US/
- Christian Copyright Licensing International
www.ccli.com/
- Digital Public Library of America (DPLA)
http://dp.la/
- Europeana
https://www.europeana.eu/portal/en
- Getty Images
www.gettyimages.com/
- LIBLICENSE Project
http://liblicense.crl.edu/
- The Public Domain Review
http://publicdomainreview.org/

MUSICAL WORKS AND SOUND RECORDINGS

- American Society of Composers, Authors & Publishers (ASCAP)
www.ascap.com/
- Broadcast Music, Inc. (BMI)
www.bmi.com/
- BZ Rights and Permissions, Inc.
www.bzrights.com
- Harry Fox Agency
www.harryfox.com
- Music Library Association (MLA)
https://www.musiclibraryassoc.org/
- Music Publishers' Association (MPA) Directory of Music Publishers
http://www.mpa.org/directory-of-music-publishers/
- Music Publishers' Association (MPA) Copyright Search Information Resource
http://www.mpa.org/content/copyright-search
- Parker Music Group
www.parkermusicgroup.net
- Recording Industry Association of America (RIAA)
www.riaa.com
- Recording Industry Sourcebook
http://isourcebook.com
- SESAC
www.sesac.com/
- Society of Composers, Authors and Music Publishers of Canada (SOCAN)
www.socan.ca/jsp/en/about/

DRAMATIC AND LITERARY WORKS

- Access © (Copyright)
www.accesscopyright.ca/
- Authors
www.authors.com/
- Authors' Licensing and Collecting Society (ALCS)
www.alcs.co.uk/
- The Authors Registry
www.authorsregistry.org/

- Baker's Plays Pioneer Drama
  www.bakersplays.com/store/index.php
- Broadway Play Publishing, Inc. (BPPI)
  www.broadwayplaypubl.com/
- Copyright Clearance Center (CCC)
  www.copyright.com/
- Copyright Licensing Agency (CLA)
  www.cla.co.uk/
- Dramatists Play Service, Inc.
  www.dramatists.com/
- Dramatic Publishing
  www.dramaticpublishing.com/
- HathiTrust
  http://www.hathitrust.org/
- Musical Theatre International (MTI)
  www.mtishows.com/
- Publications Rights Clearinghouse (PRC)
  http://nwu.org/publications-rights-clearinghouse/
- Rodgers & Hammerstein Organization
  www.rnh.com/
- Samuel French, Inc.
  www.samuelfrench.com/store/index.php
- Tams-Witmark Music Library, Inc.
  http://www.tamswitmark.com/

PHOTOGRAPHIC AND GRAPHIC WORKS

- Advertising Photographers of America
  www.apanational.org
- American Society of Picture Professionals
  www.aspp.com
- The American Society of Media Photographers
  www.asmp.org
- Graphic Artists Guild
  https://www.graphicartistsguild.org/
- List of stock photo agencies
  www.mindspring.com/~frankn/photo/stock.html
- National Press Photographers Association
  www.nnpa.org
- Professional Photographers of America
  www.ppa.com

MOTION PICTURE AND AUDIOVISUAL WORKS

- Criterion Pictures
  www.criterionpic.com/
- Internet Movie Database (IMDB)
  www.imdb.com
- Kino International
  https://www.kinolorber.com/
- Motion Picture Licensing Corporation
  www.mplc.com/
- Swank Motion Pictures, Inc.
  www.swank.com/

COMICS, CARTOONS, AND EDITORIALS

- Andrews McMeel Syndication
  http://syndication.andrewsmcmeel.com/
- The Cartoon Bank
  www.cartoonbank.com/
- CartoonStock
  www.cartoonstock.com/
  Tribune Content Agency: Comicshttps://tribunecontent-agency.com/premium-content/comics/
- EToon
  www.etoon.com
- King Features Syndicate
  www.kingfeatures.com

PROFESSIONAL ASSOCIATION LISTSERVS AND DISCUSSION GROUPS

- Art Libraries Society of North America (ARLIS/NA) Listserv
  https://www.arlisna.org/about/arlis-l
- Canadian Heritage Information Network (CHIN) Listserv
  https://www.canada.ca/en/heritage-information-network.html
- Collections Stewardship Professional Network of the American Alliance of Museums (CSAAM) Listserv
  https://www.collectionsstewardship.org/listserve/
- ImageMuse
  https://imagemuse.groups.io/g/main
- Museum Computer Network (MCN), Intellectual Property Special Interest Group (IPSIG)
  http://mcn.edu/community/special-interest-groups-sigs/intellectual-property-sig/
- Museum Intellectual Property (MUSIP)
  https://groups.io/g/musip
- Society of American Archivists (SAA) Listservs
  http://www2.archivists.org/listservs
- Visual Resources Association (VRA) Listserv
  http://vraweb.org/membership/vral/

SELECTION OF ONLINE RIGHTS AND REPRODUCTIONS REQUEST FORMS

- Brooklyn Museum
  https://brooklynmuseum.wufoo.com/forms/brooklyn-museum-image-request
- Indianapolis Museum of Art at Newfields
  https://discovernewfields.org/application/files/1515/0895/3058/Newfields_Image_Request_Form.pdf
- Indianapolis Museum of Art Archives at Newfields
  https://discovernewfields.org/application/files/9315/0827/1319/IMA_Archives_Reproduction_Request_Form.pdf
- J. Paul Getty Museum
  www.getty.edu/legal/image_request/index.html
- New Mexico Museum of Art
  http://nmartmuseum.org/education/research-and-reproductions
- The Sixth Floor Museum at Dealey Plaza
  https://www.jfk.org/the-collections/rights-reproductions-request-form/
- Spencer Museum of Art
  https://spencerart.ku.edu/image-services
- Yale University Art Gallery
  http://artgallery.yale.edu/rights-and-reproductions-request-form-new

SELECTION OF ONLINE RIGHTS AND REPRODUCTIONS FEE SCHEDULES

- Brooklyn Museum
  https://d1lfxha3ugu3d4.cloudfront.net/info/docs/Image_Service_Fee_Schedule_2016_updated.pdf
- Indianapolis Museum of Art at Newfields
  https://discovernewfields.org/application/files/8315/0733/2356/RR_FeeSchedule_Newfields_2017.pdf
- Indianapolis Museum of Art Archives at Newfields
  https://discovernewfields.org/application/files/9215/0723/9098/IMA_Archives_Reproduction_Fee_Schedule.pdf
- J. Paul Getty Museum
  www.getty.edu/legal/image_request/fees_schedule.pdf
- New Mexico Museum of Art
  http://nmartmuseum.org/assets/files/policies/Photo%20Fee%20Schedule-2017.pdf
- Spencer Museum of Art
  http://www.spencerart.ku.edu/collection/rights.shtml

2014 ONLINE IMAGE USE SURVEY

A short survey was conducted by the authors using Survey Monkey from December 11 through December 31, 2014, to attempt an informal quantification of the size of digital image files utilized by cultural institutions in online collection databases and institutional blogs. Volunteers to complete the survey were sought by posting the survey link to three listservs: Museum IP, RCAAM Listserv, and Museum Discussion List. The following data is the quantification of the replies to the questions posed to the respondents.[2]

100 TOTAL RESPONDENTS' WORK DEMOGRAPHICS:

- 72% work in a museum
  - 67%—art museums
  - 13%—history museums
  - 5%—natural history/anthropology
  - 15%—other type of museum
- 17% work in a university
  - 69%—museum/gallery
  - 8%—library
  - 3%—archive
  - 20%—other
- 11% work in another type of institution

ONLINE COLLECTION DATABASES:

- Question to Respondents:
  - Do you have a standard file size for the digital images your institution uses for its online collection database?
- General Reply:
  - Yes: 67%
  - No: 33%
  - 46 respondents self-selected to reply to the open-ended question, "Other type of standard?" to which they noted they have larger standards for images in the public domain or if they have permission from the copyright holder, but those standards were not explicitly outlined by the respondents.
- Digital Image File Specifications:
  - *maximum height (pixels):*
    - 51 respondents
    - smallest standard: 200 pixels
    - largest standard: 19000 pixels
    - average standard: 1729 pixels
    - median standard: 900 pixels

- *maximum width (pixels):*
  - 50 respondents
  - smallest standard: 200 pixels
  - largest standard: 19000 pixels
  - average standard: 1849 pixels
  - median standard: 1024 pixels
- *maximum resolution (dpi):*
  - 50 respondents
  - smallest standard: 72 dpi (36% of respondents)
  - largest standard: 2400 dpi
  - average standard: 247 dpi
  - median standard: 150 dpi

INSTITUTIONAL BLOGS

- Question to Respondents:
  - Do you have a standard file size for the digital images your institution uses on blogs?
- General Reply:
  - 86 respondents
  - Yes: 31.4%
  - No: 41.86%
  - Do Not use images: 26.74%
- Digital Image File Specifications:
  - *maximum height (pixels):*
    - 17 respondents
    - smallest standard: 350 pixels
    - largest standard: 1536 pixels
    - average standard: 934 pixels
    - median standard: 850 pixels
  - *maximum width (pixels):*
    - 20 respondents
    - smallest standard: 400 pixels
    - largest standard: 2100 pixels
    - average standard: 1030 pixels
    - median standard: 1000 pixels
  - *maximum resolution (dpi):*
    - 20 respondents
    - smallest standard: 72 dpi (73% of respondents)
    - largest standard: 300 dpi
    - average standard: 98 dpi
    - median standard: 72 dpi

2018 ONLINE IMAGE USE SURVEY

This survey was conducted using Survey Monkey from February 11 through March 12, 2018. The respondents were gathered by posting the survey link to three museum listservs: Museum IP, RCAAM Listserv, and Museum Discussion List.

86 overall respondents

1. Do you have a standard file size for the digital images your institution uses for its online collection database? (86 respondents)
   a. Yes—54.65%
   b. No—27.91%
   c. Do Not Use Images—1.16%
   d. Other—16.28%
      i. Of those selecting "other" 43% do not have an online collections database
      ii. Of those selecting "other" 21% have varying sizes depending on several factors, including the copyright right status
2. What is your standard file size for digital images for your online collection database? (Leave blank if you do not have a max/min standard) (54 respondents and 32 overall respondents left question blank)

   Largest maximum height: 4096 pixels
   Smallest maximum height: 300 pixels
   Average maximum height: 1371 pixels
   Median maximum height: 1000 pixels

   Largest maximum width: 4288 pixels
   Smallest maximum width: 300 pixels
   Average maximum width: 654 pixels
   Median maximum width: 600 pixels

   Largest minimum height: 3750 pixels
   Smallest minimum height: 0 pixels
   Average minimum height: 1022 pixels
   Median minimum height: 550 pixels

   Largest minimum width: 6000 pixels
   Smallest minimum width: 0 pixels
   Average minimum width: 1294 pixels
   Median minimum width: 550 pixels

   Largest maximum resolution: 2400 pixels
   Smallest maximum resolution: 72 pixels
   Average maximum resolution: 308 pixels
   Median maximum resolution: 300 pixels

Largest minimum resolution: 600 pixels
Smallest minimum resolution: 0 pixels
Average minimum resolution: 202 pixels
Median minimum resolution: 72 pixels

3. Do you have a standard file size for the digital images your institution uses on blogs? (85 respondents)
   a. Yes—24.71%
   b. No—57.65%
   c. Do Not Use Images—5.88%
   d. Other—11.76%
      i. Of those selecting "other" 20% do not know if their institution has a standard
      ii. Of those selecting "other" 30% do not have blogs
4. What is your standard file size for digital images on your institution uses on blogs? (Leave blank if you do not have a max/min standard) (22 respondents and 64 overall respondents left question blank)

Largest maximum height: 2000 pixels
Smallest maximum height: 475 pixels
Average maximum height: 1013 pixels
Median maximum height: 1000 pixels

Largest maximum width: 2000 pixels
Smallest maximum width: 300 pixels
Average maximum width: 894 pixels
Median maximum width: 1000 pixels

Largest minimum height: 1240 pixels
Smallest minimum height: 249 pixels
Average minimum height: 654 pixels
Median minimum height: 475 pixels

Largest minimum width: 1240 pixels
Smallest minimum width: 475 pixels
Average minimum width: 654 pixels
Median minimum width: 475 pixels

Largest maximum resolution: 1200 pixels
Smallest maximum resolution: 72 pixels
Average maximum resolution: 313 pixels
Median maximum resolution: 300 pixels

Largest minimum resolution: 1200 pixels
Smallest minimum resolution: 72 pixels
Average minimum resolution: 276 pixels
Median minimum resolution: 186 pixels

5. Have your standard files sizes changed in the last 5 years? (85 respondents)
   a. Yes—32.82%
   b. No—61.18%
6. If so, why? (35 respondents)
   - Our old website restricted images to 500 pixels on the longest edge. We transitioned to eMuseum, which gave us more flexibility and felt comfortable with the standards we decided for ourselves.
   - Change in Collections Mangers. Instituted standard for file format and dpi.
   - New norms in the field.
   - Increased institutional acceptance of fair use and willingness to take on a greater risk of using larger files online, as the repercussions from rights holders to these types of uses has been minimal, if existent at all. Also, for online collection pages there is no maximum file size (pixels or dpi) that is defined, because of Open Access the largest, high resolution files are made accessible online.
   - Standardizing for uniformity; sized up to meet users' expectations of larger, more useful images.
   - We're moving toward more of an open-access-like policy with our images in the public domain. We're committed to making our collections accessible and available to researchers, publishers, and the general public in support of scholarship, education, and personal enrichment.
   - More server space.
   - CMS, PastPerfect, was able to handle higher resolution images.
   - We allowed for higher res jpg files on the database. They were previously thumbnail size to avoid copyright issues.
   - In response to fair use and specifically VAGA's concerns about sizes used online.
   - We have only begun to formally digitize our collections in the last three years.
   - Standardized hi-res larger formats to reduce the need to re-photograph objects for research/display purposes.
   - High-res capabilities; staff support for imaging initiatives and file management.
   - We upgraded our procedure to better suit growing tech.
   - For our website, yes, because we redesigned the site to be responsive, so we need larger images now. Our

standard size for the online collection has not changed, but we are currently working on a new system for the online collection as well and will update our image size in response to the design of the site.
- Blog standards changed to reflect a new branding standard at our institution.
- We have been using 600px @ 72ppi but are considering changing to 1200px. We will be adopting a Fair Use Policy and will be Open Access this year so we're working on deciding how we want to use it.
- Internal push to share more of the collection online, but not in formats that would impact image order sales.
- Went from 200 to 600 DPI to increase clarity when printed.
- We reduced the file size due to database capacity.
- We did not have a system to capture images five years ago. At the beginning of the photo project, we established standards for resolution, if not actual image measurements.
- Generally we use more hi-res images than before thanks to the technology of our digital camera
- To meet ARS/VAGA requirements
- Collection had too many low resolution images only.
- Website redesign. ARS rider to Artstor contract influenced image size decisions at that time.
- We changed to Mimsy database and had to adhere to their standards.
- Public expectations have changed. They expect easy access and decent file sizes (at least 300dpi).
- Standardization is now implemented.
- Changed DAM (from PastPerfect-Online to CONTENTdm), hired two-year contract position for digital collections to work out more sophisticated workflows, leadership relaxed access restrictions (lifted watermark requirement on digital images).
- No, but our standard thumbnails (currently 249px max H or W) will be larger before too long, now that the AAMD document on which that 249px practice was based has been supplanted.
- With the AAMD thumbnail policy change, we increased our file sizes accordingly (from 250 to 480 in most cases).
- Demand and increased technological standards.
- We are a new institution and only recently standardized.
- Expectations of the quality of image, change in overall thinking regarding images and copyright.

7. Does your institution currently follow any of the following guidelines/codes of best practices for online image uses? (85 respondents)
   - Guidelines for The Use of Copyrighted Materials and Works of Art By Art Museums, which replaced the Association of Art Museum Directors (AAMD) Policy on the Use of "Thumbnail" Digital Images in Museum Online Initiatives—30.59%
   - College Art Association (CAA) Code of Best Practices in Fair Use for the Visual Arts—29.41%
   - Association of Research Libraries (ARL) Code of Best Practices in Fair Use for Academic and Research Libraries—4.71%
   - Visual Resources Association (VRA) Statement on the Fair Use of Images for Teaching, Research, and Study—11.76%
   - A Museum Guide to Digital Rights Management, Canadian Heritage Information Network—1.18%
   - We do not follow a specific guideline/code of best practice—29.41%
   - In-house created guidelines or standards—48.24%
   - Others—5.88%
     - Creative Commons
     - Best practices for orphans
     - Used other guidelines as templates to create one that works for our organization
     - Federal Agencies Digital Guidelines Initiative
8. Does your institution earn income from licensing images? (84 respondents)
   a. Yes—47.62%
   b. No, we have an Open Access Policy—20.24%
   c. We have a limited Open Access Policy—10.71%
   d. Other? —21.43%
      i Of those selecting "other" 33% do not license images
      ii. Of those selecting "other" 28% only charge fees to for-profit companies
9. What type of institution do you work at? (86 respondents)
   a. Art Museum—31.40%
   b. History Museum—30.23%
   c. Natural History/Anthropology Museum—3.49%
   d. Science Museum—1.16%
   e. Archive (stand-alone)—0.00%

f. Library (stand-alone)—1.16%
g. University Art Museum—16.28%
h. University History Museum—1.16%
i. University Natural History/Anthropology Museum—1.16%
j. University Science Museum—0.00%
k. University Archive—0.00%
l. University Library—1.16%
m. Other (please specify)—12.79%
i. Other museums include: general, multi-disciplinary, children's, historic site, and private foundation

NOTES

1. For a more extensive list of Open Access programs see Andrea Wallace and Douglas McCarthy, Survey of GLAM open access policies [2.0], accessed May 14, 2018, https://docs.google.com/spreadsheets/d/1WPSKJptUJ-o8SXtg00llcxq0IKJu8eO6Ege_GrLaNc/

2. See chapter 4, Online Image Use Survey, for a more detailed interpretation of the survey results.

Glossary

Appeal: The legal process by which the non-prevailing party seeks the review of a lower court's decision by a higher court to reverse the lower court's judgment or grant a new trial.

Application Program Interface (API): A set of routines, protocols, and tools that accomplish a specific task to communicate with a specific software component. A typical use in the cultural sector is to provide access to collections, metadata, and image databases with the goal of providing external users and collaborators with images and data for use in their own systems.

Appropriation: The act of taking possession of another's property; the act of incorporating pre-existing artwork or other creative material in a new work. The use of appropriated material that is protected by intellectual property laws may raise issues of infringement and fair use as well as rights of privacy or publicity.

Assignment: The transfer of ownership of specified intellectual property rights from one person or entity to another. Under US law intellectual property rights, including copyright, are freely assignable unless otherwise prohibited by contract. In some foreign intellectual property regimes, certain intellectual property rights, referred to generally as "moral rights," cannot be assigned under any circumstances. In the United States an assignment must be in writing and the assignment may be recorded with the Copyright Office.

Attribution: Credit; the act of ascribing a work (as of literature or art) to a particular author or artist. Used in the Creative Commons attribution license (CC BY) that requires only credit to the original creator when reusing a work (see Creative Commons).

Author: For copyright, the person(s) who created the copyrighted work or, under US copyright law, if the work is a work for hire, the employer, or commissioning party.

Bargain: A voluntary agreement between parties for the exchange of a specific promise or performance.

Berne Convention: Also known as the Berne Convention for the Protection of Literary and Artistic Works. An international agreement establishing copyrights relations among nations. The first Berne Convention was adopted in Berne, Switzerland, in 1886. The Berne Convention requires each signatory country to provide national treatment to copyright owners of other signatory countries. The convention requires a minimal level of copyright protection. The United States became a signatory to the Berne Convention effective March 1, 1989.

Cease and Desist: A demand, usually in writing, made by or on behalf of the presumptive holder of an intellectual property (such as copyright or trademark) or similar (such as invasion of privacy) right, to an alleged infringer to stop ("cease and desist") a use that purportedly infringes or violates a right.

Collections Management System (CMS): A computer program that facilitates the administrative responsibilities (cataloguing, accessioning, tracking loans, exhibition planning, digital image retrieval, copyright management, etc.) associated with the documentation and stewardship of a cultural institution's holdings.

Comma-Separated Values (CSV): A file format commonly used for transmitting tabular data between disparate systems.

Commission: A form of business transaction in which an artist or other creative professional is hired, usually as an independent contractor, to create a specified work for an agreed-on price and subject to other terms and conditions negotiated by the parties. The terms and conditions of a commission are often memorialized in a written commission agreement.

Common Law: Law derived from custom and judicial precedent, including opinions written by judges.

Consultant: A person or organization engaged under contract on a temporary basis to provide recommendations, specialist, or professional advice, or to assist in decision making. Generally, it is the advisory nature distinguishing the work of a consultant from other contractors.

Contract: A transaction between parties in which there is a mutual agreement to be bound and obligated to the other for the specific performance promised through the consideration given by each party, respectively.

Contractor: A person who is hired to perform specified service(s) during a specified period of time and for a specified compensation. A person's status as a contractor (rather than as an employee) has important implications under tax, employment, and intellectual property laws. Designation as a contractor depends principally on whether the person performing the work controls how, when, and with what tools the work is performed. Absent a written "work-for-hire" agreement for a work within one of nine categories enumerated in the Copyright Act, a contractor retains copyright ownership of any work created in the course of providing the contracted-for services.

Contributory Liability: When a third party is held liable for the actions of other parties based on their relationship with the actual negligence, infringement, or harm caused by knowingly encouraging, enabling, or benefitting from it.

Copyright: A system of legal protection for original works of expression that are "fixed" in a tangible medium. To be eligible for copyright protection, the work must meet certain minimum thresholds of originality and not otherwise be precluded from the scope of applicable copyright law (e.g., under US law, works created by employees of the federal government within the scope of their employment). Ideas are not eligible for copyright protection. Under current US law, copyright arises upon creation and fixation in a tangible medium, and there are no longer any formalities (such as notice and registration) required to acquire or maintain copyright. For works eligible for copyright protection, copyright laws typically grant a broad set of exclusive rights to control the use and exploitation of the work that may last for many decades. Copyright laws also typically include a certain range of exceptions to the copyright owners' exclusive rights, including an exception for fair use (in the United States) and fair dealing (in the United Kingdom and other common law countries) (see Fair Use).[1]

Copyright Administrator: The individual or institution that manages the copyright rights in a work on behalf of the work's author.

Copyright Notice: A notation attached to a creative work indicating the copyright owner of the work. The copyright notice may take a variety of forms depending on applicable law. In the United States the most common form is © [year of first publication] [name of copyright owner].

Copyright Owner: The person or entity that owns one or more of the exclusive rights of copyright in a work. Initially, the copyright owner may be: the author, the employer of the author if the work is created within the scope of the author's employment, or the person or entity commissioning the author pursuant to a valid written "work-for-hire" agreement for a work within nine categories enumerated in the Copyright Act. The copyright owner may transfer some or all the rights by way of an assignment or allow another person or entity to exercise some or all the rights pursuant to a license, which may be exclusive or nonexclusive. The copyright owner may also designate a copyright administrator to manage its copyrights on its behalf (see Rights Holder).

Copyright Registration: The process of obtaining a registration from the US Copyright Office for a copyrighted work. Although, under current US copyright law, copyright inheres in a work on its creation and fixation in a tangible medium of expression, timely registration of the copyright has certain benefits. Registration for an American work is a precondition to bringing a lawsuit for infringement. Previously, obtaining a valid copyright registration was required to maintain copyright, and failure to maintain that registration resulted in the work entering the public domain.

Core Work: The original creative work (literary, musical, dramatic, or artistic work) from which a derivative work may be made.

Creative Commons Licenses: A series of standardized prescriptive licenses made available by Creative Commons that a copyright owner may voluntarily attach to works otherwise protected by copyright, giving permission to use the work for certain purposes specified in the license without the need to contact the owner. Creative Commons licenses allow for a range of permitted uses and may impose certain requirements such as attribution (CC BY) and pass-through (CC SA "Share and ShareAlike") as follows:

- Public Domain Mark: allows any user to "mark" the work as being in the public domain
- CC0: waives all rights and places the work in the public domain
- CC BY: attribution required
- CC BY-ND: attribution required, no derivatives allowed
- CC BY-NC-SA: attribution required, noncommercial only, sharealike (allows derivatives as long as licensed under identical terms)
- CC BY-SA: attribution required, sharealike
- CC BY-NC: attribution required, noncommercial only
- CC BY-NC-ND: attribution required, noncommercial only, no derivatives[2]

Credit Line: Attribution for contribution to a creative work. The format and placement of a credit line vary depending on the type of creative work and applicable standards and practices (see Attribution).

Cultural Institutions: Includes, but is not limited to, public and private museums, libraries, archives, and historical property associations, educational institutions including colleges and universities, and all other entities engaged in the collection, preservation, interpretation, and dissemination of cultural heritage.

Damages: Monetary compensation awarded by the law to an injured party for recompense to a legal wrong. Damages may take a variety of forms, but two of the most common are:

- Actual: Measurable monetary losses the injured party actually sustained as a result of the legal wrong that can be awarded.
- Statutory: Minimum and maximum monetary award amounts that are stipulated within the applicable statute(s) in a given legal dispute and are not measured by the injured party's actual losses.

Declaratory Judgment: A form of legal action in which the plaintiff seeks a preemptive ruling from the court on the legality of a proposed action. In the copyright context, for example, a plaintiff might seek a declaratory judgment that a use not authorized by the copyright owner is a non-infringing fair use.

Defamation: Making of false public statements damaging another's reputation. Truth and opinion are defenses to a claim of defamation (see Libel and Slander).

Derivative Work: A work based upon one or more preexisting works, such as a translation, musical arrangement, dramatization, fictionalization, motion picture version, sound recording, art reproduction, abridgment, condensation, or any other form in which a work may be recast, transformed, or adapted. A work consisting of editorial revisions, annotations, elaborations, or other modifications that, as a whole, represent an original work of authorship is a "derivative work."[3] Under US copyright law, the copyright owner has the right to control the creation and distribution of derivative works.

Digital Asset Management System (DAMS): A digital program used for storing, managing, and retrieving digital assets, such as images or videos of collection objects.

Digital Millennium Copyright Act (DMCA) of 1998: Implements two 1996 treaties of the World Intellectual Property Organization. The DMCA prohibits the act of bypassing technological measures used to prevent access to copyrighted works and the creation and circulation of programs and devices or the offering of services to bypass technological measures that prevent access to copyrighted works or preclude the unauthorized exercise of exclusive copyright rights. The prohibition (which has both civil and criminal provisions) applies without regard to whether acts of infringement have occurred. The DMCA also establishes a regime for limiting damages against internet service providers and other intermediaries whose services may be used to facilitate infringements, if and to the extent that they do not have knowledge of infringement and act expeditiously to take down the infringing material.

Digital Rights Management (DRM): A group of technologies used to control the use of digital materials after sale or distribution.

Dilution: When the distinctiveness of a trademark is blurred from association with only one product in the market by other similar marks or names (see Tarnishment).

Dismissal: Cancellation of a lawsuit or a specific motion, such as for summary judgment, appeal, or by settlement.

Distribution Partner: Includes any company, service, or entity that a cultural institution may work with to share content related to collection works. Could include partnerships for documentary or commercial films.

Droit de Divulgation: The right of the author to control the public disclosure of their work through publication, performance, or sharing. This includes the right to determine if and when a work is completed and to make a work public at all and, if so, the timing of said publication. Droit de Divulgation is one of the four elements of the concept of moral rights. Countries like France specifically recognize these rights. In the United States the concepts that make up moral rights are expressed through a variety of laws, such as trademark (see Moral Rights).

Droit de Suite: A right granted to artists or their heirs in some countries like France, which allows them to receive a fee on the resale of their works of art—to collect the resale royalties (see Moral Rights).

Dublin Core: A metadata schema developed by the Dublin Core Metadata Initiative for description of analog and digital materials. The original metadata set included fifteen elements (Simple Dublin Core) to describe the "core" data about an object. Additional data elements and qualifiers (Qualified Dublin Core) allow users to expand descriptive data.[4]

Duration: The statutory term of protection for intellectual property rights.

Economic Rights: The right of a copyright owner to benefit financially from the exercise of exclusive copyright rights.

Estoppel: A judicial device by which a party is prevented, or estopped, from asserting something contrary to previous actions, statements, or what has been legally established as true. Estoppel may be used as a bar to relitigation or as an affirmative defense.

Exclusive License: An agreement by which the owner of intellectual property rights gives another party the sole and exclusive right to exploit one or more specified intellectual property rights in accordance with the specific terms and conditions specified in the license. Any rights not specifically granted in the license are presumed to be retained by the intellectual property owner. During the term of an exclusive license, the owner of the intellectual property rights may not license the rights subject to the license to any other person or entity and, depending on the scope of exclusivity, that person may also be precluded from exercising the right (see Nonexclusive License).

Fair Dealing: A term that applies to the copyright laws in member countries in the Commonwealth of Nations (formerly the British Commonwealth). Unlike fair use under US law, which relies on a four-factor balancing test to be applied by courts, fair dealing laws typically establish specific categories of use, such as news reporting or academic scholarship, which are excluded from the copyright rights of copyright owners. As such, fair dealing is generally considered less flexible than the United States concept of fair use (see Fair Use).

Fair Use: An exception in US copyright law to the exclusive rights of copyright that, under certain circumstances, allows the use of copyrighted material without authorization from the copyright owner. European copyright laws contain different statutory exceptions, described in the United Kingdom as fair dealing. Whether a particular use can be considered fair use or fair dealing depends primarily on the context and manner of the specific use. Certain uses including commentary, criticism, news reporting, research, teaching, library archiving, and scholarship may be considered fair use or fair dealing if they meet certain criteria specified in the applicable law. The US Copyright Act contains a four-factor balancing test for fair use:

1. The purpose and character of the use, including whether such use is of a commercial nature or is for nonprofit educational purposes
2. The nature of the copyrighted work
3. The amount and substantiality of the portion used in relation to the copyrighted work as a whole
4. The effect of the use upon the potential market for, or value of, the copyrighted work[5]

This four-factor test is utilized by the courts to determine whether a particular use of a copyrighted work without the copyright owner's authorization constitutes an infringement of that owner's copyright or is, instead, a permissible fair use. While there are no legally defined best practice guidelines for assessing whether certain types of uses may be reasonably justified as a fair use, many groups and organizations have developed guidelines to aid creative professionals and cultural organizations in best practices (see Appendix C: References and Resources).

File Transfer Protocol (FTP): A standard network protocol that allows users to move files from one host computer to another via the internet.

Genetic Resources (GR): Refers to genetic material of actual or potential value. Genetic material is any material of plant, animal, microbial, or other origin containing functional units of heredity. Examples include material of plant, animal or microbial origin, such as medicinal plants, agricultural crops, and animal breeds. GRs as encountered in nature are not creations of the human mind and thus they cannot be directly protected as intellectual property. However, there are intellectual property issues associated with GRs. Inventions or plant varieties based on or developed using GRs (associated with traditional knowledge or not) may be patentable or protected by plant breeders' rights.[6]

GLAM: Acronym for "Galleries, Libraries, Archives, Museums." The GLAM-Wiki initiative with Wikipedia founded to help cultural institutions share their resources with the world through collaborative projects with experienced Wikipedia editors.[7]

Impoundment: Seizure of any goods and their placement into the custody of the law for safekeeping pending the outcome of a legal action.

Imprimatur: A mark of approval or endorsement.

Indigenous Knowledge: The entire field of traditional knowledge (TK), genetic resources (GR), and traditional cultural expressions (TCE).[8]

Infringement: The use by one party of another's intellectual property in violation of applicable law. To succeed on a claim of copyright infringement, the copyright owner must demonstrate that they own the copyright in the work, that the work qualifies for copyright protection, and that the work was used in violation of the owner's exclusive rights. The defendant is responsible for asserting and proving affirmative defenses such as fair use. A person or entity found liable for copyright infringement under US copyright law may be liable for statutory damages (if registration of the work is timely) or actual damages and loss of profits plus defendant's profits arising from the infringement. If the work was timely registered with the Copyright Office, a prevailing party may be awarded attorneys' fees and court costs.

Injunction: A court order prohibiting an infringer from infringing the copyright owner's copyrights, including ceasing the infringing use and impoundment of infringing copies.[9]

Institutional Repository (IR): An online archive for collecting, preserving, and disseminating digital copies of the intellectual output of an institution, particularly a research institution. Digital media preserved in such a system may include images, audiovisual media, text, digital publications, and the like. While IRs are often password-protected systems within, for example, a university setting, Open Access may also be a goal, opening "gray" literature that might otherwise be relatively inaccessible to the broader community.

Intellectual Property (IP): A term referring to several distinct types of creations of the human mind for which a set of exclusive rights are recognized under the corresponding fields of law. Under intellectual property law, creators and/or owners of a variety of intangible assets such as musical, literary, and artistic works (in the case of copyright), certain discoveries and inventions (in the case of patents), commercially valuable information that remains secret (in the case of trade secrets), and certain words, phrases, symbols, and designs (in the case of trademarks) are granted certain exclusive rights in and to those assets. The intangible assets themselves are referred to as "intellectual property" and the rights recognized by law are referred to as "intellectual property rights."

Intellectual Property Audit (IP Audit): An evaluation of an organization's intellectual property assets. As applied to cultural institutions, an IP Audit is a process of self-evaluation that the organization consistently and continuously engages in to:

1. Assess the Intellectual Property assets for which it is responsible
2. Determine how best to manage those assets to further its mission and goals
3. Implement strategies to minimize the risks associated with the use of those assets

Intellectual Property Policy (IP Policy): A policy that governs the intellectual property of an organization and may include guidance for conducting an intellectual property audit (see Intellectual Property Audit).

International Image Interoperability Framework (IIIF): The International Image Interoperability Framework (IIIF) is a set of shared application program interface (API) specifications for interoperable functionality in digital image repositories. IIIF has the following goals to:

1. give scholars an unprecedented level of uniform and rich access to image-based resources hosted around the world
2. define a set of common application programming interfaces that support interoperability between image repositories
3. develop, cultivate, and document shared technologies, such as image servers and web clients, that provide a world-class user experience in viewing, comparing,

manipulating, and annotating images[10] (see Application Program Interface)

Internet Protocol Address (IP Address): The unique numerical label assigned to individual devices—computers, printers, etc.—that share a network for communication. This serves to identify both the host network interface and address location.

Joint Authorship: Under US copyright law, a form of copyright ownership in which multiple authors share copyright ownership in a jointly created work and, absent a contract to the contrary, each is entitled to exploit copyright ownership independent of the other owners, subject to a duty to account.

Lawsuit: The common term for a legal action taken by an individual or institution against another individual or institution where the outcome of the action may be decided by a court of law.

Legalese: A slang term for the sometimes arcane, specialized, and convoluted verbiage utilized by lawyers and legal scholars.

Liability: An obligation to do or to refrain from doing something; may also be used to refer to a party's responsibility for their conduct.

Libel: A false and malicious publication that is printed with the purpose of defaming the living party identified in the publication (see Defamation and Slander).

License: A right granted that gses one party the permission to do something that they could not legally do absent that permission. May be a contract in which the owner or administrator of specific intellectual property rights grants permission to another person to use that intellectual property for a defined purpose in accordance with the specific terms and conditions contained in the license. Any rights not specifically granted in the license are presumed to be retained by the intellectual property owner. A license may be exclusive or nonexclusive. Nonexclusive licenses may be oral as well as written and may, depending on the facts, be implied (see Exclusive License and Nonexclusive License).

Licensee: The party to which a license has been granted.

Licensing: The process by which a copyright owner grants some or all of his or her intellectual property rights to another person or entity. A copyright owner may retain a copyright administrator to negotiate and manage licensing agreements on his or her behalf.

Licensor: The party that may grant a license to a licensee.

Linked Open Data in Libraries Archives and Museums (LODLAM): Using the internet to connect related data not previously linked or using the internet to reduce the barriers to linking data currently linked using other methods. Recommended best practices for sharing, and connecting pieces of data, information, and knowledge. Linked Open Data is often used to refer to Linked Data in general rather than to Linked Data that is explicitly published under an open license. Not all Linked Data will be open and not all Open Data will be linked[11] (see Open Data).

Litigation: A legal controversy through which parties seek the use of a court to determine and enforce legal rights.

Metadata: Data describing structural data and descriptive data. An example of structural data is the type of file or size of file. An example of descriptive data is the subject matter. Metadata allows data to be sorted and filtered, searched, and discovered in an easier manner. It can be created and entered manually or created via automatic systems. For example, a camera may generate metadata about the image file it makes, and the photographer may manually add metadata to the image file.

Moral Rights: Rights arising from the relationship between an artist and his or her creative works. Moral rights are unalienable natural rights that cannot be assigned or waived by the artist and which, in some cases outside the United States, can survive the artist's death. Moral rights may include rights relating to completion, display, attribution, resale, alteration, and destruction of the work. An important moral right now recognized by most European countries is the *droit de suite* or resale royalty right. Except to a very limited extent available under the Visual Artists Rights Act, US intellectual property laws do not recognize the concept of moral rights in intellectual property (see Droit de Divulgation and Droit de Suite).

Native American Graves Protection and Repatriation Act (NAGPRA): A federal law passed in 1990. NAGPRA provides a process for museums and federal agencies to return certain American Indian cultural items—human remains, funerary objects, sacred objects, or objects of cultural patrimony—to lineal descendants and culturally affiliated Indian tribes and Native Hawaiian organizations. NAGPRA includes provisions for unclaimed and culturally unidentifiable American Indian cultural items, intentional and inadvertent discovery of American Indian cultural items on federal and tribal lands, and penalties for noncompliance and illegal trafficking. In addition, NAGPRA authorizes federal grants to Indian tribes, Native Hawaiian organizations, and museums to assist with the documentation and repatriation of American Indian cultural items and establishes the Native American Graves Protection and Repatriation Review Committee to monitor the NAGPRA process and facilitate the resolution of disputes that may arise concerning repatriation under NAGPRA.[12]

Nonexclusive License: An agreement by which the owner of intellectual property rights gives another party the nonexclusive right to exploit the specified intellectual property rights in accordance with the specific terms and conditions specified in the license. Any rights not specifically granted in the license are presumed to be retained by the intellectual property owner. During the term of a nonexclusive license, the owner of the intellectual property rights may license the same rights to other persons or entities without restriction. A nonexclusive license may be written or oral and may, in certain circumstances, be implied (see Exclusive License).

Open Access (OA): The practice of providing unrestricted access via the internet to peer-reviewed scholarly journal articles. OA is also increasingly being provided to theses, scholarly monographs, and book chapters. OA comes in two degrees:

- Gratis OA: no-cost online access
- Libre OA: Gratis OA plus some additional usage rights

Open Archives Initiative (OAI): The Open Archives Initiative develops and promotes interoperability standards that aim to facilitate the efficient dissemination of content. OAI has its roots in the open access and institutional repository movements. Continued support of this work remains a cornerstone of the Open Archives program. Over time, however, the work of OAI has expanded to promote broad access to digital resources for eScholarship, eLearning, and eScience.

Open Content: Similar to Open Access, but usually includes the right to *modify* the work, whereas in scholarly publishing it is usual to keep an article's content intact and to associate it with a fixed author or fixed group of authors.

Open Data: The concept that some data should be freely available to everyone to use and republish as they wish without restrictions from copyright, patents, or other mechanisms of Intellectual Property control (see Linked Open Data).

Open-Source Software: Computer software that is widely available without restriction in source code form. The source code and certain other rights normally reserved for copyright holders are provided under an open source license that permits users to study, change, improve, and at times also to distribute the software, generally under the terms of that license.

Oral History: A first-person account of historical or social events obtained through interviews, often taped or video recorded.

Originality: Under US copyright law, an essential element in determining whether a particular work is subject to copyright. Although a work must be original to be copyrightable, the degree of originality is very low. To meet the standard of originality, the work must be more than a "slavish" reproduction.

Orphan Work: A work that is or is presumed to be under copyright, but for which the copyright owner or copyright administrator either cannot be identified or located. The term orphan work is also sometimes used in situations where the copyright owner does not respond to a request for permission to use the work. Depending on the purpose and manner of the proposed use, use of an orphan work may be justified as a fair use. Some localities (e.g., the United Kingdom and Canada) have enacted compulsory licensing schemes with respect to the use of orphan works (see Fair Use).

Patent: Legal protection for inventions that normally have some utilitarian application, although the law also includes some limited design protection. Patent protection is different from copyright protection, and lasts for a shorter period of time. Under current US patent law, a patent lasts for twenty years and requires the patent holder to meet formalities that put the world on notice that a patent exists.[13]

Personal Rights: Certain rights pertaining to individual "personhood" including rights of privacy and publicity.

Public Display: Public display is the right of the copyright holder to control the public display of certain copyrighted works and is analogous to the right of public performance (see Public Performance). The scope of display rights is limited to the following work types:

- choreographic
- dramatic
- graphical
- literary

- musical
- pantomimes
- pictorial
- sculptural
- still images (from audiovisual works or motion pictures)

Public Domain: Works that are not subject to protection under copyright law, because:

1. they do not meet the threshold requirements for copyright protection
2. they are specifically exempt from copyright protection (e.g., works authored by employees of the US federal government in the course of their employment)
3. applicable formalities (notice and registration) to maintain protection have not been met
4. the term of copyright protection has expired

Works that are in the public domain may be freely used without permission.

Public Performance: A right of the copyright holder to control the public performance of certain copyrighted works and is analogous to the right of public display (see Public Display). The scope of performance rights is limited to the following work types:

- audiovisual
- choreographic
- dramatic
- literary
- motion pictures
- musical
- pantomimes

Publication: The distribution of copies of the work to the public by sale or other transfer of ownership, or by rental, lease, or lending. Publication also includes offering to distribute copies to a group of persons for purposes of further distribution, public performance, or public display. A public performance or a public display of a work does not by itself constitute publication.

Quitclaim: The act of assigning and transferring intellectual property rights, ownership (title), and any other interest that a person or entity has or may have in a creative work, often without any representations of ownership. The document evidencing the quitclaim may refer to certain specific rights (such as copyright in the work) or may be broadly worded to include all possible rights, title and interests in the work.

Release: Permission, usually in writing, that allows for the use of material otherwise protected under intellectual property laws; a waiver of rights. The terms of a release typically include the scope of the permitted use, the term of the use, and any limitations on the use, as well as representations, warranties, and indemnifications regarding the extent of the owner's rights and liability for their use. Examples of typical releases include:

- Appearance or Model Release: permission to use an individual's image, name, and likeness in connection with a work, such as a photograph or film
- Location Release: deals with permission to enter private property
- Materials Release: deals with creative content such as artworks, photographs, film, or video footage

Remedy: The relief provided by law with respect to an infringement or violation of legal rights. In the case of copyright infringement, the statutory remedies can include damages, injunctive relief, and impoundment of infringing copies (see Damages, Injunction, and Impoundment).

Right of Privacy: Protects private individuals against unwanted public exposure, including damage to reputation or personal dignity (e.g., emotional distress or defamation). Right of privacy also includes the collection and use of personal information. In the United States privacy rights are governed by a patchwork of federal, state, and local laws.

Right of Publicity: The right to control the commercial exploitation of elements of personhood including name, likeness, voice, image, or other identifying characteristics. Rights of publicity in the United States are creatures of state law.[14] Depending on the state, rights of publicity may survive the person's death.

Right of Reproduction: The right of the copyright owner to create any reproductions or copies of the work.

Rights and Reproductions Specialist: Refers to a contractor or employee of a cultural institution who is responsible for managing intellectual property rights, including but not limited to registrars, rights and reproductions managers, archivists, librarians, and lawyers.

Rights Holder: The individual or institution that owns the intellectual property rights in a work. The rights holder may be the author or may be another copyright owner, such as an assignee of rights or an individual who has inherited them from the author (see Copyright Owner).

Royalty: A percentage of the revenue from the sale of a product that includes copyrighted material, paid to the owner of the intellectual property.

Safe Harbor: A provision of a statute or regulation that specifies certain actions will be deemed to not violate a given rule, provision, or law.

Sampling: Use of elements of one recording mixed into a new composition or recording.

Secondary Liability: A legal action by which one party assumes the legal responsibility for the actions of another party.

Settlement: The resolution of a lawsuit, or other legal dispute, prior to a formal court judgment. Often referred to by the general public as "getting out of court."

Slander: A false and malicious statement that is spoken with the purpose of causing damage to the reputation of another (see Defamation and Libel).

Software: A collection of computer programs and related data that provides instructions for telling a computer what to do and how to do it. Refers to one or more computer program and data held in the storage of the computer for some purposes—a set of programs, procedures, algorithms, and its documentation concerned with the operation of a data processing system. Program software performs the function of the program it implements, either by directly providing instructions to the computer hardware or by serving as input to another piece of software. Software may be in object code or source code, which is readable by human beings.

Statute: A law enacted by the formal, written act of the legislature.

Stock Agency: A commercial supplier of media (e.g., still, video, or audio) and in some cases the rights associated with their use. Agencies may have a particular focus (e.g., fine arts, sports, or society) or may cover a broad range of resources.

Sublicense: A license granted by the licensee of the owner of the intellectual property. Licensees typically will not have the ability to grant a sublicense unless they are authorized to do so by the rights holder. The licensee cannot grant sublicenses that are broader than the rights in the license from the rights holder.

Summary Judgment: A form of dispositive judicial ruling on a lawsuit made when the material facts are not in dispute and the only thing the court needs to do is to apply the applicable law to the facts of the case.

Takedown Notice: A letter sent by a presumptive copyright owner, copyright administrator, or rights holder to an Internet service provider or other intermediary requesting removal (takedown) of allegedly infringing material pursuant to the Digital Millennium Copyright Act (see Digital Millennium Copyright Act [DMCA] of 1998).

Tarnishment: The unauthorized use of a trademark in such a way that it becomes associated by consumers with inferior goods or services or is portrayed in an unflattering manner, such that the trademark loses its value (see Dilution).

Thin Copyright: A legal concept relating to originality. A work may have a "thin copyright" when it is one where there are few ways to express the same underlying idea. The fewer ways to express the idea, the thinner the copyright becomes. Works with a thin copyright might include: a chart or graph showing facts and figures, or a book in the public domain republished with a new foreword.

Thumbnail: A reduced-size version of an image used as an aid in recognition and organization. While there is no legal definition for what constitutes a thumbnail, many groups and organizations have attempted to create best practices (see Appendix C: References and Resources).

Tombstone Information: Basic data about an object such as maker, date made, title, medium, credit line, etc. This type of information often appears on a wall label or in an online collection entry.

Trademark: A name, logo, slogan, color, or other unique characteristic (mark) used to identify the source and origin of goods or services. Trademark rights arise from use of a mark in connection with particular goods or services. Common law trademark rights can arise from consistent use of a particular mark in association with particular goods or services. In the United States trademarks may also be registered under state and federal law. In the United States a federally registered trademark can last perpetually as long as it is being used in connection with goods or services being sold in interstate commerce and the trademark holder meets defined formalities in the trademark law.[15]

Trade Secret: Information including, but not limited to formulas, practices, designs, or compilations of data, that has economic value from not being known to or readily ascertainable by those who could gain value from its use or disclosure and is the subject of reasonable security measures. In some jurisdictions, such secrets are referred to as confidential information or classified information.

Traditional Cultural Expression (TCE): Also called expressions of folklore, may include music, dance, art, designs, names, signs and symbols, performances, ceremonies, architectural forms, handicrafts and narratives, or many other artistic or cultural expressions.[16]

Traditional Knowledge (TK): Knowledge, know-how, skills, and practices that are developed, sustained, and passed on from generation to generation within a community, often forming part of its cultural or spiritual identity.[17]

TRIPs: The Agreement on Trade-Related Aspects of Intellectual Property Rights is an international agreement from the World Trade Organization that outlines minimum standards for the regulation of intellectual property as applicable to member nations of the World Trade Organization.[18]

Underlying Work: A single work can contain multiple layers of copyright ownership—a copyrightable work that is used in another work is referred to as the underlying work. For example, in a photograph of a sculpture, the sculpture would be referred to as the underlying work.

Vicarious Liability: Liability of one part of the actions of another, such as liability of an employer for the actions of an employee.

Visual Artists Rights Act of 1990 (VARA): Added as a provision to the US copyright law in 1990, VARA provides moral rights, parallel to copyright, for subsequently created works of visual art. VARA was enacted in connection with the U.S. ratification of the Berne Convention (see Berne Convention). For qualifying works of visual art, the artist is granted additional rights regardless of subsequent ownership of the artwork. These rights cannot be transferred, but can be waived and last only for the lifetime of the author or, for joint works, of the last surviving author.

These rights include:

- right to claim authorship
- right to prevent the use of one's name on any work the author did not create
- right to prevent use of one's name on any work that has been distorted, mutilated, or modified in a way that would be prejudicial to the author's honor or reputation
- right to prevent distortion, mutilation, or modification that would prejudice the author's honor or reputation
- authors of works of "recognized stature" may prohibit intentional or grossly negligent destruction of a work

Qualifying works of visual art are limited to paintings, drawings, prints or sculptures, existing in a single copy, in a limited edition of two hundred copies or fewer that are signed and consecutively numbered by the author; or, in the case of a sculpture, in multiple cast, carved, or fabricated sculptures of two hundred or fewer that are consecutively numbered by the author and bear the signature or other identifying mark of the author; or still photographic images produced for exhibition purposes only, existing in a single copy that is signed by the author, or in a limited edition of two hundred copies or fewer that are signed and consecutively numbered by the author.[19]

VRA Core: A data standard for the description of works of visual culture as well as the images that document them. The standard is hosted by the Network Development and MARC Standards Office of the Library of Congress in partnership with the Visual Resources Association.[20]

Waiver: The intentional and voluntary surrender of a known right.

Work for Hire: Under US copyright law, works made by an employee in the course of employment or one of nine types of works specially ordered or commissioned in writing, in either case where the employer or commissioning party is the author of the work.

World Intellectual Property Organization (WIPO): An agency of the United Nations, headquartered in Geneva, Switzerland, that assists in developing and administering intellectual property treaties and provides other services, policy, information, and cooperation. Its mission is to lead the development of a balanced and effective international intellectual property system. Its mandate, governing bodies, and procedures are set out in the WIPO Convention, which established WIPO in 1967.[21]

World Trade Organization (WTO): An organization based in Switzerland that assists in the negotiation and administration of global trade treaties and handling of intercountry disputes. Its role is to ensure the free flow of goods in a predictable and smooth manner.[22]

NOTES

1. 17 U.S.C. §§ 1 et seq.

2. "About the Licenses," Creative Commons, accessed March 8, 2018, http://creativecommons.org/licenses/.

3. 17 U.S. Code § 101.

4. Dublin Core, accessed March 8, 2018, http://dublincore.org/.

5. 17 U.S.C. § 107.

6. "Genetic Resources," World Intellectual Property Organization, accessed March 8, 2081, http://www.wipo.int/tk/en/genetic/.

7. "Wikipedia: GLAM," GLAM Wiki, accessed March 8, 2018, https://en.wikipedia.org/wiki/Wikipedia:GLAM.

8. World Intellectual Property Organization, accessed March 8, 2014, http://www.wipo.int/tk/en/.

9. 17 U.S.C. § 502.

10. "About IIIF," International Image Interoperability Framework, accessed March 8, 2018, http://iiif.io/about/.

11. "About," LODLAM Linked Open Data in Libraries Archives and Museums, accessed March 8, 2018, http://lodlam.net/about/.

12. Native American Graves Protection Act and Repatriation Act, 25 U.S.C. §§ 3001 et seq.

13. 35 U.S.C. §§ 1 et seq.

14. See, for example, Ind. Code Ann. § 32-36-1-7 (West 2014); Cal. Civ. Code § 3344 (West 2014).

15. 15 U.S.C. Ch. 22, §§ 1051 et seq.

16. "Traditional Cultural Expressions," World Intellectual Property Organization, accessed March 8 2018, http://www.wipo.int/tk/en/folklore/.

17. "Traditional Knowledge," World Intellectual Property Organization, accessed March 8, 2018, http://www.wipo.int/tk/en/tk/.

18. "Trade-Related Aspects of Intellectual Property Rights," World Trade Organization, accessed March 8, 2018, https://www.wto.org/english/tratop_e/trips_e/trips_e.htm.

19. 17 U.S.C. § 106A.

20. VRA Code," The Library of Congress, accessed March 8, 2018, https://www.loc.gov/standards/vracore/.

21. World Intellectual Property Organization, accessed March 8, 2018, http://www.wipo.int/portal/en/.

22. World Trade Organization, accessed March 8, 2018, http://www.wto.org/index.htm.

Bibliography

A Photo Editor. "Richard Prince Loses Fair Use Argument." March 11, 2011. http://aphotoeditor.com/2011/03/19/richard-prince-loses-fair-use-argument/.

Abrahamson, Jeffery A. "Tuning Up for a New Musical Age: Sound Recording Copyright Protection in a Digital Environment." *AIPLA Quarterly Journal* 25, no. 2 (1997): 181.

American Association of Museums. "Information Center Fact Sheet: Museum Licensing for Museums." 2007.

American Association of Museums' Technical Information Service. *AAM Intellectual Property Resource Pack.* Washington, DC: American Association of Museums, 2000.

American Library Association. "Digital Copyright Slider." 2012. http://librarycopyright.net/resources/digitalslider/index.html.

——. Office for Information Technology Policy. "Fair Use Evaluator." http://librarycopyright.net/resources/fairuse/index.php.

——. Office for Information Technology Policy. "Section 108 of the U.S. Copyright Code Spinner." http://librarycopyright.net/resources/spinner/index.html.

American University: Washington College of Law: Program on Information Justice and Intellectual Property. "Code of Best Practices in Fair Use for Online Video." Center for Social Media. June 2008. http://archive.cmsimpact.org/sites/default/files/online_best_practices_in_fair_use.pdf.

Aoki, Keith, James Boyle, and Jennifer Jenkins. *Bound by Law? Tales from the Public Domain.* Durham, NC: Duke Center for the Public Domain at Duke Law School, 2006.

Appiah, Kwame Anthony. "Whose Culture Is It?" *The New York Review of Books.* February 9, 2006. http://www.nybooks.com/articles/2006/02/09/whose-culture-is-it/.

Artstor Blog: Images and Ideas for Teaching and Scholarship. "Artstor to help launch the Digital Public Library of America." March 28, 2013. https://artstor.wordpress.com/2013/03/28/artstor-to-help-launch-the-digital-public-library-of-america/.

Artsy Editorial, "The Law Shaking Up the Art World," *Copyright Cortex,* April 20, 2017. https://copyrightcortex.org/tools-resources/the-law-shaking-up-the-art-world.

Associated Press. "Relatives win injunction against Mattel's Frida Kahlo Barbie," *Los Angeles Times.* April 20, 2018. http://www.latimes.com/world/la-fg-mexico-frida-court-20180420-story.html.

Association of American Publishers, Association of American University Press, Copyright Clearance Center, National Association of College Stores, and Software & Information Industry Association. *Questions & Answers on Copyright for the Campus Community.* 7th ed. 2006.

Association of Art Museum Directors. *AAMD Policy on the Use of "Thumbnail" Digital Images in Museum Online Initiatives.* New York: 2011.

——. *Guidelines for the Use of Copyright Materials and Works of Art by Art Museums.* New York: October 11, 2017

Association of Independent Video and Filmmakers, Independent Feature Project, International Documentary Association, National Alliance for Media Arts and Culture, and Women in Film and Video. "Documentary Filmmakers' Statement of Best Practices in Fair Use." Center for Media & Social Impact. June 2005. http://archive.cmsimpact.org/sites/default/files/fair_use_final.pdf/.

Association of Research Libraries. "Code of Best Practices in Fair Use for Academic and Research Libraries." January 2012. http://arl.org/storage/documents/publications/code-of-best-practices-fair-use.pdf/.

———. "ARL Urges US to Ratify Marrakesh Treaty, Improve Access to Publications for Visually Impaired." March 15, 2018. http://www.arl.org/news/arl-news/4489-arl-urges-us-to-ratify-marrakesh-treaty-improve-access-to-publications-for-visually-impaired#.WvSLs6QvzRZ.

Atkinson, Rebecca. "Should Museums Allow People to Take Photographs in Galleries?" *Museums Journal*. July 30, 2012. https://www.museumsassociation.org/museums-journal/news/30072012-poll-should-museums-allow-photography.

Aufderheide, Patricia. "Museums Put Fair Use to Work." Center for Media and Social Impact. November 18, 2015. http://archive.cmsimpact.org/blog/fair-use/museums-put-fair-use-work.

Aufderheide, Patricia, David R. Hansen, Meredith Jacob, Peter Jaszi, and Jennifer M. Urban. "Statement of Best Practices in Fair Use of Collections Containing Orphan Works for Libraries, Archives, and Other Memory Institutions." Center for Media and Social Impact. 2014. http://archive.cmsimpact.org/sites/default/files/documents/orphanworks-dec14.pdf/.

Aufderheide, Patricia, Katharine Coles, Peter Jaszi. and Jennifer Urban. "Code of Best Practices in Fair Use for Poetry." Center for Media and Social Impact. January 2011. http://archive.cmsimpact.org/sites/default/files/documents/pages/fairusepoetrybooklet_singlepg_3.pdf/.

Aufderheide, Patricia, and Peter Jaszi. *Reclaiming Fair Use: How to Put Balance Back in Copyright*. Chicago: University of Chicago Press, 2011.

Aufderheide, Patricia, Peter Jaszi, Bryan Bello, and Tijana Milosevic. "Copyright, Permissions, and Fair Use Among Visual Artists and the Academic and Museum Visual Arts Communities: An Issues Report." Report to the College Art Association, February 2014.

Baca, Murtha, ed. *Introduction to Metadata*. 2nd ed. Los Angeles: Getty Publications, 2008. http://www.getty.edu/publications/virtuallibrary/0892368969.html/.

Bailey, Jonathan. "Getty Images Changes Watermark, Tries to Change Image." *Plagiarism Today*. May 30, 2012. https://www.plagiarismtoday.com/2012/05/30/getty-images-changes-watermark-tries-to-change-image/.

———. "The Great Pinterest Divide: To Opt Out or Not." *Plagiarism Today*. February 23, 2012. https://www.plagiarismtoday.com/2012/02/23/the-great-pinterest-divide-to-opt-out-or-not/.

Bailey, Martin. "To Ban or Not to Ban Photography." *The Art Newspaper*. March 12, 2014. http://www.theartnewspaper.com/articles/to-ban-or-not-to-ban-photography/32000/.

Bason, Tamlin H. "9th Circuit: Marilyn Monroe Not Protected by California's Post-Mortem Publicity Statute." *Bloomberg BNA*. Last modified September 7, 2012. http://www.bna.com/9th-circuit-marilyn-n17179869601/.

Behrnd-Klodt, Menzi, and Christopher J. Prom, eds. *Rights in the Digital Era*. Society of American Archivists, 2015.

Berkman Center for Internet and Society. *Copyright for Librarians: The Essential Handbook*. November 8, 2012. http://cyber.law.harvard.edu/publications/2013/copyright_for_librarians/.

Binlot, Ann. "Did Bob Dylan Rip Off Classic Photos for His Gagosian Show? See the Evidence." *Artinfo*. September 27, 2011. http://www.blouinartinfo.com/news/story/38716/did-bob-dylan-rip-off-classic-photos-for-his-gagosian-show-see-the-evidence/.

Blakely, Megan, Kerry Patterson, Victoria Stobo, Andrea Wallace, and Simon Tanner. "Copyright and Cultural Memory: Digital Conference Proceedings," *Copyright Cortex*, March 22, 2017. https://copyrightcortex.org/tools-resources/copyright-cultural-memory-digital-conference-proceedings.

Bober, Phyllis Pray. "Standards and Guidelines: Copyrights and Permissions in Scholarly and Educational Publishing." College Art Association. Accessed September 21, 2014. http://www.collegeart.org/standards-and-guidelines/guidelines/educationsl-publishing-permissions.

Bosman, Julie. "Best-Selling Author Gives Away His Work." *New York Times*. September 27, 2011. https://www.nytimes.com/2011/09/27/books/paulo-coelho-discusses-aleph-his-new-novel.html.

Boyle, James. *The Public Domain: Enclosing the Commons of the Mind*. New Haven: Yale University Press, 2008.

Brehm, Allison S., and Cathy D. Lee. "Click Here to Accept the Terms of Service." *Communications Lawyer* 31 (2015).

Briston, Heather, Mark Allen Greene, Cathy Henderson, Peter Hirtle, Peter Jaszi, William Maher, Aprille Cooke McKay, Richard Pearce-Moses, and Merrilee Proffitt. "Orphan Works: Statement of Best Practices." Society of American Archivists. January 12, 2009, rev. June 17, 2009. https://www2.archivists.org/groups/intellectual-property-working-group/orphan-works-statement-of-best-practices.

Brown, Laura Clark, Judy Ruttenberg, and Kevin L. Smith. "The Triangle Research Libraries Network's Intellectual Property Rights Strategy for Digitization of Modern Manuscript Collections and Archival Record Groups." Triangle Research Libraries Network. January 2011. http://citeseerx.ist.psu.edu/viewdoc/download?doi=10.1.1.404.4255&rep=rep1&type=pdf.

Bruwelheide, Janis H. *The Copyright Primer for Librarians and Educators*. 2nd ed. Edwards Brothers, Inc., 1995.

Bryan, Susan Montoya. "Paul Frank teams up with Native American artists." *Yahoo! News*. Last modified August 16, 2013. http://news.yahoo.com/paul-frank-teams-native-american-artists-202540914.html.

Chang, RayMing. "Revisiting the Visual Artists Rights Act of 1990: A Follow-up Survey About Awareness and Waiver." *Texas Intellectual Property Law Journal* 13, no. 2 (Winter 2005): 129.

Chatters, James C. "Kennewick Man." *Newsletter of the American Anthropological Association*. 2004.

Christiansen, Rupert. "Should We Ban Photography in Museums and Galleries?" *Telegraph*. March 8, 2014. https://www.telegraph.co.uk/culture/museums/10682442/Should-we-ban-photography-in-museums-and-galleries.html.

Cohen, Noam. "A Store of images, From a Time When 'Cut and Paste' Meant Just That." *New York Times*. October 30, 2011. https://www.nytimes.com/2011/10/31/business/media/a-london-bookstore-sells-clip-art-in-an-online-world.html.

College Art Association. "Code of Best Practices in Fair Use for the Visual Arts." February 2015. http://www.collegeart.org/programs/caa-fair-use/best-practices.

———. "Orphan Works." Last modified June 2008. http://www.collegeart.org/publications/ow.

———. "Standards and Guidelines: Copyrights and Permissions in Scholarly and Educational Publishing." http://www.collegeart.org/standards-and-guidelines/guidelines/educationsl-publishing-permissions.

Copeland, Dave. "How You Could Get Sued For Using Pinterest." *ReadWrite*. February 17, 2012. http://readwrite.com/2012/02/17/how_you_could_get_sued_for_using_pinterest/.

Courtney, Julia, ed. *The Legal Guide for Museum Professionals*. Lanham, MD: Rowman & Littlefield, 2015.

Crews, Kenneth D. "Copyright Duration and the Progressive Degeneration of a Constitutional Doctrine." *Syracuse Law Review* 55 (2008): 189–250. http://papers.ssrn.com/sol3/papers.cfm?abstract_id=1656604.

———. "Museum Policies and Art Images: Conflicting Objectives and Copyright Overreaching." *Fordham Intellectual Property, Media, & Entertainment Law Journal* 22 (2012): 795.

Cuno, James. "Open Content, An Idea Whose Time Has Come." *The Getty Iris*. August 12, 2013. http://blogs.getty.edu/iris/open-content-an-idea-whose-time-has-come/.

Davis, James. "Google Art Project: Behind the Scenes: Glowy Night at the Museum." Tate Blog. February 11, 2011. http://www.tate.org/uk/context-comment/blogs/google-art-project-behind-scenes-0/.

Department for Business, Innovation and Skills, Intellectual Property Office and Baroness Neville-Rolfe DBE CMG. "UK Opens Access to 91 Million Orphan Works," press release, October 29, 2014. United Kingdom Intellectual Property Office. Accessed December 16, 2014. https://www.gov.uk/government/news/uk-opens-access-to-91-million-orphan-works.

Digital Public Library of America. "The Digital Public Library of America Policy Statement on Metadata." April 2013. https://pro.dp.la/hubs/metadata-application-profile.

Doctorow, Cory. "Little Brother German Fan-Translation." *Craphound.* November 23, 2008. https://craphound.com/news/2008/11/23/little-brother-german-fan-translation/.

Doskow, Emily. "Defamation Law Made Simple." *NOLO: Law for All.* Accessed July 22, 2014. https://www.nolo.com/legal-encyclopedia/defamation-law-made-simple-29718.html.

Esworthy, Cynthia. "A Guide to the Visual Artists Rights Act." Harvard Law School. http://www.law.harvard.edu/faculty/martin/art_law/esworthy.htm.

European Commission. "Directive 2012/28/EU of the European Parliament and the Council of 25 October 2012 on Certain Permitted Uses of Orphan Works." Accessed December 16, 2014. http://ec.europa.eu/internal_market/copyright/orphan_works/index_en.htm.

The Everywhereist, "Ten Reasons Why You Shouldn't Take Photos in Museums." January 20, 2010. http://www.everywhereist.com/ten-reasons-why-you-shouldnt-take-photos-in-museums/.

Falk, John H., and Beverly K. Sheppard. *Thriving in the Knowledge Age: New Business Models for Museums and Other Cultural Institutions.* 2006.

Ferro, Shane. "Could Prince v. Cariou Bring Down Google Search?" *Artinfo.* February 9, 2012. http://www.blouinartinfo.com/news/story/759422/could-prince-v-cariou-bring-down-google-search?qt-article_detail_popular=0/.

Fishman, Stephen. *The Public Domain: How to Find & Use Copyright-Free Writings, Music, Art & More*, 8th ed. May 2017.

Fournier, Melissa. "Opening Access to Works in the Public Domain at Yale University." Presentation at the Midwinter Virtual Meeting of the Image Resources Interest Group of the Association of College and Research Libraries, February 14, 2012. https://digitalcoffee.yale.edu/resources/presentations-and-downloads.

Frye, Brian L. "Art in the Shadow of the Law." *Kentucky Bench & Bar Magazine.* March/April 2018. https://papers.ssrn.com/sol3/papers.cfm?abstract_id=3152924.

Gerstenblith, Patty. *Art, Cultural Heritage, and the Law.* 3rd. ed. Durham, NC: Carolina Academic Press, 2012.

———. "Identity and Cultural Property: The Protection of Cultural Property in the United States." *Boston University Law Review* 75, no. 559 (1995): 578.

Gore, Emily. "The principles for establishing international & interoperable rights statements." DPLA Blog. May 11, 2015. Accessed May 26, 2015. https://dp.la/news/the-principles-for-establishing-international-interoperable-rights-statements/.

Gorgels, Peter. "Rijksmuseum Mobile First: Rijsstudio Redesign And The New Rijksmuseum App." *MW18: Museums and the Web 2018.* https://mw18.mwconf.org/paper/rijksmuseum-mobile-first-redesign-rijksstudio-the-new-rijksmuseum-app/.

Greer Martin, "Balancing Copyright and Access in Digital Collections," *Copyright Cortex*, May 18, 2016. https://copyrightcortex.org/tools-resources/balancing-copyright-access-in-digital-collections.

Grimes, William. "Museum Rules: Talk Softly, and Carry No Selfie Stick." *New York Times.* February 14, 2015. https://www.nytimes.com/2015/02/15/us/museum-rules-talk-softly-and-carry-no-selfie-stick.html?_r=0.

Halperin, Julia. "Is It About to Get Much Easier for Artists to Bring Copyright-Infringement Lawsuits?" Artinfo. January 9, 2012. http://www.blouinartinfo.com/news/story/755345/is-it-about-to-get-much-easier-for-artists-to-bring-copyright#/.

Hamma, Ken. September 15, 2011 (5:35 p.m.), comment on Taylor Green, "The Copyright Revolution at US Art Museums." *Modern Art Notes: Art-focused Journalism.* September 15, 2011. https://web.archive

s.org/web/20160518061413/http://blogs.artinfo.com/modernartnotes/2011/09/the-copyright-revolution-at-us-art-museums/.

———. "Investing for the Public." Presentation at Museum Computer Network Conference, September 7, 2006. http://mcn.edu/conferences/past-conferences/.

Hansen, David R., Berkeley Law, University of California. Samuelson Law, Technology, & Public Policy Clinic. "Orphan Works: Definitional Issues." Berkeley Digital Library Copyright Project, White Paper No. 1, December 19, 2011.

Hargrave, Josef, and Radha Mistry. "Museums in the Digital Age." *Arup*. London: Arup (2013).

Harris, Beth, and Steven Zucker. "Re-imagining museums." *Museums Association*. May 30, 2012. https://www.museumsassociation.org/comment/30052012-why-the-google-art-project-is-important.

Harris, Lesley Ellen. *Canadian Copyright Law*. 4th ed. Hoboken, NJ: John Wiley & Sons, Inc., 2014.

Healey, Jon. "The Guardian uses copyright to shush a critic of its cultural criticism." *Los Angeles Times*. June 11, 2015. http://www.latimes.com/opinion/opinion-la/la-ol-the-guardian-copyright-takedown-africa-video-20150610-story.html.

Heins, Marjorie, and Tricia Beckles. "Will Fair Use Survive? Free Expression in the Age of Copyright Control." A Public Policy Report for the Brennan Center For Justice, New York University School of Law. 2005. http://www.brennancenter.org/sites/default/files/publications/Will%20Fair%20Use%20Survive.pdf/.

Her Majesty's Government, United Kingdom. *Modernising Copyright: A modern robust and flexible framework: Government response to consultation on copyright exceptions and clarifying copyright law*. December 2012. http://copyright-debate.co.uk/wp-content/uploads/Modernising-Copyright-a-modern-robust-and-flexible-framework-Government-response.pdf.

Hill, Simon. "From J-Phone to Lumia 1020: A Complete History of the Camera Phone." *Digital Trends*. Last modified August 11, 2013. https://www.digitaltrends.com/mobile/camera-phone-history/.

Hilton, John, III, and David Wiley. "Free: Why Authors Are Giving Books Away on the Internet." *TechTrends* 54, no.2 (March 1, 2010): 43–49.

Hines, Candace. "Black Musical Traditions and Copyright Law: Historical Tensions." *Michigan Journal of Race & Law* 10 (2005): 463.

Hirtle, Peter B. "Copyright Term and the Public Domain in the United States." *Cornell University: Copyright Information Center*. Last modified January 1, 2015. https://copyright.cornell.edu/publicdomain.

Hirtle, Peter B., Emily Hudson, and Andrew T. Kenyon. *Copyright and Cultural Institutions: Guidelines for Digitization for U.S. Libraries, Archives, and Museums*. October 14, 2009. https://ecommons.cornell.edu/bitstream/handle/1813/14142/Hirtle-Copyright_final_RGB_lowres-cover1.pdf;jsessionid=719D4C9FE787ACA6739C85666E1BEA20?sequence=2.

Holdren, John P., director, to heads of executive departments and agencies, memorandum, February 22, 2013. "Increasing Access to the Result of Federally Funded Scientific Research." *Office of Science and Technology Policy*. https://obamawhitehouse.archives.gov/blog/2016/02/22/increasing-access-results-federally-funded-science.

Hollowell, Julie, and George Nicholas. "Intellectual Property Issues in Archaeology?" *Anthropology News* 45, no. 4 (April 2004).

———. "Intellectual Property Issues in Archaeological Publication: Some Questions to Consider." *Archaeologies: Journal of the World Archaeological Congress* 4, no. 2 (August 2008): 208–17.

Horejs, Jason. "Debate: Should Visitors be Allowed to Photograph Artwork in Galleries, Museums, and Art Shows?" Red Dot Blog. March 16, 2015. http://reddotblog.com/debate-should-visitors-be-allowed-to-photograph-artwork-in-galleries-museums-and-art-shows/.

Howard, Jennifer. "Supreme Court Appears Divided on Copyright Case Affecting Libraries and Publishers." *The Chronicle of Higher Education*. October 29, 2012. http://chronicle.com/article/Supreme-Court-Appears-Divided/135478/.

Hurley, Dan. "Are Selfies Changing the Museum Experience?" *WVXU.* April 3, 2018. http://wvxu.org/post/are-selfies-changing-museum-experience#stream/0.

Jaszi, Peter, and Nick Lewis. "Protection for Pre-1972 Sound Recordings under State Law and Its Impact on Use by Nonprofit Institutions: A 10-State Analysis." Washington College of Law, American University, September 2009. https://www.clir.org/pubs/reports/pub146/.

Jenkins, Henry. "If It Doesn't Spread, It's Dead (Part One): Media Viruses and Memes." *Confessions of an Aca-Fan.* February 11, 2009. http://henryjenkins.org/2009/02/if_it_doesnt_spread_its_dead_p.html.

Johnson, Stephanie G. "Visitor Photography Policy: An Exploration of Current Trends and Considerations Across American Museums." Master's research project, University of Oregon, June 4, 2014. https://scholarsbank.uoregon.edu/xmlui/handle/1794/17940.

Jones, Michael E. *Art Law: A Concise Guide for Artists, Curators, and Art Educators.* Lanham, MD: Rowman & Littlefield, 2016.

Kandiuk, Mary, and Aaron Lupton. "Digital Images in Teaching and Learning at York University: Are the Libraries Meeting the Needs of Faculty Members in Fine Arts?" *Evidence Based Library and Information Practice* 7, no. 2 (2012): 20–48. http://ejournals.library.ualberta.ca/index.php/EBLIP/article/view/12412/14059/.

Keene, Adrienne. "Paul Frank Powwow Party Update: Am I Dreaming?" Native Appropriations. Last modified September 14, 2012. http://www.nativeappropriations.com/2012/09/paul-frank-powwow-party-update-am-i-dreaming.html.

Kelly, Kristin. "Images of Works of Art in Museums: The Experience of Open Access: A Study of Eleven Museums." Report for the Andrew W. Mellon Foundation, 2013. https://www.clir.org/wp-content/uploads/sites/9/pub157.pdf.

Kels, Charles G., and Lori H. Kels. "Medical Privacy After Death: Implications of New Modifications to the Health Insurance Portability and Accountability Act Privacy Rule." *Mayo Clinic Proceedings* 8, no. 10 (October 2013): 1051–55.

Kennedy, Randy. "Artist Sues the A.P. Over Obama Image." *New York Times.* February 9, 2009. https://www.nytimes.com/2009/02/10/arts/design/10fair.html.

——. "Richard Prince Settles Copyright Suit With Patrick Cariou over Photographs." *New York Times* ArtsBeat Blog. Last modified March 18, 2014. https://artsbeat.blogs.nytimes.com/2014/03/18/richard-prince-settles-copyright-suit-with-patrick-cariou-over-photographs/?mtrref=undefined&gwh=D983A15DD7ED7FA1D7070F985E08CEB9&gwt=pay.

Kingston, Adrian, and Philip Edgar. "A review of a year of open access images at Te Papa." *MWA2015: Museums and the Web Asia 2015.* August 15, 2015. https://mwa2015.museumsandtheweb.com/paper/a-review-of-a-year-of-open-access-images-at-te-papa/.

Kuan, Christine. "Maximum Museum: Digital Images, Licensing, and the Future of Museums." Paper given on the panel session "Got Images? Hot to License, Distribute, and Leverage Collection Media" at the American Association of Museums (AAM) Annual Meeting and MuseumExpo, Minneapolis St. Paul, May 2, 2012. http://www.academia.edu/1548900/Maximum_Museum_Digital_Images_Licensing_and_the_Future_of_Museums.

Kuruvilla, Heather Hope. *A Legal Dictionary for Museum Professionals.* Lanham, MD: Rowman & Littlefield, 2016.

Landes, William M. "What has the Visual Artists Rights Act of 1990 Accomplished?" John M. Olin Law & Economics Working Paper No. 123, 2nd series, University of Chicago Law School, 2001.

Lee, Brian Angelo. "Making Sense of 'Moral Rights' in Intellectual Property." *Temple Law Review* 84 (2011).

Lehmann PLC. "The Mess at Mass MOCA." http://lehmannplc.com/article/exhibiting-unfinished-commissioned-work.

Levine, Melissa, Richard C. Adler, Justin Bonfiglio, Kristina Eden, and Brian S. Hall. *Finding the Public Domain: Copyright Review Management System Toolkit.* Michigan Publishing Services, 2016. https://quod.lib.umich.edu/c/crmstoolkit?page=home.

Library Copyright Alliance, "Library Copyright Alliance Welcome Introduction of Marrakesh Treaty

Implementation Act, S. 2559." March 15, 2018. http://www.librarycopyrightalliance.org/storage/documents/Marrakesh_Act_PR_final.pdf.

Library of Congress. "Copyright and Other Restrictions That Apply to Publication/Distribution of Images: Assessing the Risk of Using a P&P Image." https://www.loc.gov/rr/print/195_copr.html.

——. National Digital Information Infrastructure and Preservation Program. *Section 108 Study Group Report.* March 2008. http://www.section108.gov/docs/Sec108StudyGroupReport.pdf.

Liptak, Adam. "Public Domain Works Can Be Copyrighted Anew, Supreme Court Rules." *New York Times.* January 18, 2012. https://www.nytimes.com/2012/01/19/business/public-domain-works-can-be-copyrighted-anew-justices-rule.html?mtrref=undefined&gwh=39DE663B92F07D6FF9C5F40B1B5DF111&gwt=pay.

Lord, Patricia M. "Unrepatriatable: Native American Intellectual Property and Museum Digital Publication." Master's thesis, John F. Kennedy University, June 18, 2014. http://www.academia.edu/7770593/Unrepatriatable_Native_American_Intellectual_Property_and_Museum_Digital_Publication/.

Maher, Katherine, and Loic Tallon. "Wikimedia and The Met: A shared digital vision," *The MET Now at The Met Blog.* April 19, 2018. https://www.metmuseum.org/blogs/now-at-the-met/2018/wikimedia-and-the-met-digital-vision.

Malaro, Marie C. "Why Ethics?" in *Museum Governance: Mission, Ethics, Policy.* Washington, DC: Smithsonian Institution Press, 1994.

Malaro, Marie C. and Ildiko Pogány DeAngelis. *A Legal Primer on Managing Museum Collections.* 3rd ed. Washington, DC: Smithsonian Books, 2012.

Marcucci, Matthew A. "5Pointz Trial Applies Visual Artists Rights Act to Graffiti Art for First Time." *Grossman LLP Art Law Blog.* October 24, 2017. https://www.grossmanllp.com/5pointz-trial-applies-visual-artists-rights-act-t.

Margoni, Thomas. "The Digitisation of Cultural Heritage: Originality, Derivative Works and (Non) Original Photographs." *Institute for Information Law, University of Amsterdam.* December 3, 2014. https://papers.ssrn.com/sol3/papers.cfm?abstract_id=2573104.

Max Planck Institute for the History of Science. "Best Practices for Access to Images: Recommendations for Scholarly Use and Publishing." January 5, 2009. https://www.mpiwg-berlin.mpg.de/PDF/MPIWGBestPracticesRecomm.pdf.

McCarthy, Douglas. "Museums in the Digital Age: insights from Wellcome Collection," *Europeana Pro.* May 1, 2018. https://pro.europeana.eu/post/museums-in-the-digital-age-insights-from-wellcome-collection.

Miranda, Carolina A. "Why Can't We Take Pictures in Art Museums?" *ARTnews.* May 2013. http://www.artnews.com/2013/05/13/photography-in-art-museums/.

Op den Kamp, Claudy and Dan Hunter. *A History of Intellectual Property in 50 Objects.* New York: Cambridge University Press, 2018.

Pantalony, Rina Elster. "Managing Intellectual Property for Museums." World Intellectual Property Organization. 2013. http://www.wipo.int/edocs/pubdocs/en/copyright/1001/wipo_pub_1001.pdf.

Pekel, Joris. "Case Study: Rijksmuseum releases 111.000 high quality images to the public domain." *OpenGLAM.* February 27, 2013. https://openglam.org/2013/02/27/case-study-rijksmuseum-releases-111-000-high-quality-images-to-the-public-domain/#sthash.ayaUhB4q.dpuf.

Phelan, Marilyn E. *Museum Law: A Guide for Officers, Directors, and Counsel.* 4th ed. Lanham, MD: Rowman & Littlefield, 2014.

Powell, Sarah. "300,000 open images and counting…" *Auckland Museum Blog.* July 14, 2017. http://www.aucklandmuseum.com/discover/stories/blog/2017/300,000-open-images-and-counting.

Prosser, W. *Law of Torts.* 2nd ed. St. Paul, MN: West Publishing, 1955.

Rosati, Eleanora, Annsley Merelle Ward, Neil J. Wilkof, and Merpel. "Can Mattel be prevented from making its own Frida Kahlo Barbie doll?" *The IPKat.* March 10, 2018. http://ipkitten.blogspot.com/2018/03/can-mattel-be-prevented-from-making-its.html.

Ross, Jen, Ashley Beamer, and Christopher Ganley. "Digital Collections, Open Data And The Boundaries Of Openness: A Case Study From The National Galleries of Scotland." *MW18: Museum and the Web 2018.* https://mw18.mwconf.org/proposal/digital-collections-open-data-and-the-boundaries-of-openness-a-case-study-from-the-national-galleries-of-scotland/.

Rousseau, Caryn. "Art Institute of Chicago Joins Google Art Project." *Huffington Post.* Last modified June 3, 2012. http://www.huffingtonpost.com/2012/04/03/google-art-project-premie_0_n_1400734.html/.

Russell, Elizabeth T. "Learning Music Licensing." American Association of Museums. http://aam-us.org/pubs/webexclusive/licensing.cfm?renderforprint=1/.

Saez, Catherine. "Interviews: What Protection of Traditional Knowledge Means to Indigenous Peoples." Intellectual Property Watch. Last modified August 20, 2013. http://www.ip-watch.org/2013/08/20/interviews-what-protection-of-traditional-knowledge-means-to-indigenous-peoples/.

Sanderhoff, Merete. "Open access can never be bad news." *Medium.* March 6, 2017. https://medium.com/smk-open/open-access-can-never-be-bad-news-d33336aad382.

Sax, Joseph L. *Playing Darts with a Rembrandt: Public and Private Rights in Cultural Treasures.* Ann Arbor: The University of Michigan Press, 2001.

Schmidt, Antje. "MKG Collection Online: The potential of open museum collections." *Hamburger Journal für Kulturanthropologie* No. 7 (2017). https://journals.sub.uni-hamburg.de/hjk/article/view/1191.

Schuessler, Jennifer. "New York Public Library Invites a Deep Digital Dive," *Copyright Cortex*, January 6, 2016. https://copyrightcortex.org/tools-resources/new-york-public-library-invites-a-deep-digital-dive.

Seagle, Simone. "Open Access at The Met: Animating Artworks in the Collection," *The MET Collection Insights Blog,* January 30, 2018. https://www.metmuseum.org/blogs/collection-insights/2018/open-access-artwork-animations.

Shapiro, Michael S., and Brett I. Miller. In *A Museum Guide to Copyright and Trademark*, edited by Christine Steiner. Washington, DC: American Association of Museums, 1999.

Shulman, James. "Sustainable Free: Lessons Learned from the Launch of a Free Service Supporting Publishing in Art." *Liber Quarterly* 24, no. 2 (2014). https://dspace.library.uu.nl/handle/1874/300769.

Sim, Disa. "The Right to Solitude in the United States and Singapore: A Call for Fundamental Reordering." *Loyola of Los Angeles Entertainment Law Review* 22 (2002).

Simon, Nina. "Museum Photo Policies Should Be as Open as Possible." Museum 2.0. August 20, 2009. http://museumtwo.blogspot.com/2009/08/museum-photo-policies-should-be-as-open.html.

Smith, Aaron. "Smartphone Ownership 2013." *Pew Research Internet Project.* June 5, 2013. http://www.pewinternet.org/2013/06/05/smartphone-ownership-2013/.

The Smoking Gun. "Sleeping Yankees Fan Sues ESPN for Defamation." Last modified July 7, 2014. http://www.thesmokinggun.com/documents/sleeping-fan-sues-Yankees-ESPN-576321/.

Spatt, David M. "Moral Rights Survive the Sale and the Southern District." *OSLA Arts & Law* (1996). http://www.artslaw.org/moral.htm.

Spoo, Robert. "Bridgeman Art Library v. Corel Corporation: Did You Know?" *The University of Tulsa: The Rights Stuff*, no. 2. 2011.

Sprague, Robert. "Orwell was an Optimist: The Evolution of Privacy in the United States and its De-Evolution for American Employees." *John Marshall Law Review* 42, no. 1 (2008).

Steinmetz, Katy. "Is Instagram Ruining Art? One Museum Is Trying 'Photo Free' Hours." *Time.* March 17, 2018. http://time.com/5204051/smartphones-instagram-museum-art-de-young/.

Streitfeld, David. "Amazon Pulls Thousands of E-Books in Dispute." Bits Blog, *New York Times.* February 22, 2012. https://bits.blogs.nytimes.com/2012/02/22/amazon-pulls-thousands-of-e-books-in-dispute/?_r=0%2F&mtrref=undefined.

Tanner, Simon. "Reproduction Charging Models & Rights Policy for Digital Images in American Art Museums: A Mellon Foundation Study." August 2004. https://www.kdl.kcl.ac.uk/fileadmin/documents/USMuseum_SimonTanner.pdf.

United Kingdom Intellectual Property Office. "Copyright: orphan works. How to get permission to copy a creative work for which the right holder(s) cannot be found in an orphan work." May 12, 2015. https://www.gov.uk/apply-for-a-licence-to-use-an-orphan-work.

United Nations Educational, Scientific and Cultural Organization (UNESCO). Universal Copyright Convention, with Appendix Declaration relating to Articles XVII and Resolution concerning Article XI 1952, September 6, 1952, revised on July 24, 1971. 25 U.S.T. 1241 (1975). http://portal.unesco.org/en/ev.php-URL_ID=15381&URL_DO=DO_TOPIC&URL_SECTION=201.html.

Urban, Jennifer M. "How Fair Use Can Help Solve the Orphan Works Problem." *Berkeley Technology Law Journal* 27 (2012). https://scholarship.law.berkeley.edu/cgi/viewcontent.cgi?article=3200&context=facpubs.

US Copyright Office. *Circular 23: The Copyright Card Catalog and the Online Files of the Copyright Office*. 2012. https://www.copyright.gov/circs/circ23.pdf.

——. Copyright Public Information Office. *Circular 34: Copyright Protection Not Available for Names, Titles, or Short Phrases*. 2012. https://www.copyright.gov/circs/circ34.pdf.

——. *Circular 22: How to Investigate the Copyright Status of a Work*. August 2009. https://www.copyright.gov/circs/circ22.pdf.

——. "Fair Use Index." https://copyright.gov/fair-use/.

——. Office of the Register of Copyrights. *Orphan Works and Mass Digitization*. June 2015. https://copyright.gov/orphan/reports/orphan-works2015.pdf.

——. Office of the Register of Copyrights. *Resale Royalties: An Updated Analysis*. December 2013. https://copyright.gov/docs/resaleroyalty/usco-resaleroyalty.pdf.

——. "Orphan Works." Accessed November 2, 2014. https://copyright.gov/orphan/.

——. *Priorities and Special Projects of the United States Copyright Office*. October 25, 2011. https://copyright.gov/docs/priorities.pdf.

——. "Revising Section 108: Copyright Exceptions for Libraries and Archives," September 2017. https://www.copyright.gov/policy/section108/discussion-document.pdf.

——. *Waiver of Moral Rights in Visual Artworks Executive Summary*. October 24, 1996. https://www.copyright.gov/reports/exsum.html.

US Department of Health and Human Services. National Institutes of Health. *Upcoming Changes to Public Access Policy Reporting Requirements and Related to NIH Efforts to Enhance Compliance*. November 16, 2012. https://grants.nih.gov/grants/guide/notice-files/NOT-OD-12-160.html.

US Department of the Interior. National Park Service. American Indian Liaison Office. *Native American Graves Protection and Repatriation Act (NAGPRA): A Quick Guide for Preserving Native American Cultural Resources*. 2012. https://www.nps.gov/history/tribes/Documents/NAGPRA.pdf.

——. National Park Service. *FY 2015 Grant Guidelines: Native American Graves Protection and Repatriation Act (NAGPRA)*. 2015. https://www.nps.gov/nagpra/grants/FY2015/FY2015%20NAGPRA%20Grant%20Guidelines.pdf.

Tallon, Loic. "Introducing Open Access at The Met," *The MET Digital Underground Blog*. February 7, 2017. https://www.metmuseum.org/blogs/digital-underground/2017/open-access-at-the-met.

_____. "Celebrating Six Months of Open Access, plus The Met on Google BigQuery, *The MET Digital Underground Blog*. August 7, 2017. https://www.metmuseum.org/blogs/digital-underground.

_____. "Creating Access beyond metmuseum.org: The Met Collection on Wikipedia, "*The MET Now at The Met Blog*. February 7, 2018. https://www.metmuseum.org/blogs/now-at-the-met/2018/open-access-at-the-met-year-one.

Vick, Kevin K., and Jean-Paul Jassy. "Why a Federal Right of Publicity Statute is Necessary." *Communications Lawyer* 28, no. 2 (August 2011).

Wagner, Gretchen, and Allan T. Kohl. "Statement on the Fair Use of Images for Teaching, Research, and Study." Visual Resources Association (VRA). March 20, 2012. https://online.vraweb.org/cgi/viewcontent.cgi?referer=&httpsredir=1&article=1013&context=vrab/.

Wallace, Andrea, and Ronan Deazley, *Display At Your Own Risk: An Experimental Exhibition of Digital Cultural Heritage.* 2016. http://displayatyourownrisk.org.

Weil, Stephen E. "Vincible Ignorance: Museums and the Law." In *Beauty and the Beasts,* 122–42. Washington, DC: Smithsonian Institution Press, 1983.

——. "Copyrights and Wrongs." *Museum News.* July/August 1993.

Whalen, Maureen. "Developing a Rights Metadata Dictionary for Digital Surrogates." *Journal of Library Metadata* 9 (2009): 15–35.

Wilson, Lee. *The Copyright Guide: A Friendly Guide to Protecting and Profiting from Copyrights.* New York: Allworth Press, 1996.

World Intellectual Property Organization. *Berne Convention for the Protection of Literary and Artistic Works,* July 14, 1967, amended on September 28, 1979. 828 U.N.T.S. 221. http://www.wipo.int/treaties/en/text.jsp?file_id=283698.

——. *Madrid Agreement Concerning the International Registration of Marks,* April 14, 1891, amended on September 28, 1979. http://www.wipo.int/wipolex/en/wipo_treaties/text.jsp?file_id=283 530.

——. *Marrakesh Treaty to Facilitate Access to Published Works for Persons Who Are Blind, Visually Impaired or Otherwise Print Disabled.* June 27, 2013. http://www.wipo.int/treaties/en/ip/marrakesh/.

——. *Paris Convention for the Protection of Industrial Property,* March 20, 1993, amended on September 28, 1979. 24 U.S.T. 2140. http://www.wipo.int/treaties/en/text.jsp?file_id=288514.

——. *WIPO Copyright Treaty,* adopted on December 20, 1996. 36 I.L.M. 65. http://www.wipo.int/treaties/en/text.jsp?file_id=295166.

——. *WIPO Performances and Phonograms Treaty,* adopted on December 20, 1996, CRNR/DC/95. http://www.wipo.int/treaties/en/text.jsp?file_id=295578.

World Trade Organization. "Declaration on the TRIPS Agreement and Public Health," adopted November 14, 2001. World Trade Organization Ministerial Conference, Doha, November 9–14, 2001.

Wu, Katrina. "The Google Art Project: An Analysis from a Legal and Social Perspective on Copyright Implications." *Journal of the Patent and Trademark Office Society* 96, no. 4 (December 2014).

Wythe, Deborah. "Working Guidelines for the Copyright Project." *BKM Tech.* Last modified January 4, 2010. https://www.brooklynmuseum.org/community/blogosphere/2010/01/14/working-guidelines-for-the-copyright-project/.

Yale University. "Open Access to Digital Representations of Works in the Public Domain from Museum, Library, and Archive Collections." May 5, 2011. https://web.library.yale.edu/sites/default/files/files/policy_-_open_access_to_digital_representations_of_works_in_the_public_domain_from_museum_library_and_archive_collections_2011_.pdf.

Yerkovich, Sally. *A Practical Guide to Museum Ethics.* Lanham, MD: Rowman & Littlefield, 2016.

Yu, Arlene. "Little Images, Big Art." BKM Tech. Last modified January 14, 2010. https://www.brooklynmuseum.org/community/blogosphere/2010/01/14/little-images-big-art/.

Zapruder, Abraham. Letter of agreement to C.D. Jackson, publisher, *LIFE Magazine.* November 25, 1963.

Zorich, Diane. "Developing Intellectual Property Policies: A How-To Guide to Museums." *Canadian Heritage Information Network (CHIN).* 2003. https://www.canada.ca/en/heritage-information-network/services/intellectual-property-copyright/guide-developing-intellectual-property-policies.html.

Index

Page references for figures are italicized.

About the Editor

Anne M. Young heads the rights and reproductions department at the Indianapolis Museum of Art at Newfields, where she is responsible for processing all external requests for the use of visual content, obtaining permissions for internal uses of images/videos, and administering the institution's onsite photography policy. She also initiates and manages all licensing agreements with artists and/or rights holders for works in the museum's collection. Young was formerly the photographic archivist for the Kinsey Institute, Indiana University, and has worked for the Art Gallery of Ontario and George Eastman Museum. She is currently a Master of Jurisprudence candidate at Indiana University's Robert H. McKinney School of Law focusing on Intellectual Property, art, and museum law. Young previously received a Master of Arts in photographic preservation and collections management from Ryerson University and a Bachelor of Arts in art history and studio art (photography) from Indiana University. She chaired the Rights and Reproductions Professional Practices Committee of the American Alliance of Museums from 2012–2018 and was appointed to serve on the 2018–2021 term of the College Art Association's Committee on Intellectual Property. Young was the editor of the 2015 publication *Rights & Reproductions: The Handbook for Cultural Institutions,* for which she received the Visual Resources Association's Nancy DeLaurier Award in 2017.

About the Contributors

Megan P. Bryant, director of Collections & Interpretation, The Sixth Floor Museum at Dealey Plaza, is responsible for the museum's collections, education, exhibits, and intellectual property–based operations and initiatives, directing and coordinating all planning, development, management, exhibition, and access for its historic, oral history, library, and archives collections. She created the museum's rights and reproductions program to manage external use of the museum's collection of films and images related to the assassination of President John F. Kennedy. She manages the copyright and all licensing activities related to the Abraham Zapruder film of the assassination and many other films and images related to that event and administers museum uses of external intellectual property. Bryant previously served as the museum's registrar for eleven years and worked in collections management at several historic sites and museums in Illinois, Colorado, and Maine. She served as chair of RCAAM's Rights and Reproductions Information Network from 2008 through 2013.

Cherie C. Chen, registrar for Rights and Reproductions, The J. Paul Getty Museum, has been with the Getty for more than twenty years, starting shortly after the Getty Center opened to the public in 1998. She has worked in the museum registrar's office since 2002. She manages the museum's portfolio of reproduction rights for objects in the collection as well as for loans to the collection. She drafts and implements policies for managing rights and monitors compliance by internal image users. Chen also oversees the work of an assistant registrar responsible for supplying media and granting rights to outside requesters and another assistant registrar responsible for obtaining images and rights for exhibition catalogues.

Kenneth D. Crews is an attorney with Gipson Hoffman & Pancione, specializing in copyright law, particularly related to the needs of universities, colleges, libraries, museums, and other cultural institutions. Previously, Crews was the founding director of the copyright office at Columbia University in New York City. In 1994, at Indiana University, he founded the first copyright policy center based at any university. Crews has been a professor of law, information science, and business, and held a named, tenured chair at Indiana University. Crews is the author of numerous articles and technical studies and four books. *Copyright Law for Librarians and Educators: Creative Strategies and Practical Solutions* (4th Edition, forthcoming 2018) is widely considered a constructive and insightful guide to understanding and working with fair use, ownership, and other principles of copyright. Crews holds a PhD from UCLA and studied law at Washington University and history at Northwestern University.

John ffrench, director of Visual Resources, Yale University Art Gallery (YUAG), oversees workflow, design, color management, and long-term archiving of images and image data. He supervises the creation, quality control, asset management, distribution of and rights related to images of works of art for publication, study, documentation, educational programs, promotion, and other uses. He has been actively involved in the development of the YUAG/Yale Campus DAM and the creation of Yale University's Open Access policy. He worked at the Denver Art Museum in collections management for ten years before coming to the YUAG in 1999 to create the digital imaging studio. He also oversees the rights and reproductions staff responsible for clearing rights for internal publications and publicity campaigns at YUAG. On campus he founded and leads the Digital Coffee Group, a campus-wide organization established to create core standards, develop resources, and provide guidance and support for digital imaging-related technology, projects, and professionals on campus. A graduate of the Johns Hopkins University museum studies program, he focused his studies on digital technology in museums.

Walter G. Lehmann, managing partner, Lehmann PLC, has been an attorney and business consultant for more than twenty years. He has focused on helping individuals, businesses, and nonprofit organizations manage real and intellectual property assets. He has represented producers, artists, writers, museums, and nonprofit arts and cultural organizations on a wide range of legal and business matters including business organization, financing, intellectual property management, board governance, nonprofit administration, and museum collections management, policies, and ethics. Lehmann's education includes a BA in English (Williams College) and JD (William Mitchell College of Law). He also completed an MA in museum studies (George Washington University). Lehmann has served on the board of directors of numerous nonprofit organizations, including the Landis Valley Museum Associates and the North Museum of Natural History and Science, where he was also interim curator of collections. He is a past member of the Walters Art Museum Collections Committee, and currently serves on the governance committee of The M (formerly the Minnesota Museum of American Art). He has taught graduate and undergraduate courses on art and museum law at Johns Hopkins University and George Washington University, served on the faculty of the ALI-CLE Legal Issues in Museum Administration course, and as chair and vice chair of the ABA-IPL Copyright Policy Committee.

Naomi Leibowitz is associate director, Creative Strategy and Operations, at the Solomon R. Guggenheim Museum. In her previous role as rights and reproductions manager, Leibowitz standardized the museum's approach to obtaining, clearing, and paying for reproduction rights. She organized and catalogued collection rights information and negotiated blanket agreements with large rights-holding organizations such as ARS and VAGA. In addition to overseeing rights and reproductions, Leibowitz currently works alongside the Guggenheim's creative director, to provide strategic guidance and coordination on key projects across the creative departments (graphics, photography, publications, interactive, and digital media). She also currently oversees audio and video content production for the museum. Leibowitz formerly worked in publishing as a photo editor. She holds a BFA in photography and imaging from New York University's Tisch School of the Arts.

Melissa Levine, lead copyright officer and librarian, University of Michigan Library, provides guidance on all aspects of copyright policy and practice at the library. She was the principal investigator for the Copyright Review Management System (CRMS), an IMLS-supported effort to learn more about the copyright status of books in HathiTrust. At the Smithsonian Institution, she handled licensing and contract negotiations for publishing, product development, electronic rights, audiovisual media, exhibitions, and festivals. At the Library of Congress, Levine was assistant general counsel and legal advisor to the National Digital Library Project. She developed copyright and permissions policies for worldwide dissemination of collections online, advised senior management on intellectual property and interrelated business and strategic issues, worked with the US Copyright Office and other government agencies on copyright issues, and represented the Library of Congress in interagency meetings and initiatives related to copyright and digital libraries. Levine has served as acting director of the Frost Art Museum at Florida International University; associate director for finance and administration at the Wolfsonian Museum; and acting curator of the World Bank's Art program. Levine earned her BA (history and art history) from Emory University and is a graduate of the University of Miami School of Law. She was selected for the 2011 Frye Leadership Institute.

Sofía Galarza Liu, head of Collection Management, Spencer Museum of Art, University of Kanasa, oversees rights and reproductions for the museum. She worked with the university's legal counsel to establish procedures that guide how the museum handles images of works in the collection. She ensures permissions are secured for internal and external image uses, including research, publication, publicity, and promotion. She completed a two-year IMLS grant-funded project to digitize the museum's collections and was actively involved in the development of the museum's online collection and online rights and reproductions request form. She has taught courses on collection management for the University of Kansas Museum Studies Graduate Program and collection management databases for the Northern States Conservation Center. She has a BFA in the history of art and an MA in museum studies from the University of Kansas. She received training at the Getty Leadership Institute in Los Angeles in the Museum Leaders: the Next Generation program. She is an active member of the Mountain-Plains Museums Association and the American Alliance of Museums.

Michelle Gallagher Roberts, head of Registration & Collections, New Mexico Museum of Art, received her BS from Central Washington University and graduated from the University of Denver with an MA in anthropology and a specialization in museum studies. She has worked at the Foothills Art Center in Golden Colorado, the Palm Springs Art Museum, the Museum of International Folk Art, and the Museum of Indian Arts & Culture. From 2006 until present, she has been responsible for all rights and reproduction requests at the New Mexico Museum of Art. Working in museums for the past twenty years, she has worked in all aspects of registration and collections management.

Nancy Sims, Copyright Program Librarian, University of Minnesota Libraries, and attorney, is fascinated by the pervasiveness of copyright and licensing issues in everyday life. She enjoys helping individuals, groups, and organizations understand how technology choices, copyright, and related legal and policy issues may affect their work, research, art, and everyday communications. Her research interests include the attribution practices and cultural norms in various academic and artistic fields. In her current position, she provides education, information, and consultation to the university's five coordinate campuses regarding copyright in teaching, class assignments, research, and publishing. She also consults with library, education, arts, and technology organizations and institutions around the country, and occasionally provides representation for individual artists, writers, programmers, and other creators. Previously, she was an instructional technology specialist at the University of Michigan Libraries, and interned with the Electronic Frontier Foundation and Fenwick & West, LLP.

Deborah Wythe is the former head of Digital Collections and Services at the Brooklyn Museum (1986 until her retirement in 2016). Her first role was serving as museum archivist, where digitization efforts led her to initiate a cross-departmental project to research and evaluate DAM software. In 2005, she was charged with designing and heading a new department, Digital Collections and Services, which is now responsible for all imaging activities museum-wide, including the photo studio, scan lab, digital asset management, copyright clearance, outside image acquisition, and rights and reproductions. In 2008, Wythe headed a collaboration among museum counsel, professional staff, and interns to develop policies, identify works protected by copyright, contact artists and estates, and obtain nonexclusive licenses. In a commitment to transparency and access, the Brooklyn Museum provides rights information on its website for all objects in the collection. She is active in the Society of American Archivists and the Museum Computer Network. She served as editor and contributing author for *Museum Archives, An Introduction*, 2nd edition.

About the Legal Review Panel

Jeffrey P. Cunard, managing partner of Debevoise & Plimpton LLP's Washington, DC, office, leads the firm's corporate intellectual property, information technology, and e-commerce practices. He has broad experience in transactions, including software and technology licenses, joint ventures, mergers and acquisitions, and outsourcing arrangements. He is internationally recognized in the field of the internet and cyberlaw and is a member of the firm's Cybersecurity and Data Privacy practice. Cunard's practice also encompasses copyright litigation, and United States and international media and telecommunications law, including privatizations and regulatory advice.

Kenan Farrell, partner, KLF Legal Intellectual Property and Business Law Office, is an intellectual property attorney licensed in Indiana, Oregon, and prior with the United States Patent and Trademark Office. He previously taught art and museum law at his alma mater, Indiana University Robert H. McKinney School of Law. Kenan maintains both the Indiana Intellectual Property Blog and the Oregon Intellectual Property Blog.

Janet Benson Forville, associate general counsel, United States Holocaust Memorial Museum, handles copyright and trademark matters and negotiates and drafts contracts at the museum, including licenses and permissions, exhibition agreements and publishing contracts. As a part of the general counsel's office, she also provides advice on a variety of matters and prepares institution-wide policies, especially related to copyright and social media. Previously, she worked for the Business Contracting Division at the Smithsonian Institution, where she helped develop and teach a training course on the subject of copyright for nonlawyers. She began her legal career working on copyright and trademark issues as an associate at a law firm serving artists and industrial designers. Prior to receiving her law degree, she worked with Washington Area Lawyers for the Arts, and spent several years supporting business development activities at an international intellectual property firm. She received her BA in liberal arts from Virginia Tech and her JD from the College of William & Mary School of Law.

Fred Goldstein is senior vice president, general counsel and secretary, at the Los Angeles County Museum of Art (LACMA). Prior to joining LACMA in 2005, Goldstein served as the senior vice president and general counsel for the Phoenix House Foundation in New York and as a partner in the law firm of Wachtell, Lipton, Rosen and Katz. Goldstein received his JD from Yale Law School and his undergraduate degree from the University of Michigan. He has taught art and museum law at Southwestern University School of Law and has served as a member of the Executive Committee of the Entertainment Law and Intellectual Property Section of the Los Angeles County Bar Association, a trustee of the Los Angeles Copyright Society, and a director of the California Association of Museums. He is currently a member of CAM's Government Relations Committee and a director of Arts for LA.

Cara Hirsch is deputy general counsel at the Virtual Reality Company (VRC), a studio focused on the creation of content for virtual reality film and other experiences. Hirsch oversees all intellectual property matters relating to the company's business, as well as supports the company's general legal function. Prior to VRC, Hirsch was associate general counsel at the Solomon R. Guggenheim Foundation, which owns and operates the Solomon R. Guggenheim Museum in New York and the Peggy Guggenheim Collection in Venice, where she focused on intellectual property, licensing, and other general legal matters. She was also deputy general counsel for Artstor, a nonprofit organization whose mission is to use digital technology to enhance scholarship, teaching, and learning in the arts, humanities, and other fields. Among her duties at Artstor, Hirsch collaborated in refining Artstor's intellectual property and other legal strategies for the organization. She also supervised the rights review and clearance process for media collections in the Artstor Digital Library, a digital image resource that makes available to nonprofit institutions more than two million digital images in the arts, architecture, humanities, and sciences. Hirsch also worked as an associate at the law firms of Weil, Gotshal & Manges LLP and Andrews Kurth LLP, where she practiced in the field of intellectual property. She served as co-chair of the Intellectual Property Rights Committee of the Visual Resources Association from 2011 to 2014. Hirsch received her JD from Fordham University School of Law and her BA, with distinction, from the University of Michigan at Ann Arbor.

Troy B. Klyber is the intellectual property manager at the Office of the General Counsel at the Art Institute of Chicago. He acts as in-house counsel to the museum and to the School of the Art Institute of Chicago for intellectual property and technology matters. He was formerly an associate at Mayer Brown LLP. He received a JD from Georgetown University Law Center and a BS in chemical engineering from the University of Illinois at Urbana-Champaign.

Lynda Knowles has been legal counsel at the Denver Museum of Nature & Science since 2007. She is a graduate of the University of North Carolina-Chapel Hill and the University of Denver Sturm College of Law. Knowles has practiced law in the Denver area for more than fifteen years. Her experience includes intellectual property development and licensing, corporate and transactional work. She is a member of the Colorado Intellectual Property Inn of Court and most recently authored a chapter for the book *The Future of Natural History Museums* on national and international legislation affecting museums.

Pamelia Kohanchi is the deputy counsel at the Los Angeles County Museum of Art (LACMA). After working with Sidley Austin LLP in its Los Angeles real estate group, Kohanchi moved to LACMA. She handles a wide variety of legal issues affecting the museum's business, including intellectual property and licensing, corporate governance, tax, employment, trusts and estates, real estate, insurance, exhibitions and planning, acquisitions, development and philanthropy, and press and publicity. Kohanchi is a graduate of the University of California, Los Angeles, and Stanford Law School.

Robert S. Meitus, partner, Meitus Gelbert Rose LLP, serves as copyright, trademark, and entertainment counsel for a wide range of clients including recording artists, record labels, filmmakers, visual artists, authors, and business clients in a range of creative industries. His practice largely involves negotiation of agreements; work with intellectual property protection, clearance and licensing; and serving generally as business/legal counsel to numerous creative clients. Meitus has also filed numerous terminations under the US Copyright Act, is regularly involved in IP litigation, and has recently served as a panelist in the Copyright Office Music Licensing Roundtable on revisions to the current copyright law. He is the author of articles on copyright law, including, "Interpreting the Copyright Act's Section 201(c) Revision Privilege with

Respect to Electronic Media" and "Revisiting the Derivative Works Exception of the Copyright Act Thirty Years After *Mills Music*." Meitus is an adjunct professor of law at the Indiana University Maurer School of Law, regularly teaching entertainment law and an intellectual property clinical course. He received his JD from the Maurer School of Law, his MA in international and public affairs from Columbia University, and his BA from Wabash College.

Megan M. Mulford is a partner in the Intellectual Property Group and the Sports, Entertainment and Media Group at Bose McKinney & Evans LLP. She focuses her practice on copyright, trademark, and right of publicity matters, and assists clients in identifying, protecting, and licensing their intellectual property assets. Mulford has experience counseling business entities, universities, museums, authors, artists, and musicians. Mulford received her JD from the Indiana University Robert H. McKinney School of Law in 2005. While in law school, she worked as a graduate assistant for The Children's Museum of Indianapolis and the Copyright Management Center, and received a Norman Lefstein Award of Excellence for pro bono service. Mulford graduated from DePauw University in 2002 with a major in communications and a minor in art history. Away from the office, Mulford is a passionate advocate for liberal arts education and the Greek experience and actively volunteers with her alma matter, DePauw University, and her sorority, Alpha Chi Omega.

Virginia Rutledge, PIPE Arts Group, is an art historian and attorney. Formerly a curator for the Los Angeles County Museum of Art, a litigator at Cravath Swaine & Moore LLP, and vice president and general counsel of Creative Commons, she is now in private practice focusing on the contemporary arts, advising artists, collectors, dealers, and cultural organizations. She is the immediate past chair of the Art Law Committee of the New York City Bar Association, and speaks and writes frequently on art and law. Rutledge holds a JD from the University of California at Berkeley School of Law (Boalt Hall), and an MP in art history from the City University of New York's Graduate School and University Center.

Bridget Smith is associate general counsel of The New York Public Library, Astor, Lenox and Tilden Foundations. She received her JD from the University of California at Berkeley. She previously worked at Davis Polk & Wardwell LLP and served as a law clerk to the Honorable Robert L. Carter of the Southern District of New York. A Truman Scholar, she holds a BA from Wellesley College and an MPP/UP from Harvard University. Smith is a member of the New York City Bar Association's Copyright & Literary Property Committee.

Maureen Whalen, former associate general counsel, retired in 2014 from The J. Paul Getty Trust, where she specialized in acquisitions and intellectual property matters. Whalen was co-chair of the Legal Issues in Museum Administration course of study sponsored by ALI-ABA, the Smithsonian Institution and the American Association of Museums in 2008 and 2009. She was a member of the Section 108 Study Group convened by the Library of Congress in 2005. Whalen published articles on the defining and recording rights metadata in digital asset management systems, and she is a strong advocate for making high-resolution digital copies of public domain images available to the public for free. Prior to joining the trust, Whalen spent more than twenty years in the cable television industry, including more than twelve years at The Walt Disney Company. She received her undergraduate and law degrees from the State University of New York at Buffalo and an MLS from the University of California, Los Angeles.

www.ingramcontent.com/pod-product-compliance
Ingram Content Group UK Ltd.
Pitfield, Milton Keynes, MK11 3LW, UK
UKHW050649200926
475560UK00005BA/368